WORLD LITERATURE
AND THOUGHT

Volume I
The Ancient Worlds

WORLD LITERATURE AND THOUGHT

Under the General Editorship of
Donald S. Gochberg
Michigan State University

Volume I
The Ancient Worlds
Edited by Donald S. Gochberg, Surjit Singh Dulai,
Edward D. Graham, and Kenneth W. Harrow

Volume II
The Middle Periods
Edited by Donald S. Gochberg, Surjit Singh Dulai,
Edward D. Graham, Kenneth W. Harrow, Priscilla Meléndez,
and Aníbal González

Volume III
The Modern World
Edited by Donald S. Gochberg, Surjit Singh Dulai,
Edward D. Graham, Kenneth W. Harrow, Priscilla Meléndez,
and Aníbal González

Volume IV
The Twentieth Century
Edited by Donald S. Gochberg, Surjit Singh Dulai,
Edward D. Graham, Kenneth W. Harrow, Priscilla Meléndez,
and Aníbal González

WORLD LITERATURE AND THOUGHT

꩜

Volume I
The Ancient Worlds

Donald S. Gochberg, General Editor
Surjit Singh Dulai
Edward D. Graham
Kenneth W. Harrow

Harcourt Brace College Publishers
Fort Worth Philadelphia San Diego New York Orlando Austin San Antonio
Toronto Montreal London Sydney Tokyo

PUBLISHER	Christopher P. Klein
SENIOR ACQUISITIONS EDITOR	David Tatom
PRODUCT MANAGER	Steven K. Drummond
DEVELOPMENTAL EDITOR	Sue A. Lister
SENIOR PROJECT EDITOR	Laura J. Hanna
PRODUCTION MANAGER	Eddie Dawson
SENIOR ART DIRECTOR	David A. Day
TEXT DESIGN AND COMPOSITION	Seaside Publishing Services
COPY EDITOR	Stacy Simpson
INDEXER	Joyce Teague
TEXT TYPE	10/12 Adobe Garamond

Cover Images: *Horsemen and Horses,* from the Parthenon Frieze. Acropolis Museum, Athens, Greece; *Oath of the Boddhisattva Maitreya.* Marble. India, second–third century. Musee Guimet, Paris, France.

Address for Editorial Correspondence:
Harcourt Brace College Publishers, 301 Commerce Street, Suite 3700, Fort Worth, TX 76102

Address for Orders
Harcourt Brace & Company, 6277 Sea Harbor Drive, Orlando, FL 32887-6777
1-800-782-4479, or 1-800-433-0001 (in Florida)

ISBN: 0-15-500919-2
Library of Congress Catalog Number: 96-79697
Printed in the United States of America
6 7 8 9 0 1 2 3 4 5 067 9 8 7 6 5 4 3 2 1

Harcourt Brace College Publishers

Contents

۶

Introduction to the World Literature and Thought *Series*

᪥

The four volumes of *World Literature and Thought* offer a rich treasury of selections from many of the world's major civilizations. These books present a diverse array of genres and languages—from philosophical treatises to love lyrics, and from ancient Akkadian to modern English. The selections have all been chosen for their lasting historical or intellectual significance, as well as for their readability. Because of the chronological structure of the volumes, the reader can more readily understand the historical contexts of the selections. Generally, we envision these carefully edited primary documents as being of most use for college-level courses in humanities, in the history of world civilizations, and in comparative or world literature.

With such a range of possible selections available to the editors, we sought to include only works that are of interest to both the searching student and the academic specialist. We have chosen works also because they exerted a significant influence on their own and later times, frequently even well outside their original cultures. Each selection is intended to be long enough to give both a clear view of the author's ideas or narrative development and a sense of the text's literary qualities. Shorter selections—lyric poems, for example—are usually printed without any abridgment. The principles of selection and annotation are modeled after Harcourt Brace's long-established four-volume *Classics of Western Thought* series, fourth edition, 1988. Excellence has remained the essential criterion of selection.

The selections appear generally in chronological order throughout the volumes: *The Ancient Worlds* (Volume I, roughly 2000 B.C. to A.D. 500), *The Middle Periods* (Volume II, 500 to 1500), *The Modern World* (Volume III, 1500 to 1900), and *The Twentieth Century* (Volume IV). Each selection is introduced by a headnote that places the work in its historical moment, gives a brief account of the author's life (where authorship is known), and generally clarifies the significance of the particular work. Although every selection also is generously footnoted, the astute reader will certainly want to refer occasionally to a standard college desk dictionary, since we saw no need—most of the time—to annotate words found there. All necessary factual information beyond the common reader's knowledge is provided for each selection. The footnotes clarify unusual words, as well as geographical and historical allusions. Brackets within the texts indicate an insertion by one of the editors. Critical interpretations usually are left to the instructor and the reader. The instructor may also wish to use the volumes in conjunction with one of the several world history narrative-texts that are readily available. Each of the volumes contains sufficient depth to function as the primary text for an academic term; all four, or any two, could provide varied reading fare for an academic year or longer.

Scrutiny of the "Contents" for each volume will show extraordinarily varied types of literature and ideas not previously seen anywhere within a single binding. Rather than creating separate volumes for each culture or language, we have chosen to integrate the collection. The reader, therefore, can more readily make his or her own connections and distinctions. The choice of selections was the result of two years of collegial discussions among the editors. As a result of those searching conversations, we were also able to clarify similarities and relationships not usually noted among diverse literatures. Four of the six editors contributing to the full series shared many years of an interdisciplinary teaching experience in the former Department of Humanities at Michigan State University. All of the editors are both specialists in their respective fields, noted in each volumes "Preface," and seasoned generalists, used to integrating diverse fields of knowledge.

Unique to this series is the inclusion of many documents *not* usually considered "literary." The greatest concern, in fact, when we made our choices was not a selection's belletristic qualities but rather its intrinsic interest and readability. We also considered whether a potential selection carried great authority in its own time, as well as in later times and other places. Thus, for example, in Volume I we included not only five books from Homer's adventurous epic *The Odyssey*, but also a generous selection from *The Laws* of the ancient Babylonian ruler Hammurabi, which influenced the religiously-based laws of the Hebrew Bible (also included) set down at least five centuries later. Another example of the series' inclusiveness of genres, from the dozens of available examples, comes from Volume II where we included not only a significant selection from the Iranian

(Persian) national epic *Shahnama,* but also an essential sampling of Islamic theology that shows the interpenetration of the expanding Muslim religion with earlier modes of literature and thought.

To help the reader organize his or her reading, selections from the same language and era are mostly clustered together. On a larger organizational scale, each of the four volumes is divided into parts which have both chronological and thematic significance. For example in Volume I, Part One, "Foundational Patterns," the reader can see emerging some of the basic value structures—religious, legal, societal, personal—in ancient cultures as diverse as Mesopotamia, Egypt, Israel, Greece, India, and China. These were differing cultures that were, nevertheless, struggling toward the same goal of establishing a good and stable society. Another useful feature is the part called "Cultural Encounters" that concludes both Volumes II and III. Here is the literature of travel and exploration at the meeting points of contrasting cultures, often seen from the observation point of a non-Western traveller. Indeed, not only in the designated parts but throughout the four volumes, cultural encounters, parallels, and contrasts are revealed and pointed out to the reader.

Even with this vast library collected for the readers' instruction and delight, it was not possible to include worthy examples from all the civilizations and languages whose texts have survived to our day. Yet, though much has necessarily been omitted, much remains. It would, perhaps, not be vainly inappropriate to conclude this brief introduction with a paraphrase of Dr. Samuel Johnson to the effect that he who tires of the wealth of humanity and its works revealed in these volumes must surely be tired of life; for there is represented in *World Literature and Thought* all that life can offer.

Donald S. Gochberg
General Editor

Preface to
The Ancient Worlds

ༀ

This first volume of the *World Literature and Thought* series contains enduring literary and intellectual works from the major ancient civilizations of Asia, Africa, and Europe. The scope of the entire four-volume series, the criteria for choosing the selections, and the level of editorial annotation are described in the preceding "Introduction to the *World Literature and Thought* Series."

This volume starts with ancient Middle Eastern and Egyptian texts going back to the third millennium B.C. The earliest selection from Western civilization (eighth century B.C.) is an excerpt from four books of Homer's adventurous Greek epic, *The Odyssey*. From there we move east to the earliest sacred texts of India and then farther east to examine classical Chinese literature and thought. Continuing onward through a diverse array of times and places, from Rome to Ethiopia, we conclude the forty-five selections around the fifth century A.D. The wealth of material offered here should enable readers to pick those civilizations and topics that they find of greatest interest. Or readers may choose to read through the contents in the given order, aided by the many cross-references.

No rigid formula was employed in allocating the number or length of the selections for each culture, civilization, region, or language. Rather, these proportions resulted from the significance of particular selections within their own cultural context, as well as in the context of world history. The areas of editorial responsibility for Volume I are the following: Donald Gochberg: General Editor, Europe and Middle East (selections 5–7, 12–19, 33–35, 37); Surjit Dulai: South Asia (selections 8–9, 20–21, 23–25, 39–42); Edward Graham: East Asia (selections 10–11, 22, 26–32, 43–45); Kenneth Harrow: Africa (selections 1–4, 36, 38). Each of the editors is both an expert in the field appropriate to his individual selections and a seasoned teacher who has discussed his selections, as well as many others that could not be included here, with numerous university classes.

Although every selection has its own introductory headnote, these are also general introductions to each of the the three major parts of this volume: "Foundational Patterns (selections 1–11), "Searching for Traditions (selections 12–32), and "Consolidation and Empires" (selections 33–45). These introductions to the parts are intended to help the reader see more readily the structural scope of the volume. The editors hope that the students who read these selections will not only increase their knowledge of ancient civilizations but also, through the abundant records of those centuries, will better understand *their own connections and cultural debts* to the varied continents and cultures.

Donald S. Gochberg
General Editor

On the Pronunciation of the Chinese Language

꙰

Selections 10-11, 22, 26-32, and 43-45 are all translations from Chinese. Written Chinese, alone among the world's major languages, is not phonetic in its nature, but is instead basically pictographic/ideographic. The thousands of characters in which Chinese is traditionally written have no sound values that are automatically comprehensible to the reader of English, Spanish, Arabic, Russian, or any other language written in a phonetic alphabet. Those from phonetic language areas who have sought to describe Chinese literature or translate its documents for non-Chinese readers have had to devise systems of representing the sounds of Chinese. In the West these are known, collectively, as systems of "Romanization," i.e., ways of expressing the sounds of Chinese in our Roman alphabet. Many such systems have been devised, none of them wholly satisfactory.

Translations from Chinese in this volume utilize the so-called Wade-Giles system, named for the British scholars who developed it. Here are a few simple guidelines that will enable the reader to come close to capturing the sounds of the names and terms which appear in these selections.

Vowel sounds (*a, e, i, o, u*) resemble those in standard English usage, with the exception of the common vowel-consonant combination *ih*, which is pronounced like the *ir* in *fir*. Vowels occurring together are pronounced as diphthongs, for instance, *ao*, which gives a combined sound like the *ow* in *now*.

The following consonants, or consonant combinations, followed by an apostrophe in the Wade-Giles system—*ch', k', p', ts',* and *tz'*—are aspirated (accompanied by a distinct exhalation of breath) and are pronounced as they would be in any English word. Without the apostrophe following them (*un*aspirated) they have the following sound values: *ch* as *j*, *k* as hard *g*, *p* as *b*, *ts* and *tz* as *dz*. An initial *hs* is close to the English *sh*, and *j* has a sound closer to the English *r*.

On Chinese Names

‫ﻌ‬

Names of Chinese individuals present some special problems for us. Often the commonly used form of the names of China's early philosophers combines the patronymic (family name derived from the father) with the honorific Tzu, which means "master." Thus, Chuang Tzu (selection 31) means Master Chuang. Normal name usage in China, as elsewhere in East Asia, is to give the patronymic first, followed by the individual's given name or names. Thus, in Western usage, Dr. Sun Yat-sen was Dr. Sun.

On the Spelling of Indian Names

‫ﻌ‬

Many of the Indian names in this volume are spelled *phonetically*, for the ease of the reader, rather than by use of the diacritical marks often used in scholarly publication.

PART I

FOUNDATIONAL PATTERNS

இ

The selections at the beginning of *The Ancient Worlds* reveal the emergence of basic structures of value—religious, legal, societal, personal—in cultures as geographically and culturally distant from one another as ancient Greece and China, Mesopotamia, Egypt, Israel, and India. As different as those cultures were, they all, in varied ways, worked toward a good and stable society. Their visions and assumptions about such a society and its inhabitants were often expressed in radically distinct literary styles. Although precise dating is not always possible for this earliest age of written expression, the texts of Part I of this book date from before 2000 B.C. to about 500 B.C.

The first selection, *The Epic of Gilgamesh,* in its earliest form, was recorded in cuneiform (wedge-shaped) script on clay tablets in Mesopotamia, the region of the Tigris and Euphrates Rivers (mainly in modern Iraq). The first expressions of the Gilgamesh myth, now lost, may date as far back as 2500 B.C. In the version that remains, the reader can see the power of an epic hero and the greater power of the quarreling gods who have small concern for humanity. Also from Mesopotamia and, like most of the other earliest literature, similarly involved with the gods, *Inanna's Descent* (Selection 2) deals with the epic journey of a goddess into the underworld and her restoration to the world of the living. Both of these Mesopotamian narratives develop themes reflected in later Jewish and Christian literature.

The third and fourth selections date from the stable and enduring Egyptian civilization. Its writings, in the form known as hieroglyphics (picture writing), unlike the Mesopotamian tablets, were carved on the walls of temples and tombs and were, thus, very visible, although not deciphered until the early nineteenth century. In the third selection, from the Middle Kingdom of ancient Egypt, ca. 2040–1650 B.C., are presented narratives of fabulous adventures—including shipwrecks and monsters—as well as an autobiographical account of exile and return. The Middle Kingdom is also represented by temple hymns and harpers' songs, inevitably involved with concerns about the end of life. In the literature from the New Kingdom (ca. 1550–1080 B.C.), shown in Selection 4, we continue to see hymns, including hymns to the sun-god that seem almost monotheistic. *The Book of the Dead,* which follows the hymns, is concerned with rituals and beliefs about burial. However, the universal emotion of erotic love, both fulfilled and unrequited, is not forgotten by the Egyptians in the poems that follow. We end the New Kingdom's selections with further tales of dangerous adventures.

Returning to the Fertile Crescent for the fifth and sixth selections, we begin with one of the earliest recorded legal codes. *The Laws of Hammurabi,* ascribed to the most famous early ruler of Babylon (1792–1750 B.C.), are even older than the laws in the Hebrew Bible, and may have influenced that code clearly stated in the Old Testament's Book of Exodus (Selection 6).

In the seventh selection, the first in a European language (Greek, ca. 800 B.C.), we revel in the daring adventures of Homer's crafty hero, Odysseus, as he journeys home to his rocky island of Ithaka after ten years of the Greek war against the great Asian city of Troy. Here, at the origins of Western epic literature, we see a resourceful hero, flawed by his own self-glorying pride, insult the monstrous son of the sea god. This atypically thoughtless act will delay his return by nearly a decade and cause the loss of his entire crew. Even in the stories of human adventure there is the theme of subjection of all humans to powers beyond themselves.

Two other great areas of early civilization are the Indus River valley that nourished ancient India and the Yellow River valley from which grew Chinese civilization. Selections 8 through 11 are texts from these two regions. Sharing Indo-European roots with ancient Greek civilization, by 2000 B.C. Aryan culture absorbed the Indus River civilization and continued to expand through the subcontinent. The sacred hymns of the Rig Veda (Selection 8) are the oldest literature of the Indian subcontinent. The Veda evolved between about 2000 and 500 B.C. Although the Veda is, thus, much older than Hinduism, the majority religion of India, it ultimately became Hinduism's most sacred scripture, and is essential to an understanding of the religion and its history. The *Brahmanas,* a part of the *Veda* and the earliest prose works in Indian literature, develop the Vedic rituals into an exacting and rigid system. As shown in Selection 9, the treatment of ritual in the *Brahmanas* often takes the form of stories that confirm the necessity of ritual.

Finally, the Chinese cluster of Part I (Selections 10 and 11) gives us works of history and of poetry, traditionally ascribed to the editorial labors of Confucius about 500 B.C., but recording events and literature originally set down as early as 1800 B.C. Carrying the stature of "Confucian classics" and serving as formative educational texts for the ruling classes, both works included here have been influential through most of the long span of Chinese history. By accepting such works as their "classics" many ethnically and linguistically diverse peoples of eastern Asia developed into a "Chinese" cultural unity.

1

æ

THE EPIC OF GILGAMESH

riting was invented in Sumer, southern Mesopotamia, around the middle of the fourth millennium B.C. At first it was pure picture writing, but soon it was supplemented by the use of phonetic signs that permitted writing to extend to complex texts in many fields of discourse. To form the signs, the technique of impressing a stylus on the surface of clay tablets was employed, giving rise to the name cuneiform, *that is, "wedge-shaped writing." This technique was used to record the earliest written literary texts, of which the supreme example is* The Epic of Gilgamesh, *the oldest version dating back to the middle of the third millennium B.C.*

The present standard version of the epic is the product of more than one thousand years of transmission and translation. It was written in the Akkadian language and dates to around 1300 B.C., when it was recorded by the scribe Sinleqqiunninni. The oldest surviving tablets of this version date to 800 B.C.

The epic tradition in Sumer arose from works of praise sung at royal courts— praise for the gods and for the rulers. The myths and stories incorporated into the praise songs were eventually combined in various forms by different performers, which accounts for the different styles and episodes to be found in the epic.

The Epic of Gilgamesh *recounts the deeds of a famous hero-king of Mesopotamia. Gilgamesh is two-thirds god, one-third human. His mother is the minor goddess Ninsun, or "Lady Wild Cow," and, like Achilles's mother, the sea-nymph Thetis (in Homer's Greek epic* The Iliad), *it is she who oversees her son's life. His father is a king of the city of Uruk, and he has no role in the epic. Gilgamesh is presented as one who has "experienced all things"—one upon whom Uruk depends for its defense and prosperity. Yet Gilgamesh is not presented as all-virtuous. He exploits his position of power and oppresses the city's young men and women; the text seems to indicate that he takes all brides for himself on the first night of their wedding. The gods decide that a counter-figure to Gilgamesh must be found, and he is Enkidu, a wild and savage man who is tamed by a cultic harlot and brought back to Uruk. There, he and Gilgamesh fight and eventually become close friends.*

4

The epic deals with their great exploits together, the eventual death of Enkidu, and Gilgamesh's search in the afterworld for the meaning of life and death following the loss of his friend. The two episodes included here introduce the characters of Gilgamesh and Enkidu, describe their initial meeting and the final quest of Gilgamesh in the world of the spirits and gods. In his journey, Gilgamesh encounters Utanapishtim, the sole survivor of the Flood, who gives his account of that great event. (This version of the Flood story is even older than the Old Testament account found in Selection 6.) Gilgamesh reaches for the gift of immortality, but he fails the tests and must return to Uruk.

The myth echoes all the themes of praise literature and quest stories: heroic rulers whose flaws drive them to seek the home of the gods for some solution. Inevitably, the conquest of obstacle after obstacle brings the hero face to face with the divine, immortal presence, with the resultant reassertion of an ordered universe in which the divine and the human each has its own proper realm.

Despite the blank spaces left in the text, the power of Gilgamesh's emotional expression reaches us across the millennia. Like the fragmented clay tablets, the story is pieced together, enabling us to recognize eternal themes, such as that of the Flood, the loss of friendship, and the search for immortality.

TABLET I
The Legacy

He who has seen everything, *I will make known* to the lands.
I will teach about him who experienced all things, . . .
Anu[1] granted him the totality of knowledge of *all*.
He saw the secret, discovered the hidden,
he brought information of the time before the Flood.
He went on a distant journey, pushing himself to exhaustion,
but then was brought to peace.
He carved on a stone stela all of his toils,

Reprinted from *The Epic of Gilgamesh*, translated with an introduction and notes, by Maureen Gallery Kovacs with the permission of the publishers, Stanford University Press. © 1985, 1989, by the Board of Trustees of the Leland Stanford Junior University. Pp. 3–12, 15–21, and 97–108.

[1]Anu is the original sky god, the most ancient deity of Sumer, called the Father of the Gods. His sacred city was Uruk, on the Euphrates River. His temple was the *Eanna*, "House of Anu," which was, from an early period, also the temple of his daughter, Inanna (Sumerian) or Ishtar (Akkadian).

and built the wall of Uruk-Haven,[2]
the wall of the sacred Eanna Temple, the holy sanctuary.
Look at its wall which gleams like copper,
inspect its inner wall, the likes of which no one can equal!
Take hold of the threshold stone—it dates from ancient times!
Go close to Eanna Temple, the residence of Ishtar,
such as no later king or man ever equaled!
Go up on the wall of Uruk and walk around,
examine its foundation, inspect its brickwork thoroughly.
Is not even the core of the brick structure made of kiln-fired brick,
and did not the Seven Sages themselves lay out its plans?
One league city, one league palm gardens, one league lowlands, the
    open area of the Ishtar Temple,
three leagues and the open area of Uruk the wall encloses.
Find the copper tablet box,
open its lock of bronze,
undo the fastening of its secret opening.
Take and read out from the lapis lazuli tablet
how Gilgamesh went through every hardship.

Gilgamesh

Supreme over other kings, lordly in appearance,
he is the hero, born of Uruk, the goring wild bull.
He walks out in front, the leader,
and walks at the rear, trusted by his companions.
Mighty net, protector of his people,
raging flood-wave who destroys even walls of stone!
Offspring of Lugalbanda,[3] Gilgamesh is strong to perfection,
son of the august cow, Rimat-Ninsun,[4] . . . Gilgamesh is awesome to
    perfection.
It was he who opened the mountain passes,
who dug wells on the flank of the mountain.
It was he who crossed the ocean, the vast seas, to the rising sun,
who explored the world regions, seeking life.

---

[2]A praise name for the city Gilgamesh rules.

[3]One of the kings of Uruk after the Flood, the name means "young king." In Sumerian literature he is the husband of Ninsun and the father of Gilgamesh.

[4]Ninsun is the divine mother of Gilgamesh; her name means "lady, wild cow." At times her name is given as Rimat-Ninsun (*rimat* means "wild cow.") The good cow appears in Sumerian literature as the one who gives birth to kings.

It was he who reached by his own sheer strength Utanapishtim,[5] the
      Faraway,
who restored the sanctuaries that the Flood had destroyed!
. . . for teeming mankind.
Who can compare with him in kingliness?
Who can say like Gilgamesh: "I am king!"?
Whose name, from the day of his birth, was called "Gilgamesh"?
Two-thirds of him is god, one-third of him is human.
The Great Goddess Aruru[6] designed the model for his body,
she prepared his form . . .
beautiful, handsomest of men,
. . . perfect . . .
He walks around in the enclosure of Uruk,
like a wild bull he makes himself mighty, head raised over others.
There is no rival who can raise his weapon against him.
His fellows stand at the alert, attentive to his orders,
and the men of Uruk become anxious in . . .
Gilgamesh does not leave a son to his father,
day and night he arrogantly . . .
[The following lines are interpreted as rhetorical, perhaps spoken by the oppressed cit-
izens of Uruk.]
Is Gilgamesh the shepherd of Uruk-Haven,
is he the shepherd . . .
bold, eminent, knowing, and wise?
Gilgamesh does not leave a girl to her mother![7]
The daughter of the warrior, the bride of the young man,
the gods kept hearing their complaints, so
the gods of the heavens implored the Lord of Uruk [Anu]:
"You have indeed brought into being a mighty wild bull, head
      raised!
There is no rival who can raise a weapon against him.
His fellows stand at the alert, attentive to his orders,
Gilgamesh does not leave a son to his father,
day and night he arrogantly . . .
Is he the shepherd of Uruk-Haven,
is he their shepherd . . .

---

[5]A king who was allowed to survive the Flood, and then was given eternal life in a remote
corner of the world. His name means "he has found life."

[6]The mother goddess who created mankind.

[7]Or "to her betrothed."

bold, eminent, knowing, and wise?
Gilgamesh does not leave a girl to her mother!"

Enkidu[8]

The daughter of the warrior, the bride of the young man,
Anu listened to their complaints,
and the gods called out to Aruru:
  "It was you, Aruru, who created mankind,
    now create a *zikru*[9] to him.
  Let him be equal to Gilgamesh's stormy heart,
    let them be a match for each other so that Uruk may find peace!"
When Aruru heard this she created within herself the *zikru* of Anu.
Aruru washed her hands, she pinched off some clay, and threw it
        into the wilderness.
In the wilderness she created valiant Enkidu,
born of silence, endowed with strength by Ninurta.[10]
His whole body was shaggy with hair,
he had a full head of hair like a woman,
his locks billowed in profusion like Ashnan.[11]
He knew neither people nor settled living,
but wore a garment like Sumukan.[12]
He ate grasses with the gazelles,
and jostled at the watering hole with the animals;
as with animals, his thirst was slaked with mere water.

The Trapper and the Harlot

A notorious trapper
came face to face with him opposite the watering hole.
A first, a second, and a third day
he came face to face with him opposite the watering hole.

---

[8]In this Akkadian version of the epic, Enkidu is a primitive man living among wild animals until he is seduced and domesticated by a harlot. He becomes the cherished friend of King Gilgamesh. In the Sumerian epic tales about Gilgamesh he was merely the servant and companion of Gilgamesh.

[9]The Akkadian *zikru* normally means "what was ordered, commanded" or "reply, response"; the meaning here is unclear.

[10]God of War, also called "Ninurta of the Silence."

[11]The goddess of grain.

[12]The god of wild animals. (Enkidu was clothed in animal skins.)

On seeing him the trapper's face went stark with fear,
and Enkidu and his animals drew back home.
He was rigid with fear; though stock-still
his heart pounded and his face drained of color.
He was miserable to the core,
and his face looked like one who had made a long journey.
The trapper addressed his father saying:
    "Father, a certain fellow has come from the mountains.
He is the mightiest in the land,
his strength is as mighty as the meteorite of Anu!
He continually goes over the mountains,
he continually jostles at the watering place with the animals,
he continually plants his feet opposite the watering place.
I was afraid, so I did not go up to him.
He filled in the pits that I had dug,
wrenched out my traps that I had spread,
released from my grasp the wild animals.
He does not let me make my rounds in the wilderness!"
The trapper's father spoke to him saying:
    "My son, there lives in Uruk a certain Gilgamesh.
There is no one stronger than he,
he is as strong as the meteorite of Anu.
Go, set off to Uruk,
tell Gilgamesh of this man of might.
He will give you the harlot Shamhat,[13] take her with you.
The woman will overcome the fellow as if she were strong.
When the animals are drinking at the watering place
have her take off her robe and expose her sex.
When he sees her he will draw near to her,
and his animals, who grew up in his wilderness, will be alien
       to him."
He heeded his father's advice.
The trapper went off to Uruk,
he made the journey, stood inside of Uruk,
and declared to . . . Gilgamesh:
    "There is a certain fellow who has come from the mountains—
he is the mightiest in the land,
his strength is as mighty as the meteorite of Anu!
He continually goes over the mountains,

---

[13]The harlot Shamhat introduces Enkidu to human living, estranging him from the world of nature. She is probably in the service of the Temple of Ishtar.

he continually jostles at the watering place with the animals,
he continually plants his feet opposite the watering place.
I was afraid, so I did not go up to him.
He filled in the pits that I had dug,
wrenched out my traps that I had spread,
released from my grasp the wild animals.
He does not let me make my rounds in the wilderness!"
Gilgamesh said to the trapper:
    "Go, trapper, bring the harlot, Shamhat, with you.
    When the animals are drinking at the watering place
    have her take off her robe and expose her sex.
    When he sees her he will draw near to her,
    and his animals, who grew up in his wilderness, will be alien
        to him."

The Harlot

The trapper went, bringing the harlot, Shamhat, with him.
They set off on the journey, making direct way.
On the third day they arrived at the appointed place,
and the trapper and the harlot sat down at their posts.
A first day and a second they sat opposite the watering hole.
The animals arrived and drank at the watering hole,
the wild beasts arrived and slaked their thirst with water.
Then he, Enkidu, offspring of the mountains,
who eats grasses with the gazelles,
came to drink at the watering hole with the animals,
with the wild beasts he slaked his thirst with water.
Then Shamhat saw him—a primitive,
a savage fellow from the depths of the wilderness!
    "That is he, Shamhat! Release your clenched arms,
    expose your sex so he can take in your voluptuousness.
    Do not be restrained—take his energy!
    When he sees you he will draw near to you.
    Spread out your robe so he can lie upon you,
    and perform for this primitive the task of womankind!
    His animals, who grew up in his wilderness, will become alien
        to him,
    and his lust will groan over you."
Shamhat unclutched her bosom, exposed her sex, and he took in her
        voluptuousness.
She was not restrained, but took his energy.
She spread out her robe and he lay upon her,

she performed for the primitive the task of womankind.

His lust groaned over her;
for six days and seven nights Enkidu stayed aroused,
and had intercourse with the harlot
until he was sated with her charms.
But when he turned his attention to his animals,
the gazelles saw Enkidu and darted off,
the wild animals distanced themselves from his body.
Enkidu . . . his utterly depleted body,
his knees that wanted to go off with his animals went rigid;
Enkidu was diminished, his running was not as before.
But then he drew himself up, for his understanding had broadened.
Turning around, he sat down at the harlot's feet,
gazing into her face, his ears attentive as the harlot spoke.
The harlot said to Enkidu:
   "You are beautiful, Enkidu, you are become like a god.
   Why do you gallop around the wilderness with the wild
      beasts?
   Come, let me bring you into Uruk-Haven,
   to the Holy Temple, the residence of Anu and Ishtar,
   the place of Gilgamesh, who is wise to perfection,
   but who struts his power over the people like a wild bull."

To Uruk

What she kept saying found favor with him.
Becoming aware of himself, he sought a friend.
Enkidu spoke to the harlot:
   "Come, Shamhat, take me away with you
   to the sacred Holy Temple, the residence of Anu and Ishtar,
   the place of Gilgamesh, who is wise to perfection,
   but who struts his power over the people like a wild bull.
   I will challenge him . . .
   Let me shout out in Uruk: 'I am the mighty one!'
   Lead me in and I will change the order of things;
   he whose strength is mightiest is the one born in the wilderness!"
[Shamhat to Enkidu:]
   "Come, let us go, so he may see your face.
   I will lead you to Gilgamesh—I know where he will be.
   Look about, Enkidu, inside Uruk-Haven,
   where the people show off in skirted finery,
   where every day is a day for some festival,
   where the lyre and drum play continually,

where harlots stand about prettily,
exuding voluptuousness, full of laughter,
and on the couch of night the sheets are spread.
Enkidu, you who do not know how to live,
I will show you Gilgamesh, a man of extreme feelings.
Look at him, gaze at his face—
he is a handsome youth, with freshness,
his entire body exudes voluptuousness.
He has mightier strength than you,
without sleeping day or night!
Enkidu, it is your wrong thoughts you must change!
It is Gilgamesh whom Shamash[14] loves,
and Anu, Enlil,[15] and Ea[16] have enlarged his mind.[17]
Even before you came from the mountain
Gilgamesh in Uruk had dreams about you."

The Dreams

Gilgamesh got up and revealed the dream, saying to his mother:
"Mother, I had a dream last night.
Stars of the sky appeared,
and some kind of meteorite of Anu fell next to me.
I tried to lift it but it was too mighty for me,
I tried to turn it over but I could not budge it.
The land of Uruk was standing around it,
the whole land had assembled about it,
the populace was thronging around it,
the men clustered about it,
and kissed its feet as if it were a little baby.
I loved it and embraced it as a wife.
I laid it down at your feet,
and you made it compete with me."
The mother of Gilgamesh, the wise, all-knowing, said to her Lord;

---

[14]The sun god, who was god of justice and who hated evil, demons, and secret, hidden behavior, such as witchcraft.

[15]The chief deity of the Sumerian pantheon, whose name means "lord wind" and who determined human destiny.

[16]The god of the subterranean freshwater sea called the Apsu; often he is presented as a trickster.

[17]Gilgamesh's special favor and intelligence were bestowed by the gods, whereas Enkidu's "broadened understanding" was merely a result of human experience.

Rimat-Ninsun, the wise, all-knowing, said to Gilgamesh:
"As for the stars of the sky that appeared
and the meteorite of Anu which fell next to you,
you tried to lift but it was too mighty for you,
you tried to turn it over but were unable to budge it,
you laid it down at my feet,
and I made it compete with you,
and you loved and embraced it as a wife."
[This means:]
"There will come to you a mighty man, a comrade who saves
his friend—
he is the mightiest in the land, he is strongest,
his strength is mighty as the meteorite of Anu!
You loved him and embraced him as a wife;
and it is he who will repeatedly save you.
Your dream is good and propitious!"
A second time Gilgamesh said to his mother:
"Mother, I have had another dream:
At the gate of my marital chamber there lay an axe,
and people had collected about it.
The Land of Uruk was standing around it,
the whole land had assembled about it,
the populace was thronging around it.
I laid it down at your feet,
I loved it and embraced it as a wife,
and you made it compete with me."
The mother of Gilgamesh, the wise, all-knowing, said to her son;
Rimat-Ninsun, the wise, all-knowing, said to Gilgamesh:
"The axe that you saw is a man.
. . . that you love him and embrace as a wife,
but that I have compete with you."
[This means:]
"There will come to you a mighty man, a comrade who saves
his friend—
he is the mightiest in the land, he is strongest,
he is as mighty as the meteorite of Anu!"
Gilgamesh spoke to his mother saying:
"By the command of Enlil, the Great Counselor, so may it come
to pass!
May I have a friend and adviser,
a friend and adviser may I have!
You have interpreted for me the dreams about him!"
After the harlot recounted the dreams of Gilgamesh to Enkidu the two
of them made love.

TABLET II
Enkidu and the Harlot

Enkidu sits in front of her.
Shamhat pulled off her clothing,
and clothed him with one piece
while she clothed herself with a second.
She took hold of him as the gods do[18]
and brought him to the hut of the shepherds.

With the Shepherds

The shepherds gathered all around him,
they marveled to themselves:
    "How the youth resembles Gilgamesh—
    tall in stature, towering up to the battlements over the wall!
    Surely he was born in the mountains;
    his strength is as mighty as the meteorite of Anu!"
They placed food in front of him,
they placed beer in front of him;
Enkidu did not eat or drink, but squinted and stared. . . .
Enkidu scattered the wolves, he chased away the lions.
The herders could lie down in peace,
for Enkidu was their watchman.
. . . he made merry.
Then he raised his eyes and saw a man.
He said to the harlot:
    "Shamhat, have that man go away!
    Why has he come? I will call out his name!"
The harlot called out to the man
and went over to him and spoke with him.
    "Young man, where are you hurrying?
    Why this arduous pace?"
The young man spoke, saying to Enkidu:
    "They have invited me to a wedding,
    as is the custom of the people.
    . . . the selection of brides . . .
    I have heaped up tasty delights for the wedding on the cere-
        monial platter.
    For the king of Broad-Marted Uruk,
    open is the veil of the people for choosing a girl.

---

[18]Religious imagery of the period commonly shows a goddess leading a worshiper by the hand into the presence of the chief god.

For Gilgamesh, the king of Broad-Marted Uruk,
open is the veil of the people for choosing.
He will have intercourse with the 'destined wife,'
he first, the husband afterward.
This is ordered by the counsel of Anu,
from the severing of his umbilical cord it has been destined
    for him."
At the young man's speech Enkidu's face flushed with anger.
Enkidu walked in front, and Shamhat after him.

The Contest

Enkidu walked down the street of Uruk-Haven,
. . . mighty . . .
He blocked the way through Uruk the Sheepfold.
The land of Uruk stood around him,
the whole land assembled about him,
the populace was thronging around him,
the men were clustered about him,
and kissed his feet as if he were a little baby.
Suddenly a handsome young man . . .
For Ishara[19] the bed of marriage is ready,
for Gilgamesh as for a god a counterpart is set up.
Enkidu blocked the entry to the marital chamber,
and would not allow Gilgamesh to be brought in.
They grappled with each other at the entry to the marital chamber,
in the street they attacked each other, the public square of the land.
The doorposts trembled and the wall shook,
Gilgamesh bent his knees, with his other foot on the ground,
his anger abated and he turned his chest away.
After he turned his chest Enkidu said to Gilgamesh:
    "Your mother bore you ever unique,
    the wild cow of the enclosure, Ninsun,
    your head is elevated over other men,
    Enlil has destined for you the kingship over the people."

Friends

They kissed each other and became friends.

---

[19]A name of Ishtar in her cultic role during the sacred marriage rite. Ishtar (Inanna) is the goddess of love and war, daughter of Anu, lover of Tammuz; she shared the Eanna temple in Uruk with Anu. As goddess of love, the votaries of her cult had some sexual duties.

A Hero's Challenge

Gilgamesh spoke to Enkidu saying:
"What you say . . ."
"Who, my friend, can ascend to the heavens?
Only the gods can dwell forever with Shamash.
As for human beings, their days are numbered,
and whatever they keep trying to achieve is but wind!
Now you are afraid of death—
what has become of your bold strength?
I will go in front of you,
and your mouth can call out: 'Go on closer, do not be afraid!'
Should I fall, I will have established my fame.
They will say: 'It was Gilgamesh who locked in battle with
    Humbaba the Terrible!'[20]
You were born and raised in the wilderness,
a lion leaped up on you, so you have experienced it all!
I will undertake it and I will cut down the cedar.
It is I who will establish fame for eternity!
Come, my friend, I will go over to the forge
and have them cast the weapons in our presence!"
Holding each other by the hand they went over to the forge.
The craftsman sat and discussed with one another.
"We should fashion the axe . . .
The hatchet should be one talent in weight . . .
Their swords should be one talent . . .
Their armor one talent, their armor . . ."
Gilgamesh said to the men of Uruk:
"Listen to me, men . . .
"You, men of Uruk, who know . . .
I want to make myself more mighty, and will go on a distant
    journey!
I will face fighting such as I have never known,
I will set out on a road I have never traveled!
Give me your blessings! . . .
I will enter the city gate of Uruk . . .

---

[20]Humbaba is a protective demon, the guardian of the cedar forest, appointed by the god
Enlil to protect the sacred cedars. He was endowed with extraordinary power to detect
trespassers and a terror-inspiring appearance with which to drive them away. It appears
that Humbaba did not turn out to be the monstrous ogre Gilgamesh was expecting.
Humbaba's long, strange dialogues indicate that he had known Gilgamesh and Enkidu
previously.

I will devote myself to the New Year's Festival.
I will perform the New Year's ceremonies in . . .
The New Year's Festival will take place, celebrations . . .
They will keep shouting 'Hurrah!' in . . ."
Enkidu spoke to the Elders:
"What the men of Uruk . . .
Say to him that he must not go to the cedar forest—
the journey is not to be made!
A man who . . .
The guardian of the cedar forest . . ."
The noble counselors of Uruk arose and delivered their advice to
       Gilgamesh:
"You are young, Gilgamesh, your heart carries you off—
you do not know what you are talking about!
. . . gave birth to you.
Humbaba's roar is a flood,
his mouth is fire, his breath, death!
He can hear rustling in his forest one hundred leagues away!
Who would go down into his forest?
Who among even the Igigi gods[21] can confront him?
In order to keep the cedar safe, Enlil assigned him as a terror to
       human beings."
Gilgamesh listened to the statement of his noble counselors.

●   ●   ●

The Story of the Flood[22]

Gilgamesh spoke to Utanapishtim, the Faraway:
"I have been looking at you,
but your appearance is not strange—you are like me!
You yourself are not different—you are like me!
My mind was resolved to fight with you,
but instead my arm lies useless over you.
Tell me, how is it that you stand in the Assembly of the Gods,
    and have found life?"

---

[21]A group of gods who were subject to the Anunnaki (the fifty sons of Anu) and did manual labor for them.

[22]The flood story told here is an adaptation or excerpt from a version of the flood episode in the *Myth of Atrahasis*. *Atrahasis* is an epithet meaning "exceedingly attentive or wise"; it is applied to the king who survived the flood and then was given eternal life in a remote corner of the world. He is the same as Utanapishtim (another epithet meaning "he who has found life").

Utanapishtim spoke to Gilgamesh, saying:
"I will reveal to you, Gilgamesh, a thing that is hidden,
a secret of the gods I will tell you!
Shuruppak,[23] a city that you surely know,
situated on the banks of the Euphrates,
that city was very old, and there were gods inside it.
The hearts of the Great Gods moved them to inflict the flood.
Their father Anu uttered the oath of secrecy,
Valiant Enlil was their adviser,
Ninurta was their chamberlain,
Ennugi[24] was their minister of canals.
Ea, the clever prince, was under oath with them
so he repeated their talk to the reed house:
    'Reed house, reed house! Wall, wall!
    Hear, O reed house! Understand, O wall!
    O man of Shuruppak, son of Ubartutu:
    Tear down the house and build a boat!
    Abandon wealth and seek living beings!
    Spurn possessions and keep alive living beings!
    Make all living beings go up into the boat.
    The boat which you are to build,
        its dimensions must measure equal to each other:
        its length must correspond to its width.
    Roof it over like the Apsu.'[25]
I understood and spoke to my lord, Ea:
    'My lord, thus is the command which you have uttered
    I will heed and will do it.
    But what shall I answer the city, the populace, and the
        Elders?'
Ea spoke, commanding me, his servant:
    'You, well then, this is what you must say to them:
        "It appears that Enlil is rejecting me
        so I cannot reside in your city,
        nor set foot on Enlil's earth.
        I will go down to the Apsu to live with my lord, Ea,
        and upon you he will rain down abundance,
        a profusion of fowl, myriad fishes.
        He will bring to you a harvest of wealth,

---

[23]One of the most ancient cities of Sumer.

[24]A minor god or demon.

[25]The freshwater sea flowing under the earth, the domain of the god Ea.

in the morning he will let loaves of bread shower down,
and in the evening a rain of wheat!'"
Just as dawn began to glow
the land assembled around me—
the carpenter carried his hatchet,
the reed worker carried his flattening stone,
. . . the men . . .
The child carried the pitch,
the weak brought whatever else was needed.
On the fifth day I laid out her exterior.
It was a field in area,[26]
its walls were each ten times twelve cubits in height,
the sides of its top were of equal length, ten times twelve
    cubits each.
I laid out its interior structure and drew a picture of it.
I provided it with six decks,
thus dividing it into seven levels.
The inside of it I divided into nine compartments.
I drove plugs to keep out water in its middle part.
I saw to the punting poles and laid in what was necessary.
Three times thirty-six hundred units of raw bitumen I poured
    into the bitumen kiln,
three times thirty-six hundred units of pitch . . . into it,
there were three times thirty-six hundred porters of casks who
    carried vegetable oil,
apart from the thirty-six hundred units of oil which they consumed
and two times thirty-six hundred units of oil which the boatman
    stored away.
I butchered oxen for the meat,
and day upon day I slaughtered sheep.
I gave the workmen ale, beer, oil, and wine, as if it were river water,
so they could make a party like the New Year's Festival.
. . . and I set my hand to the oiling.
The boat was finished by sunset.
The launching was very difficult.
They had to keep carrying a runway of poles front to back,
until two-thirds of it had gone into the water.
Whatever I had I loaded on it:

---

[26]The boat described is clearly a cube, not like ordinary Mesopotamian boats, and is probably an allusion to the dimensions of the ziggurat, the Mesopotamian stepped temple tower.

whatever silver I had I loaded on it,
whatever gold I had I loaded on it.
All the living beings that I had I loaded on it,
I had all my kith and kin go up into the boat,
all the beasts and animals of the field and the craftsmen I had go up.
Shamash had set a stated time:[27]
    'In the morning I will let loaves of bread shower down,
    and in the evening a rain of wheat!
    Go inside the boat, seal the entry!'
That stated time had arrived.
In the morning he let loaves of bread shower down,
and in the evening a rain of wheat.
I watched the appearance of the weather—
the weather was frightful to behold!
I went into the boat and sealed the entry.
For the caulking of the boat, to Puzuramurri, the boatman,
I gave the palace together with its contents.
Just as dawn began to glow
there arose from the horizon a black cloud.
Adad[28] rumbled inside of it,
before him went Shullat and Hanish,[29]
heralds going over mountain and land.
Erragal[30] pulled out the mooring poles,
forth went Ninurta and made the dikes overflow.
The Anunnaki[31] lifted up the torches,
setting the land ablaze with their flare.
Stunned shock over Adad's deeds overtook the heavens,
and turned to blackness all that had been light.
The . . . land shattered like a . . . pot.
All day long the south wind blew . . .,
blowing fast, submerging the mountain in water,
overwhelming the people like an attack.
No one could see his fellow,

---

[27] Earlier, Ea, not Shamash, had given the stated time.

[28] The chief storm god.

[29] Minor weather gods, usually paired together, the two being heralds of Adad.

[30] Another name for Nergal, the husband of Erishkigal, and, with her, ruler of the underworld.

[31] The fifty sons of Anu, including the Seven Great Annunaki who "fixed the destinies" and who could authorize change in the constitution of the universe.

they could not recognize each other in the torrent.
The gods were frightened by the flood,
and retreated, ascending to the heaven of Anu.
The gods were cowering like dogs, crouching by the outer wall.
Ishtar shrieked like a woman in childbirth,
the sweet-voiced mistress of the gods wailed:
    'The olden days have alas turned to clay,
    because I said evil things in the Assembly of the Gods!
    How could I say evil things in the Assembly of the Gods,
    ordering a catastrophe to destroy my people?!
    No sooner have I given birth to my dear people
    than they fill the sea like so many fish!'
The gods—those of the Anunnaki—were weeping with her,
the gods humbly sat weeping, sobbing with grief,
their lips burning, parched with thirst.
Six days and seven nights
came the wind and flood, the storm flattening the land.
When the seventh day arrived, the storm was pounding,
the flood was a war—struggling with itself like a woman
           writhing in labor.
The sea calmed, fell still, the whirlwind and flood stopped up.
I looked around all day long—quiet had set in
and all the human beings had turned to clay!
The terrain was as flat as a roof.
I opened a vent and fresh air, daylight, fell upon the side of
      my nose.
I fell to my knees and sat weeping,
tears streaming down the side of my nose.
I looked around for coastlines in the expanse of the sea,
and at twelve leagues there emerged a region of land.
On Mt. Nimush the boat lodged firm,
Mt. Nimush held the boat, allowing no sway,
One day and a second Mt. Nimush held the boat, allowing no sway.
A third day, a fourth, Mt. Nimush held the boat, allowing no sway.
A fifth day, a sixth, Mt. Nimush held the boat, allowing no sway.
When a seventh day arrived
I sent forth a dove and released it.
The dove went off, but came back to me;
no perch was visible so it circled back to me.
I sent forth a swallow and released it.
The swallow went off, but came back to me.
no perch was visible, so it circled back to me,
I sent forth a raven and released it.

The raven went off, and saw the waters slither back.
It eats, it scratches, it bobs, but does not circle back to me.
Then I sent out everything in all directions and sacrificed a sheep.
I offered incense in front of the mountain-ziggurat.
Seven and seven cult vessels I put in place,
and into the fire into their bowls I poured reeds, cedar, and myrtle.
The gods smelled the savor,
the gods smelled the sweet savor,
and collected like flies over a sheep sacrifice.
Just then Beletili[32] arrived.
She lifted up the beads which Anu had made for his enjoyment:
   'You gods, as surely as I shall not forget this lapis lazuli
      around my neck,
     may I be mindful of these days, and never forget them!
     The gods may come to the incense offering,
     but Enlil may not come to the incense offering,
     because without considering he brought about the flood
     and consigned my people to annihilation.'
Just then Enlil arrived.
He saw the boat and became furious,
he was filled with rage at the Igigi gods:
   'Where did a living being escape?
   No man was to survive the annihilation!'
Ninurta spoke to valiant Enlil, saying:
   'Who else but Ea could devise such a thing?
   It is Ea who knows every machination!'
Ea spoke to the valiant Enlil, saying:
   'It is you, O valiant one, who is the sage of the gods.
   How, how could you bring about a flood without consideration?
   Charge the violation to the violator,
   charge the offense to the offender,
   but be compassionate lest mankind be cut off,
   be patient lest they be killed.
   Instead of your bringing on the flood,
   would that a lion had appeared to diminish the people!
   Instead of your bringing on the flood,
   would that a wolf had appeared to diminish the people!
   Instead of your bringing on the flood,
   would that famine had occurred to slay the land!
   Instead of your bringing on the flood,

---

[32]Another name for Aruru (see footnote 6).

would that pestilent Erra had appeared to ravage the land!
It was not I who revealed the secret of the great gods,
I only made a dream appear to Atrahasis; and thus he heard
the secret of the gods.
Now then! The deliberation should be about him!'
Enlil went up inside the boat
and, grasping my hand, made me go up.
He had my wife go up and kneel by my side.
He touched our forehead and, standing between us, he
blessed us:
'Previously Utanapishtim was a human being.
But now let Utanapishtim and his wife become like us, the gods!
Let Utanapishtim reside far away, at the mouth of the rivers.'
They took us far away and settled us at the mouth of the rivers."

A Chance at Immortality

[The Story of the Flood ends. Utanapishtim now addresses Gilgamesh again.]
"Now then, who will convene the gods on your behalf,
that you may find the life that you are seeking?
Wait! You must not lie down for six days and seven nights."
As soon as he sat down with his head between his legs
sleep, like a fog, blew upon him.
Utanapishtim said to his wife:
"Look there! The man, the youth who wanted eternal life!
Sleep, like a fog, blew over him."
His wife said to Utanapishtim the Faraway:
"Touch him, let the man awaken.
Let him return safely by the way he came.
Let him return to his land by the gate through which he left."
Utanapishtim said to his wife:
"Mankind is deceptive, and will deceive you.
Come, bake loaves for him and keep setting them by his head
and draw on the wall each day that he lay down."
She baked his loaves and placed them by his head
and marked on the wall the day that he lay down.
The first loaf was desiccated,
the second stale, the third moist, the fourth turned white, its . . .,
the fifth sprouted gray mold, the sixth is still fresh.
The seventh—suddenly he touched him and the man awoke.
Gilgamesh said to Utanapishtim:
"The very moment sleep was pouring over me
you touched me and alerted me!"

Utanapishtim spoke to Gilgamesh, saying:
>"Look over here, Gilgamesh, count your loaves!
>You should be aware of what is marked on the wall!
>Your first loaf is desiccated,
>the second stale, the third moist, your fourth turned white, its . . .
>the fifth sprouted gray mold, the sixth is still fresh.
>The seventh—at that instant you awoke!"

Gilgamesh said to Utanapishtim the Faraway:
>"O woe! What shall I do, Utanapishtim, where shall I go?
>The Snatcher has taken hold of my flesh,
>in my bedroom Death dwells,
>and wherever I set foot there too is Death!"

Home Empty-Handed

Utanapishtim said to Urshanabi, the ferryman:[33]
>"May the harbor reject you, may the ferry landing reject you!
>May you who used to walk its shores be denied its shores!
>The man in front of whom you walk, matted hair chains his
>   body,
>animal skins have ruined his beautiful skin.
>Take him away, Urshanabi, bring him to the washing place.
>Let him wash his matted hair in water like *ellu*.[34]
>Let him cast away his animal skin and have the sea carry it off,
>let his body be moistened with fine oil,
>let the wrap around his head be made new,
>let him wear royal robes worthy of him!
>Until he goes off to his city,
>until he sets off on his way,
>let his royal robe not become spotted, let it be perfectly new!"

Urshanabi took him away and brought him to the washing place.
He washed his matted hair with water like *ellu*.
He cast off his animal skin and the sea carried it off.
He moistened his body with fine oil,

---

[33]The ferryman across the river of the underworld, which separates the world of the living from the world of the dead. The name means "servant of two-thirds," a reference to his role as servant to Gilgamesh, who was two-thirds god.

[34]*Ellu* is a problematic term whose meaning suggests "shining oil" or "purification priest." A straightforward translation of the line would be, "And let him wash in water his filthy hair, as clean as possible." (Information on *ellu* was provided by the translator of the epic, Maureen Kovacs, in a letter to the editor.)

and made a new wrap for his head.
He put on a royal robe worthy of him.
Until he went away to his city,
until he set off on his way,
his royal robe remained unspotted, it was perfectly clean.
Gilgamesh and Urshanabi boarded the boat,
they cast off the *magillu*-boat,[35] and sailed away.

A Second Chance at Life

The wife of Utanapishtim the Faraway said to him:
    "Gilgamesh came here exhausted and worn out.
    What can you give him so that he can return to his land with
        honor?"
Then Gilgamesh raised a punting pole
and drew the boat to shore.
Utanapishtim spoke to Gilgamesh, saying:
    "Gilgamesh, you came here exhausted and worn out.
    What can I give you so you can return to your land?
    I will disclose to you a thing that is hidden, Gilgamesh,
    a . . . I will tell you.
    There is a plant . . . like a boxthorn,
    whose thorns will prick your hand like a rose.
    If your hands reach that plant you will become a young
        man again."
Hearing this, Gilgamesh opened a conduit to the Apsu
and attached heavy stones to his feet.
They dragged him down, to the Apsu they pulled him.
He took the plant, though it pricked his hand,
and cut the heavy stones from his feet,
letting the waves throw him onto its shores.
Gilgamesh spoke to Urshanabi, the ferryman, saying:
    "Urshanabi, this plant is a plant against decay
    by which a man can attain his survival.
    I will bring it to Uruk-Haven,
    and have an old man eat the plant to test it.
    The plant's name is 'The Old Man Becomes a Young Man.'[36]
    Then I will eat it and return to the condition of my youth."
At twenty leagues they broke for some food,

---

[35]*Magillu* is the name of a boat taken from earlier mythology.

[36]The same as the apparent meaning of the name *Gilgamesh*.

at thirty leagues they stopped for the night.
Seeing a spring and how cool its waters were,
Gilgamesh went down and was bathing in the water.
A snake smelled the fragrance of the plant,
silently came up and carried off the plant.
While going back it sloughed off its casing.
At that point Gilgamesh sat down, weeping,
his tears streaming over the side of his nose.
    "Counsel me, O ferryman Urshanabi!
    For whom have my arms labored, Urshanabi?
    For whom has my heart's blood roiled?
    I have not secured any good deed for myself,
    but done a good deed for the 'lion of the ground'![37]
    Now the high waters are coursing twenty leagues distant,
    as I was opening the conduit I turned my equipment over
                into it.
    What can I find to serve as a marker for me?
    I will turn back from the journey by sea and leave the boat by
                the shore!"

Deeds over Death

At twenty leagues they broke for some food,
at thirty leagues they stopped for the night.
They arrived in Uruk-Haven.
Gilgamesh said to Urshanabi, the ferryman:
    "Go up Urshanabi, onto the wall of Uruk and walk around.
    Examine its foundation, inspect its brickwork thoroughly—
    is not even the core of the brick structure of kiln-fired brick,
    and did not the Seven Sages themselves lay out its plan?
    One league city, one league palm gardens, one league lowlands,
                the open area of the Ishtar Temple,
    three leagues and the open area of Uruk the wall encloses."

---

[37]Perhaps "chameleon."

2

꙳

INANNA'S DESCENT

*E*vidence suggests the Sumerian myth Inanna's Descent *dates to the Third
Dynasty (ca. 2100–2000* B.C.*) of Ur, the leading city of southern
Mesopotamia. This was a period in which some of the rulers, notably the
monarch Shulgi, were concerned to preserve older literary works and to encourage the creation of new ones. With the end of this dynasty came the end of
Sumerian civilization. The schools that followed did much to preserve the older
"classics," developing a class of scholars.*

*Inanna's Descent, an epic thought to be pieced together from at least two
earlier mythic versions, belongs to that period of Sumerian civilization in which
the celebration of rulers and gods continued to be part of the creative process, a
process that doubtless dated back to the beginnings of oral literature. Inanna
plays several roles in Sumerian mythology: Goddess of love and war, she is represented in various roles, including daughter of Nanna (or Anu), sky-god and
father of the gods, and granddaughter of Enlil, chief deity of the Sumerian gods.
In* Inanna's Descent *Inanna instructs her servant to appeal to both these gods for
help, and is turned down. Her final, successful appeal is to Enki, represented here
as her father. Inanna's identity reaches beyond her parentage: she is associated
with the planet Venus, making her goddess of the morning and evening star; and
she is also associated with herd animals, hence her treatment in the underworld
as a slab of meat. Finally, she is wife to the shepherd Dumuzi, the figure who
must stand in for her as sacrifice to the forces of the underworld.*

*In this myth, Inanna descends to the underworld realm of her sister,
Ereshkigala, for obscure reasons. The first half of the narrative deals with her progressive divestment of clothes and adornments and then with her death at
Ereshkigala's command. However, Enki intervenes, and, in scenes that evoke visits to the underworld in other cultures' mythologies, such as those of the Greek
Orpheus and Demeter, his emissaries are able to revive Inanna and restore her to
the world of the living. Inanna, however, must find a substitute to take her place.
Here the second half of the myth begins: The candidate chosen by Inanna for this
task is Dumuzi, the only figure she approached who had not mourned at her*

27

absence and death. Dumuzi attempts to flee the rangers of the underworld, taking refuge at times with Inanna herself, as well as with his sister, Geshtinanna, but to no avail. He is taken off, but with the consolation that Geshtinanna will share his fate by spending six months of every year in his place.

Echoed in the later Greek myth of Persephone, and in other myths of dying and rising gods, Inanna embodies vegetative, animal, and human beings. Goddess of love and procreation, she is, at turns, a figure for dying and rising barley, the sacrificed sheep, and the star of life and death whose rival is purchased at the price of divine sacrifice.

INANNA PLANS TO TAKE OVER HADES

From the upper heaven she had her heart set on the netherworld,
the goddess had from the upper heaven her heart set on the netherworld.
Inanna had from the upper heaven her heart set on the netherworld.[1]

My lady forsook heaven, forsook earth, went down into Hades.
Inanna forsook heaven, forsook earth, went down into Hades.
Lordship she forsook, queenship she forsook, went down into Hades.

In Uruk she forsook Eanna, went down into Hades.

In Bad-Tibira she forsook Emushkalamma, went down into Hades;
in Zabalam she forsook Giguna, went down into Hades;
in Adab she forsook Eshara, went down into Hades;
in Nippur she forsook Ebaragdurgara, went down into Hades;

In Kishi she forsook Hursag-kalamma, went down into Hades;
in Akkade she forsook E-ulmash, went down into Hades.[2]

Reprinted from Thorkild Jacobsen, "Inanna's Descent" from *The Harps That Once . . .: Sumerian Poetry in Translation.* Copyright 1987, 206–232. Reprinted by permission of Yale University Press.

[1]In one of her aspects, Inanna was goddess of the planet Venus, the morning and evening star. As such, she identifies herself at the gate of Hades. However, she also represents herd animals, and thus embodies mythic qualities of the heavens above and the earth below, the abode of the dead. This is the realm of death to which Inanna goes, although, in the following paragraph, she is depicted as going down to Hades. *Hades* (really a Greek reference) is the translator's term for an abode of the dead associated with the fearsome mountains of the east, a realm apparently joined by function to the netherworld by the poem's composer.

[2]This is a list of Inanna's major cult centers and temples; this list indicates that she took a route east and then north from Uruk.

The seven powers of office she bundled,
hugged the powers, kept them handy;
fetched out the stored-away
mittu-weapon.

Kaffieh and *aghal,* the desert headdress, she put on her head;
the wig of her brow she took; held in the hand the pure yardstick and
    measuring line.
Small lapis lazuli beads she hung around her neck,
with yoked oval stone beads she covered her chest.
Gold bracelets she slipped over her hands;
and the breast-shields named "O man, come hither, come hither!" she
    drew over her chest.
With the robe of office, the robe of queenship, she covered her back;
the kohl named "O may he come, may he come!" she put on her eyes.

SHE PROVIDES AGAINST POSSIBLE FAILURE

Inanna was walking toward Hades,
her page Ninshubur[3] was walking at her side,
Holy Inanna said to Ninshubur:
    "My ever-loyal one,
    my page of fair words,
    my envoy of true words,
    I am now going down into Hades,
    if I stay gone to Hades
    set up resounding wailings for me,
    sound the tambourine[4] for me in the assemblies of administrators,
    make the rounds for me of the gods' houses,
    claw at your eyes for grief for me, claw at your mouth for me,
    claw, in the places one goes not with a man, your big belly for me!
    Dress in a one-ply garment for me like one who has no man![5]
    Wend first your foot to Enlil's temple, Ekur,
    and upon your entering Enlil's temple, Ekur,
    weep before Enlil saying:

---

[3]*Ninshubur* is the name of a god as well as a goddess. When it refers to Inanna's hand maiden and page, it is that of a goddess.

[4]An instrument typically used to accompany lamentations.

[5]That is, one who has no one responsible for her as head of a household to which she belongs. To dress in a one-ply garment was a mark of poverty and is here a sign of mourning.

'O Father Enlil! Let no man put to death your child in Hades!
Let him not mix your good silver in among Hades's dust,
   let him not cut up your good lapis lazuli in among the flint-
     arrowhead maker's stones,
   let him not split up your good boxwood in among the carpen-
     ter's lumber,
   let him not put to death in Hades the maiden Inanna!'[6]

If Enlil stands not by you in this matter, go on to Ur!

In Ur, the nation's birth-chamber,[7]
upon your entering Ekishnugal, Nanna's temple
weep before Nanna saying:
   'Father Nanna! Let no man put to death your child in Hades
   Let him not mix your good silver in among Hades's dust,
   let him not cut up your good lapis lazuli in among the flint-
     arrowhead maker's stones,
   let him not split up your good boxwood in among the carpen-
     ter's lumber,
   let him not put to death in Hades the maiden Inanna!'

If Nanna stands not by you in this matter, go on to Eridu!

Upon your entering E-engur, Enki's temple,
weep before Enki saying:
   'Father Enki! Let no man put to death your child in Hades!
   Let him not mix your good silver in among Hades's dust,
   let him not cut up your good lapis lazuli in among the flint-
     arrowhead maker's stones,
   let him not split up your good boxwood in among the carpen-
     ter's lumber,
   let him not put to death in Hades the maiden Inanna!'

Father Enki, a lord of vast intelligence,
knows the grass of life, knows the water of life.
May he make me come alive!"

Inanna was walking toward Hades,
to her page Ninshubur she said:
   "Go, Ninshubur,
   and toss not your head at my orders I have given you!"

---

[6]That is, do not treat what is valuable (silver, etc.) as merely ordinary (dust); do not treat the goddess Inanna as a mere mortal.

[7]Sumer and Akkad were united as a nation only under the Third Dynasty of Ur. Thus Ur was the "birth-chamber" of the nation.

INANNA SEEKS ENTRY INTO HADES

When Inanna had come close to Egalkurzagin,[8]
she wickedly rammed things against the door of Hades,
shouted wickedly into Hades's palace:
> "Open the house instantly! Gatekeeper, open the house instantly!
> Open the house instantly! Neti, open the house instantly, and let me
> go in to my wailing!"

Neti, chief gatekeeper,
answered holy Inanna saying:
> "And who might you be? You!"

> "I am Inanna, toward where the sun rises!"

> "If you are Inanna toward where the sun rises,
> why have you gone away to a land of no return?
> How could your heart take you on a road that he who goes it travels
> not back?"

Holy Inanna replied to him:
> "My elder sister Ereshkigala
> —to have the obsequies for Gugalanna,[9] her husband, who was
> killed,
> [and highly] viewed—
> is pouring grandiosely at his wake. That's why!"

Neti, Hades's chief gatekeeper,
answered holy Inanna saying:
> "Wait for me, Inanna, let me speak to my mistress,
> let me speak to my mistress Ereshkigala, let me make you known
> to her!"

Neti, Hades's chief gatekeeper,
went into the house to Ereshkigala, his mistress, and said to her:
> "My mistress! A single maiden,
> tall like a god, has approached Egalkurzagin;
> she wickedly rammed things against the door of Hades,
> shouted wickedly into Hades's palace,
> In Eanna she . . .,

---

[8]*Egalkurzagin* is a name for the abode of the dead. It means "lustrous mountain palace," apparently referring to the shining, snow-covered mountains.

[9]The thunderstorms of spring were regarded as a battle between a celestial lion or lion–bird and a celestial bull in which the bull was killed. The bull was called *Gugalanna*, "the great bull of heaven," and was Ereshkigala's husband.

the seven powers of office she has bundled,
has hugged the powers, kept them handy,
has fetched out the stored-away *mittu*-weapon.

Kaffieh and *aghal,* the desert headdress, she has put on her head,
the wig of her brow she has taken,
holds in the hand a pure yardstick and measuring line.
Small lapis lazuli beads she has hung around her neck,
with yoked oval stone beads she has covered her chest.
Gold bracelets she has slipped over her hands,
the breast-shield named
'O man, come hither, come hither!' she has drawn over her chest;
the kohl named
'O may he come, may he come!' she has put on her eyes.
With the robe of office. The robe of queenship, she has covered
her back!"

ERESHKIGALA DECIDES TO FACE HER

That day did Ereshkigala smite her thigh,[10] bite her lip, and cry out in
anger.
To Neti, her chief gatekeeper she said:
"Come, my Neti, Hades's chief gatekeeper,
toss not your head at the order I am to give you!
Let the bolts be drawn on Hades's seven great gates,
and let the doorleaf of the Ganzir palace [the facade of Hades] be
pushed open first
After she has entered,
crouching down, having had the clothes stripped off,[11] someone can
usher her in."

INANNA IS STRIPPED

Neti, Hades's chief gatekeeper,
obeyed his mistress's orders,
drew back the bolts on Hades's seven great gates,
and pushed open first the doorleaf of the Ganzir palace,
the facade of Hades.

---

[10]Indicating that she has arrived at a decision and probably that she is ready to have it out with Inanna.

[11]The dead are stripped of their clothes and buried crouching down. Inanna's actions would seem to indicate that she is submitting to the authority of Hades and so is on a par with mortals.

To holy Inanna he said:
  "Come, Inanna, come in through it!"
After she had entered in,
someone had slipped off her *kaffieh* and *aghal,* the desert headdress, of
    her head.

  "Why was that?"

  "Be quiet, Inanna, an office of Hades has been faultlessly performed.
  Inanna, open not your mouth against Hades's sacred functions!"

After she had entered through the second great gate,
someone had slipped off her the pure yardstick and measuring line.

  "Why was that?"

  "Be quiet, Inanna, an office of Hades has been faultlessly performed.
  Inanna, open not your mouth against Hades's sacred functions!"

After she had entered through the third great gate,
someone had slipped off her the small lapis lazuli beads of her neck.

  "Why was that?"

  "Be quiet, Inanna, an office of Hades has been faultlessly performed.
  Inanna, open not your mouth against Hades's sacred functions!"

After she had entered through the fourth great gate,
someone had slipped off her the yoked oval stone beads of her chest.

  "Why was that?"

  "Be quiet, Inanna, an office of Hades has been faultlessly performed.
  Inanna, open not your mouth against Hades's sacred functions!"

After she had entered through the fifth great gate,
someone had slipped off her the gold rings of her hands.

  "Why was that?"

  "Be quiet, Inanna, an office of Hades has been faultlessly performed.
  Inanna, open not your mouth against Hades's sacred functions!"

After she had entered through the sixth great gate,
someone had slipped off her the breast-shield named 'O man, come
    hither, come hither!'

  "Why was that?"

  "Be quiet, Inanna, an office of Hades has been faultlessly performed.
  Inanna, open not your mouth against Hades's sacred functions!"

After she had entered through the seventh great gate,
someone had slipped off her the robe of office, the robe of queenship
    off her back.

"Why was that?"

"Be quiet, Inanna, an office of Hades has been faultlessly performed.
Inanna, open not your mouth against Hades's sacred functions!"

INANNA ATTEMPTS TO USURP ERESHKIGALA'S THRONE AND IS PUNISHED

Crouching down having had the clothes stripped off, she was led in
    by a man.
Holy Ereshkigala she made get up out of her chair
and in her chair she sat down.

The Anunnaki, the seven judges, rendered judgment to her face,
their verdict was a verdict gripping the bowels,
they cried out against her, it was the call for punishment!
Killed she was, and turned into a slab of tainted meat,[12]
and the slab of tainted meat a man hung from a peg.

NINSHUBUR FOLLOWS ORDERS

When three days and three nights had gone by,
her page Ninshubur,
her page, fair of words,
her envoy, true of words,
was setting up resounding wailings for her.
The tambourine which she sounded for her in the assemblies of
    administrators,
she had made the rounds for her of the gods' houses.
She clawed at her eyes for grief for her, clawed at her mouth for her,
and in the places one goes not with a man, she clawed her big belly
    for her.
Like one who has no man, she dressed in a one-ply garment for her.

Her foot she wended first to Enlil's temple, Ekur,
and upon her entering Enlil's temple, Ekur,
wept before Enlil saying:
    "Father Enlil! Let no man put to death your child in Hades!
    Let him not mix your good silver in among Hades's dust,
        let him not cut up your good lapis lazuli in among the flint-
            arrowhead maker's stones,

---

[12]Thus indicating her association with herd animals.

let him not split up your good boxwood in among the carpenter's lumber,

let him not put to death in Hades the maiden Inanna!"

Father Enlil answered Ninshubur:

"My child craved the upper heaven, craved too the netherworld;

Inanna craved the upper heaven, craved too the netherworld;

Hades's offices, demanding offices, demanding offices, have been performed effectively.

Who has ever been reached there and reclaimed?"[13]

Father Enlil stood not by her in this matter; to Ur she went.

In Ur, the nation's birth-chamber, upon her entering Ekishnugal, Nanna's temple,

she wept before Nanna saying:

"Father Nanna! Let no man put to death your child in Hades!

Let him not mix your good silver in with Hades's dust,

let him not cut up your good lapis lazuli in among the flint-arrowhead maker's stones,

let him not split up your good boxwood in among the carpenter's lumber,

let him not put to death in Hades the maiden Inanna!"

Father Nanna answered Ninshubur:

"My child craved the upper heaven, craved too the netherworld;

Inanna craved the upper heaven, craved too the netherworld;

Hades's offices, demanding offices, demanding offices, have been performed effectively.

Who has ever been reached there and reclaimed?"

Father Nanna stood not by her in this matter. To Eridu she went.

Upon her entering E-engur, Enki's temple,

she wept before Enki saying:

"Father Enki! Let no man put to death your child in Hades!

Let him not mix your good silver in with Hades's dust,

let him not cut up your good lapis lazuli in with the flint arrowhead maker's stones,

let him not split up your good boxwood in with the carpenter's lumber,

let him not put to death in Hades the maiden Inanna!"

---

[13]Enlil here, and Nanna next, express a natural reaction to the news of Inanna. Hades lies outside the jurisdiction of the gods above, so they can do nothing. Furthermore, what has happened is in the natural order of things. The offices of Hades have been realized and performed, as is proper.

ENKI PLANS TO TRICK ERESHKIGALA INTO MAKING A RASH PROMISE

Father Enki answered Ninshubur:
> "What has been done to my child down there? She has me worried!
> What has been done to Inanna down there? She has me worried!
> What has been done to the queen of all lands down there? She has me worried!
> What has been done to heaven's holy one down there? She has me worried!"[14]

From under his fingernail he brought out dirt, and fashioned from
> it a *myrmidon.*

From under another fingernail of his he brought out dirt, and fashioned
> from it a young elegist.[15]

To the *myrmidon* he gave the grass of life,
to the young elegist he gave the water of life.
Father Enki said to the young elegist and the *myrmidon:*
> "Go! Lay the foot toward Hades!
> When you have flown like flies over the doorleaves,
> when you have wiggled like lizards past the door-pivots,
> Lo! The mother who gave birth,
> Ereshkigala, lies sick with grief for her little ones.
> Her holy shoulders no linen veils,
> her bosom, like oil cruses, has nothing drawn over it,
> her nails are like a copper rake upon her,
> her hair?—Leaks she has on her head![16]
> When she is saying 'Woe, my heart!'
> Say to her: 'You are aweary, my lady, woe your heart!'
> When she is saying: 'Woe, my liver!'
> Say to her: 'You are aweary, my lady, woe your liver!'"

---

[14]Enki is disturbed more personally and deeply than Enlil and Nanna. He thinks not just in terms of power to command, but he explores ways to achieve his goal by guile. Enki's special emotional involvement arises because he is Inanna's father. In another version of the myth, Inanna is the daughter of Nanna and granddaughter of Enlil, the first two gods Inanna's servant approached for help.

[15]The *myrmidon* is a member of the cult personnel around Inanna. along with the elegist (or poet), he is a professional mourner.

[16]Ereshkigala is presented as a typical mourner, a mother lamenting the death of her young children: she has rent her clothes, clawed herself with her nails, and pulled her hair in gestures of grief.

She will ask:

> "Who are you to whom I have spoken from my heart to your
>   hearts, from my liver to your livers
>   If you be gods, let me talk with you,
>   if you be humans, let me determine your circumstances for you!'
> Adjure her by the life's breath of heaven, by the life's breath of earth,
>   and say to her . . .
> They will offer you the river at its high water; may you not
>   accept it.
> They will offer you the field when in grain; may you not accept it.
> Say to her: 'Give us the slab of tainted meat hanging from the peg!'
> Throw on it one the grass of life, one the water of life, and may
>   Inanna rise!"

THE RUSE SUCCEEDS

The young elegist and the *myrmidon* obeyed Enki's orders.
Over the doorleaves they flew like flies,
wiggled like lizards past the door-pivots,
Lo! The mother who gave birth
Ereshkigala, lay sick with grief for her little ones.
Her holy shoulders no linen veiled,
her bosom, like oil cruses, had nothing drawn over it,
her nails were like a copper rake upon her.
Her hair?—Leaks she had on her head!

When she said "Woe, my heart!"
they said to her: "You are aweary, my lady, woe your heart!"
When she said, "Woe, my liver!"
they said to her: "You are aweary, my lady, woe your liver!"

She said to them:
  "Who are you
    to whom I have spoken from my heart to your heart, from my liver
      to your liver?
  If you be gods let me talk with you,
    if you be humans, let me determine your circumstances for you!"[17]

They adjured her by the life's breath of heaven by the life's
breath of earth and said to her . . .

---

[17]Lamenting for somebody, or with somebody, was a highly valued kindness. Ereshkigala
feels beholden to the two strangers who take pity on her in her lone mourning and she
will offer to do something for them in return.

They offered them the river at its high waters, but they accepted it not.
They offered them the field when in grain, but they accepted it not.

"Give us the slab of tainted meat hanging from the peg!"

Holy Ereshkigala replied to it, to the young elegist and the *myrmidon:*
"The slab of tainted meat is the property of your mistress!"
"Though the slab of tainted meat be the property of our mistress
        give it to us!" they said to her.

They were being given the tainted slab of meat hanging on the peg
and threw upon it, one the grass of life, one the water of life,
and Inanna rose.

THE REVIVED INANNA MUST
PROVIDE A SUBSTITUTE

Inanna was about to ascend from Hades,
but the Anunnaki laughed at it saying:
"What man has ever, ascending from Hades, ascended scot-free?
If Inanna is to ascend from Hades,
    let her give it one head in lieu of her head!"

Inanna was ascending from Hades.
Little rangers, like unto reeds for lance-shafts,
big rangers, like unto bamboo,
walked beside her.
The man in front of her, though no herald, held a staff in the hand,
the one behind her, though not an envoy, had tied a weapon unto
        the hip.

The men who followed her to him,[18]
the men who followed Inanna to him,
knew not food, knew not drink,
ate not offerings of flour strewn,
did not drink libated water,
They took the wife from a man's lap,
took the child from the wet-nurse's breast.

Inanna was ascending from Hades.

When Inanna had ascended from Hades,
her page Ninshubur threw herself at her feet;
she had sat in the dust, was dressed in dirty clothing.

---

[18]The word *him* refers to a substitute to be designated.

The rangers said to Holy Inanna:
    "Inanna, go on to your city, and let us carry her off!"

Holy Inanna answered the rangers:
    "My page, fair of words,
    my envoy true of words,
    was not letting go of my instructions,
    did not toss her head at the orders I had given!
    She set up resounding wailings for me.
    The tambourine which she sounded for me in the assemblies of
        administrators,
    she made go for me the rounds of the gods' houses.
    She clawed at her eyes for grief for me, clawed at her mouth,
    and in the places one goes not with a man, she clawed her big belly
        for me.
    Like one who has no man she dressed in a one-ply garment for me.
    To Enlil's temple, Ekur,
    to Nanna's temple in Ur, and
    to Eridu and Enki's temple,
    she went for me and had me come alive.
    How could you give me another such?"

    "Let us go for him, let us go for him, to Sigkurshaga in Umma!"

In Umma, from Sigkurshaga,
Shara[19] threw himself at her feet;
he had sat in the dust, was dressed in dirty clothing.

The rangers said to holy Inanna:
    "Inanna, go on to your city and let us carry him off!"
Holy Inanna answered the rangers:
    "My singer of songs, Shara,
    my one who clips my nails, my one who ties the hair-bunch on
        my neck,
    how could you give me another such?"
    "Let us go for him, let us go for him, to Emushkalamma in
        Bad-Tibira!"

In Bad-Tibira, from Emushkalamma,
Lulal threw himself at her feet. In his city
he had sat in the dust, was dressed in dirty clothing.
The rangers said to holy Inanna:
    "Inanna, go on to your city, and let us carry him off!"

---

[19]Shara, the city god of Umma, usually counts as Inanna's son, though here he appears
rather to be her personal servant or beautician.

Holy Inanna answered the rangers:
> "Preeminent Lulal, leading my right and left wings of the army,
> how could you give me another such?"
> "Let us go for him to the maimed apple tree in the Kullab desert!"
To the maimed apple tree in the Kullab desert they followed in
> her footsteps.

DUMUZI, FOR NOT SORROWING, IS DESIGNATED

Dumuzi had dressed in a grand garment and sat seated in grandeur.[20]

The rangers swept into his fold,
and pouring out the milk from all seven churns,
they bumped him seven strong, as if *he* were the intruder,
starting by hitting the shepherd in the face with the reed pipes
> and flutes.

She looked at him, it was a look to kill;
she gave him orders, it was an order gripping the bowels;
she called out to them, it was a call for punishment:
> "How long must you dawdle? Carry him off!"

Holy Inanna gave the shepherd Dumuzi into their hands.

They, the men who had escorted her,
the men who went for Dumuzi,
knew not food, knew not water,
ate not offerings of flour strewn,
did not drink libated water.
They bent not over to that sweet thing, a wife's loins,
they did not kiss that dainty thing, a child.
They would make a man's child get up from his knee,
would make a daughter-in-law leave the father-in-law's house.

DUMUZI ESCAPES

Dumuzi knit the brows, he burst into tears,
the lad lifted his hands heavenwards to the sun god:[21]

---

[20]Dumuzi's festive attire, contrasting so glaringly with the mourning garb he should have been wearing if he had been desolate at the loss of Inanna, triggers Inanna's jealousy and hot anger.

[21]The sun god, Utu, was the guardian of justice and fairness. He was also, as Inanna's brother, Dumuzi's brother-in-law. In this part of the composition the standard pattern is followed in which Inanna appears as the sister of Utu, both of them children of Nanna and Ningal. She is not, as in the earlier part, seen as the daughter of Enki.

"Sun god! You are my brother-in-law, I am your brother-in-law,
I carry the butter to your mother's house,[22]
I carry the milk to Ningal's house.
When you have made my hands like unto the feet of a
　　skink [lizard],
　　when you have made my feet like unto the feet of a skink,
　　let me escape from my rangers, and may they not catch me!"

[The text has a lacuna here. It must have told how the sun god granted Dumuzi's wish, changed him into a skink—and told how he escaped. Presumably he fled to Inanna in Uruk. The rangers follow.]

The little ranger opened the mouth and said to the big ranger:
　　"Come! Let us go with him to Inanna's holy loins!"[23]

The rangers entered Uruk and seized holy Inanna:
　　"Come Inanna! Get started on your journey, get going descending
　　　　into Hades!
Go to the place your heart desired, descending into Hades,
go to Ereshkigala's place descending into Hades!
May you not dress in your queenly robe, the holy robe of office,
the robe of queenship, descending into Hades!
And when you have taken off the decorous and illustrious holy
　　crown of your head, descending into Hades;
you should not take your gay wig, descending into Hades;
unstrap your shoes the 'wild-dog puppies' of your feet,
descending into Hades.
Where you are descending no . . .!"

RECAPTURE AND SECOND ESCAPE

They reviled holy Inanna, they . . . her,
and Inanna in her panic gave them Dumuzi in hand.

As for the lad, they were putting huge hobbles on his feet;
as for the lad, they were ensnaring him, were putting a neck stock on
　　his shoulders,
henzir weapons, *kibir* axes, huge copper spears, they were carrying up
　　before him,

---

[22]As the shepherd, Dumuzi naturally would supply his mother-in-law's house with these delicacies.

[23]"Holy loins" seems oddly out of place here. It may be that the ranger envisioned Dumuzi as forgiven and in Inanna's embrace. More likely, though, the phrase is a stereotypical formula, used as a standard description of movement toward Inanna in sexual circumstances.

great axes they were sharpening.
They made the lad stand up, made him sit down,
the clothes of his back they threw down, set up . . .
As for the lad, they tied his arms, and valuing his clothes at thirty
        shekels only
covered his eyes with his own clothes.

SECOND ESCAPE

The lad lifted his hands heavenward to the sun god:
    "Sun god, I am your comrade, you are a gallant, you know me!
    Your sister, whom I took to wife,
    she, having descended into Hades,
    so as to ascend from Hades,
    wants to give me to Hades as substitute.
    O sun god, you are a fair judge, let her not wrong me!

    When you have changed my hands, when you have switched
        my frame,
    let me slip out of the hands of my rangers, and may they not
        catch me!
    Like a noble serpent I shall traverse plain and hills,
    let me flee for my life to my sister Geshtinanna's place!"

The sun god accepted his tearful plea
changed his hands, switched his frame.
A noble serpent he traversed plain and hills,
like a bird in flight from a falcon's talons Dumuzi tended to his life,
fled for his life to Geshtinanna's place.

GESHTINANNA PROTECTS
HER BROTHER

Geshtinanna, looking at her brother,
clawed at her cheeks for grief, clawed at her mouth,
pulled out the pin of the front of her dress, and rent her dress with it;
over the ill-used lad she was voicing bitter lament forsooth:
    "Woe, my brother! Woe, my brother! the lad who that day was not
        wrapped for burial!
    Woe, my brother, the shepherd Ama-ushumgal-anna, the lad who
        that day was not, amid wails, wrapped for burial!
    Woe, my brother, the lad who will not wed a wife, will not have
        a child!
    Woe, my brother, who will have no comrade, will have no friend!

Woe, my brother, the lad for whom his mother will see no good
fortune!"[24]
The rangers were seeking Dumuzi, cast around for him.

The little ranger said to the big ranger:
"Rangers have no mercy, have no fathers, mothers, wives, brothers,
sisters, or children;
ever since the days the nation was founded, since heaven was
removed from earth,
you have been rangers for shoving people along,
such have no clemency or kindness, know not good and evil!

Whoever saw a man find safety for his life in a house not his own?
We will not go for him to the place of his comrade, we will not go
for him to the place of his father-in-law,
let us go for the shepherd to Geshtinanna's place!"

The gendarmes had let him slip out of their hands, they were
seeking him,
and before she had finished that wailing
the rangers followed him to Geshtinanna's place.

"Show me where your brother is!" they said to her, but she was not
giving out that information.
She came up to the wool, plucked it in the shearing place, but she was
not giving out that information.
She came up to a piece of ground, dug with her hoe there, but she
was not giving out that information.
She came up to the skins, was tying them up on the ground with her
string, but she was not giving out that information.
She was pouring out her loins' bedding of chaff, but she was not giving
out that information,
and they did not discover Dumuzi in Geshtinanna's house.
The little ranger said to the big ranger:
"Come, let us go for him to the holy sheepfold!"

---

[24]The composer of the poem apparently used a standard Geshtinanna lament in which she
mourned her brother who lay slain by bandits in the desert without decent burial and
who was still an unmarried youth without child. Here, one can see the pursuit by the
rangers as implying that Dumuzi already was dead and lying unburied in the desert.
Also, he would have to be considered engaged only, not married, to Inanna.

DUMUZI CAPTURED IN HOLY SHEEPFOLD

In his holy sheepfold they seized Dumuzi,
they surrounded him and seized him, they sought him and they
saw him.
The house protected not the lad, an axe was taken to the door,
they sharpened their hip-daggers and surrounded him in the enclosed
space.

GESHTINANNA SEEKS HIM

The sister, for the sake of her brother, tore around the city like a
circling bird.
"Let me go to my brother so ill used! I will enter any household!"
[The text has a second lacuna here. A relevant passage in a Dumuzi lament indicates that the fly told Geshtinanna that her brother was held in the brewery with the wise brewmasters. Geshtinanna must have joined her brother there. When the text resumes, the fly is mentioned, and one may conjecture that it pleaded with Inanna on Geshtinanna's behalf.]

INANNA'S EASEMENT OF TERM

The fly . . .
The maiden Inanna answered the fly:[25]
"In the beer brewery . . .,
as with the doers of equal tasks, let me determine conditions for them!"
So now, by Inanna's determining conditions, thus it verily is.

Dumuzi broke into tears thereat:
"My sister has come, she has been given into their hands together
with me!
Alas now! Her life is lost!"
[to which Inanna seems to answer:]
"You half a year only, you sister half a year only.
When you demand it she will spend the days in question.
When your sister demands it you will spend the days in question."

Holy Inanna was giving Dumuzi as substitute for herself.
O holy Ereshkigala!
Praise of you is sweet!

---

[25]The section of the tale dealing with Geshtinanna's search for Dumuzi and joining him in Hades does not belong with the myth dealing with Dumuzi as shepherd, but to another, variant group of myths in which he is god of barley and beer and brother of the goddess of the grapevine stock and its wine, Geshtinanna. Both Dumuzi and Geshtinanna at different times of the year go underground in storage as, respectively, beer and wine.

3

❦

EGYPTIAN LITERATURE OF THE MIDDLE KINGDOM

As in Sumer (Selection 2), writing appears at the dawn of Egyptian civiliza-tion as a form of picture-writing called hieroglyphics in which individual words are represented by pictorial symbols. As these symbols evolved into syllabic sounds, a sophisticated writing system developed that permitted such notations as lists of fabrics, foods, and ointments to decorate the walls of private tombs. These early forms of writing date to the first Egyptian dynasty, beginning around 3,000 B.C. (see chronology of the kingdoms below).

Eventually the tombs served as the site for the inscription of prayers for the dead, and for the earliest and most quintessential form of literature, the autobi-ography. As praise-songs for the dead, laudatory records of the life of the deceased, these early writings grew increasingly elaborate with time, joining prayers for offerings with individual accomplishments. Catalogues of the virtues of the dead person emerged in formal style, whereas the autobiographical narrative developed as freer prose.

A third literary form also emerged in the next thousand years, the instruction, a composition in which maxims are strung together, reflecting the "wisdom" of the sages. These were the first literary compositions attributed to specific authors, often those whose supposed authorship gave additional authority and prestige to the text. This is the case, for example, with biblical wisdom literature, like the Proverbs attributed to King Solomon.

For the ancient Egyptians these literary forms were highly regarded, as the art of using words well gave high status to the scribes. There was little change in the basic compositions until the time of the Middle Kingdom, around the second mil-lennium B.C. This period ushered in the classical age of Egyptian literature, and brought with it a vast number of literary works, combining narratives with cata-logues of virtues and prayers, hymns to the gods and praises to the kings. The art of fiction developed less-elevated forms of narrative: prose tales, deriving from oral sources hitherto unrecorded.

A good example of this Middle Kingdom fictional genre is "The Tale of the Shipwrecked Sailor," a seemingly simple account of an official being entertained by one of his attendants on their return home. The official is despondent, and the story meant to cheer him up deals with the miraculous adventure that befell his attendant when he was shipwrecked on an island. The story has all the appearance of a fable, with monsters, kings, and treasure spicing the tale. The geographical references, the high-flown language, and the subtle evocation of the supernatural all give the tale a deeper resonance than would appear on the surface.

The "Story of Sinuhe" is the most famous narrative of the Twelfth Dynasty. It has the qualities of high literature as it is recounted in the form of a personal autobiography composed for the tomb. It makes reference to the death of an actual ruler, Amenemhet I (1991–1962 B.C.) and to the ascension to the throne of his son, Sesostris I, and is narrated from the point of view of a courtly attendant, the "Prince, Count, Governor of the domains of the sovereign," Sinuhe. Containing a rich variety of literary modes, it is presented as a work of sophistication, not folk simplicity, with praise-songs, poetical interludes, and proverbial sayings interspersed in the account of Sinuhe's life story. Fearful for his life, Sinuhe flees Egypt and makes his fortune in foreign lands. Eventually, he returns to his homeland and dies there amidst great honors. Numerous copies of this work have been found, attesting to its widespread popularity in ancient Egypt.

During the Middle Kingdom one finds earlier forms persisting from earlier periods: monumental inscriptions, spells on coffins, didactic instructions, indexes, and especially songs and hymns that express religious values and embody cultic traditions. Although some popular songs have survived in fragments, it is mostly hymns associated with temple rites and songs accompanied by the harp, termed harper's songs, that one finds. The songs invariably are linked to the fate of the dead, while the hymns contain praise for the deities and the kings. During this period of the Middle Kingdom the reflections on death cease to be mechanical repetitions of pious hopes for a better afterlife, and, as with "The Song from the Tomb of King Intef," express sentiments echoed later in the biblical Psalms: "Heap up your joys/ Let your heart not sink!/ Follow your heart and your happiness,/ Do your things on earth as your heart commands!"

Broad Chronology of Egyptian History

The Archaic Period:	Dynasties 1–2 (ca. 3,000–2,650 B.C.)
The Old Kingdom:	Dynasties 3–8 (ca. 2650–2135 B.C.)
The Transition to the Middle Kingdom:	Dynasties 9–mid-11 (ca. 2135–2040 B.C.)
The Middle Kingdom:	Dynasties 11–14 (ca. 2040–1650 B.C.)
The Hyksos Period:	Dynasties 15–17 (ca. 1650–1550 B.C.)
The New Kingdom:	Dynasties 18–20 (ca. 1550–1080 B.C.)
The Late Period:	Dynasties 21–31 (1080–332 B.C.)

THE TALE OF THE SHIPWRECKED SAILOR[1]

The worthy attendant said: Take heart, my lord! We have reached home. The mallet has been seized, the mooring-post staked, the prow-rope placed on land. Praise is given, god is thanked, everyone embraces his fellow. Our crew has returned safely; our troops have had no loss. We have left Wawat behind, we have passed Senmut; we have returned in safety, we have reached our land. Now listen to me, my lord! I am not exaggerating. Wash yourself, pour water over your fingers. You must answer when questioned. You must speak to the king with presence of mind. You must answer without stammering! A man's mouth can save him. His speech makes one forgive him. But do as you like! It is tiresome to talk to you.

But I shall tell you something like it that happened to me. I had set out to the king's mines, and had gone to sea in a ship of a hundred and twenty cubits in length and forty cubits in width. One hundred and twenty sailors were in it of the pick of Egypt. Looked they at sky, looked they at land, their hearts were stouter than lions. They could foretell a storm before it came, a tempest before it broke.

A storm came up while we were at sea, before we could reach land. As we sailed it made a swell, and in it a wave eight cubits tall. The mast—it [the wave] struck it. Then the ship died. Of those in it not one remained. I was cast on an island by a wave of the sea. I spent three days alone, with my heart as companion. Lying in the shelter of trees I hugged the shade.

Then I stretched my legs to discover what I might put in my mouth. I found figs and grapes there, all sorts of fine vegetables, sycamore figs, unnotched and notched,[2] and cucumbers that were as if tended. Fish were there and fowl; there is nothing that was not there. I stuffed myself and put some down, because I had too much in my arms. Then I cut a fire drill, made a fire, and gave a burnt offering to the gods.

Then I heard a thundering noise and thought, "It is a wave of the sea." Trees splintered, the ground trembled. Uncovering my face, I found it was a snake that was coming. He was of thirty cubits; his beard was over two cubits long. His body

---

"The Tale of the Shipwrecked Sailor," "The Story of Sinuhe," "A Cycle of Hymns to King Sesostris III," "A Hymn to Osiris," "The Hymn to Hapy," "Three Harpers' Songs," from *Ancient Egyptian Literature,* vol. I: "The Old and Middle Kingdoms," by Miriam Lichtheim, copyright 1973 Regents of the University of California. Pp. 212–215, 223–233, 198–200, 203–209, 194, 196–197. Reprinted by permission of the University of California Press.

[1]A high official is returning from an expedition that apparently failed in its objective, for he is despondent and fearful of the reception awaiting him at court. One of his attendants exhorts him to take courage, and as an example of how a disaster may turn into a success, tells him of a marvelous adventure that happened to him years ago. At the end of the tale, however, the official remains despondent.

[2]That is, unripe and ripe figs.

was overlaid with gold; his eyebrows were of real lapis lazuli. He was bent up in front.

Then he opened his mouth to me, while I was on my belly before him. He said to me: "Who brought you, who brought you, fellow, who brought you? If you delay telling me who brought you to this island, I shall make you find yourself reduced to ashes, becoming like a thing unseen." I said: "Though you speak to me, I do not hear it; I am before you without knowing myself." Then he took me in his mouth, carried me to the place where he lived, and set me down unhurt, I being whole with nothing taken from me.

Then he opened his mouth to me, while I was on my belly before him. He said to me: "Who brought you, who brought you, fellow, who brought you to this island of the sea, whose two sides are in water?" Then I answered him, my arms bent before him. I said to him: "I had set out to the mines on a mission of the king in a ship of a hundred and twenty cubits in length and forty cubits in width. One hundred and twenty sailors were in it of the pick of Egypt. Looked they at sky, looked they at land, their hearts were stouter than lions. They could foretell a storm before it came, a tempest before it struck. Each of them—his heart was stouter, his arm stronger than his mate's. There was no fool among them. A storm came up while we were at sea, before we could reach land. As we sailed it made a swell, and in it a wave eight cubits tall. The mast—it struck it. Then the ship died. Of those in it not one remained, except myself who is here with you. I was brought to this island by a wave of the sea."

Then he said to me: "Don't be afraid, don't be afraid, fellow; don't be pale-faced, now that you have come to me. It is god who has let you live and brought you to this island of the *ka*.[3] There is nothing that is not in it; it is full of all good things. You shall pass month upon month until you have completed four months in this island. Then a ship will come from home with sailors in it whom you know. You shall go home with them, you shall die in your town.

"How happy is he who tells what he has tasted,[4] when the calamity has passed. I shall tell you something similar that happened on this island. I was here with my brothers and there were children with them. In all we were seventy-five serpents, children and brothers, without mentioning a little daughter whom I had obtained through prayer. Then a star fell, and they went up in flames through it. It so happened that I was not with them in the fire, I was not among them. I could have died for their sake when I found them as one heap of corpses.

"If you are brave and control your heart, you shall embrace your children, you shall kiss your wife, you shall see your home. It is better than everything else. You shall reach home, you shall be there among your brothers.

Stretched out on my belly I touched the ground before him; then I said to him: "I shall speak of your power to the king, I shall let him know of your great-

---

[3]Perhaps a phantom island of the spirit world.

[4]That is, experienced.

ness. I shall send you *ibi* and *hknw* oils, laudanum, *hsyt*-spice, and the incense of the temples which pleases all the gods. I shall tell what happened to me, what I saw of your power. One will praise god for you in the city before the councillors of the whole land. I shall slaughter oxen for you as burnt offering; I shall sacrifice geese to you. I shall send you ships loaded with all the treasures of Egypt, as is done for a god who befriends people in a distant land not known to the people."

Then he laughed at me for the things I had said, which seemed foolish to him. He said to me: "You are not rich in myrrh and all kinds of incense. But I am the lord of Punt,[5] and myrrh is my very own. That *hknw*-oil you spoke of sending, it abounds on this island. Moreover, when you have left this place, you will not see this island again; it will have become water."

Then the ship came, as he had foretold. I went and placed myself on a tall tree, I recognized those that were in it. When I went to report it, I found that he knew it. He said to me: "In health, in health, fellow, to your home, that you may see your children! Make me a good name in your town; that is what I ask of you." I put myself on my belly, my arms bent before him. Then he gave me a load of myrrh, *hknw*-oil, laudanum, *hsyt*-spice, *tispss*-spice, perfume, eye-paint, giraffe's tails, great lumps of incense, elephant's tusks, greyhounds, long-tailed monkeys, baboons, and all kinds of precious things.

I loaded them on the ship. Then I put myself on my belly to thank him and he said to me: "You will reach home in two months. You will embrace your children. You will flourish at home, you will be buried."

I went down to the shore near the ship; I hailed the crew which was in the ship. I gave praise on the shore to the lord of the island, those in the ship did the same. We sailed north to the king's residence. We reached the residence in two months, all as he had said. I went in to the king; I presented to him the gifts I had brought from the island. He praised god for me in the presence of the councillors of the whole land. I was made an attendant and endowed with serfs of his.

See me after I had reached land, after I saw what I had tasted! Listen to me! It is good for people to listen.

He said to me: "Don't make an effort, my friend. Who would give water at dawn to a goose that will be slaughtered in the morning?"

Colophon: It is done from beginning to end as it was found in writing, by the scribe with skilled fingers, Imenaa, son of Imeny—life, prosperity, health!

⸙

THE STORY OF SINUHE

The prince, count, governor of the domains of the sovereign in the lands of the Asiatics, true and beloved friend of the king, the attendant Sinuhe, says:

---

[5]Punt lies to the south of Egypt, presumably near the Horn of Africa (present-day Somalia).

I was an attendant who attended his lord, a servant of the royal harem, waiting on the princess, the highly praised royal wife of King Sesostris in Khenemsut, the daughter of King Amenemhet in Kanefru, Nefru, the revered.[6]

Year thirty, third month of the inundation, day seven: the god ascended to his horizon. The king of Upper and Lower Egypt, *Sehetepibre,* flew to heaven and united with the sun-disk, the divine body merging with its maker. Then the residence was hushed; hearts grieved; the great portals were shut; the courtiers were head-on-knee; the people moaned.

His majesty, however, had despatched an army to the land of the Tjemeh, with his eldest son as its commander, the good god Sesostris. He had been sent to smite the foreign lands and to punish those of Tjehenu.[7] Now he was returning, bringing captives of the Tjehenu and cattle of all kinds beyond number. The officials of the palace sent to the western border to let the king's son know the event that had occurred at the court. The messengers met him on the road, reaching him at night. Not a moment did he delay. The falcon flew with his attendants, without letting his army know it.

But the royal sons who had been with him on this expedition had also been sent for. One of them was summoned while I was standing there. I heard his voice, as he spoke, while I was in the near distance. My heart fluttered, my arms spread out, a trembling befell all my limbs. I removed myself in leaps, to seek a hiding place. I put myself between two bushes, so as to leave the road to its traveler.

I set out southward. I did not plan to go to the residence. I believed there would be turmoil and did not expect to survive it. I crossed Maaty near Sycamore; I reached Isle-of-Snefru.[8] I spent the day there at the edge of the cultivation. Departing at dawn I encountered a man who stood on the road. He saluted me while I was afraid of him. At dinner time I reached Cattle-Quay. I crossed in a barge without a rudder, by the force of the west wind. I passed to the east of the quarry, at the height of Mistress of the Red Mountain. Then I made my way northward. I reached the Walls of the Ruler, which were made to repel the Asiatics and to crush the Sand-farers. I crouched in a bush for fear of being seen by the guard on duty upon the wall.

I set out at night. At dawn I reached Peten. I halted at Isle-of-Kem-Wer. An attack of thirst overtook me; I was parched, my throat burned. I said, "This is the

---

[6]Sinuhe was in the service of Princess Nefru, the wife of Sesostris I, the latter being co-regent at the time of his father's death. Khenemsut and Kanefru are the names of the pyramids of Sesostris I and Amenemhet I. Egyptian kings were regarded as having a divine nature.

[7]Tjemeh and Tjehenu designated two distinct Libyan peoples who merged in the course of time. In this story, the terms are used interchangeably.

[8]Sinuhe is traveling south along the edge of the western desert until he crosses the Nile at a spot called the Cattle-Quay. He lands in the vicinity of the Red Mountain (today's Gebel al-Ahmar) and only then decides to flee the country and, hence, turns northward.

taste of death." I raised my heart and collected myself when I heard the lowing sound of cattle and saw Asiatics. One of their leaders, who had been in Egypt, recognized me. He gave me water and boiled milk for me. I went with him to his tribe. What they did for me was good.

Land gave me to land. I traveled to Byblos; I returned to Qedem. I spent a year and a half there. Then Ammunenshi, the ruler of Upper Retenu, took me to him, saying to me: "You will be happy with me; you will hear the language of Egypt." He said this because he knew my character and had heard of my skill, Egyptians who were with him having borne witness for me. He said to me: "Why have you come here? Has something happened at the residence?" I said to him: "King Sehetepibre departed to the horizon, and one did not know the circumstances." But I spoke in half-truths:[9] "When I returned from the expedition to the land of the Tjemeh, it was reported to me and my heart grew faint. It carried me away on the path of flight, though I had not been talked about; no one had spat in my face; I had not heard a reproach; my name had not been heard in the mouth of the herald. I do not know what brought me to this country; it is as if planned by god. As if a delta-man[10] saw himself in Yebu, a marsh-man in Nubia."

Then he said to me: "How then is that land without that excellent god, fear of whom was throughout the lands like Sakhmet[11] in a year of plague?" I said to him in reply: "Of course his son has entered into the palace, having taken his father's heritage.

> He is a god without peer,
> No other comes before him;
> He is lord of knowledge, wise planner, skilled leader,
> One goes and comes by his will.

> He was the smiter of foreign lands,
> While his father stayed in the palace,
> He reported to him on commands carried out.

> He is a champion who acts with his arm,
> A fighter who has no equal,
> When seen engaged in archery,
> When joining the melee.

> Horn-curber who makes hands turn weak,
> His foes cannot close ranks;

---

[9]That is, he pretends that the death of the old king had been reported to him when, in fact, he had only overheard a conspiratorial message and had disclaimed any knowledge of the circumstances.

[10]A man from the Nile delta.

[11]The lion goddess.

Keen-sighted he smashes foreheads,
None can withstand his presence.

Wide-striding he smites the fleeing,
No retreat for him who turns him his back;
Steadfast in time of attack,
He makes [foes] turn back and turns not his back.

Stouthearted when he sees the mass,
He lets not slackness fill his heart;
Eager at the sight of combat,
Joyful when he works his bow.

Clasping his shield he treads under foot,
No second blow needed to kill;
None can escape his arrow,
None turn aside his bow.

The bowmen flee before him,
As before the might of the goddess;
As he fights he plans the goal,
Unconcerned about all else.

Lord of grace, rich in kindness,
He has conquered through affection;
His city loves him more than itself,
Acclaims him more than its own god.

Men outdo women in hailing him,
Now that he is king;
Victor while yet in the egg,
Set to be ruler since his birth.

Augmenter of those born with him,
He is unique, god-given;
Happy the land that he rules!

Enlarger of frontiers,
He will conquer southern lands,
While ignoring northern lands,
Though made to smite Asiatics and tread on Sand-farers!

"Send to him! Let him know your name as one who inquires while being far from his majesty. He will not fail to do good to land that will be loyal to him."

He said to me: "Well then, Egypt is happy knowing that he is strong. But you are here. You shall stay with me. What I shall do for you is good."

He set me at the head of his children. He married me to his eldest daughter. He let me choose for myself of his land, of the best that was his, on his border with another land. It was a good land called Yaa. Figs were in it and grapes. It had more wine than water. Abundant was its honey, plentiful its oil. All kinds of fruit were on its trees. Barley was there and emmer,[12] and no end of cattle of all kinds. Much also came to me because of the love of me; for he had made me chief of a tribe in the best part of his land. Loaves were made for me daily, and wine as daily fare, cooked meat, roast fowl, as well as desert game. For they snared for me and laid it before me, in addition to the catch of my hounds. Many sweets were made for me, and milk dishes of all kinds.

I passed many years, my children becoming strong men, each a master of his tribe. The envoy who came north or went south to the residence stayed with me. I let everyone stay with me. I gave water to the thirsty; I showed the way to him who had strayed; I rescued him who had been robbed. When Asiatics conspired to attack the rulers of hill-countries,[13] I opposed their movements. For this ruler of Retenu made me carry out numerous missions as commander of his troops. Every hill tribe against which I marched I vanquished, so that it was driven from the pasture of its wells. I plundered its cattle, carried off its families, seized their food, and killed people by my strong arm, by my bow, by my movements and my skillful plans. I won his heart and he loved me, for he recognized my valor. He set me at the head of his children, for he saw the strength of my arms.

> There came a hero of Retenu,
> To challenge me in my tent.
> A champion was he without peer,
> He had subdued it all.
> He said he would fight with me,
> He planned to plunder me,
> He meant to seize my cattle
> At the behest of his tribe.

The ruler conferred with me and I said: "I do not know him; I am not his ally, that I could walk about in his camp. Have I ever opened his back rooms or climbed over his fence? It is envy, because he sees me doing your commissions. I am indeed like a stray bull in a strange herd, whom the bull of the herd charges, whom the longhorn attacks. Is an inferior beloved when he becomes a superior? No Asiatic makes friends with a delta-man. And what would make papyrus cleave to the mountain? If a bull loves combat, should a champion bull retreat for fear of being equaled? If he wishes to fight, let him declare his wish. Is there a god who does not know what he has ordained, and a man who knows how it will be?"

At night I strung my bow, sorted my arrows, practiced with my dagger, polished my weapons. When it dawned Retenu came. It had assembled its tribes; it had gathered its neighboring peoples; it was intent on this combat.

---

[12]A variety of wheat.

[13]Sinuhe is on the side of the "rulers of the mountainlands," from which the name *Hyksos* was derived. In our text, they are rendered "rulers of hill-countries."

He came toward me while I waited, having placed myself near him. Every heart burned for me; the women jabbered. All hearts ached for me thinking: "Is there another champion who could fight him?" He raised his battle-axe and shield, while his armful of missiles fell toward me. When I had made his weapons attack me, I let his arrows pass me by without effect, one following the other. Then, when he charged me, I shot him, my arrow sticking in his neck. He screamed; he fell on his nose; I slew him with his axe. I raised my war-cry over his back, while every Asiatic shouted. I gave praise to Mont,[14] while his people mourned him. The ruler Ammunenshi took me in his arms.

Then I carried off his goods; I plundered his cattle. What he had meant to do to me I did to him. I took what was in his tent; I stripped his camp. Thus I became great, wealthy in goods, rich in herds. It was the god who acted, so as to show mercy to one with whom he had been angry, whom he had made stray abroad. For today his heart is appeased.

> A fugitive fled his surroundings—
> I am famed at home.
> A laggard lagged from hunger—
> I give bread to my neighbor.
> A man left his land in nakedness—
> I have bright clothes, fine linen.
> A man ran for lack of one to send—
> I am rich in servants.
> My house is fine, my dwelling spacious—
> My thoughts are at the palace!

Whichever god decreed this flight, have mercy, bring me home! Surely you will let me see the place in which my heart dwells! What is more important than that my corpse be buried in the land in which I was born! Come to my aid! What if the happy event should occur?[15] May god pity me! May he act so as to make happy the end of one whom he punished! May his heart ache for one whom he forced to live abroad! If he is truly appeased today, may he hearken to the prayer of one far away! May he return one whom he made roam the earth to the place from which he carried him off!

May Egypt's king have mercy on me, that I may live by his mercy! May I greet the mistress of the land who is in the palace! May I hear the commands of her children! Would that my body were young again! For old age has come; feebleness has overtaken me. My eyes are heavy, my arms weak; my legs fail to follow. The heart is weary; death is near. May I be conducted to the city of eternity! May

---

[14]God of Thebes.

[15]That is, What if I should die abroad?

I serve the Mistress of All! May she speak well of me to her children; may she spend eternity above me![16]

Now when the majesty of King Kheperkare was told of the condition in which I was, his majesty sent word to me with royal gifts, in order to gladden the heart of this servant like that of a foreign ruler. And the royal children who were in his palace sent me their messages. Copy of the decree brought to this servant concerning his return to Egypt:

> Horus: Living in Births; the Two Ladies: Living in Births; the King of Upper and Lower Egypt: Kheperkare; the Son of Re: Sesostris, who lives forever.[17] Royal decree to the Attendant Sinhue:

> This decree of the king is brought to you to let you know: That you circled the foreign countries, going from Qedem to Retenu, land giving you to land, was the counsel of your own heart. What had you done that one should act against you? You had not cursed, so that your speech would be reproved. You had not spoken against the counsel of the nobles, that your words should have been rejected. This matter—it carried away your heart. It was not in my heart against you. This your heaven in the palace lives and prospers to this day.[18] Her head is adorned with the kingship of the land; her children are in the palace. You will store riches which they give you; you will live on their bounty. Come back to Egypt! See the residence in which you lived! Kiss the ground at the great portals, mingle with the courtiers! For today you have begun to age. You have lost a man's strength. Think of the day of burial, the passing into reveredness.

> A night is made for you with ointments and wrappings from the hand of Tait. A funeral procession is made for you on the day of burial; the mummy case is of gold, its head of lapis lazuli. The sky is above you as you lie in the hearse, oxen drawing you, musicians going before you. The dance of the mww-dancers is done at the door of your tomb; the offering-list is read to you; sacrifice is made before your offering-stone. Your tomb-pillars, made of white stone, are among those of the royal children. You shall not die abroad! Not shall Asiatics inter you. You shall not be wrapped in the skin of a ram to serve as your coffin. Too long a roaming of the earth! Think of your corpse, come back!

This decree reached me while I was standing in the midst of my tribe. When it had been read to me, I threw myself on my belly. Having touched the soil, I

---

[16]The "Mistress of All" could be either the queen or the goddess Nut.

[17]The decree begins by an evocation of the gods and the rulers.

[18]This sentence refers to the queen.

spread it on my chest.[19] I strode around my camp shouting: "What compares with this which is done to a servant whom his heart led astray to alien lands? Truly good is the kindness that saves me from death! Your *ka*[20] will grant me to reach my end, my body being at home!"

Copy of the reply to this decree:

The servant of the palace, Sinuhe, says: In very good peace! Regarding the matter of this flight which this servant did in his ignorance. It is your *ka*, O good god, lord of the Two Lands, which Re loves and which Mont, lord of Thebes, favors; and Amun, lord of Thrones-of-the-Two-Lands, and Sobk-Re, lord of Sumenu, and Horus, Hathor, Atum with his Ennead, and Sopdu-Neferbau-Semseru the Eastern Horus, and the Lady of Yemet—may she enfold your head—and the conclave upon the flood, and Min-Horus of the hill-countries, and Wereret lady of Punt, Nut, Haroeris-Re, and all the gods of Egypt and the isles of the sea—may they give life and joy to your nostrils, may they endue you with their bounty, may they give you eternity without limit, infinity without bounds! May the fear of you resound in lowlands and highlands, for you have subdued all that the sun encircles! This is the prayer of this servant for his lord who saves from the west.

The lord of knowledge who knows people knew in the majesty of the palace that this servant was afraid to say it. It is like a thing too great to repeat. The great god, the peer of Re, knows the heart of one who has served him willingly. This servant is in the hand of one who thinks about him. He is placed under his care. Your majesty is the conquering Horus; your arms vanquish all lands. May then your majesty command to have brought to you the prince of Meki from Qedem, the mountain chiefs from Keshu, and the prince of Menus from the lands of the Fenkhu. They are rulers of renown who have grown up in the love of you. I do not mention Retenu—it belongs to you like your hounds.

Lo, this flight which the servant made—I did not plan it. It was not in my heart; I did not devise it. I do not know what removed me from my place. It was like a dream. As if a delta-man saw himself in Yebu, a marsh-man in Nubia. I was not afraid; no one ran after me. I had not heard a reproach; my name was not heard in the mouth of the herald. Yet my flesh crept, my feet hurried, my heart drove me; the god who had willed this flight dragged me away. Nor am I a haughty man. He who knows his land respects men. Re has set the fear of you throughout the land, the dread of you in every foreign country. Whether I am at the residence, whether I am in this place, it is you who covers this horizon. The

---

[19]As a gesture of humility.

[20]Vital force or personality.

sun rises at your pleasure. The water in the river is drunk when you wish. The air of heaven is breathed at your bidding. This servant will hand over to the brood which this servant begot in this place. This servant has been sent for! Your majesty will do as he wishes! One lives by the breath which you give. As Re, Horus, and Hathor love your august nose, may Mont, lord of Thebes, wish it to live forever!

I was allowed to spend one more day in Yaa, handing over my possessions to my children, my eldest son taking charge of my tribe; all my possessions became his—my serfs, my herds, my fruit, my fruit trees. This servant departed southward. I halted at Horusways. The commander in charge of the garrison sent a message to the residence to let it be known. Then his majesty sent a trusted overseer of the royal domains with whom were loaded ships bearing royal gifts for the Asiatics who had come with me to escort me to Horusways. I called each one by his name, while every butler was at his task. When I had started and set sail, there was kneading and straining beside me, until I reached the city of Itj-tawy.

When it dawned, very early, they came to summon me. Ten men came and ten men went to usher me into the palace. My forehead touched the ground between the sphinxes, and the royal children stood in the gateway to meet me. The courtiers who usher through the forecourt set me on the way to the audience-hall. I found his majesty on the great throne in a kiosk of gold. Stretched out on my belly, I did not know myself before him, while this god greeted me pleasantly. I was like a man seized by darkness. My *ba*[21] was gone, my limbs trembled; my heart was not in my body; I did not know life from death.

His majesty said to one of the courtiers: "Lift him up, let him speak to me." Then his majesty said: "Now you have come, after having roamed foreign lands. Flight has taken its toll of you. You have aged, have reached old age. It is no small matter that your corpse will be interred without being escorted by bowmen. But don't act thus, don't act thus, speechless though your name was called!" Fearful of punishment, I answered with the answer of a frightened man: "What has my lord said to me, that I might answer it? It is not disrespect to the god! It is the terror which is in my body, like that which caused the fateful flight! Here I am before you. Life is yours. May your majesty do as he wishes!"

Then the royal daughters were brought in, and his majesty said to the queen: "Here is Sinuhe, come as an Asiatic, a product of nomads!" She uttered a very great cry, and the royal daughters shrieked all together. They said to his majesty: "Is it really he, O king, our lord?" Said his majesty: "It is really he!" Now having brought with them their necklaces, rattles, and *sistra*, they held them out to his majesty:[22]

---

[21]Soul.

[22]The princesses hold out the emblems sacred to Hathor and perform a ceremonial dance and song in which they beg a full pardon for Sinuhe.

Your hands upon the radiance, eternal king,
Jewels of heaven's mistress!
The Gold[23] gives life to your nostrils,
The Lady of Stars enfolds you!

Southcrown fared north, northcrown south,
Joined, united by your majesty's word.
While the cobra decks your brow,
You deliver the poor from harm.
Peace to you from Re, Lord of Lands!
Hail to you and the Mistress of All!

Slacken your bow, lay down your arrow,
Give breath to him who gasps for breath!
Give us our good gift on this good day,
Grant us the son of northwind, bowman born in Egypt!

He made the flight in fear of you,
He left the land in dread of you!
A face that sees you shall not pale,
Eyes that see you shall not fear!

His majesty said: "He shall not fear, he shall not dread! He shall be a companion among the nobles. He shall be among the courtiers. Proceed to the robing-room to wait on him!"

I left the audience-hall, the royal daughters giving me their hands. We went through the great portals, and I was put in the house of a prince. In it were luxuries: a bathroom and mirrors. In it were riches from the treasury; clothes of royal linen, myrrh, and the choice perfume of the king and of his favorite courtiers were in every room. Every servant was at his task. Years were removed from my body. I was shaved; my hair was combed. Thus was my squalor returned to the foreign land, my dress to the Sand-farers. I was clothed in fine linen; I was anointed with fine oil. I slept on a bed. I had returned the sand to those who dwell in it, the tree-oil to those who grease themselves with it.

I was given a house and a garden that had belonged to a courtier. Many craftsmen rebuilt it, and all its woodwork was made anew. Meals were brought to me from the palace three times, four times a day, apart from what the royal children gave without a moment's pause.

A stone pyramid was built for me in the midst of the pyramids. The masons who build tombs constructed it. A master draftsman designed in it. A master sculptor carved in it. The overseers of construction in the necropolis busied themselves with it. All the equipment that is placed in a tomb-shaft was supplied. Mortuary priests were given me. A funerary domain was made for me. It had

---

[23]That is, the god Hathor.

fields and a garden in the right place, as is done for a companion of the first rank. My statue was overlaid with gold, its skirt with electrum. It was his majesty who ordered it made. There is no commoner for whom the like has been done. I was in the favor of the king, until the day of landing[24] came.

Colophon: It is done from beginning to end as it was found in writing.

❧

A CYCLE OF HYMNS TO KING SESOSTRIS III[25]

I

Horus: Divine of Form; the Two Ladies: Divine of Birth; Gold-Horus: Being; the King of Upper and Lower Egypt: *Khakaure;* the Son of Re: *Sesostris*—he has seized the Two Lands in triumph.

Hail to you, *Khakaure,* our Horus, divine of form!
Land's protector who widens its borders,
Who smites foreign countries with his crown.
Who holds the Two Lands[26] in his arms' embrace,
Who subdues foreign lands by a motion of his hands.
Who slays bowmen without a blow of the club,
Shoots the arrow without drawing the string.
Whose terror strikes the bowmen in their land,
Fear of whom smites the nine bows.
Whose slaughter brought death to thousands of bowmen,
Who had come to invade his borders.
Who shoots the arrow as does Sakhmet,
When he felled thousands who ignored his might.
His majesty's tongue restrains Nubia,
His utterances make Asiatics flee.
Unique youth who fights for his frontiers,
Not letting his subjects weary themselves.
Who lets the people sleep till daylight,
The youths may slumber, his heart protects them.

---

[24]The day of death. Through its beginning and its ending, the story is given the form of the tomb-autobiography in which the narrator looks back on his completed life.

[25]Four hymns to King Sesostris III that date from the Middle Kingdom.

[26]Upper and Lower Egypt: Upper Egypt is to the south, while Lower Egypt is to the north and includes the Nile delta. This is a hymn to the red crown of Lower Egypt. The crowns of Upper and Lower Egypt are not here associated with a king but rather with the croc-odile-god Sobk, the lord of the Fayyum town of Shedyt. The papyrus on which the hymn was found dates from the Hyksos period.

Whose commands made his borders,
Whose words joined the Two Shores!

II

How the gods rejoice: you have strengthened their offerings!
How your people rejoice: you have made their frontiers!
How your forbears rejoice: you have enriched their portions!
How Egypt rejoices in your strength: you have protected its customs!
How the people rejoice in your guidance: your might has won increase
for them!
How the Two Shores rejoice in your dreadedness: you have enlarged
their holdings!
How the youths whom you levied rejoice: you have made them prosper!
How your elders rejoice: you have made them youthful!
How the Two Lands rejoice in your power: you have protected their
walls!
Chorus: Horus, extender of his borders, may you repeat eternity!

III

How great is the lord of his city: he is Re, little are a thousand other
men!
How great is the lord of his city: he is a canal that restrains the river's
flood water!
How great is the lord of his city: he is a cool room that lets a man sleep
till dawn!
How great is the lord of his city: he is a walled rampart of copper of
Sinai!
How great is the lord of his city: he is a shelter whose hold does not fail!
How great is the lord of his city: he is a fort that shields the timid from
his foe!
How great is the lord of his city: he is an overflowing shade, cool in
summertime!
How great is the lord of his city: he is a warm corner, dry in wintertime!
How great is the lord of his city: he is a mountain that blocks the storm
when the sky rages!
How great is the lord of his city: he is Sakhmet to foes who tread on his
frontier!

IV

He came to us to take the southland: the double-crown was fastened to
his head!
He came and gathered the Two Lands: he joined the sedge to the bee!

He came and ruled the black land: he took the red land to himself!
He came and guarded the Two Lands: he gave peace to the Two Shores!
He came and nourished the black land: he removed its needs!
He came and nourished the people: he gave breath to his subjects'
      throats!
He came and trampled foreign lands: he smote the bowmen who
      ignored his terror!
He came and fought on his frontier: he rescued him who had been
      robbed!
He came and showed the power of his arms: glorying in what his might
      had brought!
He came to let us raise our youths: inter our old ones by his will.

A HYMN TO OSIRIS[27]

Recitation. The Deputy-treasurer Sobk-iry, born of the lady Senu, the justified, says:

Hail, Osiris, son of Nut!
Two-horned, tall of crown,
Given crown and joy before the nine gods.
Whose awe Atum set in the heart of men, gods, spirits, and dead,
Whom rulership was given in On;
Great of presence in Djedu,
Lord of fear in Two-Mounds,[28]
Great of terror in Rostau,[29]
Lord of awe in Hnes.
Lord of power in Tenent,[30]
Great of love upon earth;
Lord of fame in the palace,
Great of glory in Abydos;

---

[27]The hymns to Osiris and to Min both are recited by the official Sobk-iry and are preceded by the prayer for offerings. Hymns to Egyptian gods consist largely of catalogues of the gods' powers, attributes, and cult centers. And since Egyptian theology associated and equated the gods with one another, their hymns too were similar. Yet each god retained some distinctive traits that are reflected in their hymns. Osiris's personality remained sharply etched owing to his fate, death at the hands of Seth—an event to which all hymns to Osiris allude.

[28]Probably a place name—not Upper or Lower Egypt.

[29]The necropolis of Giza.

[30]A sanctuary near Memphis.

Whom triumph was given before the assembled nine gods,
For whom slaughter was made in Herwer's great hall.
Whom the great powers fear,
For whom the great rise from their mats;
Fear of whom Shu has made,
Awe of whom Tefnut fashioned,
To whom the two assemblies come bowing down,[31]
For great is fear of him,
Strong is awe of him.

Such is Osiris, king of gods,
Great power of heaven,
Ruler of the living,
King of those beyond!
Whom thousands bless in Kher-aha,[32]
Whom mankind extols in On;
Who owns the choice cuts in houses-on-high,[33]
For whom sacrifice is made in Memphis.

[The text of the stela of Sobk-iry ends here. Other variants of the hymn add:]
For whom a night's feast is made in Sekhem.[34]
Whom the gods, when they see him, worship,
Whom the spirits, when they see him, adore,
Who is mourned by multitudes in this,[35]
Who is hailed by those below!

HYMN TO MIN[36]

Recitation. The Deputy-treasurer Sobk-iry, born of the lady Senu, the justified, speaks as one clean and pure:

I worship Min, I extol arm-raising Horus:
Hail to you, Min in his procession!
Tall-plumed, son of Osiris,
Born of divine Isis.
Great in Senut, might in Ipu,[37]

---

[31]The assembled sanctuaries of Upper and Lower Egypt.

[32]A locality south of Heliopolis.

[33]Another locality near Heliopolis.

[34]Letopolis, opposite Heliopolis.

[35]A reference to the god's tomb and temple at Abydos.

[36]Min is equated with Horus.

[37]Senut is a sanctuary of Min in Upper Egypt, and *Ipu* is a name for Panopolis, or Akhmim, another of Min's cult centers.

You of Coptus, Horus strong-armed,
Lord of awe who silences pride,
Sovereign of all the gods!
Fragrance laden when he comes from Medja-land,
Awe-inspiring in Nubia,
You of Utent,[38] hail and praise!

THE HYMN TO HAPY[39]

Adoration of Hapy:
Hail to you, Hapy,
Sprung from earth,
Come to nourish Egypt!
Of secret ways,
A darkness by day,
To whom his followers sing!
Who floods the fields that Re has made,
To nourish all who thirst;
Lets drink the waterless desert,
His dew descending from the sky.

Friend of Geb, lord of Nepri,
Promoter of the arts of Ptah.
Lord of the fishes,
He makes fowl stream south,
No bird falling down from heat.
Maker of barley, creator of emmer,
He lets the temples celebrate.

When he is sluggish, noses clog,
Everyone is poor;
As the sacred loaves are pared,
A million perish among men.
When he plunders, the whole land rages,
Great and small roar;
People change according to his coming,
When Khnum has fashioned him.
When he floods, earth rejoices,
Every belly jubilates,

---

[38]A region to the south of Egypt.

[39]Hapy is the personification of the Nile River. Here it is the annual inundations of the river that are celebrated with thanks and exuberance. The hymn dates from the Middle Kingdom and came to be regarded as a classic in the New Kingdom.

Every jawbone takes on laughter,
Every tooth is bared.

Food provider, bounty maker,
Who creates all that is good!
Lord of awe, sweetly fragrant,
Gracious when he comes.
Who makes herbage for the herds,
Gives sacrifice for every god.
Dwelling in the netherworld,
He controls both sky and earth.
Conqueror of the Two Lands,
He fills the stores,
Makes bulge the barns,
Gives bounty to the poor.

Grower of all delightful trees—
He has no revenue;
Barges exist by his might—
He is not hewn in stone.
Mountains cleave by his surge—
One sees no workmen, no leader,
He carries off in secrecy.

No one knows the place he's in,
His cavern is not found in books.
He has no shrines, no portions,
No service of his choice;
But youths, his children, hail him,
One greets him like a king.
Lawful, timely, he comes forth,
Filling Egypt, South and North;
As one drinks, all eyes are on him,
Who makes his bounty overflow.

He who grieved goes out in joy,
Every heart rejoices;
Sobk, Neith's child, bares his teeth,
The nine gods exult.
As he spouts, makes drink the fields,
Everyone grows vigorous.
Rich because another toils,
One has no quarrel with him;
Maker of food he's not defied,
One sets no limits for him.

Light-maker who comes from dark,
Fattener of herds,
Might that fashions all,
None can live without him.
People are clothed with the flax of his fields,
For he made Hedj-hotep[40] serve him;
He made anointing with his unguents,
For he is the like of Ptah.
All kinds of crafts exist through him,
All books of godly words,
His produce from the sedges.[41]

Entering the cavern,
Coming out above,
He wants his coming secret.
If he is heavy,[42] the people dwindle,
A year's food supply is lost.
The rich man looks concerned,
Everyone is seen with weapons,
Friend does not attend to friend.
Cloth is wanting for one's clothes,
Noble children lack their finery;
There's no eye-paint to be had,
No one is anointed.

This truth is fixed in people's hearts:
Want is followed by deceit.
He who consorts with the sea,
Does not harvest grain.
Though one praises all the gods,
Birds will not come down to deserts.
No one beats his hand with gold,
No man can get drunk on silver,
One cannot eat lapis lazuli,
Barley is foremost and strong!

Songs to the harp are made for you,
One sings to you with clapping hands;
The youths, your children hail you,
Crowds adorn themselves for you,

---

[40]The weaver-god.

[41]The papyrus plants from which books with pages were made.

[42]That is, if his rise is sluggish and insufficient.

Who comes with riches, decks the land,
Makes flourish every body;
Sustains the pregnant woman's heart,
And loves a multitude of herds.

When he rises at the residence,
Men feast on the meadows' gifts,
Decked with lotus for the nose,
And all the things that sprout from earth.
Children's hands are filled with herbs,
They forget to eat.
Good things are strewn about the houses,
The whole land leaps for joy.

When you overflow, O Hapy,
Sacrifice is made for you;
Oxen are slaughtered for you,
A great oblation is made to you.
Fowl is fattened for you,
Desert game snared for you,
As one repays your bounty.
One offers to all the gods
Of that which Hapy has provided,
Choice incense, oxen, goats,
And birds in holocaust.

Might is Hapy in his cavern,
His name unknown to those below,
For the gods do not reveal it.
You people who extol the gods,
Respect the awe his son has made,
The All-Lord who sustains the shores!
    Oh joy when you come!
    Oh joy when you come, O Hapy,
    Oh joy when you come!
    You who feeds men and herds
    With your meadow gifts!
    Oh joy when you come!
    Oh joy when you come, O Hapy!
    Oh joy when you come!

THREE HARPERS' SONGS[43]

Stela of Iki

O tomb, you were built for festivity,
You were founded for happiness!
The singer Neferhotep, born of Henu.

Stela of Nebankh from Abydos

The singer Tjeniaa says:
How firm you are in your seat of eternity,
Your monument of everlastingness!
It is filled with offerings of food,
It contains every good thing.
Your *ka* is with you,
It does not leave you,
O royal seal-bearer, great steward, Nebankh!
Yours is the sweet breath of the northwind!
So says his singer who keeps his name alive!
The honorable singer Tjeniaa, whom he loved,
Who sings to his *ka* every day.

The Song from the Tomb of King Intef

Song which is in the tomb of King Intef, the justified, in front of the singer with the harp.

He is happy, this good prince!
Death is a kindly fate.
A generation passes,
Another stays,
Since the time of the ancestors.
The gods who were before rest in their tombs,
Blessed nobles too are buried in their tombs.
[Yet] those who built tombs,

---

[43]These songs, accompanied by a harp, were carved on tomb walls and on mortuary stelae (burial stones). Their theme was death, and they contained reflections on death, but were not recited in rituals involving burial and revivification. In general, their authors praised death and the tomb, and reassured the owner of the tomb about his or her fate. Oddly enough, the third song, "The Song from the Tomb of King Intef," broke the traditional Egyptian mold and cast doubt on the reality of the afterlife and on the usefulness of tombs.

Their places are gone,
What has become of them?
I have heard the words of Imhotep and Hardedef,[44]
Whose sayings are recited whole.
What of their places?
Their walls have crumbled,
Their places are gone,
As though they had never been!
None comes from there,
To tell of their state,
To tell of their needs,
To calm our hearts,
Until we go where they have gone!

Hence rejoice in your heart!
Forgetfulness profits you,
Follow your heart as long as you live!
Put myrrh on your head,
Dress in fine linen,
Anoint yourself with oils fit for a god.
Heap up your joys,
Let your heart not sink!
Follow your heart and your happiness,
Do your things on earth as your heart commands!
When there comes to you that day of mourning,
The weary-hearted[45] hears not their mourning,
Wailing saves no man from the pit!

Refrain: Make holiday,
Do not weary of it!
Lo, none is allowed to take his goods with him,
Lo, none who departs comes back again!

---

[44]The two famous sages of the Old Kingdom who were worshiped as gods.
[45]That is, Osiris.

4

※

EGYPTIAN LITERATURE OF THE
NEW KINGDOM

The New Kingdom followed a period of turbulent conquest by a people of uncertain origin, the Hyksos. The military campaigns of King Ahmose ended the Hyksos rule around the mid-sixteenth century B.C. and reunited Egypt under a strong rule. The New Kingdom began as Ahmose and his successors took back Egypt and expanded Egyptian rule southward to Nubia and eastward to Syria and beyond. A series of proud dynasties saw great wealth and cosmopolitanism grow to new heights. Except for the brief interlude of Akhenaten, when monotheistic worship of the sun-god Aten was forced on the population, traditional belief in the pantheon of Egyptian deities continued, although expression of that belief reflected an ever-widening universalism.

The principal literary categories found in Egypt reflected these realities, building on those developed in the earlier period—private autobiographies, royal historical inscriptions, hymns and prayers, instructions, mortuary spells, and tales—by broadening their treatment and adding new themes and motifs, along with two new genres: school texts and love lyrics. We see these patterns of continuity and development in the hymns to the gods where transcendence and universalism are emphasized. A fine example is the "Hymn to the Sun-God" in which the rise to prominence of Amun, worshiped at Thebes, resulted in his assimilation to the supreme god, the sun-god Re. Re had become an all-embracing creator-god whose many names reflected the major gods and their forms: Harakhti in the morning, Khepri at midday, and Atum in the evening. Above all, he was visible as the Aten, the sun-disk. With the reign of Amenhotep III, the sun-god was worshiped as first among many gods; with his successor, Amenhotep IV (Akhenaten), he became, for one brief moment in the long history of Egypt, the sole god. In the first hymn of this chapter, we see the sun-god's attributes as supreme creator-god emphasized; in the second hymn, "The Great Hymn to the Aten," Egyptian religious praise reaches its epitome with the expression of the doctrine of one god.

In contrast to these doctrines of faith in a sky god, The Book of the Dead is concerned with the rituals performed during and after burial. The texts, written over a vast period of time, contain spells designed to bring about the resurrection of a dead person and his or her safety in the afterlife. Gathered into a collection of papyrus scrolls on which the spells were inscribed, they were made available to anyone who wished to have their name inserted into the scroll; the scroll was then buried with them. One hundred ninety-two chapters are known to exist, the most famous of which is the "Judgment of the Dead." Above all, these spells reflect the Egyptians' fascination with the problem of overcoming death and winning eternal life, thus recapitulating the dismemberment, reconstitution, and resurrection of Osiris.

Finally, secular forms of literature are expressed in love songs and prose stories. The cycle of "Love Poems" expresses love's aching pain and desire, presented in sophisticated literary form while written in simple and direct language. The tales, on the other hand, borrow from the fabulous and mythological, but are apparently imaginative works of entertainment rather than serious expressions of religious conviction. "The Two Brothers" is the story of Bata and Anubis, brothers whose names are borrowed from the gods and whose attributes are supernatural. Their adventures are connected to the myths of their namesake gods, but the emotions and narrative twists appear closer to those of fables. "The Report of Wenamun," written at the end of the New Kingdom, contains the irony and subtlety of a dying age. Whereas the earlier, triumphant theme of a voyage provided the framework for the story of Sinuhe (Selection 3), here all is danger and deception, reflecting the political decline of the period.

HYMN TO THE SUN-GOD[1]

Adoration of Amun when he rises as Harakhti by the overseer of the works of Amun, Suti, (and) the overseer of the works of Amun, Hor. They say:

Hail to you, Re, perfect each day,
Who rises at dawn without failing,
Khepri who wearies himself with toil!
Your rays are on the face, yet unknown,
Fine gold does not match your splendor;
Self-made you fashioned your body,
Creator uncreated.
Sole one, unique one, who traverses eternity,
Remote one, with millions under his care;
Your splendor is like heaven's splendor,
Your color brighter than its hues.
When you cross the sky all faces see you,
When you set you are hidden from their sight;
Daily you give yourself at dawn,
Safe is your sailing under your majesty.
In a brief day you race a course,
Hundred thousands, millions of miles;
A moment is each day to you,
It has passed when you go down.
You also complete the hours of night,
You order it without pause in your labor.
Through you do all eyes see,
They lack aim when your majesty sets.

"Hymn to the Sun-god," "The Great Hymn to the Aten," "The Book of the Dead," "Papyrus Chester Beatty I," "The Two Brothers," "The Report of Wenamun" from *Ancient Egyptian Literature,* vol. II: "The New Kingdom," by Miriam Lichtheim, copyright 1976 Regents of the University of California. Pp. 87, 96–100, 121, 123–127, 182–185, 203–211, 224–229. Reprinted by permission of the University of California Press.

[1]In the course of the Eighteenth Dynasty, the rise to prominence of Amun of Thebes resulted in his identification with the supreme god, the sun-god Re. The dominance of sun worship had turned the sun-god into the all-embracing creator-god who manifested himself in many forms and under many names. Thus he absorbed Amun and Horus, and he was Atum, Harakhti, and Khepri. His visible form, the sun-disk (Aten) became yet another manifestation of the god himself. The hymns to the sun-god by the twin brothers Suti and Hor, who lived during the reign of Amenhotep III, address the god in these various forms, and they accord a prominent place to the Aten. In this hymn, the sun-god is addressed as Amun, Harakhti, Re, and Khepri.

When you stir to rise at dawn,
Your brightness opens the eyes of the herds;
When you set in the western mountain,
They sleep as in the state of death.

THE GREAT HYMN TO THE ATEN[2]

Adoration of *Re-Harakhti-who-rejoices in lightland In-his-name-Shu-who-is-Aten,*
living forever; the great living Aten who is in jubilee, the lord of all that the Disk
encircles, lord of sky, lord of earth, lord of the house-of-Aten in Akhet-Aten; and
of the King of Upper and Lower Egypt, who lives by Maat, the Lord of the Two
Lands, *Neferkheprure, Sole-one-of-Re;* the Son of Re who lives by Maat, the Lord
of Crowns, *Akhenaten,* great in his lifetime; and his beloved great Queen, the
Lady of the Two Lands, *Nefer-nefru-Aten Nefertiti,* who lives in health and youth
forever. The Vizier, the Fanbearer on the right of the King ——— Ay; he says:[3]

Splendid you rise in heaven's lightland,
O living Aten, creator of life!
When you have dawned in eastern lightland,
You fill every land with your beauty.
You are beauteous, great, radiant,
High over every land;
Your rays embrace the lands,
To the limit of all that you made.
Being Re, you reach their limits,
You bend them for the son whom you love;
Though you are far, your rays are on earth,
Though one sees you, your strides are unseen.

When you set in western lightland,
Earth is in darkness as if in death;
One sleeps in chambers, heads covered,
One eye does not see another.
Were they robbed of their goods,
That are under their heads,
People would not remark it.
Every lion comes from its den,

---

[2]"The Great Hymn to the Aten" expresses the cosmopolitan and humanist outlook of the
New Kingdom at its purest and most sympathetic. All peoples are seen as the creatures
of the sun-god, who made them diverse in skin color, speech, and character.

[3]Though the hymn undoubtedly was composed for recitation by the king, inscribed in
the tomb of Ay, it was adapted to recitation by the courtier.

All the serpents bite;[4]
Darkness hovers, earth is silent,
As their maker rests in lightland.

Earth brightens when you dawn in lightland,
When you shine as Aten of daytime;
As you dispel the dark,
As you cast your rays,
The Two Lands are in festivity.
Awake they stand on their feet,
You have roused them;
Bodies cleansed, clothed,
Their arms adore your appearance.
The entire land sets out to work,
All beasts browse on their herbs;
Trees, herbs are sprouting,
Birds fly from their nests,
Their wings greeting your *ka*.[5]
All flocks frisk on their feet,
All that fly up and alight,
They live when you dawn for them.
Ships fare north, fare south as well,
Roads lie open when you rise;
The fish in the river dart before you,
Your rays are in the midst of the sea.

Who makes seed grow in women,
Who creates people from sperm;
Who feeds the son in his mother's womb,
Who soothes him to still his tears.
Nurse in the womb,
Giver of breath,
To nourish all that he made.
When he comes from the womb to breathe,
On the day of his birth,
You open wide his mouth,
You supply his needs.
When the chick in the egg speaks in the shell,
You give him breath within to sustain him;
When you have made him complete,
To break out from the egg,

---

[4]One of several passages that recall similar formulations in the 104th Psalm.
[5]Vital force or personality.

He comes out from the egg,
To announce his completion,
Walking on his legs he comes from it.

How many are your deeds,
Though hidden from sight,
O Sole God beside whom there is none!
You made the earth as you wished, you alone,
All peoples, herds, and flocks;
All upon earth that walk on legs,
All on high that fly on wings,
The lands of Khor and Kush,
The land of Egypt.
You set every man in his place,
You supply their needs;
Everyone has his food,
His lifetime is counted.
Their tongues differ in speech,
Their characters likewise;
Their skins are distinct,
For you distinguished the peoples.

You made Hapy in *dat*,[6]
You bring him when you will,
To nourish the people,
For you made them for yourself.
Lord of all who toils for them,
Lord of all lands who shines for them,
Aten of daytime, great in glory!
All distant lands, you make them live,
You made a heavenly Hapy descend for them;
He makes waves on the mountains like the sea,
To drench their fields and their towns.
How excellent are your ways, O Lord of eternity!
A Hapy from heaven for foreign peoples,
And all lands' creatures that walk on legs,
For Egypt the Hapy who comes from *dat*.[7]

Your rays nurse all fields,
When you shine they live, they grow for you;
You made the seasons to foster all that you made,

---

[6]The netherworld.

[7]Hapy, the inundating Nile, emerges from the netherworld to nourish Egypt, while foreign peoples are sustained by a "Nile from heaven" who descends as rain.

Winter to cool them, heat that they taste you.
You made the far sky to shine therein,
To behold all that you made;
You alone, shining in your form of living Aten,
Risen, radiant, distant, near.
You made millions of forms from yourself alone,
Towns, villages, fields, the river's course;
All eyes observe you upon them,
For you are the Aten of daytime on high.

You are in my heart,
There is no other who knows you,
Only your son, *Neferkheprure, Sole-one-of-Re,*
Whom you have taught your ways and your might.
Those on earth come from your hand as you made them,
When you have dawned they live,
When you set they die;
You yourself are lifetime, one lives by you.
All eyes are on your beauty until you set,
All labor ceases when you rest in the west;
When you rise you stir everyone for the King,
Every leg is on the move since you founded the earth.
You rouse them for your son who came from your body,
The King who lives by Maat, the Lord of the Two Lands,
Neferkheprure, Sole-one-of-Re,
The Son of Re who lives by Maat, the Lord of crowns,
Akhenaten, great in his lifetime;
And the great Queen whom he loves, the Lady of the Two Lands,
Nefer-nefru-Aten Nefertiti, living forever.

THE BOOK OF THE DEAD
Chapter 43

To Retain One's Head

Formula for not letting the head of N[8] be cut off in the necropolis.

I am the great one, son of the great one,
The fiery one, son of the fiery one,

---

[8]N is apparently the person being buried. The prayer seems to offer the deceased assurance of sharing in the rebirth of Osiris after death.

To whom his head was given after having been cut off[9]
The head of Osiris shall not be taken from him,
My head shall not be taken from me!
I am risen, renewed, refreshed,
I am Osiris!

Chapter 105

An Address to the Ka

Formula to appease the *ka* to be said by N.

Hail to you, my *ka*, my helper!
Behold, I have come before you,
Risen, animated, mighty, healthy!
I have brought incense to you,
To purify you with it,
To purify your sweat with it.

Whatever speech I made,
Whatever evil deed I did,
Be it removed from me!
For mine is that green amulet,
Fastened to the neck of Re,[10]
That makes the lightlanders green.
My *ka* greens like theirs,
My ka's food is as theirs.

O weigher on the scales,
May *maat*[11] rise to the nose of Re that day!
Do not let my head be removed from me!
For mine is an eye that sees,
An ear that hears;
For I am not an ox for slaughter,
I shall not be an offering for those above!
Let me pass by you, I am pure,
Osiris has vanquished his foes!

---

[9]The deceased identifies himself with Osiris, who was resurrected despite having been slain and dismembered by Seth.

[10]Life-giving, powerful god.

[11]The divine order.

Chapter 125

The Judgment of the Dead

The Declaration of Innocence

To be said on reaching the Hall of the Two Truths so as to purge N of any sins committed and to see the face of every god:

> Hail to you, great God, Lord of the Two Truths!
> I have come to you, my Lord,
> I was brought to see your beauty.
> I know you, I know the names of the forty-two gods,[12]
> Who are with you in the Hall of the Two Truths,
> Who live by warding off evildoers,
> Who drink of their blood,
> On that day of judging characters before Wennofer?[13]
> Lo, your name is "He-of-Two-Daughters,"
> [And] "He-of-Maat's-Two-Eyes."
> Lo, I come before you,
> Bringing Maat to you,
> Having repelled evil for you.
>
> I have not done crimes against people,
> I have not mistreated cattle,
> I have not sinned in the Place of Truth.[14]
> I have not known what should not be known,
> I have not done any harm.
> I did not begin a day by exacting more than my due,
> My name did not reach the bark of the mighty ruler.
> I have not blasphemed a god,
> I have not robbed the poor.
> I have not done what the god abhors,
> I have not maligned a servant to his master.
> I have not caused pain,
> I have not caused tears.
> I have not killed,
> I have not ordered to kill,
> I have not made anyone suffer.
> I have not damaged the offerings in the temples,

---

[12]The dead person insists that he knows the names of the gods—knowing their names meant having power over them.

[13]That is, Osiris.

[14]A term for temple and necropolis.

I have not depleted the loaves of the gods,
I have not stolen the cakes of the dead.
I have not copulated nor defiled myself.
I have not increased nor reduced the measure,
I have not diminished the arura,[15]
I have not cheated in the fields.
I have not added to the weight of the balance,
I have not falsified the plummet of the scales.
I have not taken milk from the mouth of children,
I have not deprived cattle of their pasture.
I have not snared birds in the reeds of the gods,
I have not caught fish in their ponds.
I have not held back water in its season,
I have not dammed a flowing stream,
I have not quenched a needed fire.
I have not neglected the days of meat offerings,
I have not detained cattle belonging to the god,
I have not stopped a god in his procession.

I am pure, I am pure, I am pure, I am pure!
I am pure as is pure that great heron in Hnes.
I am truly the nose of the Lord of Breath,
Who sustains all the people,
On the day of completing the Eye[16] in On,
In the second month of winter, last day,
In the presence of the lord of this land.
I have seen the completion of the Eye in On!
No evil shall befall me in this land.
In this Hall of the Two Truths;
For I know the names of the gods in it,
The followers of the great God!

The Declaration to the Forty-two Gods[17]

O Wide-of-stride who comes from On: I have not done evil.
O Flame-grasper who comes from Kheraha: I have not robbed.
O Long-nosed who comes from Khmun:[18] I have not coveted.
O Shadow-eater who comes from the cave: I have not stolen.
O Savage-faced who comes from Rostau: I have not killed people.
O Lion-Twins who come from heaven: I have not trimmed the measure.

---

[15]Unit used to measure land; equals two-thirds of an acre.

[16]The Horus Eye.

[17] Most of the forty-two gods are minor demons; only a few are major gods.

[18]Thoth of Hermopolis, a god in the shape of the long-nosed ibis.

O Flint-eyed who comes from Khem: I have not cheated.

O Fiery-one who comes backward: I have not stolen a god's property.

O Bone-smasher who comes from Hnes: I have not told lies.

O Flame-thrower who comes from Memphis: I have not seized food.

O Cave-dweller who comes from the west: I have not sulked.

O White-toothed who comes from Lakeland:[19] I have not trespassed.

O Blood-eater who comes from slaughterplace: I have not slain sacred cattle.

O Entrail-eater who comes from the tribunal: I have not extorted.

O Lord of Maat who comes from Maaty: I have not stolen bread rations.

O Wanderer who comes from Bubastis: I have not spied.

O Pale-one who comes from On: I have not prattled.

O Villain who comes from Anjdty: I have contended only for my goods.

O Fiend who comes from slaughterhouse: I have not committed adultery.

O Examiner who comes from Min's temple: I have not defiled myself.

O Chief of the nobles who comes from Imu: I have not caused fear.

O Wrecker who comes from Huy: I have not trespassed.

O Disturber who comes from the sanctuary: I have not been violent.

O Child who comes from the nome[20] of On: I have not been deaf to Maat.

O Foreteller who comes from Wensi: I have not quarreled.

O Bastet who comes from the shrine: I have not winked.

O Backward-faced who comes from the pit: I have not copulated with a boy.

O Flame-footed who comes from the dusk: I have not been false.

O Dark-one who comes from darkness: I have not reviled.

O Peace-bringer who comes from Sais: I have not been aggressive.

O Many-faced who comes from Djefet: I have not had a hasty heart.

O Accuser who comes from Utjen: I have not attacked and reviled a god.

O Horned-one who comes from Siut: I have not made many words.

O Nefertem who comes from Memphis: I have not sinned, I have not done wrong.

O Timeless-one who comes from Djedu: I have not made trouble.

O Willful-one who comes from Tjebu: I have not waded in water.

O Flowing-one who comes from Nun: I have not raised my voice.

O Commander of people who comes from his shrine: I have not cursed a god.

O Benefactor who comes from Huy: I have not been boastful.

O Nehebkau who comes from the city: I have not been haughty.

---

[19]This line refers to Sobk, the crocodile-god of Fayyum, a region south of Cairo.

[20]A province of ancient Egypt.

O High-of-head who comes from the cave: I have not wanted more
  than I had.
O Captor who comes from the graveyard: I have not cursed god in
  my town.

LOVE POEMS

A Cycle of Seven Stanzas[21]

Beginning of the says of great happiness

The one, the sister without peer,
The handsomest of all!
She looks like the rising morning star
At the start of a happy year.
Shining bright, fair of skin,
Lovely the look of her eyes,
Sweet the speech of her lips,
She has not a word too much.
Upright neck, shining breast,
Hair true lapis lazuli;
Arms surpassing gold,
Fingers like lotus buds.
Heavy thighs, narrow waist,
Her legs parade her beauty;
With graceful step she treads the ground,
Captures my heart by her movements.
She causes all men's necks
To turn about to see her;
Joy has he whom she embraces,
He is like the first of men!
When she steps outside she seems
Like that other one![22]

---

[21]The cycle consists of seven stanzas, each headed by the word *house*, which means "stanza" or "chapter," followed by a numeral. In addition, in the original language (Old Egyptian), the first line of each stanza repeats the appropriate numeral, or uses a homophone of the numeral; and the same word recurs as the final word of the stanza. Thus, the first stanza begins and ends with the word *one*, while the second begins and ends with the word *brother*, which is an Old Egyptian homophone of the numeral *two*, and so on. The stanzas are spoken by a young man and a young woman in alternating sequence; their use of the terms *brother* and *sister* would seem to indicate terms of endearment rather than a sibling relationship.

[22]The "other one" is the sun, viewed as the sole eye of heaven.

Second Stanza

My brother torments my heart with his voice,
He makes sickness take hold of me;
He is neighbor to my mother's house,
And I cannot go to him!
Mother is right in charging him thus:
"Give up seeing her!"
It pains my heart to think of him,
I am possessed by love of him.
Truly, he is a foolish one,
But I resemble him;
He knows not my wish to embrace him,
Or he would write to my mother.
Brother, I am promised to you
By the Gold[23] of women!
Come to me that I see your beauty,
Father, Mother will rejoice!
My people will hail you all together,
They will hail you, O my brother!

Third Stanza

My heart devised to see her beauty
While sitting down in her house;
On the way I met Mehy on his chariot,
With him were his young men.
I knew not how to avoid him:
Should I stride on to pass him?
But the river was the road,
I knew no place for my feet.
My heart, you are very foolish,
Why accost Mehy?
If I pass before him,
I tell him my movements;
Here, I'm yours, I say to him,
Then he will shout my name,
And assign me to the first . . .
Among his followers.[24]

---

[23]Hathor, patronness of love, was called "the Gold."

[24]This stanza is somewhat obscure. *Mehy* (meaning "flax") is the name of a prince. It is unclear what the consequences of meeting him are. Apparently, the speaker of the stanza is the young man.

Fourth Stanza

My heart flutters hastily,
When I think of my love of you;
It lets me not act sensibly,
It leaps from its place.
It lets me not put on a dress,
Nor wrap my scarf around me;
I put no paint upon my eyes,
I'm even not anointed.
"Don't wait, go there," says it to me,
As often as I think of him;
My heart, don't act so stupidly,
Why do you play the fool?
Sit still, the brother comes to you,
And many eyes as well![25]
Let not the people say of me:
"A woman fallen through love!"
Be steady when you think of him,
My heart, do not flutter!

Fifth Stanza

I praise the Golden,[26] I worship her majesty,
I extol the Lady of Heaven;
I give adoration to Hathor,
Laudations to my mistress!
I called to her, she heard my plea,
She sent my mistress to me;
She came by herself to see me,
O great wonder that happened to me!
I was joyful, exulting, elated,
When they said: "See, she is here!"
As she came, the young men bowed,
Out of great love for her.
I make devotions to my goddess,
That she grant me my sister as gift;
Three days now that I pray to her name,
Five days since she went from me!

---

[25]That is, many people will be watching you.
[26]Hathor.

Sixth Stanza

I passed before his house,
I found his door ajar;
My brother stood by his mother,
And all his brothers with him.
Love of him captures the heart
Of all who tread the path;
Splendid youth who has no peer,
Brother outstanding in virtues!
He looked at me as I passed by,
And I, by myself, rejoiced;
How my heart exulted in gladness,
My brother, at your sight!
If only the mother knew my heart,
She would have understood by now;
O Golden, put it in her heart,
Then will I hurry to my brother!
I will kiss him before his companions,
I would not weep before them;
I would rejoice at their understanding
That you acknowledge me!
I will make a feast for my goddess,
My heart leaps to go;
To let me see my brother tonight,
O happiness in passing!

Seventh Stanza

Seven days since I saw my sister,
And sickness invaded me;
I am heavy in all my limbs,
My body has forsaken me.
When the physicians come to me,
My heart rejects their remedies;
The magicians are quite helpless,
My sickness is not discerned.
To tell me "She is here" would revive me!
Her name would make me rise;
Her messenger's coming and going,
That would revive my heart!
My sister is better than all prescriptions,
She does more for me than all medicines;
Her coming to me is my amulet,

The sight of her makes me well!
When she opens her eyes my body is young,
Her speaking makes me strong;
Embracing her expels my malady—
Seven days since she went from me!

THE TWO BROTHERS[27]

It is said, there were two brothers, of the same mother and the same father. Anubis was the name of the elder, and Bata the name of the younger. As for Anubis, he had a house and a wife; and his young brother was with him as if he were a son. He was the one who made clothes for him, and he went behind his cattle to the fields. He was the one who did the plowing, and he harvested for him. He was the one who did for him all kinds of labor in the fields. Indeed, his young brother was an excellent man. There was none like him in the whole land, for a god's strength was in him.

Now when many days had passed, his young brother was tending his cattle according to his daily custom. And he returned to his house in the evening, laden with all kinds of field plants, and with milk, with wood, and with every good thing of the field. He placed them before his elder brother, as he was sitting with his wife. Then he drank and ate and went to sleep in his stable among his cattle.

Now when it had dawned and another day had come, he took foods that were cooked and placed them before his elder brother. Then he took bread for himself for the fields, and he drove his cattle to let them eat in the fields. He walked behind his cattle, and they would say to him: "The grass is good in such-and-such a place." And he heard all they said and took them to the place of good grass that they desired. Thus the cattle he tended became exceedingly fine, and they increased their offspring very much.

Now at plowing time his elder brother said to him: "Have a team of oxen made ready for us for plowing, for the soil has emerged and is right for plowing. Also, come to the field with seed, for we shall start plowing tomorrow." So he said to him. Then the young brother made all the preparations that his elder brother had told him to make.

Now when it had dawned and another day had come, they went to the field with their seed and began to plow. And their hearts were very pleased with this work they had undertaken. And many days later, when they were in the field, they had need of seed. Then he sent his young brother, saying: "Hurry, fetch us seed from the

---

[27]This is a complex and vivid tale, rich in motifs that have parallels in later literature. The two protagonists have some connection with a myth of the two gods Anubis and Bata, while the episode of Bata and his brother's wife has a remarkable similarity to the tale of Joseph and Potiphar's wife in the biblical book of Genesis.

village." His young brother found the wife of his elder brother seated braiding her hair. He said to her: "Get up, give me seed, so that I may hurry to the field, for my elder brother is waiting for me. Don't delay." She said to him: "Go, open the store-room and fetch what you want. Don't make me leave my hairdo unfinished."

Then the youth entered his stable and fetched a large vessel, for he wished to take a great quantity of seed. He loaded himself with barley and emmer and came out with it. Thereupon she said to him: "How much is what you have on your shoulder?" He said to her: "Three sacks of emmer and two sacks of barley, five in all, are on my shoulder." So he said to her. Then she spoke to him saying: "There is great strength in you. I see your vigor daily." And she desired to know him as a man. She got up, took hold of him, and said to him: "Come, let us spend an hour lying together. It will be good for you. And I will make fine clothes for you."

Then the youth became like a leopard in his anger over the wicked speech she had made to him; and she became very frightened. He rebuked her, saying: "Look, you are like a mother to me; and your husband is like a father to me. He who is older than I has raised me. What is this great wrong you said to me? Do not say it to me again! But I will not tell it to anyone. I will not let it come from my mouth to any man." He picked up his load; he went off to the field. He reached his elder brother, and they began to work at their task. When evening had come, his elder brother returned to his house. And his young brother tended his cattle, loaded himself with all things of the field, and drove his cattle before him to let them sleep in their stable in the village.

Now the wife of his elder brother was afraid on account of the speech she had made. So she took fat and grease and made herself appear as if she had been beaten, in order to tell her husband, "It was your young brother who beat me." Her husband returned in the evening according to his daily custom. He reached his house and found his wife lying down and seeming ill. She did not pour water over his hands in the usual manner; nor had she lit a fire for him. His house was in dark-ness, and she lay vomiting.

Her husband said to her: "Who has had words with you?" She said to him: "No one has had words with me except your young brother. When he came to take seed to you, he found me sitting alone. He said to me: 'Come, let us spend an hour lying together; loosen your braids.' So he said to me. But I would not listen to him. 'Am I not your mother? Is your elder brother not like a father to you?' So I said to him. He became frightened and he beat me, so as to prevent me from telling you. Now if you let him live, I shall die! Look, when he returns, do not let him live! For I am ill from this evil design which he was about to carry out in the morning."

Then his elder brother became like a leopard. He sharpened his spear and took it in his hand. Then his elder brother stood behind the door of his stable, in order to kill his young brother when he came in the evening to let his cattle enter the sta-ble. Now when the sun had set he loaded himself with all the plants of the field according to his daily custom. He returned, and as the lead cow was about to enter the stable she said to her herdsman: "Here is your elder brother waiting for you with his spear in order to kill you. Run away from him." He heard what his lead cow said, and when another went in she said the same. He looked under the door of the stable and saw the feet of his elder brother as he stood behind the door with his spear in his hand. He set his load on the ground and took off at a run so as to flee. And his elder brother went after him with his spear.

Then his young brother prayed to Pre-Harakhti, saying: "My good lord! It is you who judge between the wicked and the just!" And Pre heard all his plea; and Pre made a great body of water appear between him and his elder brother, and it was full of crocodiles. Thus one came to be on the one side, and the other on the other side. And his elder brother struck his own hand twice, because he had failed to kill him. Then his young brother called to him on this side, saying: "Wait here until dawn! When the Aten has risen, I shall contend with you before him; and he will hand over the wicked to the just! For I shall not be with you any more. I shall not be in the place in which you are. I shall go to the Valley of the Pine."

Now when it dawned and another day had come, and Pre-Harakhti had risen, one gazed at the other. Then the youth rebuked his elder brother, saying: "What is your coming after me to kill me wrongfully, without having listened to my words? For I am yet your young brother, and you are like a father to me, and your wife is like a mother to me. Is it not so that when I was sent to fetch seed for us your wife said to me: 'Come, let us spend an hour lying together'? But look, it has been turned about for you into another thing." Then he let him know all that had happened between him and his wife. And he swore by Pre-Harakhti, saying: "As to your coming to kill me wrongfully, you carried your spear on the testimony of a filthy whore!" Then he took a reed knife, cut off his phallus, and threw it into the water; and the catfish swallowed it. And he grew weak and became feeble. And his elder brother became very sick at heart and stood weeping for him loudly. He could not cross over to where his young brother was on account of the crocodiles.

Then his young brother called to him, saying: "If you recall something evil, will you not also recall something good, or something that I have done for you? Go back to your home and tend your cattle, for I shall not stay in the place where you are. I shall go to the Valley of the Pine. But what you shall do for me is to come and look after me, when you learn that something has happened to me. I shall take out my heart and place it on top of the blossom of the pine. If the pine is cut down and falls to the ground, you shall come to search for it. If you spend seven years searching for it, let your heart not be disgusted. And when you find it and place it in a bowl of cool water, I shall live to take revenge on him who wronged me. You will know that something has happened to me when one puts a jug of beer in your hand and it ferments. Do not delay at all when this happens to you."

Then he went away to the Valley of the Pine; and his elder brother went to his home, his hand on his head and smeared with dirt.[28] When he reached his house, he killed his wife, cast her to the dogs, and sat mourning for his young brother.

Now many days after this, his young brother was in the Valley of the Pine. There was no one with him, and he spent the days hunting desert game. In the

---

[28]Gestures of mourning.

evening he returned to sleep under the pine on top of whose blossom his heart was. And after many days he built a mansion for himself with his own hand in the Valley of the Pine, filled with all good things, for he wanted to set up a household.

Coming out of his mansion, he encountered the Ennead[29] as they walked about administering the entire land. Then the Ennead addressed him in unison, saying: "O Bata, Bull of the Ennead, are you alone here, having left your town on account of the wife of Anubis, your elder brother? He has killed his wife and you are avenged of all the wrong done to you." And as they felt very sorry for him, Pre-Harakhti said to Khnum:[30] "Fashion a wife for Bata, that he not live alone!" Then Khnum made a companion for him who was more beautiful in body than any woman in the whole land, for the fluid of every god was in her. Then the seven Hathors came to see her, and they said with one voice: "She will die by the knife."

He desired her very much. She sat in his house while he spent the day hunting desert game, bringing it and putting it before her. He said to her: "Do not go outdoors, lest the sea snatch you. I cannot rescue you from it, because I am a woman like you. And my heart lies on top of the blossom of the pine. But if another finds it, I shall fight with him." Then he revealed to her all his thoughts.

Now many days after this, when Bata had gone hunting according to his daily custom, the young girl went out to stroll under the pine which was next to her house. Then she saw the sea surging behind her, and she started to run before it and entered her house. Thereupon the sea called to the pine, saying: "Catch her for me!" And the pine took away a lock of her hair. Then the sea brought it to Egypt and laid it in the place of the washermen of Pharaoh. Thereafter the scent of the lock of hair got into the clothes of Pharaoh. And the king quarreled with the royal washermen, saying: "A scent of ointment is in the clothes of Pharaoh!" He quarreled with them every day, and they did not know what to do.

The chief of the royal washermen went to the shore, his heart very sore on account of the daily quarrel with him. Then he realized that he was standing on the shore opposite the lock of hair which was in the water. He had someone go down, and it was brought to him. Its scent was found to be very sweet, and he took it to Pharaoh.

Then the learned scribes of Pharaoh were summoned, and they said to Pharaoh: "As for this lock of hair, it belongs to a daughter of Pre-Harakhti in whom there is the fluid of every god. It is a greeting to you from another country. Let envoys go to every foreign land to search for her. As for the envoy who goes to the Valley of the Pine, let many men go with him to fetch her." His majesty said: "What you have said is very good." And they were sent.

Now many days after this, the men who had gone abroad returned to report to his majesty. But those who had gone to the Valley of the Pine did not return, for Bata had killed them, leaving only one of them to report to his majesty. Then his majesty sent many soldiers and charioteers to bring her back, and with them

---

[29]Nine gods.

[30]Creator god.

was a woman into whose hand one had given all kinds of beautiful ladies' jewelry. The woman returned to Egypt with her, and there was jubilation for her in the entire land. His majesty loved her very very much, and he gave her the rank of Great Lady. He spoke with her in order to make her tell about her husband, and she said to his majesty: "Have the pine felled and cut up." The king sent soldiers with their tools to fell the pine. They reached the pine, they felled the blossom on which was Bata's heart, and he fell dead at that moment.

When it had dawned and the next day had come, and the pine had been felled, Anubis, the elder brother of Bata, entered his house. He sat down to wash his hands. He was given a jug of beer, and it fermented. He was given another of wine, and it turned bad. Then he took his staff and his sandals, as well as his clothes and his weapons, and he started to journey to the Valley of the Pine. He entered the mansion of his young brother and found his young brother lying dead on his bed. He wept when he saw his young brother lying dead. He went to search for the heart of his young brother beneath the pine under which his young brother had slept in the evening. He spent three years searching for it without finding it.

When he began the fourth year, his heart longed to return to Egypt, and he said: "I shall depart tomorrow." So he said in his heart. When it had dawned and another day had come, he went to walk under the pine and spent the day searching for it. When he turned back in the evening, he looked once again in search of it and he found a fruit. He came back with it, and it was the heart of his young brother! He fetched a bowl of cool water, placed it in it, and sat down according to his daily custom.

When night had come, his heart swallowed the water, and Bata twitched in all his body. He began to look at his elder brother while his heart was in the bowl. Then Anubis, his elder brother, took the bowl of cool water in which was the heart of his young brother and let him drink it. Then his heart stood in its place, and he became as he had been. Thereupon they embraced each other, and they talked to one another.

Then Bata said to his elder brother: "Look, I shall change myself into a great bull of beautiful color, of a kind unknown to man, and you shall sit on my back. By the time the sun has risen, we shall be where my wife is, that I may avenge myself. You shall take me to where the king is, for he will do for you everything good. You shall be rewarded with silver and gold for taking me to Pharaoh. For I shall be a great marvel, and they will jubilate over me in the whole land. Then you shall depart to your village."

When it had dawned and the next day had come, Bata assumed the form which he had told his elder brother. Then Anubis, his elder brother, sat on his back. At dawn he reached the place where the king was. His majesty was informed about him; he saw him and rejoiced over him very much. He made a great offering for him, saying: "It is a great marvel." And there was jubilation over him in the entire land. Then the king rewarded his elder brother with silver and gold, and he dwelled in his village. The king gave him many people and many things, for Pharaoh loved him very much, more than anyone else in the whole land.

Now when many days had passed, he[31] entered the kitchen, stood where the lady was, and began to speak to her, saying: "Look, I am yet alive!" She said to him: "Who are you?" He said to her: "I am Bata. I know that when you had the pine felled for Pharaoh, it was on account of me, so that I should not live. Look, I am yet alive! I am a bull." The lady became very frightened because of the speech her husband had made to her. Then he left the kitchen.

His majesty sat down to a day of feasting with her. She poured drink for his majesty, and he was very happy with her. Then she said to his majesty: "Swear to me by God, saying: 'Whatever she will say, I will listen to it!'" He listened to all that she said: "Let me eat of the liver of this bull; for he is good for nothing." So she said to him. He became very vexed over what she had said, and the heart of Pharaoh was very sore.

When it had dawned and another day had come, the king proclaimed a great offering, namely, the sacrifice of the bull. He sent one of the chief royal slaughterers to sacrifice the bull. And when he had been sacrificed and was carried on the shoulders of the men, he shook his neck and let fall two drops of blood beside the two doorposts of his majesty, one on the one side of the great portal of Pharaoh, and the other on the other side. They grew into two big Persea trees, each of them outstanding. Then one went to tell his majesty: "Two big Persea trees have grown this night—a great marvel for his majesty—beside the great portal of his majesty." There was jubilation over them in the whole land, and the king made an offering to them.

Many days after this, his majesty appeared at the audience window of lapis lazuli with a wreath of all kinds of flowers on his neck. Then he mounted a golden chariot and came out of the palace to view the Persea trees. Then the lady came out on a team behind Pharaoh. His majesty sat down under one Persea tree and the lady under the other. Then Bata spoke to his wife: "Ha, you false one! I am Bata! I am alive in spite of you. I know that when you had the pine felled for Pharaoh, it was on account of me. And when I became a bull, you had me killed."

Many days after this, the lady stood pouring drink for his majesty, and he was happy with her. Then she said to his majesty: "Swear to me by God, saying: 'Whatever she will say, I will listen to it!' So you shall say." He listened to all that she said. She said: "Have the two Persea trees felled and made into fine furniture." The king listened to all that she said. After a short while his majesty sent skilled craftsmen. They felled the Persea trees of Pharaoh, and the queen, the lady, stood watching it. Then a splinter flew and entered the mouth of the lady. She swallowed it, and in a moment she became pregnant. The king ordered made of them[32] whatever she desired.

Many days after this, she gave birth to a son. One went to tell his majesty: "A son has been born to you." He was fetched, and a nurse and maids were assigned to him. And there was jubilation over him in the whole land. The king sat down

---

[31] The bull.

[32] The Persea trees.

to a feastday and held him on his lap. From that hour his majesty loved him very much, and he designated him as Viceroy of Kush. And many days after this, his majesty made him crown prince of the whole land.

Now many days after this, when he had spent many years as crown prince of the whole land, his majesty flew up to heaven.[33] Then the king[34] said: "Let my great royal officials be brought to me, that I may let them know all that has happened to me." Then his wife was brought to him. He judged her in their presence, and they gave their assent. His elder brother was brought to him, and he made him crown prince of the whole land. He spent thirty years as king of Egypt. He departed from life; and his elder brother stood in his place on the day of death.

Colophon:—It has come to a good end under the scribe of the treasury, Kagab, and the scribes of the treasury, Hori and Meremope. Written by the scribe Ennana, the owner of this book. Whoever maligns this book, Thoth will contend with him.

THE REPORT OF WENAMUN[35]

Year five,[36] fourth month of the summer, day sixteen, the day of departure of Wenamun, the Elder of the Portal of the Temple of Amun, Lord of Thrones-of-the-Two-Lands, to fetch timber for the great noble bark of Amen-Re, King of Gods, which is upon the river and is called *Amen-user-he*.[37]

On the day of my arrival at Tanis, the place where Smendes and Tentamun are,[38] I gave them the dispatches of Amen-Re, King of Gods. They had them read

---

[33]That is, the king died.

[34]The new king, Bata.

[35]The papyrus for "The Report of Wenamun" was written at the end of the Twelfth Dynasty, directly after the events that the report relates. Whether or not the report reflects an actual mission, it depicts a true historical situation and a precise moment. It is the third decade of the reign of Ramses XI, 1090–1080 B.C., during which the king yielded power to the two men who shared the effective rule of Egypt: Herihor in the south and Smendes in the north. The empire had been lost, and thus so simple an enterprise as the purchase of Lebanese timber could be depicted as a perilous adventure.

[36]The year date is reckoned by the "renaissance era" introduced by Herihor in the nineteenth year of the reign of Ramses XI.

[37]The name of the great processional boat of Amun of Thebes.

[38]Smendes, the ruler of Tanis, subsequently became the first king of the Twenty-first Dynasty. The fact that his wife, Tentamun, always is mentioned together with him suggests that she was an important person, perhaps a princess, who shared the rule with her husband.

out before them and they said: "I will do, I will do as Amen-Re, King of Gods, our lord has said."

I stayed until the fourth month of summer in Tanis. Then Smendes and Tentamun sent me off with the ship's captain, Mengebet,[39] and I went down upon the great sea of Syria in the first month of summer, day one. I arrived at Dor,[40] a Tjeker town; and Beder, its prince, had fifty loaves, one jug of wine, and one ox-haunch brought to me. Then a man of my ship fled after stealing one vessel of gold worth five *deben*, four jars of silver worth twenty *deben*, and a bag with eleven *deben* of silver; total of what he stole: gold five *deben*, silver thirty-one *deben*.

That morning when I had risen, I went to where the prince was and said to him: "I have been robbed in your harbor. Now you are the prince of this land, you are the one who controls it. Search for my money! Indeed the money belongs to Amen-Re, King of Gods, the lord of the lands. It belongs to Smendes; it belongs to Herihor, my lord, and to the other magnates of Egypt. It belongs to you; it belongs to Weret; it belongs to Mekmer; it belongs to Tjekerbaal, the prince of Byblos!"[41] He said to me: "Are you serious? Are you joking? Indeed I do not understand the demand you make to me. If it had been a thief belonging to my land who had gone down to your ship and stolen your money, I would replace it for you from my storehouse, until your thief, whatever his name, had been found. But the thief who robbed you, he is yours, he belongs to your ship. Spend a few days here with me; I will search for him."

I stayed nine days moored in his harbor. Then I went to him and said to him: "Look, you have not found my money. Let me depart with the ship captains, with those who go to sea."

[Translator's note: The next eight lines are broken. Apparently the prince advises Wenamun to wait some more, but Wenamun departs. He passes Tyre and approaches Byblos. Then he seizes thirty deben *of silver from a ship he has encountered that belongs to the Tjeker. He tells the owners that he will keep the money until his money has been found. Through this action he incurs the enmity of the Tjeker.]*

They departed and I celebrated in a tent on the shore of the sea in the harbor of Byblos. And I made a hiding place for Amun-of-the-Road[42] and placed his possessions in it. Then the prince of Byblos sent to me saying: "Leave my harbor!" I sent to him, saying: "Where shall I go? If you have a ship to carry me, let me be taken back to Egypt." I spent twenty-nine days in his harbor, and he spent it me sending to me daily to say: "Leave my harbor!"

---

[39]The captain is Syrian, and so, apparently, is the crew; but the ship is in the service of Egypt.

[40]A port town on the northern Palestinian coast, controlled by the Tjeker, one of the "sea peoples" who, having failed to invade Egypt, settled on the Palestinian coast.

[41]That is, the stolen money was intended for the persons with whom Wenamun expected to do business.

[42]The statuette that represented Amun in his role as protector of travelers.

Now while he was offering to his gods, the god took hold of a young man of his young men and put him in a trance. He said to him:[43] "Bring the god up! Bring the envoy who is carrying him! It is Amun who sent him. It is he who made him come!" Now it was while the entranced one was entranced that night that I had found a ship headed for Egypt. I had loaded all my belongings into it and was watching for the darkness, saying: "When it descends I will load the god so that no other eye shall see him."

Then the harbor master came to me, saying: "Wait until morning, says the prince!" I said to him: "Was it not you who daily took time to come to me, saying: 'Leave my harbor'? Do you now say: 'Wait this night,' in order to let the ship that I found depart, and then you will come to say: 'Go away'?" He went and told it to the prince. Then the prince sent to the captain of the ship, saying: "Wait until morning, says the prince."

When morning came, he sent and brought me up, while the god rested in the tent where he was on the shore of the sea. I found him seated in his upper chamber with his back against a window, and the waves of the great sea of Syria broke behind his head. I said to him: "Blessings of Amun!" He said to me: "How long is it to this day since you came from the place where Amun is?" I said to him: "Five whole months till now." He said to me: "If you are right, where is the dispatch of Amun that was in your hand? Where is the letter of the High Priest of Amun that was in your hand?" I said to him: "I gave them to Smendes and Tentamun." Then he became very angry and said to me: "Now then, dispatches, letters you have none. Where is the ship of pinewood that Smendes gave you? Where is its Syrian crew? Did he not entrust you to this foreign ship's captain in order to have him kill you and have them throw you into the sea? From whom would one then seek the god? And you, from whom would one seek you?" So he said to me.

I said to him: "Is it not an Egyptian ship? Those who sail under Smendes are Egyptian crews. He has no Syrian crews."[44] He said to me: "Are there not twenty ships here in my harbor that do business with Smendes? As for Sidon, that other place you passed, are there not another fifty ships there that do business with Werekter and haul to his house?"

I was silent in this great moment. Then he spoke to me, saying: "On what business have you come?" I said to him: "I have come in quest of timber for the great noble bark of Amen-Re, King of Gods. What your father did, what the father of your father did, you too will do it." So I said to him. He said to me: "True, they did it. If you pay me for doing it, I will do it. My relations carried out this business after Pharaoh had sent six ships laden with the goods of Egypt, and they had been unloaded into their storehouses. You, what have you brought for me?"

He had the daybook of his forefathers brought and had it read before me. They found entered in his book a thousand *deben* of silver and all sorts of things. He said

---

[43]That is, the man in a trance said to the prince.
[44]Wenamun claims that Syrian crews who sail for Egypt are Egyptian crews.

to me: "If the ruler of Egypt were the lord of what is mine and I were his servant, he would not have sent silver and gold to say: 'Carry out the business of Amun.' It was not a royal gift that they gave to my father! I too, I am not your servant, nor am I the servant of him who sent you! If I shout aloud to Lebanon, the sky opens and the logs lie here on the shore of the sea! Give me the sails you brought to move your ships, loaded with logs for Egypt! Give me the ropes you brought to lash the pines that I am to fell in order to make them for you ——. ——— that I am to make for you for the sails of your ships; or the yards may be too heavy and may break, and you may die in the midst of the sea. For Amun makes thunder in the sky ever since he placed Seth beside him![45] Indeed, Amun has founded all the lands. He founded them after having first founded the land of Egypt from which you have come. Thus craftsmanship came from it in order to reach the place where I am! Thus learning came from it in order to reach the place where I am![46] What are these foolish travels they made you do?"

I said to him: "Wrong! These are not foolish travels that I am doing. There is no ship on the river that does not belong to Amun. His is the sea and his the Lebanon of which you say, 'It is mine.' It is a growing ground for *Amen-user-he,* the lord of every ship. Truly, it was Amen-Re, King of Gods, who said to Herihor, my master: 'Send me!' And he made me come with this great god. But look, you have let this great god spend these twenty-nine days moored in your harbor. Did you not know that he was here? Is he not he who he was? You are prepared to haggle over the Lebanon with Amun, its lord? As to your saying, the fomer kings sent silver and gold: If they had owned life and health, they would not have sent these things. It was in place of life and health that they sent these things to your fathers! But Amen-Re, King of Gods, he is the lord of life and health, and he was the lord of your fathers! They passed their lifetimes offering to Amun. You too, you are the servant of Amun!

"If you will say 'I will do' to Amun, and will carry out his business, you will live, you will prosper, you will be healthy; you will be beneficent to your whole land and your people. Do not desire what belongs to Amen-Re, King of Gods! Indeed, a lion loves his possessions! Have your scribe brought to me that I may send him to Smendes and Tentamun, the pillars Amun has set up for the north of his land; and they will send all that is needed. I will send him to them, saying: 'Have it brought until I return to the south; then I shall refund you all your expenses.'"[47] So I said to him.

He placed my letter in the hand of his messenger; and he loaded the keel, the prow-piece, and the stern-piece, together with four other hewn logs, seven in all,

---

[45]Seth was equated with the Syrian god Baal, and both were storm gods.

[46]That is, though Egypt was created by Amun before all other lands and was thus the motherland of all the arts; the civilization of Syria is now fully grown and no longer dependent on Egypt.

[47]That is, after Wenamun has returned to Thebes, his master, Herihor, will reimburse Smendes and Tentamun.

and sent them to Egypt. His messenger who had gone to Egypt returned to me in Syria in the first month of winter, Smendes and Tentamun having sent: four jars and one *kakmen*-vessel of gold, five jars of silver, ten garments of royal linen, ten *hrd*-garments[48] of fine linen, five hundred smooth linen mats, five hundred ox-hides, five hundred ropes, twenty sacks of lentils, and thirty baskets of fish. And she had sent to me:[49] five garments of fine linen, five *hrd*-garments of fine linen, one sack of lentils, and five baskets of fish.

The prince rejoiced. He assigned three hundred men and three hundred oxen, and he set supervisors over them to have them fell the timbers. They were felled and they lay there during the winter. In the third month of summer they dragged them to the shore of the sea. The prince came out and stood by them, and he sent to me, saying: "Come!" Now when I had been brought into his presence, the shadow of his sunshade fell on me. Then Penamun, a butler of his, intervened, saying: "The shadow of Pharaoh, your lord, has fallen upon you." And he was angry with him and said: "Leave him alone."

As I stood before him, he addressed me, saying: "Look, the business my fathers did in the past, I have done it, although you did not do for me what your fathers did for mine. Look, the last of your timber has arrived and is ready. Do as I wish, and come to load it. For has it not been given to you? Do not come to look at the terror of the sea. For if you look at the terror of the sea, you will see my own! Indeed, I have not done to you what was done to the envoys of Khaemwese,[50] after they had spent seventeen years in this land. They died on the spot." And he said to his butler: "Take him to see the tomb where they lie."

I said to him: "Do not make me see it. As for Khaemwese, the envoys he sent you were men and he himself was a man. You have not here one of his envoys, though you say: 'Go and see your companions.' Should you not rejoice and have a stela made for yourself, and say on it: 'Amen-Re, King of Gods, sent me Amun-of-the-Road, his envoy, together with Wenamun, his human envoy, in quest of timber for the great noble bark of Amen-Re, King of Gods. I felled it; I loaded it; I supplied my ships and my crews. I let them reach Egypt so as to beg for me from Amun fifty years of life over and above my allotted fate.' And if it comes to pass that in another day an envoy comes from the land of Egypt who knows writing and he reads out your name on the stela, you will receive water of the west like the gods who are there."

He said to me: "A great speech of admonition is what you have said to me."[51] I said to him: "As to the many things you have said to me: If I reach the place where

---

[48] *Hrd* is an unknown term, thought by some to mean "awning" or "veil," though others point to the fact that Egyptian art never depicts the wearing of veils.

[49] Tentamun sent a personal gift to Wenamun.

[50] It is uncertain to whom the prince is referring; perhaps it was the vizier Khaemwese, who served under Ramses IX.

[51] The prince appears to be speaking ironically.

the high priest of Amun is and he sees your accomplishment, it is your accomplishment that will draw profit to you."

I sent off to the shore of the sea, to where the logs were lying. And I saw eleven ships that had come in from the sea and belonged to the Tjeker who were saying: "Arrest him! Let no ship of his leave for the land of Egypt!" Then I sat down and wept. And the secretary of the prince came out to me and said to me: "What is it?" I said to him: "Do you not see the migrant birds going down to Egypt a second time? Look at them traveling to the cool water![52] Until when shall I be left here? For do you not see those who have come to arrest me?"

He went and told it to the prince. And the prince began to weep on account of the words said to him, for they were painful. He sent his secretary out to me, bringing me two jugs of wine and a sheep. And he sent me Tentne, an Egyptian songstress who was with him, saying: "Sing for him! Do not let his heart be anxious." And he sent to me, saying: "Eat, drink; do not let your heart be anxious. You shall hear what I will say tomorrow."

When morning came, he had his assembly summoned. He stood in their midst and said to the Tjeker: "What have you come for?" They said to him: "We have come after the blasted ships that you are sending to Egypt with our enemy." He said to them: "I cannot arrest the envoy of Amun in my country. Let me send him off, and you go after him to arrest him."

He had me board and sent me off from the harbor of the sea. And the wind drove me to the land of Alasiya.[53] Then the town's people came out against me to kill me. But I forced my way through them to where Hatiba, the princess of the town was. I met her coming from one of her houses to enter another. I saluted her and said to the people who stood around her: "Is there not one among you who understands Egyptian?" And one among them said: "I understand it." I said to him: "Tell my lady that I have heard it said as far away as Thebes, the place where Amun is: 'If wrong is done in every town, in the land of Alasiya right is done.' Now is wrong done here too every day?"

She said: "What is it you have said?" I said to her: "If the sea rages and the wind drives me to the land where you are, will you let me be received so as to kill me, though I am the envoy of Amun? Look, as for me, they would search for me till the end of time. As for this crew of the prince of Byblos, whom they seek to kill, will not their lord find ten crews of yours and kill them also?" She had the people summoned and they were reprimanded. She said to me: "Spend the night
————"[54]

[52]That is, Wenamun now has been abroad for more than a year and thus is witnessing for the second time the annual flight to Egypt of migratory birds.

[53]Probably Cyprus.

[54]The remainder of the report is lost.

5

❧

Hammurabi

THE LAWS

Not only did some of the earliest heroic literature, like The Epic of Gilgamesh *(Selection 1), come from Mesopotamia, the region of the Tigris–Euphrates river valley in today's southern Iraq, but also some of the earliest legal codes. One such important practical compilation has come down to us as* The Laws *(or* Code*) of Hammurabi. The most famous ruler of the first Babylonian dynasty, Hammurabi transformed the formerly unimportant city of Babylon into a major political and cultural center, unifying Mesopotamia under his imperial rule (1792–1750 B.C.). His activities are known to us from various official inscriptions on stone monuments and clay tablets, numerous letters, and* The Laws. *The letters and* The Laws *established what modern scholars regard as the classic form of the Akkadian language, part of the ancient Semitic language family.*

Not really a "code" in the technical sense of a systematically arranged collection, The Laws *is a compilation of economic edicts on such matters as prices, wages, and debts; common (customary) law of the region; important precedents; and some innovations by Hammurabi himself. The document reflects the legal thinking and moral values of its time and may have influenced the later Covenant Code in the Old Testament's Book of Exodus, chapters 21 through 23 (see Selection 6).*

The concept of equality before the law did not exist in Hammurabi's time: aristocrats, commoners, and slaves had differing responsibilities and paid differing penalties. Slaves, for example, were lawfully mutilated for what seems to us to be merely minor offenses. Offenses of the upper classes against slaves were punished only to the extent they resulted in "property damage" to the owner. Among those of equal rank, the principle of "an eye for an eye" is stated very clearly, with no mention of the practice of imprisonment. These laws thus required swift and painful justice, perhaps based on the premise of creating a deterrent effect. They advance far beyond the primitive concept of private revenge and establish an unvarying institutionalized legal standard.

Written near the end of Hammurabi's reign, The Laws is found on stone monuments and clay tablets from his and later reigns. On the most important and complete monument, a stone slab eight feet high discovered by a French scholar in 1901, Hammurabi is shown at the top receiving the laws from the enthroned sun-god Shamash. Then follows the prologue that catalogues Hammurabi's conquests of various cities and his respect for their gods, the 282 paragraphs of the laws, and the epilogue emphasizing the significance of Hammurabi's righteous justice.

PROLOGUE

When the lofty Anu,[1] king of the Anunnaki, and Bel, lord of heaven and earth, he who determines the destiny of the land, committed the rule of all mankind to Marduk, the chief son of Ea; when they made him great among the Igigi; when they pronounced the lofty name of Babylon; when they made it famous among the quarters of the world and in its midst established an everlasting kingdom whose foundations were firm as heaven and earth—at that time, Anu and Bel called me, Hammurabi, the exalted prince, the worshiper of the gods, to cause justice to prevail in the land, to destroy the wicked and the evil, to prevent the strong from oppressing the weak, to go forth like the sun over the black-head race,[2] to enlighten the land and to further the welfare of the people. . . . When Marduk sent me to rule the people and to bring help to the country, I established law and justice in the land and promoted the welfare of the people.

From *The Code of Hammurabi, King of Babylon about 2250 B.C.,* trans. Robert Francis Harper. Chicago: University of Chicago Press, 1904. Adapted by the editor.

[1]As was customary for such official pronouncements, Hammurabi prefaces his listing of the laws with a statement of their divine authority. Here, he names several of the Mesopotamian gods, Marduk being the chief patron god of Babylon.

[2]The dark-haired Babylonians.

ON CRIMINAL LAW PROCEDURES[3]

1

If a man[4] brings an accusation against a man, and charges him with a [capital] crime, but cannot prove it, he, the accuser, shall be put to death.

2

If a man charges a man with sorcery, and cannot prove it, he who is charged with sorcery shall go to the river, into the river he shall throw himself, and if the river overcomes him, his accuser shall take to himself his house [estate]. If the river shows that man to be innocent and he comes forth unharmed, he who charged him with sorcery shall be put to death. He who threw himself into the river shall take to himself the house of his accuser.[5]

3

If a man in a case [pending judgment], bears false [threatening] witness, or does not prove the testimony that he has given, if that case be a case involving life, that man shall be put to death.

4

If a man [in a case] bears witness for grain or money [as a bribe], he shall himself bear the penalty imposed in that case.

5

If a judge pronounces a judgment, renders a decision, delivers a verdict duly signed and sealed and, afterward, alters his judgment, they shall call that judge to account for the alteration of the judgment that he had pronounced, and he shall pay twelvefold the penalty that was in said judgment; and, in the assembly, they shall expel him from his seat of judgment, and he shall not return; and with the judges in a case he shall not take his seat.

---

[3]Headings are written by the editor; paragraph numbering is by modern scholars after the 1901 discovery of the monument containing *The Laws.*

[4]There are three distinct social–legal classes noted in these laws. The first, Babylonian *awîlum,* refers to wealthy property owners and aristocrats, usually—but not always— males. For that group, the translator uses the word *man.* The second class, *muskênum,* refers to poor commoners, usually—but not always—males, here translated as "free-man." The third class, *wardum-amtum,* consists of both male and female "slaves."

[5]The Euphrates River was regarded as a god who judges. (Later, medieval Western tradition took the *opposite* position in "trial by ordeal": the accused was judged *innocent* of sorcery if he drowned and guilty if he survived being thrown in the water.)

6

If a man steals the property of a god [temple] or palace, that man shall be put to death; and he who receives from his hand the stolen [property] shall also be put to death.

•   •   •

22

If a man practices robbery and is captured, that man shall be put to death.

23

If the robber is not captured, the man who has been robbed shall, in the presence of a god, make an itemized statement of his loss, and the city and the governor, in whose province and jurisdiction the robbery was committed, shall compensate him for whatever was lost.

24

If it is a life [that is lost], the city and governor shall pay one *mana*[6] of silver to his heirs.

25

If a fire breaks out in a man's house and a man who goes to extinguish it casts his eye on the furniture of the owner of the house and takes the furniture of the owner of the house, that man shall be thrown into that fire.

•   •   •

ON BUSINESS TRANSACTIONS

107

If a merchant lends to an agent[7] and the agent returns to the merchant whatever the merchant had given him; and if the merchant denies [receiving] what the agent has given to him, that agent shall call the merchant to account in the presence of a god and witnesses; and the merchant, because he has had a dispute with his agent, shall give to him sixfold the amount that he obtained.

•   •   •

---

[6]About five hundred grams (eighteen ounces). A *mana* was divided into sixty *shekels*.

[7]A traveling salesperson.

109

If outlaws collect in the house of a wine-seller, and she does not arrest these outlaws and bring them to the palace, that wine-seller shall be put to death.

•   •   •

122

If a man gives to another silver, gold, or anything else on deposit, whatever he gives he shall show to witnesses and he shall arrange the contracts and [then] he shall make the deposit.

123

If a man gives on deposit without witnesses or contracts, and at the place of deposit they dispute with him [i.e., deny the deposit], that case has no penalty.

124

If a man gives to another silver, gold, or anything else on deposit in the presence of witnesses and the latter disputes with him [or denies it], they shall call that man to account and he shall double whatever he has disputed and repay it.

125

If a man gives anything of his on deposit and at the place of deposit, either by burglary or pillage, he suffers loss in common with the owner of the house, the owner of the house who has been negligent and has lost what was given to him on deposit shall make good [the loss] and restore [it] to the owner of the goods; the owner of the house shall institute a search for what has been lost and take it from the thief.

126

If a man has not lost anything, but says that he has lost something, or if he files a claim for loss when nothing has been lost, he shall declare his [alleged] loss in the presence of a god, and he shall double and pay for the [alleged] loss the amount for which he had made claim.

•   •   •

229

If a builder builds a house for a man and does not make its construction firm, and the house which he has built collapses and causes the death of the owner of the house, that builder shall be put to death.

230

If it causes the death of a son of the owner of the house, they shall put to death a son of that builder.

231

If it causes the death of a slave of the owner of the house, he shall give to the owner of the house a slave of equal value.

232

If it destroys property, he shall restore whatever it destroyed, and because he did not make the house that he built firm and it collapsed, he shall rebuild the house that collapsed from his own property [i.e., at his own expense].

233

If a builder builds a house for a man and does not make its construction meet the requirements and a wall falls in, that builder shall strengthen that wall at his own expense.

●　　●　　●

245

If a man hires an ox and causes its death through neglect or abuse, he shall restore an ox of equal value to the owner of the ox.

246

If a man hires an ox and he breaks its foot or cuts its hamstring, he shall restore an ox of equal value to the owner of the ox.

247

If a man hires an ox and destroys its eye, he shall pay silver to the owner of the ox to the extent of one-half of its value.

248

If a man hires an ox and breaks its horn or cuts off its tail or injures the flesh [through which] the ring [passes], he shall pay silver to the extent of one-fourth of its value.

249

If a man hires an ox and a god strikes it and it dies, the man who hired the ox shall take an oath before god and go free.

250

If a bull, when passing through the street, gores a man and brings about his death, this case has no penalty.

251

If a man's bull has been wont to gore and they have made known to him his habit of goring, and he has not protected his horns or has not tied him up, and that bull gores the son of a man and brings about his death, he shall pay one-half *mana* of silver.

• • •

ON MARRIAGE AND FAMILY

131

If a man accuses his wife and she has not been taken in lying with another man, she shall take an oath in the name of a god and she shall return to her house.

132

If the finger has been pointed at the wife of a man because of another man, and she has not been taken in lying with another man, for her husband's sake she shall throw herself into the river.[8]

• • •

136

If a man deserts his city and flees and afterwards his wife enters into another house; if that man returns and would take his wife, the wife of the fugitive shall not return to her husband because he hated his city and fled.

137

If a man sets his face to put away a concubine who has borne him children or a wife who has presented him with children, he shall return to that woman her dowry and shall give to her the income of field, garden, and goods and she shall bring up her children; from the time that her children are grown up, from whatever is given to her children, they shall give to her a portion corresponding to that of a son and the man of her choice may marry her.

138

If a man would put away his wife who has not borne him children, he shall give her money to the amount of her marriage settlement[9] and he shall make good to her the dowry[10] that she brought from her father's house and then he may put her away.

139

If there were no marriage settlement, he shall give to her one *mana* of silver for a divorce.

---

[8]That is, submit to the ordeal by water, as in Law 2.

[9]Price the man paid her family for the marriage.

[10]Money and goods the wife brought to the marriage.

140

If he be a freeman, he shall give her one-third *mana* of silver.

141

If the wife of a man who is living in his house sets her face to go out and play the part of a fool, neglect her house, belittle her husband, they shall call her to account; if her husband says "I have put her away," he shall let her go. On her departure, nothing shall be given to her for her divorce. If her husband says: "I have not put her away," her husband may take another woman. The first woman shall dwell in the house of her husband as a maid servant.

142

If a woman hates her husband and says: "Thou shalt not have me," they shall inquire into her record for her defects; and if she has been a careful mistress and is without reproach and her husband has been going about and greatly belittling her, that woman has no blame. She shall receive her dowry and shall go to her father's house.

143

If she has not been a careful mistress, has gadded about, has neglected her house, and has belittled her husband, they shall throw that woman into the water.

•   •   •

145

If a man takes a wife and she does not present him with children and he sets his face to take a concubine, that man may take a concubine and bring her into his house. That concubine shall not rank with his wife.

146

If a man takes a wife and she gives a maid servant to her husband, and that maid servant bears children and afterwards would take rank with her mistress; because she has borne children, her mistress may not sell her for money, but she may reduce her to bondage and count her among the maid servants.

147

If she has not borne children, her mistress may sell her for money.

148

If a man takes a wife and she becomes afflicted with disease, and if he sets his face to take another, he may. His wife, who is afflicted with disease, he shall not put away. She shall remain in the house which he has built and he shall maintain her as long as she lives.

149

If that woman does not elect to remain in her husband's house, he shall make good to her the dowry that she brought from her father's house and she may go.

•   •   •

194

If a man gives his son to a nurse to be suckled and that son dies in the hands of the nurse, and the nurse substitutes another son without the consent of his father and mother, they shall call her to account; and because she has substituted another son without the consent of his father or mother, they shall cut off her breast.

195

If a son strikes his father, they shall cut off his hand.

ON LIABILITY FOR ASSAULT

196

If a man destroys the eye of another man, they shall destroy his eye.

197

If one breaks a man's bone, they shall break his bone.

198

If one destroys the eye of a freeman or breaks the bone of a freeman, he shall pay one *mana* of silver.

199

If one destroys the eye of a man's slave or breaks a bone of a man's slave, he shall pay one-half his price [market value].

200

If a man knocks out a tooth of a man of his own rank, they shall knock out his tooth.

201

If one knocks out a tooth of a freeman, he shall pay one-third *mana* of silver.

202

If a man strikes [i.e., commits an assault] the person of a man who is his superior, he shall receive sixty strokes with an ox-tail whip in public.

203

If a man strikes another man of his own rank, he shall pay one *mana* of silver.

204

If a freeman strikes a freeman, he shall pay ten *shekels* of silver.

205

If a man's slave strikes a man's son, they shall cut off his ear.

206

If a man strikes another man in a quarrel and wounds him, he shall swear: "I struck him without intent," and he shall be responsible for the physician.

207

If [he] dies as the result of the stroke, he shall swear [as above], and if he is a man, he shall pay one-half *mana* of silver.

208

If [he] is a freeman, he shall pay one-third *mana* of silver.

209

If a man strikes a man's daughter and brings about a miscarriage, he shall pay ten *shekels* of silver for her miscarriage.

210

If that woman dies, they shall put his daughter to death.

211

If, through a stroke, he brings about a miscarriage to the daughter of a freeman, he shall pay five *shekels* of silver.

212

If that woman dies, he shall pay one-half *mana* of silver.

213

If he strikes the female slave of a man and brings about a miscarriage, he shall pay two *shekels* of silver.

214

If that female slave dies, he shall pay one-third *mana* of silver.

ON MEDICAL PRACTICE

215

If a physician operates on a man for a severe wound [or makes a severe wound upon a man] with a bronze lancet and saves the man's life, or if he opens an abscess [in the eye] of a man with a bronze lancet and saves that man's eye, he shall receive ten *shekels* of silver [as his fee].

216

If he is a freeman, he shall receive five *shekels*.

217

If it is a man's slave, the owner of the slave shall give two *shekels* of silver to the physician.

218

If a physician operates on a man for a severe wound with a bronze lancet and causes the man's death, or opens an abscess [in the eye] of a man with a bronze lancet and destroys the man's eye, they shall cut off his fingers.

219

If a physician operates on a slave of a freeman for a severe wound with a bronze lancet and causes his death, he shall restore a slave of equal value.

220

If he opens an abscess [in his eye] with a bronze lancet, and destroys his eye, he shall pay silver to the extent of one-half of his price.

221

If a physician sets a broken bone for a man or cures his diseased bowels, the patient shall give five *shekels* of silver to the physician.

222

If he is a freeman, he shall give three *shekels* of silver.

223

If it is a man's slave, the owner of the slave shall give two *shekels* of silver to the physician.

•   •   •

EPILOGUE

The righteous laws that Hammurabi, the wise king, established and [by which] he gave the land stable support and pure government. Hammurabi, the perfect king, am I. I was not careless, nor was I neglectful of the black-head people, whose rule Bel presented and Marduk delivered to me. I provided them with a peaceful country. I opened up difficult barriers and lent them support. With the powerful weapon that Za-má-má and Nana entrusted to me, with the breadth of vision that Ea allotted me, with the might which Marduk gave me, I expelled the enemy to the north and south; I made an end of their raids; I brought health to the land; I made the populace to rest in security; I permitted no one to molest them.

The great gods proclaimed me and I am the guardian governor, whose scepter is righteous and whose beneficent protection is spread over my city. In my bosom I carried the people of the land of Sumer and Akkad; under my protection I brought their brethren into security; in my wisdom I restrained [hid] them; that the strong might not oppose the weak, and that they should give justice to the orphan and the widow, in Babylon, the city whose turrets Anu and Bel raised; in Esagila, the temple whose foundations are firm as heaven and earth, for the pronouncing of judgments in the land, for the rendering of decisions for the land, and for the righting of wrong, my weighty words I have written upon my monument, and in the presence of my image as king of righteousness have I established. . . .

In the days that are yet to come, for all future time, may the king who is in the land observe the words of righteousness that I have written upon my monument! May he not alter the judgments of the land that I have pronounced, or the decisions of the country that I have rendered! May he not efface my statues! If that man has wisdom, if he wishes to give his land good government, let him give attention to the words that I have written upon my monument! And may this monument enlighten him as to procedure and administration, the judgments that I have pronounced, and the decisions that I have rendered for the land! And let him rightly rule his black-head people; let him pronounce judgments for them and render for them decisions! Let him root out the wicked and evildoer from his land! Let him promote the welfare of his people!

Hammurabi, the king of righteousness, whom Shamash has endowed with justice, am I. My words are weighty; my deeds are unrivaled. . . .

6

❧

THE BIBLE
OLD TESTAMENT

*T*he collection of sacred books in the Hebrew language that is known to Christians as the Old Testament is the complete Bible (Tanakh) for Jews. It is accepted by both faiths, and also by Moslems, as a divinely inspired text. Most of the Old Testament tells of the one God's dealings with his "chosen witnesses," the Jewish people—originally conceived as the descendants of the patriarch Abraham. As the biblical tradition developed, the text came to be viewed by varied believers as the revelation of God's will to all humanity. Like the Sumerian Epic of Gilgamesh (Selection 1), the Old Testament is many centuries older than Christianity. Christians view it as the essential prologue to their own additional sacred text, the New Testament (Selection 35). Through Christianity, some Jewish religious ideas were eventually spread throughout the Roman Empire. The following passages show aspects of the Jewish version of some crucial events in the developing relationship between the human and the divine; they also show the growing human comprehension of God's presence and plan.

The first five books of the Old Testament, known to Jews as the Torah ("teaching" or "law"), begin with God's creation of the universe and then focus on a garden. It is a fertile and pleasant place where man and woman enjoy the intimacy of their creator. This proper relationship is broken by an act of their proud and rebellious free will, the "original sin," followed by the first murder, committed by the first offspring of these original humans. The possibility of doing evil, then, lies deep in human nature. God's judgment, therefore, falls often upon humanity as it did when he sent a great flood that only Noah and his family survived. Thus, a theme that will run through the Jewish–Christian narrative is set forth: a recurring pattern of sin, divine judgment, punishment, and—because of the merits of only one person or a few—divine mercy.

The Hebrew people, through their founding patriarch, Abraham, are selected as the instrument of divine purpose. God establishes a special covenant (binding conditional agreement) with them. They pledge obedience to God and then, through Moses, are given God's law at Mount Sinai. With the establishment of *that law, the Jewish religion develops far beyond its tribal origins. Many Jews, however, prove unequal to God's covenantal demands. Exposed to the competing ways and faiths of neighboring peoples, some Jews follow strange gods and adopt a life contrary to God's law. God's anger is expressed through his spokesmen, the prophets (moralizing believers in the one God), who warn Jews and others in his name. Gradually, the prophets give shape and direction to the Jewish religious experience. The books named for the prophets number about half of the Old Testament books.*

In his emotional intensity, Jeremiah is the great tragic prophet. He loves his people but has to cry out against their moral and religious folly. Born to a priestly family in the kingdom of Judah in a village near Jerusalem he endured the capture of Jerusalem by the Babylonians in 587 B.C. Jeremiah saw the destruction of the Temple and Jerusalem's other sacred places as God's punishment for straying from the divine law. Many Jews then were brought into captivity in Babylon, but the prophetic tradition continued through that period of "exile" and even after many were able to return home. The return from exile was also a sign of God's mercy for his people who have repented of their earlier sinful ways. The inspired messages of the prophets mark the peak of Jewish religious literature.

GENESIS[1]
The Beginnings of History
1:1–4:16

In the beginning God created the heavens and the earth. The earth was without form and void, and darkness was upon the face of the deep; and the spirit of God was moving over the face of the waters.

[1]A Greek word meaning "origin" or "birth." Genesis is the first book of the Bible and begins with two versions of the creation story. It then tells about the expulsion from Eden of the first people, the first murder, the flood, and the Hebrew patriarchs (down to the settling of some of their descendants in Egypt). Genesis thus introduces the ancestry of the Israelites (Hebrews)—first, like all humanity, from Adam, and then, more particularly, from "Father" Abraham. Genesis also describes the covenant (conditional agreement) that God first established with Noah for all mankind, and the later, special covenant with Abraham and his descendants.

And God said, "Let there be light"; and there was light. And God saw that the light was good; and God separated the light from the darkness. God called the light day, and the darkness he called night. And there was evening and there was morning, one day.

And God said, "Let there be a firmament in the midst of the waters, and let it separate the waters from the waters." And God made the firmament and separated the waters which were under the firmament from the waters which were above the firmament. And it was so.[2] And God called the firmament heaven. And there was evening and there was morning, a second day.

And God said, "Let the waters under the heavens be gathered together into one place, and let the dry land appear." And it was so. God called the dry land earth, and the waters that were gathered together he called seas. And God saw that it was good. And God said, "Let the earth put forth vegetation, plants yielding seed, and fruit trees bearing fruit in which is their seed, each according to its kind, upon the earth." And it was so. The earth brought forth vegetation, plants yielding seed according to their own kinds, and trees bearing fruit in which is their seed, each according to its kind. And God saw that it was good. And there was evening and there was morning, a third day.

And God said, "Let there be lights in the firmament of the heavens to separate the day from the night; and let them be for signs and for seasons and for days and years, and let them be lights in the firmament of the heavens to give light upon the earth." And it was so. And God made the two great lights, the greater light to rule the day, and the lesser light to rule the night; he made the stars also. And God set them in the firmament of the heavens to give light upon the earth, to rule over the day and over the night, and to separate the light from the darkness. And God saw that it was good. And there was evening and there was morning, a fourth day.

And God said, "Let the waters bring forth swarms of living creatures, and let birds fly above the earth across the firmament of the heavens." So God created the great sea monsters and every living creature that moves, with which the waters swarm, according to their kinds, and every winged bird according to its kind. And God saw that it was good. And God blessed them, saying, "Be fruitful and multiply and fill the waters in the seas, and let birds multiply on the earth." And there was evening and there was morning, a fifth day.

And God said, "Let the earth bring forth living creatures according to their kinds: cattle[3] and creeping things and beasts of the earth according to their

---

[2]This description of God's creative action on the second day rests upon the belief that the world was created out of a watery chaos. The "firmament" was conceived as a vault, or dome, that separated the waters below from the waters above. It provided the boundary beyond which Gold dwelt.

[3]All domestic animals.

kinds." And it was so. And God made the beasts of the earth according to their kinds and the cattle according to their kinds, and everything that creeps upon the ground according to its kind. And God saw that it was good.

Then God said, "Let us make man in our image, after our likeness; and let them have dominion over the fish of the sea, and over the birds of the air, and over the cattle, and over all the earth, and over every creeping thing that creeps upon the earth."

So God created man[4] in his own image, in the image of God he created him; male and female he created them. And God blessed them, and God said to them, "Be fruitful and multiply, and fill the earth and subdue it; and have dominion over the fish of the sea and over the birds of the air and over every living thing that moves upon the earth." And God said, "Behold, I have given you every plant yielding seed which is upon the face of all the earth, and every tree with seed in its fruit; you shall have them for food. And to every beast of the earth, and to every bird of the air, and to everything that creeps on the earth, everything that has the breath of life, I have given every green plant for food." And it was so. And God saw everything that he had made, and behold, it was very good. And there was evening and there was morning, a sixth day.

Thus the heavens and the earth were finished, and all the host of them. And on the seventh day God finished his work which he had done, and he rested on the seventh day from all his work which he had done. So God blessed the seventh day and hallowed it, because on it God rested from all his work which he had done in creation.

These are the generations of the heavens and the earth when they were created.[5]

In the day that the Lord God made the earth and the heavens, when no plant of the field was yet in the earth and no herb of the field had yet sprung up—for the Lord God had not caused it to rain upon the earth, and there was no man to till the ground; but a mist went up from the earth and watered the whole face of the ground—then the Lord God formed man of dust from the ground, and breathed into his nostrils the breath of life; and man became a living being. And the Lord God planted a garden in Eden, in the east; and there he put the man whom he had formed. And out of the ground the Lord God made to grow every tree that is pleasant to the sight and good for food, the tree of life also in the midst of the garden, and the tree of the knowledge of good and evil.

A river flowed out of Eden to water the garden, and there it divided and became four rivers. The name of the first is Pishon; it is the one which flows around the whole land of Hav'ilah, where there is gold; and the gold of that land

---

[4]A Hebrew word for "man" is *adam*.

[5]A Hebrew word for "earth" is *adamah*. This sentence begins a second version of the creation story; it differs in some significant ways from the first.

is good; bdellium and onyx stone are there. The name of the second river is Gihon; it is the one which flows around the whole land of Cush. And the name of the third river is Tigris, which flows east of Assyria. And the fourth river is the Euphrates.

The Lord God took the man and put him in the garden of Eden to till it and keep it. And the Lord God commanded the man, saying, "You may freely eat of every tree of the garden; but of the tree of the knowledge of good and evil you shall not eat, for in the day that you eat of it you shall die."

Then the Lord God said, "It is not good that the man should be alone; I will make him a helper fit for him. So out of the ground the Lord God formed every beast of the field and every bird of the air, and brought them to the man to see what he would call them; and whatever the man called every living creature, that was its name. The man gave names to all cattle, and to the birds of the air, and to every beast of the field; but for the man there was not found a helper fit for him. So the Lord God caused a deep sleep to fall upon the man, and while he slept took one of his ribs and closed up its place with flesh; and the rib which the Lord God had taken from the man he made into a woman and brought her to the man. Then the man said,

> "This at last is bone of my bones
>   and flesh of my flesh;
> she shall be called Woman,
>   because she was taken out of Man."[6]

Therefore a man leaves his father and his mother and cleaves to his wife, and they become one flesh. And the man and his wife were both naked, and were not ashamed.

Now the serpent was more subtle than any other wild creature that the Lord God had made. He said to the woman, "Did God say, 'You shall not eat of any tree of the garden'?" And the woman said to the serpent, "We may eat of the fruit of the trees of the garden; but God said, 'You shall not eat of the fruit of the tree which is in the midst of the garden, neither shall you touch it, lest you die.'" But the serpent said to the woman, "You will not die. For God knows that when you eat of it your eyes will be opened, and you will be like God, knowing good and evil." So when the woman saw that the tree was good for food, and that it was a delight to the eyes, and that the tree was to be desired to make one wise, she took of its fruit and ate; and she also gave some to her husband, and he ate. Then the eyes of both were opened, and they knew that they were naked; and they sewed fig leaves together and made themselves aprons.

And they heard the sound of the Lord God walking in the garden in the cool of the day, and the man and his wife hid themselves from the presence of the Lord

---

[6]Another Hebrew word for "man" is *ish;* for "woman," *ishshah.*

God among the trees of the garden. But the Lord God called to the man, and said to him, "Where are you?" And he said, "I heard the sound of thee in the garden, and I was afraid, because I was naked; and I hid myself." He said, "Who told you that you were naked? Have you eaten of the tree of which I commanded you not to eat?" The man said, "The woman whom thou gavest to be with me, she gave me the fruit of the tree, and I ate." Then the Lord God said to the woman, "What is this that you have done?" The woman said, "The serpent beguiled me, and I ate." The Lord God said to the serpent,

> "Because you have done this,
> > cursed are you above all cattle,
> > and above all wild animals;
> upon your belly you shall go,
> > and dust you shall eat.
> > all the days of your life.
> I will put enmity between you and the woman,
> > and between your seed [descendants] and her seed;
> he shall bruise your head,
> > and you shall bruise his heel."

To the woman he said,

> "I will greatly multiply your pain in childbearing;
> > in pain you shall bring forth children,
> yet your desire shall be for your husband,
> > and he shall rule over you."

And to Adam he said,

> "Because you have listened to the voice of your wife,
> > and have eaten of the tree
> of which I commanded you,
> > 'You shall not eat of it,'
> cursed is the ground because of you;
> > in toil you shall eat of it all the days of your life;
> thorns and thistles it shall bring forth to you;
> > and you shall eat the plants of the field.
> In the sweat of your face
> > you shall eat bread
> till you return to the ground,
> > for out of it you were taken;
> you are dust,
> > and to dust you shall return."

The man called his wife's name Eve, because she was the mother of all living.[7] And the Lord God made for Adam and for his wife garments of skins, and clothed them.

Then the Lord God said, "Behold, the man has become like one of us, knowing good and evil; and now, lest he put forth his hand and take also of the tree of life, and eat, and live forever"—therefore the Lord God sent him forth from the garden of Eden, to till the ground from which he was taken. He drove out the man; and at the east of the garden of Eden he placed the cherubim,[8] and a flaming sword which turned every way, to guard the way to the tree of life.

Now Adam knew[9] Eve, his wife, and she conceived and bore Cain, saying, "I have gotten a man with the help of the Lord." And again, she bore his brother, Abel. Now Abel was a keeper of sheep, and Cain a tiller of the ground. In the course of time Cain brought to the Lord an offering of the fruit of the ground, and Abel brought of the firstlings of his flock and of their fat portions. And the Lord had regard for Abel and his offering, but for Cain and his offering he had no regard.[10] So Cain was very angry, and his countenance fell. The Lord said to Cain, "Why are you angry, and why has your countenance fallen? If you do well, will you not be accepted? And if you do not do well, sin is couching at the door; its desire is for you, but you must master it."

Cain said to Abel his brother, "Let us go out to the field." And when they were in the field, Cain rose up against his brother Abel, and killed him. Then the Lord said to Cain, "Where is Abel, your brother?" He said, "I do not know; am I my brother's keeper?" And the Lord said, "What have you done? The voice of your brother's blood is crying to me from the ground. And now you are cursed from the ground, which has opened its mouth to receive your brother's blood from your hand. When you till the ground, it shall no longer yield to you its strength; you shall be a fugitive and a wanderer on the earth." Cain said to the Lord, "My punishment is greater than I can bear. Behold, thou hast driven me this day away from the ground; and from thy face I shall be hidden; and I shall be a fugitive and a wanderer on the earth, and whoever finds me will slay me." Then the Lord said to him, "Not so! If anyone slays Cain, vengeance shall be taken on him sevenfold." And the Lord put a mark[11] on Cain, lest any who came upon him should kill him. Then Cain went away from the presence of the Lord, and dwelt in the land of Nod, east of Eden.

---

[7]Eve's name, in Hebrew, is similar to the word for "living."

[8]Winged, semi-divine creatures who served as guardians of sacred areas.

[9]That is, had sexual intercourse.

[10]The Cain and Abel story may personify a social conflict between settled farmers and nomadic shepherds. No reason is given for the Lord's acceptance only of Abel's offering.

[11]A protective mark, or emblem, perhaps like a tattoo.

The Flood

6:1–22

When men began to multiply on the face of the ground, and daughters were born to them, the sons of God saw that the daughters of men were fair; and they took to wife such of them as they chose. Then the Lord said, "My spirit shall not abide in man forever, for he is flesh, but his days shall be a hundred and twenty years." The Nephilim [giants] were on the earth in those days, and also afterward, when the sons of God came into the daughters of men, and they bore children to them.[12] These were the mighty men that were of old, the men of renown.

The Lord saw that the wickedness of man was great in the earth, and that every imagination of the thoughts of his heart was only evil continually. And the Lord was sorry that he had made man on the earth, and it grieved him to his heart. So the Lord said, "I will blot out man whom I have created from the face of the ground, man and beast and creeping things and birds of the air, for I am sorry that I have made them." But Noah found favor in the eyes of the Lord.

These are the generations of Noah. Noah was a righteous man, blameless in his generation; Noah walked with God. And Noah had three sons, Shem, Ham, and Japheth.

Now the earth was corrupt in God's sight, and the earth was filled with violence. And God saw the earth, and behold, it was corrupt; for all flesh had corrupted their way upon the earth. And God said to Noah, "I have determined to make an end of all flesh; for the earth is filled with violence through them; behold, I will destroy them with the earth. Make yourself an ark of gopher wood; make rooms in the ark, and cover it inside and out with pitch. This is how you are to make it: the length of the ark three hundred cubits,[13] its breadth fifty cubits, and its height thirty cubits. Make a roof for the ark, and finish it to a cubit above; and set the door of the ark in its side; make it with lower, second, and third decks. For behold, I will bring a flood of waters upon the earth, to destroy all flesh in which is the breath of life from under heaven; everything that is on the earth shall die. But I will establish my covenant with you; and you shall come into the ark, you, your sons, your wife, and your sons' wives with you. And of every living thing of all flesh, you shall bring two of every sort into the ark, to keep them alive with you; they shall be male and female. Of the birds according to their kinds, and of the animals according to their kinds, of every creeping thing of the

---

[12]This story of the mating of "the sons of God" with "the daughters of men" reveals the survival of an earlier, non-Hebrew mythology. Unlike those earlier myths, however, the biblical account of a divine parent does not grant semi-divine status to the offspring. The story attempts, rather, to explain the origin of a legendary race of giants.

[13]A cubit is an ancient unit of measurement based on the length of a man's forearm, usually about eighteen inches.

ground according to its kind, two of every sort shall come in to you, to keep them alive. Also take with you every sort of food that is eaten, and store it up; and it shall serve as food for you and for them." Noah did this; he did all that God commanded him.[14]

EXODUS[15]

The Covenant

19:1–20:21

On the third new moon after the people of Israel had gone forth out of the land of Egypt, on that day they came into the wilderness of Sinai. And when they set out from Reph'idim and came into the wilderness of Sinai, they encamped in the wilderness; and there Israel encamped before the mountain. And Moses went up to God, and the Lord called to him out of the mountain, saying, "Thus you shall say to the house of Jacob, and tell the people of Israel: You have seen what I did to the Egyptians, and how I bore you on eagles' wings and brought you to myself. Now therefore, if you will obey my voice and keep my covenant, you shall be my own possession among all peoples; for all the earth is mine, and you shall be to me a kingdom of priests and a holy nation.[16] These are the words which you shall speak to the children of Israel."

So Moses came and called the elders of the people, and set before them all these words which the Lord had commanded him. And all the people answered

---

[14]God then sends the flood as a punishment for human wickedness. (Many details of this biblical flood story resemble the account in the earlier *Epic of Gilgamesh* [Selection 1], with the essential difference that the biblical flood represents a single, divine, moral judgment—not the whims of many gods.) God's mercy will be shown by his saving of a righteous remnant (Noah and his family) through whom humanity can begin anew. Through Noah, God will make a covenant with all humanity that "never again shall there be a flood to destroy the earth."

[15]A Greek word meaning "a going out." The Book of Exodus tells about the departure from Egypt, around 1300 B.C., of an oppressed Hebrew community. It begins the story of their forty-year journey through the desert back to the land of their ancestors who were described in Genesis—Abraham, his son Isaac, and Isaac's son Jacob (also called Israel). The Hebrew religious and political leader was Moses. Exodus's climactic event is God's reassertion of his covenant with the Hebrew people through his giving of the law to Moses at Mount Sinai. With the establishment of this law, the Jewish religion develops a clear identity.

[16]The first part of this sentence identifies the Hebrews as God's chosen people or "own possession"—on the condition that they obey God's law. It also emphasizes that their God is also the God of "all the earth" and that the Hebrews are "a holy nation" in the sense that it is the consecrated carrier of God's word.

together and said, "All that the Lord has spoken we will do." And Moses reported the words of the people to the Lord. And the Lord said to Moses, "Lo, I am coming to you in a thick cloud, that the people may hear when I speak with you, and may also believe you forever."

Then Moses told the words of the people to the Lord. And the Lord said to Moses, "Go to the people and consecrate them today and tomorrow, and let them wash their garments, and be ready by the third day; for on the third day the Lord will come down upon Mount Sinai in the sight of all the people. And you shall set bounds for the people round about saying, 'Take heed that you do not go up into the mountain or touch the border of it; whoever touches the mountain shall be put to death; no hand shall touch him, but he shall be stoned or shot; whether beast or man, he shall not live.' When the trumpet sounds a long blast, they shall come up to the mountain." So Moses went down from the mountain to the people, and consecrated the people; and they washed their garments. And he said to the people, "Be ready by the third day; do not go near a woman."

On the morning of the third day there were thunders and lightnings, and a thick cloud upon the mountain, and a very loud trumpet blast, so that all the people who were in the camp trembled. Then Moses brought the people out of the camp to meet God; and they took their stand at the foot of the mountain. And Mount Sinai was wrapped in smoke, because the Lord descended upon it in fire; and the smoke of it went up like the smoke of a kiln, and the whole mountain quaked greatly. And as the sound of the trumpet grew louder and louder, Moses spoke, and God answered him in thunder. And the Lord came down upon Mount Sinai, to the top of the mountain; and the Lord called Moses to the top of the mountain, and Moses went up. And the Lord said to Moses, "Go down and warn the people, lest they break through to the Lord to gaze and many of them perish. And also let the priests who come near to the Lord consecrate themselves, lest the Lord break out upon them." And Moses said to the Lord, "The people cannot come up to Mount Sinai; for thou thyself didst charge us, saying, 'Set bounds about the mountain, and consecrate it.'" And the Lord said to him, "Go down, and come up bringing Aaron [Moses's brother] with you; but do not let the priests and the people break through to come up to the Lord, lest he break out against them." So Moses went down to the people and told them.

And God spoke all these words, saying,[17]

"I am the Lord your God, who brought you out of the land of
Egypt, out of the house of bondage.

"You shall have no other gods before me.

---

[17]The following "Ten Commandments" state the essence of Jewish duties to God and to the rest of humanity. The commandments were given as some basic requirements if the Hebrews were to enter into a covenant with God.

"You shall not make for yourself a graven image,[18] or any likeness of anything that is in heaven above, or that is in the earth beneath, or that is in the water under the earth; you shall not bow down to them or serve them; for I the Lord your God am a jealous God, visiting the iniquity of the fathers upon the children to the third and fourth generation of those who hate me, but showing steadfast love to thousands of those who love me and keep my commandments.

"You shall not take the name of the Lord your God in vain; for the Lord will not hold him guiltless who takes his name in vain.[19]

"Remember the sabbath day, to keep it holy. Six days you shall labor, and do all your work; but the seventh day is a sabbath to the Lord your God; in it you shall not do any work, you, or your son, or your daughter, your manservant, or your maidservant, or your cattle, or the sojourner who is within your gates; for in six days the Lord made heaven and earth, the sea, and all that is in them, and rested the seventh day; therefore the Lord blessed the sabbath day and hallowed it.

"Honor your father and your mother, that your days may be long in the land which the Lord your God gives you.

"You shall not kill.[20]

"You shall not commit adultery.

"You shall not steal.

"You shall not bear false witness against your neighbor.

"You shall not covet your neighbor's house; you shall not covet your neighbor's wife, or his manservant, or his maidservant, or his ox, or his ass, or anything that is your neighbor's."

Now when all the people perceived the thunderings and the lightnings and the sound of the trumpet and the mountain smoking, the people were afraid and trembled; and they stood afar off, and said to Moses, "You speak to us, and we will hear; but let not God speak to us, lest we die." And Moses said to the people, "Do not fear; for God has come to prove you, and that the fear of him may be before your eyes, that you may not sin."

And the people stood afar off, while Moses drew near to the thick darkness where God was.

---

[18]This second commandment, prohibiting worship of any carved statue, was unique in the ancient world.

[19]Others translate: "You shall not swear falsely by the name of the Lord your God; for the Lord will not clear one who swears falsely by his name." This third commandment prohibits both false legal testimony and every possible wrong or vain usage of God's name.

[20]Others translate: "murder." (Killing as capital punishment for crimes and during war is *not* forbidden in the Old Testament.)

The Torah, or Law[21]

20:22–23:33

And the Lord said to Moses, "Thus you shall say to the people of Israel: 'You have seen for yourselves that I have talked with you from heaven. You shall not make gods of silver to be with me, nor shall you make yourselves gods of gold. An altar of earth you shall make for me and sacrifice on it your burnt offerings and your peace offerings, your sheep and your oxen; in every place where I cause my name to be remembered I will come to you and bless you. And if you make me an altar of stone, you shall not build it of hewn stones; for if you wield your tool upon it you profane it. And you shall not go up by steps to my altar, that your nakedness be not exposed on it.'

"Now these are the ordinances which you shall set before them. When you buy a Hebrew slave, he shall serve six years, and in the seventh he shall go out free, for nothing. If he comes in single, he shall go out single; if he comes in married, then his wife shall go out with him. If his master gives him a wife and she bears him sons or daughters, the wife and her children shall be her master's and he shall go out alone. But if the slave plainly says, 'I love my master, my wife, and my children; I will not go out free,' then his master shall bring him to God, and he shall bring him to the door or the doorpost; and his master shall bore his ear through with an awl; and he shall serve him for life.

"When a man sells his daughter as a slave, she shall not go out as the male slaves do. If she does not please her master, who has designated her for himself, then he shall let her be redeemed; he shall have no right to sell her to a foreign people, since he has dealt faithlessly with her. If he designates her for his son, he shall deal with her as with a daughter. If he takes another wife to himself, he shall not diminish her food, her clothing, or her marital rights. And if he does not do these three things for her, she shall go out for nothing, without payment of money.

"Whoever strikes a man so that he dies shall be put to death. But if he did not lie in wait for him, but God let him fall into his hand, then I will appoint for you a place to which he may flee. But if a man willfully attacks another to kill him treacherously, you shall take him from my altar, that he may die.

"Whoever strikes his father or his mother shall be put to death.

"Whoever steals a man, whether he sells him or is found in possession of him, shall be put to death.

"Whoever curses his father or his mother shall be put to death.

---

[21]In addition to the basic principles established in the Ten Commandments, the Old Testament, according to traditional rabbinic count, states 603 other commandments. They regulate many details in the daily lives of the faithful. Some of these regulations can be seen in the following section. Many are based on customs of neighboring societies but reflect distinctive Jewish ethical and ritual practices.

"When men quarrel and one strikes the other with a stone or with his fist and the man does not die but keeps his bed, then if the man rises again and walks abroad with his staff, he that struck him shall be clear; only he shall pay for the loss of his time, and shall have him thoroughly healed.

"When a man strikes his slave, male or female, with a rod and the slave dies under his hand, he shall be punished. But if the slave survives a day or two, he is not to be punished; for the slave is his money.

"When men strive together, and hurt a woman with child, so that there is a miscarriage, and yet no harm follows, the one who hurt her shall be fined, according as the woman's husband shall lay upon him; and he shall pay as the judges determine. If any harm follows, then you shall give life for life, eye for eye, tooth for tooth, hand for hand, foot for foot, burn for burn, wound for wound, stripe for stripe.[22]

"When a man strikes the eye of his slave, male or female, and destroys it, he shall let the slave go free for the eye's sake. If he knocks out the tooth of his slave, male or female, he shall let the slave go free for the tooth's sake.

"When an ox gores a man or woman to death, the ox shall be stoned, and its flesh shall not be eaten; but the owner of the ox shall be clear. But if the ox has been accustomed to gore in the past, and its owner has been warned but has not kept it in, and it kills a man or a woman, the ox shall be stoned, and its owner also shall be put to death. If a ransom is laid on him, then he shall give for the redemption of his life whatever is laid upon him. If it gores a man's son or daughter, he shall be dealt with according to the same rule. If the ox gores a slave, male or female, the owner shall give to their master thirty *shekels* of silver, and the ox shall be stoned.

"When a man leaves a pit open, or when a man digs a pit and does not cover it, and an ox or an ass falls into it, the owner of the pit shall make it good; he shall give money to its owner, and the dead beast shall be his.

"When one man's ox hurts another's, so that it dies, then they shall sell the live ox and divide the price of it; and the dead beast also they shall divide. Or if it is known that the ox has been accustomed to gore in the past, and its owner has not kept it in, he shall pay ox for ox, and the dead beast shall be his.

"If a man steals an ox or a sheep, and kills it or sells it, he shall pay five oxen for an ox, and four sheep for a sheep. He shall make restitution; if he has nothing, then he shall be sold for his theft. If the stolen beast is found alive in his possession, whether it is an ox or an ass or a sheep, he shall pay double.

---

[22]No example of the actual carrying out of physical retribution, as in "eye for eye," is recorded in the Old Testament. Except in cases of intentional homicide, the principle of retribution was transformed into monetary compensation scaled to the degree of injury. Similarly, other statements of extreme punishment, such as the one for striking one's parents, have no record of enforcement in the biblical narrative.

"If a thief is found breaking in, and is struck so that he dies, there shall be no bloodguilt for him; but if the sun has risen upon him, there shall be bloodguilt for him.

"When a man causes a field or vineyard to be grazed over, or lets his beast loose and it feeds in another man's field, he shall make restitution from the best in his own field and in his own vineyard.

"When fire breaks out and catches in thorns so that the stacked grain or the standing grain or the field is consumed, he that kindled the fire shall make full restitution.

"If a man delivers to his neighbor money or goods to keep, and it is stolen out of the man's house, then, if the thief is found, he shall pay double. If the thief is not found, the owner of the house shall come near to God, to show whether or not he has put his hand to his neighbor's goods.

"For every breach of trust, whether it is for ox, for ass, for sheep, for clothing, or for any kind of lost thing, of which one says, 'This is it,' the case of both parties shall come before God; he whom God shall condemn shall pay double to his neighbor.

"If a man delivers to his neighbor an ass or an ox or a sheep or any beast to keep, and it dies or is hurt or is driven away, without anyone seeing it, an oath by the Lord shall be between them both to see whether he has not put his hand to his neighbor's property; and the owner shall accept the oath, and he shall not make restitution. But if it is stolen from him, he shall make restitution to its owner. If it is torn by beasts, let him bring it as evidence; he shall not make restitution for what has been torn.

"If a man borrows anything of his neighbor, and it is hurt or dies, the owner not being with it, he shall make full restitution. If the owner was with it, he shall not make restitution; if it was hired, it came for its hire.

"If a man seduces a virgin who is not betrothed, and lies with her, he shall give the marriage present for her, and make her his wife. If her father utterly refuses to give her to him, he shall pay money equivalent to the marriage present for virgins.

"You shall not permit a sorceress to live.

"Whoever lies with a beast shall be put to death.

"Whoever sacrifices to any god, save to the Lord only, shall be utterly destroyed.

"You shall not wrong a stranger or oppress him, for you were strangers in the land of Egypt. You shall not afflict any widow or orphan. If you do afflict them, and they cry out to me, I will surely hear their cry; and my wrath will burn, and I will kill you with the sword, and your wives shall become widows and your children fatherless.

"If you lend money to any of my people with you who is poor, you shall not be to him as a creditor, and you shall not exact interest from him. If ever you take your neighbor's garment in pledge, you shall restore it to him before the sun goes down; for that is his only covering, it is his mantle for his body; in what else shall he sleep? And if he cries to me, I will hear, for I am compassionate.

"You shall not revile God, nor curse a ruler of your people.

"You shall not delay to offer from the fullness of your harvest and from the outflow of your presses.

"The first-born of your sons you shall give to me. You shall do likewise with your oxen and with your sheep: seven days it shall be with its dam; on the eighth day you shall give it to me.[23]

"You shall be men consecrated to me; therefore you shall not eat any flesh that is torn by beasts in the field; you shall cast it to the dogs.

"You shall not utter a false report. You shall not join hands with a wicked man, to be a malicious witness. You shall not follow a multitude to do evil; nor shall you bear witness in a suit, turning aside after a multitude, so as to pervert justice; nor shall you be partial to a poor man in his suit.

"If you meet your enemy's ox or his ass going astray, you shall bring it back to him. If you see the ass of one who hates you lying under its burden, you shall refrain from leaving him with it, you shall help him to lift it up.

"You shall not pervert the justice due to your poor in his suit. Keep far from a false charge, and do not slay the innocent and righteous, for I will not acquit the wicked. And you shall take no bribe, for a bribe blinds the officials, and subverts the cause of those who are in the right.

"You shall not oppress a stranger; you know the heart of a stranger, for you were strangers in the land of Egypt.

"For six years you shall sow your land and gather in its yield; but the seventh year you shall let it rest and lie fallow, that the poor of your people may eat; and what they leave the wild beasts may eat. You shall do likewise with your vineyard, and with your olive orchard.

"Six days you shall do your work, but on the seventh day you shall rest; that your ox and your ass may have rest, and the son of your bondmaid, and the alien, may be refreshed. Take heed to all that I have said to you; make no mention of the names of other gods, nor let such be heard out of your mouth.

"Three times in the year you shall keep a feast to me.[24] You shall keep the feast of unleavened bread; as I commanded you, you shall eat unleavened bread for seven days at the appointed time in the month of Abib, for in it you came out

---

[23]In many ancient cultures first-born male children had a special value. Some religious groups, like the neighbors of the Hebrews, actually sacrificed them, but that was never a part of the Jewish religion. This passage states that first-born male oxen and sheep would be part of a sacrificial meal. Human sons, then, would be consecrated to God's service. Later in the biblical narrative (the Book of Numbers), the Jewish tribe of Levites assumes the priestly duties in place of all other Hebrew first-born males.

[24]The three festivals are known today as Passover, Shavuot, and Sukot.

of Egypt. None shall appear before me empty-handed. You shall keep the feast of harvest, of the first fruits of your labor, of what you sow in the field. You shall keep the feast of ingathering at the end of the year, when you gather in from the field the fruit of your labor. Three times in the year shall all your males appear before the Lord God.

"You shall not offer the blood of my sacrifice with leavened bread, or let the fat of my feast remain until the morning.

"The first of the first fruits of your ground you shall bring into the house of the Lord your God.

"You shall not boil a kid in its mother's milk.[25]

"Behold, I send an angel before you, to guard you on the way and to bring you to the place which I have prepared. Give heed to him and hearken to his voice, do not rebel against him, for he will not pardon your transgression; for my name is in him.

"But if you hearken attentively to his voice and do all that I say, then I will be an enemy to your enemies and an adversary to your adversaries.

"When my angel goes before you, and brings you in to the Amorites, and the Hittites, and the Per'izzites, and the Canaanites, the Hivites, and the Jeb'usites, and I blot them out, you shall not bow down to their gods, nor serve them, nor do according to their works, but you shall utterly overthrow them and break their pillars in pieces. You shall serve the Lord your God, and I will bless your bread and your water; and I will take sickness away from the midst of you. None shall cast her young or be barren in your land; I will fulfil the number of your days. I will send my terror before you, and will throw into confusion all the people against whom you shall come, and I will make all your enemies turn their backs to you. And I will send hornets before you, which shall drive out Hivite, Canaanite, and Hittite from before you. I will not drive them out from before you in one year, lest the land became desolate and the wild beasts multiply against you. Little by little I will drive them out from before you, until you are increased and possess the land. And I will set your bounds from the Red Sea to the sea of the Philistines,[26] and from the wilderness[27] to the Euphra'tes; for I will deliver the

---

[25]This prohibition against boiling a kid in its mother's milk rejects a Canaanite method of preparing a ritual sacrifice. Later generations of Jews came to consider the passage as a prohibition against the dietary mixing of any milk with meat, although it was not originally intended as a basis for dietary law.

[26]That is, from the Gulf of Akaba to the eastern coast of the Mediterranean where the Philistines lived.

[27]The Sinai and Negev deserts. This is one of several differing passages describing the extent of the future promised land. The map varies depending on whether it is stated at the time of Moses, Joshua, or the Judges. The intention of sole possession was apparently abandoned later, at the time of the Judges who succeeded Joshua.

inhabitants of the land into your hand, and you shall drive them out before you. You shall make no covenant with them or with their gods. They shall not dwell in your land lest they make you sin against me; for if you serve their gods, it will surely be a snare to you."

THE BOOK OF JEREMIAH
Jeremiah's Call and His Visions
1:1–2:19

The words of Jeremiah, the son of Hilki'ah, of the priests who were in An'athoth in the land of Benjamin, to whom the word of the Lord came in the days of Josi'ah the son of Amon, king of Judah, in the thirteenth year of his reign. It came also in the days of Jehoi'akim the son of Josi'ah, king of Judah, and until the end of the eleventh year of Zedeki'ah, the son of Josi'ah, king of Judah, until the captivity of Jerusalem in the fifth month.[28]

Now the word of the Lord came to me saying,

> "Before I formed you in the womb I knew you,
>   and before you were born I consecrated you;
>   I appointed you a prophet to the nations."

Then I said, "Ah, Lord God! Behold, I do not know how to speak, for I am only a youth." But the Lord said to me,

> "Do not say, 'I am only a youth';
> for to all to whom I send you you shall go,
> and whatever I command you you shall speak.
> Be not afraid of them,
>   for I am with you to deliver you, says the Lord."

Then the Lord put forth his hand and touched my mouth; and the Lord said to me,

> "Behold, I have put my words in your mouth.
> See, I have set you this day over nations and over kingdoms,
> to pluck up and to break down,
> to destroy and to overthrow,
> to build and to plant."

And the word of the Lord came to me, saying, "Jeremiah, what do you see?" And I said, "I see a rod of almond." Then the Lord said to me, "You have seen well, for I am watching over my word to perform it."

---

[28]Anathoth is about three miles north of Jerusalem. The references to the royal reigns include the years 627–587 B.C., although Jeremiah's activity may also have been later.

The word of the Lord came to me a second time, saying, "What do you see?" And I said, "I see a boiling pot, facing away from the north."

Then the Lord said to me, "Out of the north evil shall break forth[29] upon all the inhabitants of the land. For, lo, I am calling all the tribes of the kingdoms of the north," says the Lord, "and they shall come and everyone shall set his throne at the entrance of the gates of Jerusalem, against all its walls round about, and against all the cities of Judah. And I will utter my judgment against them,[30] for all their wickedness in forsaking me; they have burned incense to other gods, and worshiped the works of their own hands. But you, gird up your loins; arise, and say to them everything that I command you. Do not be dismayed by them, lest I dismay you before them. And I, behold, I make you this day a fortified city, an iron pillar, and bronze walls, against the whole land, against the kings of Judah, its princes, its priests, and the people of the land. They will fight against you; but they shall not prevail against you, for I am with you," says the Lord, "to deliver you."

The word of the Lord came to me, saying, "Go and proclaim in the hearing of Jerusalem, 'Thus says the Lord,

> I remember the devotion of your youth,
>> your love as a bride,
> how you followed me in the wilderness,
>> in a land not sown.
> Israel was holy to the Lord,
>> the first fruits of his harvest.
> All who ate of it became guilty;
>> evil came upon them, says the Lord.'"

Hear the word of the Lord, O house of Jacob, and all the families of the house of Israel. Thus says the Lord:

> "What wrong did your fathers find in me
>> that they went far from me,
> and went after worthlessness, and became worthless?
> They did not say, 'Where is the Lord
>> who brought us up from the land of Egypt,
> who led us in the wilderness,
>> in a land of deserts and pits,
> in a land of drought and deep darkness,
>> in a land that none passes through,
>> where no man dwells?'
> And I brought you into a plentiful land
>> to enjoy its fruits and its good things.

---

[29]A reference to the Babylonians, specifically identified later by Jeremiah.

[30]That is, against Jerusalem and Judah.

But when you came in you defiled my land,
    and made my heritage an abomination.
The priests did not say, 'Where is the Lord?'
    Those who handle the law did not know me;
the rulers transgressed against me;
    the prophets prophesied by Ba'al,[31]
    and went after things that do not profit.

Therefore I still contend with you," says the Lord,
    "and with your children's children I will contend.
For cross to the coasts of Cyprus and see,
    or send to Kedar[32] and examine with care;
    see if there has been such a thing.
Has a nation changed its god,
    even though they are no gods?
But my people have changed their glory
    for that which does not profit.
Be appalled, O heavens, at this,
    be shocked, be utterly desolate," says the Lord,
for my people have committed two evils:
    they have forsaken me,
the fountain of living waters,
    and hewed out cisterns for themselves,
broken cisterns
    that can hold no water.

Is Israel a slave? Is he a homeborn servant?
    Why then has he become a prey?
The lions have roared against him,
    they have roared loudly.
They have made his land a waste;
    his cities are in ruins, without inhabitant.[33]
Moreover, the men of Memphis and Tah'panhes[34]
    have broken the crown of your head.
Have you not brought this upon yourself
    by forsaking the Lord your God,
    when he led you in the way?

---

[31]A Canaanite god. Jeremiah is accusing the Jews of wandering from their allegiance to the one true God.

[32]In Arabia.

[33]The results of foreign invasions.

[34]Egyptian cities.

And now what do you gain by going to Egypt,
to drink the waters of the Nile?
Or what do you gain by going to Assyria,
to drink the waters of the Euphra'tes?
Your wickedness will chasten you,
and your apostasy will reprove you.
Know and see that it is evil and bitter
for you to forsake the Lord your God;
the fear of me is not in you," says the Lord God of hosts.

A Public Pronouncement and Its Consequences
19:1–20:6

Thus said the Lord, "Go, buy a potter's earthen flask and take some of the elders of the people and some of the senior priests and go out to the valley of the son of Hinnom at the entry of the Potsherd Gate,[35] and proclaim there the words that I tell you. You shall say, 'Hear the word of the Lord, O kings of Judah and inhabitants of Jerusalem. Thus says the Lord of hosts, the God of Israel, Behold, I am bringing such evil upon this place that the ears of everyone who hears of it will tingle. Because the people have forsaken me, and have profaned this place by burning incense in it to other gods whom neither they nor their fathers nor the kings of Judah have known;[36] and because they have filled this place with the blood of innocents, and have built the high places of Ba'al to burn their sons in the fire as burnt offerings to Ba'al, which I did not command or decree, nor did it come into my mind; therefore, behold, days are coming, says the Lord, when this place shall no more be called Topheth, or the valley of the son of Hinnom, but the valley of Slaughter. And in this place I will make void the plans of Judah and Jerusalem, and will cause their people to fall by the sword before their enemies, and by the hand of those who seek their life. I will give their dead bodies for food to the birds of the air and to the beasts of the earth. And I will make this city a horror, a thing to be hissed at; everyone who passes by it will be horrified and will hiss because of all its disasters. And I will make them eat the flesh of their sons and their daughters, and everyone shall eat the flesh of his neighbor in the siege and in the distress, with which their enemies and those who seek their life afflict them.'

"Then you shall break the flask in the sight of the men who go with you, and shall say to them, 'Thus says the Lord of hosts: So will I break this people and this

---

[35]One of the gates of the walled city of Jerusalem.

[36]That is, who have not proved themselves to the people. Jeremiah repeats God's condemnation of the people for forsaking him, for worshiping idols, and for offering children as sacrifices to Baal.

city, as one breaks a potter's vessel, so that it can never be mended. Men shall bury in Topheth[37] because there will be no place else to bury. Thus will I do to this place, says the Lord, and to its inhabitants, making this city like Topheth. The houses of Jerusalem and the houses of the kings of Judah—all the houses upon whose roofs incense has been burned to all the host of heaven, and drink offerings have been poured out to other gods—shall be defiled like the place of Topheth.'"

Then Jeremiah came from Topheth, where the Lord had sent him to prophesy, and he stood in the court of the Lord's house, and said to all the people: "Thus says the Lord of hosts, the God of Israel, 'Behold, I am bringing upon this city and upon all its towns all the evil that I have pronounced against it, because they have stiffened their neck, refusing to hear my words.'"

Now Pashhur the priest, the son of Immer, who was chief officer in the house of the Lord, heard Jeremiah prophesying these things. Then Pashhur beat Jeremiah the prophet, and put him in the stocks that were in the upper Benjamin Gate of the house of the Lord. On the morrow, when Pashhur released Jeremiah from the stocks, Jeremiah said to him, "The Lord does not call your name Pashhur, but Terror on every side. For thus says the Lord: 'Behold, I will make you a terror to yourself and to all your friends. They shall fall by the sword of their enemies while you look on. And I will give all Judah into the hand of the king of Babylon; he shall carry them captive to Babylon, and shall slay them with the sword. Moreover, I will give all the wealth of the city, all its gains, all its prized belongings, and all the treasures of the kings of Judah into the hand of their enemies, who shall plunder them, and seize them, and carry them to Babylon. And you, Pashhur, and all who dwell in your house, shall go into captivity; to Babylon you shall go; and there you shall die, and there you shall be buried, you and all your friends, to whom you have prophesied falsely.'"

Babylon's Fall and the Return of the Exiles
50:1–20

The word which the Lord spoke concerning Babylon, concerning the land of the Chalde'ans, by Jeremiah the prophet:

> "Declare among the nations and proclaim,
>   set up a banner and proclaim,
>   conceal it not, and say:
> 'Babylon is taken,
>   Bel is put to shame,

---

[37]A place where children were sacrificed to Baal and other Canaanite gods.

Mer'odach[38] is dismayed.
Her images are put to shame,
    her idols are dismayed.'

"For out of the north[39] a nation has come up against her, which shall make her land a desolation, and none shall dwell in it; both man and beast shall flee away.

"In those days and in that time," says the Lord, "the people of Israel and the people of Judah shall come together, weeping as they come; and they shall seek the Lord their God. They shall ask the way to Zion, with faces turned toward it, saying, 'Come, let us join ourselves to the Lord in an everlasting covenant which will never be forgotten.'

"My people have been lost sheep; their shepherds have led them astray, turning them away on the mountains; from mountain to hill they have gone, they have forgotten their fold. All who found them have devoured them, and their enemies have said, 'We are not guilty, for they have sinned against the Lord, their true habitation, the Lord, the hope of their fathers.'

"Flee from the midst of Babylon,[40] and go out of the land of the Chalde'ans, and be as he-goats before the flock. For behold, I am stirring up and bringing against Babylon a company of great nations, from the north country; and they shall array themselves against her; from there she shall be taken. Their arrows are like a skilled warrior who does not return empty-handed. Chalde'a shall be plundered; all who plunder her shall be sated," says the Lord.

"Though you rejoice, though you exult,
    O plunderers of my heritage,
though you are wanton as a heifer at grass,
    and neigh like stallions,
your mother shall be utterly shamed,
    and she who bore you shall be disgraced.
Lo, she shall be the last of the nations,
    a wilderness dry and desert.
Because of the wrath of the Lord she shall not be inhabited,
    but shall be an utter desolation;
everyone who passes by Babylon shall be appalled,
    and hiss because of all her wounds.
Set yourselves in array against Babylon round about,
    all you that bend the bow;

---

[38]Names of the city god of Babylon.

[39]Probably a reference to Persia, which conquered Babylon in 539 B.C.

[40]This passage is addressed to the captive Jews.

shoot at her, spare no arrows,
>   for she has sinned against the Lord.
Raise a shout against her round about,
>   she has surrendered;
her bulwarks have fallen,
>   her walls are thrown down.
For this is the vengeance of the Lord:
>   take vengeance on her,
>   do to her as she has done.
Cut off from Babylon the sower,
>   and the one who handles the sickle in time of harvest;
because of the sword of the oppressor,
>   everyone shall turn to his own people,
>   and everyone shall flee to his own land.

"Israel is a hunted sheep driven away by lions. First the king of Assyria devoured him, and now at last Nebuchadrez'zar, king of Babylon, has gnawed his bones. Therefore," thus says the Lord of hosts, the God of Israel, "Behold, I am bringing punishment on the king of Babylon and his land, as I punished the king of Assyria. I will restore Israel to his pasture, and he shall feed on Carmel and in Bashan, and his desire shall be satisfied on the hills of E'phraim and in Gilead.[41] In those days and in that time," says the Lord, "iniquity shall be sought in Israel, and there shall be none; and sin in Judah, and none shall be found; for I will pardon those whom I leave as a remnant."

---

[41]The northern kingdom of Israel had been conquered by the Assyrians in 722 B.C., the southern kingdom of Judah by the Babylonians in 587 B.C. This passage states that now the Jewish kingdoms will be restored and Babylon, as Assyria earlier, will be destroyed. Carmel, Bashan, Ephraim, and Gilead are areas on both sides of the Jordan River, formerly part of the northern kingdom.

7

Homer

THE ODYSSEY

Literature probably began with oral poetry. The epic is among the earliest forms of such poetry—sung by bards who memorized and modified thousands of lines. It is, typically, a long narrative poem about some great struggle (for example, a war between great powers that determines the fate of a civilization or the homecoming of a war's most famous survivor). The epic style is usually lofty and serious; the central figure is a hero whose actions affect the fate of the whole group—his crew, tribe, nation, or race. The traditional epic (also called primary, or folk, epic) was shaped and orally transmitted by a poet or poets out of historical and legendary materials about their group's past struggles and triumphs. In the Western tradition, Homer was the earliest of the great "shapers." According to ancient accounts, he lived as a professional entertainer in the early Greek settlements on the eastern edge of the Aegean Sea around the eighth century B.C. The oldest surviving epics of Western civilization, The Iliad and The Odyssey, are attributed to him. His poems certainly tell of a time long before his own, since the estimated date for the fall of the great city of Troy (Ilion) described by Homer ranges from 1280 to 1184 B.C. That catastrophic event, the root of so much myth, occurs right after The Iliad's story ends and just before The Odyssey's begins. Whatever the historical facts underlying the poems, across the centuries they have been widely admired and imitated.

The Iliad begins with a fierce dispute between Agamémnon, commander-in-chief of the Greek forces besieging the lofty walled city of Troy on the coast of Asia Minor, and his mightiest warrior, Akhilleus. The tragic slaughter among Greeks will be caused by Akhilleus's unrelenting anger against his commander and his consequent withdrawal from the fighting. Only after Akhilleus's dearest friend, Patróklos, is killed while wearing Akhilleus's armor does the wrathful hero return to the battle, where he kills the Trojan's fighting leader, Hektor. Although the epic ends with Hektor's funeral, the listener/reader knows that now Akhilleus is fated to die soon and Troy to fall.

The actual destruction of Troy was accomplished by the stratagem of the wooden horse devised by the most resourceful of all those who fought at Troy, Odysseus, "that man skilled in all ways of contending." The Odyssey is the story of his eventful homecoming. King of the rocky and steep island of Ithaka facing the western coast of Greece, Odysseus had been drafted against his will into Agamémnon's forces, but he proved to be a vital factor in the eventual Greek triumph after ten years of fighting. His homecoming will take another ten years, and he will return, alone and disguised, to find his household has been disrupted by scores of unruly young warriors who insist that his wife, faithful Penélopê, immediately marry one of them. (They had convinced themselves that Odysseus had long since perished.) These unwanted suitors also have plotted to murder Telémakhos, the infant son whom Odysseus left behind, now growing into manhood. Odysseus will take bloody revenge on those who had abused his kingdom's hospitality during his twenty years of absence. The Odyssey ends with restoration of the "proper" social order in Ithaka.

The first excerpt in the following selection is taken from Book Nine of The Odyssey. It is Odysseus's recounting of how he blinded Polyphêmos, the one-eyed monster, who had imprisoned Odysseus and some of his crew in a crude cave. Tragically for Odysseus's companions, the monster appealed to his father, Poseidon, the great god of the sea. It would, thus, be Poseidon's revenge that so long delayed Odysseus's return and caused the death of all his crew. The second excerpt in this selection, taken from Book Seventeen, tells of Odysseus's return to his home disguised as a malformed beggar for his own protection from the intruding suitors. He is recognized only by his old hound, Argos. The third excerpt, from Book Nineteen, includes the famous digression on the identifying scar of Odysseus, recognized by his old nurse as she hospitably washes the "beggar's" feet at Penélopê's command. The final excerpt, from Books Twenty-One and Twenty-Two, tells of the archery contest in which Penélopê promises to marry that man who can bend and string the hunting bow left behind by Odysseus and send an arrow through twelve aligned axe-handle sockets. To the irritated astonishment of the suitors, who were unable even to bend the bow, the recently arrived "beggar" asks to compete. It is now time for Odysseus's revenge.

Homer's original audience regarded the poems as part of their ancestral history. Thus, they already knew the main lines of the story. (Troy must fall; Akhilleus must die before Troy's destruction; Odysseus must, after many adventures, make his way home, etc.) The audience's fascination with the epics, therefore, focused on the poet's embellishment of the traditional plot—as well as on his development of character and the beauty of his language. Homer's epic poems have been translated many times from the original Greek into most of the world's languages. The following is a particularly distinguished American poetic version.

FROM BOOK NINE: NEW COASTS
AND POSEIDON'S SON

"In the next land we found were Kyklopês,
giants, louts, without a law to bless them.[1]
In ignorance leaving the fruitage of the earth in mystery
to the immortal gods, they neither plow
nor sow by hand, nor till the ground, though grain—
wild wheat and barley—grows untended, and
wine-grapes, in clusters, ripen in heaven's rain.
Kyklopês have no muster and no meeting,
no consultation or old tribal ways,
but each one dwells in his own mountain cave
dealing out rough justice to wife and child,
indifferent to what the others do.

     Well, then:
across the wide bay from the mainland
there lies a desert island, not far out,
but still not close inshore. Wild goats in hundreds
breed there; and no human being comes
upon the isle to startle them—no hunter
of all who ever tracked with hounds through forests
or had rough going over mountain trails.
The isle, unplanted and untilled, a wilderness,
pastures goats alone. And this is why:
good ships like ours with cheekpaint at the bows
are far beyond the Kyklopês. No shipwright
toils among them, shaping and building up
symmetrical trim hulls to cross the sea
and visit all the seaboard towns, as men do
who go and come in commerce over water.
This isle—seagoing folk would have annexed it
and built their homesteads on it: all good land,

---

[1]Odysseus is telling the Phaiákians, who have given him gracious hospitality on their island, what has happened to him in the ten years since the conclusion of the war at Troy. These islanders, after Odysseus finishes his exciting account, will bring him safely home to Ithaka. For their aid to Odysseus, the vengeful Poseidon will turn the Phaiákian ship to stone.

fertile for every crop in season: lush
well-watered meads along the shore, vines in profusion,
prairie, clear for the plow, where grain would grow
chin high by harvest time, and rich sub-soil.
The island cove is landlocked, so you need
no hawsers out astern, bow-stones or mooring:
run in and ride there till the day your crews
chafe to be under sail, and a fair wind blows.
You'll find good water flowing from a cavern
through dusky poplars into the upper bay.
Here we made harbor. Some god guided us
that night, for we could barely see our bows
in the dense fog around us, and no moonlight
filtered through the overcast. No look-out,
nobody saw the island dead ahead,
nor even the great landward rolling billow
that took us in: we found ourselves in shallows,
keels grazing shore: so furled our sails
and disembarked where the low ripples broke.
There on the beach we lay, and slept till morning.

When Dawn spread out her finger tips of rose
we turned out marvelling, to tour the isle,
while Zeus's shy nymph daughters[2] flushed wild goats
down from the heights—a breakfast for my men.
We ran to fetch our hunting bows and long-shanked
lances from the ships, and in three companies
we took our shots. Heaven gave us game a-plenty:
for every one of twelve ships in my squadron
nine goats fell to be shared; my lot was ten.
So there all day, until the sun went down,
we made our feast on meat galore, and wine—
wine from the ship, for our supply held out,
so many jars were filled at Ismaros
from stores of the Kikonês that we plundered.[3]
We gazed, too, at Kyklopês Land, so near,
we saw their smoke, heard bleating from their flocks.

---

[2]Nymphs are minor local goddesses. Zeus is the king of the gods with specific control of the sky and weather. He is also a patron of hospitality, a quality clearly not valued by Polyphêmos.

[3]The Kikonês at Ismaros were allies of the Trojans whom Odysseus raided on his first stop after leaving Troy.

But after sundown, in the gathering dusk,
we slept again above the wash of ripples.

When the young Dawn with finger tips of rose
came in the east, I called my men together
and made a speech to them:

       'Old shipmates, friends,
the rest of you stand by; I'll make the crossing
in my own ship, with my own company,
and find out what the mainland natives are—
for they may be wild savages, and lawless,
or hospitable and god-fearing men.'

At this I went aboard, and gave the word
to cast off by the stern. My oarsmen followed,
filing in to their benches by the rowlocks,
and all in line dipped oars in the grey sea.

As we rowed on, and nearer to the mainland,
at one end of the bay, we saw a cavern
yawning above the water, screened with laurel,
and many rams and goats about the place
inside a sheepfold—made from slabs of stone
earthfast between tall trunks of pine and rugged
towering oak trees.

       A prodigious man
slept in this cave alone, and took his flocks
to graze afield—remote from all companions,
knowing none but savage ways, a brute
so huge, he seemed no man at all of those
who eat good wheaten bread; but he seemed rather
a shaggy mountain reared in solitude.
We beached there, and I told the crew
to stand by and keep watch over the ship;
as for myself I took my twelve best fighters
and went ahead. I had a goatskin full
of that sweet liquor that Euanthês's son,
Maron, had given me. He kept Apollo's
holy grove at Ismaros;[4] for kindness
we showed him there, and showed his wife and child,

---

[4]Apollo, a son of Zeus, is the god of light, often identified with the sun, and patron of music, archery, and prophecy.

he gave me seven shining golden talents[5]
perfectly formed, a solid silver winebowl,
and then this liquor—twelve two-handled jars
of brandy, pure and fiery. Not a slave
in Maron's household knew this drink; only
he, his wife and the storeroom mistress knew;
and they would put one cupful—ruby-colored,
honey-smooth—in twenty more of water,
but still the sweet scent hovered like a fume
over the winebowl. No man turned away
when cups of this came round.

          A wineskin full
I brought along, and victuals in a bag,
for in my bones I knew some towering brute
would be upon us soon—all outward power,
a wild man, ignorant of civility.

We climbed, then, briskly to the cave. But Kyklops
had gone afield, to pasture his fat sheep,
so we looked round at everything inside:
a drying rack that sagged with cheeses, pens
crowded with lambs and kids, each in its class:
firstlings apart from middlings, and the 'dewdrops,'
or newborn lambkins, penned apart from both.
And vessels full of whey were brimming there—
bowls of earthenware and pails for milking.
My men came pressing round me, pleading:

          'Why not
take these cheeses, get them stowed, come back,
throw open all the pens, and make a run for it?
We'll drive the kids and lambs aboard. We say
put out again on good salt water!'

          Ah,
how sound that was! Yet I refused. I wished
to see the caveman, what he had to offer—
no pretty sight, it turned out, for my friends.

We lit a fire, burnt an offering,
and took some cheese to eat; then sat in silence
around the embers, waiting. When he came
he had a load of dry boughs on his shoulder

---

[5]The talent was a unit of weight; in this case, ingots of gold.

to stoke his fire at suppertime. He dumped it
with a great crash into that hollow cave,
and we all scattered fast to the far wall.
Then over the broad cavern floor he ushered
the ewes he meant to milk. He left his rams
and he-goats in the yard outside, and swung
high overhead a slab of solid rock
to close the cave. Two dozen four-wheeled wagons,
with heaving wagon teams, could not have stirred
the tonnage of that rock from where he wedged it
over the doorsill. Next he took his seat
and milked his bleating ewes. A practiced job
he made of it, giving each ewe her suckling;
thickened his milk, then, into curds and whey,[6]
sieved out the curds to drip in withy baskets,
and poured the whey to stand in bowls
cooling until he drank it for his supper.
When all these chores were done, he poked the fire,
heaping on brushwood. In the glare he saw us.

'Strangers,' he said, 'who are you? And where from?
What brings you here by sea ways—a fair traffic?
Or are you wandering rogues, who cast your lives
like dice, and ravage other folk by sea?'

We felt a pressure on our hearts, in dread
of that deep rumble and that mighty man.
But all the same I spoke up in reply:

'We are from Troy, Akhaians,[7] blown off course
by shifting gales on the Great South Sea;
homeward bound, but taking routes and ways
uncommon; so the will of Zeus would have it.
We served under Agamémnon, son of Atreus—
the whole world knows what city
he laid waste, what armies he destroyed.
It was our luck to come here; here we stand,
beholden for your help, or any gifts
you give—as custom is to honor strangers.
We would entreat you, great Sir, have a care

---

[6]The liquid part of separated milk, distinguished from the lumpy curds, which are made
into cheese.

[7]Homer's general term for the Greek forces, including those from Ithaka.

for the gods' courtesy; Zeus will avenge
the unoffending guest.'

He answered this
from his brute chest, unmoved:

'You are a ninny,
or else you come from the other end of nowhere,
telling me, mind the gods! We Kyklopês
care not a whistle for your thundering Zeus
or all the gods in bliss; we have more force by far.
I would not let you go for fear of Zeus—
you or your friends—unless I had a whim to.
Tell me, where was it, now, you left your ship—
around the point, or down the shore, I wonder?'

He thought he'd find out, but I saw through this,
and answered with a ready lie:

'My ship?
Poseidon Lord, who sets the earth a-tremble,
broke it up on the rocks at your land's end.
A wind from seaward served him, drove us there.
We are survivors, these good men and I.'

Neither reply nor pity came from him,
but in one stride he clutched at my companions
and caught two in his hands like squirming puppies
to beat their brains out, spattering the floor.
Then he dismembered them and made his meal,
gaping and crunching like a mountain lion—
everything: innards, flesh, and marrow bones.
We cried aloud, lifting our hands to Zeus,
powerless, looking on at this, appalled;
but Kyklops went on filling up his belly
with manflesh and great gulps of whey,
then lay down like a mast among his sheep.
My heart beat high now at the chance of action,
and drawing the sharp sword from my hip I went
along his flank to stab him where the midriff
holds the liver. I had touched the spot
when sudden fear stayed me: if I killed him
we perished there as well, for we could never
move his ponderous doorway slab aside.
So we were left to groan and wait for morning.

When the young Dawn with finger tips of rose
lit up the world, the Kyklops built a fire
and milked his handsome ewes, all in due order,
putting the sucklings to the mothers. Then,
his chores being all dispatched, he caught
another brace of men to make his breakfast,
and whisked away his great door slab
to let his sheep go through—but he, behind,
reset the stone as one would cap a quiver.
There was a din of whistling as the Kyklops
rounded his flock to higher ground, then stillness.
And now I pondered how to hurt him worst,
if but Athena granted what I prayed for.
Here are the means I thought would serve my turn:

a club, or staff, lay there along the fold—
an olive tree, felled green and left to season
for Kyklops' hand. And it was like a mast
a lugger of twenty oars, broad in the beam—
a deep-sea-going craft—might carry:
so long, so big around, it seemed. Now I
chopped out a six-foot section of this pole
and set it down before my men, who scraped it;
and when they had it smooth, I hewed again
to make a stake with pointed end. I held this
in the fire's heart and turned it, toughening it,
then hid it, well back in the cavern, under
one of the dung piles in profusion there.

Now came the time to toss for it: who ventured
along with me? whose hand could bear to thrust
and grind that spike in Kyklops's eye, when mild
sleep had mastered him? As luck would have it,
the men I would have chosen won the toss—
four strong men, and I made five as captain.

At evening came the shepherd with his flock,
his woolly flock. The rams as well, this time,
entered the cave: by some sheep-herding whim—
or a god's bidding—none were left outside.
He hefted his great boulder into place
and sat him down to milk the bleating ewes
in proper order, put the lambs to suck,

and swiftly ran through all his evening chores.
Then he caught two more men and feasted on them.
My moment was at hand, and I went forward
holding an ivy bowl of my dark drink,
looking up, saying:

      'Kyklops, try some wine.
Here's liquor to wash down your scraps of men.
Taste it, and see the kind of drink we carried
under our planks. I meant it for an offering
if you would help us home. But you are mad,
unbearable, a bloody monster! After this,
will any other traveler come to see you?'

He seized and drained the bowl, and it went down
so fiery and smooth he called for more:

'Give me another, thank you kindly. Tell me,
how are you called? I'll make a gift will please you.
Even Kyklopês know the wine-grapes grow
out of grassland and loam in heaven's rain,
but here's a bit of nectar and ambrosia!'

Three bowls I brought him, and he poured them down.
I saw the fuddle and flush come over him,
then I sang out in cordial tones:

      'Kyklops,
you ask my honorable name? Remember
the gift you promised me, and I shall tell you.
My name is Nohbdy: mother, father, and friends,
everyone calls me Nohbdy.'

      And he said:

'Nohbdy's my meat, then, after I eat his friends.
Others come first. There's a noble gift, now.'

Even as he spoke, he reeled and tumbled backward,
his great head lolling to one side; and sleep
took him like any creature. Drunk, hiccuping,
he dribbled streams of liquor and bits of men.

Now, by the gods, I drove my big hand spike
deep in the embers, charring it again,
and cheered my men along with battle talk
to keep their courage up: no quitting now.
The pike of olive, green though it had been,

reddened and glowed as if about to catch.
I drew it from the coals and my four fellows
gave me a hand, lugging it near the Kyklops
as more than natural force nerved them; straight
forward they sprinted, lifted it, and rammed it
deep in his crater eye, and I leaned on it
turning it as a shipwright turns a drill
in planking, having men below to swing
the two-handled strap that spins it in the groove.
So with our brand we bored that great eye socket
while blood ran out around the red hot bar.
Eyelid and lash were seared; the pierced ball
hissed broiling, and the roots popped.

      In a smithy
one sees a white-hot axehead or an adze
plunged and wrung in a cold tub, screeching steam—
the way they make soft iron hale and hard—:
just so that eyeball hissed around the spike.
The Kyklops bellowed and the rock roared round him,
and we fell back in fear. Clawing his face
he tugged the bloody spike out of his eye,
threw it away, and his wild hands went groping;
then he set up a howl for Kyklopês
who lived in caves on windy peaks nearby.
Some heard him; and they came by divers ways
to clump around outside and call:

      'What ails you,
Polyphêmos? Why do you cry so sore
in the starry night? You will not let us sleep.
Sure no man's driving off your flock? No man
has tricked you, ruined you?'

      Out of the cave
the mammoth Polyphêmos roared in answer:

'Nohbdy, Nohbdy's tricked me, Nohbdy's ruined me!'

To this rough shout they made a sage reply:

'Ah well, if nobody has played you foul
there in your lonely bed, we are no use in pain
given by great Zeus. Let it be your father,
Poseidon Lord, to whom you pray.'

So saying
they trailed away. And I was filled with laughter
to see how like a charm the name deceived them.
Now Kyklops, wheezing as the pain came on him,
fumbled to wrench away the great doorstone
and squatted in the breach with arms thrown wide
for any silly beast or man who bolted—
hoping somehow I might be such a fool.
But I kept thinking how to win the game:
death sat there huge; how could we slip away?
I drew on all my wits, and ran through tactics,
reasoning as a man will for dear life,
until a trick came—and it pleased me well.
The Kyklops's rams were handsome, fat, with heavy
fleeces, a dark violet.

Three abreast
I tied them silently together, twining
cords of willow from the ogre's bed;
then slung a man under each middle one
to ride there safely, shielded left and right.
So three sheep could convey each man. I took
the woolliest ram, the choicest of the flock,
and hung myself under his kinky belly,
pulled up tight, with fingers twisted deep
in sheepskin ringlets for an iron grip.
So, breathing hard, we waited until morning.

When Dawn spread out her finger tips of rose
the rams began to stir, moving for pasture,
and peals of bleating echoed round the pens
where dams with udders full called for a milking.
Blinded, and sick with pain from his head wound,
the master stroked each ram, then let it pass,
but my men riding on the pectoral fleece
the giant's blind hands blundering never found.
Last of them all my ram, the leader, came,
weighted by wool and me with my meditations.
The Kyklops patted him, and then he said:

'Sweet cousin ram, why lag behind the rest
in the night cave? You never linger so,
but graze before them all, and go afar
to crop sweet grass, and take your stately way
leading along the streams, until at evening

you run to be the first one in the fold.
Why, now, so far behind? Can you be grieving
over your master's eye? That carrion rogue
and his accurst companions burnt it out
when he had conquered all my wits with wine.
Nohbdy will not get out alive, I swear.
Oh, had you brain and voice to tell
where he may be now, dodging all my fury!
Bashed by this hand and bashed on this rock wall
his brains would strew the floor, and I should have
rest from the outrage Nohbdy worked upon me.'

He sent us into the open, then. Close by,
I dropped and rolled clear of the ram's belly,
going this way and that to untie the men.
With many glances back, we rounded up
his fat, stiff-legged sheep to take aboard,
and drove them down to where the good ship lay.
We saw, as we came near, our fellows' faces
shining; then we saw them turn to grief
tallying those who had not fled from death.
I hushed them, jerking head and eyebrows up,
and in a low voice told them: 'Load this herd;
move fast, and put the ship's head toward the breakers.'
They all pitched in at loading, then embarked
and struck their oars into the sea. Far out,
as far off shore as shouted words would carry,
I sent a few back to the adversary:

'O Kyklops! Would you feast on my companions?
Puny, am I, in a caveman's hands?
How do you like the beating that we gave you,
you damned cannibal? Eater of guests
under your roof! Zeus and the gods have paid you!'

The blind thing in his doubled fury broke
a hilltop in his hands and heaved it after us.
Ahead of our black prow it struck and sank
whelmed in a spuming geyser, a giant wave
that washed the ship stern foremost back to shore.
I got the longest boathook out and stood
fending us off, with furious nods to all
to put their backs into a racing stroke—
row, row, or perish. So the long oars bent
kicking the foam sternward, making head

until we drew away, and twice as far.
Now when I cupped my hands I heard the crew
in low voices protesting:

      'Godsake, Captain!
Why bait the beast again? Let him alone!'

'That tidal wave he made on the first throw
all but beached us.'

      'All but stove us in!'

'Give him our bearing with your trumpeting,
he'll get the range and lob a boulder.'

      'Aye
He'll smash our timbers and our heads together!'

I would not heed them in my glorying spirit,
but let my anger flare and yelled:

      'Kyklops,
if ever mortal man inquire
how you were put to shame and blinded, tell him
Odysseus, raider of cities, took your eye:
Laërtês's son, whose home's on Ithaka!'

At this he gave a mighty sob and rumbled:

'Now comes the weird[8] upon me, spoken of old.
A wizard, grand and wondrous, lived here—Télemos,
a son of Eurymos; great length of days
he had in wizardry among the Kyklopês,
and these things he foretold for time to come:
my great eye lost, and at Odysseus's hands.
Always I had in mind some giant, armed
in giant force, would come against me here.
But this, but you—small, pitiful, and twiggy—
you put me down with wine, you blinded me.
Come back, Odysseus, and I'll treat you well,
praying the god of earthquake to befriend you—
his son I am, for he by his avowal
fathered me, and, if he will, he may
heal me of this black wound—he and no other
of all the happy gods or mortal men.'

Few words I shouted in reply to him:
'If I could take your life I would and take

---

[8]Fate.

your time away, and hurl you down to hell!
The god of earthquake could not heal you there!'

At this he stretched his hands out in his darkness
toward the sky of stars, and prayed Poseidon:

'O hear me, lord, blue girdler of the islands,
if I am thine indeed, and thou art father:
grant that Odysseus, raider of cities, never
see his home: Laërtês's son, I mean,
who kept his hall on Ithaka. Should destiny
intend that he shall see his roof again
among his family in his father land,
far be that day, and dark the years between.
Let him lose all companions, and return
under strange sail to bitter days at home.'

In these words he prayed, and the god heard him.
Now he laid hands upon a bigger stone
and wheeled around, titanic for the cast,
to let it fly in the black-prowed vessel's track.
But it fell short, just aft the steering oar,
and whelming seas rose giant above the stone
to bear us onward toward the island.
                    There
as we ran in we saw the squadron waiting,
the trim ships drawn up side by side, and all
our troubled friends who waited, looking seaward.
We beached her, grinding keel in the soft sand,
and waded in, ourselves, on the sandy beach.
Then we unloaded all the Kyklops's flock
to make division, share and share alike,
only my fighters voted that my ram,
the prize of all, should go to me. I slew him
by the seaside and burnt his long thighbones
to Zeus beyond the stormcloud, Kronos's son,
who rules the world. But Zeus disdained my offering;
destruction for my ships he had in store
and death for those who sailed them, my companions.
Now all day long until the sun went down
we made our feast on mutton and sweet wine,
till after sunset in the gathering dark
we went to sleep above the wash of ripples.

When the young Dawn with finger tips of rose
touched the world, I roused the men, gave orders

to man the ships, cast off the mooring lines;
and filing in to sit beside the rowlocks
oarsmen in line dipped oars in the grey sea.
So we moved out, sad in the vast offing,
having our precious lives, but not our friends."

FROM BOOK SEVENTEEN:
THE BEGGAR AT THE MANOR

While he spoke[9]
an old hound, lying near, pricked up his ears
and lifted up his muzzle. This was Argos,
trained as a puppy by Odysseus,
but never taken on a hunt before
his master sailed for Troy. The young men, afterward,
hunted wild goats with him, and hare, and deer,
but he had grown old in his master's absence.
Treated as rubbish now, he lay at last
upon a mass of dung before the gates—
manure of mules and cows, piled there until
fieldhands could spread it on the king's estate.
Abandoned there, and half destroyed with flies,
old Argos lay.

                    But when he knew he heard
Odysseus's voice nearby, he did his best
to wag his tail, nose down, with flattened ears,
having no strength to move nearer his master.
And the man looked away,
wiping a salt tear from his cheek; but he
hid this from Eumaios. Then he said:

"I marvel that they leave this hound to lie
here on the dung pile;
he would have been a fine dog, from the look of him,
though I can't say as to his power and speed
when he was young. You find the same good build
in house dogs, table dogs landowners keep
all for style."

---

[9]Odysseus is approaching his own home on Ithaka, disguised by immortal Athena as an old beggar. He is accompanied by the faithful and hospitable swineherd Eumaios, but has revealed his true identity only to Telémakhos, his son.

And you replied, Eumaios:

"A hunter owned him—but the man is dead
in some far place. If this old hound could show
the form he had when Lord Odysseus left him,
going to Troy, you'd see him swift and strong.
He never shrank from any savage thing
he'd brought to bay in the deep woods; on the scent
no other dog kept up with him. Now misery
has him in leash. His owner died abroad,
and here the women slaves will take no care of him.
You know how servants are: without a master
they have no will to labor, or excel.
For Zeus who views the wide world takes away
half the manhood of a man, that day
he goes into captivity and slavery."

Eumaios crossed the court and went straight forward
into the mégaron[10] among the suitors;
but death and darkness in that instant closed
the eyes of Argos, who had seen his master,
Odysseus, after twenty years.

　　　　　　　Long before anyone else
Telémakhos caught sight of the grey woodsman
coming from the door, and called him over
with a quick jerk of his head. Eumaios's
narrowed eyes made out an empty bench
beside the one the carver used—that servant
who had no respite, carving for the suitors.
This bench he took possession of, and placed it
across the table from Telémakhos
for his own use. Then the two men were served
cuts from a roast and bread from a bread basket.

At no long interval, Odysseus came
through his own doorway as a mendicant,
humped like a bundle of rags over his stick.
He settled on the inner ash wood sill,
leaning against the door jamb—cypress timber
the skilled carpenter planed years ago
and set up with a plumbline.

---

[10]The great central hall of Odysseus's palace. The suitors often ate, slept, and were entertained there.

Now Telémakhos
took an entire loaf and a double handful
of roast meat; then he said to the forester:

"Give these to the stranger there. But tell him
to go among the suitors, on his own;
he may beg all he wants. This hanging back
is no asset to a hungry man."

The swineherd rose at once, crossed to the door,
and halted by Odysseus.

"Friend," he said,
"Telémakhos is pleased to give you these,
but he commands you to approach the suitors;
you may ask all you want from them. He adds,
your shyness is no asset to a beggar."

The great tactician, lifting up his eyes,
cried:

"Zeus aloft! A blessing on Telémakhos!
Let all things come to pass as he desires!"

Palms held out, in the beggar's gesture, he
received the bread and meat and put it down
before him on his knapsack—lowly table!—
then he fell to, devouring it. Meanwhile
the harper in the great room sang a song.
Not till the man was fed did the sweet harper
end his singing—whereupon the company
made the walls ring again with talk.

Unseen,
Athena[11] took her place beside Odysseus,
whispering in his ear:

"Yes, try the suitors.
You may collect a few more loaves, and learn
who are the decent lads, and who are vicious—
although not one can be excused from death!"

So he appealed to them, one after another,
going from left to right, with open palm,
as though his lifetime had been spent in beggary.

---

[11]Daughter of Zeus, divine personification of wisdom; she favors Odysseus above all other
mortals.

And they gave bread, for pity—wondering, though,
at the strange man. Who could this beggar be,
where did he come from? each would ask his neighbor;
till in their midst the goatherd, Melánthios,
raised his voice:

        "Hear just a word from me,
my lords who court our illustrious queen!
        This man,
this foreigner, I saw him on the road;
the swineherd, here was leading him this way;
who, what, or whence he claims to be, I could not
say for sure."

        At this, Antínoös
turned on the swineherd brutally, saying:

        "You famous
breeder of pigs, why bring this fellow here?
Are we not plagued enough with beggars,
foragers and such rats!
        You find the company
too slow at eating up your lord's estate—
is that it? So you call this scarecrow in?"

The forester replied:
        "Antínoös,
well born you are, but that was not well said.
Who would call in a foreigner?—unless
an artisan with skill to serve the realm,
a healer, or a prophet, or a builder,
or one whose harp and song might give us joy.
All these are sought for on the endless earth,
but when have beggars come by invitation?
Who puts a field mouse in his granary? My lord,
you are a hard man, and you always were,
more so than others of this company—hard
on all Odysseus's people and on me.
But this I can forget
as long as Penélopê lives on, the wise and tender
mistress of this hall; as long
as Prince Telémakhos—"

        But he broke off
at a look from Telémakhos, who said:

"Be still.
Spare me a long-drawn answer to this gentleman.
With his unpleasantness, he will forever make
strife where he can—and goad the others on."

He turned and spoke out clearly to Antínoös:

"What fatherly concern you show me! Frighten
this unknown fellow, would you, from my hall
with words that promise blows—may God forbid it!
Give him a loaf. Am I a niggard? No,
I call on you to give. And spare your qualms
as to my mother's loss, or anyone's—
not that in truth you have such care at heart:
your heart is all in feeding, not in giving."

Antínoös replied:

"What high and mighty
talk, Telémakhos! Control your temper.
If every suitor gave what I may give him,
he could be kept for months—kept out of sight!"

He reached under the table for the footstool
his shining feet had rested on—and this
he held up so that all could see his gift.

But all the rest gave alms,
enough to fill the beggar's pack with bread
and roast meat.
              So it looked as though Odysseus
had had his taste of what these men were like
and could return scot free to his own doorway—
but halting now before Antínoös
he made a little speech to him. Said he:

"Give a mite, friend. I would not say, myself,
you are the worst man of the young Akhaians.
The noblest, rather; kingly, by your look;
therefore you'll give more bread than others do.
Let me speak well of you as I pass on
over the boundless earth!
                          I, too, you know,
had fortune once, lived well, stood well with men,
and gave alms, often, to poor wanderers
like this one that you see—aye, to all sorts,
no matter in what dire want. I owned

servants—many, god knows—and all the rest
that goes with being prosperous, as they say.
But Zeus the son of Kronos brought me down.

No telling
why he would have it, but he made me go
to Egypt with a company of rovers—
a long sail to the south—for my undoing.
Up the broad Nile and in to the riverbank
I brought my dipping squadron. There, indeed,
I told the men to stand guard at the ships;
I sent patrols out—out to rising ground;
but reckless greed carried my crews away
to plunder the Egyptian farms; they bore off
wives and children, killed what men they found.
The news ran on the wind to the city, a night cry,
and sunrise brought both infantry and horsemen,
filling the river plain with dazzle of bronze;
then Zeus lord of lightning
threw my men into a blind panic; no one dared
stand against that host closing around us.
Their scything weapons left our dead in piles,
but some they took alive, into forced labor,
myself among them. And they gave me, then,
to one Dmêtor, a traveler, son of Iasos,
who ruled at Kypros. He conveyed me there.
From that place, working northward, miserably—"[12]

But here Antínoös broke in, shouting:

                    "God!
What evil wind blew in this pest?
                    Get over,
stand in the passage! Nudge my table, will you?
Egyptian whips are sweet
to what you'll come to here, you nosing rat,
making your pitch to everyone!
These men have bread to throw away on you
because it is not theirs. Who cares? Who spares
another's food, when he has more than plenty?"

With guile Odysseus drew away, then said:

---

[12]Several times in the epic Odysseus invents a convincingly detailed false tale to go with
his counterfeit identity. (Kypros is usually spelled "Cyprus.")

"A pity that you have more looks than heart.
You'd grudge a pinch of salt from your own larder
to your own handy man. You sit here, fat
on others' meat, and cannot bring yourself
to rummage out a crust of bread for me!"
Then anger made Antínoös's heart beat hard,
and, glowering under his brows, he answered:

> "Now!
You think you'll shuffle off and get away
after that impudence? Oh, no you don't!"

The stood he let fly hit the man's right shoulder
on the packed muscle under the shoulder blade—
like solid rock, for all the effect one saw.
Odysseus only shook his head, containing
thoughts of bloody work, as he walked on,
then sat, and dropped his loaded bag again
upon the doorsill. Facing the whole crowd
he said, and eyed them all:

> "One word only,
my lords, and suitors of the famous queen.
One thing I have to say.
There is no pain, no burden for the heart
when blows come to a man, and he defending
his own cattle—his own cows and lambs.
Here it was otherwise. Antínoös
hit me for being driven on by hunger—
how many bitter seas men cross for hunger!
If beggars interest the gods, if there are Furies[13]
pent in the dark to avenge a poor man's wrong, then may
Antínoös meet his death before his wedding day!"

FROM **BOOK NINETEEN:**
RECOGNITIONS AND A DREAM

And Penélopê said:[14]
"Dear guest, no foreign man so sympathetic
ever came to my house, no guest more likeable,

---

[13]Goddesses, spirits of pitiless revenge who pursue especially those who have killed kindred or have violated the laws of hospitality.

[14]Penélopê, unknowingly, is speaking to the disguised Odysseus who has just assured the despairing queen that he knows Odysseus "is alive and well and headed homeward now."

so wry and humble are the things you say.
I have an old maidservant ripe with years,
one who in her time nursed my lord. She took him
into her arms the hour his mother bore him.
Let her, then, wash your feet, though she is frail.
Come here, stand by me, faithful Eurýkleia,
and bathe—bathe your master, I almost said,
for they are of an age, and now Odysseus's
feet and hands would be enseamed like his.
Men grow old soon in hardship."

                Hearing this,
the old nurse hid her face between her hands
and wept hot tears, and murmured:

                "Oh, my child!
I can do nothing for you! How Zeus hated you,
no other man so much! No use, great heart,
O faithful heart, the rich thighbones you burnt
to Zeus who plays in lightning—and no man
ever gave more to Zeus—with all your prayers
for a green age, a tall son reared to manhood.
There is no day of homecoming for you.
Stranger, some women in some far off place
perhaps have mocked my lord when he'd be home
as now these strumpets mock you here. No wonder
you would keep clear of all their whorishness
and have no bath. But here am I. The queen
Penélopê, Ikários's daughter, bids me;
so let me bathe your feet to serve my lady—
to serve you, too.

                My heart within me stirs,
mindful of something. Listen to what I say:
strangers have come here, many through the years,
but no one ever came, I swear, who seemed
so like Odysseus—body, voice and limbs—
as you do."

                Ready for this, Odysseus answered:

"Old woman, that is what they say. All we have seen
the two of us remark how like we are,
as you yourself have said, and rightly, too."

Then he kept still, while the old nurse filled up
her basin glittering in firelight; she poured
cold water in, then hot.

But Lord Odysseus
whirled suddenly from the fire to face the dark.
The scar: he had forgotten that. She must not
handle his scarred thigh, or the game was up.
But when she bared her lord's leg, bending near,
she knew the groove at once.

An old wound
a boar's white tusk inflicted, on Parnassos[15]
years ago. He had gone hunting there
in company with his uncles and Autólykos,
his mother's father—a great thief and swindler
by Hermês's favor,[16] for Autólykos pleased him
with burnt offerings of sheep and kids. The god
acted as his accomplice. Well, Autólykos
on a trip to Ithaka
arrived just after his daughter's boy was born.
In fact, he had no sooner finished supper
than Nurse Eurýkleia put the baby down
in his own lap and said:

"It is for you, now,
to choose a name for him, your child's dear baby;
the answer to her prayers."

Autólykos replied:

"My son-in-law, my daughter, call the boy
by the name I tell you. Well you know, my hand
has been against the world of men and women;
odium and distrust I've won. Odysseus
should be his given name.[17] When he grows up,
when he comes visiting his mother's home
under Parnassos, where my treasures are,
I'll make him gifts and send him back rejoicing."

Odysseus in due course went for the gifts,
and old Autólykos and his sons embraced him

---

[15]The mountain range above Apollo's famous shrine of prophecy near Delphi on the Greek mainland.

[16]Hermês was the swift messenger of the gods who also guided the souls of the dead into the underworld. He was a trickster whose special patronage applied to merchants and thieves.

[17]The hero's Greek name means something like "causer of pain" or "causer of anger."

with welcoming sweet words; and Amphithéa,
his mother's mother, held him tight and kissed him,
kissed his head and his fine eyes.
                    The father
called on his noble sons to make a feast,
and going about it briskly they led in
an ox of five years, whom they killed and flayed
and cut in bits for roasting on the skewers
with skilled hands, with care; then shared it out.
So all the day until the sun went down
they feasted to their hearts' content. At evening,
after the sun was down and dusk had come,
they turned to bed and took the gift of sleep.

When young Dawn spread in the eastern sky
her finger tips of rose, the men and dogs
went hunting, taking Odysseus. They climbed
Parnassos's rugged flank mantled in forest,
entering amid high windy folds at noon
when Hêlios[18] beat upon the valley floor
and on the winding ocean whence he came.
With hounds questing ahead, in open order,
the sons of Autólykos went down a glen,
Odysseus in the lead, behind the dogs,
pointing his long-shadowing spear.
                    Before them
a great boar lay hid in undergrowth,
in a green thicket proof against the wind
or sun's blaze, fine soever the needling sunlight,
impervious too to any rain, so dense
that cover was, heaped up with fallen leaves.
Patter of hounds' feet, men's feet, woke the boar
as they came up—and from his woody ambush
with razor back bristling and raging eyes
he trotted and stood at bay. Odysseus,
being on top of him, had the first shot,
lunging to stick him; but the boar
had already charged under the long spear.
He hooked aslant with one white tusk and ripped out
flesh above the knee, but missed the bone.

---

[18]The sun, personified as a god who drove daily across the sky from east to west and floated back during the night in a golden cup on the ocean stream.

Odysseus's second thrust went home by luck,
his bright spear passing through the shoulder joint;
and the beast fell, moaning as life pulsed away.
Autólykos's tall sons took up the wounded,
working skillfully over the Prince Odysseus
to bind his gash, and with a rune[19] they stanched
the dark flow of blood. Then downhill swiftly
they all repaired to the father's house, and there
tended him well—so well they soon could send him,
with Grandfather Autólykos's magnificent gifts,
rejoicing, over sea to Ithaka.
His father and the Lady Antikleía
welcomed him, and wanted all the news
of how he got his wound; so he spun out
his tale, recalling how the boar's white tusk
caught him when he was hunting on Parnassos.

This was the scar the old nurse recognized;
she traced it under her spread hands, then let go,
and into the basin fell the lower leg
making the bronze clang, sloshing the water out.
Then joy and anguish seized her heart; her eyes
filled up with tears; her throat closed, and she whispered,
with hand held out to touch his chin:

      "Oh yes!
You are Odysseus! Ah, dear child! I could not
see you until now—not till I knew
my master's very body with my hands!"

Her eyes turned to Penélopê with desire
to make her lord, her husband, known—in vain,
because Athena had bemused the queen,
so that she took no notice, paid no heed.
At the same time Odysseus's right hand
gripped the old throat; his left hand pulled her near,
and in her ear he said:

      "Will you destroy me,
nurse, who gave me milk at your own breast?
Now with a hard lifetime behind I've come
in the twentieth year home to my father's island.
You found me out, as the chance was given you.
Be quiet; keep it from the others, else

---

[19]A magic spell.

I warn you, and I mean it, too,
if by my hand god brings the suitors down
I'll kill you, nurse or not, when the time comes—
when the time comes to kill the other women."

Eurýkleia kept her wits and answered him:

"Oh, what mad words are these you let escape you!
Child, you know my blood, my bones are yours;
no one could whip this out of me. I'll be
a woman turned to stone, iron I'll be.
And let me tell you too—mind now—if god
cuts down the arrogant suitors by your hand,
I can report to you on all the maids,
those who dishonor you, and the innocent."

But in response the great tactician said:

"Nurse, no need to tell me tales of these.
I will have seen them, each one, for myself.
Trust in the gods, be quiet, hold your peace."

Silent, the old nurse went to fetch more water,
her basin being all spilt.
              When she had washed
and rubbed his feet with golden oil, he turned,
dragging his bench again to the fire side
for warmth, and hid the scar under his rags.

FROM BOOK TWENTY-ONE:
THE TEST OF THE BOW

              "My lords, hear me:
suitors indeed, you commandeered this house
to feast and drink in, day and night, my husband
being long gone, long out of mind. You found
no justification for yourselves—none
except your lust to marry me. Stand up, then:
we now declare a contest for that prize.
Here is my lord Odysseus's hunting bow.
Bend and string it if you can. Who sends an arrow
through iron axe-helve[20] sockets, twelve in line?

---

[20]Axe-handle. That is, the contestant must shoot the arrow through the holes, designed
  for the insertion of the handles, in the axe-heads (or blades).

I join my life with his, and leave this place, my home,
my rich and beautiful bridal house, forever
to be remembered, though I dream it only."

Then to Eumaios:

      "Carry the bow forward.
Carry the blades."

        Tears came to the swineherd's eyes
as he reached out for the big bow. He laid it
down at the suitors' feet. Across the room
the cowherd sobbed, knowing the master's weapon.
Antínoös growled, with a glance at both:
      "Clods.
They go to pieces over nothing.
      You two, there,
why are you sniveling? To upset the woman
even more? Has she not pain enough
over her lost husband? *Sit down.*
Get on with dinner quietly, or cry about it
outside, if you must. Leave us the bow.

A clean-cut game, it looks to me.
Nobody bends that bowstave easily
in this company. Is there a man here
made like Odysseus? I remember him
from childhood: I can see him even now."

That was the way he played it, hoping inwardly
to span the great horn bow with corded gut
and drill the iron with his shot—he, Antínoös,
destined to be the first of all to savor
blood from a biting arrow at his throat,
a shaft drawn by the fingers of Odysseus
whom he had mocked and plundered, leading on
the rest, his boon companions. Now they heard
a gay snort of laughter from Telémakhos,
who said then brilliantly:

      "A queer thing, that!
Has Zeus almighty made me a half-wit?
For all her spirit, Mother has given in,
promised to go off with someone—and
is that amusing? What am I cackling for?
Step up, my lords, contend now for your prize.
There is no woman like her in Akhaia,

not in old Argos, Pylos, or Mykênê,[21]
neither in Ithaka nor on the mainland,
and you all know it without praise of mine.
Come on, no hanging back, no more delay
in getting the bow bent. Who's the winner?
I myself should like to try that bow.
Suppose I bend it and bring off the shot,
my heart will be less heavy, seeing the queen my mother
go for the last time from this house and hall,
if I who stay can do my father's feat."

He moved out quickly, dropping his crimson cloak,
and lifted sword and sword belt from his shoulders.
His preparation was to dig a trench,
heaping the earth in a long ridge beside it
to hold the blades half-bedded. A taut cord
aligned the socket rings. And no one there
but looked on wondering at his workmanship,
for the boy had never seen it done.
            He took his stand then
on the broad door sill to attempt the bow.
Three times he put his back into it and sprang it,
three times he had to slack off. Still he meant
to string that bow and pull for the needle shot.
A fourth try, and he had it all but strung—
when a stiffening in Odysseus made him check.
Abruptly then he stopped and turned and said:

"Blast and damn it, must I be a milksop
all my life? Half-grown, all thumbs,
no strength or knack at arms, to defend myself
if someone picks a fight with me.
            Take over,
O my elders and betters, try the bow,
run off the contest."

            And he stood the weapon
upright against the massy-timbered door
with one arrow across the horn aslant,
then went back to his chair. Antínoös
gave the word:

---

[21]Greek cities on the mainland.

"Now one man at a time
rise and go forward. Round the room in order;
left to right from where they dip the wine."

As this seemed fair enough, up stood Leódês
the son of Oinops. This man used to find
visions for them in the smoke of sacrifice.
He kept his chair well back, retired by the winebowl,
for he alone could not abide their manners
but sat in shame for all the rest. Now it was he
who had first to confront the bow,
standing up on the broad door sill. He failed.
The bow unbending made his thin hands yield,
no muscle in them. He gave up and said:

"Friends, I cannot. Let the next man handle it.
Here is a bow to break the heart and spirit
of many strong men. Aye. And death is less
bitter than to live on and never have
the beauty that we came here laying siege to
so many days. Resolute, are you still,
to win Odysseus's lady Penélopê?
Pit yourselves against the bow, and look
among Akhaians for another's daughter.
Gifts will be enough to court and take her.
Let the best offer win."

With this Leódês
thrust the bow away from him, and left it
upright against the massy-timbered door,
with one arrow aslant across the horn.
As he went down to his chair he heard Antínoös's
voice rising:

"What is that you say?
It makes me burn. You cannot string the weapon,
so 'Here is a bow to break the heart and spirit
of many strong men.' Crushing thought!
You were not born—you never had it in you—
to pull that bow or let an arrow fly.
But here are men who can and will."

He called out to the goatherd, Melánthios:

"Kindle a fire there, be quick about it,
draw up a big bench with a sheepskin on it,
and bring a cake of lard out of the stores.

Contenders from now on will heat and grease the bow.
We'll try it limber, and bring off the shot."

Melánthios darted out to light a blaze,
drew up a bench, threw a big sheepskin over it,
and brought a cake of lard. So one by one
the young men warmed and greased the bow for bending,
but not a man could string it. They were whipped.
Antínoös held off; so did Eurýmakhos,
suitors in chief, by far the ablest there.

Two men had meanwhile left the hall:
swineherd and cowherd, in companionship,
one downcast as the other. But Odysseus
followed them outdoors, outside the court,
and coming up said gently:

       "You, herdsman,
and you, too, swineherd, I could say a thing to you,
or should I keep it dark?

       No, no; speak,
my heart tells me. Would you be men enough
to stand by Odysseus if he came back?
Suppose he dropped out of a clear sky, as I did?
Suppose some god should bring him?
Would you bear arms for him, or for the suitors?"

The cowherd said:

       "Ah, let the master come!
Father Zeus, grant our old wish! Some courier
guide him back! Then judge what stuff is in me
and how I manage arms!"

       Likewise Eumaios
fell to praying all heaven for his return,
so that Odysseus, sure at least of these,
told them:

       "I am at home, for I am he.
I bore adversities, but in the twentieth year
I am ashore in my own land. I find
the two of you, alone among my people,
longed for my coming. Prayers I never heard
except your own that I might come again.
So now what is in store for you I'll tell you:
If Zeus brings down the suitors by my hand

I promise marriages to both, and cattle,
and houses built near mine. And you shall be
brothers-in-arms of my Telémakhos.[22]
Here, let me show you something else, a sign
that I am he, that you can trust me, look:
this old scar from the tusk wound that I got
boar hunting on Parnassos—
Autólykos's sons and I."

        Shifting his rags
he bared the long gash. Both men looked, and knew,
and threw their arms around the old soldier, weeping,
kissing his head and shoulders. He as well
took each man's head and hands to kiss, then said—
to cut it short, else they might weep till dark—

"Break off, no more of this.
Anyone at the door could see and tell them.
Drift back in, but separately at intervals
after me.

        Now listen to your orders:
when the time comes, those gentlemen, to a man,
will be dead against giving me bow or quiver.
Defy them. Eumaios, bring the bow
and put it in my hands there at the door.
Tell the women to lock their own door tight.
Tell them if someone hears the shock of arms
or groans of men, in hall or court, not one
must show her face, but keep still at her weaving.
Philoítios, run to the outer gate and lock it.
Throw the cross bar and lash it."

        He turned back
into the courtyard and the beautiful house
and took the stool he had before. They followed
one by one, the two hands loyal to him.

Eurýmakhos had now picked up the bow.
He turned it round, and turned it round
before the licking flame to warm it up,

---

[22]That is, Odysseus is promising the two loyal slaves, Eumaios and Philoítios (the cowherd), freedom from their servitude and noble status approaching that of his own son. Ironically, Eumaios was actually of royal birth, having been kidnapped by Phoenician traders and sold as a slave-child to Odysseus's father.

but could not, even so, put stress upon it
to jam the loop over the tip
   though his heart groaned to bursting.
Then he said grimly:

   "Curse this day.
What gloom I feel, not for myself alone,
and not only because we lose that bride.
Women are not lacking in Akhaia,
in other towns, or on Ithaka. No, the worst
is humiliation—to be shown up for children
measured against Odysseus—we who cannot
even hitch the string over his bow.
What shame to be repeated of us, after us!"

Antínoös said:

   "Come to yourself. You know
that is not the way this business ends.
Today the islanders held holiday, a holy day,
no day to sweat over a bowstring.
   Keep your head.
Postpone the bow. I say we leave the axes
planted where they are. No one will take them.
No one comes to Odysseus's hall tonight.
Break out good wine and brim our cups again,
we'll keep the crooked bow safe overnight,
order the fattest goats Melánthios has
brought down tomorrow noon, and offer thighbones burning
to Apollo, god of archers,
while we try out the bow and make the shot."

As this appealed to everyone, heralds came
pouring fresh water for their hands, and boys
filled up the winebowls. Joints of meat went round,
fresh cuts for all, while each man made his offering,
tilting the red wine to the gods, and drank his fill.
Then spoke Odysseus, all craft and gall:

"My lords, contenders for the queen, permit me:
a passion in me moves me to speak out.
I put it to Eurýmakhos above all
and to that brilliant prince, Antínoös. Just now
how wise his counsel was, to leave the trial
and turn your thoughts to the immortal gods! Apollo
will give power tomorrow to whom he wills.
But let me try my hand at the smooth bow!

Let me test my fingers and my pull
to see if any of the oldtime kick is there,
or if thin fare and roving took it out of me."

Now irritation beyond reason swept them all,
since they were nagged by fear that he could string it.
Antínoös answered, coldly and at length:

"You bleary vagabond, no rag of sense is left you.
Are you not coddled here enough, at table
taking meat with gentlemen, your betters,
denied nothing, and listening to our talk?
When have we let a tramp hear all our talk?
The sweet goad of wine has made you rave!
Here is the evil wine can do
to those who swig it down. Even the centaur
Eurýtion, in Peiríthoös's hall
among the Lapíthai, came to a bloody end
because of wine; wine ruined him: it crazed him,
drove him wild for rape in that great house.
The princes cornered him in fury, leaping on him
to drag him out and crop his ears and nose.
Drink had destroyed his mind, and so he ended
in that mutilation—fool that he was.
Centaurs and men made war for this,
but the drunkard first brought hurt upon himself.[23]
The tale applies to you: I promise you
great trouble if you touch that bow. You'll come by
no indulgence in our house; kicked down
into a ship's bilge, out to sea you go,
and nothing saves you. Drink, but hold your tongue.
Make no contention here with younger men."

At this the watchful queen Penélopê
interposed:

                "Antínoös, discourtesy
to a guest of Telémakhos—whatever guest—
that is not handsome. What are you afraid of?

---

[23]Antínoös, the contemptuous leading suitor, compares the foreign "beggar" to the drunken centaur (half-horse, half-man) who tried to rape the women at a wedding in the royal house of the Lapíthai, his human neighbors. The ensuing battle established the supremacy of civilized men over uncivilized beasts. Ironically, it is the suitors who have really been acting the uncivilized role.

Suppose this exile put his back into it
and drew the great bow of Odysseus—
could he then take me home to be his bride?
You know he does not imagine that! No one
need let that prospect weigh upon his dinner!
How very, very improbable it seems."

It was Eurýmakhos who answered her:

"Penélopê, O daughter of Ikários,
most subtle queen, we are not given to fantasy.
No, but our ears burn at what men might say
and women, too. We hear some jackal whispering:
'How far inferior to the great husband
her suitors are! Can't even budge his bow!
Think of it; and a beggar, out of nowhere,
strung it quick and made the needle shot!'
That kind of disrepute we would not care for."

Penélopê replied, steadfast and wary:

"Eurýmakhos, you have no good repute
in this realm, nor the faintest hope of it—
men who abused a prince's house for years,
consumed his wine and cattle. Shame enough.
Why hang your heads over a trifle now?
The stranger is a big man, well-compacted,
and claims to be of noble blood.
Ai!
Give him the bow, and let us have it out!
What I can promise him I will:
if by the kindness of Apollo he prevails
he shall be clothed well and equipped.
A fine shirt and a cloak I promise him;
a lance for keeping dogs at bay, or men;
a broadsword; sandals to protect his feet;
escort, and freedom to go where he will."

Telémakhos now faced her and said sharply:

"Mother, as to the bow and who may handle it
or not handle it, no man here
has more authority than I do—not one lord
of our own stony Ithaka nor the islands lying
east toward Elis: no one stops me if I choose
to give these weapons outright to my guest.
Return to your own hall. Tend your spindle.

Tend your loom. Direct your maids at work.
This question of the bow will be for men to settle,
most of all for me. I am master here."

She gazed in wonder, turned, and so withdrew,
her son's clearheaded bravery in her heart.
But when she had mounted to her rooms again
with all her women, then she feel to weeping
for Odysseus, her husband. Grey-eyed Athena
presently cast a sweet sleep on her eyes.

The swineherd had the horned bow in his hands
moving toward Odysseus, when the crowd
in the banquet hall broke into an ugly din,
shouts rising from the flushed young men:

       "Ho! Where
do you think you are taking that, you smutty slave?"

"What is this dithering?"

       "We'll toss you back alone
among the pigs, for your own dogs to eat,
if bright Apollo nods and the gods are kind!"

He faltered, all at once put down the bow, and stood
in panic, buffeted by waves of cries,
hearing Telémakhos from another quarter
shout:

"Go on, take him the bow!
       Do you obey this pack?
You will be stoned back to your hills! Young as I am
my power is over you! I wish to God
I had as much the upper hand of these!
There would be suitors pitched like dead rats
through our gate, for the evil plotted here!"

Telémakhos's frenzy struck someone as funny,
and soon the whole room roared with laughter at him,
so that all tension passed. Eumaios picked up
bow and quiver, making for the door,
and there he placed them in Odysseus's hands.
Calling Eurýkleia to his side he said:

       "Telémakhos
trusts you to take care of the women's doorway.
Lock it tight. If anyone inside
should hear the shock of arms or groans of men

in hall or court, not one must show her face,
but go on with her weaving."

                    The old woman
nodded and kept still. She disappeared
into the women's hall, bolting the door behind her.
Philoítios left the house now at one bound,
catlike, running to bolt the courtyard gate.
A coil of deck-rope of papyrus fiber
lay in the gateway; this he used for lashing,
and ran back to the same stool as before,
fastening his eyes upon Odysseus.

                    And Odysseus took his time,
turning the bow, tapping it, every inch,
for borings that termites might have made
while the master of the weapon was abroad.
The suitors were now watching him, and some
jested among themselves:

                    "A bow lover!"

"Dealer in old bows!"

                    "Maybe he has one like it
at home!"

                    "Or has an itch to make one for himself."

"See how he handles it, the sly old buzzard!"

And one disdainful suitor added this:

"May his fortune grow an inch for every inch he bends it!"

But the man skilled in all ways of contending,
satisfied by the great bow's look and heft,
like a musician, like a harper, when
with quiet hand upon his instrument
he draws between his thumb and forefinger
a sweet new string upon a peg: so effortlessly
Odysseus in one motion strung the bow.
Then slid his right hand down the cord and plucked it,
so the taut gut vibrating hummed and sang
a swallow's note.

                    In the hushed hall it smote the suitors
and all their faces changed. Then Zeus thundered
overhead, one loud crack for a sign.
And Odysseus laughed within him that the son

of crooked-minded Kronos had flung that omen down.
He picked one ready arrow from his table
where it lay bare: the rest were waiting still
in the quiver for the young men's turn to come.
He nocked it, let it rest across the handgrip,
and drew the string and grooved butt of the arrow,
aiming from where he sat upon the stool.

> Now flashed
arrow from twanging bow clean as a whistle
through every socket ring, and grazed not one,
to thud with heavy brazen head beyond.

> Then quietly
Odysseus said:

> "Telémakhos, the stranger
you welcomed in your hall has not disgraced you.
I did not miss, neither did I take all day
stringing the bow. My hand and eye are sound,
not so contemptible as the young men say.
The hour has come to cook their lordships' mutton—
supper by daylight. Other amusements later,
with song and harping that adorn a feast."

He dropped his eyes and nodded, and the prince
Telémakhos, true son of King Odysseus,
belted his sword on, clapped hand to his spear,
and with a clink and glitter of keen bronze
stood by his chair, in the forefront near his father.

FROM BOOK TWENTY-TWO: DEATH IN THE GREAT HALL

Now shrugging off his rags the wiliest fighter of the islands
leapt and stood on the broad door sill, his own bow in his hand.
He poured out at his feet a rain of arrows from the quiver
and spoke to the crowd:

> "So much for that. Your clean-cut game is over.
Now watch me hit a target that no man has hit before,
if I can make this shot. Help me, Apollo."

He drew to his fist the cruel head of an arrow for Antínoös
just as the young man leaned to lift his beautiful drinking cup,
embossed, two-handled, golden: the cup was in his fingers:
the wine was even at his lips: and did he dream of death?

How could he? In that revelry amid his throng of friends
who would imagine a single foe—though a strong foe indeed—
could dare to bring death's pain on him and darkness on his eyes?
Odysseus's arrow hit him under the chin
and punched up to the feathers through his throat.

Backward and down he went, letting the winecup fall
from his shocked hand. Like pipes his nostrils jetted
crimson runnels, a river of mortal red,
and one last kick upset his table
knocking the bread and meat to soak in dusty blood.
Now as they craned to see their champion where he lay
the suitors jostled in uproar down the hall,
everyone on his feet. Wildly they turned and scanned
the walls in the long room for arms; but not a shield,
not a good ashen spear was there for a man to take and throw.
All they could do was yell in outrage at Odysseus:

"Foul! to shoot at a man! That was your last shot!"
"Your own throat will be slit for this!"

   "Our finest lad is down!
You killed the best on Ithaka."

   "Buzzards will tear your eyes out!"

For they imagined as they wished—that it was a wild shot,
an unintended killing—fools, not to comprehend
they were already in the grip of death.
But glaring under his brows Odysseus answered:

"You yellow dogs, you thought I'd never make it
home from the land of Troy. You took my house to plunder,
twisted my maids to serve your beds. You dared
bid for my wife while I was still alive.
Contempt was all you had for the gods who rule wide heaven,
contempt for what men say of you hereafter.
Your last hour has come. You die in blood."

8

※

THE HYMNS OF THE RIG-VEDA

The hymns of the Rig-Veda are the first known works of literature of the Indian subcontinent. They are the oldest part of the sacred literature of the Aryans, an Indo-European people who invaded and conquered northwestern India between 2000 and 1500 B.C. In the subsequent centuries, they penetrated farther into the interior of the subcontinent, reaching its eastern edge by 500 B.C. Their religious literature evolved into a vast body of literary compositions collectively known as the Veda. With changing conditions and the mingling of Aryans with indigenous people, the Aryan religion itself changed, and by the centuries just before the beginning of the Christian era, it had developed into Hinduism, which has since remained the majority religion of India.

Aryans believed that the Veda was holy literature. Hindus, too, consider it to be their most sacred scripture. In Sanskrit, the language of the Veda, the word veda means "knowledge." Hindus believe, as did the Aryans, that the Veda is eternal and contains divine knowledge revealed to ancient seer-poets who delivered it through their inspired utterances. These utterances were preserved in memory and transmitted orally from generation to generation for centuries, with close attention to accuracy of content and pronunciation, before they came to be written down. The Veda actually consists of four individual collections, each also called a Veda. These are the Rig-Veda, the Yajur-Veda, the Sam-Veda, and the Atharva-Veda. Each of these four Vedas has two distinct parts: the first, from an earlier time, is a collection of hymns called the Samhita, and the second is a series of texts on ritual and metaphysics. The Samhita of the Rig-Veda is the oldest of the four Samhitas. It is a product of the Aryan experience, from the time when they were still in their original home in West Central Asia until the early centuries of their settlement in India. Amidst predominantly Indian material, it still contains strong memories of a primitive Indo-European past. While the later Vedic literature reflects considerable mixing of the Aryan and the non-Aryan cultures, the hymns of the Rig-Veda are almost entirely Aryan. They are also the most mytho-poetic part of the Veda. It is these qualities, the poetry as well as the antiquity of the Rig-Vedic hymns, that endow the Rig-Veda, and indeed the Veda *as a whole, with their profound significance. As observed by Max Muller, the famous nineteenth-century translator of ancient Indian literature:* "The Veda has a twofold interest: it belongs to the history of the world and to the history of India. . . . As long as man continues to take an interest in the history of his race, and as long as we collect in libraries and museums the relics of former ages, the first place in that long row of books which contains the records of the Aryan branch of mankind will belong forever to the Rig-Veda" *One should add that, within the Rig-Veda, that first place belongs to its hymns.*

As we see them in the Rig-Vedic hymns, the Aryans were cow-herding nomads. Perhaps the main reason for their movement away from their original home and the eventual invasion of India was a search for new pastures. As cattle-herders, they had little use for the towns and cities of the pre-Aryan Indus Valley civilization. Instead, the Aryans lived in the open country in makeshift dwellings, moving from place to place according to their needs for good grazing grounds. Not much advanced in the arts of civilization, the Aryans were, however, strongly equipped for fighting. They were physically large and stalwart and aggressive in character. They knew how to make bronze and fashion weapons from it. They also built fast light-wheeled chariots pulled by horses. The Aryans probably introduced the horse to India.

Sociologically, the Aryans were a tribal people held together by ties of blood and kinship, their loyalty, during their early career in India, limited to their respective tribes and to their race. They distinguished themselves from the non-Aryan Indians as people of a superior varna *("color"). In fact, they called themselves* arya, *a Sanskrit word meaning "noble." Their social and political organization was rudimentary. Although there was division of function among its members as needed on occasion, all members of a tribe were fundamentally equal and there were no strict class distinctions. By and large, all men were cattle-herders in times of peace, and all were soldiers in times of war. Priestly functions were entrusted to those who were considered able to perform them best, rather than because of a permanent class distinction. We learn about all these and other features of Aryan life from the Rig-Vedic hymns.*

Naturally, the hymns tell more about the religion of the Aryans than about any other aspect of their culture. The Aryan religion centered on their belief in numerous gods whom they worshiped with a rite called the yajna *("sacrifice"), which involved offering of food and drink to the gods, with recitations of selected hymns, often in the presence of fire. The more important* yajnas *included on-site ritual slaughter and cooking of animals offered to the gods along with libations of* soma, *an exhilarating drink made from the freshly pressed juice of a plant whose name is not known. After the ritual oblations, the worshipers themselves consumed the food and drink, believing that the gods had descended among them to partake of their offerings and rejoice with them in the blessings of life.*

As would be the case with any culture, the gods of the Aryans are personifications of important facets of their experience. Since the Aryans lived amidst nature and depended for their survival on uncontrolled nature, their gods represented these natural forces. Nature also combined with significant and memorable activities in their lives, such as war, in shaping the attributes of their gods.

The Rig-Veda *contains more than a thousand hymns. They are arranged in ten* mandalas *("circles" or "books"), each of these books, according to tradition, ascribed to one seer-poet or a family, or school, of seer-poets. Within each book, the hymns generally are arranged according to the deities to whom they are addressed. Hymns to Agni, the god of fire, generally come first; those to Indra, the god of rain and war, come next; and after them, the hymns to other gods and deified objects follow. One book, the ninth, is almost entirely devoted to the god Soma. The following selection provides a small sampling of hymns about four major deities—Indra, Agni, Soma, and Varuna—and a minor one, Ushas.*

Since Indra is the most popular god in the Rig-Veda, *we shall read the hymns dedicated to him first. The* Rig-Veda *has more hymns about him than about any other god. The Aryans found him to be a most convivial and congenial deity. He epitomizes their interests and character perfectly. He is, above all, a warrior god heroically defeating his enemies as Aryans wanted to defeat the non-Aryans. He loves to drink and goes into battle drunk with soma and followed by his army of celestial soldiers,* maruts, *also drunk. In a very large number of hymns, he fights against and cuts down into pieces a dragon named Vritra. This dragon represents the leadership of the native Indians against whom the Aryans had to fight to conquer India. Indra's weapon is* vajra, *the thunderbolt, which shows his Indo-European connection with the Greek god Zeus. The thunderbolt is also an essential part of Indra's identity as a nature god, the god of rain. By dismembering the dragon in his battle against Vritra, he brings out the sun (which symbolizes freeing of nature) and, more importantly, he frees the waters, which means that Indra brings rain. The dragon stands for the thick, black clouds blocking the sun and holding the rain as a prisoner. Furthermore, Indra's battle against the dragon also depicts—in the form of myth—a collision between two diametrically opposed cultures: the nomadic culture of the Aryans and the pre-Aryan agrarian and settled culture of India. In some of the Rig-Vedic hymns, the dragon is shown lying on a mountain slope, blocking the river waters. The dragon seems to personify the low dams that the pre-Aryans built on mountain slopes to flood the plains on either side of the rivers in order to irrigate their fields and to fertilize them with the silt from the rivers. Such use of water, however, did not suit the Aryans; creating large expanses of wetland destroyed pastures and impeded the mobility so essential to their military and political expansion. The destruction of the dragon means the destruction of the very economic basis of the pre-Aryan culture.*

Second to Indra in the number of hymns devoted to him, Agni (etymologically from the same root as "ignite"), the god of fire, is actually the most important Aryan god. He is considered the priest of gods and the god of priests. As the god of fire, he especially personifies the sacrificial fire. All important sacrifices are made in his presence or, rather, through him. He is the carrier of sacrifices to the gods and a messenger between mortals and immortals. The hymns often describe Agni as one who goes in front. This shows his high place among the gods. It also has a literal meaning, because in their eastward expansion, the Aryans burned forests before them in order to advance. As fire was considered the purest and the most purifying element, Agni was the very embodiment of purity. He had three forms: earthly as fire, atmospheric as lightning, and heavenly as the sun. For every sacrificial ritual, he had to be brought out anew by friction, with a wooden drill. He is, therefore, called the child of sticks. But he also can be born of stone, by the striking of one stone against another. Agni is, in fact, energy that resides not only in wood and forests, and in stones, rocks, and mountains, but in everything. This concept of Agni as dwelling in all things is of great significance in the evolution of Indian religious philosophy.

The god Soma is deified soma juice. His role in the pantheon parallels that of Agni in some ways. Along with Agni, he is present at important sacrifices in the form of libations of soma. He also acts as a mediator between humans and gods, bringing them even closer together than does Agni. For not only do gods come down to quaff soma with the mortals, the latter—partaking of the drink themselves—become godlike during the ritual. They believe that, in the drink they imbibe, it is Soma who enters their being and transforms mere humans into himself. It is easy to see that this belief in communion with divinity, has a basis in the actual consciousness-altering property of the substance that is soma. As a concept, Soma, like Agni, has important implications for the future evolution of Indian religious thought, where the human self is seen as essentially divine in nature and capable of uniting with the eternal and divine reality underlying all existence. In form, Soma remains closer to the liquid he personifies and is, on the whole, less of a personal being than the other main gods of the Aryans.

Older in name—because his name is connected with the Greek god of the sky, Uranus—Varuna appears in the history of Aryan religion later than Agni and Indra. His emergence reflects the stage in Indian history when the Aryans had begun to mingle with the non-Aryans, and the social and moral values based on the natural ties of blood and kinship no longer sufficed for individual and social well-being. A diversifying society needed more deliberatively formulated rules of conduct and morality for its maintenance and stability. Varuna is the guardian of right conduct and moral law. He particularly watches over the keeping of contracts, the foundation of social order. He severely punishes those guilty of breach of promise and other kinds of ethical wrongdoing. Instead of material offerings, he expects his worshipers to offer good conduct. So the worshipers approach him trembling with fear. Varuna is also the guardian of rita, *an etherlike entity that is supposed to permeate the cosmos and sustain its regular functioning, as the proper circulation of blood sustains the health of a living organism. Varuna thus applies himself to the protection of both the cosmic and the moral order—the two are inseparable from each other. Breach of the moral laws can have a disruptive effect on the cosmic order.*

The Aryan gods are mainly male and associated with phenomena in the sky. Prominent among the few female deities is Ushas, goddess of the dawn. Thus, she too is a sky god. In form, she is closer to the phenomenon she represents than to being a personalized deity. Hymns addressed to her give beautiful descriptions of the rising dawn. The Aryans' love of nature and the poetic quality of the verses, both characteristic features of the Rig-Vedic compositions, are here at their best.

Besides the hymns to gods, the following selection also includes a hymn addressed to the sacrificial horse and two hymns about the myths of creation. The hymns of creation provide an interesting contrast to the biblical account of creation found in Genesis (Selection 6). The Rig-Vedic creation myth states that the birth of the world came from the dismemberment of a primeval being, Purusha. The creation hymns, as well as the hymn to the sacrificial horse, exemplify the symbolic power of sacrifice.

INDRA
Hymn III.31

Wise, teaching, following the thought of order,[1] the sonless gained a
    grandson from his daughter.[2]
Fain, as a sire, to see his child prolific, he sped to meet her with an
    eager spirit.
The son left not his portion to the brother, he made a home to hold
    him who should gain it.
What time his parents[3] gave the priest[4] his being, of the good pair
    one acted, one promoted.
Agni was born trembling with tongue that flickered, so that the Red's
    great children[5] should be honored.

From *Hymns of the Rig-Veda*, trans. Ralph T. H. Griffith. London, 1889. Reprinted Varanasi (India): Chowkhamba Sanskrit Series Office, 1963. [Hymns III.31, 32, I.32; I.1, IV.5, 6, X.5, 51; IX.1, 3, 4; II.28, V.85, VII.87, 89; I.113; I.163; X.129; X.90].

[1]The cosmic order.

[2]The meaning is obscure. Perhaps it is a metaphorical reference to the priest whose function it is to generate the sacrificial fire with a wooden drill, the lower stick of which is considered female (hence daughter) and is producer of fire.

[3]The drill made of two sticks (parents) to produce fire by friction.

[4]Agni, the god of fire, is considered to be the priest of gods.

[5]Rays of the sun.

Great is their germ, that born of them is mighty, great the bays' lord's
approach through sacrifices.[6]

Conquering bands upon the warrior waited: they recognized great light
from out the darkness.

The conscious dawns went forth to meet his coming, and the sole master of the kine[7] was Indra.

The sages freed them from their firm-built prison: the seven priests
drove them forward with their spirit.

All holy order's pathway they discovered: he,[8] full of knowledge, shared
these deeds through worship.

When Sarama[9] had found the mountain's fissure, that vast and ancient
place she plundered thoroughly,

In the floods' van she led them forth, light-footed: she who well knew
came first unto their lowing.

Longing for friendship came the noblest singer:[10] the hill poured forth
its treasure for the pious.

The hero[11] with young followers fought and conquered, and straightway Angiras[12] was singing praises.

Peer of each noble thing, yea, all-excelling, all creatures doth he know,
he slayeth Sushna.[13]

Our leader, fain for war, singing from heaven, as friend he saved his
lovers from dishonor.

They sat them down with spirit fain for booty, making with hymns a
way to life eternal.

And this is still their place of frequent session, whereby they sought to
gain the months[14] through order.

Drawing the milk of ancient seed prolific, they joyed as they beheld
their own possession.

Their shout of triumph heated earth and heaven. When the kine
showed, they bade the heroes rouse them.

---

[6]Indra, the horse-driving (bays' lord) warrior and rain god is born of the sun's rays and
the kindling of the sacrificial fire.

[7]Literally "cows"; or, figuratively, the sun's rays.

[8]The priests performing worship.

[9]Indra's hound (female). She goes in front of the released cows or waters.

[10]The "noblest singer" stands for a group, a famous family of priests, the Angirases.

[11]Indra.

[12]See footnote 10.

[13]The name of an enemy.

[14]Monthly festivals.

Indra drove forth the kine, that Vritra-slayer,[15] while hymns of praise
rose up and gifts were offered.

For him the cow, noble and far-extending, poured pleasant juices,
bringing oil and sweetness.

They made a mansion for their father,[16] deftly provided him a great and
glorious dwelling;

With firm support parted and stayed the parents,[17] and, sitting, fixed
him there erected, mighty.

What time the ample chalice[18] had impelled him, swift waxing, vast, to
pierce the earth and heaven,—

Him in whom blameless songs are all united: all powers invincible
belong to Indra.

I crave thy powers, I crave thy mighty friendship: full many a team[19]
goes to the Vritra-slayer.

Great is the land, we seek the prince's favor. Be thou, O Maghavan,[20]
our guard and keeper.

He, having found great, splendid, rich dominion, sent life and motion
to his friends and lovers.

Indra, who shone together with the heroes, begat the song, the fire, and
sun and morning.

Vast, the house-friend, he set the waters flowing, all-lucid, widely
spread, that move together.

By the wise cleansings of the meath[21] made holy, through days and
nights they speed the swift streams onward.

To thee proceed the dark, the treasure-holders, both of them sanctified
by Surya's[22] bounty.

The while thy lovely storming friends, O Indra, fail to attain the
measure of thy greatness.

Be lord of joyous songs, O Vritra-slayer, bull dear to all, who gives the
power of living.

---

[15]An enemy slain by Indra. Vritra figures frequently, as a demon, dragon, or snake, in the
hymns to Indra.

[16]Indra.

[17]Heaven and earth.

[18]The bowl of soma juice.

[19]Hymns, sent forth like teams of horses.

[20]Another name for Indra.

[21]Soma, the holy drink.

[22]Surya is the sun as a god.

Come unto us with thine auspicious friendship, hastening, mighty one, with mighty succours.

Like Angiras I honor him with worship; and renovate old song for him the ancient.

Chase thou the many godless evil creatures; and give us, Maghavan, heaven's light to help us.

Far forth are spread the purifying waters: convey thou us across them unto safety.

Save us, our charioteer, from harm, O Indra, soon, very soon, make us win spoil of cattle.

His kine their lord hath shown, even Vritra's slayer: through the black hosts he passed with red attendants.

Teaching us pleasant things by holy order, to us hath he thrown open all his portals.

Call we on Maghavan, auspicious Indra, best hero in this fight where spoil is gathered.

The strong who listens, who gives aid in battles, who slays the Vritras, wins and gathers riches.

Hymn III.32

Drink thou this soma, Indra, lord of soma; drink thou the draught of noonday which thou lovest.

Puffing thy cheeks, impetuous, liberal giver, here loose thy two bay horses and rejoice thee.

Quaff it pure, meal-blent, mixed with milk, O Indra; we have poured forth the soma for thy rapture.

Knit with the prayer-fulfilling band of Maruts,[23] yea, with the Rudras,[24] drink till thou art sated;

Those who gave increase to thy strength and vigor, the Maruts singing forth thy might, O Indra.

Drink thou, O fair of cheek, whose hand wields thunder, with Rudras banded, at our noon libation.

They, even the Maruts who were there, excited with song the meath-created strength of Indra.

By them impelled to act he reached the vitals of Vritra, though he deemed that none might wound him.

Pleased, like a man, with our libation, Indra, drink, for enduring hero might, the soma.

---

[23]Indra's celestial soldiers.

[24]Gods of the storm.

Lord of bays, moved by sacrifice come hither: thou with the swift ones
stirrest floods and waters.

When thou didst loose the streams to run like racers in the swift
contest, having smitten Vritra

With flying weapon where he lay, O Indra, and, godless, kept the
goddesses encompassed.

With reverence let us worship mighty Indra, great and sublime, eternal,
ever-youthful,

Whose greatness the dear world-halves have not measured, no, nor
conceived the might of him the holy.

Many are Indra's nobly wrought achievements, and none of all the gods
transgress his statutes.

He beareth up this earth and heaven, and, doer of marvels, he begat the
sun and morning.

Hymn I.32

I will declare the manly deeds of Indra, the first that he achieved, the
thunder-wielder.

He slew the dragon, then disclosed the waters, and cleft the channels of
the mountain torrents.

He slew the dragon lying on the mountain: his heavenly bolt of thunder
Tvashtar[25] fashioned.

Like lowing kine in rapid flow descending the waters glided downward
to the ocean.

Impetuous as a bull, he chose the soma, and in three sacred beakers
drank the juices.

Maghavan grasped the thunder for his weapon, and smote to death this
first-born of the dragons.

When, Indra, thou hadst slain the dragons' first-born, and overcome the
charms of the enchanters,[26]

Then, giving life to sun and dawn and heaven, thou foundest not one
foe to stand against thee.

Indra, with his own great and deadly thunder smote into pieces Vritra,
worst of Vritras.

As trunks of trees, what time the axe hath felled them, low on the earth
so lies the prostrate dragon.

He, like a mad weak warrior, challenged Indra, the great impetuous
many-slaying hero.

He, brooking not the clashing of the weapons, crushed—Indra's foe—
the shattered forts in falling.

---

[25]The god of the forge and crafts.

[26]The enemies of the Aryans, and of Indra, were believed to possess the powers of magic.

Footless and handless still he challenged Indra, who smote him with his bolt between the shoulders.

Emasculate yet claiming manly vigor, thus Vritra lay with scattered limbs dissevered.

There as he lies like a bank-bursting river, the waters taking courage flow above him.

The dragon lies beneath the feet of torrents which Vritra with his greatness had encompassed.

Then humbled was the strength of Vritra's mother: Indra hath cast his deadly bolt against her.

The mother was above, the son was under, and like a cow beside her calf lay Danu.[27]

Rolled in the midst of never-ceasing currents flowing without a rest forever onward,

The waters bear off Vritra's nameless body: the foe of Indra sank to during darkness.

Guarded by Ahi[28] stood the thralls of Dasas,[29] the waters stayed like kine held by the robber.

But he, when he had smitten Vritra, opened the cave wherein the floods had been imprisoned.

A horse's tail[30] wast thou when he, O Indra, smote on thy bolt; thou, God without a second,

Thou hast won back the kine, hast won the soma; thou hast let loose to flow the seven rivers.

Nothing availed him lightning, nothing thunder, hailstorm or mist which he had spread around him:

When Indra and the dragon strove in battle, Maghavan gained the victory forever.

Whom sawest thou to avenge the dragon, Indra, that fear possessed thy heart when thou hadst slain him;

That, like a hawk affrighted through the regions, thou crossed nine-and-ninety flowing rivers?

Indra is king of all that moves and moves not, of creatures tame and horned, the thunder-wielder.

Over all living men he rules as sovereign, containing all as spokes within the felly.

---

[27]This reference to Vritra's mother suggests the matriarchal orientation of a pre-Aryan Indian civilization.

[28]The cloud-serpent holding water in.

[29]A non-Aryan people against whom the Aryans were fighting.

[30]To become a "horse's tail" means to disappear fast.

AGNI
Hymn I.1

I praise Agni, the chosen priest, god, minister of sacrifice,
The hotar,[31] lavisher of wealth.
Worthy is Agni to be praised by living as by ancient seers.
He shall bring hitherward the gods.
Through Agni man obtains wealth, yea, plenty waxing day by day,
Most rich in heroes, glorious.
Agni, the perfect sacrifice which thou encompassest about
Verily goeth to the gods.
May Agni, sapient-minded priest, truthful, most gloriously great,
The god, come hither with the gods.
Whatever blessing, Agni, thou wilt grant unto thy worshiper,
That, Angiras, is indeed thy truth.
To thee, dispeller of the night, O Agni, day by day with prayer
Bringing thee reverence, we come;
Ruler of sacrifices, guard of law eternal, radiant one,
Increasing in thine own abode.
Be to us easy of approach, even as a father to his son:
Agni, be with us for our weal.

Hymn IV.5

How shall we give with one accord oblation to Agni, to Vaisvanara[32] the
bounteous?
Great light, with full high growth hath he uplifted, and, as a pillar bears
the roof, sustains it.
Reproach not him who, God and self-reliant, vouchsafed this bounty
unto me a mortal,—
Deathless, discerner, wise, to me the simple, Vaisvanara most manly,
youthful Agni.
Sharp-pointed, powerful, strong, of boundless vigor, Agni who knows
the lofty hymn, kept secret
As the lost milch-cow's track, the doubly mighty,—he hath declared to
me this hidden knowledge.
May he with sharpened teeth, the bounteous giver, Agni, consume with
flame most fiercely glowing

---

[31]The invoking priest, one who calls the gods to enjoy the offerings.

[32]Common god of all Aryans.

Those who regard not Varuna's[33] commandments and the dear steadfast
laws of sapient Mitra.[34]

Like youthful women without brothers, straying, like dames who hate
their lords, of evil conduct,

They who are full of sin, untrue, unfaithful, they have engendered this
abysmal station.

To me, weak, innocent, thou, luminous Agni, hast boldly given as 'twere
a heavy burthen,

This Prishtha[35] hymn, profound and strong and mighty, of seven
elements, and with offered dainties.

So may our song that purifies, through wisdom reach in a moment him
the universal,

Established on the height, on earth's best station, above the beauteous
grassy skin of Prisni.[36]

Of this my speech what shall I utter further? They indicate the milk
stored up in secret

When they have thrown as 'twere the cows' stalls open. The bird[37]
protects earth's best and well-loved station.

This is the great ones'[38] mighty apparition which from of old the
radiant cow[39] hath followed.

This, shining brightly in the place of order, swift, hasting on in secret,
she discovered.

He then who shone together with his parents remembered Prisni's fair
and secret treasure,

Which, in the mother cow's most lofty station, the bull's[40] tongue, of
the flame bent forward, tasted.

With reverence I declare the law, O Agni; what is, comes by thine order,
Jatavedas.[41]

Of this, whate'er it be, thou art the sovereign; yea, all the wealth that is
in earth or heaven.

---

[33]Varuna is the god of the natural and the moral order.

[34]A god of light.

[35]Intended for midday oblations.

[36]The earth. Prisni is also the cow whose milk is used in the oblation that Agni, the bull,
devours.

[37]The sun; it flies through heaven.

[38]The sun's rays.

[39]The dawn.

[40]The bull is Agni in the form of the sun.

[41]Omniscient Agni.

What is our wealth therefrom, and what our treasure? Tell us, O
Jatavedas, for thou knowest,

What is our best course in this secret passage: we, unreproached, have
reached a place far distant.

What is the limit, what the rules, the guerdon? Like fleet-foot coursers
speed we to the contest.

When will the goddesses, the immortal's spouses, the dawns, spread over
us the sun-god's splendor?

Unsatisfied, with speech devoid of vigor, scanty and frivolous and
inconclusive,

Wherefore do they address thee here, O Agni? Let these who have no
weapons suffer sorrow.

The majesty of him the good, the mighty, aflame, hath shone for glory
in the dwelling.

He, clothed in light, hath shone most fair to look on, wealthy in
blessings, as a home shines with riches.

Hymn IV.6

Priest of our rite, stand up erect, O Agni, in the gods' service best of
sacrificers,

For over every thought thou art the ruler: thou furtherest e'en the
wisdom of the pious.

He was set down 'mid men as priest unerring, Agni, wise, welcome in
our holy synods.

Like Savitar.[42] he hath lifted up his splendor, and like a builder raised
his smoke to heaven.

The glowing ladle, filled with oil, is lifted: choosing gods' service to the
right he circles.

Eager he rises like the new-wrought pillar which, firmly set and fixed,
anoints the victims.

When sacred grass is strewn and Agni kindled, the Adhvaryu[43] rises to
his task rejoicing.

Agni the priest, like one who tends the cattle, goes three times round, as
from of old he wills it.

Agni himself, the priest, with measured motion, goes round, with sweet
speech, cheerful, true to order.

His fulgent flames run forth like vigorous horses: all creatures are
affrighted when he blazes.

---

[42]The sun as generator of life.

[43]The priest(s) who perform(s) the practical work of sacrifice.

Beautiful and auspicious is thine aspect, O lovely Agni, terrible when
spreading.

Thy splendors are not covered by darkness: detraction leaves no stain
upon thy body.

Naught hindered his production, bounteous giver: his mother and his
sire[44] were free to send him.

Then as a friend benevolent, refulgent, Agni shone forth in human
habitations.

He, Agni, whom the twice-five sisters,[45] dwelling together, in the
homes of men engendered,

Bright like a spear's tooth, wakened in the morning, with powerful
mouth and like an axe well-sharpened.

These thy bay coursers, Agni, dropping fatness, ruddy vigorous,
speeding straightly forward,

And red steeds, wonderful, of mighty muscle, are to this service of the
gods invited:

These brightly shining flames of thine, O Agni, that move forever
restless, all-subduing,

Like falcons hasting eagerly to the quarry, roar loudly like the army of
the Maruts.

To thee, O flaming God, hath prayer been offered. Let the priest laud
thee: give to him who worships.

Men have established Agni as invoker, fain to adore the glory of
the living.

Hymn X.5

He only is the sea, holder of treasures: born many a time he views the
hearts within us.

He hides him in the secret couple's bosom. The bird dwells in the
middle of the fountain.

Inhabiting one dwelling-place in common, strong stallions and the
mares have come together.

The sages guard the seat of holy order, and keep the highest names
concealed within them.

The holy pair, of wondrous power, have coupled: they formed the
infant, they who bred produced him.

The central point of all that moves and moves not, the while they wove
the sage's thread with insight.

---

[44]Earth and heaven.

[45]The priest's ten fingers that produce the fire from the drill.

For tracks of order and refreshing viands attend from ancient times the
goodly infant.

Wearing him as a mantle, earth and heaven grow strong by food of
pleasant drink and fatness.

He, calling loudly to the seven red sisters,[46] hath, skilled in sweet drink,
brought them to be looked on.

He, born of old, in middle air, hath halted, and sought and found the
covering robe of Pushan.[47]

Seven are the pathways which the wise have fashioned; to one of these
may come the troubled mortal.

He standeth in the dwelling of the highest, a pillar, on sure ground
where paths are parted.

Not being, being[48] in the highest heaven, in Aditi's bosom and in
Daksha's[49]birthplace,

Is Agni, our first-born of holy order, the milch-cow and the bull in life's
beginning.

Hymn X.51

Large was that covering, and firm of texture, folded wherein thou
enteredst the waters.[50]

One deity alone, O Jatavedas Agni, saw all thy forms in sundry places.

What god hath seen me? Who of all their number clearly beheld my
forms in many places?

Where lie, then, all the sacred logs of Agni that lead him godward,
Varuna and Mitra?

In many places, Agni Jatavedas, we sought thee hidden in the plants
and waters.

Then Yama[51] marked thee, god of wondrous splendor! Effulgent from
thy tenfold secret dwelling.

---

[46]The tongues of fire.

[47]The sun-god as giver of prosperity and protector of travelers.

[48]Both the existent and the nonexistent.

[49]Aditi and Daksha are wife and husband. The former is infinite nature and the latter the
creative power. The meaning here is that Agni is as yet undeveloped embryo and therefore is both male and female.

[50]Fearing the fate of his three brothers, who had perished in the service of the gods, Agni
once fled and hid himself in the waters. The gods discovered him and persuaded him to
return to his sacred duties.

[51]The god of the dead.

I fled in fear from sacrificial worship, Varuna, lest the gods should thus
engage me.

Thus were my forms laid down in many places. This, as my goal, I Agni
saw before me.

Come; man is pious and would fain do worship; he waits prepared: in
gloom thou, Agni, dwellest.

Make pathways leading godward clear and easy, and bear oblations with
a kindly spirit.

This goal mine elder brothers once selected, as he who drives a car the
way to travel.

So, Varuna, I fled afar through terror, as flies the wild bull from an
archer's bowstring.

We give thee life unwasting, Jatavedas, so that, employed, thou never
shalt be injured.

So, nobly born! shalt thou with kindly spirit bear to the gods their share
of men's oblations.

Grant me the first oblations and the latter, entire, my forceful share of
holy presents,

The soul of plants, the fatness of the waters, and let there be long life,
ye gods, to Agni.

Thine be the first oblations and the latter, entire, thy forceful shares of
holy presents.

Let all this sacrifice be thine, O Agni, and let the world's four regions
bow before thee.

SOMA

Hymn IX.1

In sweetest and most gladdening stream flow pure, O Soma, on thy way,
Pressed out for Indra, for his drink.

Fiend-queller, friend of all men, he hath with the wood[52] attained unto
His place, his iron-fashioned home.[53]

Be thou best Vritra-slayer, best granter of bliss, most liberal:
Promote our wealthy princes' gifts.

Flow onward with thy juice unto the banquet of the mighty gods;
Flow hither for our strength and fame.

O Indu,[54] we draw nigh to thee, with this one object day by day:

---

[52]Some wooden implement, perhaps a spoon.

[53]A metal container for the soma juice.

[54]Another name for soma, meaning "the moon," which was believed to contain the celestial nectar that it pours down through the sieve of heaven.

To thee alone our prayers are said.
By means of this eternal fleece[55] may Surya's daughter[56] purify
Thy soma that is foaming forth.
Ten sister maids[57] of slender form seize him within the press and hold
Him firmly on the final day.[58]
The virgins send him forth: they blow the skin musician-like, and fuse
The triple foe-repelling meath.
Inviolable milch-kine round about him blend for Indra's drink,
The fresh young soma with their milk.
In the wild raptures of this draught, Indra slays all the Vritras: he,
The hero, pours his wealth on us.

Hymn IX.3

Here present this immortal god flies, like a bird upon her wings,
To settle in the vats of wood.
This god, made ready with the hymn, runs swiftly through the
                    winding ways,
Inviolable as he flows.
This god while flowing is adorned, like a bay steed for war, by men
Devout and skilled in holy songs.
He, like a warrior going forth with heroes, as he flows along
Is fain to win all precious boons.
This god, as he is flowing on, speeds like a car and gives his gifts:
He lets his voice be heard of all.
Praised by the sacred bards, this god dives into waters, and bestows
Rich gifts upon the worshiper.
Away he rushes with his stream, across the regions, into heaven,
And roars as he is flowing on.
While flowing, meet for sacrifice, he hath gone up to heaven across
The regions, irresistible.
After the way of ancient time, this god, pressed out for deities,
Flows tawny to the straining-cloth.
This lord of many holy laws, even at his birth engendering strength,
Effused, flows onward in a stream.

---

[55]The filter made of wool for filtering soma juice.

[56]Faith.

[57]The priest's fingers.

[58]The day on which the soma is extracted.

Hymn IX.4

O Soma flowing on thy way, win thou and conquer high renown;
And make us better than we are.
Win thou the light, win heavenly light, and, Soma, all felicities;
And make us better than we are.
Win skillful strength and mental power. O Soma, drive away our foes;
And make us better than we are.
Ye purifiers, purify soma for Indra, for his drink:
Make thou us better than we are.
Give us our portion in the sun through thine own mental power and aids;
And make us better than we are.
Through thine own mental power and aid long may we look upon
       the sun;
Make thou us better than we are.
Well-weaponed Soma, pour to us a stream of riches doubly great;
And make us better than we are.
As one victorious, unsubdued in battle pour forth wealth to us;
And make us better than we are.
Well-weaponed Soma, pour to us a stream of riches doubly great;
And make us better than we are.
As one victorious, unsubdued in battle pour forth wealth to us;
And make us better than we are.
By worship, Pavamana![59] men have strengthened thee to prop the law:
Make thou us better than we are.
O Indu, bring us wealth in steeds, manifold, quickening all life;
And make us better than we are.

VARUNA

Hymn II.28

This praise of the self-radiant wise Aditya[60] shall be supreme o'er all
      that is in greatness.
I beg renown of Varuna the mighty, the god exceeding kind to him who
      worships.
Having extolled thee, Varuna, with thoughtful care may we have high
      fortune in thy service,

---

[59]The god Soma often is addressed as Pavamana, meaning "self-purifying." Soma juice undergoes purification as it flows through the wool that is used as a strainer.

[60]*Aditya*, meaning "son of Aditi," is a generic name for gods. It especially refers to the sun and Varuna.

Singing thy praises like the fires at coming, day after day, of mornings
  rich in cattle.
May we be in thy keeping, O thou leader wide-ruling Varuna, lord of
  many heroes.
O sons of Aditi, forever faithful, pardon us, gods, admit us to your
  friendship.
He made them flow, the Aditya, the sustainer: the rivers run by Varuna's
  commandment.
These feel no weariness, nor cease from flowing: swift have they flown
  like birds in air around us.
Loose me from sin as from a bond that binds me: may we swell, Varuna,
  thy spring of order.
Let not my thread, while I weave song, be severed, nor my work's sum,
  before the time, be shattered.
Far from me, Varuna, remove all danger: accept me graciously, thou
  holy sovereign.
Cast off, like cords that hold a calf, my troubles: I am not even mine
  eyelid's lord without thee.
Strike us not, Varuna, with those dread weapons which, Asura,[61] at thy
  bidding wound the sinner.
Let us not pass away from light to exile. Scatter, that we may live, the
  men who hate us.
O mighty Varuna, now and hereafter, even as of old, will we speak forth
  our worship.
For in thyself, invincible god, thy statutes ne'er to be moved are fixed as
  on a mountain.
Move far from me what sins I have committed: let me not suffer, king,
  for guilt of others.
Full many a morn remains to dawn upon us: in these, O Varuna, while
  we live direct us.
O king, whoever, be he friend or kinsman, hath threatened me
  affrighted in my slumber—
If any wolf or robber fain would harm us, therefrom, O Varuna, give
  thou us protection.
May I not live, O Varuna, to witness my wealthy, liberal, dear friend's
  destitution.
King, may I never lack well-ordered riches. Loud may we speak, with
  heroes, in assembly.

---

[61]Lord God. In this case, Varuna.

Hymn V.85

Sing forth a hymn sublime and solemn, grateful to glorious Varuna,
  imperial ruler,
Who hath struck out, like one who slays the victim, earth as a skin to
  spread in front of Surya.
In the tree-tops the air he hath extended, put milk in kine and vigorous
  speed in horses,
Set intellect in hearts, fire in the waters, Surya in heaven and Soma on
  the mountain.
Varuna lets the big cask, opening downward, flow through the heaven
  and earth and air's mid-region.
Therewith the universe's sovereign waters earth as the shower of rain
  bedews the barley.
When Varuna is fain for milk he moistens the sky, the land, and earth
  to her foundation.
Then straight the mountains clothe them in the rain-cloud: the
  heroes,[62] putting forth their vigor, loose them.
I will declare this mighty deed of magic, of glorious Varuna the lord
  immortal,
Who standing in the firmament hath meted the earth out with the sun
  as with a measure.
None, verily, hath ever let or hindered this the most wise god's mighty
  deed of magic,
Whereby with all their flood, the lucid rivers fill not one sea wherein
  they pour their waters.
If we have sinned against the man who loves us, have ever wronged a
  brother, friend, or comrade,
The neighbor ever with us, or a stranger, O Varuna, remove from us the
  trespass.
If we, as gamesters cheat at play, have cheated, done wrong unwittingly
  or sinned of purpose,
Cast all these sins away like loosened fetters, and, Varuna, let us be thine
  own beloved.

Hymn VII.87

Varuna cut a pathway out for Surya, and led the watery floods of rivers
  onward.
The mares[63] as in a race, speed on in order. He made great channels for
  the days to follow.

---

[62]Maruts, Indra's soldiers.

[63]The swift rivers.

The wind, thy breath, hath sounded through the region like a wild beast
    that seeks his food in pastures.
Within these two, exalted earth and heaven, O Varuna, are all the forms
    thou lovest.
Varuna's spies, sent forth upon their errand, survey the two world-halves
    well formed and fashioned.
Wise are they, holy, skilled in sacrifices, the furtherers of the praise-
    songs of the prudent.
To me who understand hath Varuna spoken, the names borne by the
    cow are three times seven.[64]
The sapient god, knowing the place's secret, shall speak as 'twere to
    teach the race that cometh.
On him three heavens rest and are supported, and the three earths are
    there in sixfold order.[65]
The wise King Varuna hath made in heaven that golden swing[66] to
    cover it with glory.
Like Varuna from heaven he sinks in Sindhu,[67] like a white-shining
    spark, a strong wild creature.
Ruling in depths and meting out the region, great saving power hath he,
    this world's controller.
Before this Varuna may we be sinless—him who shows mercy even to
    the sinner—
While we are keeping Aditi's ordinances. Preserve us evermore, ye gods,
    with blessings.

Hymn VII.89

Let me not yet, King Varuna, enter into the house of clay:[68]
Have mercy, spare me, mighty lord.
When, thunderer! I move along tremulous like a wind-blown skin,
Have mercy, spare me, mighty lord.
O bright and powerful god, through want of strength I erred and went
    astray:
Have mercy, spare me, mighty lord.

---

[64]The cow here is a personification of both speech and written language. "Three times
seven" refers to the twenty-one meters of Sanskrit poetry.

[65]Different regions of the world. Each of the three earths is seen as having two seasons.

[66]The sun.

[67]River Indus or the sea.

[68]The grave.

Thirst found thy worshiper though he stood in the midst of water-
floods:

Have mercy, spare me, mighty lord.

O Varuna, whatever the offence may be which we as men commit
against the heavenly host,

When through our want of thought we violate thy laws, punish us not,
O god, for that iniquity.

USHAS

Hymn I.113

This light is come, amid all lights the fairest; born is the brilliant, far-
extending brightness.

Night, sent away for Savitar's uprising, hath yielded up a birthplace for
the morning.

The fair, the bright is come with her white offspring;[69] to her the dark
one hath resigned her dwelling.

Akin, immortal, following each other, changing their colors both the
heavens move onward.

Common, unending is the sisters'[70] pathway; taught by the gods, alter-
nately they travel.

Fair-formed, of different hues and yet one-minded, night and dawn
clash not, neither do they tarry.

Bright leader of glad sounds, our eyes behold her; splendid in hue she
hath unclosed the portals.

She, stirring up the world, hath shown us riches: dawn hath awakened
every living creature.

Rich dawn, she sets afoot the coiled-up sleeper, one for enjoyment, one
for wealth or worship,

Those who saw little for extended vision. All living creatures hath the
dawn awakened.

One to high sway, one to exalted glory, one to pursue his gain, and one
his labor:

All to regard their different vocations, all moving creatures hath the
dawn awakened.

We see her there, the child of heaven, apparent, the young maid,
flushing in her shining raiment.

Thou sovereign lady of all earthly treasure, flush on us here, auspicious
dawn, this morning.

---

[69]The white clouds.

[70]Night and day.

She, first of endless morns to come hereafter, follows the path of morns
that have departed.

Dawn, at her rising, urges forth the living: him who is dead she wakes
not from his slumber.

As thou, dawn, hast caused Agni to be kindled,[71] and with the sun's
eye hast revealed creation.

And hast awakened men to offer worship; thou hast performed, for
gods, a noble service.

How long a time, and they shall be together,—dawns that have shone
and dawns to shine hereafter?

She yearns for former dawns with eager longing, and goes forth gladly
shining with the others.

Gone are the men who in the days before us looked on the rising of the
earlier morning.

We, we the living, now behold her brightness, and they come nigh who
shall hereafter see her.

Foe-chaser, born of law, the law's protectress, joy-giver, waker of all
pleasant voices,

Auspicious, bringing food for gods' enjoyment, shine on us here, most
bright, O dawn, this morning.

From days eternal hath dawn shone, the goddess, and shows this light
today, endowed with riches.

So will she shine on days to come; immortal she moves on in her own
strength, undecaying.

In the sky's borders hath she shone in splendor: the goddess hath
thrown off the veil of darkness.

Awakening the world with purple horses, on her well-harnessed chariot
dawn approaches.

Bringing all life-sustaining blessings with her, showing herself she sends
forth brilliant lustre.

Last of the countless mornings that have vanished, first of bright morns
to come hath dawn arisen.

Arise! The breath, the life, again hath reached us: darkness hath passed
away, and light approacheth.

She for the sun hath left a path to travel: we have arrived where men
prolong existence.

Singing the praises of refulgent mornings with his hymn's web the
priest, the poet, rises.

Shine then today, rich maid, on him who praises thee, shine down on us
the gift of life and offspring.

---

[71]Daybreak is the time for lighting sacrificial fires.

Dawns giving sons all heroes, kine and horses, shining upon the man
who brings oblations,—

These let the soma-presser gain when ending his glad songs louder than
the voice of Vayu.[72]

Mother of gods, Aditi's form of glory, ensign of sacrifice, shine forth
exalted.

Rise up, bestowing praise on our devotion: all-bounteous, make us chief
among the people.

Whatever splendid wealth the dawns bring with them to bless the man
who offers praise and worship,

Even that may Mitra, Varuna vouchsafe us, and Aditi and Sindhu, earth
and heaven.

THE SACRIFICIAL HORSE
Hymn I.163

What time, first springing into life, thou neighedst, proceeding from the
sea or upper waters,

Limbs of the deer hadst thou, and eagle pinions. O steed, thy birth is
high and must be praised.

This steed which Yama gave hath Trita[73] harnessed, and him, the first of
all, hath Indra mounted.

His bridle the Gandharva[74] grasped. O Vasus,[75] from out the sun ye
fashioned forth the courser.

Yama art thou, O horse; thou art Aditya; Trita art thou by secret
operation.

Thou art divided thoroughly from Soma.[76] They say thou hast three
bonds in heaven that hold thee.

Three bonds, they say, thou hast in heaven that bind thee, three in the
waters, three within the ocean.

To me thou seemest Varuna, O courser, there where they say is thy
sublimest birthplace.

---

[72]The god of wind.

[73]God of the remote birthplace of the sun. In this passage, *Yama* means "Agni" as a solar
deity.

[74]Gandharva is Visvavasu, a heavenly being who dwells in the region of the air and guards
the celestial soma.

[75]Means "good." Vasus are a class of gods, eight in number, who were at first personifications of natural phenomena.

[76]Perhaps here the moon, but the meaning is obscure.

Here, courser, are the places where they groomed thee, here are the
traces of thy hoofs as winner.

Here have I seen the auspicious reins that guide thee, which those who
guard the holy law keep safely.

Thyself from far I recognized in spirit,—a bird that from below flew
through the heaven.

I saw thy head still soaring, striving upward by paths unsoiled by dust,
pleasant to travel.

Here I beheld thy form, matchless in glory, eager to win thee food at
the cow's station.[77]

Whene'er a man brings thee to thine enjoyment, thou swallowest the
plants, most greedy eater.

After thee, courser, come the car, the bridegroom, the kine come after,
and the charm of maidens.

Full companies have followed for thy friendship: the pattern of thy vigor
gods have copied.

Horns[78] made of gold hath he: his feet are iron: less fleet than he,
though swift as thought, is Indra.

The gods have come that they may taste the oblation of him who
mounted, first of all, the courser.

Symmetrical in flank, with rounded haunches, mettled like heroes, the
celestial coursers

Put forth their strength, like swans in lengthened order, when they, the
steeds, have reached the heavenly causeway.

A body formed for flight hast thou, O charger; swift as the wind in
motion is thy spirit.

Thy horns are spread abroad in all directions: they move with restless
beat in wildernesses.

The strong steed hath come forward to the slaughter, pondering with a
mind directed godward.

The goat who is his kin is led before him: the sages and the singers
follow after.

The steed is come unto the noblest mansion, is come unto his father
and his mother.[79]

This day shall he approach the gods, most welcome: then he declares
good gifts to him who offers.

---

[77]The cow's station is the sacrificial altar.

[78]Used figuratively to mean "mane." The sun's rays are probably the intended meaning.

[79]Heaven and earth.

CREATION
Hymn X.129

Then was not nonexistent nor existent: there was no realm of air, no sky
beyond it.
What covered in, and where? and what gave shelter? Was water there,
unfathomed depth of water?
Death was not then, nor was there aught immortal: no sign was there,
the day's and night's divider.
That one thing, breathless, breathed by its own nature: apart from it
was nothing whatsoever.
Darkness there was: at first concealed in darkness this. All was
indiscriminated chaos.
All that existed then was void and formless: by the great power of
warmth was born that unit.
Thereafter rose desire in the beginning, desire, the primal seed and germ
of spirit.
Sages who searched the heart's thought discovered the existent's kinship
in the nonexistent.
Transversely was their severing line[80] extended: what was above it then,
and what below it?
There were begetters, there were mighty forces, free action here and
energy up yonder.
Who verily knows and who can here declare it, whence it was born and
whence comes this creation?
The gods are later than this world's production. Who knows then
whence it first came into being?
He, the first origin of this creation, whether he formed it all or did not
form it,
Whose eye controls this world in highest heaven, he verily knows it, or
perhaps he knows not.

PURUSHA (THE MACROCOSMIC PERSON)
Hymn X.90

A thousand heads hath Purusha, a thousand eyes, a thousand feet.
On every side pervading earth he fills a space ten fingers wide.
This Purusha is all that yet hath been and all that is to be;
The lord of immortality which waxes greater still by food.

---

[80]A line drawn by the ancient sages to divide the upper and lower worlds. It marked duality coming out of unity.

So mighty is his greatness; yea, greater than this is Purusha.
All creatures are one-fourth of him, three-fourths eternal life in heaven.
With three-fourths Purusha went up: one-fourth of him again was here.
Thence he strode out to every side over what eats not and what eats.
From him Viraj[81] was born; again Purusha from Viraj was born.
As soon as he was born he spread eastward and westward o'er the earth.
When gods prepared the sacrifice with Purusha as their offering,
Its oil was spring, the holy gift was autumn; summer was the wood.
They balmed as victim on the grass Purusha born in earliest time.
With him, the deities and all Sadhyas[82] and Rishis sacrificed.
From that great general sacrifice the dripping fat was gathered up.
He formed the creatures of the air, and animals both wild and tame.
From that great general sacrifice Richas and Sama-hymns were born:
Therefrom were spells and charms produced; the yajus[83] had its birth
     from it.
From it were horses born, from it all cattle with two rows of teeth:
From it were generated kine, from it the goats and sheep were born.
When they divided Purusha how many portions did they make?
What do they call his mouth, his arms? What do they call his thighs
     and feet?
The Brahman was his mouth, of both his arms was the Rajanya made.
His thighs became the Vaisya, from his feet the Sudra[84] was produced.
The moon was gendered from his mind, and from his eye the sun
     had birth;
Indra and Agni from his mouth were born, and Vayu from his breath.
Forth from his navel came mid-air; the sky was fashioned from his head;
Earth from his feet, and from his ear the regions. Thus they formed
     the worlds.
Seven fencing-sticks[85] had he, thrice seven layers of fuel were prepared,
When the gods, offering sacrifice, bound, as their victim, Purusha.
Gods, sacrificing, sacrificed the victim: these were the earliest holy
     ordinances.
The mighty ones attained the height of heaven, there where the
     Sadhyas, gods of old, are dwelling.

---

[81]The vital juice, sperm, ovum, or embryo.

[82]A class of celestial beings, probably ancient divine sacrificers.

[83]The hymns (*richas* or *yajus*) of the *Rig-Veda,* those of the *Sama-Veda,* and the compositions of the *Yajur-Veda* were created by the sacrifice of Purusha.

[84]The four social classes—the Brahmans (priests), Rajanyas (rulers–warriors), the Vaisyas (commoners), and the Sudras (menials)—were born from Purusha's sacrifice.

[85]Pieces of wood laid around the sacrificial fire to enclose it.

9

ॐ

BRAHMANAS

The Brahmanas, *the earliest prose works in Indian literature, are a series of texts about sacrificial ritual that follow the* Samhitas *("hymns") in each of the four* Vedas *(see Selection 8). The* Brahmanas *lay down the requirements for each ritual, and provide explanations and justifications for these requirements. Often, as illustrated in the following excerpts, the explanations take the form of stories.*

The title Brahmanas *comes from the word* brahman, *which, depending on whether the emphasis falls on the first or the second syllable, can mean "prayer" or "one who prays," namely, the priest. The Vedic sacrifice, as a whole, was a form of prayer. More specifically, however, the prayer consisted of the holy words from the* Veda *that the priests recited at the sacrifice. The* Brahmanas *are thus texts belonging to the priests that contain knowledge about prayer and sacrifice.*

The Brahmanas *represent a new phase in the Vedic religion, a phase known as Brahmanism and ushered in by changes in the Aryans' way of life. As the Aryans settled in India and came to interact closely with the pre-Aryan Indians in the years approaching 1000* B.C., *their society changed profoundly. It acquired the characteristics of a settled civilization. Agriculture replaced cattle-herding as the main economic activity; trade, both local and long-distance, grew significantly; and the tribe ceased to be a viable political unit. Small monarchies and republics emerged. The most far-reaching changes occurred in the social organization. In their tribal days, although there had been impromptu division of social functions according to occasion, there had been no strict class divisions among the Aryans. Now society became classified into distinct social orders, the highest order being the priests* (brahmans), *the next highest the warrior–rulers* (kashatriyas or rajaniyas), *and the third the commoners* (vaishyas). *There was a fourth category, the menials* (shudras), *who provided many essential services to the upper classes but were themselves outside the pale of society, some of them considered literally untouchable for the upper classes. Strict rules governed every individual's social and moral conduct. The rules were considered sacred and their breach a sacrilege. By following the rules themselves and enforcing them on others, the two highest orders maintained their superior position and held the commoners between them and the menials beneath them. It was a society based on power—the spiritual power of priests and the armed might of warrior–rulers.*

The Brahmanas *reflect this temper of the Brahmanic society closely. Like the rules for social and moral duties, those for the performance of sacrificial ritual are laid down here precisely and in great detail. The* Brahmanas *give clear and precise instructions about every possible aspect of the ritual—the kinds and number of priests required, the types of sacred fires to be built, prayers to be recited, offerings to be made, appropriate utensils, time and place for the sacrifice and preparation of the place, priests' fees, and the like. The performance of sacrifice is thus an extremely complex and rigidly prescribed process, which must always be performed in the exact same manner.*

Earlier, sacrifices had been much simpler. They had also been different in spirit, having the character of religious feasts where humans shared with the gods the god-given bounties. Now the sacrificial ritual was strictly solemn and impersonal. Its purpose, instead of being a thankful rejoicing, was to compel the gods and nature, by the power of sacrifice, to grant the worshipers' wishes. Sacrifice had become a formula for exacting desired results.

The explanations justifying the prescribed requirements for the Brahmanic ritual are usually long and tedious. Generally, they are not rationally convincing. This is so because the power of sacrifice was considered essentially a mystery beyond rational explanation. Its performance was believed to be an act of magic providing control over the natural and supernatural forces. In the Rig-Veda, *there is a hymn addressed to Purusha, a macrocosmic being (see Selection 8). The hymn tells the story of the creation of the world as a result of the sacrifice of this being. Different parts of his dismembered body became different parts of both the physical universe and the human social order. The rites of sacrifice prescribed in the* Brahmanas *are seen as a symbolic re-enactment of this primeval act of creation. This re-enactment is believed to renew and revitalize creation. The sacrificial ritual thus was practiced as a means of controlling and sustaining the health of both society and the cosmos.*

The emphasis on the power of ritual in the Brahmanas *reduces the stature of the gods mentioned in them. Their personalities tend to become faint, buried under the profusion of ritual formulae. Despite this, the* Brahmanas *are filled with interesting narratives about all kinds of myths and legends, which have always served as a rich source of information for the followers of the Hindu religion and inspiration for Indian writers. The two following selections from the* Jaiminiya Brahmana *are chosen to illustrate the belief in the power of prayer (or sacrifice) and the performers of prayer, the priest–sages, as well as to show the narrative quality of the* Brahmanas. *The selections also show other important aspects of Brahmanic culture besides the role of sacrificial ritual. For example, we see here the conflict between the two highest social orders, the priest–sages and the warrior–rulers, a conflict that often was resolved in a collusion between them to con-*

trol the lower classes. The first excerpt tells the story of a Brahman who revives a child run over and killed by a chariot he was driving. Later, he teaches his king's people a lesson for having given a prejudicial judgment against him. In the second excerpt, a famous sage, Cyavana, with the power of his Brahmanic knowledge, first compels a king to give him, an old man, a young daughter in marriage. Then he maneuvers to make two gods restore his youth.

JAIMINIYA BRAHMANA
3.94–96

The Charioteer and the Vanishing Fire

Vrsa, the son of Jana, was the domestic priest [Purohita] of King Triyaruna, son of Trivrsan of the Iksvakus.[1] Now in the old days the domestic priest would hold the reins in the chariot for the king in order to watch out for the king, so that he would not do any harm. As the two of them [Vrsa and Triyaruna] were driving along, they cut down with the wheel of the chariot the son of a Brahmin,[2] a little boy playing in the road. One of the two [the king] had driven the horses forward, while the other [the priest] had tried to pull them to one side, but they came on so hard that he could not pull them aside. And so they had cut down the boy. They argued with each other about it: "You are the one who murdered him." "No, you are the one who murdered him." Vrsa threw down the reins, stepped down from the chariot, and said, "*You* are the murderer." "No," said the king, "the one who holds the reins is the driver of the chariot. You are the murderer." "No," said the priest, "I tried to pull back to avoid him, but you drove the horses on. You are the murderer."

Finally they said, "Let us ask," and they went to ask the Iksvakus. The Iksvakus said, "The one who holds the reins is the driver. You are the murderer," and they accused Vrsa the priest. He prayed, "Let me get out of this; let me find help and a way out. Let that boy come to life." He saw[3] this chant and brought the boy to life with it, saying, "For your skill, which brings the sap of life—." Now, the "sap of life" is the life's breath; and so with this verse he put the life's breath back in the

---

From *Tales of Sex and Violence: Folklore, Sacrifice, and Danger in the Jaiminiya Brahmana* by Wendy Doniger O'Flaherty, University of Chicago, 1985. Copyright 1985 by the University of Chicago, Chicago and reprinted with their permission. [Pp. 64–67, 81–83].

[1]The name of a people, the subjects of King Triyaruna.

[2]A variation of "Brahman," a priest.

[3]Saw in his mind's eye.

child. And he continued, "—and for the chariot-horse, which is the drink—the lovely, much-desired, enlivening, enriching, inspiring drink—we pray today." Now, the "drink" is the man; and so with this verse he revived him. For this is a chant that cures and makes restoration. And it is also a chant that gives you what you want. Whoever praises with this chant gets whatever he wants.

But Vrsa was angry, and he went to Jana [his father] and said, "They gave a false and prejudiced judgment against me." Then the power went out of the fire of the Iksvakus: if they placed food on the fire in the evening, by morning it still had not been cooked; and if they placed food on the fire in the morning, the same thing happened to it [by evening]. Then they said, "We have displeased a Brahmin and treated him with dishonor. That is why the power has gone out of our fire. Let us invite him back." They invited him, and he came back, just like a Brahmin summoned by a king. As he arrived, he prayed, "Let me see this power of the fire." He saw this chant and sang it over the fire. Then he saw this: "The wife of Triyaruna is a flesh-eating ghoul [Pisaci]. She is the one who has covered the fire with a cushion and sits on it." Then he spoke these verses [from the *Rg Veda*]:[4] "The young mother secretly keeps the boy tightly swathed and does not give him to the father. The people no longer see before them his altered face, hidden by the charioteer. Who is the boy that you are carrying, young woman? The chief queen, not the stepmother, gave him birth, for the embryo grew for many autumns. I saw him born when his mother bore him. Agni[5] shines forth with a high light; by his power he makes all things manifest. He overpowers the godless forces of evil magic; he sharpens his two horns to gore the demons. Let Agni's bellowings reach to heaven as piercing weapons to destroy the demons. His angry glare breaks forth in ecstasy of Soma. The obstacles of the godless cannot hold him back."

As Vrsa finished saying these verses, the power of the fire ran up into her[6] and burnt her all up. Then they dispersed that power of the fire properly, here and there [in each house], and the fire cooked for them properly.

3.120–129

The Rejuvenation of Cyavana

Cyavana, the son of Bhrgu,[7] said to his sons, "I know the *Brahmana of the Vastupa.*[8] Therefore put me down on the sacrificial place [*vastu*] and go away on

---

[4]An alternate spelling for *Rig-Veda.*

[5]Fire. Also the god of fire.

[6]"Her" refers to fire. The meaning here is that the power of fire returned to it.

[7]Progenitor of the Bhrigus, a famous family of sages. He was believed to be the son of Varuna, the god of the cosmic and the moral order.

[8]The name of a *Brahmana,* literally the *Brahmana of the Place of Sacrifice.*

the thrice-returning[9] departure." They said, "We cannot do that, for people will cry out against us and revile us, saying, 'They are abandoning their father.'" "No," he said, "by this means you will be better off, and by this I hope to become young again. Leave me and go forth." As he gave them this command, they placed him at the fountain of youth on the Sarasvati River,[10] and they went forth on the thrice-returning departure. As he was left behind, he wished, "Let me become young again, and find a young girl for a wife, and sacrifice with a thousand [cows]."

Cyavana saw this hymn and praised with it, and at that moment Saryata[11] the Manava [descendant of Manu[12]] settled down with his clan near him. The young boys who were cowherds and shepherds smeared Cyavana with mud and with balls of dust and cowshit and ashes.[13] Cyavana then produced a condition among the Saryatis[14] so that no one recognized anyone else: a mother did not know her son, nor a son his mother. Saryata said [to his people], "Have you seen anything around here that could have caused this state of affairs?" They said to him, "Nothing but this: there is an old man on his last legs lying there. The boys who are cowherds and shepherds smeared him today with mud and balls of shit and dust and ashes. This has happened because of that."

Saryata said, "That was Cyavana, the son of Bhrgu, who knows the *Brahmana of the Vastupa*. His sons have left him in the sacrificial place and gone away." Then Saryata ran up to Cyavana and said, "Honor to you, great sage; have mercy, sir, on the Saryatis." Now, Saryata had a beautiful daughter named Sukanya ["Lovely Maiden"]. Cyavana said, "Give me Sukanya." "No," said the king, "mention anything else of value." But Cyavana said, "No, I know the *Brahmana of the Vastupa*. Put her down beside me today at evening, and go away with your clan." They said, "Let us discuss this, and then we will give you our answer." They held a council together and said, "We might obtain a few treasures with her, two or three at the most, but this way we will obtain everything with her. Hell, let's give her to him." They gave her to him, but they said to her, "My dear girl, this is a worn-out old man, who will not be able to run after you. As soon as we have harnessed the horses, run after us right away."

And so, when they had harnessed the horses, she stood up and was about to run after the clan, but Cyavana said, "Serpent, come and help your friend to save

---

[9]The meaning is obscure. Perhaps it means a gainful journey.

[10]An actual, as well as a mythical, river. It was believed to have in it the fountain of youth.

[11]The name of a king or a chief.

[12]The first man, the mythical ancestor of all humankind.

[13]Smearing one's body with dirt and ashes has been a practice of Indian ascetics from the ancient times to the present. It is supposed to give the practitioner an inner power.

[14]The subjects of Sarayata.

his life." And a black snake rose up right against her as she was about to go. When she saw it, she sat right down again.

The two Asvins,[15] who have no share in the soma[16] offerings, happened to be wandering about there. They came to Sukanya and said, "My dear girl, this is an old man, not whole, not fit to be a husband. Be our wife." "No," she said, "I will be the wife of the man to whom my father gave me." Then they went away, but Cyavana had overheard them, and he said to Sukanya, "My dear girl, what was all that noise about?" She said, "Two men—the handsomest men I have ever seen—came to me and said, 'My dear girl, this is an old man, not whole, not fit to be a husband. Be our wife.'" "And what did *you* say?" "'No,' said I, 'I will be the wife of the man to whom my father gave me.'"

Cyavana was very pleased about that. He told her, "Those were the two Asvins; they will come tomorrow and speak to you in the same way. Now, you say to them, '*You* are the ones who are not whole; for though you are gods, you do not drink the soma.' Then they will ask you, 'Who can see to it that we may share in the soma?' 'My husband,' you say. This is my hope of becoming young again."

The next day, the two Asvins came and said the same thing, and she said, "You are not whole; for though you are gods, you do not drink the soma. My husband is whole, for he drinks the soma." They said, "Who can see to it that we may share in the soma?" "My husband," said she. Then they said to him, "Sage, sir, make us share the soma." "All right," said he, "and you make me young again." They drew him down into the fountain of youth of the Sarasvati River.

He said, "My dear girl, we will all come out looking the same; by this sign, you will know me." They did all come out looking the same, the handsomest men in the world; but she recognized him and could tell them apart. "This is my husband," she said, and they said to him, "Sage, we have granted your desire: you have become young again. Now teach us so that we may share the soma." And he sent them to Dadhyanc.[17]

Now, Indra[18] had threatened to cut off the head of Dadhyanc if he told anyone the secret of the sacrifice: how the sacrifice is made whole when the head is cut off. The Asvins gave Dadhyanc the head of a horse, through which he told them the secret of the sacrifice. Indra cut off that head, and then the Asvins replaced Dadhyanc's head. Thus the Asvins became sharers in the soma.

---

[15]Twin gods, half-human and half-horse in form, known for their handsomeness.

[16]Juice of an unknown plant poured as a libation to gods at the time of ritual sacrifices. It was a consciousness-altering substance.

[17]A mythical sage.

[18]A major Aryan and Hindu god. In his early history he was a god of war and rain. Later he became a king in the heavens (see Selection 8).

10

⚘

THE BOOK OF HISTORY

Consciousness of history and the search for meaning in the past have always been prominent features of Chinese thought. Not only this selection, but the others that represent early Chinese experience frequently allude to the persons and events of early history, in many cases specifically to the actions described in this selection.

The Shu ching, ("book of history" or "book of documents") was accepted for thousands of years in China as the record of the legendary founders of the Chinese state early in the third millennium B.C. and of the earliest dynasties, dating from around 1800 B.C. Editing of the book itself was ascribed to the philosopher Confucius (551–479 B.C.). Scholars now question the reliability of its accounts and detect many later additions. To Confucius (Selection 26) and his disciples, however, and even to those who disagreed with them on matters of moral and political belief, there was no doubt that—as we see in the first excerpt—it was true that the Emperor Yao of the Hsia Dynasty had passed over his own son in order to identify, test, and elevate to the throne a humble but competent man. To Confucius there was no doubt that the Hsia Dynasty lost the "mandate of Heaven," the moral approval and support of the powers above, and that it was replaced by the Shang Dynasty that gained and, in time, lost the mandate to the Chou Dynasty. There also was no doubt that one of the heroes of the early Chou Dynasty was the emperor's brother, the Duke of Chou, who is seen in the second excerpt scrupulously carrying out the religious rites connected with building a capital city for the new dynasty.

The skepticism of modern scholars about these early documents as history can be misleading as we try to grasp their influence in Chinese history. To the Chinese, history is "philosophy teaching by example." History provides examples of good rulers doing the right things for the right reasons and, thereby, bringing blessings and prosperity on their people. In other instances, history shows the destructive consequences of selfish, corrupt, or merely thoughtless behavior on the part of rulers. The important "truth" of these documents is, then, their moral truth. The books' heroes are heroic, not because they are powerful but because they are virtuous—their power flows from that virtue. In the late centuries B.C. The

Book of History *took its place among the five "Confucian classics," along with* The Book of Songs *(Selection 11),* The Book of Changes, The Book of Rites, *and* The Spring and Autumn Annals.

❧

FROM THE "CANON OF YAO" *AND* THE "CANON OF SHUN"

Examining into antiquity, we find that the Emperor Yao[1] was called Fang-hsun. He was reverent, intelligent, accomplished, sincere, and mild. He was sincerely respectful and capable of modesty. His light covered the four extremities of the empire and extended to Heaven above and the earth below. He was able to make bright his great virtue, and bring affection to the nine branches of the family. When the nine branches of the family had become harmonious, he distinguished and honored the hundred clans. When the hundred clans had become illustrious, he harmonized the myriad states. The numerous people were amply nourished and prosperous and became harmonious. Then he charged [his counsellors] Hsi and Ho with reverence to follow august Heaven and calculate and delineate the sun, the moon, and the other heavenly bodies, and respectfully to give the people the seasons. . . .

The emperor said: "Ah, you Hsi and Ho, the year has 366 days, and by means of an intercalary month you must fix the four seasons and complete the year. If you earnestly regulate all the functionaries, the achievements will all be glorious." The emperor said: "Who will carefully attend to this? I will raise him up and employ him."

Fang Ch'i said: "Your heir-son Chu is enlightened."

The emperor said: "Alas, he is deceitful and quarrelsome; will he do?" . . .

The emperor said: Oh, you, Chief of the Four Mountains, I have been on the throne for seventy years. If you can carry out the mandate, I shall resign my position to you."

From *Sources of Chinese Tradition,* Vol. I, ed. Wm. Theodore DeBary, Wing-tsit Chan, and Burton Watson, 1960, © Columbia University Press, New York. Reprinted with permission of the publisher.

[1]It seems probable that *The Book of History* sought to give historical reality to mythic heroic figures common to the early legends of most peoples, often crediting each with specific culture achievements, such as Yao's development of the calendar. Traditional dating, which gives him a 101-year reign, from 2357 to 2256 B.C., should provoke some skepticism. The reign of his successor, Shun, dates from 2255–2206 B.C.

The Chief of the Four Mountains said: "I have not the virtue. I would only disgrace the high position."

The emperor said: "Promote someone who is already illustrious, or raise up someone who is humble and mean."

They all said to the emperor: "There is an unmarried man in a low position called Shun of Yu."

The emperor said: "Yes, I have heard of him. What is he like?"

The chief said: "He is the son of a blind man. His father is stupid, his mother is deceitful, his half-brother Hsiang is arrogant. Yet he has been able to live in harmony with them and to be splendidly filial. He has controlled himself and has not come to wickedness."

The emperor said: "I will try him; I will wive him and observe his behavior towards my two daughters." He gave orders and sent down his two daughters to the bend of the Kuei River to be wives in the House of Yu. The emperor said: "Be reverent!"

● ● ●

The emperor said: "Come, you Shun, in the affairs on which you have been consulted, I have examined your words; your words have been accomplished and capable of yielding fine results for three years. Do you ascend the imperial throne." Shun considered himself inferior in virtue and was not pleased. But in the first month, the first day, he accepted the abdication of Yao in the Temple of the Accomplished Ancestor. . . . Then he made *lei* sacrifice to the Lord-on-High; he made *yin* sacrifice to the six venerable ones; he made *wang* sacrifice to mountains and rivers, and he made comprehensive sacrifices to all the spirits.[2] . . . In the second month of the year he went around the east to the fiefs, and came to the venerable T'ai Mountain[3] where he made burnt offering; he made *wang* sacrifice successively to mountains and rivers and he gave audience to the eastern princes. He put into accord the seasons, the months, and the proper days. He made uniform the pitchpipes, the measures of length, the measures of capacity, and the weights. . . . He delimited the twelve provinces and raised altars on twelve mountains and he deepened the rivers.

---

[2]Chronicle segments of *The Book of History* are almost always specific about the sacrificial rites—usually offerings of animals or produce accompanied by prayer—which these heroic figures of the past performed on great occasions. Although the significance of such ritual acts changed over time, becoming less a matter of literal belief and more a matter of respect and good form, ritual behavior continued to be emphasized in the Confucian tradition, one of the marks of the gentleman and one of the key duties of the ruler.

[3]Mount T'ai *(T'ai Shan)*, in modern Shantung Province, is still considered a sacred mountain, visited every year by hundreds of thousands of pilgrims who climb to the shrines at its peak. (The ancient religious structures have recently been joined by a TV transmitter mast.)

FROM THE "ANNOUNCEMENT OF THE DUKE OF SHAO"

In the second month, third quarter, sixth day *i-wei*,[4] the king in the morning proceeded from Chou and arrived in Feng. The Grand Guardian, the Duke of Shao, preceded the Duke of Chou[5] to inspect the site. In the third month, the day *mou-shen*, the third day after the first appearance of the new moon on *ping-wu*, the Grand Guardian arrived in the morning at Lo and consulted the tortoise oracle[6] about the site. When he had obtained the oracle he planned and laid out the city.[7] On the third day *keng-hsu*, the Grand Guardian with all the Yin[8] people started work on the emplacements at the bend of the Lo River, and on the fifth day *chia-yin* the emplacements were determined. The next day *i-mao*, the Duke of Chou arrived in the morning at Lo and thoroughly inspected the plans for the new city. On the third day *ting-ssu*, he sacrificed two oxen as victims on the suburban altar, and on the next day *mou-wu* he sacrificed to the God of the Soil in the new city one ox, one sheep, and one pig. On the seventh day *chia-tzu* the Duke of Chou by written documents gave charges to all the rulers of the states of Hou, Tien, and Nan zones in the Yin realm. When orders had been given to the Yin multitude they

---

[4]The binomial terms by which days are identified in this passage relate to the sixty-day cycle that was basic to Chinese calendar reckoning.

[5]The Duke of Chou was almost certainly an historical figure, and if traditional dating for the dynasty is correct, he must have flourished in the late twelfth and early eleventh centuries B.C. As younger brother of the first king of Chou, he was in a position to take power for himself when the king died, leaving an infant son. But the duke sacrificed personal ambition to family devotion and statesmanship, and worked successfully to preserve and strengthen the state for his young nephew. His selfless devotion to good government later made him the great moral hero of antiquity for the Confucians.

[6]Many systems of divination were used in early China, usually in an attempt to determine the approval or disapproval of the divine ancestors for proposed major acts of the ruler. The system referred to here involved carving the characters for a question into the flat bottom section of a tortoise shell, then breaking the shell by applying a heated metal rod to it. The diviners interpreted the ancestors' reply from the way the crack ran across the inscription on the shell. Discovery and deciphering of these oracle bones has given modern archaeologists a great deal of information about Shang and early Chou history and about the development of Chinese as a written language.

[7]On or near the present site of Loyang, near the confluence of the Lo and Yellow Rivers in modern Honan Province. Loyang often served as a capital city for later dynasties as well.

[8]Yin is an alternate name for Shang, the dynasty that the Chou had just overthrown. Much is made in this passage of the moral righteousness of this change in the locus of power, and about the "mandate of Heaven" as something to be lost by corrupt rulers and gained by virtuous newcomers. But the point is also being made that the *subjects* of the old dynasty have not been dispossessed, and their willing participation in building the new capital is a sign of their acquiescence to the new regime.

arose with vigor to do their work. The Grand Guardian then together with all the ruling princes of the states went out and took gifts and entered again and gave them to the Duke of Chou.

The Duke of Chou said: "I salute and bow down my head and I extol the king and your Grace. I make an announcement to all the Yin and managers of affairs. Oh, august Heaven, the Lord-on-High, has changed his principal son [the ruler] and this great state Yin's mandate. Now that the king has received the mandate, unbounded is the grace, but also unbounded is the solicitude. Oh, how can he be but careful! Heaven has removed and made an end to the great state Yin's mandate. There are many former wise kings of Yin in Heaven, and the later kings and people here managed their mandate. But in the end [under the last king] wise and good men lived in misery so that, leading their wives and carrying their children, wailing and calling to Heaven, they went to where no one could come and seize them. Oh, Heaven had pity on the people of the four quarters, and looking with affection and giving its mandate, it employed the zealous ones [the leaders of Chou]. May the king now urgently pay careful attention to his virtue. Look at the ancient predecessors, the lords of Hsia; Heaven indulged them and cherished and protected them. They strove to comprehend the obedience to Heaven; but in these times they have lost their mandate. Now a young son is the successor; may he not neglect the aged elders. Then he will comprehend our ancient men's virtue, nay still more it will occur that he is able to comprehend and endeavor to follow Heaven. . . . May the king come and take over the work of the Lord-on-High, and himself manage the government in the center of the land. I, Tan, say: Having made the great city, he shall from here be a counterpart to august Heaven. He shall carefully sacrifice to the upper and lower spirits, and from here centrally govern. . . . We should not fail to mirror ourselves in the lords of Hsia; we likewise should not fail to mirror ourselves in the lords of Yin.[9] We do not presume to know and say that the lords of Hsia undertook Heaven's mandate so as to have it for so-and-so many years; we do not presume to know and say that it could not have been prolonged. It was that they did not reverently attend to their virtue, and so they prematurely renounced their mandate. We do not presume to know and say that the lords of Yin received Heaven's mandate for so-and-so many years; we do not know and say that it could not have been prolonged. It was that they did not reverently attend to their virtue and so they prematurely threw away their mandate. Now the king has succeeded to and received their mandate. We should then also remember the mandates of these two states and in succeeding to them equal their merits. . . . Being king, his position will be that of a leader in virtue; the small people will then imitate him in all the world. . . . May those above and below [the king and his servants] labor and be anxiously careful. May they say: We have received Heaven's mandate, may it grandly equal the span of years of the lords of Hsia and not miss the span of years of the lords of Yin."

9In other words, we should learn the lessons of history and not repeat the mistakes of the past.

11

THE BOOK OF SONGS

The cornerstone document of Chinese literature is a collection of 305 lyric poems called the Shi ching, literally "song-word scripture," variously translated as the "book of odes" or "book of songs." These songs originated in the early centuries of the Chou Dynasty, roughly between 1100 and 600 B.C. This was a society dominated by an emperor and a powerful feudal-warrior nobility, resting on the productive base of peasant farmers, with its locus in the North China Plain and the Yellow River valley. The Book of Songs brings together a mixture ranging from peasant folk songs to those that celebrate great events in the lives of the feudal and imperial families. We have the words of these songs but have no idea of the music that undoubtedly was essential to their considerable vitality.

Tradition has it that the original collection numbered some three thousand songs, and that the philosopher Confucius, around 500 B.C., selected roughly a tenth of these as exemplary lyrics, giving shape to the book as we know it now. Verification of this is problematic, as are all the old beliefs regarding Confucius's role in creating the four other "Confucian classics." It is true, however, that Confucius knew these poems and quoted them to his disciples approvingly and in ways that suggest that they knew them too. These poems came to be regarded as a repository of insight into the human condition and as metaphors for proper relationships within family, society, and state. As a classic of the emerging Confucian tradition, The Book of Songs survived the book-burning of 213 B.C. during the Ch'in Dynasty. As the basis of moral and literary instruction for China's governing class, The Book of Songs was committed to memory by every candidate for public office down to the early years of the twentieth century, and it came to provide much of the currency of quotation in conversation and writing for more than two thousand years, much as the Bible has done in the West.

The allegorical interpretations that Confucian moralists gave the songs—for example, that poems of love between man and woman are metaphors for the proper relationship between subject and ruler—tended to obscure the original intent of many of these lyrics. Although this, like all poetry, loses much in the translation, we are at least free to see these songs for what they were and to catch something of the passions that brought them into being. We can share the yearn-

ing of the young woman (poem 45) separated from her lover for a day that seems eternal, share the feudal retainer's admiration for his lord (poem 119), and share the pain of separation as a young soldier leaves his family to go to war (poem 124).

The songs deal with such central concerns of early Chou Dynasty life as warfare and hunting, praise of the great leaders of the dynasty, protest against the injustice of feudal and imperial officials, and the rituals of ancestor veneration and agriculture. More than a third of these lyrics concern love, courtship, and marriage. They give us a broad range of voices and experiences, from those of young peasant men and women deeply in love and sometimes deeply hurt by love, to the stately grace and beauty of a noblewoman on her wedding journey. Although we know that all of these anonymous poems were edited later by male scholars, we still clearly hear women's voices in them, for almost the last time in a literate culture that would deny any significant place to women as writers for two and a half millennia.

This is symbolic poetry, relying heavily on nature for its sources. Nature symbolism is universal in lyric poetry, but the Western tradition commonly works it into a simile; for instance in Robert Burns's:

> *O, my luve's like a red, red rose,*
> *That's newly sprung in June.*

Characteristically, The Book of Songs *employs what has been called "elliptical symbolism," in which the human component is simply set beside the natural, rarely stating a "like" or "as." In the opening couplet of the first poem in these selections we hear a woman exclaim:*

> *Sun in the east!*
> *This lovely man . . .*

The sun is not likened to the man, but is a metaphor for him. However, the matter is more complex than straightforward A-as-metaphor-for-B. In some cases, the relationship between human and natural object is one of contrast. In poem 66, for instance, we again hear a woman's voice and again encounter the sun as symbol:

> *Oh sun, ah moon*
> *That shine upon the earth below,*
> *A man like this*
> *Will not stand firm to the end.*

Here, however, the constancy of sun and predictability of moon are set against the inconstancy of the man.

The songs have no individual titles, and so are usually numbered. In these selections we have followed the thematic arrangement and numbering of the translator, the great British scholar, Sir Arthur Waley. However, we also have indicated the number assigned by an early Chinese scholar named Mao, whose arrangement is considered the standard reference.

ᚹ

4 (MAO NO. 99)

Sun in the east!
This lovely man
Is in my house.
Is in my home.
His foot is upon my doorstep.

Moon in the east!
This lovely man
Is in my bower,
Is in my bower,
His foot is upon my threshold.

10 (MAO NO. 147)

That the mere glimpse of a plain cap
Could harry me with such longing,
Cause pain so dire!

That the mere glimpse of a plain coat
Could stab my heart with grief!
Enough! Take me with you to your home.

That a mere glimpse of plain leggings
Could tie my heart in tangles!
Enough! Let us two be one.

17 (MAO NO. 20)

Plop fall the plums; but there are still seven.
Let those gentlemen that would court me
Come while it is lucky!

Plop fall the plums; but there are still three.
Let any gentlemen who would court me
Come before it is too late!

From *The Book of Songs*, Arthur Waley, trans., Grove Press, Inc., New York, 1937.

Plop fall the plums; in shallow baskets we lay them.
Any gentleman who would court me
Had better speak while there is time.

22 (MAO NO. 42)

Of fair girls the loveliest
Was to meet me at the corner of the wall.
But she hides and will not show herself;
I scratch my head, pace up and down.

Of fair girls the prettiest
Gave me a red flute.
The flush of that red flute
Is pleasure at the girl's beauty.

She has been in the pastures and brought for me rush wool,
Very beautiful and rare.
It is not you that are beautiful;
But you were given by a lovely girl.

24 (MAO NO. 76)

I beg of you, Chung Tzu,
Do not climb into our homestead,
Do not break the willows we have planted.
Not that I mind about the willows,
But I am afraid of my father and mother.
Chung Tzu I dearly love;
But of what my father and mother say
Indeed I am afraid.

I beg of you, Chung Tzu,
Do not climb over our wall,
Do not break the mulberry trees we have planted.
Not that I mind about the mulberry trees,
But I am afraid of my brothers.
Chung Tzu I dearly love;
But of what my brothers say
Indeed I am afraid.

I beg of you, Chung Tzu,
Do not climb into our garden,
Do not break the hard-wood we have planted.
Not that I mind about the hard-wood,
But I am afraid of what people will say.
Chung Tzu I dearly love;
But of all that people will say
Indeed I am afraid.

26 (MAO NO. 96)

The Lady:[1] The cock has crowed;
It is full daylight.

The Lover: It was not the cock that crowed,
It was the buzzing of those green flies.

The Lady: The eastern sky glows;
It is broad daylight.

The Lover: That is not the glow of dawn,
But the rising moon's light.
The gnats fly drowsily;
It would be sweet to share a dream with you.

The Lady: Quick! Go home!
Lest I have cause to hate you!

28 (MAO NO. 41)

Cold blows the northern wind,
Thick falls the snow.
Be kind to me, love me,
Take my hand and go with me.
Yet she lingers, yet she havers [talks aimlessly]!
There is no time to lose.

The north wind whistles,
Whirls the falling snow.
Be kind to me, love me,
Take my hand and go home with me.
Yet she lingers, yet she havers!
There is no time to lose.

Nothing is redder than the fox,
Nothing is blacker than the crow.[2]
Be kind to me, love me,
Take my hand and ride with me.
Yet she lingers, yet she havers!
There is no time to lose.

45 (MAO NO. 72)

Oh, he is plucking cloth-creeper,
For a single day I have not seen him;
It seems like three months!

---

[1]The Chinese original gives no indication of who speaks what lines in this Romeo-and-Juliet-like dialogue.

[2]That is, "there is no love truer than mine."

Oh, he is plucking southernwood,
For a single day I have not seen him;
It seems like three autumns!

Oh, he is plucking mugwort,
For a single day I have not seen him;
It seems like three years!

56 (MAO NO. 81)

If along the highroad
I caught hold of your sleeve,
Do not hate me;
Old ways take time to overcome.

If along the highroad
I caught hold of your hand,
Do not be angry with me;
Friendship takes time to overcome.

63 (MAO NO. 23)

In the wilds there is a dead doe;
With white rushes we cover her.[3]
There was a lady longing for the spring;
A fair knight seduced her.

In the wood there is a clump of oaks,
And in the wilds a dead deer
With white rushes well bound;
There was a lady fair as jade.

"Heigh, not so hasty, not so rough;
Heigh, do not touch my handkerchief.
Take care, or the dog will bark."

66 (MAO NO. 29)

Oh sun, ah, moon
That shine upon the earth below,
A man like this
Will not stand firm to the end.
How can such a one be true?
Better if he had never noticed me.

---

[3]In other words, if one finds a dead doe in the woods, one covers her with rush leaves. The knight has "killed" the lady's virginity and should treat her with at least as much respect and should "cover" his deed by marrying her.

O sun, ah, moon
That cover the earth below,
A man like this
Will not deal kindly to the end.
How can such a one be true?
Better if he had not requited me.

O sun, ah, moon
That rise out of the east,
A man like this,
Of whom no good word is said,
How can he be true?
I wish I could forget him.

Oh sun, ah, moon
That from the east do rise,
Heigh, father! Ho, mother,
You have nurtured me to no good end.
How should he be true?
He requited me, but did not follow up.

86 (MAO NO. 57)

A splendid woman and upstanding;
Brocade she wore, over an unlined coat,
Daughter of the Lord of Ch'i,[4]
Wife of the Lord of Wei,
Sister of the Crown Prince of Ch'i,
Called sister-in-law by the Lord of Hsing,
Calling the Lord of T'an her brother-in-law.

Hands white as rush-down,
Skin like lard,
Neck long and white as the tree-grub,
Teeth like melon seeds,
Lovely head, beautiful brows.
Oh, the sweet smile dimpling,
The lovely eyes so black and white.

---

[4]This court ode celebrates an aspect of one of the most famous marriages of the age, which took place in 757 B.C. The bride, whose name was Chuang Chiang, apparently escorted by an honor guard of her fiancé's men, is making the traditional wedding journey from her parents' home to the great estate where she will be married and will live. An elegant formal costume and artificially white cosmetics were customary among upper-class Chinese women for centuries, and survive in modified form today among the *geisha* in Japan. The fish of the last strophe are symbols of good luck and fertility.

This splendid lady takes her ease;
She rests where the fields begin.
Her four steeds prance,
The red trappings flutter.
Screened by fans of pheasant-feather she is led to court.
Oh, you Great Officers, retire early,
Do not fatigue our lord.

Where the water of the river, deep and wide,
Flows northward in strong course,
In the fish-net's swish and swirl
Sturgeon, snout-fish leap and lash.
Reeds and sedges tower high.
All her ladies are tall-coifed;
All her knights, doughty men.

96 (MAO NO. 67)

My lord is all a-glow.
In his left hand he holds the reed-organ,
With his right he summons me to make free with him.
Oh, the joy!

My lord is carefree.
In his left hand he holds the dancing plumes,
With his right he summons me to sport with him.
Oh, the joy!

103 (MAO NO. 187)

O oriole, yellow bird,
Do not settle on the corn,
Do not peck at my millet.
The people of this land
Are not minded to nurture me.
I must go back, go home,
To my own land and kin.[5]

O oriole, yellow bird,
Do not settle on the mulberries,
Do not peck my sorghum.

---

[5]The theme of this poem is parallel to that of the Book of Ruth in the Bible, and reminds one of the lines from John Keat's poem "To a Nightingale":

"... the self-same song that found a path
Through the sad heart of Ruth, when sick for home,
She stood in tears amid the alien corn."

With the people of this land
One can make no covenant.
I must go back, go home,
To where my brothers are.

O oriole, yellow bird,
Do not settle on the oaks,
Do not peck my wine-millet.
With the people of this land
One can come to no understanding.
I must go back, go home
To where my own men are.

119 (MAO NO. 80)

His furs of lamb's wool so glossy!
Truly he is steadfast and tough.
That great gentleman
Would give his life rather than fail his lord.

His furs of lamb's wool, facings of leopard's fur!
He is very martial and strong.
That great gentleman
Is the upholder of right in this land.

His furs of lamb's wool so splendid,
His three festoons so gay!
That great gentleman
Is the first in all our land.

124 (MAO NO. 110)

I climb that wooded hill
And look toward where my father is.
My father is saying, "Alas, my son is on service;
Day and night he knows no rest.
Grant that he is being careful of himself,
So that he can come back and not be left behind!"

I climb that bare hill
And look toward where my mother is.
My mother is saying, "Alas, my young one is on service;
Day and night he gets no sleep.
Grant that he is being careful of himself,
So that he may come back and not be cast away."

I climb that ridge
And look toward where my elder brother is.
My brother is saying, "Alas, my young brother is on service.
Day and night he toils.
Grant that he is being careful of himself,
So that he may come back and not die."

127 (MAO NO. 185)

Minister of War,
We are the king's claws and fangs.
Why should you roll us on from misery to misery,
Giving us no place to stop in or take rest?

Minister of War,
We are the king's claws and teeth.
Why should you roll us from misery to misery,
Giving us no place to come to and stay?

Minister of War,
Truly you are not wise.
Why should you roll us from misery to misery?
We have mothers who lack food.

130 (MAO NO. 234)

What plant is not faded?
What day do we not march?
What man is not taken
To defend the four bounds?

What plant is not wilting?
What man is not taken from his wife?
Alas for us soldiers,
Treated as though we were not fellow men!

Are we buffaloes, are we tigers
That our home should be these desolate wilds?
Alas for us soldiers,
Neither by day nor night can we rest!

The fox bumps and drags
Through the tall, thick grass.
Inch by inch we move our barrows
As we push them along the track.

158 (MAO NO. 291)

Very sharp, the good shares[6]
At work on the southern acre.
Now they sow the many sorts of grain,
The seeds that hold moist life.
Here come provisions for you
Carried in baskets, in hampers.
Their dinner is fine millet,
Their rush-hats finely plaited,
Their hoes cut deep
To clear away thistle and smartweed:
"Where thistle and smartweed lie rotting,
Millet grows apace."
It rustles at the reaping,
Nods heavy at the stacking,
It is piled high as a wall,
Is as even as the teeth of a comb.
All the barns are opened:
"When all the barns are brim full,
Wife and child will be at peace."
We kill this black-muzzled bull.
Oh, crooked is its horn!
We shall succeed, we shall continue,
Continue the men of old.

182 (MAO NO. 182)

What of the night?
The night is not yet spent.
The torches in the courtyard are alight.
But my lord has come;
Tinkle, tinkle go his harness-bells.

What of the night?
The night is not yet old.
The torches in the courtyard are bright.
But my lord has come;
Twit, twit go the bells.

---

[6]This planting song describes in some detail the rather wasteful process of clearing and planting fields typical of the agricultural practice of the day. The crop is millet, the staple grain of north China in early times. A bountiful harvest to come is foreseen and what are probably old peasant sayings are repeated. The respect for tradition and importance of sacrificial ritual connected with crop planting commended such songs to the Confucian scholars.

What of the night?
The night nears dawn.
The torches in the courtyard gleam.
My lord has come;
I can see his banners.

184 (MAO NO. 175)

The red bow[7] is unstrung,
When one is given it, one puts it away.
I have a lucky guest;
To the depths of my heart I honor him.
The bells and drums are all set;
The whole morning I feast him.

The red bow is unstrung,
When one is given it, one stores it.
I have a lucky guest;
To the depths of my heart I delight in him.
The bells and drums are all set;
The whole morning I ply him.

The red bow is unstrung,
When one is given it, one puts it in its press.
I have a lucky guest;
To the depths of my heart I love him.
The bells and drums are all set;
The whole morning I drink pledges with him.

205 (MAO NO. 280)

Blind men, blind men[8]
In the courtyard of Chou.

---

[7]The bow was the principal weapon of feudal lords and their knights in Chou Dynasty China. Red, the color of honor, suggests this bow was a gift from the speaker's emperor or feudal lord, signifying valorous conduct. The bow is thus treated as a "guest," much as one in our society would celebrate the receipt of a medal, but the symbolism seems to suggest that the man who bestowed the bow is also, metaphorically at least, present as a "guest."

[8]Musicians in early China were often blind men. We know from many of the songs, and from the later writings of Confucius and his followers, that music played a central role in family and state rituals. Archaeologists in recent years have recovered and restored several sets of the bronze chimes described here, so that the tones, though not the actual music, of these instruments is known. The last three lines indicate another important idea associated with many of these clan and family rituals: that the spirits of the departed ancestors "attended" as honored guests.

We have set up the cross-board, the stand,
With the upright hooks, the standing plumes.
The little and big drums are hung for beating;
The tambourines and stone-chimes, the mallet-box and scraper.
All is ready, and they play.
Pan-pipes and flute are ready and begin.
Sweetly blend the tones,
Solemn the melody of their bird-music.
The ancestors are listening;
As our guests they have come,
To gaze long upon their victories.

215 (MAO NO. 267)

The charge that Heaven gave
Was solemn, was forever.
And, ah, most glorious
King Wen[9] in plenitude of power!
With blessing he has whelmed us;
We need but gather them in.
High favors has King Wen vouchsafed to us;
May his descendants hold them fast.

232 (MAO NO. 157)

Broken were our axes
And chipped our hatchets.
But since the Duke of Chou[10] came to the East
Throughout the kingdom all is well.
He has shown compassion to us people,
He has greatly helped us.

Broken were our axes
And chipped our hoes.
But since the Duke of Chou came to the East
The whole land has been changed.
He has shown compassion to us people,
He has greatly blessed us.

---

[9]King Wen was ruler of the Chou people at the time they undertook to supplant the
Shang. His son, Wu, was the first emperor of the Chou Dynasty. This dynastic song
touches on the theme of the "mandate of Heaven."

[10]See Selection 10, *The Book of History.* The elliptical symbolism of the broken tools refers
to the sad condition of society before the duke instituted the reforms that have been
associated with his name ever since.

Broken were our axes
And chipped our chisels.
But since the Duke of Chou came to the East
All the kingdoms are knit together.
He has shown compassion to us people,
He has been a great boon to us.

276 (MAO NO. 113)

Big rat, big rat,
Do not gobble our millet!
Three years we have slaved for you,
Yet you take no notice of us.
At last we are going to leave you
And go to that happy land;
Happy land, happy land,
Where we shall have our place.

Big rat, big rat,
Do not gobble our corn!
Three years we have slaved for you,
Yet you give us no credit.
At last we are going to leave you
And go to that happy kingdom;
Happy kingdom, happy kingdom,
Where we shall get our due.

Big rat, big rat,
Do not eat our rice shoots!
Three years we have slaved for you.
Yet you did nothing to reward us.
At last we are going to leave you
And go to those happy borders;
Happy borders, happy borders,
Where no sad songs are sung.

277 (MAO NO. 119)

Tall stands that pear tree;
Its leaves are fresh and fair.
But alone I walk, in utter solitude.
True indeed, there are other men;
But they are not like children of one's own father.
Heigh, you that walk upon the road,
Why do you not join me?
A man that has no brothers,
Why do you not help him?

Tall stands that pear tree;
Its leaves grow very thick.
Alone I walk and unbefriended.
True indeed, there are other men;
But they are not like people of one's own clan.
Heigh, you that walk upon the road,
Why do you not join me?
A man that has no brothers,
Why do you not help him?

286 (MAO NO. 206)

Don't escort the big chariot;
You will only make yourself dusty.
Don't think about the sorrows of the world;
You will only make yourself wretched.

Don't escort the big chariot;
You won't be able to see for dust.
Don't think about the sorrows of the world;
Or you will never escape from your despair.

Don't escort the big chariot;
You'll be stifled with dust.
Don't think about the sorrows of the world;
You will only load yourself with care.

PART
II

SEARCHING FOR
TRADITIONS

⅔❦

In Selections 12 through 32 we see further development of the traditions that emerged in the selections in Part I, as well as the creation of new forms of written expression. In Western literary genres alone, for example (in addition to Homer's heroic epics, excerpted in Selection 7), there can now be seen lyric poems (Selection 12), theatrical dramas (Selection 13), historical narratives (Selections 14 and 15), social commentary (Selection 16), and philosophical argument (Selections 18 and 19). The selections in Part II of this book date from the seventh to the third centuries B.C.

In the large Greek cluster (Selections 12 through 19) that begins Part II, we read the short lyrics of Sappho (Selection 12) with their intense and intimate feelings. The Greek contribution to drama is seminal and, as an example of this, Sophocles's fifth-century B.C. tragedy *Antigone* is reprinted uncut in Selection 13. In *Antigone* the heroine pits her strong will and religious obligation against the power of government. A new definition of history as the written record of contemporary events—rather than the older poetic glorification of epic heroes—emerged in the West with Herodotus (Selection 14), who wrote of the Greek national effort to turn back a great invading army from Asia (the Persian Wars). This prose narrative by Herodotus is, in a sense, also of epic proportions, but he attempts to be both objective and rationally analytical—a very different intention from that of earlier poets. Thucydides (Selection 15) follows the analytical example of Herodotus, the "Father of History" in the West, but applies his narrative talents to a more tragically intimate military and political conflict, the Peloponnesian War among the Greek city-states at the end of the fifth century B.C. That conflict among cousins was ultimately to destroy the institution of the Greek city-state *(polis)*, even glorious Athens, as an independent political unit. Xenophon (Selection 16) described Athens's great rival, Sparta, the rigidly militaristic *polis* that he most admired. After the defeat of Athens in the Peloponnesian War and the end of its territorial expansion, philosophical discourse flourished. Its most famous proponents—even into modern times—are Plato and Aristotle (Selections 17 through 19). Plato devoted himself to developing the philosophy of his beloved teacher Socrates, whose defense of his teachings before an Athenian jury Plato recorded as the *Apology* in Selection 17. Spurred especially by the fate of Socrates, Plato and Aristotle were both concerned with defining the most effective kinds of government, of political leaders, and of citizens (Selections 18 and 19).

As the focus of this book moves east to India, we read the *Upanishads* in Selection 20, the last and the most philosophical part of the *Veda,* written around 700 to 300 B.C. In their subject and goal, the attainment of true reality, the *Upanishads* bear a remarkable resemblance to the philosophy of Plato in his "Allegory of the Cave," in Selection 18. Also originating in India is the humanistic religious philosophy of Buddha (Selection 21), who was born in the sixth century B.C. His views were to spread throughout Asia and, eventually, the world, becoming especially significant in China (Selection 22).

Although the title of this volume refers to the plural *worlds* of the ancient period, it is important not to overlook the travelers who ventured between those worlds separated by hazardous distances. Their accounts influenced all who could read their languages and, thus, shaped their public's perceptions of cultures other than their own. Megasthenes, for example, was an ambassador from a former general of Alexander the Great to the court of the Indian Emperor Chandragupta Maurya, who reigned from around 320 to 298 B.C. Thus, we see a Greek writer who journeyed across the width of the Middle East, perhaps several times, to write an account of India, where he lived for many years. His account of that distant land, *Indika,* in Selection 23, was much quoted and copied by later Greek and Roman historians. Also in India, not long after Megasthene's sojourn there, Kautilya wrote a shrewd treatise on the acquisition and preservation of political power, *Arthashastra,* in Selection 24, almost two millennia before the Italian Machiavelli was to enunciate the same realistic principles for the West. The last selection in Part II of this book from the great civilization of ancient India is excerpted from the vast epic known as the *Mahabharata* (Selection 25). Like Homer's *Iliad* and *Odyssey*, it deals with heroic conflicts, good and evil, suffering and destruction, and the interplay of human and divine forces.

A large cluster of Chinese writings, Selections 26 through 32, ends Part II. The cluster begins with some of the collected teachings of Confucius, born around 551 B.C. His views of appropriate human behavior, both personal and political, have dominated Chinese discussion of those topics for the last two and a half millennia, even into the Marxist/Maoist era of the twentieth century. However, as other selections in this cluster demonstrate, Confucius stood at the beginning of a three-century period that produced a wide variety of speculation among Chinese philosophers about human nature and conduct. Some of these philosophers elaborated Confucius's original teaching, while others disagreed with him radically. The great dialogue represented in Selections 26 through 32 lies at the heart of Chinese classical philosophy.

12

❦

Sappho

LYRIC POETRY

In ancient Greece, lyric poetry originally referred to poetry sung to the accompaniment of the lyre, a string instrument that was plucked like the modern harp. The sound box at the bottom of the lyre was first constructed from the shell of a tortoise. Eventually, lyric poetry developed the association with intense personal feelings that it has to this day. Although many lyric poems were composed in Greece from very early times, most of them have been lost. The scraps that survive are contained either as excerpted quotations within the works of other ancient authors or exist in the remains of ancient Egyptian scrolls made out of papyrus that were discovered in the early twentieth century. (After Alexander the Great's conquests in the fourth century B.C., Greek culture spread to Egypt, where great libraries were established.) The great age of personal lyric poetry came just after the period of the heroic Homeric epics (see Selection 7) and just before the poetry of the drama (see Selection 13) and the development of prose for historical narrative and philosophical argument (see Selections 14 through 19).

Sappho, then and now, is the most admired of the Greek lyric poets. (Plato was to call her the "tenth Muse.") Born in the late seventh century B.C., she lived most of her life on the Greek island of Lesbos in the Aegean Sea near the coast of Asia Minor. Married and the mother of a daughter, her lyrics are chiefly concerned with the intimate world of personal relationships, especially among a circle of upper-class young women, possibly her students. (Hence, the modern usage of the term lesbian comes from the name of Sappho's island, although there are no explicit references to sexual activities in the surviving fragments.) Aristocratic women, apparently, had their own intense framework of communal functions and festivals, probably prior to their later lives as wives and mothers.

❦

THE LYRIC POEM[1]

Come, holy tortoise shell,
my lyre, and become a poem.

TO ANACTORIA

Some say a formation of horsemen, infantry,
or ships is the loveliest thing on the black
earth, but I maintain it is whatever
a person loves.

It is perfectly easy to make this clear
to everyone. Helen, who far surpassed
the human race in beauty, deserted
her excellent husband

and went sailing off to Troy with never
a thought for her child or her own dear parents.[2]
Love led her astray. . . .
[Three lines are lost.]

. . . reminds me now of Anactoria,
who is far away.

I would rather see her graceful walk
and the fire in her eyes than all the chariots
the Lydians[3] own or their army marching
in heavy armor.

"The Lyric Poem" and "Epitaph" from *Sappho and the Greek Lyric Poets* by Willis Barnstone, translator, pp. 65 and 92. Copyright © 1962, 1967, 1988 by Willis Barnstone. Reprinted by permission of Schocken Books, published by Pantheon Books, a division of Random House, Inc. Other lyrics from *Early Greek Lyric Poetry*, David Mulroy, translator (Ann Arbor: The University of Michigan Press, 1992), pp. 90, 92, 95, 98. Copyright © the University of Michigan, 1992.

[1]The titles are editorial additions and were not part of Sappho's rediscovered poems.

[2]In Greek myth, Helen, queen of Sparta, on the mainland of Greece, ran away with Paris, prince of Troy, on the coast of Asia Minor. This love affair, brought about by the goddess of love, Aphrodite, was the immediate cause of the Trojan War that Homer described in *The Iliad* and *The Odyssey*.

[3]Well known to the Greeks, Lydia was a rich country in western Asia Minor.

INVOCATION TO APHRODITE

Immortal Aphrodite, enthroned in splendor,
Zeus's[4] cunning child, I pray,
make me no slave to regrets,
madam, and sorrows,
but visit me now, if ever before
you heard my voice from far away,
heeded and came, leaving your father's
palace of gold

in a chariot harnessed to sparrows, lovely
and swift, who guided you through the aether
from sky to black earth with their wings
constantly flapping.

They arrived without warning. I saw your heavenly
face smiling at me, O blessed.
You asked what I suffered from this time, why
I was calling again,

and what in my frenzied soul I wanted
the most to happen. "Whom shall I
persuade to take you back, O Sappho?
Who does you wrong?

"Does she run from you now? She will soon pursue.
She accepts no gifts? Soon she will give them.
She is not in love? She will be soon,
however reluctant."

Come to me now again. Free me
from painful emotion. Make the things
my heart craves happen. Be
my comrade-in-arms.

LOVESICKNESS

To me the man who happens to sit
opposite you seems like a god
as bending close he listens and replies
to your sweet voice

and fetching laughter; such exchange
makes my heart pound with alarm.
Let me so much as glimpse you, my voice
fails me completely.

---

[4]Zeus was king of the gods.

My tongue is broken; a subtle flame
instantly courses beneath my skin.
No vision is left in my eyes. A whirring
fills my ears.

Cold sweat flows. Trembling
shakes my entire frame. I grow
paler than grass and feel as though
I have nearly died.

TO AN UNEDUCATED RIVAL

You will soon be dead and buried and no one will ever
mention you again, because you disdain the roses
of Pierian song.[5] Flown from here you will wander
with corpses in twilight, unnoticed even in Hell.

EPITAPH

Here is the dust of Timas who unmarried
was led into Persephone's dark bedroom,[6]
and when she died her girlfriends took sharp
iron knives and cut off their soft hair.

---

[5]Pieria is a region on the northern slopes of Mount Olympus, which the Greeks thought
to have been the birthplace of the Muses, patron goddesses of the arts, and, therefore,
inspirers of human creativity. The peak itself contained the palaces of Zeus and his
immortal court.

[6]Persephone was queen of the underworld, where souls went after death. The authorship
of this lyrical epitaph has been disputed.

13

❧

Sophocles

ANTIGONE

Dramatic tragedy represents the chief literary achievement of Athens in the Golden Age and one of the noblest products of the human imagination. Its development was encouraged by the extraordinary awareness and maturity of outlook that characterized the Athenian populace in the sixth and fifth centuries B.C. Poets of genius (like Sappho in the preceding selection) found an audience of comparable taste and feeling, and those who wrote tragedies had a favorable climate in which to present both their interpretations of Hellenic traditions and ideals and their own insights into the nature of human life and destiny. Of these dramatists the three considered supreme were Aeschylus, Sophocles, and Euripides. They were the only Greek tragedians to have some of their works preserved complete—to the benefit of later generations.

Throughout his long life, Sophocles (ca. 496–406 B.C.) had every advantage: an aristocratic education, wealth, good looks, success, and, above all, the inspiration of living in Athens during the Golden Age. He is said to have been victorious twenty-four times in the great annual dramatic competitions. Unfortunately, of the more than 120 plays he wrote, only seven survive. The most famous of these deal with the mythical story of Oedipus, that king of the great city Thebes who unknowingly killed his father and married his mother, who then bore him four children. Early in our own century, Sigmund Freud, the founder of psychoanalysis, labeled the "Oedipus complex"—a son's love for his mother and rivalry with his father—one of the most powerful human instinctual drives.

Since the Oedipus legend was already well known to Sophocles's audience, their interest lay in watching the main characters' responses to the working out of their inevitable fates. As interpreted by Sophocles, the legend deals with the relationship of humans to the divine order. Since, to Sophocles, divine order and justice were considered identical, King Oedipus—who had unintentionally broken the moral code guaranteed by the Olympian gods—is made to suffer horribly.

Whether or not his punishment is justified by human standards is irrelevant to the judgment of the gods. It is their will that humans should know themselves and thus realize their limitations.

The play that comes first in the plot sequence (of Sophocles's three surviving plays on the Oedipus story) is Oedipus the King. *At its conclusion, the self-blinded Oedipus, having come to know the moral code through suffering, emerges a wiser man, more aware of life's meaning than he ever had been as a confident, proud ruler. The next surviving play in the development of the myth is* Oedipus at Colonus, *written at the end of Sophocles's long life. It describes how the aged Oedipus arrives at Colonus, a hamlet within the political rule of Athens, after many years of homeless wandering. There, amidst peals of thunder, he finally is welcomed into a mystical reunion with the gods.*

Just before he dies at Colonus, Oedipus curses his son, Polynices, who came to him for support in his effort to regain the Theban throne from Eteocles, his younger brother. (Only Oedipus's daughters, Antigone and Ismene, remained loyal to their father in his painful wandering.) Polynices, nevertheless, chooses to continue his attack against his native city, raising an army in Argos, whose princess he had married. As his angry father prophesied, the two brothers kill each other during the unsuccessful attack. As the play Antigone *opens, Creon, formerly brother-in-law (and uncle) to Oedipus, rules Thebes. He issues a proclamation that Eteocles is to be buried with full honors as a defender of the city but that his brother, who attacked the city with foreign forces, is to be left unburied and exposed. This prohibition of proper burial strikes at the heart of Greek family and religious obligations.* Antigone *is the earliest written of Sophocles's three surviving "Theban plays," but it concludes the tragically interwoven plot.*

Acceptance of divine law and of human limitations was not the private viewpoint of Sophocles alone. The sentiments of the Chorus, whose dramatic role was to comment on the action and to express general opinion, show that the belief that human beings should know themselves as well as the gods' demands was part of the consciousness of Athenian citizens. The miracle of Periclean Athens was based in part on the result of this belief: faith that each individual has the potential to face harsh realities, even the prospect of ultimate doom, with courage and dignity. The suffering of such men as Oedipus and Creon—stirring the emotions of pity and fear—and their recognition of their own mistakes are evidence of such potential and are the essence of tragedy. The Greek attitude, then, was one of awe and wonder at the uniqueness of humans and their inherent moral capacity for achieving harmony with the divine will. This attitude is the core of the philosophy that came to be known as humanism.

⟡

ANTIGONE

CHARACTERS

Antigone, daughter of Oedipus and Jocasta
Ismene, sister of Antigone
A Chorus of old Theban citizens and their **Leader**
Creon, king of Thebes, uncle of Antigone and Ismene
A Sentry
Haemon, son of Creon and Eurydice
Tiresias, a blind prophet
A Messenger
Eurydice, wife of Creon
Guards, attendants, and **a boy**

TIME AND SCENE

The royal house of Thebes. It is still night, and the invading armies of Argos have just been driven from the city. Fighting on opposite sides, the sons of Oedipus, Eteocles and Polynices, have killed each other in combat. Their uncle, Creon, is now king of Thebes.

Enter Antigone, slipping through the central doors of the palace. She motions to her sister, Ismene, who follows her cautiously toward an altar at the center of the stage.

ANTIGONE

My own flesh and blood—dear sister, dear Ismene,
how many griefs our father Oedipus handed down!
Do you know one, I ask you, one grief
that Zeus will not perfect for the two of us
while we still live and breathe? There's nothing,
no pain—our lives are pain—no private shame,
no public disgrace, nothing I haven't seen
in your griefs and mine. And now this:
an emergency decree, they say, the Commander

has just declared for all of Thebes.
What, haven't you heard? Don't you see?
The doom reserved for enemies
marches on the ones we love the most.

ISMENE

Not I, I haven't heard a word, Antigone.
Nothing of loved ones,
no joy or pain has come my way, not since
the two of us were robbed of our two brothers,
both gone in a day, a double blow—
not since the armies of Argos vanished,
just this very night. I know nothing more,
whether our luck's improved or ruin's still to come.

ANTIGONE

I thought so. That's why I brought you out here,
past the gates, so you could hear in private.

ISMENE

What's the matter? Trouble, clearly . . .
you sound so dark, so grim.

ANTIGONE

Why not? Our own brothers' burial!
Hasn't Creon graced one with all the rites,
disgraced the other? Eteocles, they say,
has been given full military honors,
rightly so—Creon's laid him in the earth
and he goes with glory down among the dead.
But the body of Polynices, who died miserably—
why, a city-wide proclamation, rumor has it,
forbids anyone to bury him, even mourn him.
He's to be left unwept, unburied, a lovely treasure
for birds that scan the field and feast to their heart's content.

Such, I hear, is the martial law our good Creon
lays down for you and me—yes, me, I tell you—
and he's coming here to alert the uninformed
in no uncertain terms,
and he won't treat the matter lightly. Whoever
disobeys in the least will die, his doom is sealed:
stoning to death inside the city walls!

There you have it. You'll soon show what you are,
worth your breeding, Ismene, or a coward—
for all your royal blood.

ISMENE

> My poor sister, if things have come to this,
> who am I to make or mend them, tell me,
> what good am I to you?

ANTIGONE

> Decide.
> Will you share the labor, share the work?

ISMENE

> What work, what's the risk? What do you mean?

ANTIGONE

Raising her hands.

> Will you lift up his body with these bare hands
> and lower it with me?

ISMENE

> What? You'd bury him—
> when a law forbids the city?

ANTIGONE

> Yes!
> He is my brother and—deny it as you will—
> your brother too.
> No one will ever convict me for a traitor.

ISMENE

> So desperate, and Creon has expressly—

ANTIGONE

> No,
> he has no right to keep me from my own.

ISMENE

> Oh my sister, think—
> think how our own father died, hated,[1]
> his reputation in ruins, driven on
> by the crimes he brought to light himself
> to gouge out his eyes with his own hands—
> then mother . . . his mother and wife, both in one,
> mutilating her life in the twisted noose—
> and last, our two brothers dead in a single day,
> both shedding their own blood, poor suffering boys,
> battling out their common destiny hand-to-hand.

---

[1]Sophocles wrote *Antigone* earlier than his other two surviving plays on the Oedipus myth—even though *Antigone* deals with a later development in the story. Ismene's description here of Oedipus's death, therefore, differs from that in *Oedipus at Colonus* where the aged tragic figure finally achieves harmonious reconciliation with the gods.

Now look at the two of us, left so alone . . .
think what a death we'll die, the worst of all
if we violate the laws and override
the fixed decree of the throne, its power—
we must be sensible. Remember we are women,
we're not born to contend with men. Then too,
we're underlings, ruled by much stronger hands,
so we must submit in this, and things still worse.

I, for one, I'll beg the dead to forgive me—
I'm forced, I have no choice—I must obey
the ones who stand in power. Why rush to extremes?
It's madness, madness.

ANTIGONE
                              I won't insist,
no, even if you should have a change of heart,
I'd never welcome you in the labor, not with me.
So, do as you like, whatever suits you best—
I'll bury him myself.
And even if I die in the act, that death will be a glory.
I'll lie with the one I love and loved by him—
an outrage sacred to the gods! I have longer
to please the dead than please the living here:
in the kingdom down below I'll lie forever.
Do as you like, dishonor the laws
the gods hold in honor.

ISMENE
                              I'd do them no dishonor . . .
but defy the city? I have no strength for that.

ANTIGONE
You have your excuses, I am on my way.
I'll raise a mound for him, for my dear brother.

ISMENE
Oh Antigone, you're so rash—I'm so afraid for you!

ANTIGONE
Don't fear for me. Set your own life in order.

ISMENE
Then don't, at least, blurt this out to anyone.
Keep it a secret. I'll join you in that, I promise.

ANTIGONE
Dear god, shout it from the rooftops. I'll hate you
all the more for silence—tell the world!

ISMENE

So fiery—and it ought to chill your heart.

ANTIGONE

I know I please where I must please the most.

ISMENE

Yes, if you can, but you're in love with impossibility.

ANTIGONE

Very well then, once my strength gives out
I will be done at last.

ISMENE

You're wrong from the start,
you're off on a hopeless quest.

ANTIGONE

If you say so, you will make me hate you,
and the hatred of the dead, by all rights,
will haunt you night and day.
But leave me to my own absurdity, leave me
to suffer this—dreadful thing. I'll suffer
nothing as great as death without glory.

Exit to the side.

ISMENE

Then go if you must, but rest assured,
wild, irrational as you are, my sister,
you are truly dear to the ones who love you.

Withdrawing to the palace.

*Enter a Chorus, the old citizens of Thebes, chanting
as the sun begins to rise.*

CHORUS

Glory!—great beam of the sun, brightest of all
that ever rose on the seven gates of Thebes,
        you burn through night at last!
                Great eye of the golden day,
mounting the Dirce's[2] banks you throw him back—
the enemy out of Argos, the white shield, the man of bronze—
he's flying headlong now
                the bridle of fate stampeding him with pain!

        And he had driven against our borders,
        launched by the warring claims of Polynices—
        like an eagle screaming, winging havoc
        over the land, wings of armor

---

[2]A river near Thebes.

shielded white as snow,
a huge army massing,
crested helmets bristling for assault.

He hovered above our roofs, his vast maw gaping
closing down around our seven gates,
his spears thirsting for the kill
but now he's gone, look,
before he could glut his jaws with Theban blood
or the god of fire put our crown of towers to the torch.
He grappled the Dragon none can master—Thebes—
the clang of our arms like thunder at his back!

Zeus[3] hates with a vengeance all bravado,
the mighty boasts of men. He watched them
coming on in a rising flood, the pride
of their golden armor ringing shrill—
and brandishing his lightning
blasted the fighter just at the goal,
rushing to shout his triumph from our walls.

Down from the heights he crashed, pounding down on the earth!
And a moment ago, blazing torch in hand—
mad for attack, ecstatic
he breathed his rage, the storm
of his fury hurling at our heads!
But now his high hopes have laid him low
and down the enemy ranks the iron god of war
deals his rewards, his stunning blows—Ares
rapture of battle, our right arm in the crisis.

Seven captains marshaled at seven gates
seven against their equals, gave
their brazen trophies up to Zeus,
god of the breaking rout of battle,
all but two: those blood brothers,
one father, one mother—matched in rage,
spears matched for the twin conquest—
clashed and won the common prize of death.

But now for Victory![4] Glorious in the morning,
joy in her eyes to meet our joy

---

[3]King of the gods. He holds court on Mount Olympus and has special charge of the sky
and such related phenomena as lightning and thunder.

[4]Victory, here, is a winged young goddess.

         she is winging down to Thebes,
our fleets of chariots wheeling in her wake—
    Now let us win oblivion from the wars,
thronging the temples of the gods
in singing, dancing choirs through the night!
        Lord Dionysus, god of the dance
        that shakes the land of Thebes, now lead the way!

             Enter Creon from the palace, attended by his guard.

        But look, the king of the realm is coming,
        Creon, the new man for the new day,
        whatever the gods are sending now . . .
        what new plan will he launch?
        Why this, this special session?
        Why this sudden call to the old men
        summoned at one command?

CREON

             My countrymen,
the ship of state is safe. The gods who rocked her,
after a long, merciless pounding in the storm,
have righted her once more.
            Out of the whole city
I have called you here alone. Well I know,
first, your undeviating respect
for the throne and royal power of King Laius.
Next, while Oedipus steered the land of Thebes,
and even after he died, your loyalty was unshakable,
you still stood by their children. Now then,
since the two sons are dead—two blows of fate
in the same day, cut down by each other's hands,
both killers, both brothers stained with blood—
as I am next in kin to the dead,
I now possess the throne and all its powers.

Of course you cannot know a man completely,
his character, his principles, sense of judgment,
not till he's shown his colors, ruling the people,
making laws. Experience, there's the test.
As I see it, whoever assumes the task,
the awesome task of setting the city's course,
and refuses to adopt the soundest policies
but fearing someone, keeps his lips locked tight,
he's utterly worthless. So I rate him now,
I always have. And whoever places a friend
above the good of his own country, he is nothing:

I have no use for him. Zeus my witness,
Zeus who sees all things, always—
I could never stand by silent, watching destruction
march against our city, putting safety to rout,
nor could I ever make that man a friend of mine
who menaces our country. Remember this:
our country *is* our safety.
Only while she voyages true on course
can we establish friendships, truer than blood itself.
Such are my standards. They make our city great.

Closely akin to them I have proclaimed,
just now, the following decree to our people
concerning the two sons of Oedipus.
Eteocles, who died fighting for Thebes,
excelling all in arms: he shall be buried,
crowned with a hero's honors, the cups we pour[5]
to soak the earth and reach the famous dead.

But as for his blood brother, Polynices,
who returned from exile, home to his father-city
and the gods of his race, consumed with one desire—
to burn them roof to roots—who thirsted to drink
his kinsmen's blood and sell the rest to slavery:
that man—a proclamation has forbidden the city
to dignify him with burial, mourn him at all.
No, he must be left unburied, his corpse
carrion for the birds and dogs to tear,
an obscenity for the citizens to behold!

These are my principles. Never at my hands
will the traitor be honored above the patriot.
But whoever proves his loyalty to the state:
I'll prize that man in death as well as life.

LEADER
If this is your pleasure, Creon, treating
our city's enemy and our friend this way . . .
The power is yours, I suppose, to enforce it
with the laws, both for the dead and all of us,
the living.

CREON
                      Follow my orders closely then,
be on your guard.

---

[5]Libations (liquid offerings) to the gods, usually wine poured on the ground.

LEADER

We're too old.

Lay that burden on younger shoulders.

CREON

No, no,

I don't mean the body—I've posted guards already.

LEADER

What commands for us then? What other service?

CREON

See that you never side with those who break my orders.

LEADER

Never. Only a fool could be in love with death.

CREON

Death is the price—you're right. But all too often
the mere hope of money has ruined many men.

A Sentry enters from the side.

SENTRY

My lord,

I can't say I'm winded from running, or set out
with any spring in my legs either—no sir,
I was lost in thought, and it made me stop, often,
dead in my tracks, wheeling, turning back,
and all the time a voice inside me muttering,
"Idiot, why? You're going straight to your death."
Then muttering, "Stopped again, poor fool?
If somebody gets the news to Creon first,
what's to save your neck?"

And so,

mulling it over, on I trudged, dragging my feet,
you can make a short road take forever . . .
but at last, look, common sense won out,
I'm here, and I'm all yours,
and even though I come empty-handed
I'll tell my story just the same, because
I've come with a good grip on one hope,
what will come will come, whatever fate—

CREON

Come to the point!
What's wrong—why so afraid?

SENTRY

First, myself, I've got to tell you,
I didn't do it, didn't see who did—
Be fair, don't take it out on me.

CREON

You're playing it safe, soldier,
barricading yourself from any trouble.
It's obvious, you've something strange to tell.

SENTRY

Dangerous too, and danger makes you delay
for all you're worth.

CREON

Out with it—then dismiss!

SENTRY

All right, here it comes. The body—
someone's just buried it, then run off . . .
sprinkled some dry dust on the flesh,
given it proper rites.

CREON

What?
What man alive would dare—

SENTRY

I've no idea, I swear it.
There was no mark of a spade, no pickaxe there,
no earth turned up, the ground packed hard and dry,
unbroken, no tracks, no wheel ruts, nothing,
the workman left no trace. Just at sunup
the first watch of the day points it out—
it was a wonder! We were stunned . . .
a terrific burden too, for all of us, listen:
you can't see the corpse, not that it's buried,
really, just a light cover of road-dust on it,
as if someone meant to lay the dead to rest
and keep from getting cursed.
Not a sign in sight that dogs or wild beasts
had worried the body, even torn the skin.

But what came next! Rough talk flew thick and fast,
guard grilling guard—we'd have come to blows
at last, nothing to stop it; each man for himself
and each the culprit, no one caught red-handed,
all of us pleading ignorance, dodging the charges,
ready to take up red-hot iron in our fists,
go through fire, swear oaths to the gods—
"I didn't do it, I had no hand in it either,
not in the plotting, not the work itself!"

Finally, after all this wrangling came to nothing,
one man spoke out and made us stare at the ground,
hanging our heads in fear. No way to counter him,
no way to take his advice and come through
safe and sound. Here's what he said:
"Look, we've got to report the facts to Creon,
we can't keep this hidden." Well, that won out,
and the lot fell to me, condemned me,
unlucky as ever, I got the prize. So here I am,
against my will and yours too, well I know—
no one wants the man who brings bad news.

LEADER
                    My king,
ever since he began I've been debating in my mind,
could this possibly be the work of the gods?

CREON
                    Stop—
before you make me choke with anger—the gods!
You, you're senile, must you be insane?
You say—why it's intolerable—say the gods
could have the slightest concern for that corpse?
Tell me, was it for meritorious service
they proceeded to bury him, prized him so? The hero
who came to burn their temples ringed with pillars,
their golden treasures—scorch their hallowed earth
and fling their laws to the winds.
Exactly when did you last see the gods
celebrating traitors? Inconceivable!

No, from the first there were certain citizens
who could hardly stand the spirit of my regime,
grumbling against me in the dark, heads together,
tossing wildly, never keeping their necks beneath
the yoke, loyally submitting to their king.
These are the instigators, I'm convinced—
they've perverted my own guard, bribed them
to do their work.
                    Money! Nothing worse
in our lives, so current, rampant, so corrupting.
Money—you demolish cities, root men from their homes,
you train and twist good minds and set them on
to the most atrocious schemes. No limit,
you make them adept at every kind of outrage,
every godless crime—money!

Everyone—
the whole crew bribed to commit this crime,
they've made one thing sure at least:
sooner or later they will pay the price.

Wheeling on the Sentry.

You—
I swear to Zeus as I still believe in Zeus,
if you don't find the man who buried that corpse,
the very man, and produce him before my eyes,
simple death won't be enough for you,
not till we string you up alive
and wring the immorality out of you.
Then you can steal the rest of your days,
better informed about where to make a killing.
You'll have learned, at last, it doesn't pay
to itch for rewards from every hand that beckons.
Filthy profits wreck most men, you'll see—
they'll never save your life.

SENTRY

Please,
may I say a word or two, or just turn and go?

CREON

Can't you tell? Everything you say offends me.

SENTRY

Where does it hurt you, in the ears or in the heart?

CREON

And who are you to pinpoint my displeasure?

SENTRY

The culprit grates on your feelings,
I just annoy your ears.

CREON

Still talking?
You talk too much! A born nuisance—

SENTRY

Maybe so,
but I never did this thing, so help me!

CREON

Yes, you did—
what's more, you squandered your life for silver!

SENTRY

Oh it's terrible when the one who does the judging
judges things all wrong.

CREON

Well now,
you just be clever about your judgments—
if you fail to produce the criminals for me,
you'll swear your dirty money brought you pain.

Turning sharply, reentering the palace.

SENTRY

I hope he's found. Best thing by far.
But caught or not, that's in the lap of fortune;
I'll never come back, you've seen the last of me.
I'm saved, even now, and I never thought,
I never hoped—
dear gods, I owe you all my thanks!

Rushing out.

CHORUS

Numberless wonders
terrible wonders walk the world but none the match for man—
that great wonder crossing the heaving gray sea,
driven on by the blasts of winter
on through breakers crashing left and right,
holds his steady course
and the oldest of the gods he wears away—
the Earth, the immortal, the inexhaustible—
as his plows go back and forth, year in, year out
with the breed of stallions[6] turning up the furrows.

And the blithe, light-headed race of birds he snares,
the tribes of savage beasts, the life that swarms the depths—
with one fling of his nets
woven and coiled tight, he takes them all,
man the skilled, the brilliant!
He conquers all, taming with his techniques
the prey that roams the cliffs and wild lairs,
training the stallion, clamping the yoke across
his shaggy neck, and the tireless mountain bull.

And speech and thought, quick as the wind
and the mood and mind for law that rules the city—
all these he has taught himself
and shelter from the arrows of the frost
when there's rough lodging under the cold clear sky

---

[6]Refers to mules, the sterile offspring from the union of horses and donkeys—still the traditional work-animals of Greek farmers.

and the shafts of lashing rain—
              ready, resourceful man!
                 Never without resources
never an impasse as he marches on the future—
only Death, from Death alone he will find no rescue
but from desperate plagues he has plotted his escapes.

Man the master, ingenious past all measure
past all dreams, the skills within his grasp—
     he forges on, now to destruction
now again to greatness. When he weaves in
the laws of the land, and the justice of the gods
that binds his oaths together
         he and his city rise high—
            but the city casts out
that man who weds himself to inhumanity
thanks to reckless daring. Never share my hearth
never think my thoughts, whoever does such things.

            Enter Antigone from the side, accompanied by the Sentry.
      Here is a dark sign from the gods—
      what to make of this? I know her,
      how can I deny it? That young girl's Antigone!
      Wretched, child of a wretched father,
      Oedipus. Look, is it possible?
      They bring you in like a prisoner—
      why? did you break the king's laws?
      Did they take you in some act of mad defiance?

SENTRY
    She's the one, she did it single-handed—
    we caught her burying the body. Where's Creon?
                         Enter Creon from the palace.

LEADER
    Back again, just in time when you need him.

CREON
    In time for what? What is it?

SENTRY
         My king,
there's nothing you can swear you'll never do—
second thoughts make liars of us all.
I could have sworn I wouldn't hurry back
(what with your threats, the buffeting I just took),
but a stroke of luck beyond our wildest hopes,
what a joy, there's nothing like it. So,

back I've come, breaking my oath, who cares?
I'm bringing in our prisoner—this young girl—
we took her giving the dead the last rites.
But no casting lots this time; this is *my* luck,
my prize, no one else's.
                    Now, my lord,
here she is. Take her, question her,
cross-examine her to your heart's content.
But set me free, it's only right—
I'm rid of this dreadful business once for all.

CREON

Prisoner! Her? You took her—where, doing what?

SENTRY

Burying the man. That's the whole story.

CREON

                    What?
You mean what you say, you're telling me the truth?

SENTRY

She's the one. With my own eyes I saw her
bury the body, just what you've forbidden.
There. Is that plain and clear?

CREON

What did you see? Did you catch her in the act?

SENTRY

Here's what happened. We went back to our post,
those threats of yours breathing down our necks—
we brushed the corpse clean of the dust that covered it,
stripped it bare . . . it was slimy, going soft,
and we took to high ground, backs to the wind
so the stink of him couldn't hit us;
jostling, baiting each other to keep awake,
shouting back and forth—no napping on the job,
not this time. And so the hours dragged by
until the sun stood dead above our heads,
a huge white ball in the noon sky, beating,
blazing down, and then it happened—
suddenly, a whirlwind!
Twisting a great dust-storm up from the earth,
a black plague of the heavens, filling the plain,
ripping the leaves off every tree in sight,
choking the air and sky. We squinted hard
and took our whipping from the gods.

And after the storm passed—it seemed endless—
there, we saw the girl!
And she cried out a sharp, piercing cry,
like a bird come back to an empty nest,
peering into its bed, and all the babies gone . . .
Just so, when she sees the corpse bare
she bursts into a long, shattering wail
and calls down withering curses on the heads
of all who did the work. And she scoops up dry dust,
handfuls, quickly, and lifting a fine bronze urn,
lifting it high and pouring, she crowns the dead
with three full libations.

        Soon as we saw
we rushed her, closed on the kill like hunters,
and she, she didn't flinch. We interrogated her,
charging her with offenses past and present—
she stood up to it all, denied nothing. I tell you,
it made me ache and laugh in the same breath.
It's pure joy to escape the worst yourself,
it hurts a man to bring down his friends.
But all that, I'm afraid, means less to me
than my own skin. That's the way I'm made.

CREON

Wheeling on Antigone.

      You,
with your eyes fixed on the ground—speak up.
Do you deny you did this, yes or no?

ANTIGONE

I did it. I don't deny a thing.

CREON

To the Sentry.

You, get out, wherever you please—
you're clear of a very heavy charge.

He leaves; Creon turns back to Antigone.

You, tell me briefly, no long speeches—
were you aware a decree had forbidden this?

ANTIGONE

Well aware. How could I avoid it? It was public.

CREON

And still you had the gall to break this law?

ANTIGONE
Of course I did. It wasn't Zeus, not in the least,
who made this proclamation—not to me.
Nor did that Justice, dwelling with the gods
beneath the earth, ordain such laws for men.
Nor did I think your edict had such force
that you, a mere mortal, could override the gods,
the great unwritten, unshakable traditions.
They are alive, not just today or yesterday:
they live forever, from the first of time,
and no one knows when they first saw the light.

These laws—I was not about to break them,
not out of fear of some man's wounded pride,
and face the retribution of the gods.
Die I must, I've known it all my life—
how could I keep from knowing?—even without
your death sentence ringing in my ears.
And if I am to die before my time
I consider that a gain. Who on earth,
alive in the midst of so much grief as I,
could fail to find his death a rich reward?
So for me, at least, to meet this doom of yours
is precious little pain. But if I had allowed
my own mother's son to rot, an unburied corpse—
that would have been an agony! This is nothing.
And if my present actions strike you as foolish,
let's just say I've been accused of folly
by a fool.

LEADER
                    Like father like daughter,
passionate, wild . . .
she hasn't learned to bend before adversity.

CREON
No? Believe me, the stiffest stubborn wills
fall the hardest; the toughest iron,
tempered strong in the white-hot fire,
you'll see it crack and shatter first of all.
And I've known spirited horses you can break
with a light bit—proud, rebellious horses.
There's no room for pride, not in a slave,
not with the lord and master standing by.

This girl was an old hand at insolence
when she overrode the edicts we made public.
But once she'd done it—the insolence,
twice over—to glory in it, laughing,
mocking us to our face with what she'd done.
I'm not the man, not now: she is the man
if this victory goes to her and she goes free.

Never! Sister's child or closer in blood
than all my family clustered at my altar
worshiping Guardian Zeus—she'll never escape,
she and her blood sister, the most barbaric death.
Yes, I accuse her sister of an equal part
in scheming this, this burial.

To his attendants.

           Bring her here!
I just saw her inside, hysterical, gone to pieces.
It never fails: the mind convicts itself
in advance, when scoundrels are up to no good,
plotting in the dark. Oh but I hate it more
when a traitor, caught red-handed,
tries to glorify his crimes.

ANTIGONE

Creon, what more do you want
than my arrest and execution?

CREON

Nothing. Then I have it all.

ANTIGONE

Then why delay? Your moralizing repels me,
every word you say—pray god it always will.
So naturally all I saw repels you too.
           Enough.
Give me glory! What greater glory could I win
than to give my own brother decent burial?
These citizens here would all agree,

To the Chorus.

they'd praise me too
if their lips weren't locked in fear.

Pointing to Creon.

Lucky tyrants—the perquisites of power!
Ruthless power to do and say whatever pleases *them.*

CREON

You alone, of all the people in Thebes,
see things that way.

ANTIGONE

They see it just that way
but defer to you and keep their tongues in leash.

CREON

And you, aren't you ashamed to differ so from them?
So disloyal!

ANTIGONE

Not ashamed for a moment,
not to honor my brother, my own flesh and blood.

CREON

Wasn't Eteocles a brother too—cut down, facing him?

ANTIGONE

Brother, yes, by the same mother, the same father.

CREON

Then how can you render his enemy such honors,
such impieties in his eyes?

ANTIGONE

He'll never testify to that,
Eteocles dead and buried.

CREON

He will—
if you honor the traitor just as much as him.

ANTIGONE

But it was his brother, not some slave that died—

CREON

Ravaging our country!—
but Eteocles died fighting in our behalf.

ANTIGONE

No matter—Death longs for the same rites for all.

CREON

Never the same for the patriot and the traitor.

ANTIGONE

Who, Creon, who on earth can say the ones below
don't find this pure and uncorrupt?

CREON

Never. Once an enemy, never a friend,
not even after death.

ANTIGONE

I was born to join in love, not hate—
that is my nature.

CREON

Go down below and love,
if love you must—love the dead! While I'm alive,
no woman is going to lord it over me.

Enter Ismene from the palace, under guard.

CHORUS
> Look,
> Ismene's coming, weeping a sister's tears,
> loving sister, under a cloud . . .
> her face is flushed, her cheeks streaming.
> Sorrow puts her lovely radiance in the dark.

CREON
> You—
> in my own house, you viper, slinking undetected,
> sucking my life-blood! I never knew
> I was breeding twin disasters, the two of you
> rising up against my throne. Come, tell me,
> will you confess your part in the crime or not?
> Answer me. Swear to me.

ISMENE
> I did it, yes—
> if only she consents—I share the guilt,
> the consequences too.

ANTIGONE
> No,
> Justice will never suffer that—not you,
> you were unwilling. I never brought you in.

ISMENE
> But now you face such dangers. . . . I'm not ashamed
> to sail through trouble with you,
> make your troubles mine.

ANTIGONE
> Who did the work?
> Let the dead and the god of death bear witness!
> I've no love for a friend who loves in words alone.

ISMENE
> Oh no, my sister, don't reject me, please,
> let me die beside you, consecrating
> the dead together.

ANTIGONE
> Never share my dying,
> don't lay claim to what you never touched.
> My death will be enough.

ISMENE
> What do I care for life, cut off from you?

ANTIGONE
> Ask Creon. Your concern is all for him.

ISMENE
>Why abuse me so? It doesn't help you now.

ANTIGONE
>>You're right—
>if I mock you, I get no pleasure from it,
>only pain.

ISMENE
>>Tell me, dear one,
>what can I do to help you, even now?

ANTIGONE
>Save yourself. I don't grudge you your survival.

ISMENE
>Oh no, no, denied my portion in your death?

ANTIGONE
>You chose to live, I chose to die.

ISMENE
>>Not, at least,
>without every kind of caution I could voice.

ANTIGONE
>Your wisdom appealed to one world—mine, another.

ISMENE
>But look, we're both guilty, both condemned to death.

ANTIGONE
>Courage! Live your life. I gave myself to death,
>long ago, so I might serve the dead.

CREON
>They're both mad, I tell you, the two of them.
>One's just shown it, the other's been that way
>since she was born.

ISMENE
>>True, my king,
>the sense we were born with cannot last forever . . .
>commit cruelty on a person long enough
>and the mind begins to go.

CREON
>>Yours did,
>when you chose to commit your crimes with her.

ISMENE
>How can I live alone, without her?

CREON
>>Her?
>Don't even mention her—she no longer exists.

ISMENE
>What? You'd kill your own son's bride?

CREON
> Absolutely:
there are other fields for him to plow.

ISMENE
> Perhaps,
but never as true, as close a bond as theirs.

CREON
> A worthless woman for my son? It repels me.

ISMENE
> Dearest Haemon, your father wrongs you so!

CREON
> Enough, enough—you and your talk of marriage!

ISMENE
> Creon—you're really going to rob your son of Antigone?

CREON
> Death with do it for me—break their marriage off.

LEADER
> So, it's settled then? Antigone must die?

CREON
> Settled, yes—we both know that.

> *To the guards.*

Stop wasting time. Take them in.
From now on they'll act like women.
Tie them up, no more running loose;
even the bravest will cut and run,
once they see Death coming for their lives.

> *The guards escort Antigone and Ismene into the palace.*
> *Creon remains while the old citizens form their chorus.*

CHORUS
> Blest, they are the truly blest who all their lives
> have never tasted devastation. For others, once
> the gods have rocked a house to its foundations
> > the ruin will never cease, cresting on and on
> from one generation on throughout the race—
> like a great mounting tide
> driven on by savage northern gales,
> > surging over the dead black depths
> roiling up from the bottom dark heaves of sand
> and the headlands, taking the storm's onslaught full-force,
> roar, and the low moaning
> > > echoes on and on
> > > > and now
> as in ancient times I see the sorrows of the house,
> the living heirs of the old ancestral kings,

piling on the sorrows of the dead
    and one generation cannot free the next—
some god will bring them crashing down,
the race finds no release.
And now the light, the hope
      springing up from the late last root
in the house of Oedipus, that hope's cut down in turn
by the long, bloody knife swung by the gods of death
by a senseless word
        by fury at the heart.

      Zeus,
yours is the power, Zeus, what man on earth
can override it, who can hold it back?
Power that neither Sleep, the all-ensnaring
    no, nor the tireless months of heaven
can ever overmaster—young through all time,
mighty lord of power, you hold fast
    the dazzling crystal mansions of Olympus.
And throughout the future, late and soon
as through the past, your law prevails:
no towering form of greatness
      enters into the lives of mortals
      free and clear of ruin.
      True,
our dreams, our high hopes voyaging far and wide
bring sheer delight to many, to many others,
    delusion, blithe, mindless lusts
and the fraud steals on one slowly . . . unaware
till he trips and puts his foot into the fire.
    He was a wise old man who coined
the famous saying: "Sooner or later
foul is fair, fair is foul
to the man the gods will ruin"—
    He goes his way for a moment only
      free of blinding ruin.

        Enter Haemon from the palace.
Here's Haemon now, the last of all your sons.
Does he come in tears for his bride,
his doomed bride, Antigone—
bitter at being cheated of their marriage?

CREON
We'll soon know, better than seers could tell us.

Turning to Haemon.

Son, you've heard the final verdict on your bride?
Are you coming now, raving against your father?
Or do you love me, no matter what I do?

HAEMON

Father, I'm your *son* . . . you in your wisdom
set my bearings for me—I obey you.
No marriage could ever mean more to me than you,
whatever good direction you may offer.

CREON

Fine, Haemon.
That's how you ought to feel within your heart,
subordinate to your father's will in every way.
That's what a man prays for: to produce good sons—
households full of them, dutiful and attentive,
so they can pay his enemy back with interest
and match the respect their father shows his friend.
But the man who rears a brood of useless children,
what has he brought into the world, I ask you?
Nothing but trouble for himself, and mockery
from his enemies laughing in his face.
Oh Haemon,
never lose your sense of judgment over a woman.
The warmth, the rush of pleasure, it all goes cold
in your arms, I warn you . . . a worthless woman
in your house, a misery in your bed.
What wound cuts deeper than a loved one
turned against you? Spit her out,
like a mortal enemy—let the girl go.
Let her find a husband down among the dead.

Imagine it: I caught her in naked rebellion,
the traitor, the only one in the whole city.
I'm not about to prove myself a liar,
not to my people, no, I'm going to kill her!
That's right—so let her cry for mercy, sing her hymns
to Zeus who defends all bonds of kindred blood.
Why, if I bring up my own kin to be rebels,
think what I'd suffer from the world at large.
Show me the man who rules his household well:
I'll show you someone fit to rule the state.
That good man, my son,
I have every confidence he and he alone

can give commands and take them too. Staunch
in the storm of spears he'll stand his ground,
a loyal, unflinching comrade at your side.

But whoever steps out of line, violates the laws
or presumes to hand out orders to his superiors,
he'll win no praise from me. But that man
the city places in authority, his orders
must be obeyed, large and small,
right and wrong.
                    Anarchy—
show me a greater crime in all the earth!
She, she destroys cities, rips up houses,
breaks the ranks of spearmen into headlong rout.
But the ones who last it out, the great mass of them
owe their lives to discipline. Therefore
we must defend the men who live by law,
never let some woman triumph over us.
Better to fall from power, if fall we must,
at the hands of a man—never be rated
inferior to a woman, never.

LEADER
                    To us,
unless old age has robbed us of our wits,
you seem to say what you have to say with sense.

HAEMON
Father, only the gods endow a man with reason,
the finest of all their gifts, a treasure.
Far be it from me—I haven't the skill,
and certainly no desire, to tell you when,
if ever, you make a slip in speech . . . though
someone else might have a good suggestion.

Of course it's not for you,
in the normal run of things, to watch
whatever men say or do, or find to criticize.
The man in the street, you know, dreads your glance,
he'd never say anything displeasing to your face.
But it's for me to catch the murmurs in the dark,
the way the city mourns for this young girl.
"No woman," they say, "ever deserved death less,
and such a brutal death for such a glorious action.
She, with her own dear brother lying in his blood—
she couldn't bear to leave him dead, unburied,

food for the wild dogs or wheeling vultures.
Death? She deserves a glowing crown of gold!"
So they say, and the rumor spreads in secret,
darkly . . .

I rejoice in your success, father—
nothing more precious to me in the world.
What medal of honor brighter to his children
than a father's growing glory? Or a child's
to his proud father? Now don't, please,
be quite so single-minded, self-involved,
or assume the world is wrong and you are right.
Whoever thinks that he alone possesses intelligence,
the gift of eloquence, he and no one else,
and character too . . . such men, I tell you,
spread them open—you will find them empty.

No,
it's no disgrace for a man, even a wise man,
to learn many things and not to be too rigid.
You've seen trees by a raging winter torrent,
how many sway with the flood and salvage every twig,
but not the stubborn—they're ripped out, roots and all.
Bend or break. The same when a man is sailing:
haul your sheets too taut, never give an inch,
you'll capsize, go the rest of the voyage
keel up and the rowing-benches under.

Oh give way. Relax your anger—change!
I'm young, I know, but let me offer this:
it would be best by far, I admit,
if a man were born infallible, right by nature.
If not—and things don't often go that way,
it's best to learn from those with good advice.

LEADER
You'd do well, my lord, if he's speaking to the point,
to learn from him,

Turning to Haemon.

and you, my boy, from him.
You both are talking sense.

CREON
So,
men our age, we're to be lectured, are we?—
schooled by a boy his age?

HAEMON

Only in what is right. But if I seem young,
look less to my years and more to what I do.

CREON

Do? Is admiring rebels an achievement?

HAEMON

I'd never suggest that you admire treason.

CREON

Oh?—

isn't that just the sickness that's attacked her?

HAEMON

The whole city of Thebes denies it, to a man.

CREON

And is Thebes about to tell me how to rule?

HAEMON

Now, you see? Who's talking like a child?

CREON

Am I to rule this land for others—or myself?

HAEMON

It's no city at all, owned by one man alone.

CREON

What? The city *is* the king's—that's the law!

HAEMON

What a splendid king you'd make of a desert island—
you and you alone.

CREON

To the Chorus.

This boy, I do believe,
is fighting on her side, the woman's side.

HAEMON

If you are a woman, yes;
my concern is all for you.

CREON

Why, you degenerate—bandying accusations,
threatening me with justice, your own father!

HAEMON

I see my father offending justice—wrong.

CREON

Wrong?
To protect my royal rights?

HAEMON

Protect your rights?

When you trample down the honors of the gods?

CREON

You, you soul of corruption, rotten through—

woman's accomplice!

HAEMON

That may be,

but you'll never find me accomplice to a criminal.

CREON

That's what *she* is,

and every word you say is a blatant appeal for her—

HAEMON

And you, and me, and the gods beneath the earth.

CREON

You'll never marry her, not while she's alive.

HAEMON

Then she'll die . . . but her death will kill another.

CREON

What, brazen threats? You go too far!

HAEMON

What threat?

Combating your empty, mindless judgments with a word?

CREON

You'll suffer for your sermons, you and your empty wisdom!

HAEMON

If you weren't my father, I'd say you were insane.

CREON

Don't flatter me with Father—you woman's slave!

HAEMON

You really expect to fling abuse at me

and not receive the same?

CREON

Is that so!

Now, by heaven, I promise you, you'll pay—

taunting, insulting me! Bring her out,

that hateful—she'll die now, here,

in front of his eyes, beside her groom!

HAEMON

No, no, she will never die beside me—

don't delude yourself. And you will never

see me, never set eyes on my face again.
Rage your heart out, rage with friends
who can stand the sight of you.

Rushing out.

LEADER

Gone, my king, in a burst of anger.
A temper young as his . . . hurt him once,
he may do something violent.

CREON

Let him do—
dream up something desperate, past all human limit!
Good riddance. Rest assured,
he'll never save those two young girls from death.

LEADER

Both of them, you really intend to kill them both?

CREON

No, not her, the one whose hands are clean;
you're quite right.

LEADER

But Antigone—
what sort of death do you have in mind for her?

CREON

I'll take her down some wild, desolate path
never trod by men, and wall her up alive
in a rocky vault, and set out short rations,
just a gesture of piety
to keep the entire city free of defilement.[7]
There let her pray to the one god she worships:
Death—who knows?—may just reprieve her from death.
Or she may learn at last, better late than never,
what a waste of breath it is to worship Death.

Exit to the palace.

CHORUS

Love, never conquered in battle
Love the plunderer laying waste the rich!
Love standing the night-watch
guarding a girl's soft cheek,

---

[7]Creon here changes his earlier proclamation of death by stoning. He decides that death by slow starvation while entombed or, possibly, suicide, would save Thebes from the "defilement" of blood-guilt.

you range the seas, the shepherds' steadings off in the wilds—
not even the deathless gods can flee your onset,
nothing human born for a day—
whoever feels your grip is driven mad.
                         Love
you wrench the minds of the righteous into outrage,
swerve them to their ruin—you have ignited this,
this kindred strife, father and son at war
                         and Love alone the victor—
warm glance of the bride triumphant, burning with desire!
Throned in power, side-by-side with the mighty laws!
Irresistible Aphrodite,[8] never conquered—
Love, you mock us for your sport.
                         Antigone is brought from the palace under guard.
            But now, even I'd rebel against the king,
            I'd break all bounds when I see this—
            I fill with tears, can't hold them back,
            not any more . . . I see Antigone make her way
            to the bridal vault where all are laid to rest.

ANTIGONE

Look at me, men of my fatherland,
      setting out on the last road
looking into the last light of day
the last I'll ever see . . .
the god of death who puts us all to bed
takes me down to the banks of Acheron[9] alive—
      denied my part in the wedding-songs,
no wedding-song in the dusk has crowned my marriage—
I go to wed the lord of the dark waters.

CHORUS

            Not crowned with glory, crowned with a dirge,
            you leave for the deep pit of the dead.
            No withering illness laid you low,
            no strokes of the sword—a law to yourself,
            alone, no mortal like you, ever, you go down
            to the halls of Death alive and breathing.

---

[8]Goddess of sexual love and fertility.

[9]One of the rivers of the underworld over which the dead souls must cross.

ANTIGONE

But think of Niobe[10]—well I know her story—
    think what a living death she died,
Tantalus's daughter, stranger queen from the east:
there on the mountain heights, growing stone
binding as ivy, slowly walled her round
and the rains will never cease, the legends say
the snows will never leave her . . .
    wasting away, under her brows the tears
showering down her breasting ridge and slopes—
a rocky death like hers puts me to sleep.

CHORUS

But she was a god, born of gods,
and we are only mortals born to die.
And yet, of course, it's a great thing
for a dying girl to hear, just hear
she shares a destiny equal to the gods,
during life and later, once she's dead.

ANTIGONE

O you mock me!
Why, in the name of all my fathers' gods
why can't you wait till I am gone—
    must you abuse me to my face?
O my city, all your fine rich sons!
And you, you springs of the Dirce,
holy grove of Thebes where the chariots gather,
    you at least, you'll bear me witness, look,
unmourned by friends and forced by such crude laws
I go to my rockbound prison, strange new tomb—
    always a stranger, O dear god,
    I have no home on earth and none below,
        not with the living, not with the breathless dead.

CHORUS

You went too far, the last limits of daring—
smashing against the high throne of Justice!
    Your life's in ruins, child—I wonder . . .
do you pay for your father's terrible ordeal?

---

[10]A mythological queen of Thebes who boasted that she had more children than the goddess Leto, who had only two (the divine twins Apollo and Artemis, whose father was Zeus). For her pride, Apollo and Artemis killed all Niobe's children. Niobe wept until she turned into a stone column on a mountain whose melting snows represent her "tears"—always flowing.

ANTIGONE

There—at last you've touched it, the worst pain
the worst anguish! Raking up the grief for father
    three times over, for all the doom
that's struck us down, the brilliant house of Laius.
O mother, your marriage-bed
the coiling horrors, the coupling there—
    you with your own son, my father—doomstruck mother!
Such, such were my parents, and I their wretched child.
I go to them now, cursed, unwed, to share their home—
    I am a stranger! O dear brother, doomed
in your marriage—your marriage murders mine,[11]
    your dying drags me down to death alive!

                               Enter Creon.

CHORUS

Reverence asks some reverence in return—
but attacks on power never go unchecked,
    not by the man who holds the reins of power.
Your own blind will, your passion has destroyed you.

ANTIGONE

No one to weep for me, my friends,
no wedding-song—they take me away
in all my pain . . . the road lies open, waiting.
Never again, the law forbids me to see
the sacred eye of day. I am agony!
No tears for the destiny that's mine,
no loved one mourns my death.

CREON

              Can't you see?
If a man could wail his own dirge *before* he dies,
he'd never finish.

                                 To the guards.

              Take her away, quickly!
Wall her up in the tomb, you have your orders.
Abandon her there, alone, and let her choose—
death or a buried life with a good roof for shelter.
As for myself, my hands are clean. This young girl—

---

[11]Antigone refers to Polynices's marriage to a princess of Argos that enabled him to raise the Argive forces that attacked Thebes. There might also be a deeper reference to the marriage of Oedipus, Antigone's father–brother, and its inevitably disastrous consequences.

dead or alive, she will be stripped of her rights,
her stranger's rights,[12] here in the world above.

ANTIGONE

O tomb, my bridal-bed—my house, my prison
cut in the hollow rock, my everlasting watch!
I'll soon be there, soon embrace my own,
the great growing family of our dead
Persephone[13] has received among her ghosts.

I,

the last of them all, the most reviled by far,
go down before my destined time's run out.
But still I go, cherishing one good hope:
my arrival may be dear to father,
dear to you, my mother,
dear to you, my loving brother, Eteocles—
When you died I washed you with my hands,
I dressed you all, I poured the cups
across your tombs. But now, Polynices,
because I laid your body out as well,
this, this is my reward. Nevertheless
I honored you—the decent will admit it—
well and wisely too.

Never, I tell you,
if I had been the mother of children
or if my husband died, exposed and rotting—
I'd never have taken this ordeal upon myself,
never defied our people's will. What law,
you ask, do I satisfy with what I say?
A husband dead, there might have been another.
A child by another too, if I had lost the first.
But mother and father both lost in the halls of Death,
no brother could ever spring to light again.

For this law alone I held you first in honor.
For this, Creon, the king, judges me a criminal
guilty of dreadful outrage, my dear brother!
And now he leads me off, a captive in his hands,
with no part in the bridal-song, the bridal-bed,
denied all joy of marriage, raising children—
deserted so by loved ones, struck by fate,
I descend alive to the caverns of the dead.

---

[12]Creon implies that he already had stripped Antigone of her rights as a Theban citizen.
[13]Queen of the underworld.

What law of the mighty gods have I transgressed?
Why look to the heavens any more, tormented as I am?
Whom to call, what comrades now? Just think,
my reverence only brands me for irreverence!
Very well: if this is the pleasure of the gods,
once I suffer I will know that I was wrong.
But if these men are wrong, let them suffer
nothing worse than they mete out to me—
these masters of unjustice!

LEADER

Still the same rough winds, the wild passion
raging through the girl.

CREON

To the guards.

                    Take her away.
You're wasting time—you'll pay for it too.

ANTIGONE

Oh god, the voice of death. It's come, it's here.

CREON

True. Not a word of hope—your doom is sealed.

ANTIGONE

            Land of Thebes, city of all my fathers—
            O you gods, the first gods of the race![14]
            They drag me away, now, no more delay.
            Look on me, you noble sons of Thebes—
            the last of a great line of kings,
            I alone, see what I suffer now
            at the hands of what breed of men—
            all for reverence, my reverence for the gods!

                    She leaves under guard; the Chorus gathers.

CHORUS

            Danaë, Danaë[15]—
    even she endured a fate like yours,
        in all her lovely strength she traded

---

[14]The Theban royal house traced its ancestry ultimately to the Olympian gods.

[15]In this ode, the Chorus searches for parallels to Antigone's approaching entombment. The references, not always clear to the modern reader, must have been familiar to Sophocles's original audience. Danaë was the only child of Acrisius, king of Argos. He feared a prophecy that his grandson would cause his death, so he shut his daughter in a bronze vault. Zeus, in the form of a golden rain shower, impregnated her and she gave birth to the hero, Perseus, who would, eventually, by throwing a discus at an athletic competition, cause the accidental death of his grandfather.

the light of day for the bolted brazen vault—
buried within her tomb, her bridal-chamber,
wed to the yoke and broken.
   But she was of glorious birth
      my child, my child
and treasured the seed of Zeus within her womb,
the cloudburst streaming gold!
     The power of fate is a wonder,
     dark, terrible wonder—
     neither wealth nor armies
     towered walls nor ships
     black hulls lashed by the salt
     can save us from that force.

The yoke tamed him too
   young Lycurgus[16] flaming in anger
king of Edonia, all for his mad taunts
Dionysus clamped him down, encased
in the chain-mail of rock
    and there his rage
       his terrible flowering rage burst—
sobbing, dying away . . . at last that madman
came to know his god—
     the power he mocked, the power
     he taunted in all his frenzy
     trying to stamp out
     the women strong with the god—
     the torch, the raving sacred cries—
     enraging the Muses who adore the flute.
And far north where the Black Rocks
    cut the sea in half
and murderous straits
split the coast of Thrace
   a forbidding city stands
where once, hard by the walls
the savage Ares thrilled to watch
a king's new queen, a Fury rearing in rage
   against his two royal sons—
     her bloody hands, her dagger-shuttle

---

[16]King of the barbarous Thracians, he attempted to suppress the wild worship of
Dionysus, god of wine and ecstasy, and—in this version of the myth—was imprisoned
by the god in a rocky cave, where he went mad.

stabbing out their eyes—cursed, blinding wounds—
their eyes blind sockets screaming for revenge![17]

They wailed in agony, cries echoing cries
      the princes doomed at birth . . .
and their mother doomed to chains,
walled off in a tomb of stone—
    but she traced her own birth back
to a proud Athenian line and the high gods
and off in caverns half the world away,
born of the wild North Wind
    she sprang on her father's gales,
      racing stallions up the leaping cliffs—
child of the heavens. But even on her the Fates
the gray everlasting Fates rode hard
my child, my child.[18]

        Enter Tiresias, the blind prophet, led by a boy.

TIRESIAS
             Lords of Thebes,
I and the boy have come together,
hand in hand. Two see with the eyes of one . . .
so the blind must go, with a guide to lead the way.

CREON
What is it, old Tiresias? What news now?

TIRESIAS
I will teach you. And you obey the seer.

CREON
           I will,
I've never wavered from your advice before.

TIRESIAS
And so you kept the city straight on course.

CREON
I owe you a great deal, I swear to that.

TIRESIAS
Then reflect, my son: you are poised,
once more, on the razor-edge of fate.

---

[17]Cleopatra, daughter of an Athenian princess and the North Wind, married the king of Thrace and bore him two sons. They were blinded by the king's second wife, who then entombed mother and sons. Ares, the god of war, sometimes associated with Thrace, watched the savage blinding.

[18]The Chorus is speaking to Antigone, "my child," after pointing out the similarities between her fate and earlier personal fates.

CREON
> What is it? I shudder to hear you.

TIRESIAS
> You will learn
> when you listen to the warnings of my craft.
> As I sat on the ancient seat of augury,[19]
> in the sanctuary where every bird I know
> will hover at my hands—suddenly I heard it,
> a strange voice in the wingbeats, unintelligible,
> barbaric, a mad scream! Talons flashing, ripping,
> they were killing each other—that much I knew—
> the murderous fury whirring in those wings
> made that much clear!
> I was afraid,
> I turned quickly, tested the burnt sacrifice,
> ignited the altar at all points—but no fire,
> the god in the fire never blazed.
> Not from those offerings . . . over the embers
> slid a heavy ooze from the long thighbones,
> smoking, sputtering out, and the bladder
> puffed and burst—spraying gall into the air—
> and the fat wrapping the bones slithered off
> and left them glistening white. No fire!
> The rites failed that might have blazed the future
> with a sign. So I learned from the boy here;
> he is my guide, as I am guide to others.
> And it's you—
> your high resolve that sets this plague on Thebes.
> The public altars and sacred hearths are fouled,
> one and all, by the birds and dogs with carrion
> torn from the corpse, the doomstruck son of Oedipus!
> And so the gods are deaf to our prayers, they spurn
> the offerings in our hands, the flame of holy flesh.
> No birds cry out an omen clear and true—
> they're gorged with the murdered victim's blood and fat.
> Take these things to heart my son, I warn you.
> All men make mistakes, it is only human.
> But once the wrong is done, a man
> can turn his back on folly, misfortune too,

---

[19]A place where blind Tiresias, chief prophet of Thebes for generations, listened to the
birds and, through the boy, observed them for signs of the gods' will.

if he tries to make amends, however low he's fallen,
and stops his bullnecked ways. Stubbornness
brands you for stupidity—pride is a crime.
No, yield to the dead!
Never stab the fighter when he's down.
Where's the glory, killing the dead twice over?

I mean you well. I give you sound advice.
It's best to learn from a good adviser
when he speaks for your own good:
it's pure gain.

CREON

                Old man—all of you! So,
you shoot your arrows at my head like archers at the target—
I even have *him* loosed on me, this fortune-teller.
Oh his ilk has tried to sell me short
and ship me off for years. Well,
drive your bargains, traffic—much as you like—
in the gold of India, silver-gold of Sardis.
You'll never bury that body in the grave,
not even if Zeus's eagles rip the corpse
and wing their rotten pickings off to the throne of god!
Never, not even in fear of such defilement
will I tolerate his burial, that traitor.
Well I know, we can't defile the gods—
no mortal has the power.

                No,
reverend old Tiresias, all men fall,
it's only human, but the wisest fall obscenely
when they glorify obscene advice with rhetoric—
all for their own gain.

TIRESIAS

Oh god, is there a man alive
who knows, who actually believes . . .

CREON

                What now?
What earth-shattering truth are you about to utter?

TIRESIAS

. . . just how much a sense of judgment, wisdom
is the greatest gift we have?

CREON

                Just as much, I'd say,
as a twisted mind is the worst affliction going.

TIRESIAS

You are the one who's sick, Creon, sick to death.

CREON

I am in no mood to trade insults with a seer.

TIRESIAS

You have already, calling my prophecies a lie.

CREON

Why not?
You and the whole breed of seers are mad for money!

TIRESIAS

And the whole race of tyrants lusts to rake it in.

CREON

This slander of yours—
are you aware you're speaking to the king?

TIRESIAS

Well aware. Who helped you save the city?[20]

CREON

You—
you have your skills, old seer, but you lust for injustice!

TIRESIAS

You will drive me to utter the dreadful secret in my heart.

CREON

Spit it out! Just don't speak it out for profit.

TIRESIAS

Profit? No, not a bit of profit, not for you.

CREON

Know full well, you'll never buy off my resolve.

TIRESIAS

Then know this too, learn this by heart!
The chariot of the sun will not race through
so many circuits more, before you have surrendered
one born of your own loins, your own flesh and blood,
a corpse for corpses given in return, since you have thrust
to the world below a child sprung for the world above,
ruthlessly lodged a living soul within the grave—
then you've robbed the gods below the earth,
keeping a dead body here in the bright air,
unburied, unsung, unhallowed by the rites.

---

[20]Tiresias, according to one legend, advised Creon that Thebes, once attacked, could be
saved only by the death of Creon's son, Megareus, who did, in fact, die while defending
the city. Later in the play, Megareus's death will be blamed on Creon by his dying wife,
Eurydice.

You, you have no business with the dead,
nor do the gods above—this is violence
you have forced upon the heavens.
And so the avengers, the dark destroyers late
but true to the mark, now lie in wait for you,
the Furies[21] sent by the gods and the god of death
to strike you down with the pains that you perfected!

There. Reflect on that, tell me I've been bribed.
The day comes soon, no long test of time, not now,
that wakes the wails for men and women in your halls.
Great hatred rises against you—
cities in tumult, all whose mutilated sons
the dogs have graced with burial, or the wild beasts,
some wheeling crow that wings the ungodly stench of carrion
back to each city, each warrior's hearth and home.

These arrows for your heart! Since you've raked me
I loose them like an archer in my anger,
arrows deadly true. You'll never escape
their burning, searing force.

> *Motioning to his escort.*

Come, boy, take me home.
So he can vent his rage on younger men,
and learn to keep a gentler tongue in his head
and better sense than what he carries now.

> *Exit to the side.*

LEADER

The old man's gone, my king—
terrible prophecies. Well I know,
since the hair on this old head went gray,
he's never lied to Thebes.

CREON

I know it myself—I'm shaken, torn.
It's a dreadful thing to yield . . . but resist now?
Lay my pride bare to the blows of ruin?
That's dreadful too.

LEADER

But good advice,
Creon, take it now, you must.

---

[21]Vengeful goddesses who especially pursue those who commit murder within their own families.

CREON

What should I do? Tell me . . . I'll obey.

LEADER

Go! Free the girl from the rocky vault
and raise a mound for the body you exposed.

CREON

That's your advice? You think I should give in?

LEADER

Yes, my king, quickly. Disasters sent by the gods
cut short our follies in a flash.

CREON

Oh it's hard,
giving up the heart's desire . . . but I will do it—
no more fighting a losing battle with necessity.

LEADER

Do it now, go, don't leave it to others.

CREON

Now—I'm on my way! Come, each of you,
take up axes, make for the high ground,
over there, quickly! I and my better judgment
have come round to this—I shackled her,
I'll set her free myself. I am afraid . . .
it's best to keep the established laws
to the very day we die.

Rushing out, followed by his entourage.
The Chorus clusters around the altar.

CHORUS

God of a hundred names![22]
Great Dionysus!
Son and glory of Semele! Pride of Thebes—
Child of Zeus whose thunder rocks the clouds—
Lord of the famous lands of evening—
King of the Mysteries!
King of Eleusis, Demeter's plain
her breasting hills that welcome in the world—
Great Dionysus!
Bacchus, living in Thebes

---

[22]The Chorus ecstatically calls on Dionysus (Bacchus, Iacchus), the wine god closely
linked with Thebes. It rejoices that Creon has seen his error and (mistakenly) assumes
that all will be healed by the god's frenzied ceremony.

the mother-city of all your frenzied women—
          Bacchus
      living along the Ismenus's rippling waters
standing over the field sown with the Dragon's teeth!

You—we have seen you through the flaring smoky fires,
      your torches blazing over the twin peaks
where nymphs of the hallowed cave climb onward
                fired with you, your sacred rage—
we have seen you at Castalia's running spring
and down from the heights of Nysa crowned with ivy
the greening shore rioting vines and grapes
          down you come in your storm of wild women
        ecstatic, mystic cries—
          Dionysus—
down to watch and ward the roads of Thebes!
First of all cities, Thebes you honor first
you and your mother, bride of the lightning—
come, Dionysus! Now your people lie
in the iron grip of plague,
come in your racing, healing stride
          down Parnassus's slopes
or across the moaning straits.
          Lord of the dancing—
dance, dance the constellations breathing fire!
Great master of the voices of the night!
Child of Zeus, God's offspring, come, come forth!
Lord, king, dance with your nymphs, swirling, raving
arm-in-arm in frenzy through the night
      they dance you, Iacchus—
          Dance, Dionysus
giver of all good things!

                        Enter a Messenger from the side.

MESSENGER
          Neighbors,
friends of the house of Cadmus and the kings,
there's not a thing in this life of ours
I'd praise or blame as settled once for all.
Fortune lifts and Fortune fells the lucky
and unlucky every day. No prophet on earth
can tell a man his fate. Take Creon:
there was a man to rouse your envy once,
as I see it. He saved the realm from enemies;

taking power, he alone, the lord of the fatherland,
he set us true on course—flourished like a tree
with the noble line of sons he bred and reared . . .
and now it's lost, all gone.

Believe me,

when a man has squandered his true joys,
he's good as dead, I tell you, a living corpse.
Pile up riches in your house, as much as you like—
live like a king with a huge show of pomp,
but if real delight is missing from the lot,
I wouldn't give you a wisp of smoke for it,
not compared with joy.

LEADER

What now?

What new grief do you bring the house of kings?

MESSENGER

Dead, dead—and the living are guilty of their death!

LEADER

Who's the murderer? Who is dead? Tell us.

MESSENGER

Haemon's gone, his blood spilled by the very hand—

LEADER

His father's or his own?

MESSENGER

His own . . .

raging mad with his father for the death—

LEADER

Oh great seer,

you saw it all, you brought your word to birth!

MESSENGER

Those are the facts. Deal with them as you will.

As he turns to go, Eurydice enters from the palace.

LEADER

Look, Eurydice. Poor woman, Creon's wife,
so close at hand. By chance perhaps,
unless she's heard the news about her son.

EURYDICE

My countrymen,

all of you—I caught the sound of your words
as I was leaving to do my part,
to appeal to queen Athena with my prayers.
I was just loosing the bolts, opening the doors,
when a voice filled with sorrow, family sorrow,

struck my ears, and I fell back, terrified,
into the women's arms—everything went black.
Tell me the news, again, whatever it is . . .
sorrow and I are hardly strangers;
I can bear the worst.

MESSENGER

         I—dear lady,
I'll speak as an eye witness. I was there.
And I won't pass over one word of the truth.
Why should I try to soothe you with a story,
only to prove a liar in a moment?
Truth is always best.

         So,
I escorted your lord, I guided him
to the edge of the plain where the body lay,
Polynices, torn by the dogs and still unmourned.
And saying a prayer to Hecate of the Crossroads,[23]
Pluto[24] too, to hold their anger and be kind,
we washed the dead in a bath of holy water
and plucking some fresh branches, gathering . . .
what was left of him, we burned them all together
and raised a high mound of native earth, and then
we turned and made for that rocky vault of hers,
the hollow, empty bed of the bride of Death.

And far off, one of us heard a voice,
a long wail rising, echoing
out of that unhallowed wedding-chamber;
he ran to alert the master and Creon pressed on,
closer—the strange, inscrutable cry came sharper,
throbbing around him now, and he let loose
a cry of his own, enough to wrench the heart,
"Oh god, am I the prophet now? going down
the darkest road I've ever gone? My son—
it's *his* dear voice, he greets me! Go, men,
closer, quickly! Go through the gap,
the rocks are dragged back—
right to the tomb's very mouth—and look,
see if it's Haemon's voice I think I hear,
or the gods have robbed me of my senses."

---

[23]A goddess of the underworld, often worshiped at crossroads.
[24]Another name of Hades, lord of the underworld.

The king was shattered. We took his orders,
went and searched, and there in the deepest,
dark recesses of the tomb we found her . . .
hanged by the neck in a fine linen noose,
strangled in her veils—and the boy,
his arms flung around her waist,
clinging to her, wailing for his bride,
dead and down below, for his father's crimes
and the bed of his marriage blighted by misfortune.
When Creon saw him, he gave a deep sob,
he ran in, shouting, crying out to him,
"Oh my child—what have you done? what seized you,
what insanity? what disaster drove you mad?
Come out, my son! I beg you on my knees!"
But the boy gave him a wild burning glance,
spat in his face, not a word in reply,
he drew his sword—his father rushed out,
running as Haemon lunged and missed!—
and then, doomed, desperate with himself,
suddenly leaning his full weight on the blade,
he buried it in his body, halfway to the hilt.
And still in his senses, pouring his arms around her,
he embraced the girl and breathing hard,
released a quick rush of blood,
bright red on her cheek glistening white.
And there he lies, body enfolding body . . .
he has won his bride at last, poor boy,
not here but in the houses of the dead.

Creon shows the world that of all the ills
afflicting men the worst is lack of judgment.

                              Eurydice turns and reenters the palace.

LEADER

What do you make of that? The lady's gone,
without a word, good or bad.

MESSENGER

           I'm alarmed too
but here's my hope—faced with her son's death,
she finds it unbecoming to mourn in public.
Inside, under her roof, she'll set her women
to the task and wail the sorrow of the house.
She's too discreet. She won't do something rash.

LEADER

I'm not so sure. To me, at least,
a long, heavy silence promises danger,
just as much as a lot of empty outcries.

MESSENGER

We'll see if she's holding something back,
hiding some passion in her heart.
I'm going in. You may be right—who knows?
Even too much silence has its dangers.

> *Exit to the palace. Enter Creon from the side,*
> *escorted by attendants carrying Haemon's body on a bier.*

LEADER

The king himself! Coming toward us,
look, holding the boy's head in his hands.
Clear, damning proof, if it's right to say so—
proof of his own madness, no one else's,
          no, his own blind wrongs.

CREON

        Ohhh,
so senseless, so insane . . . my crimes,
my stubborn, deadly—
Look at us, the killer, the killed,
father and son, the same blood—the misery!
My plans, my mad fanatic heart,
my son, cut off so young!
Ai, dead, lost to the world,
not through your stupidity, no, my own.

LEADER

       Too late,
too late, you see what justice means.

CREON

      Oh I've learned
through blood and tears! Then, it was then,
when the god came down and struck me—a great weight
shattering, driving me down that wild savage path,
ruining, trampling down my joy. Oh the agony,
    the heartbreaking agonies of our lives.

> *Enter the Messenger from the palace.*

MESSENGER

    Master,
what a hoard of grief you have, and you'll have more.
The grief that lies to hand you've brought yourself—

Pointing to Haemon's body.

the rest, in the house, you'll see it all too soon.

CREON

What now? What's worse than this?

MESSENGER

The queen is dead.
The mother of this dead boy . . . mother to the end—
poor thing, her wounds are fresh.

CREON

No, no,
harbor of Death, so choked, so hard to cleanse!—
why me? why are you killing me?
Herald of pain, more words, more grief?
I died once, you kill me again and again!
What's the report, boy . . . some news for me?
My wife dead? O dear god!
Slaughter heaped on slaughter?

The doors open; the body of Eurydice is brought out on her bier.

MESSENGER

See for yourself:
now they bring her body from the palace.

CREON

Oh no,
another, second loss to break the heart.
What next, what fate still waits for me?
I just held my son in my arms and now,
look, a new corpse rising before my eyes—
wretched, helpless mother—O my son!

MESSENGER

She stabbed herself at the altar,
then her eyes went dark, after she'd raised
a cry for the noble fate of Megareus, the hero
killed in the first assault, then for Haemon,
then with her dying breath she called down
torments on your head—you killed her sons.

CREON

Oh the dread,
I shudder with dread! Why not kill me too?—
run me through with a good sharp sword?
Oh god, the misery, anguish—
I, I'm churning with it, going under.

MESSENGER

Yes, and the dead, the woman lying there,
piles the guilt of all their deaths on you.

CREON

How did she end her life, what bloody stroke?

MESSENGER

She drove home to the heart with her own hand,
once she learned her son was dead . . . that agony.

CREON

And the guilt is all mine—
can never be fixed on another man,
no escape for me. I killed you,
I, god help me, I admit it all!

To his attendants.

Take me away, quickly, out of sight.
I don't even exist—I'm no one. Nothing.

LEADER

Good advice, if there's any good in suffering.
Quickest is best when troubles block the way.

CREON

Kneeling in prayer.

Come, let it come!—that best of fates for me
that brings the final day, best fate of all.
Oh quickly, now—
so I never have to see another sunrise.

LEADER

That will come when it comes;
we must deal with all that lies before us.
The future rests with the ones who tend the future.

CREON

That prayer—I poured my heart into that prayer!

LEADER

No more prayers now. For mortal men
there is no escape from the doom we must endure.

CREON

Take me away, I beg you, out of sight.
A rash, indiscriminate fool!
I murdered you, my son, against my will—
you too, my wife . . .
              Wailing wreck of a man,
whom to look to? where to lean for support?

Desperately turning from Haemon to Eurydice on their biers.

Whatever I touch goes wrong—once more
a crushing fate's come down upon my head.

The Messenger and attendants lead Creon into the palace.

CHORUS

Wisdom is by far the greatest part of joy,
and reverence toward the gods must be safeguarded.
The mighty words of the proud are paid in full
with mighty blows of fate, and at long last
those blows will teach us wisdom.

The old citizens exit to the side.

14

ૐ

Herodotus

THE HISTORIES

D ramatic tragedy (exemplified by Sophocles's Antigone, Selection 13) was a
leading cultural endeavor that flourished during the fifth century B.C., the
Golden Age of Athens. That same century also saw the emergence of history (the
written record of contemporary events—in prose) as a new way of preserving the
deeds of mankind from oblivion (as contrasted to epic poetry, like The Epic of
Gilgamesh *and* The Odyssey, *Selections 1 and 7). The appearance of historical
writing might have been a result of applying the Greek tradition of rational
inquiry to the human story, much the same way that nature-philosophers applied
rational inquiry to the physical world. However, the immediate inspiration for
this earliest surviving prose work of Western literature was patriotic: the great
Greek national effort of the Persian Wars (490–445 B.C.).*

Herodotus (ca. 484–425 B.C.) has been called the Father of History because
he was the first to explore with clarity the causes of human actions in a prose narrative of great scope expressed with consummate literary skill. He was born in
Asia Minor at Halicarnassus—a Greek city chafing under Persian control. After
an unsuccessful revolt by the inhabitants, Herodotus, as a young man, went into
exile; thereafter, although he loved Athens as his adopted home and was much
acclaimed there for his recitations, he spent much of his life wandering through
the Mediterranean lands and even into Egypt, Babylonia, and the regions north
of the Black Sea.

It was during these long travels that Herodotus set out to record the leading
events of the Persian Wars. His main object was to describe the rival worlds of
Greece and Persia as seen through a single mind; for this purpose he put together vast and varied materials he gathered on his travels. He was the first to make
past events the object of research and verification. This bold and original undertaking he called historiai ("researches" or "inquiries") set down to "preserve the
memory of the past by putting on record the astonishing achievements both of our

own and of other peoples; and more particularly, to show how they [Greeks and Persians] came into conflict." Judged by modern standards of historical scholarship, his Histories *might seem unsatisfactory; after all, he often had to depend on unreliable sources. It is, however, a work of striking breadth and tolerance, as the following episodes suggest. Even in the patriotic saga of the Greek stand at Thermopylae, Herodotus treats the Persian enemies and their culture with the respect due a great rival.*

Herodotus wrote his Histories *for recitation before a public audience, not to be read privately; for it was as a public teller of tales that he made his living. Like Homer before him, therefore, his writing reflected commonly held ethical and heroic values. Herodotus kept in mind the need to hold the interest and approval of his listening audience, usually Athenians. "Thus Athens went from strength to strength and proved . . . how noble a thing freedom is." The heroic resistance at the pass of Thermopylae, however, which climaxes the following excerpt, features the soldierly skill and determination of the Spartan warriors, the great Greek rivals to Athenian military glory.*

Clearly, Herodotus, like his audience, believed in the prophetic power of oracles. They often demonstrate, as does the whole of the Histories, *a basic moral sequence found in much world literature: prosperity–pride–ruin. Herodotus's view of this divine balancing of human affairs is evident in his introduction: "I will proceed with my history, telling the story as I go along of small cities no less than of great. For most of those which were great are small today; and those which used to be small were great in my own time. Knowing therefore, that human prosperity never abides long in the same place, I shall pay attention to both alike."*

Xerxes[1] at first was not at all interested in invading Greece but began his reign by building up an army for a campaign in Egypt. But Mardonius—the son of Gobryas and Darius's sister and thus cousin to the king—who was present in court and had more influence with Xerxes than anyone else in the country, used constantly to talk to him on the subject. "Master," he would say, "the Athenians have done us great injury, and it is only right that they should be punished for their crimes. By all means finish the task you already have in hand; but when you

Herodotus, *The Histories*, trans. Aubrey de Sélincourt, rev. A. R. Burn (London: Penguin Books, 1954, rev. 1972), pp. 442–447, 452–453, 456–457, 458–459, 464–466, 475–477, 511–515, 517–520. Copyright © the Estate of Aubrey de Sélincourt, 1954; copyright © A. R. Burn, 1972. Reproduced by permission of Penguin Books Ltd.

[1]King of Persia from 485 to 465 B.C. who invaded Greece in 480 B.C.

have tamed the arrogance of Egypt, then lead an army against Athens. Do that, and your name will be held in honor all over the world, and people will think twice in future before they invade your country." And to the argument for revenge he would add that Europe was a very beautiful place; it produced every kind of garden tree; the land there was everything that land should be—it was, in short, too good for anyone in the world except the Persian king. Mardonius's motive for urging the campaign was love of mischief and adventure and the hope of becoming governor of Greece himself; and after much persistence he persuaded Xerxes to make the attempt. Certain other occurrences came to his aid. In the first place, messengers arrived from the Aleuadae in Thessaly[2] (the Aleuadae were the Thessalian reigning family) with an invitation to Xerxes, promising zealous assistance; at the same time the Pisistratidae[3] in Susa spoke to the same purpose and worked upon him even more strongly through the agency of an Athenian named Onomacritus, a collector of oracles, who had arranged and edited the oracles of Musaeus.[4] The Pisistratidae had made up their quarrel with him before coming to Susa. He had been expelled from Athens by Hipparchus[5] for inserting in the verses of Musaeus a prophecy that the islands off Lemnos would disappear under water—Lasus of Hermione had caught him in the very act of the forgery. Before his banishment he had been a close friend of Hipparchus. Anyway, he went to Susa; and now, whenever he found himself in the king's presence, the Pisistratidae would talk big about his wonderful powers and he would recite selections from his oracles. Any prophecy which implied a setback to the Persian cause he would carefully omit, choosing for quotation only those which promised the brightest triumphs, describing to Xerxes how it was fore-ordained that the Hellespont should be bridged by a Persian, and how the army would march from Asia into Greece. Subjected, therefore, to this double pressure, from Onomacritus's oracles on the one side, and the advice of the Pisistratidae and Aleuadae on the other, Xerxes gave in and allowed himself to be persuaded to undertake the invasion of Greece.

First, however, in the year after Darius's death, he sent an army against the Egyptian rebels and decisively crushed them; then, having reduced the country to a condition of worse servitude than it had ever been in the previous reign, he

---

[2]A region of northeastern Greece; its leading family conspired with Xerxes.

[3]A clan of Athenian exiles, descended from Pisistratus, a famous tyrant of Athens, who died in 527 B.C. Some of the banished clan lived in Susa, the capital city of the Persian Empire.

[4]A mythical Greek poet to whom a collection of oracles (authoritative prophecies) was attributed.

[5]Younger son of Pisistratus, assassinated in 514 B.C. He had ruled Athens jointly with his older brother.

turned it over to his brother Achaemenes, who long afterwards, while he was still governor, was killed by a son of Psammetichus, a Libyan.

After the conquest of Egypt, when he was on the point of taking in hand the expedition against Athens, Xerxes called a conference of the leading men in the country, to find out their attitude towards the war and explain to them his own wishes. When they met, he addressed them as follows: "Do not suppose, gentlemen, that I am departing from precedent in the course of action I intend to undertake. We Persians have a way of living, which I have inherited from my predecessors and propose to follow. I have learned from my elders that ever since Cyrus[6] deposed Astyages and we took over from the Medes the sovereign power we now possess, we have never yet remained inactive. This is God's guidance, and it is by following it that we have gained our great prosperity. Of our past history you need no reminder; for you know well enough the famous deeds of Cyrus, Cambyses, and my father Darius, and their additions to our empire. Now I myself, ever since my accession, have been thinking how not to fall short of the kings who have sat upon this throne before me, and how to add as much power as they did to the Persian empire. And now at last I have found a way to win for Persia not glory only but a country as large and as rich as our own—indeed richer than our own[7]—and at the same time to get satisfaction and revenge. That, then, is the object of this meeting—that I may disclose to you what it is that I intend to do. I will bridge the Hellespont[8] and march an army through Europe into Greece, and punish the Athenians for the outrage they committed upon my father and upon us.[9] As you saw, Darius himself was making his preparations for war against these men; but death prevented him from carrying out his purpose. I therefore on his behalf, and for the benefit of all my subjects, will not rest until I have taken Athens and burnt it to the ground, in revenge for the injury which the Athenians without provocation once did to me and my father. These men, you remember, came to Sardis with Aristagoras the Milesian, a subject of ours, and burnt the temples and sacred groves; and you know all too well how they served our troops under Datis and Artaphernes,[10] when they landed upon Greek soil. For these reasons I have now prepared to make war upon them, and, when I con-

---

[6]Founder of the Persian Empire (559–529 B.C.), father of Cambyses.

[7]Xerxes greatly overstates the size and wealth of the Greek city-states.

[8]The strait separating Europe from Asia, near the site of ancient Troy.

[9]In 499 B.C., some ethnic Greeks on the coast of Asia Minor revolted against Darius, their Persian king. With the aid of Athenian infantry, the rebels burned the city of Sardis. Focusing his revenge on Athens, Darius invaded Greece in 490 B.C. but was defeated at Marathon near Athens. He died while preparing a new invasion that his son, Xerxes, would now push forward.

[10]Persian commanders in the failed campaign of 490 B.C.

sider the matter, I find several advantages in the venture; if we crush the Athenians and their neighbors in the Peloponnese,[11] we shall so extend the empire of Persia that its boundaries will be God's own sky, so that the sun will not look down upon any land beyond the boundaries of what is ours. With your help I shall pass through Europe from end to end and make it all one country. For if what I am told is true, there is not a city or nation in the world which will be able to withstand us, once these are out of the way. Thus the guilty and the innocent alike shall bear the yoke of servitude.

"If, then, you wish to gain my favor, each one of you must present himself willingly and in good heart on the day which I shall name; whoever brings with him the best equipped body of troops I will reward with those marks of distinction held in greatest value by our countrymen. That is what you must do; but so that I shall not appear to consult only my own whim, I will throw the whole matter into open debate, and ask any of you who may wish to do so, to express his views."

The first to speak after the king was Mardonius. "Of all Persians who have ever lived," he began, "and of all who are yet to be born, you, my lord, are the greatest. Every word you have spoken is true and excellent, and you will not allow the wretched Ionians[12] in Europe to make fools of us. It would indeed be an odd thing if we who have defeated and enslaved the Sacae, Indians, Ethiopians, Assyrians, and many other great nations for no fault of their own, but merely to extend the boundaries of our empire, should fail now to punish the Greeks who have been guilty of injuring us without provocation. Have we anything to fear from them? The size of their army? Their wealth? The question is absurd; we know how they fight; we know how slender their resources are. People of their race we have already reduced to subjection—I mean the Greeks of Asia, Ionians, Aeolians, and Dorians.[13] I myself before now have had some experience of these men, when under orders from your father I invaded their country; and I got as far as Macedonia—indeed almost to Athens itself—without a single soldier daring to oppose me. Yet, from what I hear, the Greeks are pugnacious enough, and start fights on the spur of the moment without sense or judgment to justify them. When they declare war on each other, they go off together to the smoothest and levellest bit of ground they can find, and have their battle on it—with the result that even the victors never get off without heavy losses, and as for the losers— well, they're wiped out. Now surely, as they all talk the same language, they ought

---

[11]A peninsula, the southern part of Greece.

[12]Greek "tribal" group that included those in Asia Minor who revolted against their Persian lords in 499 B.C. and their kinsmen in Athens, the source of Ionian power.

[13]All three tribal groups—Ionian, Aeolian, and Dorian—had some of their population migrate to Asia Minor, where they had become subjects of the Persian Empire.

to be able to find a better way of settling their differences: by negotiation, for instance, or an interchange of views—indeed by anything rather than fighting. Or if it is really impossible to avoid coming to blows, they might at least employ the elements of strategy and look for a strong position to fight from. In any case, the Greeks, with their absurd notions of warfare, never even thought of opposing me when I led my army to Macedonia.

"Well then, my lord, who is likely to resist you when you march against them with the millions of Asia at your back, and the whole Persian fleet? Believe me, it is not in the Greek character to take so desperate a risk. But should I be wrong and they be so foolish as to do battle with us, then they will learn that we are the best soldiers in the world. Nevertheless, let us take this business seriously and spare no pains; success is never automatic in this world—nothing is achieved without trying."

Xerxes's proposals were made to sound plausible enough by these words of Mardonius, and when he stopped speaking there was a silence. For a while nobody dared to put forward the opposite view, until Artabanus, taking courage from the fact of his relationship to the king—he was a son of Hystaspes and therefore Xerxes's uncle—rose to speak. "My lord," he said, "without a debate in which both sides of a question are expressed, it is not possible to choose the better course. All one can do is to accept whatever it is that has been proposed. But grant a debate, and there is a fair choice to be made. We cannot assess the purity of gold merely by looking at it: we test it by rubbing it on other gold—then we can tell which is the purer. I warned your father—Darius my own brother—not to attack the Scythians,[14] those wanderers who live in a cityless land. But he would not listen to me. Confident in his power to subdue them he invaded their country, and before he came home again many fine soldiers who marched with him were dead. But you, my lord, mean to attack a nation greatly superior to the Scythians: a nation with the highest reputation for valor both on land and at sea. It is my duty to tell you what you have to fear from them: you have said you mean to bridge the Hellespont and march through Europe to Greece. Now suppose—and it is not impossible—that you were to suffer a reverse by sea or land, or even both. These Greeks are said to be great fighters—and indeed one might well guess as much from the fact that the Athenians alone destroyed the great army we sent to attack them under Datis and Artaphernes. Or, if you will, suppose they were to succeed upon one element only—suppose they fell upon our fleet and defeated it, and then sailed to the Hellespont and destroyed the bridge: then, my lord, you would indeed be in peril. It is no special wisdom of my own that makes me argue as I do; but just such a disaster as I have suggested did, in fact, very nearly overtake us when your father bridged the Thracian Bosphorus and the Danube to take his army into Scythia. You will remember how on that occasion the Scythians

---

[14]Fierce nomadic tribes living north of the Black Sea.

went to all lengths in their efforts to induce the Ionian guard to break the Danube bridge, and how Histiaeus, the lord of Miletus, merely by following the advice of the other Ionian despots instead of rejecting it, as he did, had it in his power to ruin Persia. Surely it is a dreadful thing even to hear said, that the fortunes of the king once wholly depended upon a single man.

"I urge you, therefore, to abandon this plan; take my advice and do not run any such terrible risk when there is no necessity to do so. Break up this conference; turn the matter over quietly by yourself, and then, when you think fit, announce your decision. Nothing is more valuable to a man than to lay his plans carefully and well; even if things go against him, and forces he cannot control bring his enterprise to nothing, he still has the satisfaction of knowing that it was not his fault—the plans were all laid; if, on the other hand, he leaps headlong into danger and succeeds by luck—well, that's a bit of luck indeed, but he still has the shame of knowing that he was ill prepared.

"You know, my lord, that amongst living creatures it is the great ones that God [Zeus] smites with his thunder, out of envy of their pride. The little ones do not vex him. It is always the great buildings and the tall trees which are struck by lightning. It is God's way to bring the lofty low. Often a great army is destroyed by a little one, when God in his envy puts fear into the men's hearts, or sends a thunderstorm, and they are cut to pieces in a way they do not deserve. For God tolerates pride in none but himself. Haste is the mother of failure—and for failure we always pay a heavy price; it is in delay our profit lies—perhaps it may not immediately be apparent, but we shall find it, sure enough, as time goes on. . . .

"This, my lord, is the advice I offer you. . . ."

After Xerxes had made his decision to fight, he had a third dream. The Magi[15] were consulted about its significance and expressed the opinion that it portended the conquest of the world and its total subjection to Persia. In the dream, Xerxes had imagined himself crowned with olive, of which the branches spread all over the earth; then the crown had suddenly vanished from his head. After the Magi's favorable interpretation, all the Persian nobles who had attended the conference hurried home to their respective provinces; and as every one of them hoped to win the reward which Xerxes had offered, no pains were spared in the subsequent preparations, and Xerxes, in the process of assembling his armies, had every corner of the continent ransacked. For the four years following the conquest of Egypt the mustering of troops and the provision of stores and equipment continued, and towards the close of the fifth Xerxes, at the head of his enormous force, began his march.

The army was indeed far greater than any other in recorded history. . . .

There was not a nation in Asia that he did not take with him against Greece; save for the great rivers there was not a stream his army drank from that was not

---

[15]Persian priest-prophets.

drunk dry. Some nations provided ships, others formed infantry units; from some cavalry was requisitioned, from others horse-transports and crews; from others, again, warships for floating bridges, or provisions and naval craft of various kinds. . . .

In Sardis Xerxes's first act was to send representatives to every place in Greece except Athens and Sparta with a demand for earth and water and a further order to prepare entertainment for him against his coming. This renewed demand for submission was due to his confident belief that the Greeks who had previously refused to comply with the demand of Darius would now be frightened into complying with his own. It was to prove whether or not he was right that he took this step.

He then prepared to move forward to Abydos, where a bridge had already been constructed across the Hellespont from Asia to Europe. Between Sestos and Madytus in the Chersonese there is a rocky headland running out into the water opposite Abydos. It was here not long afterwards that the Greeks under Xanthippus the son of Ariphron took Artaÿctes the Persian governor of Sestos, and nailed him alive to a plank—he was the man who collected women in the temple of Protesilaus at Elaeus and committed various acts of sacrilege. This headland was the point to which Xerxes's engineers carried their two bridges from Abydos—a distance of seven furlongs.[16] One was constructed by the Phoenicians using flax cables, the other by the Egyptians with papyrus cables. The work was successfully completed, but a subsequent storm of great violence smashed it up and carried everything away. Xerxes was very angry when he learned of the disaster, and gave orders that the Hellespont should receive three hundred lashes and have a pair of fetters [leg shackles] thrown into it. I have heard before now that he also sent people to brand it with hot irons. He certainly instructed the men with the whips to utter, as they wielded them, the barbarous and presumptuous words: "You salt and bitter stream, your master lays this punishment upon you for injuring him, who never injured you. But Xerxes the King will cross you, with or without your permission. No man sacrifices to you, and you deserve the neglect by your acid and muddy waters." In addition to punishing the Hellespont Xerxes gave orders that the men responsible for building the bridges should have their heads cut off. The men who received these invidious orders duly carried them out, and other engineers completed the work. . . .

No sooner had the troops begun to move than the sun vanished from his place in the sky and it grew dark as night, though the weather was perfectly clear and cloudless. Xerxes, deeply troubled, asked the Magi to interpret the significance of this strange phenomenon, and was given to understand that God meant to foretell to the Greeks the eclipse of their cities—for it was the sun which gave

---

[16]A furlong is a unit of distance equal to 220 yards, an eighth of a mile. (The translator here has converted Greek into English measurements.)

warning of the future to Greece, just as the moon did to Persia. Having heard this Xerxes continued the march in high spirits.

The army, however, had not gone far when Pythius the Lydian, in alarm at the sign from heaven, was emboldened by the presents he had received to come to Xerxes with a request. "Master," he said, "there is a favor I should like you to grant me—a small thing, indeed, for you to perform, but to me of great importance, should you consent to do so." Xerxes, who thought the request would be almost anything but what it actually turned out to be, agreed to grant it and told Pythius to say what it was he wanted. This generous answer raised Pythius's hopes, and he said, "My lord, I have five sons, and it happens that every one of them is serving in your army in the campaign against Greece. I am an old man, Sire, and I beg you in pity to release from service one of my sons—the eldest—to take care of me and my property. Take the other four—and may you return with your purpose accomplished."

Xerxes was furiously angry. "You miserable fellow," he cried, "have you the face to mention your son, when I, in person, am marching to the war against Greece with my sons and brothers and kinsmen and friends—*you,* my slave, whose duty it was to come with me with every member of your house, including your wife? Mark my words: it is through the ears you can touch a man to pleasure or rage—let the spirit which dwells there hear good things, and it will fill the body with delight; let it hear bad, and it will swell with fury. When you did me good service, and offered more, you cannot boast that you were more generous than I; and now your punishment will be less than your impudence deserves. Yourself and four of your sons are saved by the entertainment you gave me; but you shall pay with the life of the fifth, whom you cling to most."

Having answered Pythius in these words Xerxes at once gave orders that the men to whom such duties fell should find Pythius's eldest son and cut him in half and put the two halves one on each side of the road, for the army to march out between them. The order was performed. . . .

From the European shore Xerxes watched his troops coming over under the whips. The crossing occupied seven days and nights without a break. There is a story that some time after Xerxes had passed the bridge, a native of the country thereabouts exclaimed: "Why, O God, have you assumed the shape of a man of Persia, and changed your name to Xerxes, in order to lead everyone in the world to the conquest and devastation of Greece? You could have destroyed Greece without going to that trouble."

After the whole army had reached the European shore and the forward march had begun, an extraordinary thing occurred—a mare gave birth to a hare. Xerxes paid no attention to this omen, though the significance of it was easy enough to understand. Clearly it meant that he was to lead an army against Greece with the greatest pomp and circumstance, and then to come running for his life back to the place he started from. There had previously been another strange and ominous occurrence in Sardis, when a mule dropped a foal with a double set of sexual organs, male and female—the former uppermost. Xerxes, however, ignored both omens and continued his march at the head of the army. . . .

As nobody has left a record, I cannot state the precise number of men provided by each separate nation, but the grand total, excluding the naval contingent, turned out to be 1,700,000.[17] The counting was done by first packing ten thousand men as close together as they could stand and drawing a circle round them on the ground; they were then dismissed, and a fence, about navel-high, was constructed round the circle; finally other troops were marched into the area thus enclosed and dismissed in their turn, until the whole army had been counted. After the counting, the army was reorganized in divisions according to nationality. . . .

Having sailed from one end to the other of the line of anchored ships, Xerxes went ashore again and sent for Demaratus,[18] the son of Ariston, who was accompanying him in the march to Greece. "Demaratus," he said, "it would give me pleasure at this point to put to you a few questions. You are a Greek, and a native, moreover, of by no means the meanest or weakest city in that country—as I learn not only from yourself but from the other Greeks I have spoken with. Tell me, then—will the Greeks dare to lift a hand against me? My own belief is that all the Greeks and all the other western peoples gathered together would be insufficient to withstand the attack of my army—and still more so if they are not united. But it is your opinion upon this subject that I should like to hear."

"My lord," Demaratus replied, "is it a true answer you would like, or merely an agreeable one?"

"Tell me the truth," said the king: "and I promise that you will not suffer by it." Encouraged by this Demaratus continued: "My lord, you bid me speak nothing but the truth, to say nothing which might later be proved a lie. Very well then; this is my answer: poverty is my country's inheritance from of old, but valor she won for herself by wisdom and the strength of law. By her valor Greece now keeps both poverty and bondage at bay.

"I think highly of all Greeks of the Dorian lands, but what I am about to say will apply not to all Dorians, but to the Spartans only. First then, they will not under any circumstances accept terms from you which would mean slavery for Greece; secondly, they will fight you even if the rest of Greece submits. Moreover, there is no use in asking if their numbers are adequate to enable them to do this; suppose a thousand of them take the field—then that thousand will fight you; and so will any number, greater than this or less."

---

[17]Herodotus's figure is impossibly huge. The estimates of modern scholars are, nevertheless, still impressive. They range from one hundred thousand to four hundred thousand combatants in the Persian army, and from seven hundred to one thousand ships in the navy.

[18]A former king of Sparta who had been dethroned by his own countrymen on a false charge of illegitimacy.

Xerxes laughed. "My dear Demaratus," he exclaimed, "what an extraordinary thing to say! Do you really suppose a thousand men would fight an army like mine? Now tell me, would *you*, who were once, as you say, king of these people, be willing at this moment to fight ten men single-handed? I hardly think so; yet, if things in Sparta are really as you have described them, then, according to your laws, you as king ought to take on a double share—so that if every Spartan is a match for ten men of mine, I should expect you to be a match for twenty. Only in that way can you prove the truth of your claim. But if you Greeks, who think so much of yourselves, are all of the size and quality of those I have spoken with when they have visited my court—and of yourself, Demaratus—there is some danger of your words being nothing but an empty boast. But let me put my point as reasonably as I can—how is it possible that a thousand men, or ten thousand, or fifty thousand, should stand up to an army as big as mine, especially if they were not under a single master, but all perfectly free to do as they pleased? Suppose them to have five thousand men: in that case we should be more than a thousand to one! If, like ours, their troops were subject to the control of a single man, then possibly for fear of him, in spite of the disparity in numbers, they might show some sort of factitious courage, or let themselves be whipped into battle; but, as every man is free to follow his fancy, it is not conceivable that they should do either. Indeed, my own opinion is that even on equal terms the Greeks could hardly face the Persians alone. We, too, have this thing that you were speaking of—I do not say it is common, but it does exist; for instance, amongst the Persians in my bodyguard there are men who would willingly fight with three Greeks together. But you know nothing of such things, or you could not talk such nonsense."

"My lord," Demaratus answered, "I knew before I began that if I spoke the truth you would not like it. But, as you demanded the plain truth and nothing less, I told you how things are with the Spartans. Yet you are well aware that I now feel but little affection for my countrymen, who robbed me of my hereditary power and privileges and made me a fugitive without a home—whereas your father welcomed me at his court and gave me the means of livelihood and somewhere to live. Surely it is unreasonable to reject kindness; any sensible man will cherish it. Personally I do not claim to be able to fight ten men—or two; indeed I should prefer not even to fight with one. But should it be necessary—should there be some great cause to urge me on—then nothing would give me more pleasure than to stand up to one of those men of yours who claim to be a match for three Greeks. So it is with the Spartans; fighting singly, they are as good as any, but fighting together they are the best soldiers in the world. They are free—yes—but not entirely free; for they have a master, and that master is Law, which they fear much more than your subjects fear you. Whatever this master commands, they do; and his command never varies: it is never to retreat in battle, however great the odds, but always to stand firm, and to conquer or die. If, my lord, you think that what I have said is nonsense—very well; I am willing henceforward to hold my tongue. This time I spoke because you forced me to speak. In any case, I pray that all may turn out as you desire."

Xerxes burst out laughing at Demaratus's answer, and good-humoredly let him go.

After the conversation I have recorded above, Xerxes . . . continued his march through Thrace towards Greece.

•   •   •

The position, then, was that Xerxes was lying with his force at Trachis in Malian territory, while the Greeks occupied the pass[19] known locally as Pylae—though Thermopylae is the common Greek name. Such were the respective positions of the two armies, one being in control of all the country from Trachis northward, the other of the whole mainland to the south. The Greek force which here await-ed the coming of Xerxes was made up of the following contingents: three hun-dred heavy-armed infantry from Sparta, five hundred from Tegea, five hundred from Mantinea, one hundred twenty from Orchomenus in Arcadia, one thousand from the rest of Arcadia; from Corinth there were four hundred; from Phlius, two hundred; and from Mycenae, eighty. In addition to these troops from the Peloponnese, there were the Boeotian contingents of seven hundred from Thespiae and four hundred from Thebes. The Locrians of Opus and the Phocians had also obeyed the call to arms, the former sending all the men they had, the lat-ter one thousand. The other Greeks had induced these two towns to send troops by a message to the effect that they themselves were merely an advance force, and that the main body of the confederate [allied] army was daily expected; the sea, moreover, was strongly held by the fleet of Athens and Aegina and the other naval forces. Thus there was no cause for alarm—for, after all, it was not a god who threatened Greece, but a man, and there neither was nor ever would be a man who was not born with a good chance of misfortune—and the greater the man, the greater the misfortune. The present enemy was no exception; he too was human, and was sure to be disappointed of his great expectations.

The appeal succeeded, and Opus and Phocis sent their troops to Trachis. The contingents of the various states were under their own officers, but the most respected was Leonidas the Spartan, who was in command of the whole army. Leonidas traced his descent directly back to Heracles,[20] through Anaxandrides and Leon (his father and grandfather), Anaxander, Eurycrates, Polydorus, Alcamenes,

---

[19]The width of the pass, the distance between a high cliff and the sea, was only about four-teen yards.

[20]It was common for aristocrats to trace their lineage back to a famous hero. For a Spartan warrior, Heracles (the Roman Hercules) would have been an especially important ances-tor as he was noted for his strength, courage, and endurance. (Note Xenophon's descrip-tion of the Spartan code of values in Selection 16).

Teleches, Archelaus, Agesilaus, Doryssus, Labotas, Echestratus, Agis, Eurysthenes, Aristodemus, Aristomachus, Cleodaeus—and so to Hyllus, who was Heracles's son. He had come to be king of Sparta quite unexpectedly, for as he had two elder brothers, Cleomenes and Dorieus, he had no thought of himself succeeding to the throne. Dorieus, however, was killed in Sicily, and when Cleomenes also died without an heir, Leonidas found himself next in the succession. He was older than Cleombrotus, Anaxandrides's youngest son, and was, moreover, married to Cleomenes's daughter. The three hundred men whom he brought on this occasion to Thermopylae were chosen by himself, all fathers of living sons. He also took with him the Thebans I mentioned, under the command of Leontiades, the son of Eurymachus. The reason why he made a special point of taking troops from Thebes, and from Thebes only, was that the Thebans were strongly suspected of Persian sympathies, so he called upon them to play their part in the war in order to see if they would answer the call, or openly refuse to join the confederacy. They did send troops, but their secret sympathy was nevertheless with the enemy. Leonidas and his three hundred were sent by Sparta in advance of the main army, in order that the sight of them might encourage the other confederates to fight and prevent them from going over to the enemy, as they were quite capable of doing if they knew that Sparta was hanging back; the intention was, when the Carneia[21] was over (for it was that festival which prevented the Spartans from taking the field in the ordinary way), to leave a garrison in the city and march with all the troops at their disposal. The other allied states proposed to act similarly; for the Olympic festival happened to fall just at this same period. None of them ever expected the battle at Thermopylae to be decided so soon—which was the reason why they sent only advance parties there.

The Persian army was now close to the pass, and the Greeks, suddenly doubting their power to resist, held a conference to consider the advisability of retreat. It was proposed by the Peloponnesians generally that the army should fall back upon the Peloponnese and hold the Isthmus; but when the Phocians and Locrians expressed their indignation at this suggestion, Leonidas gave his voice for staying where they were and sending, at the same time, an appeal for reinforcements to the various states of the confederacy, as their numbers were inadequate to cope with the Persians.

During the conference Xerxes sent a man on horseback to ascertain the strength of the Greek force and to observe what the troops were doing. He had heard before he left Thessaly that a small force was concentrated here, led by the Lacedaemonians [Spartans] under Leonidas of the house of Heracles. The Persian rider approached the camp and took a thorough survey of all he could see—which was not, however, the whole Greek army; for the men on the further side of the wall which, after its reconstruction, was now guarded, were out of sight. He did,

---

[21]Spartan harvest festival.

nonetheless, carefully observe the troops who were stationed on the outside of the wall. At that moment these happened to be Spartans, and some of them were stripped for exercise, while others were combing their hair. The Persian spy watched them in astonishment; nevertheless he made sure of their numbers, and of everything else he needed to know, as accurately as he could, and then rode quietly off. No one attempted to catch him, or took the least notice of him.

Back in his own camp he told Xerxes what he had seen. Xerxes was bewildered; the truth, namely that the Spartans were preparing themselves to die and deal death with all their strength, was beyond his comprehension, and what they were doing seemed to him merely absurd. Accordingly, he sent for Demaratus, the son of Ariston, who had come with the army, and questioned him about the spy's report, in the hope of finding out what the behavior of the Spartans might mean. "Once before," Demaratus said, "when we began our march against Greece, you heard me speak of these men. I told you then how I saw this enterprise would turn out, and you laughed at me. I strive for nothing, my lord, more earnestly than to observe the truth in your presence; so hear me once more. These men have come to fight us for possession of the pass, and for that struggle they are preparing. It is the common practice of the Spartans to pay careful attention to their hair when they are about to risk their lives. But I assure you that if you can defeat these men and the rest of the Spartans who are still at home, there is no other people in the world who will dare to stand firm or lift a hand against you. You have now to deal with the finest kingdom in Greece, and with the bravest men."

Xerxes, unable to believe what Demaratus said, asked further how it was possible that so small a force could fight with his army. "My lord," Demaratus replied, "treat me as a liar, if what I have foretold does not take place." But still Xerxes was unconvinced.

For four days Xerxes waited, in constant expectation that the Greeks would make good their escape; then, on the fifth, when still they had made no move and their continued presence seemed mere impudent and reckless folly, he was seized with rage and sent forward the Medes and Cissians[22] with orders to take them alive and bring them into his presence. The Medes charged, and in the struggle which ensued many fell; but others took their places, and in spite of terrible losses refused to be beaten off. They made it plain enough to anyone, and not least to the king himself, that he had in his army many men, indeed, but few soldiers. All day the battle continued; the Medes, after their rough handling, were at length withdrawn and their place was taken by Hydarnes and his picked Persian troops—the King's Immortals—who advanced to the attack in full confidence of bringing the business to a quick and easy end. But, once engaged, they were no more successful than the Medes had been; all went as before, the two armies fight-

---

[22]Allies of the Persians.

ing in a confined space, the Persians using shorter spears than the Greeks and having no advantage from their numbers.

On the Spartan side it was a memorable fight; they were men who understood war pitted against an inexperienced enemy, and amongst the feints they employed was to turn their backs on a body and pretend to be retreating in confusion, whereupon the enemy would pursue them with a great clatter and roar; but the Spartans, just as the Persians were on them, would wheel and face them and inflict in the new struggle innumerable casualties. The Spartans had their losses too, but not many. At last the Persians, finding that their assaults upon the pass, whether by divisions or by any other way they could think of, were all useless, broke off the engagement and withdrew. Xerxes was watching the battle from where he sat; and it is said that in the course of the attacks three times, in terror for his army, he leapt to his feet.

Next day the fighting began again, but with no better success for the Persians, who renewed their onslaught in the hope that the Greeks, being so few in number, might be badly enough disabled by wounds to prevent further resistance. But the Greeks never slackened; their troops were ordered in divisions corresponding to the states from which they came, and each division took its turn in the line except the Phocian, which had been posted to guard the track over the mountains. So when the Persians found that things were no better for them than on the previous day, they once more withdrew. —

How to deal with the situation Xerxes had no idea; but just then, a man from Malis, Ephialtes, the son of Eurydemus, came, in hope of a rich reward, to tell the king about the track which led over the hills to Thermopylae—and thus he was to prove the death of the Greeks who held the pass.[23] . . .

The Greeks at Thermopylae had their first warning of the death that was coming with the dawn from the seer Megistias, who read their doom in the victims of sacrifice;[24] deserters, too, came in during the night with news of the Persian flank movement, and lastly, just as day was breaking, the look-out men came running from the hills. In council of war their opinions were divided, some urging that they must not abandon their post, others the opposite. The result was that the army split: some dispersed, contingents returning to their various cities, while others made ready to stand by Leonidas. It is said that Leonidas himself dismissed them, to spare their lives, but thought it unbecoming for the Spartans under his command to desert the post which they had originally come to guard.

---

[23] The track led *around* the pass to the rear of the Greek forces. (Ephialtes came from the local region. Some ten years later, when he had returned from his place of refuge, Ephialtes was assassinated.)

[24] Cattle and sheep were the most common victims of the ritual sacrifice to the gods of the Greeks. Seers told the future by examining the slaughtered animals' entrails.

I myself am inclined to think that he dismissed them when he realized that they had no heart for the fight and were unwilling to take their share of the danger; at the same time honor forbade that he himself should go. And indeed by remaining at his post he left a great name behind him, and Sparta did not lose her prosperity, as might otherwise have happened; for right at the outset of the war the Spartans had been told by the Delphic oracle[25] that either their city must be laid to waste by the foreigner or a Spartan king be killed. . . .

I believe it was the thought of this oracle, combined with his wish to lay up for the Spartans a treasure of fame in which no other city should share, that made Leonidas dismiss those troops; I do not think that they deserted, or went off without orders, because of a difference of opinion. Moreover, I am strongly supported in this view by the case of the seer Megistias, who was with the army—an Acarnanian, said to be of the clan of Melampus—who foretold the coming doom from his inspection of the sacrificial victims. He quite plainly received orders from Leonidas to quit Thermopylae, to save him from sharing the army's fate. He refused to go, but he sent his only son, who was serving with the forces.

Thus it was that the confederate troops, by Leonidas's orders, abandoned their posts and left the pass, all except the Thespians and the Thebans who remained with the Spartans.[26] The Thebans were detained by Leonidas as hostages very much against their will; but the Thespians of their own accord refused to desert Leonidas and his men, and stayed, and died with them. They were under the command of Demophilus the son of Diadromes.

In the morning Xerxes poured a libation to the rising sun, and then waited till it was well up before he began to move forward. This was according to Ephialtes's instructions, for the way down from the ridge is much shorter and more direct than the long and circuitous ascent.[27] As the Persian army advanced to the assault, the Greeks under Leonidas, knowing that they were going to their deaths, went out into the wider part of the pass much further than they had done before; in the previous days' fighting they had been holding the wall and making sorties from behind it into the narrow neck, but now they fought outside the narrows. Many of the invaders fell; behind them the company commanders plied their whips indiscriminately, driving the men on. Many fell into the sea and were drowned, and still more were trampled to death by their friends. No one could

---

[25]Delphi, on the Greek mainland, was the site of the ancient world's most famous oracle. Questioners would come there seeking advice on matters concerning religious ritual, morality, and the course of the future.

[26]Some modern estimates number the total Greek forces under Leonidas, including his three hundred Spartans, at about seven thousand men. Before the final stand, when most of the units were allowed to march away, 1,100 stayed with the Spartans.

[27]The instructions allowed time for the troops guided by Ephialtes to reach the rear of the Greek force at about the same time as the main Persian frontal attack.

count the number of the dead. The Greeks, who knew that the enemy were on their way round by the mountain track and that death was inevitable, put forth all their strength and fought with fury and desperation. By this time most of their spears were broken, and they were killing Persians with their swords.

In the course of that fight Leonidas fell, having fought most gallantly, and many distinguished Spartans with him—their names I have learned, as those of men who deserve to be remembered; indeed, I have learned the names of all the three hundred. Amongst the Persian dead, too, were many men of high distinction, including two brothers of Xerxes. . . .

There was a bitter struggle over the body of Leonidas; four times the Greeks drove the enemy off, and at last by their valor rescued it. So it went on, until the troops with Ephialtes were close at hand; and then, when the Greeks knew that they had come, the character of the fighting changed. They withdrew again into the narrow neck of the pass, behind the wall, and took up a position in a single compact body—all except the Thebans—on the little hill at the entrance to the pass, where the stone lion in memory of Leonidas stands today. Here they resisted to the last, with their swords, if they had them, and, if not, with their hands and teeth, until the Persians, coming on from the front over the ruins of the wall and closing in from behind, finally overwhelmed them with missile weapons.

Of all the Spartans and Thespians who fought so valiantly the most signal proof of courage was given by the Spartan Dieneces. It is said that before the battle he was told by a native of Trachis that, when the Persians shot their arrows, there were so many of them that they hid the sun. Dieneces, however, quite unmoved by the thought of the strength of the Persian army, merely remarked: "This is pleasant news that the stranger from Trachis brings us: if the Persians hide the sun, we shall have our battle in the shade." . . .

The dead were buried where they fell, and with them the men who had been killed before those dismissed by Leonidas left the pass. Over them is this inscription, in honor of the whole force:

> Four thousand here from Pelops's land
> Against three million once did stand.

The Spartans have a special epitaph; it runs:

> Go tell the Spartans, you who read:
> We took their orders, and are dead.

[Editor's note: After the battle at Thermopylae the Persians continued their advance. The Athenians evacuated their city which was captured by the Persians who burned down the temples on the Acropolis (the high citadel which dominated the city). In the following months, however, there was a great naval battle in the narrow waters between the island of Salamis and the mainland; there was also a major land battle near Plataea (in 479 B.C.). On both occasions the Persians were totally routed. After those battles never again did a Persian military force threaten the European mainland.]

15

※

Thucydides

HISTORY OF THE PELOPONNESIAN WAR

*T*he Persian Wars, described in Herodotus's account of the heroic Greek stand
  at Thermopylae (Selection 14), were the prelude to Greek glory; the
Peloponnesian War (431–404 B.C.), fought mainly between the major Greek
city–states of Athens and Sparta, brought only suffering and disaster. In the years
following the final victory over the Persians in 479 B.C., democratic Athens
expanded into an imperial power by using the financial contributions from other
city–states, intended for the common defence of Greece, to build up the powerful
Athenian navy and its own economic prosperity. Thus, the conflict with Sparta,
which had the stronger army, was "inevitable" (the historian Thucydides tells us)
because of "the growth of Athenian power and the fear which this caused in
Sparta."

The task of recording and analyzing that bitter struggle of Greek against
Greek fell to Thucydides (ca. 460–400 B.C.). Born in Athens to an aristocratic
and wealthy family, Thucydides was chosen in 424 B.C. to command a fleet
against the Spartans in the northern Aegean Sea. For allowing himself to be out-
maneuvered and defeated by the enemy, he was exiled and did not return to
Athens until 404 B.C. Thucydides thus had ample opportunity to observe the
Peloponnesian War from both sides; he spent his twenty years of exile in various
parts of Greece, recording the tragedy of his own times. Behind his narrative lay
the deeper purpose of searching for an answer to the following question: Why had
Athens, with the fairest prospects of victory, been beaten? Thucydides's History
is, in essence, an analysis of the causes of the Athenian defeat; hence, it has been
well described as a study in the pathology of imperialism and war. It is, in a sense,
a moral history of the Peloponnesian War.

Thucydides's own reflections on issues and motives are found in the forty or more "set speeches" for which the History is famous. These speeches—which appear as direct quotations from the individual participants, but were actually composed by Thucydides—represent a common device in ancient Greek literature. They show the importance of the spoken word in Greek culture. Thucydides, describing his method, stated that "while keeping as closely as possible to the general sense of the words that were actually used, [I] . . . make the speakers say what, in my opinion, was called for by each situation."

The first excerpt contains the most famous speech of the History—the "Funeral Oration" by Pericles, the leading Athenian statesman, in honor of those who died in the war's first campaign. Like Abraham Lincoln's "Gettysburg Address," which bears many similarities to Pericles's speech, it is both an appeal to patriotism and a reasoned explanation of a free and open democracy's superiority to rival forms of government. It represents Pericles's ideal view of what he wished the Athenian citizenry to be.

In the summer following the public funeral, a dreadful plague broke out among the people crowded inside the walls of Athens. The besieged city lost more than a fourth of its inhabitants, a blow from which it never fully recovered. (Pericles died in the following year from the lingering effects of the plague.) Thucydides, too, was a victim, but he recovered. His medical and sociological description of the plague's symptoms and results, included here, is remarkable for its scientific objectivity.

Thucydides says he composed his History (which breaks off, unfinished, with the events of 411 B.C.) so that its readers could "understand clearly the events which happened in the past and which (human nature being what it is) will, at some time or other and in much the same ways, be repeated in the future." It was written "to last forever." The History is impartial and reflective, conveying both the Periclean ideals favored by Thucydides—civilized reason, individual excellence, and democratic moderation—and the war's later moral degeneration and disillusionment. That degeneration resulted in the sacrifice of those ideals to the demands of imperial power and, ultimately, to the brutal facts of everyday survival.

There is in Thucydides's writing none of the sentiment or supernaturalism that make the recitations of Herodotus so entertaining. In fact, Thucydides is contemptuous of oracles and theories of divine causation. Lovers of his objectivity, insight, and explanations of human history entirely in human terms have hailed him as the supreme historian of all time.

PERICLES'S FUNERAL ORATION [430 B.C.]

In the same winter[1] the Athenians, following their annual custom, gave a public funeral for those who had been the first to die in the war. These funerals are held in the following way: two days before the ceremony the bones of the fallen are brought and put in a tent which has been erected, and people make whatever offerings they wish to their own dead. Then there is a funeral procession in which coffins of cypress wood are carried on wagons. There is one coffin for each tribe, which contains the bones of members of that tribe. One empty bier is decorated and carried in the procession: this is for the missing, whose bodies could not be recovered. Everyone who wishes to, both citizens and foreigners, can join in the procession, and the women who are related to the dead are there to make their laments at the tomb. The bones are laid in the public burial-place, which is in the most beautiful quarter outside the city walls. Here the Athenians always bury those who have fallen in war. The only exception is those who died at Marathon,[2] who, because their achievement was considered absolutely outstanding, were buried on the battlefield itself.

When the bones have been laid in the earth, a man chosen by the city for his intellectual gifts and for his general reputation makes an appropriate speech in praise of the dead, and after the speech all depart. This is the procedure at these burials, and all through the war, when the time came to do so, the Athenians followed this ancient custom. Now, at the burial of those who were the first to fall in the war Pericles, the son of Xanthippus, was chosen to make the speech. When the moment arrived, he came forward from the tomb and, standing on a high platform, so that he might be heard by as many people as possible in the crowd, he spoke as follows:

"Many of those who have spoken here in the past have praised the institution of this speech at the close of our ceremony. It seemed to them a mark of honor to our soldiers who have fallen in war that a speech should be made over them. I do not agree. These men have shown themselves valiant in action, and it would be enough, I think, for their glories to be proclaimed in action, as you have just seen it done at this funeral organized by the state. Our belief in the courage and manliness of so many should not be hazarded on the goodness or badness of one man's speech. Then it is not easy to speak with a proper sense of balance, when a man's listeners find it difficult to believe in the truth of what one is saying. The man

---

Thucydides, *History of the Peloponnesian War,* trans. Rex Warner (London: Penguin Books, 1954), pp. 143–156. Copyright © Rex Warner, 1954. Reproduced by permission of Penguin Books Ltd.

[1]431–430 B.C.

[2]The site, twenty-six miles from Athens, where a Greek force, mainly Athenians, defeated the first Persian invasion in 490 B.C.

who knows the facts and loves the dead may well think that an oration tells less than what he knows and what he would like to hear: others who do not know so much may feel envy for the dead, and think the orator over-praises them, when he speaks of exploits that are beyond their own capacities. Praise of other people is tolerable only up to a certain point, the point where one still believes that one could do oneself some of the things one is hearing about. Once you get beyond this point, you will find people becoming jealous and incredulous. However, the fact is that this institution was set up and approved by our forefathers, and it is my duty to follow the tradition and do my best to meet the wishes and the expectations of every one of you.

"I shall begin by speaking about our ancestors, since it is only right and proper on such an occasion to pay them the honor of recalling what they did. In this land of ours there have always been the same people living from generation to generation up till now, and they, by their courage and their virtues, have handed it on to us, a free country. They certainly deserve our praise. Even more so do our fathers deserve it. For to the inheritance they had received they added all the empire we have now, and it was not without blood and toil that they handed it down to us of the present generation. And then we ourselves, assembled here today, who are mostly in the prime of life, have, in most directions, added to the power of our empire and have organized our state in such a way that it is perfectly well able to look after itself both in peace and in war.

"I have no wish to make a long speech on subjects familiar to you all: so I shall say nothing about the warlike deeds by which we acquired our power or the battles in which we or our fathers gallantly resisted our enemies, Greek or foreign. What I want to do is, in the first place, to discuss the spirit in which we faced our trials and also our constitution and the way of life which has made us great. After that I shall speak in praise of the dead, believing that this kind of speech is not inappropriate to the present occasion, and that this whole assembly, of citizens and foreigners, may listen to it with advantage.

"Let me say that our system of government does not copy the institutions of our neighbors. It is more the case of our being a model to others, than of our imitating anyone else. Our constitution is called a democracy because power is in the hands not of a minority but of the whole people. When it is a question of settling private disputes, everyone is equal before the law; when it is a question of putting one person before another in positions of public responsibility, what counts is not membership of a particular class, but the actual ability which the man possesses. No one, so long as he has it in him to be of service to the state, is kept in political obscurity because of poverty. And, just as our political life is free and open, so is our day-to-day life in our relations with each other. We do not get into a state with our next-door neighbor if he enjoys himself in his own way, nor do we give him the kind of black looks which, though they do no real harm, still do hurt people's feelings. We are free and tolerant in our private lives; but in public affairs we keep to the law. This is because it commands our deep respect.

"We give our obedience to those whom we put in positions of authority, and we obey the laws themselves, especially those which are for the protection of the oppressed, and those unwritten laws which it is an acknowledged shame to break.

"And here is another point. When our work is over, we are in a position to enjoy all kinds of recreation for our spirits. There are various kinds of contests and sacrifices regularly throughout the year; in our own homes we find a beauty and a good taste which delight us every day and which drive away our cares. Then the greatness of our city brings it about that all the good things from all over the world flow in to us, so that to us it seems just as natural to enjoy foreign goods as our own local products.

"Then there is a great difference between us and our opponents, in our attitude towards military security. Here are some examples: Our city is open to the world, and we have no periodical deportations in order to prevent people observing or finding out secrets which might be of military advantage to the enemy. This is because we rely, not on secret weapons, but on our own real courage and loyalty. There is a difference, too, in our educational systems. The Spartans, from their earliest boyhood, are submitted to the most laborious training in courage; we pass our lives without all these restrictions, and yet are just as ready to face the same dangers as they are. Here is a proof of this: When the Spartans invade our land, they do not come by themselves, but bring all their allies with them; whereas we, when we launch an attack abroad, do the job by ourselves, and, though fighting on foreign soil, do not often fail to defeat opponents who are fighting for their own hearths and homes. As a matter of fact none of our enemies has ever yet been confronted with our total strength, because we have to divide our attention between our navy and the many missions on which our troops are sent on land. Yet, if our enemies engage a detachment of our forces and defeat it, they give themselves credit for having thrown back our entire army; or, if they lose, they claim that they were beaten by us in full strength. There are certain advantages, I think, in our way of meeting danger voluntarily, with an easy mind, instead of with a laborious training, with natural rather than with state-induced courage. We do not have to spend our time practicing to meet sufferings which are still in the future; and when they are actually upon us we show ourselves just as brave as these others who are always in strict training. This is one point in which, I think, our city deserves to be admired. There are also others:

"Our love of what is beautiful does not lead to extravagance; our love of the things of the mind does not make us soft. We regard wealth as something to be properly used, rather than as something to boast about. As for poverty, no one need be ashamed to admit it: the real shame is in not taking practical measures to escape from it. Here each individual is interested not only in his own affairs but in the affairs of the state as well: even those who are mostly occupied with their own business are extremely well-informed on general politics—this is a peculiarity of ours: we do not say that a man who takes no interest in politics is a man who minds his own business; we say that he has no business here at all. We

Athenians, in our own persons, take our decisions on policy or submit them to proper discussions: for we do not think that there is an incompatibility between words and deeds; the worst thing is to rush into action before the consequences have been properly debated. And this is another point where we differ from other people. We are capable at the same time of taking risks and of estimating them before hand. Others are brave out of ignorance; and, when they stop to think, they begin to fear. But the man who can most truly be accounted brave is he who best knows the meaning of what is sweet in life and of what is terrible, and then goes out undeterred to meet what is to come.

"Again, in questions of general good feeling there is a great contrast between us and most other people. We make friends by doing good to others, not by receiving good from them. This makes our friendship all the more reliable, since we want to keep alive the gratitude of those who are in our debt by showing continued goodwill to them: whereas the feelings of one who owes us something lack the same enthusiasm, since he knows that, when he repays our kindness, it will be more like paying back a debt than giving something spontaneously. We are unique in this. When we do kindnesses to others, we do not do them out of any calculations of profit or loss: we do them without afterthought, relying on our free liberality. Taking everything together then, I declare that our city is an education to Greece, and I declare that in my opinion each single one of our citizens, in all the manifold aspects of life, is able to show himself the rightful lord and owner of his own person, and do this, moreover, with exceptional grace and exceptional versatility. And to show that this is no empty boasting for the present occasion, but real tangible fact, you have only to consider the power which our city possesses and which has been won by those very qualities which I have mentioned. Athens, alone of the states we know, comes to her testing time in a greatness that surpasses what was imagined of her. In her case, and in her case alone, no invading enemy is ashamed at being defeated, and no subject can complain of being governed by people unfit for their responsibilities. Mighty indeed are the marks and monuments of our empire which we have left. Future ages will wonder at us, as the present age wonders at us now. We do not need the praises of Homer, or of anyone else whose words may delight us for the moment, but whose estimation of facts will fall short of what is really true. For our adventurous spirit has forced an entry into every sea and into every land; and everywhere we have left behind us everlasting memorials of good done to our friends or suffering inflicted on our enemies.

"This, then, is the kind of city for which these men, who could not bear the thought of losing her, nobly fought and nobly died. It is only natural that every one of us who survive them should be willing to undergo hardships in her service. And it was for this reason that I have spoken at such length about our city, because I wanted to make it clear that for us there is more at stake than there is for others who lack our advantages; also I wanted my words of praise for the dead to be set in the bright light of evidence. And now the most important of these words has been spoken. I have sung the praises of our city; but it was the courage and gallantry of these men, and of people like them, which made her splendid. Nor would you find it true in the case of many of the Greeks, as it is true of them, that no words can do more than justice to their deeds.

"To me it seems that the consummation which has overtaken these men shows us the meaning of manliness in its first revelation and in its final proof. Some of them, no doubt, had their faults; but what we ought to remember first is their gallant conduct against the enemy in defence of their native land. They have blotted out evil with good, and done more service to the commonwealth than they ever did harm in their private lives. No one of these men weakened because he wanted to go on enjoying his wealth: no one put off the awful day in the hope that he might live to escape his poverty and grow rich. More to be desired than such things, they chose to check the enemy's pride. This, to them, was a risk most glorious, and they accepted it, willing to strike down the enemy and relinquish everything else. As for success or failure, they left that in the doubtful hands of Hope, and when the reality of battle was before their faces, they put their trust in their own selves. In the fighting, they thought it more honorable to stand their ground and suffer death than to give in and save their lives. So they fled from the reproaches of men, abiding with life and limb the brunt of battle; and, in a small moment of time, the climax of their lives, a culmination of glory, not of fear, were swept away from us.

"So and such they were, these men—worthy of their city. We who remain behind may hope to be spared their fate, but must resolve to keep the same daring spirit against the foe. It is not simply a question of estimating the advantages in theory. I could tell you a long story (and you know it as well as I do) about what is to be gained by beating the enemy back. What I would prefer is that you should fix your eyes every day on the greatness of Athens as she really is, and should fall in love with her. When you realize her greatness, then reflect that what made her great was men with a spirit of adventure, men who knew their duty, men who were ashamed to fall below a certain standard. If they ever failed in an enterprise, they made up their minds that at any rate the city should not find their courage lacking to her, and they gave to her the best contribution that they could. They gave her their lives, to her and to all of us, and for their own selves they won praises that never grow old, the most splendid of sepulchres—not the sepulchre in which their bodies are laid, but where their glory remains eternal in men's minds, always there on the right occasion to stir others to speech or to action. For famous men have the whole earth as their memorial: it is not only the inscriptions on their graves in their own country that mark them out; no, in foreign lands also, not in any visible form but in people's hearts, their memory abides and grows. It is for you to try to be like them. Make up your minds that happiness depends on being free, and freedom depends on being courageous. Let there be no relaxation in face of the perils of the war. The people who have most excuse for despising death are not the wretched and unfortunate, who have no hope of doing well for themselves, but those who run the risk of a complete reversal in their lives, and who would feel the difference most intensely, if things went wrong for them. Any intelligent man would find a humiliation caused by his own slackness more painful to bear than death, when death comes to him unperceived, in battle, and in the confidence of his patriotism.

"For these reasons I shall not commiserate with those parents of the dead, who are present here. Instead I shall try to comfort them. They are well aware that they have grown up in a world where there are many changes and chances. But this is good fortune—for men to end their lives with honor, as these have done, and for you honorably to lament them: their life was set to a measure where death and happiness went hand in hand. I know that it is difficult to convince you of this. When you see other people happy you will often be reminded of what used to make you happy too. One does not feel sad at not having some good thing which is outside one's experience: real grief is felt at the loss of something which one is used to. All the same, those of you who are of the right age must bear up and take comfort in the thought of having more children. In your own homes these new children will prevent you from brooding over those who are no more, and they will be a help to the city, too, both in filling the empty places, and in assuring her security. For it is impossible for a man to put forward fair and honest views about our affairs if he has not, like everyone else, children whose lives may be at stake. As for those of you who are now too old to have children, I would ask you to count as gain the greater part of your life, in which you have been happy, and remember that what remains is not long, and let your hearts be lifted up at the thought of the fair fame of the dead. One's sense of honor is the only thing that does not grow old, and the last pleasure, when one is worn out with age, is not, as the poet said, making money,[3] but having the respect of one's fellow men.

"As for those of you here who are sons or brothers of the dead, I can see a hard struggle in front of you. Everyone always speaks well of the dead, and, even if you rise to the greatest heights of heroism, it will be a hard thing for you to get the reputation of having come near, let alone equalled, their standard. When one is alive, one is always liable to the jealousy of one's competitors, but when one is out of the way, the honor one receives is sincere and unchallenged.

"Perhaps I should say a word or two on the duties of women to those among you who are now widowed. I can say all I have to say in a short word of advice. Your great glory is not to be inferior to what God has made you, and the greatest glory of a woman is to be least talked about by men, whether they are praising

---

[3]A reference to that worldly view exemplified by a well-known remark of Simonides (ca. 556–468 B.C.), a famous poet and businessman. When criticized for his love of money, he replied that, since he had been deprived by old age of all other pleasures, he could still be comforted by profit.

you or criticizing you. I have now, as the law demanded, said what I had to say. For the time being our offerings to the dead have been made, and for the future their children will be supported at the public expense by the city, until they come of age. This is the crown and prize which she offers, both to the dead and to their children, for the ordeals which they have faced. Where the rewards of valor are the greatest, there you will find also the best and bravest spirits among the people. And now, when you have mourned for your dear ones, you must depart."

THE PLAGUE [430 B.C.]

In this way the public funeral was conducted in the winter that came at the end of the first year of the war. At the beginning of the following summer the Peloponnesians[4] and their allies, with two-thirds of their total forces as before, invaded Attica,[5] again under the command of the Spartan King Archidamus, the son of Zeuxidamus. Taking up their positions, they set about the devastation of the country.

They had not been many days in Attica before the plague first broke out among the Athenians. Previously attacks of the plague had been reported from many other places in the neighborhood of Lemnos[6] and elsewhere, but there was no record of the disease being so virulent anywhere else or causing so many deaths as it did in Athens. At the beginning the doctors were quite incapable of treating the disease because of their ignorance of the right methods. In fact mortality among the doctors was the highest of all, since they came more frequently in contact with the sick. Nor was any other human art or science of any help at all. Equally useless were prayers made in the temples, consultation of oracles, and so forth; indeed, in the end people were so overcome by their sufferings that they paid no further attention to such things.

The plague originated, so they say, in Ethiopia in upper Egypt, and spread from there into Egypt itself and Libya and much of the territory of the King of Persia. In the city of Athens it appeared suddenly, and the first cases were among the population of Piraeus,[7] where there were no wells at that time, so that it was supposed by them that the Peloponnesians had poisoned the reservoirs. Later, however, it appeared also in the upper city, and by this time the deaths were greatly increasing in number. As to the question of how it could first have come about

---

[4]The Peloponnesian peninsula forms the south of Greece; its dominant city-state was Sparta.

[5]The mountainous region around Athens, Attica's chief city.

[6]An island in the Aegean Sea colonized by kinsmen of the Athenians.

[7]The chief port of Athens, five miles from the central city.

or what causes can be found adequate to explain its powerful effect on nature, I must leave that to be considered by other writers, with or without medical experience. I myself shall merely describe what it was like, and set down the symptoms, knowledge of which will enable it to be recognized, if it should ever break out again. I had the disease myself and saw others suffering from it.

That year, as is generally admitted, was particularly free from all other kinds of illness, though those who did have any illness previously all caught the plague in the end. In other cases, however, there seemed to be no reason for the attacks. People in perfect health suddenly began to have burning feelings in the head; their eyes became red and inflamed; inside their mouths there was bleeding from the throat and tongue, and the breath became unnatural and unpleasant. The next symptoms were sneezing and hoarseness of voice, and before long the pain settled on the chest and was accompanied by coughing. Next the stomach was affected with stomach-aches and with vomitings of every kind of bile that has been given a name by the medical profession, all this being accompanied by great pain and difficulty. In most cases there were attacks of ineffectual retching, producing violent spasms; this sometimes ended with this stage of the disease, but sometimes continued long afterwards. Externally the body was not very hot to the touch, nor was there any pallor: the skin was rather reddish and livid, breaking out into small pustules and ulcers. But inside there was a feeling of burning, so that people could not bear the touch even of the lightest linen clothing, but wanted to be completely naked, and indeed most of all would have liked to plunge into cold water. Many of the sick who were uncared for actually did so, plunging into the water-tanks in an effort to relieve a thirst which was unquenchable; for it was just the same with them whether they drank much or little. Then all the time they were afflicted with insomnia and the desperate feeling of not being able to keep still.

In the period when the disease was at its height, the body, so far from wasting away, showed surprising powers of resistance to all the agony, so that there was still some strength left on the seventh or eighth day, which was the time when, in most cases, death came from the internal fever. But if people survived this critical period, then the disease descended to the bowels, producing violent ulcerations and uncontrollable diarrhoea, so that most of them died later as a result of the weakness caused by this. For the disease, first settling in the head, went on to affect every part of the body in turn, and even when people escaped its worst effects, it still left its traces on them by fastening upon the extremities of the body. It affected the genitals, the fingers, and the toes, and many of those who recovered lost the use of these members; some, too, went blind. There were some also who, when they first began to get better, suffered from a total loss of memory, not knowing who they were themselves and being unable to recognize their friends.

Words indeed fail one when one tries to give a general picture of this disease; and as for the sufferings of individuals, they seemed almost beyond the capacity of human nature to endure. Here in particular is a point where this plague showed itself to be something quite different from ordinary diseases: though there were many dead bodies lying about unburied, the birds and animals that eat human flesh either did not come near them or, if they did taste the flesh, died of it afterwards. Evidence for this may be found in the fact that there was a complete disappearance of all birds of prey: they were not to be seen either round the bodies or anywhere else. But dogs, being domestic animals, provided the best opportunity of observing this effect of the plague.

These, then, were the general features of the disease, though I have omitted all kinds of peculiarities which occurred in various individual cases. Meanwhile, during all this time there was no serious outbreak of any of the usual kinds of illness; if any such cases did occur, they ended in the plague. Some died in neglect, some in spite of every possible care being taken of them. As for a recognized method of treatment, it would be true to say that no such thing existed: what did good in some cases did harm in others. Those with naturally strong constitutions were no better able than the weak to resist the disease, which carried away all alike, even those who were treated and dieted with the greatest care. The most terrible thing of all was the despair into which people fell when they realized that they had caught the plague; for they would immediately adopt an attitude of utter hopelessness, and, by giving in in this way, would lose their powers of resistance. Terrible, too, was the sight of people dying like sheep through having caught the disease as a result of nursing others. This indeed caused more deaths than anything else. For when people were afraid to visit the sick, then they died with no one to look after them; indeed, there were many houses in which all the inhabitants perished through lack of any attention. When, on the other hand, they did visit the sick, they lost their own lives, and this was particularly true of those who made it a point of honor to act properly. Such people felt ashamed to think of their own safety and went into their friends' houses at times when even the members of the household were so overwhelmed by the weight of their calamities that they had actually given up the usual practice of making laments for the dead. Yet still the ones who felt most pity for the sick and the dying were those who had had the plague themselves and had recovered from it. They knew what it was like and at the same time felt themselves to be safe, for no one caught the disease twice, or, if he did, the second attack was never fatal. Such people were congratulated on all sides, and they themselves were so elated at the time of their recovery that they fondly imagined that they could never die of any other disease in the future.

A factor which made matters much worse than they were already was the removal of people from the country into the city,[8] and this particularly affected the incomers. There were no houses for them, and, living as they did during the hot season in badly ventilated huts, they died like flies. The bodies of the dying

---

[8]This was done because of the war raging outside the city's walls.

were heaped one on top of the other, and half-dead creatures could be seen staggering about in the streets or flocking around the fountains in their desire for water. The temples in which they took up their quarters were full of the dead bodies of people who had died inside them. For the catastrophe was so overwhelming that men, not knowing what would happen next to them, became indifferent to every rule of religion or of law. All the funeral ceremonies which used to be observed were now disorganized, and they buried the dead as best they could. Many people, lacking the necessary means of burial because so many deaths had already occurred in their households, adopted the most shameless methods. They would arrive first at a funeral pyre that had been made by others, put their own dead upon it and set it alight; or, finding another pyre burning, they would throw the corpse that they were carrying on top of the other one and go away.

In other respects also Athens owed to the plague the beginnings of a state of unprecedented lawlessness. Seeing how quick and abrupt were the changes of fortune which came to the rich who suddenly died and to those who had previously been penniless but now inherited their wealth, people now began openly to venture on acts of self-indulgence which before then they used to keep dark. Thus they resolved to spend their money quickly and to spend it on pleasure, since money and life alike seemed equally ephemeral. As for what is called honor, no one showed himself willing to abide by its laws, so doubtful was it whether one would survive to enjoy the name for it. It was generally agreed that what was both honorable and valuable was the pleasure of the moment and everything that might conceivably contribute to that pleasure. No fear of god or law of man had a restraining influence. As for the gods, it seemed to be the same thing whether one worshiped them or not, when one saw the good and the bad dying indiscriminately. As for offences against human law, no one expected to live long enough to be brought to trial and punished: instead everyone felt that already a far heavier sentence had been passed on him and was hanging over him, and that before the time for its execution arrived it was only natural to get some pleasure out of life.

This, then, was the calamity which fell upon Athens, and the times were hard indeed, with men dying inside the city and the land outside being laid waste.

16

꤮

Xenophon

THE GOVERNMENT OF SPARTA

T*he heroic stand at Thermopylae of the three hundred Spartans (described by
Herodotus in Selection 14) was a clear fulfillment of the code under which
they had been reared. Sparta had admirers beyond its own borders, particularly
among aristocrats and the wealthy. In the late fifth century B.C. pro-Spartan, anti-
democratic sentiment was strong among followers of the Athenian philosopher
Socrates and among supporters of the reactionary government set up in Athens by
the victorious Spartans after the disastrous Peloponnesian War (431–404 B.C.).
That war, so well described by Thucydides in the preceding selection, set the Greek
city-states against each other, with Athens and Sparta as the primary antagonists.*

*One of the followers of Socrates was Xenophon (ca. 428–354 B.C.), an aristo-
cratic property-holding Athenian. After the downfall of the reactionary party, he
was among those Greeks who, in 401 B.C., joined the mercenary army of a prince
who claimed the throne of Persia. The collapse of this expedition led to a perilous
retreat of hundreds of miles through Persian territory to the Black Sea and safety.
Later, Xenophon campaigned under the king of Sparta against the Persians.
During his long absence from Athens, he was declared an exile and his property
was confiscated. For the next twenty years, Xenophon lived in retirement on a
country estate near Olympia given him by the Spartans, whom he greatly admired.
With ample opportunity to observe it directly, he fully embraced the value the
Spartans placed on their social organization and customs. He enjoyed his years as
a country gentleman on Spartan-held territory, hunting and writing vigorously.*

Xenophon's best-known work is the Anabasis *("March Up Country"), a spirited account of the long retreat, of which he had been the leader. He also wrote
three books about Socrates, and a history continuing from where Thucydides left
off in his* History of the Peloponnesian War. *His* Government of Sparta, *reprint-*

ed here in part, is perhaps the most detailed account of the Spartan way of life available to us. We can see clearly the rigid, proud conservatism of a society where "senators" had to be at least sixty years of age and members of the citizens' assembly (a merely consultative body) had to be at least thirty.

The influence of Sparta, in proportion to its population, is quite astonishing. In 480 B.C., when King Leonidas fought the Persians at Thermopylae, there were only about eight thousand Spartan citizens; by the time Xenophon settled in their territory, less than a century later, there were only about two thousand.

Not long after Xenophon's death, this regimented society—whose creation is attributed to Lycurgus, an ancient (and probably legendary) lawgiver—broke down forever. Perhaps this occurred precisely because of that same soldierly, stubborn inflexibility that Xenophon regards as a unique asset. For example, the Spartans regarded themselves as a unique race whose code forbade intermarrying with other groups. This attitude eventually contributed to the steady decline in the number of Spartan citizens. In any case, enactment of that code, which Xenophon sees as the basic foundation of Spartan greatness, can be dated at about 600 B.C. (The original reason for the code may very well have been the Spartans' need to control their helots [serfs], who vastly outnumbered their citizen-masters.) Certainly, the rigid Spartan code of Lycurgus is in marked contrast to the Athenian ideals of democratic openness described in the preceding selection by Pericles/Thucydides.

Of all the distinction won by Sparta at Thermopylae and, later, in the Peloponnesian War, nothing remained but an aristocratic warrior tradition. It was a tradition, however, destined for a long life. Through Xenophon and Plato, and later Plutarch (the Roman biographer), the Spartan ideal of breeding and discipline passed on to the ruling classes of Europe, whose education, from the fifteenth to the mid-twentieth centuries, was based on the Greek and Roman classics.

LAWS AND CUSTOMS OF SPARTANS
The Regulations of Lycurgus Respecting Marriage and the Treatment of Children

Reflecting once how Sparta, one of the least populous of states, had proved the most powerful and celebrated city in Greece, I wondered by what means this result had been produced. When I proceeded, however, to contemplate the institutions of the Spartans, I wondered no longer.

Xenophon, *The Government of Lacedaemon,* in *Xenophon's Minor Works,* trans. J. S. Watson (London: Bell [Bohn Classical Library], 1878), 204–209, 212–221. Adapted by the editor.

Lycurgus, who made the laws[1] for them, by obedience to which they have flourished, I not only admire, but consider to have been in the fullest sense a wise man; for he rendered his country preeminent in prosperity, not by imitating other states, but by making laws contrary to those of most governments.

With regard, for example, to the procreation of children, that I may begin from the beginning, other people feed their young women, who are about to produce offspring, and who are of the class regarded as well brought up, on the most moderate quantity of vegetable food possible, and on the least possible quantity of meat, while they either keep them from wine altogether, or allow them to use it only when mixed with water; and as the greater number of the men engaged in trades are sedentary, so the rest of the Greeks think it proper that their young women should sit quietly and spin wool. But how can we expect that women thus treated should produce a vigorous progeny? Lycurgus, on the contrary, thought that female slaves were competent to furnish clothes; and, considering that the production of children was the noblest duty of the free, he enacted, in the first place, that the female should practice bodily exercises no less than the male sex; and he then appointed for the women contests with one another, just as for the men, expecting that when both parents were rendered strong, a stronger offspring would be born from them.

Observing, too, that the men of other nations, when women were united to husbands, associated with their wives during the early part of their intercourse without restraint, he made enactments quite at variance with this practice; for he ordained that a man should think it a shame to be seen going in to his wife, or coming out from her. When married people meet in this way, they must feel stronger desire for the company of one another, and whatever offspring is produced must thus be rendered far more robust than if the parents were satiated with each other's society.

In addition to these regulations, he also took from the men the liberty of marrying when each of them pleased, and appointed that they should contract marriages only when they were in full bodily vigor, deeming this injunction also conducive to the production of an excellent offspring. Seeing also that if old men chanced to have young wives, they watched their wives with the utmost strictness, he made a law quite opposed to this feeling; for he appointed that an old man should introduce to his wife whatever man in the prime of life he admired for his corporeal and mental qualities, in order that she might have children by him. If, again, a man was unwilling to associate with his wife, and yet was desirous of having proper children, he made a provision also with respect to him, that whatever woman he saw likely to have offspring, and of good disposition, he might, on obtaining the consent of her husband, have children by her. Many similar per-

---

[1] These laws of Sparta had not been written down, but were learned and practiced from generation to generation.

missions he gave; for the women are willing to have two families, and the men to receive brothers to their children, who are equal to them in birth and standing, but have no claim to share in their property.

Let him who wishes, then, consider whether Lycurgus, in thus making enactments different from those of other legislators, in regard to the procreation of children, secured for Sparta a race of men eminent for size and strength.

On the Training and Education of Children

Having given this account of the procreation of children, I wish also to detail the education of those of both sexes. Of the other Greeks, those who say that they bring up their sons best set slaves over them to take charge of them, as soon as the children can understand what is said to them, and send them, at the same time, to schoolmasters, to learn letters, and music, and the exercises of the palaestra.[2] They also render their children's feet delicate by the use of sandals, and weaken their bodies by changes of clothes; and as to food, they regard their appetite as the measure of what they are to take. But Lycurgus, instead of allowing each citizen to set slaves as guardians over his children, appointed a man to have the care of them all, one of those from whom the chief magistrates are chosen; and he is called the paedonomus. He invested this man with full authority to assemble the boys, and, if he found that any one was negligent of his duties, to punish him severely. He assigned him also some of the grown-up boys as whip-carriers, that they might inflict whatever punishment was necessary; so that great dread of disgrace, and great willingness to obey, prevailed among them.

Instead, also, of making their feet soft with sandals, he enacted that they should harden them by going without sandals; thinking that, if they exercised themselves in this state, they would go up steep places with far greater ease, and descend declivities with greater safety; and that they would also leap, and skip, and run faster unshod, if they had their feet inured to doing so, than shod. Instead of being rendered effeminate, too, by a variety of dresses, he made it a practice that they should accustom themselves to one dress throughout the year; thinking that they would thus be better prepared to endure cold and heat.

As to food, he ordained that they should exhort the boys to take only such a quantity as never to be oppressed with overeating, and not to be strangers to living somewhat frugally; supposing that, being thus brought up, they would be the better able, if they should be required, to support toil under a scarcity of supplies, would be the more likely to persevere in exertion, should it be imposed on them, on the same quantity of provisions, and would be less desirous of sauces, more easily satisfied with any kind of food, and pass their lives in greater health. He also considered that the fare which rendered the body slender would be more

---

[2]A public area used for athletic training.

conducive to increasing its stature than that which expanded it with nutriment. Yet that the boys might not suffer too much from hunger, Lycurgus, though he did not allow them to take what they wanted without trouble, gave them liberty to steal certain things to relieve the cravings of nature; and he made it honorable to steal as many cheeses as possible. That he did not give them leave to form schemes for getting food because he was at a loss what to allot them, I suppose no one is ignorant; as it is evident that he who designs to steal must be wakeful during the night, and use deceit, and lay plots; and, if he would gain anything of consequence, must employ spies. All these things, therefore, it is plain that he taught the children from a desire to render them more dexterous in securing provisions, and better qualified for warfare.

Someone may say, "Why, then, if he thought it honorable to steal, did he inflict a great number of whiplashes on him who was caught in the act?" I answer that in other things which men teach, they punish him who does not follow his instructions properly; and that the Spartans accordingly punished those who were detected as having attempted to steal in an improper manner. These boys he gave in charge to others to whip them at the altar of Diana Orthia; designing to show by this enactment that it is possible for a person, after enduring pain for a short time, to enjoy pleasure with credit for a long time. It is also shown by this punishment that, where there is need of activity, the inert person benefits himself the least, and occasions himself most trouble.

In order, too, that the boys, in case of the paedonomus being absent, may never be in want of a leader, he appointed that whoever of the citizens may happen at any time to be present is to assume the direction of them, and to enjoin whatever he may think advantageous for them, and punish them if they do anything wrong. By doing this, Lycurgus has also succeeded in rendering the boys much more modest; for neither boys nor men respect anyone so much as their rulers. And that if, on any occasion, no full-grown man happen to be present, the boys may not even in that case be without a leader, he ordained that the most active of the grown-up youths take the command of each band; so that the boys there are never without a superintendent.

It appears to me that I must say something also of the boys as objects of affection; for this has likewise some reference to education. Among the other Greeks, a man and boy either form a union, as among the Boeotians, and associate together, or, as among the Eleians, the men gain the favor of the youths by means of attentions bestowed upon them; but there are some of the Greeks who prohibit the suitors for the boys' favors from having the least conversation with them. But Lycurgus, acting contrary to all these people also, thought proper, if any man, being himself such as he ought to be, admired the disposition of a youth, and made it his object to render him a faultless friend, and to enjoy his society, to bestow praise upon him, and regarded this as the most excellent kind of education; but if any man showed that his affection were fixed only on the bodily attractions of a youth, Lycurgus, considering this as most unbecoming, appointed that at Sparta suitors for the favors of boys should abstain from intimate connection with them, not less strictly than parents abstain from such intercourse with their children, or children of the same family from that with one another. That such a state of things is disbelieved by some, I am not surprised; for in most states the laws are not at all averse to the love of youths; but Lycurgus, for his part, took such precautions with reference to it.

● ● ●

Meals Taken in Public: On Temperance

The employments which Lycurgus appointed for each period of life have now been almost all specified. What mode of living he instituted for all the citizens, I will next endeavor to explain.

Lycurgus, then, having found the Spartans, like the other Greeks, taking their meals at home, and knowing that most were guilty of excess at them, caused their meals to be taken in public, thinking that his regulations would thus be less likely to be transgressed. He appointed them such a quantity of food that they should neither be overfed nor feel stinted. Many extraordinary supplies are also furnished from what is caught in hunting, and for these the rich sometimes contribute bread; so that the table is never without provisions, as long as they design the meal to last, and yet is never expensive.

Having put a stop likewise to all unnecessary drinking, which weakens alike the body and the mind, he gave permission that everyone should drink when he was thirsty, thinking that the drink would thus be most healthful and most pleasant. When they take their meals together in this manner, how can anyone ruin either himself or his family by gluttony or drunkenness? In other states, equals in age generally associate together, and with them modesty has but very little influence; but Lycurgus, at Sparta, mixed citizens of different ages, so that the younger are for the most part instructed by the experience of the older. It is a custom at these public meals, that whatever anyone has done to his honor in the community is related; so that insolence, or disorder from intoxication, or any indecency in conduct or language, has there no opportunity of showing itself. The practice of taking meals away from home is also attended with these advantages, that the people are obliged to walk in taking their departure homewards, and to be careful that they may not stagger from the effects of wine, knowing that they will not remain where they dined, and that they must conduct themselves in the night just as in the day; for it is not allowable for anyone who is still liable to military duty to walk with a torch.

As Lycurgus observed, too, that those who, after taking food, exercise themselves, become well-complexioned, plump, and robust, while those who are inactive are puffy, unhealthy-looking, and feeble, he did not neglect to give attention to that point; and as he perceived that when anyone engages in labor from his own inclination, he proves himself to have his body in efficient condition, he ordered that the oldest in each place of exercise should take care that those belonging to it should never be overcome by taking too much food. With regard to this matter, he appears to me to have been by no means mistaken; for no one would easily find men more healthy, or more able-bodied, than the Spartans; for they exercise themselves alike in their legs, in their hands, and in their shoulders.

Rules Regarding Children, Slaves, and Property

In the following particulars, also, he made enactments contrary to the usage of most states; for in other communities each individual has the control over his own children, and servants, and property; but Lycurgus, wishing to order things so that the citizens might enjoy some advantage from one another, unattended with any reciprocal injury, ordained that each should have authority not only over his own children, but over those of others. But when a person is conscious that his fellow citizens are fathers of the children over whom he exercises authority, he must exercise it in such a way as he would wish it to be exercised over his own. If a boy, on any occasion, receive blows from another boy, and complain of that boy to his father, it is considered dishonorable in the father not to inflict additional blows on his son. Thus they trust to one another to impose nothing disgraceful on the children.

He enacted also that a person might use his neighbor's servants, if he had need of them. He introduced, too, a community of property in hunting-dogs; so that those who require them call on their owner to hunt, who, if he is not at leisure to hunt himself, cheerfully sends them out. They use horses also in like manner; for whoever is sick, or wants a vehicle, or desires to go to some place speedily, takes possession of a horse, if he sees one anywhere, and, after making proper use of it, restores it.

Nor, in regard to the following point, did he allow that which is customary among other people should be practiced among his countrymen. For when men, from being overtaken by night in hunting, are in want of provisions, unless they have previously furnished themselves with them, he directed that, in such a case, those who have partaken of what they need, leave the rest ready for use, and that those who require a supply, having opened the seals, and taken as much as they want, seal the remainder up again and leave it. As they share thus, then, with one another, those who possess but little participate, whenever they are in need, in all the produce of the country.

Restrictions on the Employments of the Spartans

The following practices, too, Lycurgus established in Sparta, at variance with those of the rest of Greece. In other communities all gain as much by traffic[3] as

---

[3]That is, by commerce.

they can; one cultivates land, another trades by sea, another engages in general commerce, another maintains himself by art. But at Sparta, Lycurgus prohibited free men from having any connection with traffic, and enjoined them to consider as their only occupation whatever secures freedom to states. How, indeed, could wealth be eagerly sought in a community where he had appointed that the citizens should contribute equally to their necessary maintenance, and should take their meals in common, and had thus provided that they should not desire wealth with a view to sensual gratifications? Nor had they, moreover, to get money for the sake of clothing; for they think themselves adorned, not by expensive raiment, but by a healthy personal appearance. Nor have they to gather money for the purpose of spending it on those who eat with them, since he has made it more honorable for a person to serve his neighbors by bodily exertion, than by putting himself to pecuniary expense; making it apparent that the one proceeds from the mind, and the other from fortune.

From acquiring money by unjust means, he prohibited them by such methods as the following. He instituted, in the first place, such a kind of money, that, even if but ten minae[4] came into a house, it could never escape the notice either of masters or of servants; for it would require much room, and a carriage to convey it. In the next place, gold and silver are searched after, and, if they are discovered anywhere, the possessor of them is punished. How, then, could gain by traffic be an object of pursuit, in a state where the possession of money occasions more pain than the use of it affords pleasure?

Obedience to the Magistrates and Laws

That at Sparta the citizens pay the strictest obedience to the magistrates [officials] and laws, we all know. I suppose, however, that Lycurgus did not attempt to establish such an excellent order of things, until he had brought the most powerful men in the state to be of the same mind with regard to it. I form my opinion on this consideration, that, in other states, the more influential men are not willing even to appear to fear the magistrates, but think that such fear is unbecoming free men; but in Sparta, the most powerful men not only put themselves under the magistrates, but even count it an honor to humble themselves before them, and to obey, when they are called upon, not walking, but running; supposing that if they themselves are the first to pay exact obedience, others will follow their example; and such has been the case. It is probable, also, that the chief men established offices of the Ephors[5] in conjunction with Lycurgus, as they must have been certain that obedience is of the greatest benefit, alike in a state, and in an

---

[4]Large iron coins (really weights) of the Spartans.

[5]A five-man board, elected annually by the citizens, that had nearly unlimited executive powers, except command in war.

army, and in a family; and they doubtless considered that the greater power magistrates have, the greater effect will they produce on the citizens in enforcing obedience. The Ephors, accordingly, have full power to impose a fine on whomsoever they please, and to exact the fine without delay; they have power also to degrade magistrates even while they are in office, and to put them in prison, and to bring them to trial for their life. Being possessed of such authority, they do not, like the magistrates in other states, always permit those who are elected to offices to rule during the whole year as they choose, but, like despots and officials in gymnastic contests, punish on the instant whomsoever they find acting at all contrary to the laws.

Though there were many other excellent contrivances adopted by Lycurgus, to induce the citizens to obey the laws, the most excellent of all appears to me to be, that he did not deliver his laws to the people until he had gone, in company with the most eminent of his fellow citizens, to Delphi, and consulted the god[6] whether it would be more beneficial and advantageous for Sparta to obey the laws which he had made. As the god replied that it would be more beneficial in every way, he at once delivered them, deciding that it would be not only illegal, but impious, to disobey laws sanctioned by the oracle.

Infamy and Penalties of Cowardice

It is deserving of admiration, too, in Lycurgus, that he made it a settled principle in the community, that an honorable death is preferable to a dishonorable life; for whoever pays attention to the subject will find that fewer of those who hold this opinion die than of those who attempt to escape danger by flight. Hence we may say with truth that safety attends for a much longer period on valor than on cowardice; for valor is not only attended with less anxiety and greater pleasure, but is also more capable of assisting and supporting us. It is evident, too, that good report [reputation] accompanies valor; for almost everybody is willing to be in alliance with the brave.

How he contrived that such sentiments should be entertained, it is proper not to omit to mention. He evidently, then, intended a happy life for the brave, and a miserable one for the cowardly. In other communities, when a man acts as a coward, he merely brings on himself the name of coward, but the coward goes to the same market, and sits or takes exercise, if he pleases, in the same place with the brave men; at Sparta, however, everyone would be ashamed to admit a coward into the same tent with him, or to allow him to be his opponent in a match at wrestling. Frequently, too, a person of such character, when they choose opposite parties to play at ball, is left without any place; and in forming a chorus he is thrust into the least honorable position. On the road he must yield the way to

---

[6]Apollo, god of prophecy, whose most famous oracular shrine was at Delphi.

others, and at public meetings he must rise up, even before his juniors. His female relatives he must maintain at home, and they too must pay the penalty of his cowardice, since no man will marry them. He is also not allowed to take a wife, and must at the same time pay the customary fine for being a bachelor. He must not walk about with a cheerful expression, or imitate the manners of persons of blameless character; else he will have to receive whipping from his betters. Since, then, such disgrace is inflicted on cowards, I do not at all wonder that death is preferred at Sparta to a life so dishonorable and infamous.

Honors Paid to Old Age: Encouragement of Virtue

Lycurgus seems to me to have provided also, with great judgment, how virtue might be practiced even to old age; for by adding to his other enactments the choice of senators at an advanced stage of life,[7] he caused honor and virtue not to be disregarded even in old age.

It is worthy of admiration in him, too, that he attached consideration to the old age of the well-deserving; for by making the old men arbiters in the contest for superiority in mental qualifications, he rendered their old age more honorable than the vigor of those in the meridian of life. This contest is deservedly held in the greatest esteem among the people, for gymnastic contests are attended with honor, but they concern only bodily accomplishments; the contest for distinction in old age involves a decision respecting merits of the mind. In proportion, therefore, as the mind is superior to the body, so much are contests for mental eminence more worthy of regard than those concerning bodily superiority.

Is it not highly worthy of admiration, also, in Lycurgus, that when he saw that those who are disinclined to practice virtue are not qualified to increase the power of their country, he obliged all the citizens of Sparta to cultivate every kind of virtue publicly. As private individuals, accordingly, who practice virtue, are superior in it to those who neglect it, so Sparta is naturally superior in virtue to all other states, as it is the only one that engages in a public cultivation of honor and virtue. Is it not also deserving of commendation that, when other states punish any person that injures another, Lycurgus inflicted no less punishment on anyone that openly showed himself unconcerned with becoming as good a man as possible? He thought, as it appears, that by those who make others slaves, or rob them, or steal anything, the individual sufferers only are injured, but that by the unprincipled and cowardly whole communities are betrayed; so that he appears to me to have justly imposed the heaviest penalties on such characters.

He also imposed on his countrymen an obligation, from which there is no exception, of practicing every kind of political virtue; for he made the privileges

---

[7]The twenty-eight senators, along with the two hereditary kings, formed the principal law-making body of Sparta (the Council of Elders); the senators were elected for life and had to be over sixty years of age.

of citizenship equally available to all those who observed what was enjoined by the laws, without taking any account either of weakness of body or scantiness of means; but if anyone was too indolent to perform what the laws prescribed, Lycurgus appointed that he should be no longer counted in the number of equally privileged citizens.

That these laws are extremely ancient is certain; for Lycurgus is said to have lived in the time of the Heracleidae;[8] but, ancient as they are, they are still very new to other communities; for, what is the most wonderful of all things, all men extol such institutions, but no state thinks proper to imitate them.

Of the Spartan Army

The regulations which I have mentioned are beneficial alike in peace and in war; but if anyone wishes to learn what he contrived better than other legislators with reference to military proceedings, he may attend to the following particulars.

In the first place, then, the Ephors proclaim the age limits for the citizen draft to the army; artisans (non-citizens) are also called by the same order to serve supplying the troops. For the Spartans provide themselves in the field with an abundance of all those things which people use in a city; and of whatever instruments an army may require in common, orders are given to bring some on wagons, and others on beasts of burden, as by this arrangement anything left behind is least likely to escape notice.

For engagements in the field he made the following arrangements. He ordered that each soldier should have a purple robe and a brazen shield; for he thought that such a dress had least resemblance to that of women, and was excellently adapted for the field of battle, as it is soonest made splendid, and is longest in growing soiled. He permitted also those above the age of puberty to let their hair grow, as he thought that they thus appeared taller, more manly, and more terrifying in the eyes of the enemy. . . .

---

[8]Children of the legendary Greek hero Heracles.

17

❧

Plato

APOLOGY

Neither Socrates nor Jesus, in Western eyes the most famous and most beloved teachers of the ancient world, are known through their own writings. For our knowledge of both we must depend mainly on the works of disciples. In the case of the Greek Socrates, our primary source is Plato, in whose written dialogues (discussions) the Athenian sage is the dominant figure.

Socrates (469–399 B.C.) was born and raised in Athens during the "Golden Age" and, later in his life, fought bravely in the Peloponnesian War (431–404 B.C.) that ended the glory of his city. He lived in an age that was, like our own, one of intellectual and moral unrest. In Athens many time-honored values and opinions were being subjected to radical criticism and revaluation, especially by a group of skeptical, relativistic teachers known as the Sophists. Socrates, although not a Sophist himself, contributed to the shaking of popular beliefs by challenging them with everyone he met; this questioning of tradition was largely responsible for his being brought to trial and put to death.

Socrates's place in history does not come from this negative influence. Unlike the Sophists he had no doubt at all that absolute, unchanging truth exists. A usable reflection or vision of that absolute truth, he maintained, is already in the possession of everyone, hidden under smug self-satisfaction and narrow prejudices, and needs only to be liberated by rigorous examination and testing of opinion. His "Socratic method" was aimed at revealing the eternal principles of human conduct, upon which personal happiness and social stability depend. This means of truth-seeking, the action of mind upon mind, is called dialectic. It assumes that real truth is there to be found through honest and systematic intellectual argument.

In the following selection, the Apology, we see Socrates defending himself in court, at the age of seventy, before a typically large jury of 501 male citizens. (Athenian legal custom required that the trial take only a single day and that the *accused person act as his own defense lawyer.) Plato was present and, therefore, we may trust that his account of the speech gives a reasonably accurate picture of the genuine Socrates—perhaps somewhat idealized by Plato's own admiration. We do not have a record of his accusers' speeches.*

The accusers charged that Socrates did not believe in the official gods of the city but rather invented his own gods, and that he corrupted the Athenian youth, urging them to believe as he did. Socrates, with calm defiance, not only dealt with the charges but also used the trial as yet another opportunity to explain the truth-seeking mission to which his life had been devoted. (The meaning in Greek of the root word for "apology" does not carry the word's modern meaning of an expression of regret; it means, rather, an explanation and justification of one's actions.)

[To the jury:]
"How you, O Athenians, have been affected by my accusers, I cannot tell; but I know that they almost made me forget who I was—so persuasively did they speak; and yet they have hardly uttered a word of truth. But of the many falsehoods told by them, there was one which quite amazed me;—I mean when they said that you should be upon your guard and not allow yourselves to be deceived by the force of my eloquence. To say this, when they were certain to be detected as soon as I opened my lips and proved myself to be anything but a great speaker, did indeed appear to me most shameless—unless by the force of eloquence they mean the force of truth; for if such is their meaning, I admit that I am eloquent. But in how different a way from theirs! Well, as I was saying, they have scarcely spoken the truth at all; from me you shall hear the whole truth, but not delivered after their manner in a set oration duly ornamented with fine words and phrases. No, by heaven! I shall use the words and arguments which occur to me at the moment, for I am confident in the justice of my cause: at my time of life I ought not to be appearing before you, O men of Athens, in the character of a boy inventing falsehoods—let no one expect it of me. And I must particularly beg of you to grant me this favor:—If I defend myself in my accustomed manner, and you hear me using the words which many of you have heard me using habitually in the agora,[1] at the tables of the money-changers, and elsewhere, I would ask you not to be surprised, and not to interrupt me on this account. For I am more than seventy years of age, and appearing now for the first time before a court of law, I

Plato, *Apology*, in *The Dialogues of Plato*, trans. Benjamin Jowett (Oxford: Clarendon Press, 1953), 341–356, 360–366. Adapted by the editor.

[1]The marketplace, a favorite social center of the citizens.

am quite a stranger to the language of the place; and therefore I would have you regard me as if I were really a stranger, whom you would excuse if he spoke in his native tongue, and after the fashion of his country:—Am I making an unfair request of you? Never mind the manner, which may or may not be good; but think only of the truth of my words, and give heed to that: let the speaker speak truly and the judge decide justly.

"And first, I have to reply to the older charges and to my first accusers,[2] and then I will go on to the later ones. For of old I have had many accusers, who have accused me falsely to you during many years; and I am more afraid of them than of Anytus[3] and his associates, who are dangerous, too, in their own way. But far more dangerous are the others, who began when most of you were children, and took possession of your minds with their falsehoods, telling of one Socrates, a wise man, who speculated about the heaven above, and searched into the earth beneath, and made the worse appear the better cause.[4] The men who have besmeared me with this tale are the accusers whom I dread; for their hearers are apt to fancy that such inquirers do not believe in the existence of the gods. And they are many, and their charges against me are of ancient date, and they were made by them in the days when some of you were more impressionable than you are now—in childhood, or it may have been in youth—and the cause went by default, for there was none to answer. And hardest of all, I do not know and cannot tell the names of my accusers; unless in the chance case of a comic poet.[5] All who from envy and malice have persuaded you—some of them having first convinced themselves—all this class of men are most difficult to deal with; for I cannot have them up here, and cross-examine them, and therefore I must simply fight with shadows in my own defence, and argue when there is no one who answers. I will ask you then to take it from me that my opponents are of two kinds; one recent, the other ancient: and I hope that you will see the propriety of

---

[2]Socrates had been much criticized for many years before his trial; here, he states that he will deal first with the old falsehoods that created the prejudices that are the real cause of the current charges against him.

[3]Anytus, Meletus, and Lycon were the three men pressing charges against Socrates. (Anytus was a wealthy merchant whose son was intellectually gifted and wished to be a follower of Socrates. Anytus had angrily refused and insisted his son go into the family's business. The young man—according to tradition—became an alcoholic.)

[4]Socrates was accused by some of being a natural philosopher (physical scientist) who speculated, or theorized, about the material nature of the universe—and was thought, therefore, to be an atheist. He was also accused of being a Sophist, a teacher of public speaking who taught people to argue their law cases without regard for truth. Actually, he had lost interest in natural philosophy decades earlier and had never been a Sophist.

[5]Aristophanes, whose satirical comedy *The Clouds* (423 B.C.) portrayed Socrates as a ridiculous fake who had contempt for religion and tradition.

my answering the latter first, for these accusations you heard long before the others, and much oftener.

"Well, then, I must make my defence, and endeavor to remove from your minds in a short time a slander which you have had a long time to take in. May I succeed, if to succeed be for my good and yours, or likely to avail me in my cause! The task is not an easy one; I quite understand the nature of it. And so leaving the event with God, in obedience to the law I will now make my defence.

"I will begin at the beginning, and ask what is the accusation which has given rise to the slander of me, and in fact has encouraged Meletus to prefer this charge against me. Well, what do the slanderers say? They shall be my prosecutors, and this is the information they swear against me: 'Socrates is an evil-doer; a meddler who searches into things under the earth and in heaven, and makes the worse appear the better cause, and teaches the aforesaid practices to others.' Such is the nature of the accusation: it is just what you have yourselves seen in the comedy of Aristophanes, who has introduced a man whom he calls Socrates, swinging about and saying that he walks on air, and talking a deal of nonsense concerning matters of which I do not pretend to know either much or little—not that I mean to speak disparagingly of anyone who is a student of natural philosophy. May Meletus never bring so many charges against me as to make me do that! But the simple truth is, O Athenians, that I have nothing to do with physical speculations. Most of those here present are witnesses to the truth of this, and to them I appeal. Speak then, you who have heard me, and tell your neighbors whether any of you have ever known me hold forth in few words or in many upon such matters. . . . You hear their answer. And from what they say of this part of the charge you will be able to judge of the truth of the rest.

"As little foundation is there for the report that I am a teacher, and take money;[6] this accusation has no more truth in it than the other. Although, if a man were really able to instruct mankind, to receive money for giving instruction would, in my opinion, be an honor to him. . . .

"I dare say, Athenians, that someone among you will reply, 'Yes, Socrates, but what *is* your occupation? What is the origin of these accusations which are brought against you; there must have been something strange which you have been doing? All these rumors and this talk about you would never have arisen if you had been like other men: tell us, then, what is the cause of them, for we should be sorry to judge hastily of you.' Now I regard this as a fair challenge, and I will endeavor to explain to you the reason why I am called wise and have such an evil fame. Please to attend then. And although some of you may think that I am joking, I declare that I will tell you the entire truth. Men of Athens, this reputation of mine has come from a certain sort of wisdom which I possess. If you

---

[6]The Sophists often charged high fees. Socrates, on the other hand, charged no fees at all for his philosophical questioning.

ask me what kind of wisdom, I reply, wisdom such as may perhaps be attained by man, for to that extent I am inclined to believe that I am wise; whereas the persons of whom I was speaking have a kind of superhuman wisdom,[7] which I know not how to describe, because I have it not myself; and he who says that I have, speaks falsely, and is taking away my character. And here, O men of Athens, I must beg you not to interrupt me, even if I seem to say something extravagant. For the word which I will speak is not mine. I will refer you to a witness who is worthy of credit; that witness shall be the god of Delphi[8]—he will tell you about my wisdom, if I have any, and of what sort it is. You must have known Chaerephon; he was early a friend of mine, and also a friend of yours, for he shared in the recent exile of the people, and returned with you.[9] Well, Chaerephon, as you know, was very impetuous in all his doings, and he went to Delphi and boldly asked the oracle to tell him whether—as I was saying, I must beg you not to interrupt—he actually asked the oracle to tell him whether anyone was wiser than I was, and the Pythian prophetess answered that there was no man wiser. Chaerephon is dead himself; but his brother, who is in court, will confirm the truth of what I am saying.

"Why do I mention this? Because I am going to explain to you why I have such an evil name. When I heard the answer, I said to myself, 'What can the god mean? And what is the interpretation of his riddle?' for I know that I have no wisdom, small or great. What then can he mean when he says that I am the wisest of men? And yet he is a god, and cannot lie; that would be against his nature. After long perplexity, I thought of a method of trying the question. I reflected that if I could only find a man wiser than myself, then I might go to the god with a refutation in my hand. I should say to him, 'Here is a man who is wiser than I am; but you said that I was the wisest.' Accordingly I went to one who had the reputation for wisdom, and observed him—his name I need not mention, he was a politician; and in the process of examining him and talking with him, this, men of Athens, was what I found. I could not help thinking that he was not really wise, although he was thought wise by many, and still wiser by himself; and thereupon I tried to explain to him that he thought himself wise, but was not really wise; and the consequence was that he hated me, and his enmity was shared by several who were present and heard me. So I left him, saying to myself as I went away: 'Well, although I do not suppose that either of us knows anything really worth knowing, I am at least wiser than this fellow—for he knows nothing, and thinks that

---

[7]Socrates, with his customary ironic (sarcastic) humor, is speaking here of the Sophists.

[8]Apollo's most famous temple was at Delphi, about seventy-five miles northwest of Athens; the Pythia, Apollo's priestess, there uttered the god's oracles (divine statements).

[9]Five years before Socrates's trial, after the defeat of Athens ended the Peloponnesian War in 404 B.C., the "Thirty Tyrants" drove the democratic leadership of Athens (including Socrates's friend Chaerephon) into exile. The democracy was restored in 403 B.C.

he knows; I neither know nor think that I know.' In this one little point, then, I seem to have the advantage of him. Then I went to another who had still higher pretensions to wisdom, and my conclusion was exactly the same. Whereupon I made another enemy of him, and of many others besides him.

"Then I went to one man after another, being not unconscious of the enmity which I provoked, and I lamented and feared this: but necessity was laid upon me,—the word of God [Apollo], I thought, ought to be considered first. And I said to myself, 'Go I must to all who appear to know, and find out the meaning of the oracle.' And I swear to you, Athenians,—for I must tell you the truth—the result of my mission was just this: I found that the men most in repute were nearly the most foolish; and that others less esteemed were really closer to wisdom. I will tell you the tale of my wanderings and of the 'Herculean' labors, as I may call them, which I endured only to find at last the oracle irrefutable. After the politicians, I went to the poets; tragic, dithyrambic, and all sorts. And there, I said to myself, you will be instantly detected; now you will find out that you are more ignorant than they are. Accordingly, I took them some of the most elaborate passages in their own writings, and asked what was the meaning of them—thinking that they would teach me something. Will you believe me? I am ashamed to confess the truth, but I must say that there is hardly a person present who would not have talked better about their poetry than they did themselves. So I learned that not by wisdom do poets write poetry, but by a sort of genius and inspiration; they are like diviners [prophets] or soothsayers who also say many fine things, but do not understand the meaning of them. The poets appeared to me to be much in the same case; and I further observed that upon the strength of their poetry they believed themselves to be the wisest of men in other things in which they were not wise. So I departed, conceiving myself to be superior to them for the same reason that I was superior to the politicians.

"At last I went to the skilled craftsmen, for I was conscious that I knew nothing at all, as I may say, and I was sure that they knew many fine things; and here I was not mistaken, for they did know many things of which I was ignorant, and in this they certainly were wiser than I was. But I observed that even the good craftsmen fell into the same error as the poets;—because they were good workmen they thought that they also knew all sorts of high matters, and this defect in them overshadowed their wisdom; and therefore I asked myself on behalf of the oracle, whether I would like to be as I was, neither having their knowledge nor their ignorance, or like them in both; and I made answer to myself and to the oracle that I was better off as I was.

"This inquiry has led to my having many enemies of the worst and most dangerous kind, and has given rise also to many imputations, including the name of 'wise'; for my hearers always imagine that I myself possess the wisdom which I find wanting in others. But the truth is, O men of Athens, that God only is wise; and by his answer he intends to show that the wisdom of men is worth little or nothing; although speaking of Socrates, he is only using my name by way of illustration, as if he said, 'He, O men, is the wisest, who, like Socrates, knows that his wisdom is in truth worth nothing.' And so I go about the world, obedient to the god, and search and make inquiry into the wisdom of anyone, whether citizen or stranger, who appears to be wise; and if he is not wise, then in vindication of the oracle I show him that he is not wise; and my occupation quite absorbs me, and I have had no time to do anything useful either in public affairs or in any concern of my own, but I am in utter poverty by reason of my devotion to the god.

"There is another thing:—young men of the richer classes, who have not much to do, come about me of their own accord; they like to hear people examined, and they often imitate me, and proceed to do some examining themselves; there are plenty of persons, as they quickly discover, who think that they know something, but really know little or nothing; and then those who are examined by them instead of being angry with themselves are angry with me: 'This confounded Socrates,' they say; 'this villainous misleader of youth!'—and then if somebody asks them, 'Why, what evil does he practice or teach?' they do not know, and cannot tell; but in order that they may not appear to be at a loss, they repeat the ready-made charges which are used against all philosophers about teaching things up in the clouds and under the earth, and having no gods, and making the worse appear the better cause; for they do not like to confess that their pretense of knowledge has been detected—which is the truth; and as they are numerous and ambitious and energetic, and speak vehemently with persuasive tongues, they have filled your ears with their loud and inveterate slanders. And this is the reason why my three accusers, Meletus and Anytus and Lycon, have set upon me. . . .

"I have said enough in my defence against the first class of my accusers; I turn to the second class. They are headed by Meletus, that good man and true lover of his country, as he calls himself. Against these, too, I must try to make a defence:— Let their affidavit be read: it contains something of this kind: It says that Socrates is a doer of evil, inasmuch as he corrupts the youth, and does not receive the gods whom the state receives, but has a new religion of his own. Such is the charge; and now let us examine the particular counts. He says that I am a doer of evil, and corrupt the youth; but I say, O men of Athens, that Meletus is a doer of evil, in that he is playing a solemn farce, recklessly bringing men to trial from a pretended zeal and interest about matters in which he really never had the smallest interest. And the truth of this I will endeavor to prove to you.

"Come hither, Meletus, and let me ask a question of you. You attach great importance to the improvement of youth?"

"Yes, I do."

"Tell the judges, then, who is their improver; for you must know, as you take such interest in the subject, and have discovered their corrupter, and are citing and accusing me in this court. Speak, then, and tell the judges who is the improver of youth:—Observe, Meletus, that you are silent, and have nothing to say. But is this not rather disgraceful, and a very considerable proof of what I was saying, that you have no interest in the matter? Speak up, friend, and tell us who their improver is."

"The laws."

"But that, my good sir, is not my question: Can you not name some person—whose first qualification will be that he knows the laws?"[10]

"The judges, Socrates, who are present in court."

"What, do you mean to say, Meletus, that they are able to instruct and improve youth?"

"Certainly they are."

"What, all of them, or some only and not others?"

"All of them."

"Truly, that is good news! There are plenty of improvers, then. And what do you say of the audience,—do they improve them?"

"Yes, they do."

"And the senators?"

"Yes, the senators improve them."

"But perhaps the members of the assembly corrupt them?—or do they too improve them?"

"They improve them."

"Then every Athenian improves and elevates them; all with the exception of myself; and I alone am their corrupter? Is that what you affirm?"

"That is what I stoutly affirm."

"I am very unfortunate if you are right. But suppose I ask you a question: Is it the same with horses? Does one man do them harm and all the world good? Is not the exact opposite the truth? One man is able to do them good, or at least very few;—the trainer of horses, that is to say, does them good, but the ordinary man does them harm if he has to do with them? Is not that true, Meletus, of horses, or of any other animals? Most assuredly it is; whether you and Anytus say yes or no. Happy indeed would be the condition of youth if they had one corrupter only, and all the rest of the world were their benefactors. But you, Meletus, have sufficiently shown that you never had a thought about the young: your carelessness is plainly seen in your not caring about the very things which you bring against me. . . .

"It will be very clear to you, Athenians, as I was saying, that Meletus has never had any care, great or small, about the matter. But still I should like to know,

---

[10]In the following series of questions, Socrates, as part of his right to cross-examine his accuser, playfully uses his logical method *(dialectic)* to make the angrily squirming Meletus look foolish. Meletus is first forced, by Socrates's questions, to define the "improver of youth" as all the "judges" (the entire jury of 501); then as the non-voting "audience"; then as the "senators" (the Council of 500 that drafted the laws and supervised their carrying out); and finally, as the "assembly" (all the adult male citizens, who voted approval of the laws of Athens).

Meletus, in what way I am affirmed to corrupt the young. I suppose you mean, as I infer from your indictment, that I teach them not to acknowledge the gods which the state acknowledges, but some other new divinities or spiritual agencies in their stead. These are the lessons by which I corrupt the youth, as you say."

"Yes, that I say emphatically."

"Then, by the gods, Meletus, of whom we are speaking, tell me and the court, in somewhat plainer terms, what you mean! For I do not as yet understand whether you affirm that I teach other men to acknowledge some gods, and therefore that I do believe in gods, and am not an entire atheist—this you do not lay to my charge,—but only you say that they are not the same gods which the city recognizes—the charge is that they are different gods. Or, do you mean that I am an atheist simply, and a teacher of atheism?"

"I mean the latter—that you are a complete atheist."

"What an extraordinary statement! Why do you think so, Meletus? Do you mean that I do not believe in the god-head of the sun or moon, like the rest of mankind?"[11]

"I assure you, judges, that he does not: for he says that the sun is stone, and the moon earth."

"Friend Meletus, do you think that you are accusing Anaxagoras?[12] Have you such a low opinion of the judges, that you fancy them so illiterate as not to know that these doctrines are found in the books of Anaxagoras the Clazomenian, which are full of them? And so, in fact, the youth are said to be taught them by Socrates, when they can be bought in the book-market for one drachma[13] at the most; and they might pay their money, and laugh at Socrates if he pretends to father these extraordinary views. And so, Meletus, you really think that I do not believe in any god?"

"I swear by Zeus that you verily believe in none at all."

"Nobody will believe you, Meletus, and I am pretty sure that you do not believe yourself. I cannot help thinking, men of Athens, that Meletus is reckless and impudent, and that he has brought this indictment in a spirit of mere wantonness and youthful bravado. Has he not compounded a riddle, thinking to try me? He said to himself:—'I shall see whether the wise Socrates will discover my facetious self-contradiction, or whether I shall be able to deceive him and the rest of them.' For he certainly does appear to me to contradict himself in the

---

[11]Apollo was the sun-god, Artemis the moon goddess. Whether or not those two divine personalities were meant in Socrates's question, reverence for the sun and moon themselves was expected of all Greeks.

[12]A natural philosopher from Clazomenae, a town in Asia Minor. Condemned for impiety, he was forced to leave Athens partly because of his materialist, anti-supernatural views of the sun and moon.

[13]A Greek coin of small value.

indictment as much as if he said that Socrates is guilty of not believing in the gods, and yet of believing in them—but this is not like a person who is in earnest.

"I should like you, O men of Athens, to join me in examining what I conceive to be his inconsistency; and do you, Meletus, answer. And I must remind the audience of my request that they would not make a disturbance if I speak in my accustomed manner.

"Did ever man, Meletus, believe in the existence of human things, and not of human beings? . . . I wish, men of Athens, that he would answer, and not be always trying to get up an interruption. Did ever any man believe in horsemanship, and not in horses? Or in flute-playing, and not in flute-players? My friend, no man ever did; I answer to you and to the court, as you refuse to answer for yourself. But now please to answer the next question: Can a man believe in the existence of things spiritual and divine, and not in spirits or demigods?"

"He cannot."

"How lucky I am to have extracted that answer, by the assistance of the court! But then you swear in the indictment that I teach and believe in divine or spiritual things (new or old, no matter for that); at any rate, I believe in spiritual things,—so you say and swear in the affidavit; and yet if I believe in them, how can I help believing in spirits or demigods;—must I not? To be sure I must; your silence gives consent. Now what are spirits or demigods? Are they not either gods or the sons of gods?"

"Certainly they are."

"But this is what I call the facetious riddle invented by you: the demigods or spirits are gods, and you say first that I do not believe in gods, and then again that I do believe in gods; that is, if I believe in demigods. For if the demigods are the illegitimate sons of gods, whether by nymphs, or by other mothers, as some are said to be—what human being will ever believe that there are no gods when there are sons of gods? You might as well affirm the existence of mules, and deny that of horses and asses.[14] Such nonsense, Meletus, could only have been intended by you to make trial of me. You have put this into the indictment because you could think of nothing real of which to accuse me. But no one who has a particle of understanding will ever be convinced by you that a man can believe in the existence of things divine and superhuman, and the same man refuse to believe in gods and demigods and heroes.

"I have said enough in answer to the charge of Meletus: any elaborate defence is unnecessary. You know well the truth of my statement that I have incurred many violent enmities; and this is what will be my destruction if I am destroyed;—not Meletus, nor yet Anytus, but the envy and detraction of the world, which has been the death of many good men, and will probably be the death of many more; there is no danger of my being the last of them.

---

[14]A mule is a sterile work animal produced by the mating of a mare with a male donkey (jackass).

"Someone will say: 'And are you not ashamed, Socrates, of a course of life which is likely to bring you to an untimely end?' To him I may fairly answer: 'There you are mistaken: a man who is good for anything ought not to calculate the chance of living or dying; he ought only to consider whether in doing anything he is doing right or wrong—acting the part of a good man or of a bad.' . . .

"Strange, indeed, would be my conduct, O men of Athens, if I who, when I was ordered by the generals whom you chose to command me at Potidaea and Amphipolis and Delium,[15] remained where they placed me, like any other man, facing death—if now, when, as I conceive and imagine, God orders me to fulfil the philosopher's mission of searching into myself and other men, I were to desert my post through fear of death, or any other fear; that would indeed be strange, and I might justly be arraigned in court for denying the existence of the gods, if I disobeyed the oracle because I was afraid of death, fancying that I was wise when I was not wise. For the fear of death is indeed the pretense of wisdom, and not real wisdom, being a pretense of knowing the unknown; and no one knows whether death, of which men are afraid because they apprehend it to be the greatest evil, may not be the greatest good. Is not this ignorance of a disgraceful sort, the ignorance which is the conceit that a man knows what he does not know? And in this respect only I believe myself to differ from men in general, and may perhaps claim to be wiser than they are:—that whereas I know but little of the world below,[16] I do not suppose that I know: but I do know that injustice and disobedience to a better, whether God or man, is evil and dishonorable, and I will never fear or avoid a possible good rather than a certain evil. And therefore if you let me go now, and . . . if you say to me, 'Socrates, this time we will not mind Anytus, and you shall be let off, but upon one condition: that you are not to inquire and speculate in this way any more, and that if you are caught doing so again you shall die.' If this was the condition on which you let me go, I should reply: 'Men of Athens, I honor and love you; but I shall obey God rather than you, and while I have life and strength I shall never cease from the practice and teaching of philosophy,' exhorting any one of you whom I meet and saying to him after my manner: 'You, my friend,—a citizen of the great and mighty and wise city of Athens,—are you not ashamed of heaping up the largest amount of money and honor and reputation, and caring so little about wisdom and truth and the greatest improvement of the soul, which you never regard nor heed at all?' And if the person with whom I am arguing, says, 'Yes, but I do care'; then I shall not leave him nor let him go at once, but proceed to interrogate and examine and cross-examine him, and if I think that he has no virtue in him but only says that he has, I shall reproach him with undervaluing the most precious, and overvaluing the less. And I shall repeat the same words to everyone whom I meet, young and old, citizen and alien, but especially to you citizens,

---

[15]Sites of battles (430–422 B.C.) during the Peloponnesian War where Socrates fought as an Athenian infantryman.

[16]The afterlife, thought by the Greeks to be in an underground place called Hades.

inasmuch as you are my brethren. . . . This is my teaching, and if it corrupts the young, it is mischievous; but if anyone says that this is not my teaching, he is speaking an untruth. Wherefore, O men of Athens, I say to you, do as Anytus bids or not as Anytus bids, and either acquit me or not; but whichever you do, understand that I shall never alter my ways, not even if I have to die many times.

"Men of Athens, do not interrupt,[17] but hear me; I begged you before to listen to me without interruption, and I beg you now to hear me to the end. I have something more to say, at which you may be inclined to cry out; but I believe that to hear me will be good for you, and therefore I beseech you to restrain yourselves. I would have you know, that if you kill such an one as I am, you will injure yourselves more than you will injure me. Nothing will injure me, not Meletus nor yet Anytus—they cannot, for a bad man is not permitted to injure a better than himself. I do not deny that Anytus may, perhaps, kill him, or drive him into exile, or deprive him of civil rights; and he may imagine, and others may imagine, that he is inflicting a great injury upon him: but there I do not agree. For the evil of doing as he is doing—the evil of seeking unjustly to take the life of another—is far greater.

"And now, Athenians, I am not going to argue for my own sake, as you may think, but for yours, that you may not sin against God by condemning me, who am his gift to you. For if you kill me you will not easily find a successor to me, who, if I may use such a ludicrous figure of speech, am a sort of gadfly,[18] given to the state by God; and the state is a great and noble horse who is tardy in his motions owing to his very size, and requires to be stirred into life. I am that gadfly which God has attached to the state, and all day long and in all places am always fastening upon you, arousing and persuading and reproaching you. You will not easily find another like me, and therefore I would advise you to spare me. I dare say that you may feel out of temper (like a person who is suddenly awakened from sleep), and you think that you might easily strike me dead as Anytus advises, and then you would sleep on for the remainder of your lives, unless God in his care of you sent you another gadfly. When I say that I am given to you by God, the proof of my mission is this:—if I had been like other men, I should not have neglected all my own concerns or patiently seen the neglect of them during all these years, and have been doing yours, coming to you individually like a father or elder brother, exhorting you to regard virtue; such conduct, I say, would be unlike human nature. . . .

"Someone may wonder why I go about in private giving advice and busying myself with the concerns of others, but do not venture to come forward in public and advise the state. I will tell you why. You have heard me speak at different times

---

[17]Apparently, Socrates is now speaking over noises from the crowd, as he directly defies the city's power in stating that he will never alter his ways.

[18]A fly that bites and annoys horses and livestock.

and places of a superhuman oracle or sign which comes to me, and is the divinity which Meletus ridicules in the indictment. This sign, which is a kind of voice, first began to come to me when I was a child; from time to time it forbids me to do something which I am going to do, but never commands anything. This is what deters me from being a politician. And rightly, as I think. For I am certain, O men of Athens, that if I had engaged in politics, I should have perished long ago, and done no good either to you or to myself. And do not be offended at my telling you the truth: for the truth is, that no man who sets himself firmly against you or any other multitude, honestly striving to keep the state from many lawless and unrighteous deeds, will save his life; he who will fight for the right, if he would live even for a brief space, must have a private station and not a public one. . . .

[Editor's note: At the end of his defence, in which—contrary to accepted custom— Socrates refused to appeal to the sympathetic emotions of the jury, he was found guilty. The vote was 280 to 221. In the next phase of the trial, the prosecution and the convicted person each propose a penalty. *The jury must then vote for one or the other penalty.]*

"There are many reasons why I am not grieved, O men of Athens, at the vote of condemnation. I expected it, and am only surprised that the votes are so nearly equal; for I had thought that the majority against me would have been far larger; but now, had thirty votes gone over to the other side, I should have been acquitted. . . .

"And so he [Meletus] proposes death as the penalty. And what shall I propose on my part, O men of Athens? Clearly that which is my due. And what is my due? What ought I to have done to me, or to pay—a man who has never had the wit to keep quiet during his whole life; but has been careless of what the many care for—wealth, and family interests, and military offices, and speaking in the assembly, and magistracies, and plots, and parties. Reflecting that I was really too honest a man to be a politician and live, I did not go where I could do no good to you or to myself; but where I could do privately the greatest good (as I affirm it to be) to every one of you, thither I went, and sought to persuade every man among you that he must look to himself, and seek virtue and wisdom before he looks to his private interests, and look to the state before he looks to the interests of the state; and that this should be the order which he observes in all his actions. What shall be done to such an one? Doubtless some good thing, O men of Athens, if he has his reward; and the good should be of a kind suitable to him. What would be a reward suitable to a poor man who is your benefactor, and who desires leisure that he may instruct you? There can be no reward so fitting as a full pension in the Prytaneum,[19] O men of Athens, a reward which he deserves far more than the citizen who has won the prize at Olympia in the horse or chariot

---

[19]The place where benefactors of Athens and winners of the athletic contests at Olympia were entertained as guests.

race, whether the chariots were drawn by two horses or by many. For I am in want, and he has enough; and he only gives you the appearance of happiness, and I give you the reality. And if I am to estimate the penalty fairly, I should say that maintenance in the Prytaneum is the just return.

"Perhaps you think that I am braving you in what I am saying now, as in what I said before about the tears and prayers. But this is not so. I speak rather because I am convinced that I never intentionally wronged anyone, although I cannot convince you—the time has been too short; if there were a law at Athens, as there is in other cities, that a capital cause should not be decided in one day, then I believe that I should have convinced you. But I cannot in a moment refute great slanders; and, as I am convinced that I never wronged another, I will assuredly not wrong myself. I will not say of myself that I deserve any evil, nor propose any penalty. Why should I? Because I am afraid of the penalty of death which Meletus proposes? When I do not know whether death is a good or an evil, why should I propose a penalty which would certainly be an evil? Shall I say imprisonment? And why should I live in prison, and be the slave of the magistrates of the year? . . . Or shall the penalty be a fine, and imprisonment until the fine is paid? There is the same objection. I should have to lie in prison, for money I have none, and cannot pay. And if I say exile (and this may possibly be the penalty which you will affix), I must indeed be blinded by the love of life, if I am so irrational as to expect that when you, who are my own citizens, cannot endure my discourses and arguments, and have found them so grievous and odious that you will have no more of them, others are likely to endure them. No indeed, men of Athens, that is not very likely. And what a life should I lead, at my age, wandering from city to city, ever changing my place of exile, and always being driven out! For I am quite sure that wherever I go, there, as here, the young men will flock to listen to me; and if I drive them away, their elders will drive me out at their request; and if I let them come, their fathers and friends will drive me out for their sakes.

"Someone will say: 'Yes, Socrates, but cannot you hold your tongue, and then you may go into a foreign city, and no one will interfere with you?' Now I have great difficulty in making you understand my answer to this. For if I tell you that to do as you say would be a disobedience to God, and therefore that I cannot hold my tongue, you will not believe that I am serious; and if I say again that daily to discourse about virtue, and of those other things about which you hear me examining myself and others, is the greatest good of man, and that the unexamined life is no life for a human being, you are still less likely to believe me. Yet I say what is true, although a thing of which it is hard for me to persuade you. Also, I have never been accustomed to think that I deserve to suffer any harm. Had I money I might have estimated the offense at what I was able to pay, and not have been much the worse. But I have none, and therefore I must ask you to proportion the fine to my means. Well, perhaps I could afford a mina,[20] and therefore I propose

---

[20]A valuable coin, probably equal to one hundred drachmas.

that penalty: Plato, Crito, Critobulus, and Apollodorus, my friends here, bid me say thirty minas, and they will be the sureties. Let thirty minas be the penalty; for which sum they will be ample security to you.

[Editor's note: The jury, insulted by Socrates's suggestion that he be rewarded for his service to Athens, voted for the death penalty, 360 to 141.]

"Not much time will be gained, O Athenians, in return for the evil name which you will get from the detractors of the city, who will say that you killed Socrates, a wise man; for they will call me wise, even though I am not wise, when they want to reproach you. If you had waited a little while, your desire would have been fulfilled in the course of nature. For I am far advanced in years, as you may perceive, and not far from death. I am speaking now not to all of you, but only to those who have condemned me to death. And I have another thing to say to them: You think that I was convicted because I had no words of the sort which would have procured my acquittal—I mean, if I had thought fit to leave nothing undone or unsaid. Not so; the deficiency which led to my conviction was not of words—certainly not. But I had not the boldness nor impudence nor inclination to address you as you would have liked me to do, weeping and wailing and lamenting, and saying and doing many things, such indeed as you have been accustomed to hear from others, but I maintain to be unworthy of myself. I thought at the time that I ought not to do anything common or mean when in danger: nor do I now repent the style of my defence; I would rather die having spoken after my manner, than speak in your manner and live. For neither in war nor yet at law ought I or any man to use every way of escaping death. Often in battle there can be no doubt that if a man will throw away his arms, and fall on his knees before his pursuers, he may escape death; and in other dangers there are other ways of escaping death, if a man has the hardihood to say and do anything. The difficulty, my friends, is not to avoid death, but to avoid unrighteousness; for that runs faster than death. I am old and move slowly, and the slower runner has overtaken me; my accusers are keen and quick, and the faster runner, who is wickedness, has overtaken them. And now I depart hence condemned by you to suffer the penalty of death,—they too go to their ways condemned by the truth to suffer the penalty of villainy and wrong; and I must abide by my award—let them abide by theirs. I suppose that these things may be regarded as fated—and I think that they are well.

"And now, O men who have condemned me, I would fain prophesy to you; for I am about to die, and in the hour of death men are gifted with prophetic power. And I prophesy to you who are my murderers, that immediately after my departure punishment far heavier than you have inflicted on me surely awaits you. Me you have killed because you wanted to escape the accuser, and not to give an account of your lives. But that will not be as you suppose: far otherwise. For I say that there will be more accusers of you than there are now, accusers whom hitherto I have restrained: and as they are younger they will be more severe with you, and you will be more offended at them. If you think that by killing men you will stop all censure of your evil lives, you are mistaken; that is not a way of escape which is either very possible, or honorable; the easiest and the noblest way is not to be disabling others, but to be improving yourselves. This is the prophecy which I utter before my departure to the judges who have condemned me.

"Friends, who would have acquitted me; I would like also to talk with you about the thing which has come to pass, while the magistrates are busy, and before I go to the place at which I must die. Stay then a little, for we may as well talk with one another while there is time. You are my friends, and I should like to show you the meaning of this event which has happened to me. O my judges— for you I may truly call judges—I should like to tell you of a wonderful circumstance. Hitherto the divine faculty of which my inner voice is the source has constantly been in the habit of opposing me even about trifles, if I was going to make a slip or error in any matter; and now as you see there has come upon me that which may be thought, and is generally believed to be, the last and worst evil. But the oracle made no sign of opposition, either when I was leaving my house in the morning, or when I was on my way to the court, or while I was speaking, at anything which I was going to say; and yet I have often been stopped in the middle of a speech, but now in nothing I either said or did touching the matter in hand has the oracle opposed me. What do I take to be the explanation of this silence? I will tell you. It is an intimation that what has happened to me is a good, and therefore those of us who think that death is an evil must be in error. I have this conclusive proof; the customary sign would surely have opposed me had I been going to evil and not to good.

"Let us reflect in another way, and we shall see that there is great reason to hope that death is a good; for one of two things—either death is a state of nothingness and utter unconsciousness, or, as men say, there is a change and migration of the soul from this world to another. Now if you suppose that there is no consciousness, but a sleep like the sleep of him who is undisturbed even by dreams, death will be an unspeakable gain. For if a person were to select the night in which his sleep was undisturbed even by dreams, and were to compare with this the other days and nights of his life, and then were to tell us how many days and nights he had passed in the course of his life better and more pleasantly than this one, I think that any man, I will not say a private man, but even the great king will not find many such days or nights, when compared with the others. Now if death be of such a nature, I say that to die is gain; for eternity is then only a single night. But if death is the journey to another place, and there, as men say, all the dead abide, what good, O my friends and judges, can be greater than this? If indeed when the pilgrim arrives in the world below, he is delivered from our earthly professors of justice, and finds the true judges who are said to give judgment there . . . and other sons of God who were righteous in their own life, that pilgrimage will be worth making. What would not a man give if he might converse with Orpheus and Musaeus and Hesiod and Homer?[21] Nay, if this be true,

---

[21]Orpheus and Musaeus were poets in ancient mythological accounts; Hesiod and Homer (Selection 7) were historical figures—Greek poets of the eighth century B.C.

let me die again and again. . . . Above all, I shall then be able to continue my search into true and false knowledge; as in this world, so also in the next; and I shall find out who is wise, and who pretends to be wise, and is not. . . . In another world they do not put a man to death for asking questions: assuredly not. For besides being happier than we are, they will be immortal, if what is said is true.

"Wherefore, O judges, be of good cheer about death, and know of a certainty that no evil can happen to a good man, either in life or after death, and that he and his are not neglected by the gods. Nor has my own approaching end happened by mere chance; I see clearly that the time had arrived when it was better for me to die and be released from trouble; therefore the oracle gave no sign, and therefore also I am not at all angry with my condemners, or with my accusers. But although they have done me no harm, they intended it; and for this I may properly blame them.

"Still I have a favor to ask of them. When my sons are grown up, I would ask you, O my friends, to punish them; I would have you trouble them, as I have troubled you, if they seem to care about riches, or anything, more than about virtue; or if they pretend to be something when they are really nothing—then reprove them, as I have reproved you, for not caring about that for which they ought to care, and thinking that they are something when they are really nothing. And if you do this, I shall have received justice at your hands, and so will my sons.

"The hour of departure has arrived, and we go our ways—I to die, and you to live. Which is better God only knows."

18

⚜

Plato

REPUBLIC

To Plato (ca. 429–347 B.C.), Socrates's most brilliant disciple, the trial and death of the master came as a profound shock (see Selection 17). Born a member of the Athenian ruling class, Plato grew up in an atmosphere of war and revolution. In 404 B.C., at the end of the Peloponnesian War, he saw the discredited Athenian democracy go down in ruin. He then looked to a government by aristocrats to achieve order and justice, only to be disillusioned by the incompetence of those installed with the support of the victorious Spartans. Those aristocrats came to be known as the "Thirty Tyrants." The death of his revered master in 399 B.C. under a restored democracy turned the youthful Plato from the anticipation of a life of public service, normal for an Athenian aristocrat, to the teaching and application of the Socratic ideals. About 387 B.C., after a prolonged absence following Socrates's death, he returned to Athens and gathered about himself a community of young disciples, teaching them the principles of his beloved teacher.

The basic human problem, it seemed to Plato, was this: How can society be reconstituted so that all individuals may experience happiness and justice? To guide and inspire a careful inquiry into this problem, Plato established a school, known as the Academy, in a grove of olive trees on the outskirts of Athens. (The school's name came from the fact that the grove was sacred to a mythological hero, Academus.) The mission of the Academy was the training of philosopher–statesmen who, Plato hoped, would someday govern Athens; for he believed that only when a city–state was governed by such men could it achieve justice. Soon, however, the Academy became not only a pan-Hellenic center for study and research, but a magnet for philosophers throughout the Mediterranean world; it was to remain such for almost a thousand years (until its forced closing by the Christian emperor Justinian, A.D. 529).

There, until his death, Plato taught and developed the thought of Socrates and continued to write the dialogues (discussions) in which he almost always portrayed Socrates as the principal speaker, even when he sometimes developed ideas beyond any that Socrates had stated. Prominent among these approximately twenty-five philosophical dialogues is the Republic, *from which the following passage is taken. Although the Spartan laws and customs are taken as an imperfect working model (see Selection 16), the* Republic's *central thesis is that governing is a task only for those qualified; that the impartial lover of truth, the philosopher, alone is qualified to govern; and that until philosophy and political power meet in one authority, there will be no end to human misery.*

The Republic *is a discussion of great intellectual richness and breadth; and as it is probably Plato's most widely read work, it has exercised a profound influence. To many it is perceived as only a utopian or visionary program, the first of its kind in Western literature. To others—perhaps reflecting upon the social disturbances, "democratic" political stupidities, and mass sufferings of the modern age—it is regarded as the greatest work of political philosophy ever written.*

The Republic *is concerned with the nature of justice and how a just social order may be realized. Socrates, the main speaker, develops the true meaning of justice and describes an ideal society in which justice has been made real. The following parable, the famous "Allegory of the Cave" that begins Book VII of the* Republic *illustrates the key function of philosophers as educators and governors. Socrates is portrayed here speaking to Glaucon, Plato's older brother, on the difference between philosophers and unenlightened men. The parable notes the difficulty philosophers will have in returning to the world of everyday affairs after they have experienced knowledge of "the Good." Nevertheless, Socrates asserts, in the truly just state, civic leadership will be the duty of those philosophers. We see here Plato's view of the alienation of most people—not from God or society, but from Plato's concept of reality.*

❧

ALLEGORY OF THE CAVE

"And now," I said, "let me show in a parable how far our nature is enlightened or unenlightened:—Behold! Human beings housed in an underground cave, which has a long entrance open towards the light and as wide as the interior of the cave; here they have been from their childhood, and have their legs and necks chained, so that they cannot move and can only see before them, being prevented by the chains from turning round their heads. Above and behind them a fire is blazing at a distance, and between the fire and the prisoners there is a raised way; and you

---

Plato, *Republic*, in *The Dialogues of Plato*, trans. Benjamin Jowett (Oxford: Clarendon Press, 1953), from Book VII. Adapted by the editor.

will see, if you look, a low wall built along the way, like the screen which marionette players have in front of them, over which they show the puppets."

"I see."

"And do you see," I said, "men passing along the wall carrying all sorts of vessels, and statues and figures of animals made of wood and stone and various materials, which appear over the wall? While carrying their burdens, some of them, as you would expect, are talking, others silent."

"You have shown me a strange image, and they are strange prisoners."

"Like ourselves," I replied, "for in the first place do you think they have seen anything of themselves, and of one another, except the shadows which the fire throws on the opposite wall of the cave?"

"How could they do so," he asked, "if throughout their lives they were never allowed to move their heads?"

"And of the objects which are being carried in like manner they would only see the shadows?"

"Yes," he said.

"And if they were able to converse with one another, would they not suppose that the things they saw were the real things?"

"Very true."

"And suppose further that the prison had an echo which came from the other side, would they not be sure to fancy when one of the passers-by spoke that the voice which they heard came from the passing shadow?"

"No question," he replied.

"To them," I said, "the truth would be literally nothing but the shadows of the images."

"That is certain."

"And now look again, and see in what manner they would be released from their bonds, and cured of their error, whether the process would naturally be as follows. At first, when any of them is liberated and compelled suddenly to stand up and turn his neck round and walk and look towards the light, he will suffer sharp pains; the glare will distress him, and he will be unable to see the realities of which in his former state he had seen the shadows; and then conceive someone saying to him that what he saw before was an illusion, but that now, when he is approaching nearer to being and his eye is turned towards more real existence, he has a clearer vision—what will be his reply? And you may further imagine that his instructor is pointing to the objects as they pass and requiring him to name them—will he not be perplexed? Will he not fancy that the shadows which he formerly saw are truer than the objects which are now shown to him?"

"Far truer."

"And if he is compelled to look straight at the firelight, will he not have a pain in his eyes which will make him turn away to take refuge in the objects of vision which he can see, and which he will conceive to be in reality clearer than the things which are now being shown to him?"

"True," he said.

"And suppose once more, that he is reluctantly dragged up that steep and rugged ascent, and held fast until he is forced into the presence of the sun itself, is he not likely to be pained and irritated? When he approaches the light his eyes will be dazzled, and he will not be able to see anything at all of what are now called realities."

"Not all in a moment," he said.

"He will require to grow accustomed to the sight of the upper world. And first he will see the shadows best, next the reflections of men and other objects in the water, and then the objects themselves; and, when he turned to the heavenly bodies and the heaven itself, he would find it easier to gaze upon the light of the moon and the stars at night than to see the sun or the light of the sun by day?"

"Certainly."

"Last of all he will be able to see the sun, not turning aside to the illusory reflections in the water, but gazing directly at it in its own proper place, and contemplating it as it is."

"Certainly."

"He will then proceed to argue that this is what gives the seasons and the years, and is the guardian of all that is in the visible world, and in a certain way the cause of all things which he and his fellows have been accustomed to behold?"

"Clearly," he said, "he would arrive at this conclusion after what he had seen."

"And when he remembered his old dwelling place, and the wisdom of the cave and his fellow prisoners, do you not suppose that he would be happy about the change, and pity them?"

"Certainly, he would."

"And if they were in the habit of awarding honors among themselves on those who were quickest to observe the passing shadows and to remark which of them went before and which followed after and which were together, and who were best able from these observations to forecast the future, do you think that he would be eager for such honors and glories, or envy those who attained honor and sovereignty among those men? Would he not say with Homer, 'Better to be a serf, laboring for a landless master,'[1] and to endure anything, rather than think as they do and live after their manner?"

"Yes," he said, "I think that he would consent to suffer anything rather than live in this miserable manner."

"Imagine once more," I said, "such a one coming down suddenly out of the sunlight, and being replaced in his old seat; would he not be certain to have his eyes full of darkness?"

---

[1] In Homer's epic poem *The Odyssey* (Selection 7), the soul of the dead Achilles in Hades states to the living Odysseus that he would rather be the lowliest slave on earth than the king of the departed souls in the underworld of Hades.

"To be sure," he said.

"And if there were a contest, and he had to compete in measuring the shadows with the prisoners who had never moved out of the cave, while his sight was still weak, and before his eyes had become steady (and the time which would be needed to acquire this new habit of sight might be very considerable), would he not make himself ridiculous? Men would say of him that he had returned from the place above with his eyes ruined; and that it was better not even to think of ascending; and if anyone tried to loose another and lead him up to the light, let them only catch the offender, and they would put him to death."[2]

"No question," he said.

"This entire allegory," I said, "you may now fit, dear Glaucon, to the previous argument; the prison-house is the world of sight, the light of fire is the power of the sun, and you will not misunderstand me if you interpret the journey upwards to be the ascent of the soul into the intellectual world according to my surmise, which, at your desire, I have expressed—whether rightly or wrongly God knows. But, whether true or false, my opinion is that in the world of knowledge the essential Form of Goodness appears last of all, and is seen only with an effort; although, when seen, it is inferred to be the universal author of all things beautiful and right, parent of light and of the lord of light in the visible world, and the immediate and supreme source of reason and truth in the intellectual; and that this is the power upon which he who would act rationally either in public or private life must have his eye fixed."

"I agree," he said, "as far as I am able to understand you."

"Moreover," I said, "you must agree once more, and not wonder that those who attain to this vision are unwilling to take any part in human affairs; for their souls are ever hastening into the upper world where they desire to dwell; which desire of theirs is very natural, if our allegory may be trusted."

"Yes, very natural."

"And is there anything surprising in one who passes from divine contemplations to the evil state of man, appearing grotesque and ridiculous; if, while his eyes are blinking and before he has become accustomed to the surrounding darkness, he is compelled to fight in courts of law, or in other places, about the images or the shadows of images of justice, and must strive against some rival about opinions of these things which are entertained by men who have never yet seen the true justice?"

"Anything but surprising," he replied.

"Anyone who has common sense will remember that the bewilderments of the eyes are of two kinds and arise from two causes, either from coming out of the light or from going into the light, and, judging that the soul may be affected in the same way, will not give way to foolish laughter when he sees anyone whose vision is per-

---

[2]As happened to Socrates (Selection 17).

plexed and weak; he will first ask whether that soul of man has come out of the brighter life and is unable to see because unaccustomed to the dark, or having turned from darkness to the day is dazzled by excess of light. And he will count the one happy in his condition and state of being, and he will pity the other; or, if he have a mind to laugh at the soul which comes from below into the light, this laughter will not be quite so laughable as that which greets the soul which returns from above out of the light into the cave."

"That," he said, "is a very just distinction."

"But then, if I am right, certain professors of education must be wrong when they say that they can put a knowledge into the soul which was not there before, like sight into blind eyes."

"They undoubtedly say this," he replied.

"Whereas our argument shows that the power and capacity of learning exists in the soul already; and that just as if it were not possible to turn the eye from darkness to light without the whole body, so too the instrument of knowledge can only by the movement of the whole soul be turned from the world of becoming to that of being, and learn by degrees to endure the sight of being, and of the brightest and best of being, or in other words, of the Good."

"Very true." . . .

"Then," I said, "the business of us who are the founders of the State will be to compel the best minds to attain that knowledge which we have already shown to be the greatest of all, namely, the vision of the Good; they must make the ascent which we have described; but when they have ascended and seen enough we must not allow them to do as they do now."

"What do you mean?"

"They are permitted to remain in the upper world, refusing to descend again among the prisoners in the cave, and partake of their labors and honors, whether they are worth having or not."

"But is not this unjust?" he said, "Ought we to give them a worse life, when they might have a better?"

"You have again forgotten, my friend," I said, "the intention of our law, which does not aim at making any one class in the State happy above the rest; it seeks rather to spread happiness over the whole State, and to hold the citizens together by persuasion and necessity, making each share with others any benefit which he can confer upon the State; and the law aims at producing such citizens, not that they may be left to please themselves, but that they may serve in binding the State together."

"True," he said, "I had forgotten."

"Observe, Glaucon, that we shall do no wrong to our philosophers but rather make a just demand, when we oblige them to watch over and care for the other citizens; we shall explain to them that in other States, men of their class are not obliged to share in the toils of politics: and this is reasonable, for they grow up spontaneously, against the will of the governments in their several States; and things which grow up of themselves, and are indebted to no one for their nurture, cannot fairly be expected to pay dues for a care they have never received. But we have brought you into the world to be rulers of the hive, kings of yourselves and of the other citizens, and have educated you far better and more perfectly than they have been educated, and you are better able to share in the double duty. Wherefore each of you, when his turn comes, must go down to rejoin his companions, and acquire with them the habit of seeing things in the dark. As you acquire that habit, you will see ten thousand times better than the inhabitants of the cave, and you will know what the several images are and what they represent, because you have seen the beautiful and just and good in their reality. And thus our State, which is also yours, will be a reality and not a dream only, and will be administered in a spirit unlike that of other States, in which men fight with one another about shadows only and are distracted in the struggle for power, which in their eyes is a great good. Whereas the truth is that the State in which those who are to govern have least ambition to do so is always the best and most peacefully governed, and the State in which they are most eager, the worst."

"Quite true," he replied.

"And will our pupils, when they hear this, refuse to take their turn at the toils of State, when they are allowed to spend the greater part of their time with one another in the heavenly light?"

"Impossible," he answered, "for they are just men, and the commands which we impose upon them are just. But there can be no doubt that every one of them will take office as a stern necessity, contrary to the spirit of our present rulers of State."

"Yes, my friend," I said, "and there lies the point. You must contrive for your future rulers another and a better life than that of a ruler, and then you may have a well-ordered State; for only in the State which offers this, will they rule who are truly rich, not in gold, but in virtue and wisdom, which are the true blessings of life. Whereas if men who are destitute and starved of such personal goods go to the administration of public affairs, thinking to enrich themselves at the public expense, order there can never be; for they will be fighting about office, and the civil and domestic conflicts which thus arise will be the ruin of the rulers themselves and of the whole State."

"Most true," he replied.

"And the only life which looks down upon the life of political ambition is that of true philosophy. Do you know of any other?"

"Indeed, I do not," he said.

"And those who govern should not be in love with power. For, if they do there will be rival lovers, and they will fight."

"No question."

"Whom, then, will you compel to become guardians of the State? Surely those who excel in judgment of the means by which a State is administered, and who at the same time have other honors and another and better life than that of politics?"

"None but these," he replied. . . .

19

❧

Aristotle

POLITICS

The Greek polis *(city–state) and its culture were the affair of a small minor-*
ity of privileged citizens who, ideally, placed honor and the esteem of their
fellow citizens above power and profit. This fact is abundantly reflected in the
writings of Xenophon and Plato, who held anti-democratic views (see Selections
16, 17, and 18). Aristotle (384–322 B.C.) also had, by modern definition, few
democratic sympathies. Born at Stagira in Macedonia, north of Greece, he grew
up in Macedonian court circles where his father was physician to the king. From
the age of seventeen until the death of Plato, twenty years later, Aristotle studied
in Athens under the master at the Academy. Later, he spent three years as court
tutor to the young Alexander, who would inherit the Macedonian throne. In 335
B.C., after Alexander had become king and began his vast conquests in Greece
and the Middle East, Aristotle established a rival school to the Academy, his
famous Lyceum. During the next dozen years, he taught there, while producing
a wealth of writings. Upon Alexander's death in 323 B.C. Aristotle was forced by
the anti-Macedonian party to flee Athens; he died in exile a year later.

Throughout his works, which systematically covered all the fields of human
knowledge—both theoretical and practical—Aristotle was concerned (as was his
teacher Plato) with the search for reality, for objective truth. Aristotle, however,
was more down-to-earth than Plato; he tried to show that material objects are no
less real than Plato's world of ideal "Forms." Aristotle tested his value-judgments
by comparing them to things in the material world, rather than by describing an
ideal vision as did Plato (see Selection 18). Aristotle's surviving writings consist
mainly of notes, or summaries, of his lectures, intended for the use of students at
the Lyceum. Unfortunately, none of his highly polished "Platonic style" dialogues,
or other works intended for a general readership, survives.

In his writings on both ethics and politics Aristotle held that they were com-
plementary ways of going about the same thing: attainment of the good life and,

therefore, happiness for those "high-minded" individuals capable of attaining it. He believed that human beings are "political [social] animals" and that their moral character could be perfected only in the community life of the polis. *But what kind of* polis? *The selection that follows is from* Politics; *it gives a portion of Aristotle's view of the "best form of the state." The state's purpose would* not *be rule by the many, equality for all, or a high material standard of life, but rather promotion of the good life only for its "high-minded" citizens. In fact, his model political community, like all Greek city–states and most of the world prior to the modern age, depended upon the institution of slave labor. Aristotle believed that many individuals were not capable of governing themselves through reason and, therefore, were "slaves by nature."*

Despite the unprecedented glories of the polis *in such humanistic endeavors as the arts, philosophy, and the beginnings of democracy, nowhere are the limits of Greek political theory better demonstrated than in Aristotle's inability to project his thinking beyond the actualities of his own time and place. (Indeed, he is supposed to have studied the varied constitutions of 158 Greek city–states before composing the* Politics.) *Despite his learning and logical power, he did not realize that the day of the small city–state had passed. Aristotle lacked the wide-ranging imagination and practical political skills of his pupil Alexander, whose expansionist career and integrationist policy pointed dramatically to the emergence of the great leader and the imperial state.*

[SLAVERY BY LAW AND BY NATURE]

Let us first speak of master and slave, looking to the needs of practical life and also seeking to attain some better theory of their relation than exists at present. For some are of opinion that the rule of a master is a science, and that the management of a household, and the mastership of slaves, and the political and royal rule,. . . are all the same. Others affirm that the rule of a master over slaves is contrary to nature, and that the distinction between slave and freeman exists by law only, and not by nature; and being an interference with nature is therefore unjust.

Property is a part of the household, and the art of acquiring property is a part of the art of managing the household; for no man can live well, or indeed live at all, unless he be provided with necessaries. And as in the arts which have a definite sphere the workers must have their own proper instruments for the accomplishment of their work, so it is in the management of a household. Now instru-

Aristotle, *The Politics of Aristotle,* trans. Benjamin Jowett. 2 vols. Oxford, 1885, Book I, chaps. 4–7, Book VII, chaps. 4–9. Adapted by the editor..

ments are of various sorts; some are living, others lifeless; in the rudder, the pilot of a ship has a lifeless, in the look-out man, a living instrument; for in the arts the servant is a kind of instrument. Thus, too, a possession is an instrument for maintaining life. And so, in the arrangement of the family, a slave is a living possession, and property a number of such instruments; and the servant is himself an instrument which takes precedence of all other instruments. For if every instrument could accomplish its own work, obeying or anticipating the will of others, like the statues of Daedalus, or the tripods of Hephaestus, which, says the poet,[1] "of their own accord entered the assembly of the Gods"; if, in like manner, the shuttle would weave and the plectrum[2] touch the lyre without a hand to guide them, chief workmen would not need servants, nor masters slaves. Here, however, another distinction must be drawn; the instruments commonly so called are instruments of production, whilst a possession is an instrument of action. The shuttle, for example, is not only of use; but something else is made by it, whereas of a garment or of a bed there is only the use. Further, as production and action are different in kind, and both require instruments, the instruments which they employ must likewise differ in kind. But life is action and not production, and therefore the slave is the minister of action. Again, a possession is spoken of as a part is spoken of; for the part is not only a part of something else, but wholly belongs to it; and this is also true of a possession. The master is only the master of the slave; he does not belong to him, whereas the slave is not only the slave of his master, but wholly belongs to him. Hence we see what is the nature and office of the slave; he who is by nature not his own but another's man, is by nature a slave; and he may be said to be another's man, who, being a human being, is also a possession. And a possession may be defined as an instrument of action, separable from the possessor.

But is there anyone thus intended by nature to be a slave, and for whom such a condition is expedient and right, or rather is not all slavery a violation of nature?

There is no difficulty in answering this question, on grounds both of reason and of fact. For that some should rule and others be ruled is a thing not only necessary, but expedient; from the hour of their birth, some are marked out for subjection, others for rule.

And there are many kinds both of rulers and subjects (and that rule is the better which is exercised over better subjects—for example, to rule over men is better than to rule over wild beasts; for the work is better which is executed by better workmen, and where one man rules and another is ruled, they may be said to

---

[1] In his epic poem *The Iliad* (Book XVIII), Homer tells of twenty three-legged tables built by Hephaestus, divine craftsman of Olympus. He fitted golden wheels to all their legs so that they could run by themselves to a meeting of the gods and amaze the company by running home again.

[2] A small, thin, ivory or metal piece used to pluck a stringed instrument like a lyre.

have a work); for in all things which form a composite whole and which are made up of parts, whether continuous or discontinuous,[3] a distinction between the ruling and the subject element comes to light. Such a duality exists in living creatures, but not in them only; it originates in the constitution of the universe; even in things which have no life there is a ruling principle, as in a musical harmony. But we are wandering from the subject. We will therefore restrict ourselves to the living creature, which, in the first place, consists of soul and body: and of these two, the one is by nature the ruler, and the other the subject. But then we must look for the intentions of nature in things which retain their nature, and not in things which are corrupted. And therefore we must study the man who is in the most perfect state both of body and soul, for in him we shall see the true relation of the two; although in bad or corrupted natures the body will often appear to rule over the soul, because they are in an evil and unnatural condition. At all events we may firstly observe in living creatures both a master's and a constitutional rule; for the soul rules the body with a master's rule, whereas the intellect rules the appetites with a constitutional and royal rule. And it is clear that the rule of the soul over the body, and of the mind and the rational element over the passionate, is natural and expedient; whereas the equality of the two or the rule of the inferior is always hurtful. The same holds good of animals in relation to men; for tame animals have a better nature than wild, and all tame animals are better off when they are ruled by man; for then they are preserved. Again, the male is by nature superior, and the female inferior; and the one rules, and the other is ruled; this principle, of necessity, extends to all mankind. Where then there is such a difference as that between soul and body, or between men and animals (as in the case of those whose business is to use their body, and who can do nothing better), the lower sort are by nature slaves, and it is better for them as for all inferiors that they should be under the rule of a master. For he who can be, and therefore is, another's and he who participates in rational principle enough to recognize, but not to act upon, such a principle, is a slave by nature. Whereas the lower animals cannot even recognize a principle; they obey their instincts. And indeed the use made of slaves and of tame animals is not very different; for both with their bodies minister to the needs of life. Nature would like to distinguish between the bodies of freemen and slaves, making the slaves strong for servile labor, the other upright, and although useless for such bodily services, useful for political life in the arts both of war and peace. But the opposite often happens—that some have the souls and others have the bodies of freemen. And doubtless if men differed from one another in the mere forms of their bodies as much as the statues of the Gods do from men, all would acknowledge that the inferior class should be slaves of the superior. And if this is true of the body, how much more just that a similar dis-

---

[3]For example, mind and body form a continuous combination (one living being); master and slave form a discontinuous combination.

tinction should exist in the soul? But the beauty of the body is seen, whereas the beauty of the soul is not seen. It is clear, then, that some men are by nature free, and others slaves, and that for these latter slavery is both expedient and right.

But that those who take the opposite view have in a certain way right on their side, may be easily seen. For the words *slavery* and *slave* are used in two senses. There is a slave or slavery by law as well as by nature. The law of which I speak is a sort of convention—the law by which whatever is taken in war is supposed to belong to the victors. But this right many jurists impeach, as they would an orator who brought forward an unconstitutional measure: they detest the notion that, because one man has the power of doing violence and is superior in brute strength, another shall be his slave and subject. Even among philosophers there is a difference of opinion. The origin of the dispute, and what makes the views invade each other's territory, is as follows: in some sense virtue, when furnished with means, has actually the greatest power of exercising force: and as superior power is only found where there is superior excellence of some kind, power seems to imply virtue, and the dispute to be simply one about justice (for it is due to one party identifying justice with goodwill,[4] while the other identifies it with the mere rule of the stronger). If these views are thus set out separately, the other views have no force or plausibility against the view that the superior in virtue ought to rule, or be master. Others, clinging, as they think, simply to a principle of justice (for law and custom are a sort of justice), assume that slavery in accordance with the custom of war is justified by law, but at the same moment they deny this. For what if the cause of the war be unjust? And again, no one would ever say that he is a slave who is unworthy to be a slave. Were this the case, men of the highest rank would be slaves and the children of slaves if they or their parents chance to have been taken captive and sold. Wherefore Greeks do not like to call Greeks slaves, but confine the term to barbarians.[5] Yet, in using this language, they really mean the natural slave of whom we spoke at first; for it must be admitted that some are slaves everywhere, others nowhere. The same principle applies to nobility. Greeks regard themselves as noble everywhere, and not only in their own country, but they deem the barbarians noble only when at home, thereby implying that there are two sorts of nobility and freedom, the one absolute, the other relative. The Helen of Theodectes[6] says: "Who would presume to call me servant who am on both sides sprung from the stem of the Gods?" What does this mean but that they distinguish freedom and slavery, noble and humble birth, by the two principles of good and evil? They think that as men and animals beget

---

[4]That is, mutual goodwill, which is held to be incompatible with the relation of master and slave.

[5]*Barbarians* is a term often used to mean simply "non-Greeks."

[6]Theodectes was a Greek tragic poet of the fourth century B.C. He wrote of Helen, whose seduction started the Trojan War. Her father was Zeus, king of the Olympian gods.

men and animals, so from good men a good man springs. But this is what nature, though she may intend it, cannot always accomplish.

We see then that there is some foundation for this difference of opinion, and that all are not either slaves by nature or freemen by nature, and also that there is in some cases a marked distinction between the two classes, rendering it expedient and right for the one to be slaves and the others to be masters: the one practicing obedience, the others exercising the authority and lordship which nature intended them to have. The abuse of this authority is injurious to both; for the interests of part and whole, of body and soul, are the same, and the slave is a part of the master, a living but separated part of his bodily frame. Hence, where the relation of master and slave between them is natural they are friends and have a common interest, but where it rests merely on law and force the reverse is true.

The previous remarks are quite enough to show that the rule of a master is not a constitutional rule, and that all the different kinds of rule are not, as some affirm, the same with each other. For there is one rule exercised over subjects who are by nature free, another over subjects who are by nature slaves. The rule of a household is a monarchy, for every house is under one head: whereas constitutional rule is a government of freemen and equals. The master is not called a master because he has knowledge, but because he is of a certain character, and the same remark applies to the slave and the freeman. Still there may be a science for the master and science for the slave. The science of the slave would be such as the man of Syracuse taught, who made money by instructing slaves in their ordinary duties. And such a knowledge may be carried further, so as to include cookery and similar menial arts. For some duties are of the more necessary, others of the more honorable sort; as the proverb says, "slave before slave, master before master." But all such branches of knowledge are servile. There is likewise a science of the master, which teaches the use of slaves; for the master as such is concerned, not with the acquisition, but with the use of them. Yet this so-called science is not anything great or wonderful; for the master need only know how to order that which the slave must know how to execute. Hence those who are in a position which places them above toil have overseers who attend to their households while they occupy themselves with philosophy or with politics. But the art of acquiring slaves, I mean of justly acquiring them, differs both from the art of the master and the art of the slave, being a skill of hunting or war. Enough of the distinction between master and slave.

●   ●   ●

[THE SIZE OF THE STATE]

In what has preceded I have discussed other forms of government; in what remains the first point to be considered is what should be the conditions of the ideal or perfect state; for the perfect state cannot exist without a due supply of the means of life. And therefore we must presuppose many purely imaginary conditions, but nothing impossible. There will be a certain number of citizens, a country in which to place them, and the like. As the weaver or shipbuilder or any other skilled craftsman must have the material proper for his work (and in proportion as this is better prepared, so will the result of his art be nobler), so the statesman or legislator must also have the materials suited to him.

First among the materials required by the statesman is population: he will consider what should be the number and character of the citizens, and then what should be the size and character of the country. Most persons think that a state in order to be happy ought to be large; but even if they are right, they have no idea what is a large and what a small state. For they judge of the size of the city by the number of the inhabitants; whereas they ought to regard, not their number, but their power. A city too, like an individual, has a work to do; and that city which is best adapted to the fulfillment of its work is to be deemed greatest, in the same sense of the word *great* in which Hippocrates[7] might be called greater, not as a man, but as a physician, than someone else who was taller. And even if we reckon greatness by numbers, we ought not to include everybody, for there must always be in cities a multitude of slaves and foreigners; but we should include those only who are members of the state, and who form an essential part of it. The number of the latter is a proof of the greatness of a city; but a city which produces numerous craftsmen and comparatively few soldiers cannot be great, for a great city is not to be confused with a populous one. Moreover, experience shows that a very populous city can rarely, if ever, be well governed; since all cities which have a reputation for good government have a limit of population. We may argue on grounds of reason, and the same result will follow. For law is order, and good law is good order; but a very great multitude cannot be orderly: to introduce order into the unlimited is the work of a divine power—of such a power as holds together the universe. Beauty is realized in number and magnitude, and the state which combines magnitude with good order must necessarily be the most beautiful. To the size of states there is a limit, as there is to other things, plants, animals, implements; for none of these retain their natural power when they are too large or too small, but they either wholly lose their nature, or are spoiled. For example, a ship which is only a span long will not be a ship at all, nor a ship a quarter of a mile long; yet there may be a ship of a certain size, either too large or too small, which will still be a ship, but bad for sailing. In like manner a state when composed of too few is not, as a state ought to be, self-sufficing; when of too many, though self-sufficing in all mere necessities, as a nation may be, it is not a state, being almost incapable of constitutional government. For who can be the general of such a vast multitude, or who the herald, unless he have the voice of a Stentor?[8]

---

[7]A famous Greek physician of the fifth century B.C.

[8]A herald in Homer's *Iliad,* known for his powerful voice.

A state, then, only begins to exist when it has attained a population sufficient for a good life in the political community: it may indeed, if it somewhat exceed this number, be a greater state. But, as I was saying, there must be a limit. What should be the limit will be easily ascertained by experience. For both governors and governed have duties to perform; the special functions of a governor are to command and to judge. But if the citizens of a state are to judge and to distribute offices according to merit, then they must know each other's characters; where they do not possess this knowledge, both the election to offices and the decision of lawsuits will go wrong. When the population is very large they are settled randomly, which clearly ought not to be. Besides, in an over-populous state foreigners and resident aliens will readily acquire the rights of citizens, for who will find them out? Clearly then the best limit of the population of a state is the largest number which suffices for the purposes of life, and can be taken in at a single view. Enough concerning the size of a state.

Much the same principle will apply to the territory of the state: everyone would agree in praising the territory which is most entirely self-sufficing; and that must be the territory which is all-producing, for to have all things and to lack nothing is sufficiency. In size and extent it should be such as may enable the inhabitants to live at once temperately and liberally in the enjoyment of leisure. Whether we are right or wrong in laying down this limit we will inquire more precisely hereafter, when we have occasion to consider what is the right use of property and wealth: a matter which is much disputed, because men are inclined to rush into one of two extremes, some into stinginess, others into luxury.

It is not difficult to determine the general character of the territory which is required (there are, however, some points on which military authorities should be heard); it should be difficult of access to the enemy, and easy of escape to the inhabitants. Further, we require that the land as well as the inhabitants of whom we were just now speaking should be taken in at a single view, for a country which is easily seen can be easily protected. As to the position of the city, if we could have what we wish, it should be well situated in regard both to sea and land. This then is one principle, that it should be a convenient center for the protection of the whole region; the other is, that it should be suitable for receiving the fruits of the soil, and also for the bringing in of timber and any other products that are easily transported.

[THE IMPORTANCE OF THE SEA]

Whether a communication with the sea is beneficial to a well-ordered state or not is a question which has often been asked. It is argued that the introduction of strangers brought up under other laws, and the increase of population, will be adverse to good order; the increase arises from their using the sea and having a crowd of merchants coming and going, and is harmful to good government. Apart from these considerations, it would be undoubtedly better, both with a

view to safety and to the provision of necessaries, that the city and territory should
be connected with the sea; the defenders of a country, if they are to maintain
themselves against an enemy, should be easily relieved both by land and by sea.
. . . Moreover, it is necessary that they should import from abroad what is not
found in their own country, and that they should export what they have in excess;
for a city ought to be a market, not indeed for the interest of others, but for her
own interest.

Those who make themselves a market for the world only do so for the sake of
revenue, and if a state ought not to desire profit of this kind it ought not to have
such a trading center. Nowadays we often see in countries and cities dockyards
and harbors very conveniently placed outside the city, but not too far off; and
they are kept in dependence by walls and similar fortifications. Cities thus situated reap the benefits from their ports; and any harm which is likely to accrue may
be easily guarded against by the laws, which will pronounce and determine who
may hold communication with one another, and who may not.

There can be no doubt that the possession of a moderate naval force is advantageous to a city; the city should be formidable not only to its own citizens but to
some of its neighbors, or, if necessary, able to assist them by sea as well as by land.
The proper number or magnitude of this naval force is relative to the character of
the state; for if her function is to take a leading part in politics, her naval power
should be commensurate with the scale of her enterprises. The population of the
state need not be much increased, since there is no necessity that the sailors
should be citizens. The marines who have the control and command will be
freemen, and belong also to the infantry; and wherever there is a dense population of resident aliens and farmers, there will always be sailors more than enough.
Of this we see instances at the present day. The city of Heraclea,[9] for example,
although small in comparison with many others, can furnish a considerable fleet.
Such are our conclusions respecting the territory of the state, its harbors, its town,
its relations to the sea, and its maritime power.

[THE CHARACTER OF THE CITIZENS]

Having spoken of the number of the citizens, we will proceed to speak of what
should be their character. This is a subject which can be easily understood by anyone who casts his eye on the more celebrated states of Hellas,[10] and generally on
the distribution of races in the habitable world. Those who live in a cold climate
and in Europe are full of spirit, but lacking in intelligence and skill; and therefore
they retain comparative freedom, but have no political organization, and are incapable of ruling over others. The natives of Asia [the Middle East] are intelligent

---

[9]A small Greek city in southern Italy.

[10]The Greek world.

and inventive, but they are lacking in spirit, and therefore they are always in a state of subjection and slavery. But the Hellenic nation, which is situated between them, is likewise intermediate in character, being high-spirited and also intelligent. Hence it continues free, and is the best-governed of any nation, and, if it could be formed into one state, would be able to rule the world.[11] There are also similar differences in the different tribes of Hellas; for some of them are of a one-sided nature, and are intelligent or courageous only, while in others there is a happy combination of both qualities. And clearly those whom the legislator will most easily lead to virtue may be expected to be both intelligent and courageous. Some say that the protectors of the state should be friendly towards those whom they know, fierce towards those whom they do not know. Now, passion is the quality of the soul which produces friendship and enables us to love; notably the spirit within us is more stirred against our friends and acquaintances than against those who are unknown to us, when we think that we are despised by them—for which reason Archilochus,[12] complaining of his friends, very naturally addresses his soul in these words, "For surely thou art plagued on account of friends."

The power of command and the love of freedom are in all men based upon this quality, for passion is commanding and invincible. Nor is it right to say that the protectors should be fierce towards those whom they do not know, for we ought not to be out of temper with anyone; and a lofty spirit is not fierce by nature, but only when excited against evil-doers. And this, as I was saying before, is a feeling which men show most strongly towards their friends if they think they have received a wrong at their hands: as indeed is reasonable; for, besides the actual injury, they seem to be deprived of a benefit by those who owe them one. Hence the saying, "Cruel is the strife of brethren," and again, "They who love in excess also hate in excess."

Thus we have nearly determined the number and character of the citizens of our state, and also the size and nature of their territory. I say "nearly," for we ought not to require the same minuteness in theory as in the facts that come to us through sense-perceptions. . . .

[THE ESSENTIAL PARTS OF THE STATE]

Now, whereas happiness is the highest good, being a realization and perfect practice of virtue, which some can attain, while others have little or none of it, the various qualities of men are clearly the reason why there are various kinds of states

---

[11]Aristotle's most famous pupil, Alexander of Macedonia, organized an Hellenic army that conquered a vast territory, stretching from Greece to India. Alexander's mixing of nations ("races") in his empire was criticized by Aristotle. (After Alexander's death, his empire was divided among his generals.)

[12]Greek poet of the seventh century B.C.

and many forms of government. For different men seek after happiness in different ways and by different means, and so make for themselves different modes of life and forms of government. We must see also how many things are indispensable to the existence of a state, for what we call the parts of a state will be found among the indispensables. Let us then enumerate the functions of a state, and we shall easily find what we want.

First, there must be food; secondly, arts, for life requires many instruments; thirdly, there must be arms, for the members of a community have need of them, and in their own hands, too, in order to maintain authority both against disobedient subjects and against external assailants; fourthly, there must be a certain amount of revenue, both for internal needs, and for the purposes of war; fifthly, or rather first, there must be a care of religion, which is commonly called worship; sixthly, and most necessary of all, there must be a power of deciding what is for the public interest, and what is just in men's dealings with one another.

These are the services which every state may be said to need. For a state is not a mere aggregate of persons, but a union of them sufficing for the purposes of life; and if any of these things be lacking, it is as we maintain impossible that the community can be absolutely self-sufficing. A state then should be framed with a view to the fulfillment of these functions. There must be farmers to procure food, and skilled craftsmen, and a warlike and a wealthy class, and priests, and judges to decide what is necessary and expedient.

[WHO SHALL BE CITIZENS]

Having determined these points, we have in the next place to consider whether all ought to share in every sort of occupation. Shall every man be at once farmer, craftsman, legislator, judge, or shall we suppose the several occupations just mentioned assigned to different persons? Or, thirdly, shall some employments be assigned to individuals and others common to all? The same arrangement, however, does not occur in every constitution; as we were saying, all may be shared by all, or not all by all, but only by some. From this arises the differences of constitutions, for in democracies all share in all; in oligarchies the opposite practice prevails. Now, since we are here speaking of the best form of government, that is, that under which the state will be most happy (and happiness, as has been already said, cannot exist without virtue), it clearly follows that in the state which is best governed and possesses men who are just absolutely, and not merely relatively to the principle of the constitution, the citizens[13] must not lead the life of mechanics or tradesmen, for such a life is ignoble, and harmful to virtue. Neither must they be

---

[13]Male citizens alone exercised political power; citizenship in Greece was normally limited to those born of citizens.

farmers, since leisure is necessary both for the development of virtue and the performance of political duties.

Again, there is in a state a class of warriors, and another of legislators who advise and determine matters of law, and these seem in a special manner parts of a state. Now, should these two classes be distinguished, or are both functions to be assigned to the same persons? Here again there is no difficulty in seeing that both functions will in one way belong to the same, in another, to different persons. To different persons insofar as these employments are suited to different times of life, for the one requires wisdom and the other strength. But on the other hand, since it is an impossible thing that those who are able to use or to resist force should be willing to remain always in subjection, from this point of view the persons are the same; for those who carry arms can always determine the fate of the constitution. It remains therefore that both functions should be entrusted by the ideal constitution to the same persons—not, however, at the same time, but in the order prescribed by nature, who has given to young men strength and to older men wisdom. Such a distribution of duties will be practical and also just, and is founded upon a principle of conformity to merit. Besides, the ruling class should be the owners of property, for they are citizens, and the citizens of a state should be in good circumstances; whereas mechanics or any other class which is not a producer of virtue have no power in the state. This follows from our first principle, for happiness cannot exist without virtue, and a city is not to be termed happy in regard to a portion of the citizens, but in regard to them all. And clearly property should be in their hands, since the farmers will of necessity be slaves or barbarian aliens.

Of the classes enumerated there remain only the priests, and the manner in which their office is to be regulated is obvious. No farmer or mechanic should be appointed to it; for the gods should receive honor from the citizens only. Now since the body of the citizens is divided into two classes, the warriors and the legislators, and it is fitting that the worship of the gods should be duly performed, and also a rest provided in their service for those who from age have given up active life, to the old men of these two classes should be assigned the duties of priesthood.

We have shown what are the necessary conditions, and what the parts of a state: farmers, craftsmen, and laborers of all kinds are necessary to the existence of states, but the essential parts[14] of the state are the warriors and legislators. And these are distinguished severally from one another, the distinction being in some cases permanent, in others not.

---

[14]The active *citizen* elements that, strictly speaking, constitute the state.

20

UPANISHADS

The Upanishads *are the third and concluding part of the* Veda. *They follow the* Brahmanas *in each of the four* Vedas *(see Selections 8 and 9). The most spiritual part of the sacred scriptures of the Hindus, the* Upanishads *have always received high praise from philosophers of varied cultures for the profound knowledge they contain. For example, the nineteenth-century German philosopher Arthur Schopenhauer says that their reading "has been the consolation of my life, and will be of my death." The Indian Nobel laureate, Rabindranath Tagore, describes the* Upanishads *as "some of the most sacred words that have ever issued from the human mind."*

The Upanishads *exceed a hundred in number, although only about a dozen are considered principal, or "classic." The earliest of them date back to ca. 700 B.C. and the latest could have appeared as late as 300 B.C. They vary greatly in length, the shortest of them being barely two pages long, and the longest more than a hundred pages.*

The word Upanishad *comes from the Sanskrit* upa *("near"),* ni *("down"), and* shad *("sit"). It refers to pupils sitting down respectfully near a teacher to listen closely to the teacher's lessons. Nearness implies that the teacher gave the lessons in strict confidence, and only to those pupils who were worthy of them because of their innate ability and prior preparation for learning. The* Upanishads *are so named because they are works of instruction that were believed to impart knowledge of a very special kind, a mystery known only to those who experienced it themselves and who chose to initiate into that mystery elite pupils qualified to understand it. Because of the nature of their content, the* Upanishads *are sometimes called secret books. They were not meant for indiscriminate dissemination among the uninitiated.*

The authors and teachers of the Upanishads *were ascetics who had withdrawn from society to live a contemplative life in the forest. In the quietude of the forest, they pondered the problems of deepest concern regarding human existence and the world. In addressing these problems, they were reacting against the Brahmanic establishment (see Selection 9). Their reaction was part of an ascetic movement that swept India from the end of the eighth century B.C. onward. The movement included many different types of ascetics (individuals who practice self-denial) who were in agreement on one fundamental point: they all found the basis and values of Brahmanism unsatisfactory.*

The Brahmanic culture was based on the performance of religious rituals as the visible means for maintaining the natural and social orders. The aims of the Brahmanic religion were materialistic, i.e., the pursuit of worldly goods. Most ascetics considered ritual—at least when the externals of its performance were seen as self-sufficient—meaningless. As to their motives, the ascetics renounced all worldly things and sought a moral and religious basis for religion.

Departing in this manner from Brahmanism, the Upanishads, *however, did not reject it totally. Rather, they expanded the Brahmanic tradition by adding to it a spiritual view of human and universal existence. For this reason, the* Upanishads *are known as an orthodox reaction against Brahmanism as distinct from several unorthodox schools of thought, such as Buddhism (see Selection 21), which arose out of the ascetic movement and did not accept the authority of Brahmanism and the* Veda. *In turn, Brahmanism eventually assimilated the* Upanishads *into the Vedic canon and accorded them and their spiritual message the highest place in it. Comprising the concluding part of the* Veda, *the* Upanishads *are also often seen as the end of the* Veda *in a more profound sense. Most students of Indian philosophy and religion across the world, Hindu and non-Hindu alike, consider the* Upanishads *to be the final and logical culmination of Vedic thought. After the Vedic period, all major movements in the intellectual history of India, from the ancient to modern times, were in one way or another indebted to the* Upanishads.

As the utterances of individuals contemplating in solitude at different times and places, the Upanishads *as a body of literature, are not fully uniform in content. Instead, they often are marked by inconsistencies from one* Upanishad *to another or even within one* Upanishad. *However, they all contain the same basic ideas. Their essential subject is the nature of reality. They all observe that what appears to be real in our ordinary perceptions of the world is not truly so. In these perceptions, it is we who attribute reality to what actually does not exist. We are caught in an illusion. This illusion also applies to our perception of ourselves. Our selves, as we ordinarily know them, are not real. In thinking them to be real, we are caught in false and illusory identities.*

The Upanishads *further observe that true reality does exist, but it lies beyond ordinary human consciousness. We must transcend this consciousness to be able to perceive true reality. In their ideas about reality and appearance, the* Upanishads *remarkably resemble the* Dialogues *of the ancient Greek philosopher Plato (see Selection 18—Plato's "Allegory of the Cave"). Since true reality is known only when one reaches it, it cannot be fully described for those who do not yet know it. The* Upanishads *mention some of reality's attributes only in an effort to suggest some idea of its nature for the limited understanding of humans. These attributes are described as follows. True reality exists absolutely; that is, it exists by itself and not relative to anything else, and there is absolutely no doubt about its existence. This reality is the ultimate foundation of all being. Everything in the universe comes out of the true reality and is eventually reabsorbed into it. This reality is eternal; it has always existed and always will. It is spiritual in character; that is, it is not like non-conscious matter, but is rather a state of consciousness, in fact, a state of omniscience. It is also a state of eternal joy. Above all, this reality is the* only *true reality. There is no other. All that is real is one. The* Upanishads *call this reality Brahman. With the emphasis on the second syllable, the word means "a priest"; when the emphasis is on the first syllable, the word means "reality").*

The Upanishads *also say that beyond an individual's illusory self, the real self exists. It is called Atman. Since all reality is one, Atman and Brahman are essentially identical. They have different names only because of a difference in their frames of reference, one (Atman) being reality from the standpoint of the individual and the other (Brahman) from the standpoint of the universe. This equation between an individual's true self and the reality of the universe is the fundamental postulate of the* Upanishads.

According to the Upanishads, *the highest goal that a person can have in life is to know the Atman. Knowledge here does not mean mere intellectual perception but rather a total personal experience of what is known. To know the Atman is to become the Atman, i.e., to realize one's true self. Until such self-realization is achieved, a person remains bound to a continuous cycle of death, rebirth, and death again; the good or bad quality of life in this transmigration from life to life is determined by one's karma (the consequences of one's good or bad deeds).*

The following excerpts illustrate the central message of the Upanishads. *The first excerpt shows the transition in the Vedic religion from the sacrificial ritual of Brahmanism to the world-view of the* Upanishads. *The sacrificial horse, which we saw connected with the cosmos in the* Brahmanas *(see Selection 8), here becomes the cosmos itself, like the all-pervading reality, Brahman. The second excerpt is a complete* Upanishad. *The* katha *(recitation) of the title implies that the study of this* Upanishad *leads to self-realization and liberation from the cycle of life and death. The second excerpt also illustrates the use of dialogue—here between Death and the boy Naciketas—and analogy as characteristic devices of exposition in the* Upanishads.

BRIHAD-ARANYAKA UPANISHAD (I.1.1)
The World as a Sacrificial Horse

Om![1] Verily, the dawn is the head of the sacrificial horse; the sun, his eye; the wind, his breath; universal fire (Agni Vaisvanara), his open mouth. The year is the body (atman) of the sacrificial horse; the sky, his back; the atmosphere, his belly; the earth, the under part of his belly; the quarters, his flanks; the intermediate quarters, his ribs; the seasons, his limbs; the months and half-months, his joints; days and nights, his feet; the stars, his bones; the clouds, his flesh. Sand is the food in his stomach; rivers are his entrails. His liver and lungs are the mountains; plants and trees, his hair. The orient is his fore part; the occident, his hind part. When he yawns, then it lightens. When he shakes himself, then it thunders. When he urinates, then it rains. Voice, indeed, is his voice.

Verily, the day arose for the horse as the sacrificial vessel which stands before. Its place is the eastern sea.

Verily, the night arose for him as the sacrificial vessel which stands behind. Its place is the western sea. Verily, these two arose on both sides of the horse as the two sacrificial vessels.[2]

Becoming a steed, he carried the gods; a stallion, the Gandharvas;[3] a courser, the demons; a horse, men.[4] The sea, indeed, is his relative. The sea is his place.

From *The Thirteen Upanishads* trans. by Robert Ernest Hume, Oxford University Press, 1921. [Pp. 73–74, 341–361.]

[1]In the Upanishads and in Indian religions in general, "om" is considered to be the original sound of the universe. In the Upanishads, it is equated with Brahman. Utterance of the sound and meditation on it are used as methods of achieving unity with Brahman.

[2]Literally, the vessels associated with the sacrificial ritual are containers for libations to be offered to the gods. Here they are given a symbolic meaning: the vessels are the Bay of Bengal to the east and the Arabian Sea to the west of the Indian subcontinent, respectively the directions in which day and night begin. The symbolic meaning of the vessels signifies the identification of the sacrificial horse with its geographical surroundings, the world, and the cosmos.

[3]Gandharvas are a class of demigods of a low order. They are spirits of a hazy moral status, existing on the fringes of the heavenly world and, in the stories about them, sometimes have associations with demons and ghouls, although themselves they are not demonic or ghoulish in character. In one role, they are celestial musicians. They are said to exercise a powerful attraction over women.

[4]Becoming one with the cosmos, the sacrificial horse is seen as the carrier of the cosmos and is given different names—stallion, etc.—with reference to the different beings (such as the Gandharvas) it carries.

KATHA UPANISHAD
First Valli[5]

Prologue: Naciketas Devoted to Death

Now verily, with zeal did Vajasravasa give his whole possession [as a religious gift]. He had a son, Naciketas by name.

Into him, boy as he was, while the sacrificial gifts were being led up, faith entered. He thought to himself:

> "Their water drunk, their grass eaten,
> Their milk milked, barren!—
> Joyless certainly are those worlds
> He goes to, who gives such [cows]!"[6]

Then he said to his father: "Papa, to whom will you give me?"—a second time—a third time.

To him then he said: "To Death I give you!"[7]

Naciketas in the House of Death

[Naciketas reflects:]
> "Of many I go as the first.
> Of many I go as an intermediate.
> What, pray, has Yama [Death] to be done
> That he will do with me today?[8]

---

[5]Section or chapter.

[6]The cows that Vajasravasa gives away for sacrifice are old and useless. Having drunk their water, eaten their food, and given milk for a lifetime, they are now at the end of their life and are barren. Naciketas feels that the gifts fulfil the letter of the ritualistic requirement and not its spirit. The giver of such an empty gift will go to a joyless world.

[7]In his sincerity about religious obligations, Naciketas wishes to offer himself as a gift instead of the cows. As he repeatedly asks his father to whom will he give him, the latter, sensing a criticism of himself, gets angry and tells his son to go to hell.

[8]Being an obedient son, Naciketas takes his father's words seriously. He carries out the command promptly like a best (first) or at least as a fairly good (intermediate) son or pupil. He wonders what duty toward Yama, the god of death, his father aims to perform by sending him to the god. The implication is that Naciketas believes that his father must have his reasons for what he has told him to do. Going as an intermediate also means that Naciketas realizes that he is not the last person to die. There will be others after him as there have been before. He shares the common destiny of all mortals. So there is no cause for lamentation.

"Look forward, how [fared] the former ones.
Look backward; so [will] the after ones.
Like grain a mortal ripens!
Like grain he is born hither again!"[9]

Warning on the Neglect of a Brahman Guest

[Voice:]

"As fire, enters
A Brahman guest into houses.
They make this the quieting thereof:—
Fetch water, Vaivasvata![10]

"Hope and expectation, intercourse and pleasantness,
Sacrifices and meritorious deeds, sons and cattle, all—
This he snatches away from the man of little understanding
In whose home a Brahman remains without eating."

Three Boons[11] Offered to Naciketas

[Death (Yama), returning from a three-day absence and finding that Naciketas has not received the hospitality which is due to a Brahman, says:]

"Since for three nights thou hast abode in my house
Without eating, O Brahman, a guest to be reverenced,
Reverence be to thee, O Brahman! Well-being be to me!
Therefore in return choose three boons!"

Naciketas's First Wish: Return to an Appeased Father on Earth

[Naciketas:]

"With intent appeased, well-minded, with passion departed,
That Gautama[12] toward me may be, O Death;
That cheerfully he may greet me, when from thee dismissed—
This of the three as boon the first I choose!"

---

[9]Like grain, human beings die and are reborn again and again. The doctrine of the transmigration of self is assumed here.

[10]This and the next verse are words of admonition to Yama (Death) as a Brahman's host. A Brahman guest is like a fire that can burn unless properly quieted. People offer the guest the water of hospitality to calm the fire down. When Naciketas arrives at Yama's house, Yama happens to be away. Naciketas has to wait for him to return for three nights without eating. *Vaivasvata,* meaning "son of the sun," is another name for Yama.

[11]Boons, here, are wishes granted by gods.

[12]An honorific epithet Naciketas uses for his father. Naciketas's first wish is for his father to cease being angry with him and to receive him cheerfully on his return home.

[*Death:*]

"Cheerful as formerly will he be—
Auddalaki Aruni,[13] from me dismissed.
Happily will he sleep o' nights, with passion departed,
When he has seen thee from the mouth of Death released."

Naciketas's Second Wish: An Understanding of the Naciketas Sacrificial Fire That Leads to Heaven

[*Naciketas:*]

"In the heavenly world is no fear whatsoever.
Not there art thou. Not from old age does one fear.
Over both having crossed—hunger, and thirst too—
Gone beyond sorrow, one rejoices in the heaven-world.

"Thyself, O Death, understandest the heavenly fire.[14]
Declare it to me who have faith.
Heaven-world people partake of immortality.
This I choose with boon the second."

[*Death:*]

"To thee I do declare, and do thou learn it of me—
Understanding about the heavenly fire, O Naciketas!
The attainment of the infinite world, likewise too its establishment—
Know thou that as set down in the secret place [of the heart]."

[*Narrator:*]

"He told him of that fire as the beginning of the world,
What bricks, and how many, and how [built].
And he too repeated that, as it was told.[15]
Then, pleased with him, the great soul again said to him:"

[*Death resumes:*]

"A further boon I give thee here today.
By thy name indeed shall this fire be [known].
This multifold garland, too, accept.[16]

"Having kindled a triple Naciketas-fire,[17] having attained union with
the three,[18]

---

[13]A genealogical name for Naciketas.

[14]The sacrificial fire that enables one to go to heaven.

[15]That is, Naciketas learned the lesson given by Yama and repeated it after Yama.

[16]Yama tells Naciketas that the sacrificial fire that he has taught him about will be named after Naciketas. Yama calls the second boon he is granting a many-shaped garland.

[17]That is, having lighted it three times.

[18]The three are father, mother, and teacher.

Performing the triple work,[19] one crosses over birth and death.
By knowing the knower of what is born from Brahma,[20] the god to be
    praised,[21]
[And] by revering [him], one goes forever to this peace.

"Having kindled a triple Naciketas-fire, having known this triad,
He who knowing thus builds up the Naciketas-fire—
He, having cast off in advance the bonds of death,
With sorrow overpassed, rejoices in the heaven-world.

"This, O Naciketas, is thy heavenly fire,
Which thou didst choose with the second boon.
As thine, indeed, will folks proclaim this fire,
The third boon, Naciketas, choose!"

Naciketas's Third Wish: Knowledge Concerning the Effect of Dying

[Naciketas:]

"This doubt that there is in regard to a man deceased:
'He exists,' say some; 'He exists not,' say others—
This would I know, instructed by thee!
Of the boons this is boon the third."

[Death:]

"Even the gods had doubt as to this of yore:
For truly, it is not easily to be understood. Subtle is this matter.
Another boon, O Naciketas, choose!
Press me not! Give up this one for me!"

This Knowledge Preferable to the Greatest Earthly Pleasures

[Naciketas:]

"Even the gods had doubt, indeed, as to this,
And thou, O Death, sayest that it is not easily to be understood.
And another declarer of it the like of thee is not to be obtained.
No other boon the equal of it is there at all."

[Death:]

"Choose centenarian sons and grandsons,
Many cattle, elephants, gold, and horses.
Choose a great abode of earth.
And thyself live as many autumns as thou desirest.

---

[19]Sacrifice, study of the scriptures, and alms-giving.

[20]An alternate spelling for Brahman, the ultimate reality.

[21]Agni, the god of fire. Could also mean any living being, for every creature is born of Brahman.

"This, if thou thinkest an equal boon,
Choose—wealth and long life!
A great one on earth, O Naciketas, be thou.
The enjoyer of thy desires I make thee.

"Whate'er desires are hard to get in the mortal world—
For all desires at pleasure make request.
These lovely maidens with chariots, with lyres—
Such [maidens], indeed, are not obtainable by men—
By these, from me bestowed, be waited on!
O Naciketas, question me not regarding dying!"

[Naciketas:]

"Ephemeral things! That which is a mortal's, O End-maker,
Even the vigor of all the powers, they wear away.
Even a whole life is slight indeed.
Thine be the vehicles! Thine be the dance and song!

"Not with wealth is a man to be satisfied.
Shall we take wealth, if we have seen thee?
Shall we live so long as thou shalt rule?
—This, in truth, is the boon to be chosen by me.

"When one has come into the presence of undecaying immortals,
What decaying mortal, here below, that understands,
That meditates upon the pleasures of beauty and delight,
Would delight in a life over-long?

"This thing whereon they doubt, O Death:
What there is in the great passing-on—tell us that!
This boon, that has entered into the hidden—
No other than that does Naciketas choose."

Second Valli

The Failure of Pleasure and of Ignorance:
The Wisdom of the Better Knowledge

[Death:]

"The better is one thing, and the pleasanter quite another.[22]
Both these, of different aim, bind a person.
Of these two, well is it for him who takes the better;
He fails of his aim who chooses the pleasanter.

"Both the better and the pleasanter come to a man.
Going all around the two, the wise man discriminates.

---

[22]That is, what is good is different from what is pleasant.

The wise man chooses the better, indeed, rather than the pleasanter.
The stupid man, from getting-and-keeping, chooses the pleasanter.

"Thou indeed, upon the pleasant and pleasantly appearing desires
Meditating, hast let them go, O Naciketas.
Thou art not one who has taken that garland of wealth
In which many men sink down.

"Widely opposite and asunder are these two:
Ignorance and what is known as 'knowledge.'
I think Naciketas desirous of obtaining knowledge!
Many desires rend thee not.

"Those abiding in the midst of ignorance,
Self-wise, thinking themselves learned,
Running hither and thither, go around deluded,
Like blind men led by one who is himself blind."

Heedlessness the Cause of Rebirth

[Death:]

"The passing-on is not clear to him who is childish,
Heedless, deluded with the delusion of wealth.
Thinking 'This is the world! There is no other!'—
Again and again he comes under my control."[23]

The Need for a Competent Teacher of the Soul

[Death:]

"He[24] who by many is not obtainable even to hear of,
He whom many, even when hearing, know not—
Wonderful is the declarer,[25] proficient the obtainer of Him!
Wonderful the knower, proficiently taught![26]

"Not, when proclaimed by an inferior man, is He
To be well understood, [though] being manifoldly considered.
Unless declared by another,[27] there is no going thither;
For He is inconceivably more subtle than what is of subtle measure.

---

[23]That is, he is born and dies again and again.

[24]The true Self.

[25]The teacher who knows the self and teaches about it.

[26]The pupil who learns well from the teacher.

[27]Other than the "inferior" man; that is, the appropriate teacher.

"Not by reasoning is this thought to be attained.

Proclaimed by another, indeed, it is for easy understanding, dearest
      friend!—

This which thou hast attained! Ah, thou art of true steadfastness!

May there be for us a questioner the like of thee, O Naciketas!"

Steadfast Renunciation and Self-Meditation Required

[Naciketas:]

"I know that what is known as treasure is something inconstant.

For truly, that which is steadfast is not obtained by those who are
      unsteadfast.

Therefore the Naciketas-fire has been built up by me,

And with means which are inconstant I have obtained that which is
      constant."

[Death:]

"The obtainment of desire, the foundation of the world,

The endlessness of will, the safe shore of fearlessness,

The greatness of praise, the wide extent, the foundation (having seen),

Thou, O Naciketas, a wise one, hast with steadfastness let [these] go!

"Him who is hard to see, entered into the hidden,

Set in the secret place [of the heart], dwelling in the depth, primeval—

By considering Him as God, through the Yoga-study[28] of what pertains
      to self,

The wise man leaves joy and sorrow behind."

The Absolutely Unqualified Soul

[Death:]

"When a mortal has heard this and fully comprehended,

Has torn off what is concerned with the right, and has taken Him as
      the subtle,

Then he rejoices, for indeed he has obtained what is to be rejoiced in.

I regard Naciketas a dwelling open [for Atman[29]].

"Apart from the right and apart from the unright,

Apart from both what has been done and what has not been done here,

Apart from what has been and what is to be—

What thou seest as that, speak that!"

---

[28] *Yoga* means "union." It refers to the union of the ordinary self with the true self, the
Atman or Brahman. It is also the name of the method that leads to such union.
Sometimes *Yoga* means "Brahman" itself.

[29] The true Self.

The Mystic Syllable "Om"[30] as an Aid

[Naciketas is unable to mention that absolutely unqualified object. Death continues to explain:]

"The word which all the *Vedas* rehearse,
And which all austerities proclaim,
Desiring which men live the life of religious studentship—
That word to thee I briefly declare.

"That is *Om!*

"That syllable, truly, indeed, is Brahma!
That syllable indeed is the supreme!
Knowing that syllable, truly, indeed,
Whatever one desires is his!

"That is the best support.
That is the supreme support.
Knowing that support,
One becomes happy in the Brahma-world."

The Eternal Indestructible Soul

[Death:]

"The wise one [i.e., the soul, the atman, the self] is not born, nor dies.
This one has not come from anywhere, has not become anyone.
Unborn, constant, eternal, primeval, this one
Is not slain when the body is slain.

"If the slayer think to slay,
If the slain think himself slain,
Both these understand not.
This one slays not, nor is slain."

The Soul Revealed to the Unstriving Elect

[Death:]

"More minute than the minute, greater than the great,
Is the Soul (Atman) that is set in the heart of a creature here.
One who is without the active will beholds Him, and becomes freed
            from sorrow—
When through the grace of the Creator he beholds the greatness of
            the Soul (Atman)."

---

[30]See Footnote 1 above.

His Paradoxical Characteristics

[Death:]

> "Sitting, He proceeds afar;
> Lying, He goes everywhere.
> Who else than I is able to know
> The god who rejoices and rejoices not?

> "Him who is the bodiless among bodies,
> Stable among the unstable,
> The great, all-pervading Soul (Atman)—
> On recognizing Him, the wise man sorrows not."

The Conditions of Knowing Him

[Death:]

> "This Soul (Atman) is not to be obtained by instruction,
> Nor by intellect, nor by much learning.
> He is to be obtained only by the one whom He chooses;
> To such a one that Soul (Atman) reveals His own person.

> "Not he who has not ceased from bad conduct,
> Not he who is not tranquil, not he who is not composed,
> Not he who is not of peaceful mind
> Can obtain Him by intelligence."

The All-Comprehending Incomprehensible

[Death:]

> "He for whom the priesthood and the nobility
> Both are as food,
> And death is as a sauce—[31]
> Who really knows where He is?

Third Valli

The Universal and the Individual Soul

There are two that drink of righteousness in the world of good deeds;
Both are entered into the secret place [of the heart], and in the highest
     upper sphere.
Brahma-knowers speak of them as "light" and "shade,"[32]

---

[31] He (the Self) reabsorbs into Himself (eats) the created world, which includes the social reality, including its class structure, as well as death.

[32] The universal, i.e., the supreme self ("light") and the individual soul ("shade").

And so do householders who maintain the five sacrificial fires,[33] and
those too who perform the triple Naciketas-fire.

The Naciketas Sacrificial Fire as an Aid

This which is the bridge for those who sacrifice,
And which is the highest imperishable Brahma
For those who seek to cross over to the fearless farther shore—
The Naciketas-fire may we master!

Parable of the Individual Soul in a Chariot

Know thou the soul [atman, self] as riding in a chariot,
The body as the chariot.
Know thou the intellect as the chariot-driver,
And the mind as the reins.

The senses, they say, are the horses;
The objects of sense, what they range over.
The self combined with senses and mind
Wise men call "the enjoyer."

He who has not understanding,
Whose mind is not constantly held firm—
His senses are uncontrolled,
Like the vicious horses of a chariot-driver.

He, however, who has understanding,
Whose mind is constantly held firm—
His senses are under control,
Like the good horses of a chariot-driver.[34]

Intelligent Control of the Soul's Chariot Needed
to Arrive beyond Reincarnation

He, however, who has not understanding,
Who is unmindful and ever impure,
Reaches not the goal,
But goes on to reincarnation.

He, however, who has understanding,
Who is mindful and ever pure,
Reaches the goal
From which he is born no more.

---

[33]Holy fires that householders, as distinct from ascetics, customarily maintain.

[34]Here is another example of a similarity to the ideas of Plato, the ancient Greek philosopher, who wrote of the soul as a charioteer (reason) who must control the horses of both
the higher human qualities and the unruly lower appetites.

He, however, who has the understanding of a chariot-driver,
A man who reins in his mind—
He reaches the end of his journey,
That highest place of Vishnu.[35]

The Order of Progression to the Supreme Person

Higher than the senses are the objects of sense.
Higher than the objects of sense is the mind;
And higher than the mind is the intellect.
Higher than the intellect is the Great Self (Atman).

Higher than the Great Self is the Unmanifest.
Higher than the Unmanifest is the Person.[36]
Higher than the Person there is nothing at all.
That is the goal. That is the highest course.

The Subtle Perception of the All-Pervading Soul

Though He is hidden in all things,
That Soul (Atman, Self) shines not forth.
But he is seen by subtle seers
With superior, subtle intellect.

The Yoga Method—of Suppression

An intelligent man should suppress his speech and his mind.
The latter he should suppress in the Understanding Self.
The understanding he should suppress in the Great Self [intellect].
That he should suppress in the Tranquil Self.

Exhortation to the Way of Liberation from Death

Arise ye! Awake ye!
Obtain your boons[37] and understand them!
A sharpened edge of a razor, hard to traverse,
A difficult path is this—poets declare!

What is soundless, touchless, formless, imperishable,
Likewise tasteless, constant, odorless,
Without beginning, without end, higher than the great, stable—
By discerning that, one is liberated from the mouth of death.

---

[35]A Vedic and Hindu god. He started as a sun god and later became the preserver of creation, one of the three central gods of Hinduism. Here, he is seen as an all-pervading god, as Brahman.

[36]The infinite and as yet unformed primeval being.

[37]Answers to one's questions.

The Immortal Value of This Teaching

The Naciketas tale,
Death's immemorial teaching—
By declaring and hearing this, a wise man
Is magnified in the Brahma-world.

If one recites this supreme secret
In an assembly of Brahmans,
Or at a time of the ceremony for the dead, devoutly—
That makes for immortality!
　　—That makes for immortality!

Fourth Valli

The Immortal Soul Not to Be Sought through Outward Senses

The Self-existent pierced the openings [of the senses] outward;
Therefore one looks outward, not within himself.
A certain wise man, while seeking immortality,
Introspectively beheld the Soul (Atman) face to face.

The childish go after outward pleasures;
They walk into the net of widespread death.
But the wise, knowing immortality,
Seek not the stable among things which are unstable here.

Yet the Agent in All the Senses, in Sleeping and in Waking

That by which [one discerns] form, taste, smell,
Sound, and mutual touches—
It is with that indeed that one discerns.
What is there left over here!
This verily, is that!
　　By recognizing as the great pervading Soul (Atman)
　　That whereby one perceives both
　　The sleeping state and the waking state,
　　The wise man sorrows not.

The Universal Soul (Atman), Identical with the Individual and with All Creation

He who knows this experiencer[38]
As the living Soul (Atman) near at hand,

---

[38]The Self, the ultimate experiencer of all that exists.

Lord of what has been and of what is to be—
He does not shrink away from Him.
This, verily, is that!
    He who was born of old from austerity,
    Was born of old from the waters,[39]
    Who stands entered into the secret place [of the heart],
    Who looked forth through beings—
This, verily, is that!
    She who arises with life,
    Aditi[40] (infinity), maker of divinity,
    Who stands entered into the secret place [of the heart],
    Who was born forth through beings—
This, verily, is that!
    Fire (Agni), the all-knower, hidden away in the two fire-sticks[41]
    Like the embryo well borne by pregnant women,
    Worthy to be worshiped day by day
        By watchful men with oblations—
This, verily, is that!
    Whence the sun rises,
    And where it goes to rest—
    On Him all the gods are founded;
    And no one ever goes beyond it.
This, verily, is that!

Failure to Comprehend the Essential Unity of Being Regarded as the Cause of Reincarnation

Whatever is here, that is there.
What is there, that again is here.
He[42] obtains death after death
Who seems to see a difference here.

By the mind, indeed, is this [realization] to be attained:
There is no difference here at all!
He goes from death to death
Who seems to see a difference here.

---

[39]These are references to creation myths where the first created, and creator, divine being is born out of heat (austerity) or the ocean of infinite, unformed reality.

[40]Aditi is the mother of gods. Here, the term is used in the sense of "mother nature" (life).

[41]A reference to the production of the sacrificial fire by friction with a drill made of two wood sticks.

[42]One who fails to see the unity of all that exists.

The Eternal Lord Abiding in One's Self

A Person of the measure of a thumb[43]
Stands in the midst of one's self (Atman),
Lord of what has been and of what is to be.
One does not shrink away from Him.
This, verily, is that!
A Person of the measure of a thumb,
Like a light without smoke,
Lord of what has been and what is to be.
He alone is today, and tomorrow too.

The Result of Seeing Multiplicity or Else Pure Unity

As water rained upon rough ground
Runs to waste among the hills,
So he who sees qualities separately,[44]
Runs to waste after them.

As pure water poured forth into pure
Becomes the very same,
So becomes the soul (atman), O Gautama,
Of the seer who has understanding.

Fifth Valli

The Real Soul of the Individual and of the World

By ruling over the eleven-gated citadel[45]
Of the unborn, the un-crooked-minded one,
One sorrows not.
But when liberated [from the body], he is liberated indeed.
This, verily, is that!
The swan [i.e., sun] in the clear, the Vasu[46] in the atmosphere,
The priest by the altar, the guest in the house,
In man, in broad space, in the right,[47] in the sky,

---

[43]The Self is described as being the size of a thumb only because it dwells in the heart. Actually, it is infinite, being the same as Brahman.

[44]Sees things as separate from one another because of their apparently differing properties (qualities).

[45]The citadel is the human body with its eleven orifices—eyes, ears, mouth, etc.

[46]*Vasu* means "that which permeates everything."

[47]The right is the cosmic entity, or law, that sustains the orderly working of the universe.

Born in water, born in cattle, born in the right, born in rock,
    is the right, the great!

Upwards the out-breath he leadeth.
The in-breath inwards he casts.
The dwarf[48] who is seated in the middle
All the gods reverence!

When this incorporate one that stands in the body
Is dissolved,
And is released from the body,
What is there left over here?
This, verily, is that!
    Not by the out-breath and the in-breath
    Doth any mortal whatsoever live.
    But by another do men live—
    Even that whereon both these depend.

The Appropriate Embodiment of the Reincarnating Soul

Come! I will declare this to you:
The hidden, eternal Brahma;
And how, after it reaches death,
The soul (atman) fares, O Gautama!

Some go into a womb
For the embodiment of a corporeal being.
Others go into a stationary thing
According to their deeds (karma), according to their knowledge.

One's Real Person, the Same as the World-Ground

He who is awake in those that sleep,
The Person who fashions desire after desire—
That indeed is the pure. That is Brahma.
That indeed is called the immortal.
On it all the worlds do rest;
And no one soever goes beyond it.
This, verily, is that!

The Unitary World-Soul, Imminent Yet Transcendent

As the one fire has entered the world
And becomes corresponding in form to every form,

---

[48]The Self, seen as small in size. See Footnote 43 above.

So the one Inner Soul of all things
Is corresponding in form to every form, and yet is outside.

As the one wind has entered the world
And becomes corresponding in form to every form,
So the one Inner Soul of all things
Is corresponding in form to every form, and yet is outside.

As the sun, the eye of the whole world,
Is not sullied by the external faults of the eyes,
So the one Inner Soul of all things
Is not sullied by the evil in the world, being external to it.

The Indescribable Bliss of Recognizing the World-Soul in One's Own Soul

The Inner Soul of all things, the One Controller,
Who makes his one form manifold—
The wise who perceive Him as standing in oneself,
They, and no others, have eternal happiness!

Him who is the Constant among the inconstant, the Intelligent among
        intelligences,
The One among many, who grants desires—
The wise who perceive Him as standing in oneself,
They, and no others, have eternal peace!

"This is it!"—thus they recognize
The highest, indescribable happiness.
How, now, shall I understand "this"?
Does it shine [of itself] or does it shine in reflection?

The Self-Luminous Light of the World

The sun shines not there, nor the moon and stars,
These lightnings shine not, much less this (earthly) fire!
After Him, as He shines, doth everything shine,
This whole world is illumined with His light.

Sixth Valli

The World-Tree Rooted in Brahma

Its root is above, its branches below—
This eternal fig-tree!
That (root) indeed is the Pure. That is Brahma.
That indeed is called the Immortal.

On it all the worlds do rest,
And no one soever goes beyond it.
This, verily, is that!

The Great Fear

This whole world, whatever there is,
Was created from and moves in Life.[49]
The great fear, the upraised thunderbolt—[50]
They who know that, become immortal.

From fear of Him fire doth burn.
From fear the sun gives forth heat.
From fear both Indra[51] and Wind,
And Death as fifth, do speed along.

Degrees of Perception of the Soul (Atman)

If one has been able to perceive [Him] here on earth
Before the dissolution of the body,
According to that [knowledge] he becomes fitted
For embodiment in the world-creations.[52]

As in a mirror, so is it seen in the body (atman);
As in a dream, so in the world of the fathers;
As if in water, so in the world of the Gandharvas *(genii)*;[53]
As if in light and shade, so in the world of Brahma.

The Gradation up to the Supersensible Person

The separate nature of the senses,
And that their arising and setting
Is of things that come into being apart [from himself],
The wise man recognizes, and sorrows not.

Higher than the senses is the mind;
Above the mind is the true being.
Over the true being is the Great Self [intellect];
Above the Great Self is the Unmanifest.

---

[49]Life, here, means Brahman.

[50]The thunderbolt is an image for the power of Brahman which instills fear in everything, i.e., makes everything work.

[51]Indra is a Vedic and Hindu god. In his early career, he is the god of rain and war. Later, he becomes a king in the heavens.

[52]The created worlds.

[53]An order of spirits, generally noble but ranking not very high in the celestial hierarchy.

Higher than the Unmanifest, however, is the Person (Purusha),
All-pervading and without any mark whatever.
Knowing which, a man is liberated
And goes to immortality.

His form is not to be beheld.
No one soever sees Him with the eye.
He is framed by the heart, by the thought, by the mind.
They who know that become immortal.

The Method of Yoga, Suppressive of the Lower Activity

When cease the five
[Sense-]knowledges, together with the mind,
And the intellect stirs not—
That, they say, is the highest course.

This they consider as Yoga—
The firm holding back of the senses.
Then one becomes undistracted.
Yoga, truly, is the origin and the end.

The Soul Incomprehensible except as Existent

Not by speech, not by mind,
Not by sight can He be apprehended.
How can He be comprehended
Otherwise than by one's saying "He is?"

He can indeed be comprehended by the thought "He is"
And by [admitting] the real nature of both [his comprehensibility and
            his incomprehensibility].
When he has been comprehended by the thought "He is,"
His real nature manifests itself.

A Renunciation of All Desires and Attachments
the Condition of Immortality

When are liberated[54] all
The desires that lodge in one's heart,
Then a mortal becomes immortal!
Therein he reaches Brahma!

When are cut all
The knots of the heart here on earth,

---

[54]Given up, renounced.

Then a mortal becomes immortal!
—Thus far is the instruction.

The Passage of the Soul from the Body to Immortality—or Elsewhere

There are a hundred and one channels of the heart.
One of these passes up to the crown of the head.
Going up by it, one goes to immortality.
The others are for departing in various directions.

A Person of the measure of a thumb is the inner soul,
Ever seated in the heart of creatures.
Him one should draw out from one's own body
Like an arrow-shaft out from a reed, with firmness.
Him one should know as the Pure, the Immortal—
   Yea, Him one should know as the Pure, the Immortal.

This Teaching, the Means of Attaining Brahma and Immortality

Then Naciketas, having received this knowledge
Declared by Death, and the entire rule of Yoga,
Attained Brahma and became free from passion, free from death,
And so may any other who knows this in regard to the Soul (Atman).

21

॰৯

Buddhist Sources: Ashvaghosha

THE LIFE OF BUDDHA

Buddha (ca. 560–480 B.C.) was the founder of Buddhism, one of the world's major religions. His real name was Siddhartha Gautama, the latter being the name of his clan. He acquired the honorific name Buddha (the "wise one") after he attained enlightenment (perfect wisdom) and began to preach his gospel. The impact that Buddha's teaching made on the world is, perhaps, equalled only by that if Jesus's teaching (Selection 35). In the words of the distinguished scholar of Indian history, A. L. Basham, "Even if judged by his posthumous effects on the world at large, he was certainly the greatest man to have been born in India." The expanse of the religion he founded stretched, at one time or another, from Afghanistan in the west to China and Japan in the north and east. During its history, Buddhism has thus covered, next to Christianity, the largest area of the world, and has had one of the largest followings of any religion.

Buddha's original teaching was simple and intended for the common people. Like the Upanishads, his teaching largely arose out of a reaction against the sacrificial and social ritualism of Brahmanism (see Selections 9 and 20). However, unlike the Upanishads, Buddha did not recognize the authority of the Veda. His doctrine also differed from the Upanishads in its orientation and purpose. Whereas the main subject of the Upanishads is the goal of union with the eternal ultimate reality beyond the transitory nature of the ordinary world, Buddha's concerns focussed on the human condition and answers to its problems within the ordinary world. He founded his religion on the observation that human life (for that matter, any form of life) was riddled with suffering. To live was to be in a state of suffering, Buddha pointed out. He dismissed questions about such subjects as the ultimate reality, and the existence of God(s) or the soul, as irrelevant to the immediate situation. The only sensible question, he thought, was how to find a solution to the problem of suffering.

Buddha's teaching was thus pragmatic in its approach. As it aimed to alleviate suffering, it was also social in spirit. Furthermore, since the goals of this teaching could be understood and attained through the use of common sense and reason, rather than requiring some suprarational perceptions, such as the mystical experience of the Upanishads, *it was rational in character. The path that Buddha preached for the attainment of the goals of his religion was that of appropriate moral conduct. This path is known as the Middle Way, because Buddha advocated moderation between the extremes of self-denial, on the one hand, and over-indulgence in worldly pleasures on the other. In this respect, Buddha's ideal resembles the "golden mean" of Aristotle, the Greek philosopher, whose practical rationalism shares a similarity with Buddha's philosophy. Buddha called the goal of his religion Nirvana, by which he meant the cessation of suffering and the attainment of tranquility of the mind, rather than perfect bliss. With such modest purposes in mind, Buddha established an order of traveling disciples and sent them across India to elevate its people's moral life.*

In the centuries following the death of Buddha, Buddhism in India mingled with the Vedic religion and Hinduism and was eventually absorbed by them. As it spread to other countries of Asia, it assimilated numerous elements of local religions and philosophies, becoming, in the process, many kinds of Buddhism. These different kinds of Buddhism were divided into two main schools of thought, the Hinayana *("Lesser Vehicle") and the* Mahayana *("Greater Vehicle"), so named because each was viewed as serving the spiritual needs of an elite and the mass of common people, respectively. The Hinayana, the earlier of the two schools to arise, was a monastic and highly philosophical religion, its central feature being the view of Nirvana as the extinction of the self and any sense of one's individuality. In the Mahayana, Buddhism became a salvationist religion in which Buddha was seen as God and savior, and the worship of Buddha became the means of reaching Nirvana, which itself was conceived of as a heavenly place.*

The two schools and their various sects produced a vast body of Buddhist literature in many different languages. The two principal languages, however, remained the Indian languages Sanskrit and Pali. Although Buddhism eventually died in India, it flourished in the rest of Asia. We know about the history of Buddhism in India mainly from the Buddhist works preserved or written in other Asian countries. In these sources, the story of Buddha's life and his original teachings is so deeply buried under embellishments of myth, miracles, and sectarian differences, that it is nearly impossible to know the actual facts. However, the following facts are reasonably certain.

Siddhartha Gautama, later known as Buddha, was born the son of a ruler of a small kingdom in northeastern India. From his very early life, he had an exceptionally compassionate nature. He was deeply moved and disturbed by the sight of pain or suffering in any living being. His father, concerned about the prince's well-being as his prospective successor, kept him guarded in the luxury of the palace to shield him from the unpleasantness and pain of the outside world. As the prince grew up, the king had him married, surrounded him with pleasurable distractions, and still kept him guarded in the palace. But the prince managed to go into town and see what are known as the "Four Signs" leading to his renunciation of his princely life. He saw an old man, a diseased man, and a dead man, which impressed upon him the unavoidable and unhappy conditions of human existence. Then he saw an ascetic, who, the prince was told, had found a way out of these conditions. As a result of this experience, Siddhartha left home, his wife, and his son, and became an ascetic, seeking wisdom that would provide a solution for the problem of suffering. Following the usual discipline of ascetics, he practiced severe self-denial until his body was reduced to mere skin and bone. He realized that extreme bodily denial was not the right path to wisdom, so he adopted a more moderate discipline and meditated with determination until he achieved perfect knowledge of truth. He preached the path to enlightenment he had discovered to his disciples throughout India. They carried it to the world.

The two excerpts in this selection pertain, respectively, to the story of Buddha's life and to his first sermon, containing the "Four Holy (Noble) Truths," that he preached after his enlightenment. The first excerpt is taken from the Buddhacarita *("The Acts of Buddha") by Ashvaghosha, a first-century* A.D. *Indian poet of the Sanskrit language.* Buddhacarita *is the earliest and in many ways the finest complete biography of Buddha. It has the merit of being free from sectarian bias. It is not known to which school Ashvaghosha belonged. The biography shows the influence of the ideas of both the Hinayana and the Mahayana schools.*

The second excerpt is taken from Samyutta Nikaya *("Connected Group") in the Pali language, which contains pronouncements on connected topics and is a major canonical work of the Hinayana school. The excerpt is a statement of the "Four Holy Truths," accepted by all schools of thought in Buddhism as the most fundamental teaching of Buddhism. The four truths are the following: life is full of suffering; suffering comes from excessive craving; the way to cessation of suffering is control of craving; craving is controlled by following the eightfold path of conduct prescribed by Buddha.*

༄

ASHVAGHOSHA'S *BUDDICARITA*, (1, 3–13, 15)
The Legend of the Buddha Shakyamuni[1]
The Birth of the Bodhisattva[2]

There lived once upon a time a king of the Shakyas, a scion of the solar race,[3] whose name was Shuddhodana. He was pure in conduct, and beloved of the Shakyas like the autumn-moon. He had a wife, splendid, beautiful, and steadfast, who was called the Great Maya, from her resemblance to Maya the Goddess.[4] These two tasted of love's delights, and one day she conceived the fruit of her womb, but without any defilement, in the same way in which knowledge joined to trance bears fruit.[5] Just before her conception she had a dream. A white king elephant seemed to enter her body, but without causing her any pain. So Maya, queen of that god-like king, bore in her womb the glory of his dynasty. But she remained free from the fatigues, depressions, and fancies which usually accompany pregnancies. Pure herself, she longed to withdraw into the pure forest, in the loneliness of which she could practice trance. She set her heart on going to Lumbini, a delightful grove, with trees of every kind, like the grove of Citraratha in Indra's Paradise.[6] She asked the king to accompany her, and so they left the city, and went to that glorious grove.

When the queen noticed that the time of her delivery was approaching, she went to a couch overspread with an awning, thousands of waiting-women look-

---

From *Buddhist Scriptures*, trans. Edward Conze (London: Penguin Books, 1959), pp. 35–56; 186–187. Reproduced by permission of Penguin Books, Ltd.

[1]That is, "the sage of the Shakya tribe." (The historical Buddha was, in fact, a member of this tribe.)

[2]A Buddha-to-be: Siddhartha before he achieved enlightenment. Bodhisattva also refers to any spiritually advanced person who is close to and capable of achieving Nirvana, or to one of a number of divine beings devoted to relieving the suffering of those caught in the world of *samsara* (the cycle of transmigration from life to life).

[3]Believed to have been descended from the sun-god.

[4]In one sense, *Maya* simply means the "illusory, unreal world." But Maya is also a goddess who personifies the world and its physical reality. She is the Indian counterpart of the Greek goddess of nature, Cybele, who was sometimes identified with the Roman goddess Maia.

[5]That is, the same way in which the mind in the state of trance perceives truth unobtrusively.

[6]Here is one of the frequent examples showing the mingling of the Vedic and Hindu mythologies with Buddhism. Indra is a Vedic and Hindu god. In Hinduism, he is a king in the heavens. Citraratha, a *gandharva* (member of a class of demigods), is entrusted with supervisory duties in Indra's heaven.

ing on with joy in their hearts. The propitious constellation of Pushya shone brightly when a son was born to the queen, for the weal of the world. He came out of his mother's side, without causing her pain or injury. His birth was as miraculous as that of Aurva, Prithu, Mandhatri, and Kakshivat,[7] heroes of old who were born respectively from the thigh, from the hand, the head, or the armpit. So he issued from the womb as befits a Buddha. He did not enter the world in the usual manner, and he appeared like one descended from the sky. And since he had for many aeons been engaged in the practice of meditation,[8] he now was born in full awareness, and not thoughtless and bewildered as other people are. When born, he was so lustrous and steadfast that it appeared as if the young sun had come down to earth. And yet, when people gazed at his dazzling brilliance, he held their eyes like the moon. His limbs shone with the radiant hue of precious gold, and lit up the space all around. Instantly he walked seven steps, firmly and with long strides. In that he was like the constellation of the Seven Seers.[9] With the bearing of a lion he surveyed the four quarters, and spoke these words full of meaning for the future: "For enlightenment I was born, for the good of all that lives. This is the last time that I have been born into this world of becoming."[10]

•   •   •

The Bodhisattva's Youth and Marriage

Queen Maya could not bear the joy which she felt at the sight of her son's majesty, which equalled that of the wisest seers. So she went to heaven, to dwell there. Her sister, his aunt, then brought up the prince as if he were her own son. And the prince grew up, and became more perfect every day.

His childhood passed without serious illness, and in due course he reached maturity. In a few days he acquired the knowledge appropriate to his station in life, which normally it takes years to learn. Since the king of the Shakyas had, however, heard from Asita, the great seer, that the supreme beatitude would be the prince's future goal, he tried to tie him down by sensual pleasures, so that he might not go away into the forest. He selected for him from a family of long-standing unblemished reputation a maiden, Yashodhara by name, chaste and outstanding for her beauty, modesty, and good breeding, a true goddess of fortune in the shape of a woman. And the prince, wondrous in his flashing beauty, took his

---

[7]Mythological heroes who also had similarly miraculous births.

[8]A belief generally held by all Buddhists that Buddha, before his life in sixth- to fifth-century B.C. India, had many earlier lives during which he practiced meditation and made spiritual progress.

[9]The constellation *Ursa Major* ("Big Dipper"). The seven seers (stars) in it are believed to be the mind-born sons of the Hindu creator god, Brahma.

[10]That is, he will become free from the cycle of birth, death, and rebirth.

delight with the bride chosen for him by his father, as it is told of Indra and Shaci[11] in the Ramayana.[12]

The monarch, however, decided that his son must never see anything that could perturb his mind, and he arranged for him to live in the upper storeys of the palace, without access to the ground. Thus he passed his time in the upper part of the palace, which was as brilliantly white as rain clouds in autumn, and which looked like a mansion of the gods shifted to the earth. It contained rooms suited to each season, and the melodious music of the female attendants could be heard in them. This palace was as brilliant as that of Shiva on Mount Kailasa.[13] Soft music came from the gold-edged tambourines which the women tapped with their finger-tips, and they danced as beautifully as the choicest heavenly nymphs. They entertained him with soft words, tremulous calls, wanton swayings, sweet laughter, butterfly kisses, and seductive glances. Thus he became a captive of these women who were well versed in the subject of sensuous enjoyment and indefatigable in sexual pleasure. And it did not occur to him to come down from the palace to the ground, just as people who in reward for their virtues live in a palace in heaven are content to remain there, and have no desire to descend to the earth.

In the course of time the fair-bosomed Yashodhara bore to the son of Shuddhodana a son, who was named Rahula. It must be remembered that all the Bodhisattvas, those beings of quite incomparable spirit, must first of all know the taste of the pleasures which the senses can give. Only then, after a son has been born to them, do they depart to the forest. Through the accumulated effects of his past deeds the Bodhisattva possessed in himself the root cause of enlightenment, but he could reach it only after first enjoying the pleasures of the senses.

The Awakening

In the course of time the women told him how much they loved the groves near the city, and how delightful they were. So, feeling like an elephant locked up inside a house, he set his heart on making a journey outside the palace. The king heard of the plans of his dearly beloved son, and arranged a pleasure excursion which would be worthy of his own affection and royal dignity, as well as of his son's youth. But he gave orders that all the common folk with any kind of affliction should be kept away from the royal road, because he feared that they might agitate the prince's sensitive mind. Very gently all cripples were driven away, and all those who were crazy, aged, ailing, and the like, and also all wretched beggars. So the royal highway became supremely magnificent.

---

[11]The wife of the god Indra. She is known for her exceptional beauty.

[12]One of the two great epic poems of India.

[13]Shiva is one of the three supreme gods of Hinduism, the other two being Brahma and Vishnu. In one of his aspects, Shiva dwells with his family in a celestial mansion on top of a high mountain peak, Kailasa, probably based on the Himalayas.

The citizens jubilantly acclaimed the prince. But the Gods of the Pure Abode,[14] when they saw that everyone was happy as if in paradise, conjured up the illusion of an old man, so as to induce the king's son to leave his home. The prince's charioteer explained to him the meaning of old age. The prince reacted to this news like a bull when a lightning-flash crashes down near him. For his understanding was purified by the noble intentions he had formed in his past lives and by the good deeds he had accumulated over countless aeons. In consequence his lofty soul was shocked to hear of old age. He sighed deeply, shook his head, fixed his gaze on the old man, surveyed the festive multitude, and, deeply perturbed, said to the charioteer: "So that is how old age destroys indiscriminately the memory, beauty, and strength of all! And yet with such a sight before it the world goes on quite unperturbed. This being so, my son, turn round the horses, and travel back quickly to our palace! How can I delight to walk about in parks when my heart is full of fear of aging?" So at the bidding of his master's son the charioteer reversed the chariot. And the prince went back into his palace, which now seemed empty to him, as a result of his anxious reflections.

On a second pleasure excursion the same gods created a man with a diseased body. When this fact was explained to him, the son of Shuddhodana was dismayed, trembled like the reflection of the moon on rippling water, and in his compassion he uttered these words in a low voice: "This then is the calamity of disease, which afflicts people! The world sees it, and yet does not lose its confident ways. Greatly lacking in insight it remains gay under the constant threat of disease. We will not continue this excursion, but go straight back to the palace! Since I have learned of the danger of illness, my heart is repelled by pleasures and seems to shrink into itself."

On a third excursion the same gods displayed a corpse, which only the prince and his charioteer could see being borne along the road. The charioteer again explained the meaning of this sight to the prince. Courageous though he was, the king's son, on hearing of death, was suddenly filled with dismay. Leaning his shoulder against the top of the chariot rail, he spoke these words in a forceful voice: "This is the end which has been fixed for all, and yet the world forgets its fears and takes no heed! The hearts of men are surely hardened to fears, for they feel quite at ease even while traveling along the road to the next life. Turn back the chariot! This is no time or place for pleasure excursions. How could an intelligent person pay no heed at a time of disaster, when he knows of his impending destruction?"

Withdrawal from the Women

From then onwards the prince withdrew from contact with the women in the palace, and in answer to the reproaches of Udayin, the king's counsellor, he

---

[14]The highest heaven.

explained his new attitude in the following words: "It is not that I despise the objects of sense, and I know full well that they make up what we call the 'world.' But when I consider the impermanence of everything in this world, then I can find no delight in it. Yes, if this triad of old age, illness, and death did not exist, then all this loveliness would surely give me great pleasure. If only this beauty of women were imperishable, then my mind would certainly indulge in the passions, though, of course, they have their faults. But since even women attach no more value to their bodies after old age has drunk them up, to delight in them would clearly be a sign of delusion. If people, doomed to undergo old age, illness, and death, are carefree in their enjoyment with others who are in the same position, they behave like birds and beasts. And when you say that our holy books tell us of gods, sages, and heroes who, though high-minded, were addicted to sensuous passions, then that by itself should give rise to agitation, since they also are now extinct. Successful high-mindedness seems to me incompatible with both extinction and attachment to sensory concerns, and appears to require that one is in full control of oneself. This being so, you will not prevail upon me to devote myself to ignoble sense pleasures, for I am afflicted by ill and it is my lot to become old and to die. How strong and powerful must be your own mind, that in the fleeting pleasures of the senses you find substance! You cling to sense-objects among the most frightful dangers, even while you cannot help seeing all creation on the way to death. By contrast I become frightened and greatly alarmed when I reflect on the dangers of old age, death, and disease. I find neither peace nor contentment, and enjoyment is quite out of the question, for the world looks to me as if ablaze with an all-consuming fire. If a man has once grasped that death is quite inevitable, and if nevertheless greed arises in his heart, then he must surely have an iron will not to weep in this great danger, but to enjoy it." This discourse indicated that the prince had come to a final decision and had combated the very foundations of sensuous passion. And it was the time of sunset.

The Flight

Even amidst the allure of the finest opportunities for sensuous enjoyment the Shakya king's son felt no contentment, and he could not regain a feeling of safety. He was, in fact, like a lion hit in the region of the heart by an arrow smeared with a potent poison. In the hope that a visit to the forest might bring him some peace, he left his palace with the king's consent, accompanied by an escort of ministers' sons, who were chosen for their reliability and their gift for telling entertaining stories. The prince rode out on the good horse Kanthaka, which looked splendid, for the bells of its bit were of fresh gold and its golden trappings beautiful with waving plumes. The beauties of the landscape and his longing for the forest carried him deep into the countryside. There he saw the soil being ploughed, and its surface, broken with the tracks of the furrows, looked like rippling water. The ploughs had torn up the sprouting grass, scattering tufts of grass here and there, and the land was littered with tiny creatures who had been killed and injured, worms, insects, and the like. The sight of all this grieved the prince as deeply as if he had witnessed the slaughter of his own kinsmen. He observed the ploughmen, saw how they suffered from wind, sun, and dust, and how the oxen were worn down by the labor of drawing. And in the supreme nobility of his mind he performed an act of supreme pity. He then alighted from his horse and walked gently and slowly over the ground, overcome with grief. He reflected on the generation and the passing of all living things, and in his distress he said to himself: "How pitiful all this!"

His mind longed for solitude, he withdrew from the good friends who walked behind him, and went to a solitary spot at the foot of a rose-apple tree. The tree's lovely leaves were in constant motion, and the ground underneath it salubrious and green like beryl. There he sat down, reflected on the origination and passing away of all that lives, and then he worked on his mind in such a way that, with this theme as a basis, it became stable and concentrated. When he had won through to mental stability, he was suddenly freed from all desire for sense-objects and from cares of any kind. He had reached the first stage of trance, which is calm amidst applied and discursive thinking. In his case it had already at this stage a supramundane purity. He had obtained that concentration of mind which is born of detachment, and is accompanied by the highest rapture and joy, and in this state of trance his mind considered the destiny of the world correctly, as it is: "Pitiful, indeed, that these people who themselves are helpless and doomed to undergo illness, old age, and destruction, should, in the ignorant blindness of their self-intoxication, show so little respect for others who are likewise victims of old age, disease, and death! But now that I have discerned this supreme dharma,[15] it would be unworthy and unbecoming if I, who am so constituted, should show no respect for others whose constitution is essentially the same as mine." When he thus gained insight into the fact that the blemishes of disease, old age, and death vitiate the very core of this world, he lost at the same moment all self-intoxication, which normally arises from pride in one's own strength, youth, and vitality. He now was neither glad nor grieved; all doubt, lassitude, and sleepiness disappeared; sensuous excitements could no longer influence him; and hatred and contempt for others were far from his mind.

The Apparition of a Mendicant

As this understanding, pure and dustless, grew farther in his noble soul, he saw a man glide towards him, who remained invisible to other men, and who appeared in the guise of a religious mendicant. The king's son asked him: "Tell me who you are," and the answer was: "O Bull among men, I am a recluse who, terrified by

---

[15]*Dharma* has several meanings, the most common of which is "the righteous path." The word also means "the cosmic, or the social, moral law." In some contexts, as in this sentence, it means "reality."

birth and death, have adopted a homeless life to win salvation. Since all that lives is to extinction doomed, salvation from this world is what I wish, and so I search for that most blessed state in which extinction is unknown. Kinsmen and strangers mean the same to me, and greed and hate for all this world of sense have ceased to be. Wherever I may be, that is my home—the root of a tree, a deserted sanctuary, a hill or wood. Possessions I have none, no expectations either. Intent on the supreme goal, I wander about, accepting any alms I may receive." Before the prince's very eyes he then flew up into the sky. For he was a denizen of the heavens, who had seen other Buddhas in the past, and who had come to him in this form so as to remind him of the task before him.

When that being had risen like a bird into the sky, the best of men was elated and amazed. Then and there he intuitively perceived the dharma, and made plans to leave his palace for the homeless life. And soon after returning to his palace he decided to escape during the night. The gods knew of his intention, and saw to it that the palace doors were open. He descended from the upper part of the palace, looked with disgust upon the women lying about in all kinds of disorderly positions, and unhesitatingly went to the stables in the outermost courtyard. He roused Chandaka, the groom, and ordered him quickly to bring the horse Kanthaka. "For I want to depart from here today, and win the deathless state!"

The Dismissal of Chandaka

They rode off, till they came to a hermitage, where the prince took off his jewels, gave them to Chandaka and dismissed him with this message to his father, King Shuddhodana: "So that my father's grief may be dispelled, tell him that I have gone to this penance grove for the purpose of putting an end to old age and death, and by no means because I yearn for paradise, or because I feel no affection for him, or from moody resentment. Since I have left for the homeless life with this end in view, there is no reason why he should grieve for me. Some day in any case all unions must come to an end, however long they may have lasted. It is just because we must reckon with perpetual separation that I am determined to win salvation, for then I shall no more be torn away from my kindred. There is no reason to grieve for me who have left for the homeless life so as to quit all grief. Rather should one grieve over those who greedily cling to those sensuous passions in which all grief is rooted. My father will perhaps say that it was too early for me to leave for the forest. But then there is no such thing as a wrong season for dharma, our hold on life being so uncertain. This very day therefore I will begin to strive for the highest good—that is my firm resolve! Death confronts me all the time—how do I know how much of life is still at my disposal?"

The charioteer once more tried to dissuade the prince, and received this reply: "Chandaka, stop this grief over parting from me! All those whom birth estranged from the oneness of dharma must one day go their separate ways. Even if affection should prevent me from leaving my kinsfolk just now of my own accord, in due course death would tear us apart, and in that we would have no say. Just think of my mother, who bore me in her womb with great longing and with many pains. Fruitless proves her labor now. What am I now to her, what she to me? Birds settle on a tree for a while, and then go their separate ways again. The meeting of all living beings must likewise inevitably end in their parting. Clouds meet and then they fly apart again, and in the same light I see the union of living beings and their parting. This world passes away, and disappoints all hopes of everlasting attachment. It is therefore unwise to have a sense of ownership for people who are united with us as in a dream—for a short while only, and not in fact. The coloring of their leaves is connate to trees, and yet they must let it go; how much more must this apply to the separation of disparate things! This being so, you had better go away now, and cease, my friend, from grieving! But if your love for me still holds you back, go now to the king, and then return to me. And, please, give this message to the people in Kapilavastu[16] who keep their eyes on me: "Cease to feel affection for him, and hear his unshakable resolve: 'Either he will extinguish old age and death, and then you shall quickly see him again; or he will go to perdition, because his strength has failed him and he could not achieve his purpose.'"

The Practice of Austerities

From then onwards the prince led a religious life, and diligently studied the various systems practiced among ascetics and yogins.[17] After a time the sage, in search of a lonely retreat, went to live on the bank of the river Nairanjana, the purity of which appealed to that of his own valor. Five mendicants had gone there before him to lead a life of austerity, in scrupulous observance of their religious vows, and proud of their control over the five senses. When the monks saw him there, they waited upon him in their desire for liberation, just as the objects of sense wait upon a lordly man to whom the merits of his past lives have given wealth, and the health to enjoy them. They greeted him reverently, bowed before him, followed his instructions, and placed themselves as pupils under his control, just as the restless senses serve the mind. He, however, embarked on further austerities, and particularly on starvation as the means which seemed most likely to put an end to birth and death. In his desire for quietude he emaciated his body for six years, and carried out a number of strict methods of fasting, very hard for men to endure. At mealtimes he was content with a single jujube fruit, a single sesamum seed, and a single grain of rice—so intent he was on winning the further, the unbounded, shore of Samsara. The bulk of his body was greatly reduced by this self-torture, but by way of compensation his psychic power grew correspondingly more and more. Wasted away though he was, his glory and majesty remained unimpaired, and his sight gladdened the eyes of those who looked upon him. It was as welcome to them as the full moon in autumn to the white lotuses

---

[16]The town of Buddha's birth in present-day southern Nepal.

[17]Practitioners of the spiritual discipline *yoga*.

that bloom at night. His fat, flesh, and blood had all gone. Only skin and bone remained. Exhausted though he was, his depth seemed unexhausted, like that of the ocean itself.

After a time, however, it became clear to him that this kind of excessive self-torture merely wore out his body without any useful result. Impelled both by his dread of becoming and by his longing for Buddhahood, he reasoned as follows: "This is not the dharma which leads to dispassion, to enlightenment, to emancipation. That method which some time ago I found under the rose-apple tree, that was more certain in its results. But those meditations cannot be carried out in this weakened condition; therefore I must take steps to increase again the strength of this body. When that is worn down and exhausted by hunger and thirst, the mind in its turn must feel the strain, that mental organ which must reap the fruit. No, inward calm is needed for success! Inward calm cannot be maintained unless physical strength is constantly and intelligently replenished. Only if the body is reasonably nourished can undue strain on the mind be avoided. When the mind is free from strain and is serene, then the faculty of transic concentration can arise in it. When thought is joined to transic concentration, then it can advance through the various stages of trance. We can then win the dharmas which finally allow us to gain that highest state, so hard to reach, which is tranquil, ageless, and deathless. And without proper nourishment this procedure is quite impossible."

Nandabala's Gift

His courage was unbroken, but his boundless intellect led him to the decision that from now on again he needed proper food. In preparation for his first meal he went into the Nairanjana River to bathe. Afterwards he slowly and painfully worked his way up the river bank, and the trees on the slope reverently bent low their branches to give him a helping hand. At the instigation of the deities, Nandabala, daughter of the overseer of the cowherds, happened to pass there, her heart bursting with joy. She looked like the foamy blue waters of the Yamuna River, with her blue dress, and her arms covered with blazing white shells. When she saw him, faith further increased her joy, her lotus eyes opened wide, she prostrated herself before him, and begged him to accept milk-rice from her. He did, and his meal marked the most fruitful moment of her life. For himself, however, he gained the strength to win enlightenment. Now that his body had been nourished, the Sage's bodily frame became fully rounded again. But the five mendicants left him, because they had formed the opinion that he had now quite turned away from the holy life—just as in the Samkhya system the five elements leave the thinking soul once it is liberated.[18] Accompanied only by his resolution, he

---

[18]Samkhya is one of the main schools of Indian philosophy. According to this school, the human soul, in its worldly existence, is trapped in five elements, from which it must release itself to achieve purity and freedom. The five elements are ether, air, fire, water, and earth.

proceeded to the root of a sacred fig-tree, where the ground was carpeted with green grass. For he was definitely determined to win full enlightenment soon.

The incomparable sound of his footsteps woke Kala,[19] a serpent of high rank, who was as strong as a king elephant. Aware that the great Sage had definitely determined on enlightenment, he uttered this eulogy: "Your steps, O Sage, resound like thunder reverberating in the earth; the light that issues from your body shines like the sun. No doubt that you today will taste the fruit you so desire! The flocks of blue jays which are whirling round up in the sky show their respect by keeping their right sides towards you;[20] the air is full of gentle breezes. It is quite certain that today you will become a Buddha."

The Sage thereupon collected fresh grass from a grass cutter, and, on reaching the foot of the auspicious great tree, sat down and made a vow to win enlightenment. He then adopted the cross-legged posture, which is the best of all because so immovable, the limbs being massive like the coils of a sleeping serpent. And he said to himself: "I shall not change this my position so long as I have not done what I set out to do!" Then the denizens of the heavens felt exceedingly joyous, the herds of beasts, as well as the birds, made no noise at all, and even the trees ceased to rustle when struck by the wind: for the Lord had seated himself with his spirit quite resolved.

The Defeat of Mara[21]

Because the great Sage, the scion of a line of royal seers, had made his vow to win emancipation, and had seated himself in the effort to carry it out, the whole world rejoiced—but Mara, the inveterate foe of the true dharma, shook with fright. People address him gladly as the God of Love, the one who shoots with flower-arrows, and yet they dread this Mara as the one who rules events connected with a life of passion, as one who hates the very thought of freedom. He had with him his three sons—Flurry, Gaiety, and Sullen Pride—and his three daughters—Discontent, Delight, and Thirst. These asked him why he was so disconcerted in his mind. And he replied to them with these words: "Look over there at that sage,

---

[19]Serpents (known as *nagas*) figure prominently in Indian mythology. Usually they are noble beings like Kala mentioned here. The word *kala* also means "time." That meaning is significant in the context of the benign purpose that Buddha's quest for enlightenment had in regard to the temporal world. The joy of nature—represented by the whirling of the blue jays and the blowing of the gentle breeze, as noticed by Kala—testifies to this meaning.

[20]A matter of etiquette while going around a person, place, or object one respects.

[21]Mara is the Buddhist counterpart of the Satan of Christian tradition. He is the incarnation of lust, sensuality, and pride. He is identified below with the Hindu god of love, Kama, who shoots arrows made of flowers to make his targets fall helplessly in love. Love here is seen as an evil passion.

clad in the armor of determination, with truth and spiritual virtue as his weapons, the arrows of his intellect drawn ready to shoot! He has sat down with the firm intention of conquering my realm. No wonder that my mind is plunged in deep despondency! If he should succeed in overcoming me, and could proclaim to the world the way to final beatitude, then my realm would be empty today, like that of the king of Videha[22] of whom we hear in the epics that he lost his kingdom because he misconducted himself by carrying off a Brahmin's daughter. But so far he has not yet won the eye of full knowledge. He is still within my sphere of influence. While there is time I therefore will attempt to break his solemn purpose, and throw myself against him like the rush of a swollen river breaking against the embankment!"

But Mara could achieve nothing against the Bodhisattva, and he and his army were defeated, and fled in all directions—their elation gone, their toil rendered fruitless, their rocks, logs, and trees scattered everywhere. They behaved like a hostile army whose commander had been slain in battle. So Mara, defeated, ran away together with his followers. The great seer, free from the dust of passion, victorious over darkness's gloom, had vanquished him. And the moon, like a maiden's gentle smile, lit up the heavens, while a rain of sweet-scented flowers, filled with moisture, fell down on the earth from above.

The Enlightenment

Now that he had defeated Mara's violence by his firmness and calm, the Bodhisattva, possessed of great skill in transic meditation, put himself into trance, intent on discerning both the ultimate reality of things and the final goal of existence. After he had gained complete mastery over all the degrees and kinds of trance: In the first watch of the night he recollected the successive series of his former births. "There was I so and so; that was my name; deceased from there I came here"—in this way he remembered thousands of births, as though living them over again. When he had recalled his own births and deaths in all these various lives of his, the Sage, full of pity, turned his compassionate mind towards other living beings, and he thought to himself: "Again and again they must leave the people they regard as their own, and must go on elsewhere, and that without ever stopping. Surely this world is unprotected and helpless, and like a wheel it turns round and round." As he continued steadily to recollect the past thus, he came to the definite conviction that this world of Samsara is as unsubstantial as the pith of a plantain tree.

Second to none in valor, he then, in the second watch of the night, acquired the supreme heavenly eye, for he himself was the best of all those who have sight. Thereupon with the perfectly pure heavenly eye he looked upon the entire world, which appeared to him as though reflected in a spotless mirror. He saw that the

---

[22]A character in the two great Sanskrit epics, the *Ramayana* and the *Mahabharata*.

decease and rebirth of beings depend on whether they have done superior or inferior deeds. And his compassionateness grew still further. It became clear to him that no security can be found in this flood of Samsaric existence, and that the threat of death is ever-present. Beset on all sides, creatures can find no resting place. In this way he surveyed the five places of rebirth with his heavenly eye. And he found nothing substantial in the world of becoming, just as no core of heartwood is found in a plantain tree when its layers are peeled off one by one.

Then, as the third watch of that night drew on, the supreme master of trance turned his meditation to the real and essential nature of this world: "Alas, living beings wear themselves out in vain! Over and over again they are born, they age, die, pass on to a new life, and are reborn! What is more, greed and dark delusion obscure their sight, and they are blind from birth. Greatly apprehensive, they yet do not know how to get out of this great mass of ill." He then surveyed the twelve links of conditioned co-production,[23] and saw that, beginning with ignorance, they lead to old age and death, and, beginning with the cessation of ignorance, they lead to the cessation of birth, old age, death, and all kinds of ill.

When the great seer had comprehended that where there is no ignorance whatever, there also the karma-formations are stopped—then he had achieved a correct knowledge of all there is to be known, and he stood out in the world as a Buddha. He passed through the eight stages of transic insight,[24] and quickly reached their highest point. From the summit of the world downwards he could detect no self anywhere.[25] Like the fire, when its fuel is burned up, he became tranquil. He had reached perfection, and he thought to himself: "This is the authentic way on which in the past so many great seers, who also knew all higher and all lower things, have traveled on to ultimate and real truth. And now I have obtained it!"

At that moment, in the fourth watch of the night, when dawn broke and all the ghosts that move and those that move not went to rest, the great seer took up the position which knows no more alteration, and the leader of all reached the state of all-knowledge. When, through his Buddhahood, he had cognized this

---

[23]A highly philosophical doctrine of the Theravada sect of Hinayana Buddhism. It describes the "chain of causation" of being. The chain has twelve links; they all arise simultaneously, the root cause of their arising being ignorance. The twelve links are: ignorance, karma formations (the consequences of one's actions), consciousness, name and form, sense-fields, contact, feelings, craving, grasping, becoming, birth, and decay and death (along with sorrow, lamentation, pain, sadness, and despair). Basically, the doctrine sets forth the contingent nature of all consciousness and being, the idea that everything is dependent for its origination on something outside itself and has no individuality of its own.

[24]The eight steps of the fourth holy truth reached in the state of trance. (See "The Four Holy Truths" in the last excerpt of this selection.)

[25]The Hinayana doctrine that the notion of the individual self is false.

fact, the earth swayed like a woman drunken with wine, and sky shone bright with the Siddhas[26] who appeared in crowds in all the directions, and the mighty drums of thunder resounded through the air. Pleasant breezes blew softly, rain fell from a cloudless sky, flowers and fruits dropped from the trees out of season—in an effort, as it were, to show reverence for him. Mandarava flowers and lotus blossoms, and also water lilies made of gold and beryl, fell from the sky on to the ground near the Shakya sage, so that it looked like a place in the world of the gods. At that moment no one anywhere was angry, ill, or sad; no one did evil, none was proud; the world became quite quiet, as though it had reached full perfection. Joy spread through the ranks of those gods who longed for salvation; joy also spread among those who lived in the regions below. Everywhere the virtuous were strengthened, the influence of dharma increased, and the world rose from the dirt of the passions and the darkness of ignorance. Filled with joy and wonder at the Sage's work, the seers of the solar race who had been protectors of men, who had been royal seers, who had been great seers, stood in their mansions in the heavens and showed him their reverence. The great seers among the hosts of invisible beings could be heard widely proclaiming his fame. All living things rejoiced and sensed that things went well. Mara alone felt deep displeasure, as though subjected to a sudden fall.

For seven days he dwelt there—his body gave him no trouble, his eyes never closed, and he looked into his own mind. He thought: "Here I have found freedom," and he knew that the longings of his heart had at last come to fulfilment. Now that he had grasped the principle of causation, and finally convinced himself of the lack of self in all that is, he roused himself again from his deep trance, and in his great compassion he surveyed the world with his Buddha-eye, intent on giving it peace. When, however, he saw on the one side the world lost in low views and confused efforts, thickly covered with the dirt of the passions, and saw on the other side the exceeding subtlety of the dharma of emancipation, he felt inclined to take no action. But when he weighed up the significance of the pledge to enlighten all beings he had taken in the past, he became again more favorable to the idea of proclaiming the path to peace. Reflecting in his mind on this question, he also considered that, while some people have a great deal of passion, others have but little. As soon as Indra and Brahma,[27] the two chiefs of those who dwell in the heavens, had grasped the Sugata's[28] intention to proclaim the path to peace, they shone brightly and came up to him, the weal of the world their concern. He remained there on his seat, free from all evil and successful in his aim.

---

[26]*Siddha* means "perfected." The Siddhas are human beings who, because of their saintly lives, have become pure and perfect, acquiring a semi-divine status and enjoying many supernatural powers.

[27]One of the supreme gods of Hinduism. He is the creator god.

[28]Another name for Buddha.

The most excellent dharma which he had seen was his most excellent companion. His two visitors gently and reverently spoke to him these words, which were meant for the weal of the world: "Please do not condemn all those that live as unworthy of such treasure! Oh, please engender pity in your heart for beings in this world! So varied is their endowment, and while some have much passion, others have only very little. Now that you, O Sage, have yourself crossed the ocean of the world of becoming, please rescue also the other living beings who have sunk so deep into suffering! As a generous lord shares his wealth, so may also you bestow your own virtues on others! Most of those who know what for them is good in this world and the next, act only for their own advantage. In the world of men and in heaven it is hard to find anyone who is impelled by concern for the weal of the world." Having made this request to the great seer, the two gods returned to their celestial abode by the way they had come. And the sage pondered over their words. In consequence he was confirmed in his decision to set the world free.

Then came the time for the alms-round, and the World-Guardians of the four quarters[29] presented the seer with begging-bowls. Gautama accepted the four, but for the sake of his dharma he turned them into one. At that time two merchants of a passing caravan came that way. Instigated by a friendly deity, they joyfully saluted the seer, and, elated in their hearts, gave him alms. They were the first to do so.

After that the sage saw that Arada and Udraka Ramaputra[30] were the two people best equipped to grasp the dharma. But then he saw that both had gone to live among the gods in heaven. His mind thereupon turned to the five mendicants. In order to proclaim the path to peace, thereby dispelling the darkness of ignorance, just as the rising sun conquers the darkness of night, Gautama betook himself to the blessed city of Kashi,[31] to which Bhimaratha gave his love, and which is adorned with the Varanasi River and with many splendid forests. Then, before he carried out his wish to go into the region of Kashi, the Sage, whose eyes were like those of a bull, and whose gait like that of an elephant in rut, once more fixed his steady gaze on the root of the Bodhi-tree,[32] after he had turned his entire body like an elephant.

---

[29]The guardians of the four quarters of the world: Yama, the god of death, in the south; Indra, the heavenly king, in the east; Kubera, the god of wealth, in the north; and Varuna, the god of the moral order, in the west.

[30]Two individuals known for their spiritual accomplishments. Buddha considered them fit to receive his teaching, but they had already departed from the world.

[31]Kashi (modern Benares or Varanasi) is the holy city of India, associated in legend with one Bhimaratha.

[32]The tree of wisdom (Bodhi) under which Buddha reached enlightenment.

The Meeting with the Mendicant

He had fulfilled his task, and now, calm and majestic, went on alone, though it seemed that a large retinue accompanied him. A mendicant, intent on dharma, saw him on the road, and in wonderment folded his hands and said to him: "The senses of others are restless like horses, but yours have been tamed. Other beings are passionate, but your passions have ceased. Your form shines like the moon in the night-sky, and you appear to be refreshed by the sweet savor of a wisdom newly tasted. Your features shine with intellectual power, you have become master over your senses, and you have the eyes of a mighty bull. No doubt that you have achieved your aim. Who then is your teacher, who has taught you this supreme felicity?" But he replied: "No teacher have I. None need I venerate, and none must I despise. Nirvana have I now obtained, and I am not the same as others are. Quite by myself, you see, have I the dharma won. Completely have I understood what must be understood, though others failed to understand it. That is the reason why I am a Buddha. The hostile forces of defilement I have vanquished. That is the reason why I should be known as one whose self is calmed. And, having calmed myself, I now am on my way to Varanasi, to work the weal of fellow-beings still oppressed by many ills. There shall I beat the deathless dharma's drum, unmoved by pride, not tempted by renown. Having myself crossed the ocean of suffering, I must help others to cross it. Freed myself, I must set others free. This is the vow which I made in the past when I saw all that lives in distress." In reply the mendicant whispered to himself, "Most remarkable, indeed!" And he decided that it would be better not to stay with the Buddha. He accordingly went his way, although repeatedly he looked back at him with eyes full of wonderment, and not without some degree of longing desire.

• • •

Turning the Wheel of Dharma

Since the mendicants thus refused to believe in the truth found by the Tathagata,[33] he, who knew the path to enlightenment to be different from the practice of austerities, expounded to them the path from his direct knowledge of it: "Those foolish people who torment themselves, as well as those who have become attached to the domains of the senses, both these should be viewed as faulty in their method, because they are not on the way to deathlessness. These so-called austerities but confuse the mind which is overpowered by the body's exhaustion. In the resulting stupor one can no longer understand the ordinary things of life, how much less the way to the truth which lies beyond the senses.

---

[33]Another name for Buddha, meaning "one who is in the state of *tathata,*" which, in turn, paradoxically, means "the void and the absolute reality."

The minds of those, on the other hand, who are attached to the worthless sense-objects, are overwhelmed by passion and darkening delusion. They lose even the ability to understand the doctrinal treatises, still less can they succeed with the method which by suppressing the passions leads to dispassion. So I have given up both these extremes, and have found another path, a middle way. It leads to the appeasing of all ill, and yet it is free from happiness and joy."

The Buddha then expounded to the five mendicants the holy eightfold path, and the four holy truths [see the following excerpt].

"And so I came to the conviction that suffering must be comprehended, its cause given up, its stopping mastered, and this path developed. Now that I have comprehended suffering, have given up its cause, have realized its stopping, and have developed this path—now I can say that my organ of spiritual vision has been opened. As long as I had not seen these four divisions of the holy real truth, so long did I not claim to be emancipated, so long did I not believe I had done what was to be done. But when I had penetrated the holy truths, and had thereby done all that had to be done: then I did claim to be emancipated, then I did see that I had reached my goal."

THE FOUR HOLY TRUTHS
[*Samyutta Nikaya,* 5.421 ff.]

What then is the holy truth of ill? Birth is ill, decay is ill, sickness is ill, death is ill. To be conjoined with what one dislikes means suffering. To be disjoined from what one likes means suffering. Not to get what one wants, also that means suffering. In short, all grasping at any of the five Skandhas[34] involves suffering.

What then is the holy truth of the origination of ill? It is that craving which leads to rebirth, accompanied by delight and greed, seeking its delight now here, now there, i.e., craving for sensuous experience, craving to perpetuate oneself, craving for extinction.[35]

What then is the holy truth of the stopping of ill? It is the complete stopping of that craving, the withdrawal from it, the renouncing of it, throwing it back, liberation from it, non-attachment to it.

What then is the holy truth of the steps which lead to the stopping of ill? It is this holy eightfold path, which consists of right views, right intentions, right speech, right conduct, right livelihood, right effort, right mindfulness, right concentration.

---

[34]Skandhas are the five passing and impermanent conditions: form, or the physical body; feelings; idea or understanding; will; and pure consciousness. What is known as the soul, according to Buddhism, has no unity but is rather a loose aggregate of the Skandhas.

[35]That is, even the quest for extinction, if it becomes a craving, is cause of suffering.

22

❧

Buddhist Sources

THE DIAMOND SUTRA

The term sutra has come to have a range of meanings in the context of Buddhist literature, from its narrowest definition as the sermons and discourses of the Buddha, to its widest definition as any Buddhist scripture. The word in the Sanskrit language originally meant "a thread," and the contents of most of the sutras are "threaded" or strung together as narratives or portions of a doctrinal explanation. Those sutras that fall into the first category—sermons and discourses of the Gautama Buddha (see Selection 21)—were reputedly written down by one of the Buddha's ten great disciples, Ananda. They each characteristically begin with the formula "Thus have I heard," identify the place where the Buddha gave this sermon, and close with another formula to the effect that all who had heard these words "were filled with joy at his teaching, and, taking it sincerely to heart . . . went their ways."

The Diamond Sutra, which is substantially reproduced here, is one of the best known and most influential of these works. While Buddhism originated in Nepal and India, and for the first centuries of its development tended to spread toward the West, its greatest triumph as a missionary religion was ultimately in the Far East: China and the countries directly influenced by Chinese civilization—Japan, Korea, and Vietnam. Whereas Buddhism ceased to play a major role in the religious and cultural life of India, it became interwoven into the fabric of all life and culture in the Far East as well as in Southeast Asia.

The Diamond of the Perfection of Transcendental Wisdom, to give it its full designation, probably was of Indian origin. It belongs to the literature of the Mahayana tradition of Buddhism, one of the two great divisions of the religion that came about toward the end of the first century A.D. This suggests that its origin, at least in this form, was much later than the life of the Gautama Buddha. Tradition has it that it was translated from Sanskrit into Chinese by the great missionary scholar–monk Kumarajiva about A.D. 400. The Diamond Sutra was *a powerful factor in the spread of Buddhism in China and the zone of Chinese cultural influence. The oldest extant printed book in the world is a Chinese text of* The Diamond Sutra, *printed from carved wooden blocks in the ninth century.*

Mahayana Buddhism (represented here), far more than the Hinayana school, which forms the other branch of the divided Buddhist religion, is a popular faith that holds out to all human beings the hope of "salvation"—release from endless cycles of rebirth and death—through enlightenment. The sutras were written to be pleasant to read or hear, and relatively easy to recite. As the text of the following document (translated from Chinese) indicates, such reading and recitation was thought to convey great merit. The discourse between the Buddha and his disciple Subhuti seems to proceed slowly and to be characterized by frequent repetition. Yet the effect of the discourse is cumulative and progressive. The most basic Buddhist philosophical beliefs—the illusory nature of being, of ego, of all apparent perception—are, indeed, hard for the conventional Western mind to accept. The sutra leads the reader or hearer, step by often-repeated step, toward familiarity with these difficult concepts and eventually toward acceptance of them as the higher reality. And, by coupling their revelation with the hope of release from our imprisonment in this false non-world, the sutra makes the acceptance of these "hard" truths ultimately a matter of joy.

SECTION I: THE CONVOCATION OF THE ASSEMBLY

Thus have I heard. Upon a time Buddha sojourned in Anathapindika's Park by Shravasti[1] with a great company of *bhikshus,*[2] even twelve hundred and fifty.

One day, at the time for breaking fast, the world-honored [the Buddha] enrobed, and carrying his bowl made his way into the great city of Shravasti to beg for his food. In the midst of the city he begged from door to door according to rule. This done, he returned to his retreat and took his meal. When he had finished he put away his robe and begging bowl, washed his feet, arranged his seat, and sat down.

From *The Diamond Sutra* and *The Sutra of Hui Neng,* translated by A. F. Price and Wong Mou-Lam. Reprinted by arrangement with Shambhala Publications, Inc., P.O. Box 308, Boston, MA, 02117.

[1]Located in northern India, near the border with Nepal. In Buddhist lore it is known as the "City of Wonders."

[2]Begging monks of the order founded by the Gautama Buddha. Nuns of the order were called *bhikshunis.*

SECTION II: SUBHUTI MAKES A REQUEST

Now in the midst of the assembly was the Venerable Subhuti. Forthwith he arose, uncovered his right shoulder, knelt upon his right knee, and, respectfully raising his hands with palms joined, addressed Buddha thus: "World-honored one, it is most precious how mindful the Tathagata[3] is of all the Bodhisattvas,[4] protecting and instructing them so well! World-honored one, if good men and good women seek the consummation of incomparable enlightenment, by what criteria should they abide and how should they control their thoughts?"

Buddha said: "Very good, Subhuti! Just as you say, the Tathagata is ever-mindful of all the Bodhisattvas, protecting and instructing them well. Now listen and take my words to heart: I will declare to you by what criteria good men and good women seeking the consummation of incomparable enlightenment should abide, and how they should control their thoughts."

Said Subhuti: "Pray, do, world-honored one. With joyful anticipation we long to hear."

SECTION III: THE REAL TEACHING OF THE GREAT WAY

Buddha said: "Subhuti, all the Bodhisattva-Heroes should discipline their thoughts as follows: All living creatures of whatever class, born from eggs, from wombs, from moisture, or by transformation, whether with form or without form, whether in a state of thinking or exempt from thought-necessity, or wholly beyond all thought realms—all these are caused by me to attain unbounded liberation nirvana.[5] Yet when vast, uncountable, immeasurable numbers of beings have thus been liberated, verily no being has been liberated. Why is this, Subhuti? It is because no Bodhisattva who is a real Bodhisattva cherishes the idea of ego-entity, a personality, a being, or a separated individuality."

SECTION IV: EVEN THE MOST BENEFICENT PRACTICES ARE RELATIVE

"Furthermore, Subhuti, in the practice of charity a Bodhisattva should be detached. That is to say, he should practice charity without regard to appearances;

---

[3]One of the many names for Buddha, one that denotes a realization of Buddha's closeness to ultimate truth. *The Diamond Sutra* gradually reveals the meaning of Tathagata, culminating in the dialogue in Section XIV below.

[4]An advanced devotee of Buddhism, one who has approached enlightenment.

[5]Nirvana is the goal of Buddhist enlightenment. A difficult concept to define, it is best understood as the final liberation not only from the physical self, but from the ego. Some Buddhists employed the analogy of a drop of rain "returning" to the sea, absorbed again into its element, losing all individuality.

without regard to sound, odor, touch, flavor, or any quality. Subhuti, thus should the Bodhisattva practice charity without attachment. Wherefore? In such a case his merit is incalculable.

"Subhuti, what do you think? Can you measure all the space extending eastward?"

"No, world-honored one, I cannot."

"Then can you, Subhuti, measure all the space extending southward, westward, northward, or in any other direction, including nadir and zenith?"

"No, world-honored one, I cannot."

"Well, Subhuti, equally incalculable is the merit of the Bodhisattva who practices charity without any attachment to appearances. Subhuti, Bodhisattvas should persevere one-pointedly in this instruction."

SECTION V: UNDERSTANDING THE ULTIMATE PRINCIPLE OF REALITY

"Subhuti, what do you think? Is the Tathagata to be recognized by some material characteristic?"

"No, world-honored one; the Tathagata cannot be recognized by any material characteristic. Wherefore? Because the Tathagata has said that material characteristics are not, in fact, material characteristics."

Buddha said: "Subhuti, wheresoever are material characteristics there is delusion; but whoso perceives that all characteristics are in fact no-characteristics, perceives the Tathagata."

• • •

SECTION VII: GREAT ONES, PERFECT BEYOND LEARNING, UTTER NO WORDS OF TEACHING

"Subhuti, what do you think? Has the Tathagata attained the consummation of incomparable enlightenment? Has the Tathagata a teaching to enunciate?"

Subhuti answered: "As I understand Buddha's meaning, there is no formulation of truth called consummation of incomparable enlightenment. Moreover, the Tathagata has no formulated teaching to enunciate. Wherefore? Because the Tathagata has said that truth is uncontainable and inexpressible.[6] It neither *is* nor is it *not*."

---

[6]Compare this assertion about the inexpressibility of ultimate truth with that of the Chinese Taoist classic, the *Tao Te Ching* (Selection 30). As Buddhism was introduced from India into China in the early centuries A.D., it made an especially strong appeal to Taoists, whose own beliefs predisposed them to understand and accept such ideas.

Thus it is that this unformulated principle is the foundation of the different systems of all the sages.

SECTION VIII: THE FRUITS OF MERITORIOUS ACTION

"Subhuti, what do you think? If anyone filled three thousand galaxies of worlds with the seven treasures[7] and gave all away in gifts of alms, would he gain great merit?"

Subhuti said: "Great indeed, world-honored one! Wherefore? Because merit partakes of the character of no-merit, the Tathagata characterized the merit as great."

Then Buddha said: "On the other hand, if anyone received and retained even only four lines of this discourse and taught and explained them to others, his merit would be the greater. Wherefore? Because, Subhuti, from this discourse issue forth all the Buddhas and the consummation of the incomparable enlightenment teachings of all the Buddhas.

"Subhuti, what is called 'the religion given by Buddha' is not, in fact, Buddha-religion."[8]

●　　●　　●

SECTION XII: VENERATION OF THE TRUE DOCTRINE

"Furthermore, Subhuti, you should know that wheresoever this discourse is proclaimed, by even so little as four lines, that place should be venerated by the whole realms of gods, men and Titans, as though it were a Buddha-shrine. How much more is this so in the case of one who is able to receive and retain the whole and read and recite it throughout!

"Subhuti, you should know that such an one attains the highest and most wonderful truth. Wheresoever this sacred discourse may be found, there should you comport yourself as though in the presence of Buddha and disciples worthy of honor."

---

[7] Agate, cornelian, crystal, gold, lapis-lazuli, pearls, silver.

[8] This paradox, apparently, can be explained by reference to the previous section (VII) of the sutra. Teaching, even the teaching of the Buddha, cannot encompass truth, but only can help one to set foot on the path toward enlightenment.

SECTION XIII: HOW THIS TEACHING
SHOULD BE RECEIVED AND RETAINED

At that time Subhuti addressed Buddha, saying: "World-honored one, by what name should this discourse be known, and how should we receive and retain it?"

Buddha answered: "Subhuti, this discourse should be known as 'The Diamond[9] of the Perfection of Transcendental Wisdom'—thus should you receive and retain it. Subhuti, what is the reason herein? According to the Buddha-teaching the perfection of transcendental wisdom is not really such. 'Perfection of Transcendental Wisdom' is just the name given to it. Subhuti, what do you think? Has the Tathagata a teaching to enunciate?"

Subhuti replied to Buddha: "World-honored one, the Tathagata has nothing to teach."

"Subhuti, what do you think? Would there be many molecules in the composition of three thousand galaxies of worlds?"

Subhuti said: "Many, indeed, world-honored one!"

"Subhuti, the Tathagata declares that all these molecules are not really such; they are called 'molecules.' Furthermore, the Tathagata declares that the world is not really a world; it is called 'a world.'

"Subhuti, what do you think? May the Tathagata be perceived by the thirty-two physical peculiarities[10] of an outstanding sage?"

"No, world-honored one, the Tathagata may not be perceived by these thirty-two marks. Wherefore? Because the Tathagata has explained that the thirty-two marks are not really such; they are called 'the thirty-two marks.'"

"Subhuti, if, on the one hand, a good man or a good woman sacrifices as many lives as the sand-grains of the Ganges, and, on the other hand, anyone receives and retains even only four lines of this discourse, and teaches and explains them to others, the merit of the latter will be the greater."

SECTION XIV: PERFECT PEACE LIES IN
FREEDOM FROM CHARACTERISTIC
DISTINCTIONS

Upon the occasion of hearing this discourse Subhuti had an interior realization of its meaning and was moved to tears. Whereupon he addressed Buddha thus: "It

---

[9]The choice of the title "Diamond" suggests not only the brilliance of the gem, but its hardness and power to cut through all other material, in this case to cut through false perceptions of the world.

[10]A set of characteristics listed in Hindu scriptures. While we see Buddhism as a religion distinct from Hinduism because of the historical course it took, the Gautama Buddha came out of the same tradition as Hinduism. He was a deep believer in its doctrines, and doubtless thought of himself as a reformer rather than as a rebel.

is a most precious thing, world-honored one, that you should deliver this supremely profound discourse. Never have I heard such an exposition since of old my eye of wisdom first opened. World-honored one, if anyone listens to this discourse in faith with a pure, lucid mind, he will thereupon conceive an idea of fundamental reality. We should know that such an one establishes the most remarkable virtue. World-honored one, such an idea of fundamental reality is not, in fact, a distinctive idea; therefore the Tathagata teaches: 'Idea of Fundamental Reality' is merely a name.

"World-honored one, having listened to this discourse, I receive and retain it with faith and understanding. This is not difficult for me, but in ages to come—in the last five hundred years,[11] if there be men coming to hear this discourse who receive and retain it with faith and understanding, they will be persons of most remarkable achievement. Wherefore? Because they will be free from the idea of ego-entity, free from the idea of a personality, free from the idea of a being, and free from the idea of a separated individuality. And why? Because the distinguishing of an ego-entity is erroneous. Likewise the distinguishing of a personality, or a being, or a separated individuality is erroneous. Consequently, those who have left behind every phenomenal distinction are called Buddhas all."

Buddha said to Subhuti: "Just as you say! If anyone listens to this discourse and is neither filled with alarm nor awe nor dread, be it known that such an one is of remarkable achievement. Wherefore? Because, Subhuti, the Tathagata teaches that the first perfection, the perfection of charity, is not, in fact, the first perfection; such is merely a name.

"Subhuti, the Tathagata teaches likewise that the perfection of patience is not the perfection of patience: such is merely a name. Why so? It is shown thus, Subhuti: When the Rajah of Kalinga mutilated my body,[12] I was at that time free from the idea of ego-entity, a personality, a being, and a separated individuality. Wherefore? Because then when my limbs were cut away piece by piece, had I been bound by the distinctions aforesaid, feelings of anger and hatred would have been aroused within me. Subhuti, I remember that long ago, some time during my last past five hundred mortal lives, I was an ascetic practicing patience. Even then I was free from those distinctions of separated selfhood. Therefore, Subhuti, Bodhisattvas should leave behind all phenomenal distinctions and awaken the thought of the consummation of incomparable enlightenment by not allowing the mind to depend on notions evoked by the sensible world—by not allowing the mind to depend upon notions evoked by sounds, odors, flavors, touch-contacts, or any qualities. The mind should be kept independent of any thoughts which arise within it. If the mind depends upon anything it has no sure haven. This is why Buddha teaches that the mind of a Bodhisattva should not accept the

---

[11]Time references seem confusing, but what is meant here is the present age and the future.

[12]An event in one of the hundreds of former incarnations of the Buddha.

appearance of things as a basis when exercising charity. Subhuti, as Bodhisattvas practice charity for the welfare of all living beings they should do it in this manner. Just as the Tathagata declares that characteristics are not characteristics, so he declares that all living beings are not, in fact, living beings.

"Subhuti, the Tathagata is he who declares that which is true; he who declares that which is fundamental; he who declares that which is ultimate. He does not declare that which is deceitful, nor that which is monstrous. Subhuti, that truth to which the Tathagata has attained is neither real nor unreal.

"Subhuti, if a Bodhisattva practices charity with mind attached to formal notions he is like unto a man groping sightless in the gloom; but a Bodhisattva who practices charity with mind detached from any formal notions is like unto a man with open eyes in the radiant glory of the morning, to whom all kinds of objects are clearly visible.

"Subhuti, if there be good men and good women in future ages, able to receive, read, and recite this discourse in its entirety, the Tathagata will clearly perceive and recognize them by means of his Buddha-knowledge; and each one of them will bring immeasurable and incalculable merit to fruition."

• • •

SECTION XVI: PURGATION THROUGH SUFFERING THE RETRIBUTION FOR PAST SINS

"Furthermore, Subhuti, if it be that good men and good women, who receive and retain this discourse, are downtrodden, their evil destiny is the inevitable retributive result of sins committed in their past mortal lives.[13] By virtue of their present misfortunes, the reacting effects of their past will be, thereby, worked out, and they will be in a position to attain the consummation of incomparable enlightenment.

"Subhuti, I remember the infinitely remote past before Dipankara Buddha.[14] There were eighty-four thousand myriads of multimillions of Buddhas and to all these I made offerings; yes, all these I served without the least trace of fault. Nevertheless, if anyone is able to receive, retain, study, and recite this discourse at the end of the last five hundred-year period, he will gain such merit that mine in the service of all the Buddhas could not be reckoned as one-hundredth part of it,

---

[13]The doctrine of karma, which is common to several schools of Indian thought, holds that one's status in each life is a projection forward of the good or evil one has done in previous existences. Buddhism accepted this doctrine but pointed the way to an eventual escape from the "wheel of reincarnation," by the achievement of enlightenment (Buddhahood) and attainment of Nirvana.

[14]Another earlier incarnation of the Buddha.

not even one-thousandth part of it, not even one thousand myriad multimillionth part of it—indeed, no such comparison is possible.

"Subhuti, if I fully detailed the merit gained by good men and good women coming to receive, retain, study, and recite this discourse in the last period, my hearers would be filled with doubt and might become disordered in mind, suspicious and unbelieving. You should know, Subhuti, that the significance of this discourse is beyond conception; likewise the fruit of its rewards is beyond conception."

● ● ●

SECTION XXV: THE ILLUSION OF EGO

"Subhuti, what do you think? Let no one say the Tathagata cherishes the idea: I must liberate all living beings. Allow no such thought, Subhuti. Wherefore? Because in reality there are no living beings to be liberated by the Tathagata. If there were living beings for the Tathagata to liberate, he would partake in the idea of selfhood, personality, entity, and separate individuality.

"Subhuti, although the common people accept the ego as real, the Tathagata declares that ego is not different from non-ego. Subhuti, whom the Tathagata referred to as 'common people' are not really common people; such is merely a name."

● ● ●

SECTION XXXII: THE DELUSION OF APPEARANCES

"Subhuti, someone might fill innumerable worlds with the seven treasures and give all away in gifts of alms, but if any good man or good woman awakens the thought of enlightenment and takes only four lines of this discourse, reciting, using, receiving, retaining, and spreading them abroad and explaining them for the benefit of others, it will be far more meritorious.

"Now in what manner may he explain them to others? By detachment from appearances—abiding in real truth. So I tell you—

> Thus shall ye think of all this fleeting world;
> A star at dawn, a bubble in a stream;
> A flash of lightning in a summer cloud;
> A flickering lamp, a phantom, and a dream."

When Buddha finished this discourse the venerable Subhuti, together with the *bhikshus, bhikshunis*, lay-brothers and sisters, and the whole realms of gods, men, and Titans, were filled with joy by his teaching, and, taking it sincerely to heart they went their ways.

23

৯৳

Megasthenes

INDIKA

Megasthenes is well known to students of Indian history as the preeminent ancient Greek writer who wrote a geographical, social, and cultural account of India around the last years of the fourth and the early years of the third century B.C. His work, called Indika, illustrates the intellectual interaction between the Graeco-Roman world and India in ancient times. Greek historians had begun to take interest in and write about the Indian subcontinent from the mid-sixth century B.C. onward. The Histories of Herodotus (ca. 484–425 B.C.), who is known as the "father of history," (see Selection 14) included a treatment of some aspects of Indian geography and culture. When Alexander the Great (356–323 B.C.) set out to conquer the world, he took with him many learned men to record his achievements and to describe the countries he would pass through or conquer. His invasion of India (327–325 B.C.), therefore, produced a rich crop of descriptive and narrative literature about India. Continuing in this tradition of writing about India, Megasthenes surpassed all his predecessors. In the words of its nineteenth-century German editor, E. A. Schwanbeck, Megasthenes's Indika is "the culmination of the knowledge which the ancients ever acquired of India. . . ."

Megasthenes was an envoy of Seleucus Nicator (ca. 358–281 B.C.) a former general of Alexander the Great, who, after Alexander's death, appropriated the Asian part of the empire created by him. Seleucus sent Megasthenes as his ambassador to the court of the Indian emperor Chandragupta Maurya (reigned ca. 320–298 B.C.). Chandragupta was a contemporary of Alexander the Great. Many historians believe that he spent some time with the great conqueror during his campaign in India. After Alexander's departure, Chandragupta built the first great Indian empire. His territories stretched from eastern India through present-day Afghanistan and touched the eastern boundary of the Seleucid empire (named after Seleucus Nicator).

Megasthenes spent many years in India at the Mauryan capital, Pataliputra, on one or several embassies. During his stay there, he gathered knowledge about the country and its people, both from personal observation and from resource persons, most of them brahmans. Thus equipped, he wrote a panoramic account of India covering a vast range of subjects in great detail. To quote Schwanbeck again, he "described the country, its soil, climate, animals, and plants, its government and religion, the manners of its people and their arts,—in short, the whole of Indian life from king to the remotest tribe; and he has scanned every object with a mind sound and unprejudiced, without overlooking even trifling and minute circumstances." His work left a powerful influence on all the later Greek and Roman historians writing about India. Whether they praised Megasthenes's work or criticized it, in fact, they always treated it as the most authoritative source of information about India. Several of them wrote their own Indikas *based on his work. The original text of Megasthenes's* Indika *has itself been lost, but his successors copied, quoted, and summarized it so often and at such great length that it has been almost entirely recovered from their use of it in their own writings. Thus resurrected and existing only in the form of fragments culled from these authors, it is a mine of information about Mauryan society and culture.*

Yet there is a side to Megasthenes's Indika *for which he has often drawn adverse criticism. It is pointed out that the book contained much fabulous and incredible material, such as the descriptions of certain peoples and animals in the excerpts "Of Some Wild Beasts of India," "Of Fabulous Races," and "Of Gold-Digging Ants" in the following selection. This aspect of the book, however, is explained by two factors. First, Megasthenes, essentially a very realistic writer, was to some extent still writing in the vein of the earlier Greek historians, such as Herodotus, who often made lavish use of the exotic and fantastic in order to entertain their audiences. Writing about a distant land and addressing audiences nurtured on the stories of these earlier historians, Megasthenes also succumbed to the same tendency to provide for this taste for the strange and marvelous. A second, and more important, reason for the fantastic side of his* Indika *is that Megasthenes, as noted above, received a considerable part of his information from the custodians of the cultural establishment, the brahmans. Quite understandably, their descriptions of the world beyond the boundaries of the mainstream culture were biased. Their ethnocentrism and imagination demonized this world, filling it with impossible and monstrous peoples, animals, and even vegetation. Megasthenes recorded what he was told, along with what he saw for himself. The presence of the fantastic in Megasthenes's* Indika *does not detract from its value as a picture of the time and place he wrote about. His forays into the impossible rather add a subtle dimension to his work. They mirror an aspect of the imaginative side of the Indian reality, a side which is found in much of the narrative literature of the country, such as, for instance, the epics. Moreover, the fantastic element in the book has a special interest and charm of its own.*

The excerpts in this selection provide a sampling of the wide variety of subject matter in Megasthenes's Indika. *They are derived from fragments of the book as cited or summarized in their works by numerous Greek and Roman authors who came after Megasthenes. These separate fragments, collected by Schwanbeck in 1846 and later translated into English by J. W. McCrindle, are here adapted for readability.*

ॐ

OF THE FERTILITY OF THE LAND

In addition to cereals, there grows throughout India much millet, which is kept well watered by the profusion of river-streams, and much pulse of different sorts, and rice also, and what is called bosporum,[1] as well as many other plants useful for food, of which most grow spontaneously. The soil yields, moreover, not a few other edible products fit for the subsistence of animals, about which it would be tedious to write. It is accordingly affirmed that famine has never visited India, and that there has never been a general scarcity in the supply of nourishing food. For, since there is a double rainfall in the course of each year,—one in the winter season, when the sowing of wheat takes place as in other countries, and the second at the time of the summer solstice, which is the proper season for sowing rice and bosporum, as well as sesamum[2] and millet—the inhabitants of India almost always gather in two harvests annually; and even should one of the sowings prove more or less abortive they are always sure of the other crop. The fruits, moreover, of spontaneous growth, and the esculent roots which grow in marshy places and are of varied sweetness, afford abundant sustenance for man. . . .

OF SOME WILD BEASTS OF INDIA

The largest tigers are found among the Prasii,[3] being nearly twice the size of the lion, and so strong that a tame tiger led by four men having seized a mule by the hinder leg overpowered it and dragged it to him. The monkeys are larger than the

---

Adapted by Surjit S. Dulai from J. W. McCrindle, ed., *Ancient India as Described by Megasthenes and Arrian* (Calcutta: Chuckervertty, Chatterjee & Co., Ltd., 1926; reprinted from the *Indian Antiquary,* 1876–1877), pp. 30–31, 54, 65, 67–69, 79–80, 86–89, 94–95, 101–102, 117–118.

[1]A grain, resembling wheat, that grows in summer.

[2]The sesame plant.

[3]A people living in the eastern part of India in the region around Pataliputra, the capital of Chandragupta Maurya.

largest dogs; they are white except in the face, which is black, though the contrary is observed elsewhere. Their tails are more than two cubits in length.[4] They are very tame, and not of a malicious disposition, so that they neither attack man nor steal. Stones are dug up which are of the color of frankincense, and sweeter than figs or honey. In some parts of the country there are serpents two cubits long which have membranous wings like bats. They fly about by night, when they let fall drops of urine or sweat, which blister the skin of persons not on their guard with putrid sores. There are also winged scorpions of an extraordinary size. Ebony[5] grows there. There are also dogs of great strength and courage, which will not let go their hold till water is poured into their nostrils. They bite so eagerly that the eyes of some become distorted, and the eyes of others fall out. Both a lion and a bull were held fast by a dog. The bull was seized by the muzzle, and died before the dog could be taken off.

OF THE CITY PATALIPUTRA

At the meeting of the river Ganges and another is situated Palibothra,[6] a city eighty stadia in length and fifteen in breadth.[7] It is of the shape of a parallelogram, and is girded with a wooden wall, pierced with loopholes for the discharge of arrows. . . . A ditch encompassed it all round, which was six hundred feet in breadth and thirty cubits in depth, and the wall was crowned with 570 towers and had four-and-sixty gates. . . . All the Indians are free, and not one of them is a slave. The Lakedaemonians[8] and the Indians are here so far in agreement. The Lakedaemonians, however, hold the Helots[9] as slaves, and these Helots do servile labor; but the Indians do not even use aliens as slaves, and much less a countryman of their own.[10]

---

[4]The cubit was an ancient unit of measurement. Originally, it was equal to the length of the forearm from the tip of the middle finger to the elbow (from seventeen to twenty-two inches).

[5]A tropical tree having hard, heavy, durable, dark wood.

[6]Pataliputra, the capital of the Mauryan empire. It was located on the site of present-day Patna, in the state of Bihar in eastern India.

[7]Stadia is the plural of stadium, an ancient Greek unit of distance. It was equal to the length of the course for foot races in a stadium, approximately 607 feet.

[8]Citizens of the ancient Greek city–state of Sparta.

[9]Helots, serfs belonging to the state, were the lowest class of Sparta. Of different tribal stock than the Spartans, they could not become citizens.

[10]This statement of Megasthenes is not true. He presents here too favorable a view of Indian society, which definitely included slavery.

OF THE MANNERS OF THE INDIANS

The Indians all live frugally, especially when in camp. They dislike a great undisciplined multitude, and consequently they observe good order. Theft is of very rare occurrence. Megasthenes says that those who were in the camp of Sandrakottos,[11] wherein lay 400,000 men, found that the thefts reported on any one day did not exceed the value of two hundred drachmas,[12] and this among a people who have no written laws, but are ignorant of writing,[13] and must therefore in all the business of life trust to memory. They live, nevertheless, happily enough, being simple in their manners and frugal. They never drink wine except at sacrifices.[14] Their beverage is a liquor composed from rice instead of barley, and their food is principally a rice-pottage. The simplicity of their laws and their contracts is proved by the fact that they seldom go to law. They have no suits about pledges or deposits, nor do they require either seals or witnesses, but make their deposits and confide in each other. Their houses and property they generally leave unguarded. These things indicate that they possess good, sober sense; but other things they do which one cannot approve: for instance, that they eat always alone, and that they have no fixed hours when meals are to be taken by all in common, but each one eats when he feels inclined. The contrary custom would be better for the ends of social and civil life.

Their favorite mode of exercising the body is by friction, applied in various ways, but especially by passing smooth ebony rollers over the skin. Their tombs are plain, and the mounds raised over the dead lowly. In contrast to the general simplicity of their style, they love finery and ornament. Their robes are worked in gold, and ornamented with precious stones, and they wear also flowered garments made of the finest muslin. Attendants walking behind hold up umbrellas over them: for they have a high regard for beauty, and avail themselves of every device to improve their looks. Truth and virtue they hold alike in esteem. Hence they accord no special privileges to the old unless they possess superior wisdom. They marry many wives, whom they buy from their parents, giving in exchange a yoke of oxen. Some they marry hoping to find in them willing helpmates; and others for pleasure and to fill their houses with children. . . .

---

[11]Greeks referred to Chandragupta Maurya by this name.

[12]A silver coin of ancient Greece.

[13]This observation attributed to Megasthenes is not correct, since, by his time, writing was definitely used by such classes as priests and merchants.

[14]The drink was probably soma juice. See Selection 8 from the *Rig-Veda*.

OF FABULOUS RACES

On a mountain called Nulo there live men whose feet are turned backward, and who have eight toes on each foot; while on many of the mountains there lives a race of men having heads like those of dogs, who are clothed with the skins of wild beasts, whose speech is barking, and who, being armed with claws, live by hunting and fowling. . . .

There is a race of men among the Nomadic Indians who instead of nostrils have merely orifices, whose legs are contorted like snakes. . . . There is also a race living on the very confines of India on the east, near the source of the Ganges, the Astomi,[15] who have no mouth; who cover their body, which is all over hairy, with the soft down found upon the leaves of trees; and who live merely by breathing, and the perfume inhaled by the nostrils. They eat nothing, and they drink nothing. They require merely a variety of odors of roots and of flowers and of wild apples. The apples they carry with them when they go on a distant journey, that they may always have something to smell. Too strong an odor would readily kill them.

Beyond the Astomi, in the remotest part of the mountains, the Trispithami and the Pygmies are said to have their abode. They are each three spans in height—that is, not more than seven-and-twenty inches. . . .

OF THE ADMINISTRATION OF PUBLIC AFFAIRS

Of the great officers of state, some have charge of the market, others of the city, others of the soldiers. Some superintend the rivers, measure the land, as is done in Egypt,[16] and inspect the sluices by which water is let out from the main canals into their branches, so that everyone may have an equal supply of it. The same persons have charge also of the huntsmen, and are entrusted with the power of rewarding or punishing them according to their deserts. They collect the taxes, and superintend the occupations connected with the land, as those of the wood-cutters, the carpenters, the blacksmiths, and the miners. They construct roads, and at every ten stadia set up a pillar to show the by-roads and distances. Those who have charge of the city are divided into six bodies of five each. The members of the first look after everything relating to the industrial arts. Those of the second attend to the entertainment of foreigners. To these they assign lodgings, and they keep watch over their modes of life by means of those persons whom they

---

[15]The Astomi, as well as the Trispithami and the Pygmies that are mentioned next, have little basis in reality.

[16]Ancient Egypt had an elaborate system of irrigation and distribution of water that was controlled by the state.

give to them for assistants. They escort them on the way when they leave the country, or, in the event of their dying, forward their property to their relatives. They take care of them when they are sick, and if they die, bury them. The third body consists of those who inquire when and how births and deaths occur, with the view not only of levying a tax, but also in order that births and deaths among both high and low may not escape the cognizance of government. The fourth class superintends trade and commerce. Its members have charge of weights and measures, and see that the products in their season are sold by public notice. No one is allowed to deal in more than one kind of commodity unless he pays a double tax. The fifth class supervises manufactured articles, which they sell by public notice. What is new is sold separately from what is old, and there is a fine for mixing the two together. The sixth and last class consists of those who collect the tenths of the prices of the articles sold. Fraud in the payment of this tax is punished with death.

Such are the functions which these bodies separately discharge. In their collective capacity they have charge both of their special departments, and also of matters affecting the general interest, as the keeping of public buildings in proper repair, the regulation of prices, the care of markets, harbors, and temples. Next to the city magistrates there is a third governing body, which directs military affairs. This also consists of six divisions, with five members to each. One division is appointed to cooperate with the admiral of the fleet, another with the superintendent of the bullock-trains which are used for transporting engines of war, food for the soldiers, provender for the cattle, and other military requisites. They supply servants who beat the drum, and others who carry gongs; grooms also for the horses, and mechanists and their assistants. To the sound of the gong they send out foragers to bring in grass, and by a system of rewards and punishments ensure the work being done with despatch and safety. The third division has charge of the foot-soldiers, the fourth of the horses, the fifth of the war-chariots, and the sixth of the elephants. There are royal stables for the horses and elephants, and also a royal magazine for the arms, because the soldier has to return his arms to the magazine, and his horse and his elephant to the stables. They use the elephants without bridles. The chariots are drawn on the march by oxen, but the horses are led along by a halter, that their legs may not be galled and inflamed, nor their spirits damped by drawing chariots. In addition to the charioteer, there are two fighting men who sit up in the chariot beside him. The war-elephant carries four men—three who shoot arrows, and the driver.

OF THE USE OF HORSES AND ELEPHANTS

When it is said that an Indian by springing forward in front of a horse can check his speed and hold him back, this is not true of all Indians, but only of such as have been trained from boyhood to manage horses; for it is a practice with them to control their horses with bit and bridle, and to make them move at a measured pace and in a straight course. They neither, however, gall their tongue by the use of spiked muzzles, nor torture the roof of their mouth. The professional trainers break them in by forcing them to gallop round and round in a ring, especially when they see them refractory. Such as undertake this work require to have a strong hand as well as a thorough knowledge of horses. The greatest proficients test their skill by driving a chariot round and round in a ring; and in truth it would be no trifling feat to control with ease a team of four high-mettled steeds when whirling round in a circle. The chariot carries two men who sit beside the charioteer. The war-elephant, either in what is called the tower, or on his bare back in truth, carries three fighting men. . . .

OF GOLD-DIGGING ANTS

Among the Derdai,[17] a great tribe of Indians, who inhabit the mountains on the eastern borders, there is an elevated plateau about three thousand stadia in circuit. Beneath the surface there are mines of gold, and here accordingly are found the ants which dig for that metal. They are not inferior in size to wild foxes. They run with amazing speed, and live by the produce of the chase. The time when they dig is winter. They throw up heaps of earth, as moles do, at the mouth of the mines. The gold-dust has to be subjected to a little boiling. The people of the neighborhood, coming secretly with beasts of burden, carry this off. If they came openly the ants would attack them, and pursue them if they fled, and would destroy both them and their cattle. So, to effect the robbery without being observed, they lay down in several different places pieces of the flesh of wild beasts, and when the ants are by this device dispersed they carry off the gold-dust. . . .

OF THE SARMANES[18]

The philosophers who are held in most honor . . . live in the woods, where they subsist on leaves of trees and wild fruits, and wear garments made from the bark of trees. They abstain from sexual intercourse and from wine. They communicate with the kings, who consult them by messengers regarding the causes of things, and who through them worship and supplicate the deity. Next in honor to them are the physicians, since they are engaged in the study of the nature of man. They are simple in their habits, but do not live in the fields. Their food consists of rice and barley-meal, which they can always get for the mere asking, or receive from

---

[17]A tribal people who lived in the mountains in northwestern India by the banks of the river Indus.

[18]Megasthenes mentions two classes of philosophers, brahmans and sarmanes. The latter were ascetics who had renounced the world. According to some historians, they were associated with Buddhism.

those who entertain them as guests in their houses. By their knowledge of pharmacy they can make marriages fruitful, and determine the sex of the offspring. They effect cures rather by regulating diet than by the use of medicines. The remedies most esteemed are ointments and plasters. All others they consider to be in a great measure pernicious in their nature. This class and the other class practice fortitude, both by undergoing active toil, and by the endurance of pain, so that they remain for a whole day motionless in one fixed attitude.

OF ELEPHANTS

The elephant, when feeding at large, ordinarily drinks water, but when undergoing the fatigues of war is allowed wine,—not that sort, however, which comes from the grape, but another which is prepared from rice. The attendants even go in advance of their elephants and gather them flowers; for they are very fond of sweet perfumes, and they are accordingly taken out to the meadows, there to be trained under the influence of the sweetest fragrance. The animal selects the flowers according to their smell, and throws them as they are gathered into a basket which is held out by the trainer. This being filled, and harvest-work, so to speak, completed, he then bathes, and enjoys his bath with all the zest of a consummate voluptuary. On returning from bathing he is impatient to have his flowers, and if there is delay in bringing them he begins roaring, and will not taste a morsel of food till all the flowers he gathered are placed before him. This done, he takes the flowers out of the basket with his trunk and scatters them over the edge of his manger, and makes by this device their fine scent be, as it were, a relish to his food. He strews also a good quantity of them as litter over his stall, for he loves to have his sleep made sweet and pleasant. . . .

24

꒰

Kautilya

ARTHASHASTRA

A rthashastra *("science of politics") is an ancient Indian treatise on the art of government written in Sanskrit and traditionally attributed to Kautilya, who lived in northern India around 300 B.C. It is a work of major importance in the history of world political thought. Because of its subject, the acquisition and preservation of political power, and because of the shrewd and unscrupulous methods it often advocates for the attainment and maintenance of that power, Arthashastra is frequently compared to that much later work of the Italian Renaissance, Niccolo Machiavelli's* The Prince *(1513). Just as, in the Western world, Machiavelli is a synonym for cunning and lack of moral compunction in politics, in India, Kautilya or Chanakya (another name by which he is known) is a byword for similarly unscrupulous qualities of character. This description, although justified to a degree, is not totally accurate for either writer. Despite the moral dubiousness of the advice it contains, the aims of the* Arthashastra *are not utterly devoid of a genuine concern for orderly government in the interest of the citizens of a state. It is, in fact, a landmark in the evolution of Indian political theory and practice because of its realism and freedom from sentimentality. For its subject matter, it parallels other ancient works on law and politics, namely,* The Laws of Hammurabi *from Mesopotamia (Selection 5), Plato's* Republic, *and Aristotle's* Politics *(Selections 18 and 19) from ancient Greece.*

The authorship and date of the Arthashastra *are not absolutely certain. Some scholars have questioned even the historical existence of Kautilya. The most obvious evidence of his existence is that Kautilya is cited, by himself or another author, throughout the* Arthashastra *as the final authority on all aspects of politics. Most of the material in the book reflects the political reality of the time of Chandragupta Maurya (reigned ca. 320 B.C. –297 B.C.), the founder of the first great empire of India. Kautilya usually is identified with a Brahman mentor of Chandragupta who astutely guided him in his rise to power and served as his chief minister. The* Arthashastra *is considered to be mainly, though not entirely, Kautilya's work. It synthesizes treatments of the science of government from the centuries before his time and even contains accretions from as late as five centuries after him. For all practical purposes, however, it is customary, and appropriate, to consider Kautilya as the primary author of the* Arthashastra.

The Sanskrit word artha *means "material wealth." In the Hindu system of values,* artha *is one of the four ends of human life, the other three being* dharma *("performance of religious duties"),* kama *("engagement in pleasurable activities"), and* moksha *("spiritual self-realization"). Of these four ends,* dharma *is of the highest importance. However,* dharma *cannot exist without the material resources for human existence. As the ultimate source of material wealth is land, the occupation of land is essential for the maintenance of society and* dharma *in it. The occupation and control of land, termed* territory *in ancient Indian politics, is the function of politics. Hence politics occupies a position of fundamental importance in the management of not only* artha *but in human affairs as a whole; also important is the study, or science* (shastra), *of politics.* Artha shastra *as a branch of learning emerged several centuries before Kautilya. Numerous authors handed down their precepts on the science of politics. Kautilya incorporated these into his work and, dealing with the subject on a vast scale, established it as an independent and full-fledged discipline.*

Kautilya's Arthashastra *deals with the subject of government in a most exhaustive manner. It contains one hundred and fifty chapters in fifteen books. The work has a clearly laid-out plan, introduced as a table of contents in Book I, followed systematically in the body of the work, and recapitulated in the last book. Kautilya develops his subject logically. He begins with a statement of the purpose and genesis of government, describes the proper manner of establishing its operations (giving at the same time a description of these operations in minute detail), and recommending measures to ensure the stability of the state and the enhancement of its power. He lays down both the theory and practice of politics, heavily emphasizing practice.*

The contents of the Arthashastra *may be divided broadly into two parts, one dealing with the state in its internal affairs, and the other with external affairs. The areas considered under internal affairs include the state bureaucracy, agriculture and other economic activities, law and order, revenue, taxes, and the treasury. Subjects examined under external affairs include diplomatic relations, alliances, or hostile maneuvers—including war—against foreign powers. The department of spying, a most prominent branch of the government in the* Arthashastra, *is vitally concerned with both domestic and foreign affairs. So, naturally, is the army.*

Although the Arthashastra *refers in passing to other forms of government, the only system of government it proposes is monarchy. Kautilya traces the genesis of monarchy in a social contract intended for the protection of the weak against the strong. He also says that the first person entrusted with kingship was of divine descent. The king in the* Arthashastra *is expected to acquire the qualities of character appropriate for kingship, but he is not of divine origin. Still, it is assumed that, because he is a king, he is endowed with the divine right to rule; it is as if kingship confers divinity rather than being derived from it. Kautilya recommends stratagems to give the king an aura of divinity. He suggests, for example, that the king surround himself with images of gods on public occasions to make him appear to be a god himself.*

Kautilya considers the well-being of the king as supremely important. One reason for this evaluation is that on the king's well-being depends the well-being of the state and its people. Therefore, a king must provide a just government. The Arthashastra *proposes a strict but humane system of justice. The laws governing "sexual intercourse with immature girls," in the excerpt below, for example, is a good illustration of this balanced approach. But by and large, however, the* Arthashastra *is primarily concerned with the interests of the king and his government rather than the welfare of the people. Public welfare is sought not so much for its own sake, but because a prosperous and orderly society benefits the king and best assures the stability of his government. The underlying motivation of the king's government in the* Arthashastra *is calculated profit for the king and the enhancement of his power. If conformity to moral principles and duty toward his subjects suit the king's interests, morality and duty should be followed. Otherwise the king and his government should dispense with principles and be concerned only with what is expedient. If necessary, they may do so ruthlessly. For example, Kautilya advises that, to replenish the depleted royal treasury, the state should confiscate private property, extort money from people by various excuses, and even defraud individuals of their money by inveigling them into deceitful partnerships. Although such measures are approved only in extreme situations, they show that the state in the* Arthashastra *is based on power and control, and all means for the attainment and maintenance of power and control in the state, no matter how unfair or devious, are justifiable.*

The most devious and powerful tool of control is the use of a vast network of spies. As we can see in the excerpt "The Institution of Spies," the state keeps under secret surveillance people at all levels of society, from the queens, the king's sons and his ministers, to the general populace. The state also spies closely on the affairs of neighboring kings and their people. Spies not only gather vital information, but also actively engage in the removal of people considered undesirable by murder, sabotage, and other similar means. They operate in such large numbers and in so many different guises that no one can escape their eyes or feel secure against them. The world of the Arthashastra *is, thus, so filled with mistrust, intrigue, and treachery that its atmosphere resembles that of an incredible tale of horrors. In defense of Kautilya, it may be said that his work reflects a time when, because of the anarchy that prevailed under inept kings and because of the invasion of India by Alexander the Great (327–325 B.C.), intrigue and treachery were the order of the day. Counter-intrigue and espionage were necessary to render the country secure from internal or foreign threats. The scale and the range of the spying activities described in the* Arthashastra *is also due, perhaps, to a scholar's obsession with completeness, a feature of Kautilya's writing evident in other areas covered by his work. The* Arthashastra *is not a portrayal of an actual situation, but a scholarly treatise on government.*

Perhaps the most interesting political theories in the Arthashastra, *included in the following excerpts, are the theories of the "Elements of Sovereignty," the "Circles of States," and the "Sixfold Policy." The first of these theories divides sovereignty into eight elements, seven of which—the king, the minister, the country, the fort, the treasury, the army, and the friend—are its limbs. The eighth element of sovereignty is the enemy. Kautilya describes the qualities of all these elements. The second theory deals with a state's relations with foreign powers. It sees the circles of states as consisting of three states in each in a total complex of twelve states. In the third theory, Kautilya gives directions as to how a king should choose one of the six possible policies toward the states in his immediate circle, as well as in the farther circles, to his maximum advantage.*

ARTHASHASTRA
Book I.1
This Arthashastra and the Earlier Arthashastras

This *Arthashastra* is made as a compendium of almost all the *Arthashastras*, which, in view of acquisition and maintenance of the earth, have been composed by ancient teachers.[1]

Book I.4
The End of Sciences: Varta and Dandaniti

Agriculture, cattle-breeding, and trade constitute *Varta*. It is most useful in that it brings in grains, cattle, gold, forest-produce, and free labor.[2] It is by means of the treasury and the army obtained solely through Varta that the king can hold under his control both his and his enemy's party.

Adapted by Surjit S. Dulai from R. Shamasastry, trans., *Kautilya's Arthashastra* (Mysore: Sri Raghuveer Printing Press; first published 1915), pp. 1, 8, 11–12, 19–22, 258–260, 279–281, 287–289, 290–291, 293.

[1]Kautilya here makes explicit his use of earlier treatments of the science of politics.

[2]Cultivators were expected to provide free labor to the state.

That sceptre on which the well-being and progress of the sciences of Anvikshaki,[3] the triple *Vedas*,[4] and Varta depend is known as *Danda* ["punishment"]. That which treats of Danda is the law of punishment or science of government *(dandaniti)*.

It is a means to make acquisitions, to keep them secure, to improve them, and to distribute among the deserving the profits of improvement. It is on this science of government that the course of the progress of the world depends.

"Hence," says my teacher,[5] "whoever is desirous of the progress of the world shall ever hold the sceptre raised. Never can there be a better instrument than the sceptre to bring people under control."

"No," says Kautilya; for whoever imposes severe punishment becomes repulsive to the people; while he who awards mild punishment becomes contemptible. But whoever imposes punishment as deserved becomes respectable. For punishment, when awarded with due consideration, makes the people devoted to righteousness and to works productive of wealth and enjoyment; while punishment, when ill-awarded under the influence of greed and anger owing to ignorance, excites fury even among hermits and ascetics dwelling in forests, not to speak of householders.

But when the law of punishment is kept in abeyance, it gives rise to such disorder as is implied in the proverb of fishes;[6] for in the absence of a magistrate, the strong will swallow the weak; but under his protection the weak resist the strong.

Book I.7

Restraint of the Organs of Sense: The Life of a Saintly King

Hence by overthrowing the aggregate of the six enemies,[7] he shall restrain the organs of sense; acquire wisdom by keeping company with the aged;[8] see through his spies; establish safety and security by being ever active; maintain his subjects in the observance of their respective duties by exercising authority; keep up his personal discipline by receiving lessons in the sciences; and endear himself to the people by bringing them in contact with wealth and doing good to them.

---

[3]The ancient Indian systems of philosophy.

[4]The three *Vedas*—*Rig-Veda, Sam-Veda,* and *Yajur-Veda*—which are considered by Hindus to be the most sacred scriptures (see Selections 8 and 20).

[5]Kautilya's *Arthashastra* frequently cites earlier authorities, e.g., "my teacher," on various aspects of the subject of politics, followed by Kautilya's own position.

[6]The well-known proverb that the big fish eat the little fish.

[7]The six enemies are lust, anger, greed, vanity, haughtiness, and excessive enjoyment.

[8]The aged are the learned and wise teachers of the sciences.

Thus with his organs of sense under his control, he shall keep away from hurting the women and property of others; avoid not only lustfulness, even in dream, but also falsehood, haughtiness, and evil proclivities; and keep away from unrighteous and uneconomical transactions.

Not violating righteousness and economy, he shall enjoy his desires. He shall never be devoid of happiness. He may enjoy in an equal degree the three pursuits of life—charity, wealth, and desire—which are interdependent upon each other. Any one of these three, when enjoyed to an excess, hurts not only the other two, but also itself.

Kautilya holds that wealth, and wealth alone, is important, inasmuch as charity and desire depend upon wealth for their realization.

Those teachers and ministers who keep him from falling a prey to dangers, and who, by striking the hours of the day as determined by measuring shadows,[9] warn him of his careless proceedings even in secret, shall invariably be respected.

Sovereignty[10] is possible only with assistance. A single wheel can never move. Hence he shall employ ministers and hear their opinion.

Book I.12

The Institution of Spies: Creation of Wandering Spies

Those orphans who are to be necessarily fed by the state and are put to study science, palmistry, sorcery, the duties of the various orders of religious life, legerdemain [sleight of hand or "magic"], and the reading of omens and augury [divination of omens], are classmate spies, or spies learning by social intercourse.

Such brave desperados of the country who, reckless of their own life, confront elephants or tigers in fight mainly for the purpose of earning money are termed fire-brands or fiery spies.

Those who have no trace of filial affection left in them and who are very cruel and indolent are poisoners.

A poor widow of Brahman caste, very clever, and desirous to earn her livelihood, is a woman ascetic. Honored in the king's harem, such a woman shall frequent the residences of the king's prime ministers.[11]

The same rule shall apply to women with shaved head,[12] as well as to those of Shudra caste.[13] All these are wandering spies.

---

[9]A method of measuring time by the length of shadows cast by the sun.

[10]Sovereignty here means more than kingship. It includes other elements of the state. See the excerpt "The Elements of Sovereignty" later in this selection.

[11]Prime minister here means a high-ranking minister, not literally the prime minister.

[12]Beggar women usually had shaved heads.

[13]Shudra is the lowest caste in Hindu society.

Of these spies, those who are of good family, loyal, reliable, well-trained in the art of putting on disguises appropriate to countries and trades, and possessed of knowledge of many languages and arts, shall be sent by the king to spy in his own country the movements of his ministers, priests, commanders of the army, the heir-apparent, the door-keepers, the officer-in-charge of the harem, the magistrate, the collector-general,[14] the chamberlain, the commissioner, the city constable, the officer-in-charge of the city, the superintendent of transactions, the superintendent of manufactories, the assembly of councillors, heads of departments, the commissary-general,[15] and officers in charge of fortifications, boundaries, and wild tracts.

Fiery spies, such as are employed to hold the royal umbrella, vase, fan, and shoes, or to attend at the throne, chariot, and conveyance, shall espy the public character of these officers.

Classmate spies shall convey this information (i.e., that gathered by the fiery spies) to the institutes of espionage.[16]

Poisoners, such as a sauce-maker, a cook, procurer of water for bathing, shampooer, the bed-maker, a barber, toilet-maker, a water-servant; servants such as have taken the appearance of a hump-backed person, a dwarf, a pigmy, the dumb, the deaf, the idiot, the blind;[17] artisans such as actors, dancers, singers, players on musical instruments, buffoons, and a bard; as well as women, shall espy the private character of these officers.

A beggar woman shall convey this information to the institute of espionage.

The immediate officers of the institutes of espionage shall, by making use of signs or writing, set their own spies in motion to ascertain the validity of the information.

Neither the institutes of espionage nor they (the wandering spies) shall know each other. . . .

Merchant spies inside forts; saints and ascetics in the suburbs of forts; the cultivator and the recluse in country parts; herdsmen in the boundaries of the country; in forests, forest-dwellers and chiefs of wild tribes shall be stationed to ascertain the movements of enemies. All these spies shall be very quick in the despatch of their work.

Spies set up by foreign kings shall also be found out by local spies; spies by spies of like profession.

---

[14]Head of the department of revenue collection.

[15]Head of the administration of law and order.

[16]Kautilya recommends the establishment of institutes of spying in addition to a network of wandering spies.

[17]Kautilya asserts that the disabled and the deformed who frequent public places, usually as beggars, are well-suited for recruitment as spies.

Book V.3

Sexual Intercourse with Immature Girls

He who defiles a maiden of equal caste before she has reached her maturity shall have his hand cut off or pay a fine of four hundred panas,[18] if the maiden dies in consequence, the offender shall be put to death.

He who defiles a maiden who has attained maturity shall have his middle finger cut off or pay a fine of two hundred panas, besides giving an adequate compensation to her father.

No man shall have sexual intercourse with any woman against her will.

He who defiles a willing maiden shall pay a fine of fifty-four panas, while the maiden herself shall pay a fine of half the amount.

When a man impersonates another man who has already paid the nuptial fee to a woman, he shall have his hand cut off or pay a fine of four hundred panas, besides making good the nuptial fee.

No man who has connection with a maiden that has passed seven menses and has not yet succeeded in marrying her, though she has been betrothed to him, shall either be guilty or pay any compensation to her father; for her father has lost his authority over her in consequence of having deprived her so long of the result of her menses.

If is no offence for a man of equal caste and rank to have connection with a maiden who has been unmarried three years after her first menses. Nor is it an offence for a man, even of different caste,[19] to have connection with a maiden who has spent more than three years after her first menses and has no jewelry on her person; for taking possession of paternal property (under such circumstances) shall be regarded as theft. . . .

No man shall have sexual intercourse with any woman against her will.

If a person substitutes in marriage another maiden for the one he has before shown, he shall, if the substitute is of the same rank, be fined one hundred panas; and two hundred panas if she is of a lower rank. The substituted maiden shall be fined fifty-four panas, while the offender shall also be compelled to return both the nuptial fee and the amount of expenditure (incurred by the bridegroom). . . . A woman who, of her own accord, yields herself to a man, shall be a slave to the king. . . .

He who carries off a maiden by force shall be fined two hundred panas; if the maiden thus carried off has golden ornaments on her person the highest punishment shall be imposed. If a number of persons abduct a maiden, each of them shall be punished as above. . . .

---

[18]The pana was an ancient Indian coin.

[19]Illegitimate sexual relations with a person of a caste different from one's own were normally considered a greater offence than those with a person of one's own caste.

When a man defiles the daughter of his own male or female slave, he shall not only pay a fine of twenty-four panas, but also provide the maiden with an adequate nuptial fee and jewelry.

Book V.4

The Conduct of a Courtier

Whoever possesses enough experience of the world and its affairs may, through the influence of an interested friend, seek the favor of a king who is endowed with amiable qualities and is possessed of all the elements of sovereignty.[20] He may court the favor of any king, provided he thinks: Just as I am in need of a patron, so is this king possessed of a taste for good advice and is of amiable character. He may even court the favor of such a king as is poor and destitute of the elements of sovereignty, but never of such a one as is of a depraved character. . . .

Having obtained admittance to an amiable king, he shall give the king instructions in science. Absence of contradiction from the king will render his position secure. When his opinion is sought about present or future schemes needing much thought and consideration, he may boldly and sensibly, and with no fear of contradiction from the assembly of ministers, pronounce his opinion so as to be in harmony with the principles of righteousness and economy. When required, he may answer questions on points of righteousness and economy and tell the king:

"Following the rule that there should be no delay in putting down by force even a strong confederacy of wicked people, you should apply force against the wicked, if they have a strong support; do not despise my advice, character and secrets; and by means of gestures I shall prevent you from inflicting punishments on anyone, when you are going to do so either willfully or under provocation."

With such agreements with the king, he (a courtier) may enter on the duty assigned to him. He shall sit by the side of, and close to, the king, and far from the seat of another courtier. He shall avoid speaking slyly against the opinion of any member of the assembly; he shall never make incredible or false statements; nor loud laughter with no cause for jest, and loud noise and spittle. He shall also avoid talking to another in secret. . . .

Without losing the opportune moments, he should speak of the king's interest; of his own interests when in company with persons friendly to him; and of others' interests in a suitable time and place, and in conformity to the principles of righteousness and economy.

When asked, he should tell the king what is both good and pleasing, but not what is bad, though pleasing; if the king is pleased to listen, he may secretly tell what, though unpleasant, is good. . . .

Self-protection shall be the first and constant thought of a wise man; for the life of a man under the service of a king is aptly compared to life in fire; whereas

---

[20]That is, suited for all aspects of the work of the state.

fire burns a part or the whole of the body, if at all, the king has the power either to destroy or to advance the whole family, consisting of sons and wives of his servants.

Book VI.1

The Elements of Sovereignty

The king, the minister,[21] the country, the fort, the treasury, the army, the friend,[22] and the enemy are the elements of sovereignty.

Of these, the best qualities of the king are:

Born of a high family, godly, possessed of valor, seeing through the medium of aged persons, virtuous, truthful, not of a contradictory nature, grateful, having large aims, highly enthusiastic, not addicted to procrastination, powerful to control his neighboring kings, of resolute mind, having an assembly of ministers of no mean quality, and possessed of a taste for discipline—these are the qualities of an inviting nature.

Inquiry, hearing, perception, retention in memory, reflection, deliberation, inference and steadfast adherence to conclusions are the qualities of the intellect.

Valor, determination of purpose, quickness, and probity are the aspects of enthusiasm.

Possessed of a sharp intellect, strong memory, and keen mind; energetic; powerful; trained in all kinds of arts; free from vice; capable of paying in the same coin by way of awarding punishments or rewards; possessed of dignity; capable of taking remedial measures against dangers; possessed of foresight; ready to avail himself of opportunities when afforded in respect of place, time, and manly efforts; clever enough to discern the causes necessitating the cessation of treaty or war with an enemy, or to lie in wait keeping treaties, obligations or pledges, or to avail himself of his enemy's weak points; making jokes with no loss of dignity or secrecy; never brow-beating and casting haughty and stern looks; free from passion, anger, greed, obstinacy, fickleness, haste, and back-biting habits; talking to others with a smiling face; and observing customs as taught by aged persons—such is the nature of self-possession.

The qualifications of a minister[23] have been described in the beginning, middle, and at the close of the work.

---

[21]The chief minister.

[22]Friend here means a foreign power who is an ally.

[23]Elsewhere, Kautilya describes these qualifications as follows: "Native; born of high family; influential; well-trained in arts; possessed of foresight; wise; of strong memory; bold; eloquent; skillful; intelligent; possessed of enthusiasm, dignity, and endurance; pure in character; affable; firm in loyal devotion; endowed with excellent conduct, strength, health, and bravery; free from procrastination and fickle-mindedness; affectionate; and free from such qualities as excite hatred and enmity. . . ."

Possessed of capital cities both in the center and the extremities of the kingdom, productive of subsistence not only to its own people, but also to outsiders on occasions of calamities, repulsive to enemies, powerful enough to put down neighboring kings, free from miry, rocky, uneven, and desert tracts, as well as from conspirators, tigers, wild beasts, and large tracts of wilderness, beautiful to look at, containing fertile lands, mines, timber and elephant forests, and pasture grounds, artistic, containing hidden passages, full of cattle, not depending upon rain for water, possessed of land and waterways, rich in various kinds of commercial articles, capable of bearing the burden of a vast army and heavy taxation, inhabited by agriculturists of good and active character, full of intelligent masters and servants, and with a population noted for its loyalty and good character—these are the qualities of a good country.

The excellent qualities of forts have already been described.[24]

Justly obtained either by inheritance or by self-acquisition, rich in gold and silver, filled with an abundance of big gems of various colors and of gold coins, and capable to withstand calamities of long duration, is the best treasury.

Coming down directly from father and grandfather of the king; ever strong; obedient; happy in keeping their sons and wives well contented; not averse to making a long sojourn; ever and everywhere invincible; endowed with the power of endurance; trained in fighting various kinds of battles; skillful in handling various forms of weapons; ready to share in the weal or woe of the king, and consequently not falling foul with him; and purely composed of soldiers of Kshatriya caste,[25] is the best army.

Coming down directly from father and grandfather, long-standing, open to conviction, never falling foul, and capable of making preparations for war quickly and on a large scale, is the best friend.

Not born of a royal family, greedy, possessed of a mean assembly of ministers, with disloyal subjects, ever doing unrighteous acts, of loose character, addicted to mean pleasures, devoid of enthusiasm, trusting to fate, indiscreet in action, powerless, helpless, impotent and ever injurious, is the worst enemy. Such an enemy is easily uprooted.

Excepting the enemy, these seven elements, possessed of their excellent characteristics are said to be the limb-like elements of sovereignty.

A wise king can make even the poor and miserable elements of his sovereignty happy and prosperous; but a wicked king will surely destroy the most prosperous and loyal elements of his kingdom.

Hence a king of unrighteous character and of vicious habits will, though he is an emperor, fall prey either to the fury of his own subjects or to that of his enemies.

---

[24]Elsewhere, Kautilya gives a very elaborate description of the location, layout, and building of forts, too long to be quoted here.

[25]The warrior caste, the second highest in the Hindu classification of society.

But a wise king, trained in politics, will, though he possesses a small territory, conquer the whole earth with the help of the best-fitted elements of his sovereignty, and will never be defeated.

Book VI.2

The Circles of States

The king who, being possessed of good character and best-fitted elements of sovereignty, is the fountain of policy, is termed the conqueror.

The king who is situated anywhere immediately on the circumference of the conqueror's territory is termed the enemy.

The king who is likewise situated close to the enemy, but separated from the conqueror only by the enemy, is termed the friend of the conqueror.

A neighboring foe of considerable power is styled an enemy; and when he is involved in calamities or has taken himself to evil ways, he becomes assailable; and when he has little or no help, he becomes destructible; otherwise (i.e., when he is provided with some help), he deserves to be harassed or reduced. Such are the aspects of an enemy.

In front of the conqueror and close to his enemy, there happen to be situated kings, such as the conqueror's friend; next to him, the enemy's friend; and next to the last, the conqueror's friend; and next, the enemy's friend's friend.

In the rear of the conqueror, there happen to be situated a rearward enemy, a rearward friend, an ally of the rearward enemy, and an ally of the rearward friend.

That foe who is equally of high birth and occupies a territory close to that of the conqueror is a natural enemy; while he who is merely antagonistic and creates enemies to the conqueror is a factitious enemy.

He whose friendship is derived from father and grandfather, and who is situated close to the territory of the immediate enemy of the conqueror is a natural friend; while he whose friendship is courted for self-maintenance is an acquired friend.

The king who occupies a territory close to both the conqueror and his immediate enemy in front and who is capable of helping both the kings, whether united or disunited, or of resisting either of them individually, is termed a *Madhyama* ["mediatory"] king.

He who is situated beyond the territory of any of the above kings, and who is very powerful and capable of helping the enemy, the conqueror, and the Madhyama king, together or individually, or of resisting any of them individually, is a neutral king—these are the (twelve) primary kings.

The conqueror, his friend, and his friend's friend are the three primary kings constituting a circle of states. As each of these three kings possesses the five elements of sovereignty, such as the minister, the country, the fort, the treasury, and the army, a circle of states consists of eighteen elements. Thus, it needs no commentary to understand that the (three) circles of states having the enemy (of the conqueror), the Madhyama king, or the neutral king at the center of each of the three circles, are different from that of the conqueror. Thus there are four primary circles of states, twelve kings, sixty elements of sovereignty, and seventy-two elements of states.

Each of the twelve primary kings shall have their elements of sovereignty, power and end. Strength is power, and happiness is the end.

Strength is of three kinds: power of deliberation is intellectual strength; the possession of a prosperous treasury and a strong army is the strength of sovereignty; and martial power is physical strength.

The end is also of three kinds: that which is attainable by deliberation is the end of deliberation; that which is attainable by the strength of sovereignty is the end of sovereignty; and that which is to be secured by perseverance is the end of martial power.

The possession of power and happiness in a greater degree makes a king superior to another; in a less degree, inferior; and in an equal degree, equal. Hence a king shall always endeavor to augment his power and elevate his happiness.

Book VII.1

The Sixfold Policy

The circle of states is the source of the sixfold policy.

My teacher says that peace, war, observance of neutrality, marching, alliance, and making peace with one and waging war with another are the six forms of state policy. . . .

Kautilya holds that, as their respective conditions differ, the forms of policy are six.

Of these, agreement with pledges is peace; offensive operation is war; indifference is neutrality; making preparations is marching; seeking the protection of another is alliance; and making peace with one and waging war with another is termed a double policy. These are the six forms.

Whoever is inferior to another shall make peace with him; whoever is superior in power shall wage war; whoever thinks, "No enemy can hurt me, nor am I strong enough to destroy my enemy," shall observe neutrality; whoever is possessed of necessary means shall march against his enemy; whoever is devoid of necessary strength to defend himself shall seek the protection of another; whoever thinks that help is necessary to work out an end shall make peace with one and wage war with another. Such is the aspect of the six forms of policy.

Of these, a wise king shall observe that form of policy which, in his opinion, enables him to build forts, to construct buildings and commercial roads, to open new plantations and villages, to exploit mines and timber and elephant forests, and at the same time to harass similar works of his enemy.

25

楽

Vyasa

MAHABHARATA

Like ancient Greece, ancient India also produced two great epic poems, the Ramayana *and the* Mahabharata. *The kernel of the latter poem existed probably as early as 500 B.C. in a fluid oral tradition, but it did not grow into its present form until the first or second century A.D. Maha of the title, meaning "great" in Sanskrit (the language of these Indian epics), refers to a great war that is the focus of the* Mahabharata. Bharata *is both an old name for India and the name of a legendary king, the ancestor of a noble line of kings. In Sanskrit tradition, India is called "the land of the Bharatas."* Mahabharata *thus means the "great war of India" or the "great war of the descendants of Bharata." The* Mahabharata *is by far the longest poem ever written in the entire history of the world. In its shortest version, it contains 88,000 couplets in eighteen books, which makes it more than seven times the combined size of Homer's* Iliad *and* Odyssey. *Noteworthy for its size, the* Mahabharata *commands still greater attention as a major work of the world's literature for the universality of its central themes as well as for its purely literary qualities. Its central themes are war and peace, wisdom and virtue, heroism and chivalry, the problem of evil and the universal scale of destruction caused by it, and the interplay of human and cosmic forces in the conflict between good and evil. All these themes together depict the beauty, grandeur, and pathos of the human condition.*

This portrayal is effected through a masterful delineation of all the main characters and vivid descriptions of the epic events. Although the basic narrative is heavily burdened with digressions and didactic material, by itself it matches the very best in the world's epic narratives, including the Iliad. *Both the* Iliad *and the* Mahabharata *are products of their respective cultures, but they also depict universal realities of the human condition. It is significant that the British film director Peter Brook made a film version of the* Mahabharata *in 1989 using an interna-*

tional cast and emphasizing its universal meaning. The Mahabharata *is from India, but, like the* Iliad, *it is also for the world.*

Tradition ascribes the Mahabharata *to the sage Vyasa who figures in the epic as its author and as a major character in its action. However, like the other characters in the story, Vyasa is a figure of legend only. The authorship of the epic actually belongs to many different and unknown hands. The war of the story perhaps had a historical basis in a political–military conflict in northern India that probably occurred some time around 1000* B.C. *A cycle of narrative poems grew around the exploits of the warriors involved in this conflict and, over time, became embellished with myth and legend, with the thread of a high moral purpose woven into them. During the last five centuries before the Christian era, these stories, now attributed to Vyasa, came to be gathered as a single work in the form of the* Mahabharata.

It was a time when—as a result of a synthesis of all the previous movements and phases of Indian culture, from the time of the Indus Valley civilization to the rise of Buddhism (see Selection 21), and of the various cults of both Aryan and non-Aryan origin—an all-embracing religion of India, to be known as Hinduism, evolved and was reaching its final definition. The Mahabharata *incorporated the teachings and practices of this rising religion as did the other Sanskrit epic, the* Ramayana, *and many other works of this era's religion and literature. Interpolations containing legendary, mythical, philosophical, theological, cultic, and morally edifying materials from all possible directions continued to pour into the epic through the early centuries of the Christian era. Thus the* Mahabharata *became part of the body of literature of Hinduism proper—as distinct from the* Veda *(Selection 8), which, although considered most sacred in Hinduism, is actually the literature of its earliest origins only. As a work of well-formulated Hinduism, the* Mahabharata *is most important. Because of its expanse and inclusiveness, it is known as the "encyclopedia of Hinduism."*

The Mahabharata *is a story of conflict within a royal family, the Kurus. It is a conflict between one hundred Kauravas and five Pandavas who are, respectively, the sons of two Kuru brothers, Dhrtarastra, who is older, and Pandu, who is king, because Dhrtarastra was born blind. Technically, the sons of Pandu, the Pandavas, are fathered by gods. From the eldest to the youngest, Yudhisthira, Bhima, Arjuna, and the twins, Nakula and Sahadeva, are, respectively, the sons of Dharma, the god of righteousness; Vayu, the god of wind; Indra, a king among the gods; and the Asvins, the twin horse-gods that pull the Sun-god's chariot. Unknown to them until the end of the story, the Pandavas also have a step-brother, Karna, fathered by the Sun-god on their mother, Kunti, before she was married. She abandoned him as an infant and he was found and raised by a chariot driver.*

Pandu dies young and Dhrtarastra takes over the reigns of government as regent. The Pandavas and Kauravas complete their education under the accomplished teacher Drona. At their graduation tournament, Karna also shows up to participate. He alone is superior in warlike skills to Arjuna, who otherwise is the greatest archer and warrior of the epic. Karna is denied the right to partici-

pate because, seen as the son of a chariot driver, he is considered lowborn. Duryodhana, the eldest Kaurava, jealous of the Pandavas' valor and fighting skills, befriends Karna and installs him as a member of the warrior class by designating him as the king of a territory under him. Karna remains devoted to Duryodhana until the end of his life.

The Pandavas come of age to take over the reign from Dhrtarastra. But Duryodhana does not allow Dhrtarastra to hand it over to the cousins. To avoid trouble between the cousins, Dhrtarastra sends the Pandavas temporarily away from the capital, Hastinapur. In the town to which they go, Duryodhana arranges to have a house built for them from flammable materials, and he plans to burn them in it. The Pandavas learn about the plan and escape through a tunnel. Keeping their escape secret, they go around disguised as Brahmans. In their wanderings they come to the kingdom of Pancala where the king, Drupada, is holding the husband-choosing rite for his daughter, Draupadi. Arjuna wins Draupadi's hand by performing the feat of archery set as a condition for it. Referring to Draupadi as they return with her to their lodgings, the Pandavas tell Kunti that they have brought the alms for the day. (Disguised as Brahmans, they live on alms.) Because she has not seen them yet, Kunti tells the Pandavas to share whatever they have brought. So Draupadi becomes the wife of the five brothers.

Since the Pandavas now have a powerful ally in Drupada, Duryodhana lets Dhrtarastra give them a portion of the kingdom. They turn it into a very prosperous and powerful kingdom in its own right. Duryodhana writhes with jealousy. His cunning maternal uncle, Sakuni, suggests to him to invite Yudhisthira to a game of dice. Yudhisthira cannot refuse the invitation because of his weakness for gambling and feels that his sense of honor would be harmed if he refused a challenge. Sakuni, adept at dicing, plays on behalf of Duryodhana, and he cheats. Yudhisthira loses everything—his kingdom, his brothers, himself, and Draupadi. Duryodhana orders his brother, Duhsasana, to bring Draupadi into the royal hall. Duhsasana drags her in and proceeds to disrobe her in the assembly. She is saved because, as her clothing is removed, miraculously other layers of it continue to appear under it endlessly. But she and Bhima vow vengeance for the indignity.

It is a condition of the game that the losing side will spend thirteen years in exile before their kingdom will be returned to them. When the Pandavas ask for their kingdom after thirteen years, Duryodhana refuses to comply with the agreement. Wise men, particularly Krsna (pronounced "Krishna"), who is god in human form and recognized as the foremost statesman, try to persuade Duryodhana to be just, but they all fail. There is no alternative but war. As the armies of the Kauravas and Pandavas stand face to face, Arjuna suddenly does not want to fight, because he feels that the greatest kingdom is not worth spilling the blood of so many kin and friends. At this point Krsna, who has become his charioteer, gives Arjuna the sermon known as the Bhagvad Gita ("song of the lord") in which he convinces Arjuna to fight without worrying about the consequences, because it is his duty as a member of the warrior class to fight. In the war, all the Kauravas and both the armies are destroyed. All the Pandavas survive, although they find it necessary to break some rules of the warrior's code in order to win. Eventually, the victors and the vanquished come together in heaven.

This narrative and the digressions from it together provide, by example and discourse, extensive lessons in the precepts, practice, and religious lore of Hinduism. Underlying all these lessons is the concept of dharma, *the foundation of the Hindu view of life. The word* dharma *is derived from the root* dhra, *meaning "to support or sustain." In an ultimate sense,* dharma *is the universal moral law that sustains the cosmic order. In a narrower sense, it means the practice of righteousness and virtue in human conduct. In a still more immediate, and most specific, sense,* dharma *stands for the set of duties and obligations required in Hinduism, according to a person's place in society. Adherence to these duties and obligations is believed to hold the fabric of society together. Although this requirement applies to all segments of society, the* Mahabharata *focuses on the* dharma *of the warrior–ruler class. In the most important episode of the epic, the* Bhagvad Gita, Krsna *convinces Arjuna that Arjuna must fight, regardless of consequences, because such is his duty as a member of the warrior–ruler class. From a critical standpoint, one can say that, in his sermon, Krsna does not emphasize the righteousness of the* cause *for which Arjuna must fight but rather the righteousness of fighting as such, because it is his occupation and duty as a warrior to fight. The* Mahabharata *thus largely suited the interests of the elite. It represents an ethic that espouses the use of armed might as righteous conduct, and, at the same time, enjoins the lower classes to keep their place in the social order. Consequently, the* Mahabharata *justifies the maintenance of a status quo, with an elite that controls society by force of military might.*

However, there also exists in the Mahabharata *the concept of righteousness of a much higher order than the mere performance and justification of one's social duties. The Pandavas exemplify this righteousness in general, and Yudhisthira personifies it almost totally. In their opposition to the wrong done by the Kauravas, he never compromises his integrity, except once when he participates in the scheme to make Drona think that his son is dead, a lie that causes Drona's death. The message of the* Mahabharata *is that moral goodness, as embodied in the characters of Yudhisthira and his younger brothers, ultimately triumphs over evil, such as that represented by the Kauravas. A moral law that governs the working of the universe makes such an outcome inevitable. When evil becomes too powerful for human beings to overcome, it requires divine intervention for its eradication. In the epic, Krsna is God in human form. Although he does not fight physically, he is on the Pandavas' side. They are, therefore, bound to win.*

It is interesting to note that the Indian statesman Mahatma Gandhi (1869–1948), famous for his political philosophy of nonviolence, derived his inspiration from the Mahabharata. *His philosophy mandated fighting against the evils of injustice and oppression, but strictly forbade the use of any physical force in the fight. It advocated, instead, the use only of moral force in the form of a courageous, but nonviolent, stand for truth and justice. Gandhi believed that moral force is far more powerful than physical force and that it inevitably leads to victory.*

The following excerpts present, in the briefest possible manner, the most essential events in the action of the Mahabharata. *The first excerpt describes the education of the princes and the appointment of Karna as a king; the second tells how Draupadi becomes the Pandavas' wife; the third describes the game of dice in which Yudhisthira loses everything and, hence, is the turning point of the story; the fourth contains the central message of the epic as delivered by Krsna to Arjuna (from the* Bhagvad Gita); *the fifth deals with the fall of Bhisma; and the last four with the deaths of Drona, Duhsasana, Karna, and Duryodhana. All excerpts, except the last three, are drawn from the Poona edition of the* Mahabharata *in Sanskrit. The last three excerpts are derived from the P. C. Roy edition of the epic.*

ADI PARVA
Book I, Chapters 121 and 127

The Education of Princes

Anxious to give his grandsons a superior education, Bhisma[1] inquired about tutors who were brave and well skilled in the science of arms. He decided that the preceptor of the Kurus should be strong, intelligent, and illustrious, and complete master of the science of arms.

When he heard that a stranger had arrived [in Hastinapura], Bhisma knew that this must be Drona and decided that he was the right tutor for his grandsons.[2] Welcoming Drona, he asked him why he had come to Hastinapura. Drona

---

From *The Mahabharata* translated by Chakravarthi V. Narasimhan. Copyright © 1965 by Columbia University Press. Reprinted with permission of the publisher. Pp. 24, 35–37, 50–55, 56, 122–125, 136–138, 157–159, 163, 164–166, 172–174. .

[1]Bhisma is the patriarch of the Kuru clan. He is Dhrtarastra and Pandu's step-uncle, who, to enable his father, Santanu, to remarry, vowed that he never would claim the throne and would remain celibate for life so that he would have no children to dispute the throne with the children of his step-brothers. Santanu's prospective wife demanded this condition before agreeing to marry him. In Sanskrit, *Bhisma* means "the terrible." He is so called because of his strength and determination. He is the greatest warrior in the epic. He cannot be killed except by his own choice.

[2]Drona is a Brahman. He is the most accomplished teacher of the art of warfare. In his childhood, he was a friend of Prince Drupada of the kingdom of Pancala. When the latter became king, he ignored Drona. It becomes Drona's mission to take revenge on Drupada for the indignity. To that end, he looks for the right pupils whom he will train to bring Drupada to his knees.

told him everything. Bhisma then appointed Drona as the preceptor [tutor] and gave him various gifts. He presented his grandsons, including the sons of Pandu, according to custom, and handed them over to Drona, who accepted them all as his pupils.

Drona called them aside when they saluted him, and said privately to them: "O princes, in my heart I have one special yearning; promise me that you will fulfil it when you have become proficient in arms." To these words the Kuru princes made no reply. Arjuna, however, gave his promise.

Thereupon Drona taught Arjuna how to fight from the back of a horse, on an elephant, on a chariot, or on the ground, in single combat, or in a crowd. He taught him how to fight with the club, the sword, the spear, and the dart. Two of Drona's pupils, Duryodhana and Bhima, became highly proficient in club fighting; Asvatthama surpassed the others in the mysteries of the science of arms;[3] the twins Nakula and Sahadeva outshone everybody in swordsmanship; Yudhisthira was the first among car-warriors.[4]

Arjuna reigned supreme in every field; he excelled all in intelligence, in concentration, in strength, and in zest, and was famous unto the limits of the ocean as the foremost of car-warriors. He was unequaled not only in the use of arms but also in his love and regard for his preceptor. Though all the royal pupils received the same instruction, yet the mighty Arjuna by his excellence became the only Atiratha among all the princes. The wicked sons of Dhrtarastra became jealous of Bhima's strength and Arjuna's many accomplishments.

When the sons of Dhrtarastra and Pandu had thus become proficient in arms, Drona said to King Dhrtarastra, "O king, your sons have completed their studies. Permit them to display their skill." The king replied, with joy in his heart: "O Drona, O best of Brahmanas,[5] great is your achievement!" By order of the king, the masons built a huge arena according to the rules, with a grandstand for the king and the royal ladies. Then, with Yudhisthira at their head, the heroic princes followed each other in the order of their age and began to display their wonderful skill in arms.

At the command of the preceptor, the youthful Arjuna, equipped with leather protector for the finger, his quiver full of arrows, bow in hand, and wearing golden armor, performed the initial rites of propitiation and entered the arena like the evening cloud reflecting the rays of the setting sun. His very entrance caused a stir among the spectators. When they had calmed down a little, Arjuna displayed before his preceptor his easy mastery of arms and his great skill in the use of the sword, the bow, and the club.

---

[3]Asvatthama is Drona's son. Later in the action, the false news of his death will cause Drona's death.

[4]A champion warrior who fought from a horse-drawn chariot.

[5]An alternative spelling for *Brahman*, "a member of the priestly order."

While the spectators were watching Arjuna's feats in wide-eyed wonder, that conqueror of hostile cities, Karna, entered the spacious arena. The entire assembly of people remained motionless, staring at the newcomer. Curious to know his name, they asked one another in agitation, "Who is he?" Then, in a voice deep as thunder, Karna, foremost of eloquent men, said to Arjuna, whom he did not know to be his brother: "O Arjuna, I shall repeat before these spectators all that you have just done. Do not be surprised." Thus challenged, Arjuna was abashed and angry, but Duryodhana was touched with affection for the challenger. With the permission of Drona, the powerful Karna, ever fond of battle, duplicated all the feats that Arjuna had displayed a little earlier.

Thereupon Duryodhana with his brothers embraced Karna with joy and spoke to him thus: "O mighty hero, welcome to you! Your arrival is our good fortune. The entire Kuru kingdom and I myself are at your service." Karna replied, "I desire only your friendship."

Karna then challenged Arjuna to a duel. When the two heroes were ready with their great bows, Krpa,[6] the son of Saradvata, who knew all the rules governing such duels, said: "O mighty hero, tell us of your father and mother, of your family, and of the royal line which you adorn. It is only after knowing your lineage that Arjuna can decide whether or not to fight with you." Duryodhana announced, "O preceptor, it is said that royalty may be claimed by three classes of men, namely, by a person of noble birth, by a hero, and by a leader of soldiers. If Arjuna is unwilling to engage in a duel with one who is not a king, I shall install Karna at once as the king of Anga."[7]

Without delay the mighty car-warrior Karna was seated on a golden seat, and crowned as the king of Anga by those learned in the rites, with unhusked rice, flowers, waterpots, gold, and much wealth.[8] When the cheers subsided, Karna said to the Kaurava king, Duryodhana, "What can I give you compared with your gift of a kingdom? O great king, I shall do your bidding." Duryodhana replied, "I seek only your friendship." Then Karna said, "So be it!" They thereupon joyfully embraced each other and felt very happy.

Having obtained Karna, Duryodhana forgot his fears aroused by Arjuna's skill in arms. The heroic Karna, accomplished in arms, spoke words of comfort to Duryodhana. Yudhisthira too was impressed with the conviction that there was no bowman on earth like Karna.

● ● ●

---

[6]Pronounced "Kripa"; Drona's brother-in-law, his wife's brother.

[7]A kingdom in the Kurus' territory.

[8]These are the ingredients used in the rite of coronation.

Book I, Chapters 176–182

Pandavas Win Draupadi

The Pandavas at last arrived in the Pancala country. After seeing the city, they took up their residence in a potter's shed. King Drupada had always cherished a secret desire to give his daughter Draupadi in marriage to Arjuna, the son of Pandu, but he never spoke of it. Having Arjuna in mind, the Pancala king caused a very rigid bow to be made. He then erected a device in the sky and set up above it a golden target.

King Drupada made the following announcement: "Whoever is able to string this bow and then with these arrows to shoot the mark above the device will obtain my daughter." This proclamation of Drupada's was published far and wide, and in response to it all the kings came there, including Duryodhana and the Kurus, accompanied by Karna. There came also many illustrious sages desirous of seeing the svayamvara.[9]

Seated in the arena along with the Brahmanas, the Pandavas observed the unequaled prosperity of the Pancala king. When the arena became absolutely quiet, Dhrstadyumna[10] stood in the center of the stage and said in a majestic voice, "Hearken, O ye assembled kings—here is the bow, these are the arrows, and there is the target. You have to shoot the target through the aperture in the device with these fine and sharp arrows. Truly I say, whosoever, being of noble birth, handsome, and strong, performs this difficult feat shall obtain today for his bride my sister Draupadi; I do not speak falsely." After giving this pledge to the assembled kings, Dhrstadyumna turned to his sister, and informed her of the names, the lineage, and the accomplishments of the assembled kings.

"O blessed girl!" said Dhrstadyumna. "All the Ksatriyas[11] celebrated in the world have gathered here on your account. These heroes will try to shoot the target for you. Among them, O fortunate girl, you shall take as your husband him who is able to shoot the target."

Meanwhile the young princes present, decked with earrings, bragged to one another; and each of them, believing himself to be the most skilled in arms, stood up arrogantly flaunting his weapons. But when they tried to perform the prescribed feat, those mighty princes were unable to bend that rigid bow and were

---

[9]Literally, "husband-choosing," a ceremony held for the purpose of finding a husband for a woman. Customarily, the ceremony involved the passing of an ordeal by the prospective husband in order to be accepted in marriage.

[10]Drupada's son. He and his sister, Draupadi, were both born out of a fire sacrifice performed by Drupada. Drupada's aim in begetting children was to take vengeance on Drona. Draupadi becomes the cause of the war in which Drona dies. It is her brother who kills him.

[11]Members of the warrior class.

all tossed to the ground, where they lay motionless. Their bracelets shattered and their earrings crushed, they gave vent to exclamations of woe, having lost their hope of obtaining Draupadi.

When all the kings had failed in their attempts to string the bow, the large-hearted Arjuna rose from the midst of the Brahmanas. While the assembled Brahmanas were talking among themselves, Arjuna came to the bow and stood there like a mountain. He first walked round the bow in due form. Then, bowing his head, he lifted the bow and strung it in an instant. He took up the five arrows, shot the target through the aperture, and felled it to the ground. Thereupon a great tumult rose in the sky and also a great clamor in the arena, while the celestials showered divine flowers on Arjuna's head.

King Drupada was delighted at the feat of the unknown Brahmana, and desired him to assist him with his army. When he announced his wish and intention of bestowing his daughter on that high-souled Brahmana, the assembled kings, all filled with rage, exchanged glances. Those powerful princes, with arms like iron maces, rose in a body and rushed upon Drupada with their weapons to kill him. Seeing all those princes surging toward him in anger and armed with bows and arrows, Drupada sought refuge with the Brahmanas. Bhima and Arjuna at once arose to resist the kings advancing upon Drupada like mad elephants, and fought them fearlessly. In the course of the fight, Bhima overcame Salya[12] in single combat. Seeing that feat of Bhima, the Lord Krsna surmised that both of them were the sons of Kunti. He persuaded the princes to desist, saying, "She has been won fairly." Those heroes among men, Bhima and Arjuna, who had been severely injured by their enemies, at last emerged from the crowd, looking resplendent, and followed by Draupadi.

Meanwhile, at home, Kunti began to fear various evils that might have befallen her sons, since they did not return even though it was past the time for alms. Out of her love for her sons, Kunti thought that something terrible must have happened to them.

It was late in the afternoon when Arjuna, attended by many Brahmanas and with a Brahmana preceding him, entered the humble potter's shed, like the sun emerging from the clouds. Those best of men, Bhima and Arjuna, then came to their mother, and represented Draupadi to her as the "alms" they had obtained that day.[13] Kunti, who was inside the room, did not see her sons or Draupadi. She therefore replied from within, "Share equally, all of you, whatever you have got." A moment later she came out, saw the maiden, and exclaimed, "Alas! What have I said?"

•　　•　　•

---

[12]King of Madra. He is the brother of Pandu's younger wife, Madri. In the war, he will be Karna's charioteer.

[13]Disguised as Brahmans, the Pandavas lived on alms.

SABHA PARVA
Book II, Chapters 53, 54, 58–63, and 65–70

The Dice Game

Sakuni[14] said, "O king, here are people gathered to capacity in this hall and ready to play. O Yudhisthira, now is the time to cast the dice and to agree on the rules of the game." "I have vowed that I shall not refuse to play if I am challenged," replied Yudhisthira. "O king, destiny is powerful and I am in its grip. Tell me, whom should I take on in this assembly? Who among these players can match my stakes? Answer me, and then let the game begin."

Duryodhana said, "O king, I shall furnish the gems and riches needed for stakes and my uncle, Sakuni, will play on my behalf." Yudhisthira replied, "It seems to me that it is wrong for one to play for another. I am sure even you will accept that. However, let it be as you wish." He continued, "O king, this expensive chain, rich with gems and adorned with the finest gold, and obtained from the ocean, this is my stake. What is the stake with which you will match it? I am going to win this stake." So saying, he cast the dice. Then Sakuni, who knew the secret of gambling, grabbed the dice. He cast them and then said to Yudhisthira, "I have won."

Yudhisthira said, "You won that stake by cheating. Fie on you, O Sakuni! Let us play staking thousands. I now stake these hundred jars, each filled with a thousand gold coins." They played, and again Sakuni claimed, "I have won." When the game had gone on for a while and Yudhisthira had lost again and again, Sakuni said, "O Yudhisthira, you have lost the greater part of the wealth of the Pandavas. Tell me if you have any assets left." Yudhisthira said, "O king, my city, my kingdom, my lands, the property that does not belong to the Brahmanas, and the subjects who are not Brahmanas—these are my remaining assets. With this as my stake, O king, I shall now play against you." Once more Sakuni cheated when casting the dice and said to Yudhisthira, "I have won."

Having lost all his wealth, Yudhisthira said, "This dark young man with crimson eyes, who looks like a lion and is endowed with mighty shoulders, Nakula, is now my stake." Thereupon, Sakuni cast the dice again and claimed that he had won. Yudhisthira then said, "Sahadeva dispenses justice and has earned a reputation for wisdom throughout the world; though he does not deserve this and is dear to me, I shall stake him." Again Sakuni cheated when casting the dice, and told Yudhisthira, "I have won."

"O king," said Sakuni, "I have won both the sons of Madri,[15] who are dear to you. Apparently Bhima and Arjuna are even dearer to you, since you do not

---

[14]Sakuni is the king of Gandhara. He is Duryodhana's maternal uncle and is adept at throwing dice.

[15]Nakula and Sahadeva. They are the twin sons of Pandu's younger wife, Madri.

wish to stake them." Thus taunted, Yudhisthira said, "I shall now stake Arjuna who enables us to sail through a battle like a boat, who is the conqueror of enemies, who is a vigorous prince, and the hero of the world." Having heard this, Sakuni again cheated when casting the dice, and told Yudhisthira, "I have won."

"O king," Yudhisthira said, "I shall now offer as my stake Bhima, our leader, who leads us single-handed in battle, who has straight eyes and close-set eyebrows, who has the shoulders of a lion and who never forgives an insult, whose strength is unmatched among humans, who is foremost among club-fighters, and who destroys his enemies." Sakuni, cheating while casting the dice, again said to Yudhisthira, "I have won."

Yudhisthira then said, "The only person left is myself, dear to my brothers. If I, too, am won we shall accept our misfortune and the lot of the vanquished." Having heard this, Sakuni cheated again when casting the dice, and told Yudhisthira, "I have won."

Sakuni then said, "There is one stake left that has not been won as yet—your beloved queen. Stake Draupadi, the daughter of the Pancala king, and win back freedom along with her." "O wretch," replied Yudhisthira, "I shall now stake the slender-waisted and beautiful Draupadi, the princess of Pancala, and play with you." When Yudhisthira said these words, the assembled elders voiced their disapproval. But, flushed with victory and mad with conceit, Sakuni cast the dice once more and said, "I have won."

• • •

His eyes red with anger, Prince Duhsasana[16] rose at his brother's words, and entered the residence of those great car-warriors, the Pandavas. There he said to the Princess Draupadi, "Come, O Pancali, you have been won. Discard your shyness and look at Duryodhana. O lady whose eyes are like lotus petals, respect the Kurus, who have won you fairly, and enter the hall." On hearing these words, the miserable Draupadi rose up in sorrow and, covering her pale face with her hands, she ran to the ladies' quarters in the palace of the old king. Thereupon Duhsasana ran after her in hot pursuit, roaring in anger, and caught hold of her by her long, blue, wavy tresses. He roughly dragged the defenceless Draupadi by her hair to the hall, while she quivered pitiably like a plantain tree in a storm.

With her hair dishevelled and her dress in disarray, the bashful Draupadi said deliberately, in anger, "O shame! The moral standards of the Bharatas[17] and of

---

[16]A younger brother of Duryodhana. At Duryodhana's command, he will drag Draupadi into the gambling hall after Yudhisthira has lost her in the game of dice.

[17]*Bharata* is a term of address used for all the Kuru kings. Sometimes it is used for any great king. Bharata was a legendary royal ancestor of the Kurus.

the Ksatriya code[18] have perished. In this hall everybody assembled looks on while the bounds of virtue are transgressed." So saying, she looked at her helpless husbands. While she was thus invoking virtue, Duhsasana shook her with even greater force, repeatedly calling her a slave and laughing aloud. Except for Duryodhana, Duhsasana, Sakuni, and Karna, all those present felt very sad on seeing Draupadi thus dragged into the hall.

Bhima then said to Yudhisthira, "All the tribute and other wealth you took from the king of Kasi,[19] all the gems the other kings presented to you, our chariots, our armor and weapons, our kingdom, and even our own selves, have all been lost in gambling. None of this provoked my anger, since you are our lord. But I think you went too far when you played with Draupadi as a stake."

Meanwhile, the evil Duhsasana began to pull at Draupadi's clothes, intending to disrobe her by force in the middle of the hall. But as her clothes were thus being pulled off, many similar clothes appeared in their place. There were loud acclamations from all the kings who saw that most miraculous spectacle.

Then Bhima swore in a loud voice in the presence of those kings, with his lower lip trembling in anger, and squeezing one hand in the other, "O kings, O men, listen to these my words which have never yet been uttered by any man and which will never be said by anyone else. If I do not drink the blood of this sinful, lowborn wretch Duhsasana in battle after rending apart his chest, let me forego the path of my ancestors!" Hearing his vow, which astonished everybody, many in the hall acclaimed Bhima vigorously and condemned Duhsasana. When finally a mass of clothes was heaped in the midst of the assembly, Duhsasana, tired and abashed, gave up his evil design and sat down.

Draupadi then said, "I, who was seen only in the svayamvara arena[20] by the assembled kings, and was never seen elsewhere in public, have been brought by force to the assembly hall today. I think that these are evil times when the Kurus allow their daughter-in-law to be thus tormented. O Kauravas, say whether this wife of Yudhisthira, born like him of a royal family, is a slave or not. I shall accept your verdict."

Upon this, Duryodhana said to Yudhisthira, "Bhima, Arjuna, and the twins are subject to your command. Reply to Draupadi's question, whether you deem her won or not." Having said this, and with the purpose of encouraging Karna

---

[18]Ksatriyas, members of the warrior class, were expected to live by a code that included such behavior as fair play, truthfulness and honesty, and chivalry toward women and the fallen enemy.

[19]The name of a city in India. It is present-day Benares. In the epic, it is a state subjugated by the Pandavas.

[20]The arena where a woman, for whom the rite of husband-choosing is performed, appeared. It is also the place where suitors appeared in order to meet the condition of selection.

and annoying Bhima, before Draupadi's very eyes Duryodhana bared his left thigh. Bhima then vowed, "Let me forego the regions of my ancestors if I do not break that thigh of yours in the great battle that is to come."

• • •

Then the defeated Pandavas prepared to go to the forest. They wore upper garments of deerskin, according to the compact. When the Pandavas were leaving the hall, the foolish Duryodhana imitated the gait of Bhima who walked like a lion. Bhima said, "I shall kill Duryodhana, and Arjuna shall slay Karna, while Sahadeva will kill the deceitful Sakuni. I shall kill the evil Duryodhana in a club-fight. I shall stand with my foot on his head while he lies on the ground. Like a lion I shall drink the blood of the sinful Duhsasana, who is brave only in words."

BHISMA PARVA
Book VI, Chapters 23–25, 33, and 40–41

Krsna's Sermon to Arjuna (known as the Bhagvad Gita)

Then Arjuna, whose flag bore the figure of an ape, looked at the Kauravas drawn up in battle array; as the fighting was about to begin, he took up his bow and said to Krsna, "I wish to see my opponents who are eager for battle and whom I have to fight in the great struggle. Station my chariot, O Krsna, between the two armies!" As requested by Arjuna, Krsna drove the chariot to a position between the two armies.

Arjuna saw his closest kinsmen, related to him as father or grandfather, uncle or brother, son or grandson, preceptor as well as companion and friend, on both sides. Overcome by this sight, he said in sorrow and compassion, "O Krsna, when I see my own people ready to fight and eager for battle, my limbs shudder, my mouth is dry, my body shivers, and my hair stands on end. Furthermore, I see evil portents, and I can see no good in killing my own kinsmen. It is not right and proper that we should kill our own kith and kin, the Kauravas. How can we be happy if we slay our own people?" Having said these words, Arjuna threw away his bow and arrows, and sat down sorrowfully on the seat of his car.

When he observed that Arjuna was overcome with compassion and that tears were welling up in his eyes, Krsna said these words to him who was thus troubled and dejected: "O Arjuna, why have you become so depressed in this critical hour? Such dejection is unknown to noble men; it does not lead to the heavenly heights, and on earth it can only cause disgrace. Do not yield to cowardice, for it is not worthy of you. Cast away this faintness of heart and arise."

Arjuna said, "O Krsna, how can I strike with my arrows people like the grandsire Bhisma and the preceptor Drona, who are worthy of my respect?" After such reflection, he finally told Krsna, "I will not fight."

Krsna smiled at Arjuna, so troubled in mind and dejected in spirit, and said, "You grieve for those for whom you should not grieve. The wise do not lament the dead or pine for the living. Anyone who believes that this kills, or thinks that this is killed, fails to understand that one neither kills nor is killed. The embodied soul merely casts off old bodies and enters new ones, just as a person discards used garments and puts on new clothes.

"The soul that lives in every human body is eternal and immortal," Krsna went on to say. "Therefore do not grieve for any creature. As a Ksatriya, your duty is to fight a righteous battle. This is the highest good for you, and you should not falter at this hour. Such a fight is an open door to heaven, and happy are they who engage in such a battle. Either you will win a victory and enjoy the earth, or be killed and go to heaven. Therefore arise, O Arjuna, and be determined to fight. Get ready for battle without thought of pleasure and pain, gain and loss, victory and defeat. In this way, you will not incur any sin. Remember that you have a right to action alone, but not to the fruits thereof. Be not motivated by the desire for the fruits of action. At the same time, do not pursue a policy of inaction.

"O Arjuna," he continued, "in this world I have taught a twofold way of life: the way of knowledge for men who engage in contemplation, and the way of works for men of action. One cannot maintain even one's physical life without action. Therefore, do your allotted work regardless of results, for men attain the highest good by doing work without attachment to its results. Resign yourself to me and fix your consciousness in the self, without desire or egoism, and then fight, freed from your fever."

Arjuna replied, "My confusion has been dispelled by this supreme discourse concerning the self, which you have given me out of your grace." Krsna said, "I am Time itself, grown mature, capable of destroying the world, and now engaged in subduing it. Even without your effort, all the opposing warriors shall cease to exist. Therefore arise and win great glory, conquer your enemies, and enjoy a prosperous kingdom. They are already slain by me, and you, O Arjuna, are merely the occasion. Kill Drona, Bhisma, Jayadratha,[21] Karna, and all the other great warriors whom I have already doomed. Do not fear, but fight and conquer your enemies in battle."

"O Lord," said Arjuna, "I desire to know the true nature of renunciation and of relinquishment." Krsna replied, "The wise understand *renunciation* to mean 'the 'giving up of those works which are prompted by desire.' *Relinquishment* means 'the abandonment of the fruits of all works.' It is not right to renounce one's duty, but when one performs a prescribed duty, with detachment and without thought of the fruit thereof, that is *relinquishment*. Courage, vigor, resourcefulness, steadfastness in battle, generosity, and leadership are the natural duties of a Ksatriya.

"The Lord dwells in the hearts of all men and causes them to turn round by his power as if they were mounted on a machine," Krsna concluded. "Seek shelter

---

[21]Son-in-law of Dhrtarastra and the king of Sindhus. He kills Abhimanyu, Arjuna's son by his marriage to Krsna's sister. Jayadratha takes Abhimanyu at a disadvantage. Arjuna vows to kill Jayadratha and fulfils that vow.

in him with your whole being, and you shall attain supreme peace and the eternal station by his grace." "My bewilderment is gone," said Arjuna. "By your grace, O Krsna, I have been made to realize my true duties. My doubts have been dispelled and I stand ready to do your bidding."

• • •

Book VI, Chapters 104–106, 112, and 114

Bhisma's Fall

The tenth day of the battle dawned. Soon afterwards the Pandavas, to the sound of drums and cymbals and the blare of conches, set forth to give battle, placing Sikhandi[22] in front. But the Pandava army was torn into pieces by Bhisma, who let loose his shafts by hundreds and thousands. The Pandavas seemed incapable of defeating in battle the great bowman Bhisma who resembled the Destroyer himself (Shiva, the god of destruction).

Beholding the prowess of Bhisma in battle, Arjuna said to Sikhandi, "Proceed towards the grandsire! Do not entertain the slightest fear of Bhisma today. I shall dislodge him from his excellent car by means of my sharp arrows." Thus urged by Partha,[23] Sikhandi rushed at Bhisma.

Approaching Bhisma, Sikhandi struck him in the center of the chest with ten broad-headed arrows. Bhisma did not retaliate but looked at Sikhandi with wrath, as if he would consume the Pancala prince with that look.

Then all the Pandavas, placing themselves behind Sikhandi, attacked Bhisma in that battle repeatedly from all sides. Sikhandi himself, protected as he was by the diadem-decked Arjuna, pierced Bhisma with ten shafts. And he struck Bhisma's charioteer with other arrows and cut off his standard with one well-aimed shaft. Then Bhisma took up another bow that was tougher, which was cut off by Arjuna with three sharp shafts. Indeed, the ambidextrous Arjuna, excited with rage, cut off one by one all the bows that Bhisma took up.

When his bows were thus cut off, Bhisma, excited with rage, took up a dart that was capable of riving a hill, and hurled it at Arjuna's car. Seeing it coursing

---

[22]Sikhandi is Bhisma's sworn enemy, Amba, reborn to kill Bhisma, who once forcibly carried her and her two sisters for his step-brother, Vicitraviria, to marry them. Asking to be spared because she was in love with another man, Amba was let go. However, the man she loved would not accept her because she had been abducted by another man. So Amba returned to Bhisma and implored him to marry her. Vowed to celibacy, Bhisma refused her request. She took an oath to kill Bhisma for the humiliation for which she held him responsible. She died and was reborn as Drupada's daughter, Sikhandini. She became a man temporarily by exchanging her sex with a yaksha (yakshas are semi-divine beings of a low order) in order to kill Bhisma.

[23] Another name for Arjuna.

towards him like the blazing bolt of heaven, Arjuna fixed five sharp broad-headed arrows on his bowstring. And with those five arrows he cut into five fragments that dart hurled by Bhisma, which fell down like a flash of lightning separated from a mass of clouds.

Beholding his dart cut off, Bhisma became filled with rage. Soon he calmed down a little, and began to reflect. And he said to himself, "With only a single bow I could slay all the Pandavas, if the mighty Visnu[24] himself were not their protector. Moreover, I will not fight with the Pandavas because of the femininity of Sikhandi. Formerly, when my father married Satyavati,[25] he gave me two boons [wishes], that I should be incapable of being slain in battle and that my death should depend on my own choice. I think this is the proper hour for me to wish my own death."

Ascertaining this to be the resolve of the great Bhisma, the Rsis[26] and the Vasus[27] stationed in the firmament said, "O son, we approve of your resolve. Act accordingly and withdraw from battle!" When they had said these words, a fragrant and auspicious breeze began to blow. The celestial cymbals were sounded, and a shower of flowers fell upon Bhisma.

Then Arjuna, drawing his Gandiva bow,[28] pierced the son of Ganga[29] with twenty-five arrows. Once more he drew closer to Bhisma and cut off his bow. Bhisma took up another bow that was stronger. However, within the twinkling of an eye, Arjuna cut that bow into three fragments with three broad-headed shafts.

After that, Bhisma, the son of Santanu, no longer desired to battle with Arjuna. Deeply pierced by Arjuna with keen shafts, Bhisma addressed Duhsasana with a smile, saying, "These arrows coursing towards me in one continuous line are surely not Sikhandi's. Except for Arjuna, all other kings united together cannot cause me pain!"

Bhisma had slain ten thousand warriors on that day, the tenth day of the battle, and now he stood on the field with his vitals pierced. There was not a space even two fingers wide in all his body that was free from arrow wounds. A little before sunset the heroic Bhisma fell down from his car on the field, with his head towards the east, in the very sight of the Kauravas. When he fell, loud lamentations of "Alas!" and "Oh!" were heard everywhere, among the kings and among

---

[24]A major Hindu god (pronounced "Vishnu"). Krsna is an incarnation of Vsnu in human form.

[25]Bhisma's stepmother, Santanu's second wife, and Dhrtrastra and Pandu's paternal grandmother.

[26]Sages who have become immortal and dwell in heaven.

[27]A particular class of minor gods whose number is usually eight. Bhisma is a vasu born in the world as a punishment for a transgression.

[28]Arjuna's bow that he received from the god Shiva.

[29]Goddess of the river Ganga, or Ganges; King Santanu's first wife and Bhisma's mother.

the celestials in heaven. The heroic combatants of both armies laid down their weapons and withdrew from battle. Meanwhile Bhisma betook himself to yoga as taught in the great *Upanishads*[30] and remained quiet, engaged in prayer.

● ● ●

DRONA PARVA
Book VII, Chapters 159, 161, 164, and 165
Drona's Death

Meanwhile Drona caused great carnage among the Pancalas. Seeing the Pandavas thus afflicted by the shafts of Drona and overcome by fear, the wise Krsna who was ever devoted to their welfare said to Arjuna, "This foremost of all car-warriors cannot be vanquished in battle, not even by the very gods with Indra at their head! Hence you must put aside fair means, and adopt some contrivance for gaining victory, so that Drona may not slay us all in battle. I think he will cease to fight if his son Asvatthama should fall. Let some man, therefore, tell him that Asvatthama has been slain in battle."

Arjuna did not relish this suggestion of Krsna's, though others approved of it. Yudhisthira himself accepted it very reluctantly. Then the mighty Bhima, having slain with a mace a huge elephant, named Asvatthama, approached Drona on the battlefield, and—not without some embarrassment—exclaimed aloud, "Asvatthama has been slain!"

Meanwhile, Krsna grew seriously concerned because Drona, foremost of warriors, was capable of sweeping all the Pandavas off the face of the earth. He said to King Yudhisthira, "If Drona, roused to anger, fights for even half a day, I tell you truly, your army will be annihilated. Save us then from Drona! Under such circumstances, falsehood is preferable to truth. By telling a lie to save a life, one is not touched by sin."

Bhima supported Krsna's argument. He said, "Drona did not believe my words. To ensure our victory, accept Krsna's advice. Tell Drona that his son is no more. If you say so, Drona will believe you and will never fight thereafter, since you are famed for your truthfulness in the three worlds."

Urged thus by Bhima and induced by the counsels of Krsna, and also because of the inevitability of destiny, Yudhisthira gave in. Fearing to tell a downright lie, but earnestly desirous of victory, Yudhisthira added indistinctly that the elephant was slain. Before this, Yudhisthira's car had stayed at the height of four fingers above the surface of the earth; after he had uttered that lie, his vehicles and animals touched the earth.

Hearing those words of Yudhisthira's, the mighty car-warrior Drona was afflicted with grief for the reported death of his son, and lost all desire to live.

---

[30]See Selection 20, *Upanishads.*

Already he was feeling a sense of guilt for fighting against the high-souled Pandavas. Hearing now of the death of his son, he became deeply depressed and filled with anxiety. Thus, when Dhrstadyumna approached him, Drona had no mind to fight as before.

Seeing that Drona was filled with great anxiety and almost deprived of his senses by grief, Dhrstadyumna, the hero who had been obtained by King Drupada at a great sacrifice from the bearer of sacrificial libations expressly for Drona's destruction, rushed at him. He took up a formidable bow and fixed on it a fierce and fiery arrow, resembling a snake of virulent poison, intent on killing Drona. But the invincible Drona cut off all the weapons, and all the bows of his antagonist, with the sole exception of his mace and sword.

Then Bhima, in a great rage, approached Drona's chariot and deliberately said these words to him: "Wretched are the Brahmanas who, not content with the advocations of their own order, have become well versed in arms, and taken to fighting. But for them the Ksatriya order would not have been thus exterminated. Nonviolence to all creatures is said to be the highest of all virtues. The Brahmana is the root of all virtue. You, Drona, are supposed to be the best of Brahmanas. And yet you fight, while your son lies dead on the field of battle, unknown to you and behind your back. Yudhisthira the just has told you this. It behoves you not to doubt this fact."

Thus addressed by Bhima, Drona laid aside his bow. Deciding to give up all his weapons, the virtuous man called for Karna, Krpa, and Duryodhana. He repeated his son's name loudly. Laying aside his weapons, he sat down on the platform of his car, and devoted himself to yoga. Seizing this opportunity, Dhrstadyuma took up his sword and, jumping down from his vehicle, rushed quickly against Drona, among loud exclamations of woe from all sides.

Drona himself remained in a supremely tranquil state. Arjuna pleaded with Dhrstadyumna, saying, "O son of Drupada, seize the preceptor alive, do not slay him!" All the troops also cried out, "He should not be slain!" Arjuna, in particular, moved by pity, pleaded repeatedly that his life should be spared. Disregarding, however, the protests of Arjuna as well as those of all the kings, Dhrstadyumna slew Drona on the platform of his car.

Upon the fall of Drona, the Kaurava warriors, already sorely afflicted by the enemy's arrows, became leaderless. Broken and routed, and filled with grief, they gathered listlessly around Duryodhana, bewailing their loss.

● ● ●

KARNA PARVA
Book VIII, Chapters 29, 42, 60, and 61

Bhima Kills Duhsasana

Fighting fiercely, Prince Duhsasana achieved many difficult feats in that duel. With a single shaft he cut off Bhima's bow; with six shafts he pierced Bhima's driver.

Then, without losing a moment he pierced Bhima himself with many shafts discharged with great speed and power, while Bhima hurled his mace at the prince. With that weapon, from a distance of ten bow-lengths, Bhima forcibly dislodged Duhsasana from his car. Struck by the mace, and thrown to the ground, Duhsasana began to tremble. His charioteer and all his steeds were slain, and his car, too, was smashed to pieces by Bhima's weapon.

Then Bhima remembered all the hostile acts of Duhsasana towards the Pandavas. Jumping down from his car, he stood on the ground, looking steadily on his fallen foe. Drawing his keen-edged sword, and trembling with rage, he placed his foot upon the throat of Duhsasana and, ripping open the breast of his enemy, drank his warm lifeblood, little by little. Then, looking at him with wrathful eyes, he said, "I consider the taste of this blood superior to that of my mother's milk, or honey, or ghee,[31] or wine, or excellent water, or milk, or curds, or buttermilk."

All those who stood around Bhima and saw him drink the blood of Duhsasana fled in terror, saying to each other, "This one is no human being!" Bhima then said, in the hearing of all those heroes, "O wretch among men, here I drink your lifeblood. Abuse us once more now, 'Beast, beast,' as you did before!"

• • •

Book VIII, Chapters 66 and 67

The Death of Karna

Fleeing in the face of Arjuna's onslaught, the broken divisions of the Kauravas saw Arjuna's weapon swelling with energy and careering like lightning. But Karna destroyed that fiery weapon of Arjuna with his own weapon of great power which he had obtained from Parasurama.[32] The encounter between Arjuna and Karna became very fierce. They attacked each other with arrows like two fierce elephants attacking each other with their tusks.

Karna then fixed on his bowstring the keen, blazing, and fierce shaft which he had long polished and preserved with the object of destroying Arjuna. Placing in position that shaft of fierce energy and blazing splendor, that venomous weapon which had its origin in the family of Airavata[33] and which lay within a golden quiver covered by sandal dust, Karna aimed it at Arjuna's head. When he saw Karna aim that arrow, Salya said, "O Karna, this arrow will not succeed in hitting Arjuna's neck! Aim carefully, and discharge another arrow that may succeed in

---

[31]Melted and clarified butter.

[32]A legendary Brahman sage and warrior who once, in a war with Ksatriyas, decimated them. He knew the art of weaponry better than any other man. Pretending to be a Brahman, Karna served him and received a weapon from him. When Parasurama found out that Karna was a Ksatriya, he put a curse on him that, in time of dire need, he would forget the mantra (the words to be recited) for the weapon.

[33]A mythical serpent.

striking the head of your enemy!" His eyes burning in wrath, Karna replied, "O Salya, Karna never aims an arrow twice!"

Thereupon Karna carefully let loose that mighty snake in the form of an arrow, which he had worshiped for many long years, saying, "You are slain, O Arjuna!" Seeing the snake aimed by Karna, Krsna, strongest among the mighty, exerted his whole strength and pressed down Arjuna's chariot with his feet into the earth. When the car itself had sunk into the ground the steeds, too, bent their knees and laid themselves down upon the earth. The arrow then struck and dislodged Arjuna's diadem, that excellent ornament celebrated throughout the earth and the heavens.

The snake said, "O Krsna! Know me as one who has been wronged by Arjuna. My enmity towards him stems from his having slain my mother!"

Then Krsna said to Arjuna, "Slay that great snake which is your enemy." Thus urged by Krsna, Arjuna asked, "Who is this snake that advances of his own accord against me, as if right against the mouth of Garuda?"[34] Krsna replied, "While you were worshiping the fire-god at the Khandava forest, this snake was ensconced within his mother's body, which was shattered by your arrows." As the snake took a slanting course across the sky, Arjuna cut it to pieces with six keen shafts, so that it fell down on the earth.

Then, because of the curse of the Brahmana, Karna's chariot wheel fell off, and his car began to reel.[35] At the same time, he forgot the invocation for the weapon he had obtained from Parasurama. Unable to endure these calamities, Karna waved his arms and began to rail at righteousness, saying, "They that are conversant with virtue say that righteousness protects the righteous! But today righteousness does not save me."

Speaking thus, he shed tears of wrath, and said to Arjuna, "O Pandava! Spare me for a moment while I extricate my wheel from the earth! You are on your car while I am standing weak and languid on the ground. It is not fair that you should slay me now! You are born in the Ksatriya order. You are the scion of a high race. Recollect the teachings of righteousness, and give me a moment's time!"

Then, from Arjuna's chariot, Krsna said, "It is fortunate, O Karna, that you now remember virtue. It is generally true that those who are mean rail at providence when they are afflicted by distress, but forget their own misdeeds. You and Duryodhana and Duhsasana and Sakuni caused Draupadi, clad in a single garment, to be brought into the midst of the assembly. On that occasion, O Karna, this virtue of yours was not in evidence! When Sakuni, skilled in dicing, vanquished Yudhisthira who was unacquainted with it, where was this virtue of yours? Out of covetousness, and relying on Sakuni, you again summoned the Pandavas to a game of dice. Whither then had this virtue of yours gone?"

---

[34]An Indian eagle. Vsnu rides the Garuda.

[35]Karna had once accidentally killed the sacrificial cow of a Brahman who, therefore, put a curse on him, "Your wheel shall fall into a hole."

When Krsna thus taunted Karna, Arjuna became filled with rage. Remembering the incidents to which Krsna alluded, he blazed with fury and, bent upon Karna's speedy destruction, took out of his quiver an excellent weapon. He then fixed on his bow that unrivalled arrow, and charged it with mantras. Drawing his bow Gandiva, he quickly said, "Let this shaft of mine be a mighty weapon capable of speedily destroying the body and heart of my enemy. If I have ever practiced ascetic austerities, gratified my preceptors, and listened to the counsels of well-wishers, let this sharp shaft, so long worshiped by me, slay my enemy Karna by that truth!"

Having uttered these words, Arjuna discharged for the destruction of Karna, that terrible shaft, that blazing arrow fierce and efficacious as a rite prescribed in the Atharva of Angiras,[36] and invincible against the god of death himself in battle. Thus sped by that mighty warrior, the shaft endowed with the energy of the sun caused all the points of the compass to blaze with light. The head of the commander of the Kaurava army, splendid as the sun, fell like the sun disappearing in the blood-red sunset behind the western hills. Cut off by Arjuna's arrow and deprived of life, the tall trunk of Karna, with blood gushing from every wound, fell down like the thunder-riven summit of a mountain of red chalk with crimson streams running down its sides after a shower of rain.

Then from the body of the fallen Karna a light, passing through the atmosphere, illumined the sky. This wonderful sight was seen by all the warriors on the battlefield. After the heroic Karna was thus thrown down and stretched on the earth, pierced with arrows and bathed in blood, Salya, the king of the Madras, withdrew with Karna's car. The Kauravas, afflicted with fear, fled from the field, frequently looking back on Arjuna's lofty standard which blazed in splendor.

• • •

SALYA PARVA
Chapters 57–60
The Death of Duryodhana

The duel then began. Duryodhana and Bhima fought like two bulls attacking each other with their horns. The clash of their maces produced loud peals like those of thunderbolts. After the fierce and terrible battle had lasted for some time, both contenders were exhausted. They rested for some time and then, taking up their maces, they once again began to ward off each other's attacks.

While the fight was thus raging between those two heroes, Arjuna said to Krsna, "Who, in your opinion, is the better of these two? What is their respective merit? Tell me this, O Krsna!"

---

[36]*Atharva-Veda* is the last of the four *Vedas*. Angiras is the name of a sage or a family of sages to whom the *Vedas* were revealed. See Selection 8.

Krsna replied, "They are equally well instructed. Bhima is possessed of greater strength while Duryodhana has greater skill and has practiced harder. If he fights fairly, Bhima will never succeed in gaining victory. If, however, he fights unfairly, he will surely be able to kill Duryodhana. At the time of the gambling, Bhima promised to break the thighs of Duryodhana with his mace in battle. Let him now fulfil his vow. Let him, by deception, kill the Kuru king who is the master of deception! If Bhima does not kill him by unfair means, the son of Dhrtarastra will surely retain the kingdom!"

Thereupon Arjuna, before Bhima's sight, struck his own left thigh. Understanding that sign, Bhima began to move about with his mace raised, making many kinds of maneuvers. Seeing the energetic and angry Bhima rushing towards him and desiring to thwart his blow, Duryodhana thought of the maneuver called avasthana, and prepared to jump upwards.

Bhima fully understood the object of his opponent. Rushing at him, with a loud roar, he fiercely hurled his mace at Duryodhana's thighs, as the latter jumped into the air. The mace, hurled by Bhima, broke the thighs of Duryodhana, and he fell down, so that the earth resounded.

Having struck Duryodhana down, Bhima approached the Kuru chief and said, "O wretch, formerly you laughed at Draupadi who had only one bit of cloth in the midst of the assembly, and you called us cows. Bear now the consequences of that insult." Saying this, he kicked the head of his fallen foe with his left foot.

Balarama[37] became highly incensed when he saw Duryodhana thus brought down by a blow aimed at his thighs. Raising his arms, he sorrowfully said in the midst of those kings, "Oh, fie on Bhima, that in such a fair fight a blow should have been inflicted below the navel! Never before has such a foul blow been seen in an encounter with the mace!

"Having unfairly killed the righteous King Duryodhana," Balarama continued, "Bhima shall be known in the world as an unfair fighter! The righteous Duryodhana, on the other hand, shall acquire eternal blessedness!"

Krsna then said to Yudhisthira, "O king of virtue, why do you permit such a wrong act? Why do you suffer the head of the insensible and fallen Duryodhana to be thus kicked by Bhima with his foot? Conversant as you are with the rules of morality, why do you look on this deed with indifference?"

Yudhisthira said, "O Krsna, Bhima's action in angrily touching the head of the fallen king with his foot does not please me, nor am I glad at this extermination of my race! But remember how we were cheated by the sons of Dhrtarastra! Remember too the many harsh words they addressed to us, and how they sent us in exile into the forest. On account of all those things Bhima has been nursing a great grief in his heart! Bearing all this in mind, O Krsna, I looked on his actions with indifference!"

---

[37]Krsna's brother, who taught Bhima and Duryodhana to fight with the mace.

26

𝆕

Confucius

THE ANALECTS

Confucius has dominated the intellectual, moral, social, and political land-scape of China and much else of East Asia for more than two millennia. For most of China's imperial history (roughly 200 B.C.–A.D. 1900) one can character-ize its condition as that of a Confucian state and society. Despite criticism and even outright condemnation from recent Marxist/Maoist ideologues, his humanis-tic views of character and behavior are so interwoven with language and custom as to constitute a permanent element in the Chinese, and more broadly, the East Asian scene. Yet for this very reason, the historical Confucius is difficult to isolate from the mass of myth, reinterpretation, and sometimes deliberate misinterpreta-tion, which has built up over the centuries. In this respect, the memory of Confucius and the record of his original teaching have suffered a fate analogous to that of other great moral/religious teachers, such as Socrates, the Buddha, and Christ (see Selections 17, 21, 22, and 35).

Tradition holds that he was born in the state of Lu, now part of Shantung Province, in 551 B.C. The fact that this small domain was a separate state sym-bolizes the chronic and worsening condition of a disintegrating feudal kingship, the Chou Dynasty (1122?—256 B.C.), characterized by rivalry and instability well before Confucius's time and sliding toward its bloody last two centuries, known in Chinese history as the Warring States Period. His family name was Kung, to which were often added the honorifics Fu and Tzu; from these elements, seventeenth-century European scholars, writing in Latin, derived the name Confucius now common in the West. Evidently he came from the class of knights (shih), principally soldiers and government functionaries in the service of feudal princes. He was one of a number of such men seeking employment as advisers or ministers among the feudal states, each of whom developed a philosophy of con-duct and governance as the basis of their claim to be heard and followed. Thus was *born out of the chaos of the times and the competition among these wandering* shih *what came to be called the Hundred Schools, a number not to be taken literally. As a result of this competition, the three centuries after 500 B.C. in China became one of the richest periods in human history for the articulation of diverse moral and political philosophies.*

Confucius's own quest took him to a number of feudal courts, where he was usually treated with respect but where he received no significant employment and encountered no prince willing to adopt his central premise, that the moral rectitude of the ruler was the most effective tool of government. Along the way, however, he began to influence a circle of young men and, by the time he returned to Lu, probably in 484 B.C., he had emerged as a great teacher. He died in Lu about fifteen years later, leaving a following of disciples, some of whose names we know.

Confucius, or the Sage, as he came to be called later, left no written record of his life and teaching. However, the surviving disciples compiled a record of their conversations with him, called the Lun Yu *or "sayings," a work now generally known in English as* The Analects. *It is divided into twenty books, each subdivided into numbered chapters, some only a sentence or two in length. In its present form, it is the product of an "official" edition compiled during the Han Dynasty, some four centuries after Confucius's death. Modern scholars recognize the combining of diverse elements in this work, some representing conflicting interpretations among the disciples, some apparently infiltrations from others among the Hundred Schools. Nevertheless, for centuries the entire* Lun Yu *was crucial in the education of the literate governing classes in China, Japan, and Korea, so that even its internal inconsistencies became part of the Confucian tradition.*

Confucius's primary aim as a teacher during his lifetime, and the main focus of his thought as it survives in The Analects, *was to lead his disciples to understand and aspire to the character of the* chun tzu, *which we translate as "the gentleman," but which has clearly the overtone of the superior man, one fit to lead state and society. In the historical references, fragments from* The Book of Songs *(Selection 11), and epigrams through which the Sage answered his disciples' questions about character and conduct, he often contrasted the gentleman, not with the* evil *person, but with the* ordinary one.

The Master said, "The gentleman understands what is moral. The small man understands what is profitable" (III, 16).

The gentleman manifests—in thoughts, words, and actions—a number of traits, chief among which are the following: benevolence, devotion to one's parents, respect for the forms of ritual and good manners, and steadfastness of character. These virtuous qualities are governed by an understanding of the tao, *the true path, or "way," to righteousness. Confucius believed that certain historical figures, especially the founders of the Chou Dynasty, exemplified these desired virtues (see Selection 10,* The Book of History). *He insisted that his disciples know their history, as well as their poetry, for history contained essential lessons regarding desirable and undesirable conduct—above all because it presented the evidence that good government by good men was possible.*

꾸

1, 3: The Master said, "It is rare, indeed, for a man with cunning words and an ingratiating face to be benevolent."

I, 6: The Master said, "A young man should be a good son at home and an obedient young man abroad, sparing of speech but trustworthy in what he says, and should love the multitude at large but cultivate the friendship of his fellow men. If he has any energy to spare from such action, let him devote it to making himself cultivated."[1]

I, 15: Tzu-kung[2] said, "'Poor without being obsequious, wealthy without being arrogant.' What do you think of this saying?"

The Master said, "That will do, but better still, 'Poor yet delighting in the way, wealthy yet observant of the rites.'"

Tzu-kung said, "The *Odes* [i.e., *Book of Songs*] say,

'Like bone cut, like horn polished,
Like jade carved, like stone ground.'

Is not what you have said a case in point?"

II, 1: The Master said, "The rule of virtue can be compared to the Pole Star which commands the homage of the multitude of stars without leaving its place."

From Confucius, *The Analects,* D. C. Lau, trans. (Penguin Classics, 1979) copyright © D. C. Lau, 1979. Reprinted with permission of the publisher.

[1]Cultivation means, for Confucius, study of the Chinese classics, such as *The Book of History* and *The Book of Songs* (Selections 10 and 11), and the art of effective expression of ideas.

[2]Tzu-kung was a disciple of Confucius, one of roughly twenty-five named in *The Analects.* Although no attempt has been made here to distinguish them as their names appear in these selections, the importance of these men is worth noting, not only as their different characters and intellects appear in *The Analects,* but because they were the ones who wrote down and later assembled the sayings of their great teacher.

II, 3: The Master said, "Guide them by edicts, keep them in line with punishments, and the common people will stay out of trouble but will have no sense of shame. Guide them by virtue, keep them in line with the rites, and they will, besides having a sense of shame, reform themselves."

II, 4: The Master said, "At fifteen I set my heart on learning; at thirty I took my stand; at forty I came to be free from doubts; at fifty I understood the Decree of Heaven; at sixty my ear was attuned; at seventy I followed my heart's desire without overstepping the line."

II, 7: Tzu-yu asked about being filial. The Master said, "Nowadays for a man to be filial means no more than that he is able to provide his parents with food. Even hounds and horses are, in some way, provided with food. If a man shows no reverence, where is the difference?"

II, 13: Tzu-kung asked about the gentleman. The Master said, "He puts his words into action before allowing his words to follow his action."

II, 17: The Master said, "Yu, shall I tell you what it is to know? To say you know when you know, and to say you do not when you do not, that is knowledge."

III, 3: The Master said, "What can a man do with the rites who is not benevolent? What can a man do with music who is not benevolent?"

III, 17: Tzu-kung wanted to do away with the sacrificial sheep at the announcement of the new moon. The Master said, "Ssu, you are loath to part with the price of the sheep, but I am loath to see the disappearance of the rite."

IV, 2: The Master said, "One who is not benevolent cannot remain long in straitened circumstances, nor can he remain long in easy circumstances. The benevolent man is attracted to benevolence because he feels at home in it. The wise man is attracted to benevolence because he finds it to his advantage."

IV, 8: The Master said, "He has not lived in vain who dies the day he is told about the way."

IV, 15: The Master said, "Ts'an! There is one single thread binding my way together."
Tseng Tzu assented.
After the Master had gone out, the disciples asked, "What did he mean?"
Tseng Tzu said, "The way of the Master consists in doing one's best and in using oneself as a measure to gauge others. That is all."

IV, 18: The Master said, "In serving your father and mother you ought to dissuade them from doing wrong in the gentlest way. If you see your advice being ignored, you should not become disobedient but remain reverent. You should not complain even if in so doing you wear yourself out."

V, 16: The Master said of Tzu-ch'an that he had the way of the gentleman on four counts: he was respectful in the manner he conducted himself; he was reverent in the service of his lord; in caring for the common people, he was generous; and, in employing their services, he was just.

VI, 20: The Master said, "To be fond of something is better than merely to know it, and to find joy in it is better than merely to be fond of it."

VI, 28: The Master went to see Nan Tzu.[3] Tzu-lu was displeased. The Master swore: "If I have done anything improper, may Heaven's curse be on me, may Heaven's curse be on me!"

VII, 1: The Master said, "I transmit but do not innovate; I am truthful in what I say and devoted to antiquity. I venture to compare myself to Old P'eng."[4]

VII, 8: The Master said, "I never enlighten anyone who has not been driven to distraction by trying to understand a difficulty or who has not got into a frenzy trying to put his ideas into words.

"When I have pointed out one corner of a square to anyone and he does not come back with the other three, I will not point it out to him a second time."

VII, 19: The Governor of She asked Tzu-lu about Confucius. Tzu-lu did not answer. The Master said, "Why did you not simply say something to this effect: He is the sort of man who forgets to eat when he tries to solve a problem that has been driving him to distraction, who is so full of joy he forgets his worries, and who does not notice the onset of old age?"

VII, 30: The Master said, "Is benevolence really far away? No sooner do I desire it than it is here."

---

[3] Wife of the Duke of Wei, a woman of scandalous reputation.

[4] Old P'eng's identity is now lost. Confucius's self-identification as a transmitter, rather than an innovator, gave powerful impetus to the following two and a half millennia of respect for tradition and mistrust of new ideas. Yet this is one of the great ironies of the Confucian legacy, for it's clear that he was, in fact, shaping a new vision of political life to replace the feudal system so obviously disintegrating in his time.

VII, 37: The Master said, "The gentleman is of easy mind, while the small man is always full of anxiety."

VIII, 8: The Master said, "Be stimulated by the *Odes* [*Book of Songs*], take your stand on the rites and be perfected by music."

VIII, 9: The Master said, "The common people can be made to follow a path but not to understand it."

IX, 14: The Master wanted to settle among the nine barbarian tribes of the east. Someone said, "But could you put up with their uncouth ways?" The Master said, "Once a gentleman settles amongst them, what uncouthness will there be?"

X, 7: In periods of purification, he invariably wore a house robe made of the cheaper sort of material [i.e., linen].

In periods of purification, he invariably changed to a more austere diet and, when at home, did not sit in his usual place.

X, 11: Even when a meal consisted only of coarse rice and vegetable broth, he invariably made an offering from them and invariably did so solemnly.

XI, 12: Chi-lu asked how the spirits of the dead and the gods should be served. The Master said, "You are not able even to serve man. How can you serve the spirits?"

"May I ask about death?"

"You do not understand even life. How can you understand death?"

XII, 2: Chung-kung asked about benevolence. The Master said, "When abroad, behave as though you were receiving an important guest. When employing the services of the common people, behave as though you were officiating at an important sacrifice. Do not impose on others what you, yourself, do not desire.[5] In this way you will be free from ill will whether in a state or in a noble family."

Chung-kung said, "Though I am not quick, I shall direct my efforts towards what you have said."

XII, 7: Tzu-kung asked about government. The Master said, "Give them enough food, give them enough arms, and the common people will have trust in you."

---

[5]This is one among several instances in which Confucius sets forth the idea of reciprocity as a basis for benevolent action. The parallel with the New Testament's "Golden Rule" in Matthew 7:12 (Selection 35) is striking.

Tzu-kung said, "If you had to give up one of these three, which should one give up first?"

"Give up arms."

Tzu-kung said, "If one had to give up one of the remaining two, which should one give up first?"

"Give up food. Death has always been with us since the beginning of time, but when there is no trust, the common people have nothing to stand on."

XII, 11: Duke Ching of Ch'i asked Confucius about government. Confucius answered, "Let the ruler be a ruler, the subject a subject, the father a father, the son a son." The duke said, "Splendid! Truly, if the ruler be not a ruler, the subject not a subject, the father not a father, the son not a son, then even if there be grain, would I get to eat it?"

XII, 19: Chi K'ang Tzu asked Confucius about government, saying, "What would you think if, in order to move closer to those who possess the way, I were to kill those who do not follow the way?"

Confucius answered, "In administering your government, what need is there for you to kill? Just desire the good yourself and the common people will be good. The virtue of the gentleman is like the wind; the virtue of the small man is like grass. Let the wind blow over the grass and it is sure to bend."

XII, 22: Fan Ch'ih asked about benevolence. The Master said, "Love your fellow men."

He asked about wisdom. The Master said, "Know your fellow men." Fan Ch'ih failed to grasp his meaning. The Master said, "Raise the straight and set them over the crooked. This can make the crooked straight."

Fan Ch'ih withdrew and went to see Tzu-hsia, saying, "Just now I went to see the Master and asked about wisdom. The Master said, 'Raise the straight and set them over the crooked. This can make the crooked straight.' What did he mean?"

Tzu-hsia said, "Rich, indeed is the meaning of these words. When Shun[6] possessed the empire, he raised Kao Yao from the multitude and by so doing put those who were not benevolent at a great distance. When T'ang possessed the empire, he raised Yi Yin from the multitude and by so doing put those who were not benevolent at a great distance."

XIV, 23: The Master said, "The gentleman gets through to what is up above; the small man gets through to what is down below."

---

[6]All those referred to in this passage are, like Shun, idealized rulers of earlier times whose chronicles are told in *The Book of History* (Selection 10).

XIV, 30: The Master said, "It is not the failure of others to appreciate your abilities that should trouble you, but rather your own lack of them."

XV, 8: The Master said, "To fail to speak to a man who is capable of benefiting is to let a man go to waste. To speak to a man who is incapable of benefiting is to let one's words go to waste. A wise man lets neither men nor words go to waste."

XV, 21: The Master said, "What the gentleman seeks, he seeks within himself; what the small man seeks, he seeks in others."

XV, 38: The Master said, "In serving one's lord, one should approach one's duties with reverence and consider one's pay as of secondary importance."

XVI, 8: Confucius said, "The gentleman stands in awe of three things. He is in awe of the Decree of Heaven. He is in awe of great men. He is in awe of the words of sages. The small man, being ignorant of the Decree of Heaven, does not stand in awe of it. He treats great men with insolence and the words of sages with derision."

XVII, 23: Tzu-lu said, "Does the gentleman consider courage a supreme quality?" The Master said, "For the gentleman it is morality that is supreme. Possessed of courage but devoid of morality, a gentleman will make trouble, while a small man will be a brigand."

XIX, 24: Shu-sun Wu-shu made defamatory remarks about Chung-ni [Confucius]. Tzu-kung said, "He is simply wasting his time. Chung-ni cannot be defamed. In other cases, men of excellence are like hills which one can climb over. Chung-ni is like the sun and the moon which one has no way of climbing over. Even if someone wanted to cut himself off from them, how could this detract from the sun and the moon? It would merely serve the more to show that he [the defamer] did not know his own measure."

27

꙳

THE BOOK OF RITES

The two short documents excerpted in this reading were written by Confucian thinkers, perhaps as late as the third and second centuries B.C. However, through the then-common Chinese tendency of attributing writings to earlier times, both came to be included in canonical versions of the Li chi, the otherwise genuinely ancient Book of Rites, one of the five Confucian classics. Both of the following documents represent major aspects of Confucian thought, and can be seen now as milestones on the road to making Confucianism a more systematic philosophy. Their importance was considerable in the age when Confucianism was becoming the official philosophy of the Han Dynasty (206 B.C.–A.D. 220) and was even more so during the Confucian revival more than a thousand years later.

The title Ta hsueh, or "great learning," suggests higher learning accessible to the advanced student, and the essay was in fact aimed at rulers and ministers more than at a general readership. It stresses self-cultivation as the basis of a process of moral refinement and strengthening. In the passage presented here we see a reliance on what some have called "chain-link" reasoning and others have likened to ripples extending outward from a stone tossed into water. These linked ideas form the basis of an "eight-step program": investigating, extending knowledge, achieving sincerity of will, rectifying the mind, cultivating personal life, regulating the family, ordering the state, and bringing peace to the world. The great strength of this teaching (in the context of emerging Confucian thought) is its stress on logical ordering of cause and result, on putting first things first in the movement from right moral thought to effective moral action. Its weakness is its over-reliance on self-cultivation in the naive belief that the ruler's moral perfection is the only problem to be solved.

The Chinese title of the other work, Chung yung, meaning, literally, "that which is central and that which is ordinary or normal," is usually translated as "the doctrine of the mean." At one level, this title refers to that balance in the human mind reflected in sincere motivations and harmonious actions. But "the *mean" also connotes here the larger idea that this desirable harmony of human character is a reflection of, indeed a part of, a universal harmony. That most pervasive of all Chinese philosophical terms, the Tao or "way," is invoked in this discussion, and is depicted not merely as a path to right conduct but as a cosmic principle. It is this aspect of the "Doctrine of the Mean" that makes it a major step toward defining a metaphysical or spiritual dimension of Confucianism; it was this which made this essay attractive to Taoists and later to Chinese Buddhists. Hence, the "Doctrine of the Mean" became an influential document in the great Neo-Confucian synthesis of the twelfth and later centuries A.D.*

꒰꜀

"THE GREAT LEARNING"

The way of learning to be great consists in manifesting the clear character, loving the people, and abiding in the highest good.

Only after knowing what to abide in can one be calm. Only after having been calm can one be tranquil. Only after having achieved tranquillity can one have a peaceful repose. Only after having peaceful repose can one begin to deliberate. Only after deliberation can the end be obtained. Things have their roots and branches. Affairs have their beginnings and their ends. To know what is first and what is last will lead one near the way.

The ancients who wished to manifest their clear character to the world would first bring order to their states. Those who wished to bring order to their states would first regulate their families. Those who wished to regulate their families would first cultivate their personal lives. Those who wished to cultivate their personal lives would first rectify their minds. Those who wished to rectify their minds would first make their wills sincere. Those who wished to make their wills sincere would first extend their knowledge. The extension of knowledge consists in the investigation of things. When things are investigated, knowledge is extended; when knowledge is extended, the will becomes sincere; when the will is sincere, the mind is rectified; when the mind is rectified, the personal life is cultivated; when the personal life is cultivated, the family will be regulated; when the family is regulated, the state will be in order; and when the state is in order, there will be peace throughout the world. From the Son of Heaven down to the common people, all must regard cultivation of the personal life as the root, or foundation. There is never a case where the root is in disorder and yet the branches are in order. There has never been a case when what is treated with great importance becomes a matter of slight importance or what is treated with slight importance becomes of great importance. . . .

FROM THE CHAPTERS OF COMMENTARY IN "THE GREAT LEARNING"

Chapter 7

What is meant by saying that cultivation of the personal life depends on the rectification of the mind is that when one is affected by wrath to any extent, his mind will not be correct. When one is affected by fear to any extent, his mind will not be correct. When he is affected by fondness to any extent, his mind will not be correct. When he is affected by worries and anxieties, his mind will not be correct. When the mind is not present, we look but do not see, listen but do not hear, and eat but do not know the taste of food. This is what is meant by saying that the cultivation of the personal life depends on the rectification of the mind.

Chapter 8

What is meant by saying that the regulation of the family depends on the cultivation of the personal life is this: Men are partial toward those for whom they have affection and whom they love, partial toward those whom they despise and dislike, partial toward those whom they fear and revere, partial toward those whom they pity and for whom they have compassion, and partial toward those whom they do not respect. Therefore there are few people in the world who know what is bad in those whom they love and what is good in those whom they dislike. Hence it is said, "People do not know the faults of their sons and do not know the bigness of their seedlings." This is what is meant by saying that if the personal life is not cultivated, one cannot regulate his family.

Chapter 9

What is meant by saying that in order to govern the state it is necessary first to regulate the family is this: There is no one who cannot teach his own family and yet can teach others. Therefore the superior man, without going beyond his family, can bring education into completion in the whole state. Filial piety is that with which one serves his ruler. Brotherly respect is that with which one serves his elders, and deep love is that with which one treats the multitude. The "Announcement of K'ang"[1] says, "Act as if you were watching over an infant." If a mother sincerely and earnestly looks for what the infant wants, she may not hit

---

[1]Reference is to a passage from *The Book of History* (see Selection 10).

the mark but she will not be far from it. A young woman has never had to learn about nursing a baby before she marries. When the individual families have become humane, then the whole country will be aroused toward humanity. When the individual families have become compliant, then the whole country will be aroused toward compliance. When one man is greedy or avaricious, the whole country will be plunged into disorder. Such is the subtle, incipient, activating force of things. . . .

Chapter 10

What is meant by saying that the peace of the world depends on the order of the state is this: When the ruler treats the elders with respect, the people will be aroused toward filial piety. When the ruler treats the aged with respect, then the people will be aroused toward brotherly respect. When the ruler treats compassionately the young and the helpless, then the common people will not follow the opposite course. Therefore the ruler has a principle with which, as with a measuring square,[2] he may regulate his conduct.

What a man dislikes in his superiors, let him not show it in dealing with his inferiors; what he dislikes in those in front of him, let him not show it in preceding those who are behind; what he dislikes in those behind him, let him not show it in following those in front of him; what he dislikes in those on the right, let him not apply it to those on the left; and what he dislikes in those on the left, let him not apply it to those on the right. This is the principle of the measuring square.

THE DOCTRINE OF THE MEAN
Chapter 1

What Heaven [*T'ien*, "nature"] imparts to man is called human nature. To follow our nature is called the way. Cultivating the way is called education. The way cannot be separated from us for a moment. What can be separated from us is not the way. Therefore the superior man is cautious over what he does not see and apprehensive over what he does not hear. There is nothing more visible than what is hidden and nothing more manifest than what is subtle. Therefore the superior man is watchful over himself when he is alone.

Before the feelings of pleasure, anger, sorrow, and joy are aroused, it is called equilibrium. When these feelings are aroused and each and all attain all due measure and degree, it is called harmony. Equilibrium is the great foundation of the

---

[2]The measuring square is a favorite metaphor of the full document. This passage, in which Confucius's notion of reciprocity is restated by elaboration, makes it clear that the "measuring square" is oneself: One should act as one wants to be acted upon.

world, and harmony its universal path. When equilibrium and harmony are realized to the highest degree, heaven and earth will attain their proper order and all things will flourish.

• • •

Chapter 20

Confucius said, . . . "There are five universal ways [in human relations], and the way by which they are practiced is three. The five are those governing the relationship between ruler and minister, between father and son, between husband and wife, between elder and younger brothers, and those in the intercourse between friends. These five are the universal paths in the world. Wisdom, humanity, and courage, these three are the universal virtues. The way by which they are practiced is one.

"Some are born with knowledge [of these virtues]. Some learn it through study. Some learn it through hard work. But when the knowledge is acquired, it comes to the same thing. Some practice them naturally and easily. Some practice them for their advantage. Some practice them with effort and difficulty. But when the achievement is made, it comes to the same thing."

Confucius said, "Love of learning is akin to wisdom. To practice with vigor is akin to humanity. To know to be shameful is akin to courage. He who knows these three things knows how to cultivate his personal life. Knowing how to cultivate his personal life, he knows how to govern other men. And knowing how to govern other men, he knows how to govern the empire, its states, and the families.

"There are nine standards by which to administer the empire, its states, and the families. They are: cultivating the personal life, honoring the worthy, being affectionate to relatives, being respectful toward the great ministers, identifying oneself with the welfare of the whole body of officers, treating the common people as one's own children, attracting the various artisans, showing tenderness to strangers from far countries, and extending kindly and awesome influence on the feudal lords. If the ruler cultivates his personal life, the way will be established. If he honors the worthy, he will not be perplexed. If he is affectionate to his relatives, there will be no grumbling among his uncles and brothers. If he respects the great ministers, he will not be deceived. If he identifies himself with the whole body of officers, then the officers will repay him heavily for his courtesies. If he treats the common people as his own children, then the masses will exhort one another [to do good]. If he attracts the various artisans, there will be sufficiency of wealth and resources in the country. If he shows tenderness to strangers from far countries, people from all quarters of the world will flock to him. And if he extends kindly and awesome influence over the feudal lords, then the world will stand in awe of him."

• • •

Chapter 22

Only those who are absolutely sincere can fully develop their nature. If they can fully develop their nature, then they can fully develop the nature of others. If they can fully develop the nature of others, they can then fully develop the nature of things. If they can fully develop the nature of things, they can then assist in the transforming and nourishing process of heaven and earth. If they can assist in the transforming process of heaven and earth, they can thus form a trinity with heaven and earth.

Chapter 23

The next in order are those who cultivate to the utmost a particular goodness. Having done this, they can attain to the possession of sincerity. As there is sincerity, there will be its expression. As it is expressed, it will become conspicuous. As it becomes conspicuous, it will become clear. As it becomes clear, it will move others. As it moves others, it changes them. As it changes them, it transforms them. Only those who are absolutely sincere can transform others.

● ● ●

Chapter 26

Therefore absolute sincerity is ceaseless. Being ceaseless, it is lasting. Being lasting, it is evident. Being evident, it is infinite. Being infinite, it is extensive and deep. Being extensive and deep, it is high and brilliant. It is because it is extensive and deep that it contains all things. It is because it is high and brilliant that it overshadows all things. It is because it is infinite and lasting that it can complete all things. In being extensive and deep, it is a counterpart of earth. In being high and brilliant, it is a counterpart of heaven. In being infinite and lasting, it is unlimited. Such being its nature, it becomes prominent without any display, produces changes without motion, and accomplishes its ends without action.

28

꒚

Mencius

THE MENCIUS

In China, for the century and a half after the death of Confucius (479 B.C.), the rivalry among numerous feudal principalities resolved itself and became a struggle for supremacy among a handful of larger states. This was the aptly named Warring States Period of Chinese history. Yet this time of ruthless leaders, who fit the model defined by Machiavelli in Italy eighteen centuries later (see Volume 3), produced one of the most effective spokespersons for humane and ethical government in the history of the world's political thought—Mencius. Mencius himself declared that "the people have never suffered more under tyrannical government than today." The realm of political thought diverged into a wide spectrum of doctrines and philosophical rivalries regarding government and society. While the fifth through third centuries B.C. were the Warring States Period in the life of the state, they were also the period of the Hundred Schools in the history of Chinese philosophy. This name signifies not a literal number of schools that existed at the time, but rather a period of remarkable creativity in Chinese thought. Just as the roughly contemporary period in the Greek world laid the foundation for most subsequent Western philosophy, the period of the Hundred Schools is the basis from which Chinese culture and life have been enriched ever since.

Like Confucius, Mencius was a wandering scholar and teacher who spent his adult life in a vain effort to influence one or another of the feudal courts. We know less about Mencius than we know about Confucius, but Mencius probably lived between 371 and 289 B.C., and he was a pupil of a man who studied under Confucius's grandson Tzu-ssu. Western scholars Latinized his name, Meng Tzu (master Meng), into the form we now use, Mencius. What we know of his thought is almost entirely contained in a book of his sayings, The Mencius, evidently compiled by his disciples. Mencius's arguments use more analogy and anecdote than do Confucius's Analects. As the result of his own style of teaching and of the *literary skill of those who set down and edited his thought,* The Mencius *stands as one of the most effective pieces of prose writing in all of Chinese literature, undoubtedly contributing to its lasting influence.*

Clearly, he is the greatest figure in the Confucian tradition after Confucius himself. It is Mencius who makes the classic argument that human nature is inherently *inclined to goodness, and that government only deserves to survive if it has a ruler who reflects the principles of human-heartedness* (jen) *and righteousness* (i). *Although this "idealistic Confucianism" became, in time, the central and official doctrine of China's Confucian state and society, it emerged in Mencius's teaching from controversy with other philosophers from among the Hundred Schools. Confucius's own views on human nature, as seen in* The Analects, *are by no means as clear-cut as Mencius believed them to be.*

Mencius argued that human thought and spirit are located in the heart, which is naturally disposed to an innocent goodness, and that the erosion of this goodness as it encounters the evils of the world can be checked and even reversed by good example and education. "A great man," he says, "is one who retains the heart of a newborn babe." Mencius felt that this inclination toward righteousness and benevolence is the property of all mankind, and appears wherever family relationships are correct—sons are loving and subordinate to fathers, wives to husbands, younger brothers to elder brothers. But the superiors in these obviously hierarchical relationships must respond with love, compassion, and responsibility. The rightly ordered family was, in Mencius's view, both the basis for society and the model for the state. The paternalism of the Confucian/Mencian family became the justification for the superior position in society of the "gentleman," and for the benevolent exercise of power by the ruler.

This paternalism, the basis of a ruler's claim to govern with the "mandate of heaven," carried responsibilities that reached well beyond the ruler's personal moral excellence. Like a father, the ruler had to educate his children (i.e., his subjects), make sure they were not hungry or ragged or homeless, and were not engaged in any but the most necessary warfare. Such a ruler would win the love, loyalty, and obedience of his subjects as no tyrant ever could. Relying even more heavily than Confucius on the figures of China's early history, Mencius repeatedly cited such "sage rulers" as Yao, Shun, and the self-effacing sage counselor the Duke of Chou (see Selection 10, The Book of History*). The reign of these "sage rulers" Mencius offered as proof that humane rule not only is possible, but is the only truly successful basis for governance. He also cited, however, those kings of the past who forfeited the love and loyalty of their subjects through tyranny or moral degeneracy, who lost the mandate of heaven and destroyed their dynasties. To Mencius, it was clear that rulers who departed from the path of humane government deserved to be overthrown: in short, he argued that a right of revolution resided with the people.*

BOOK I, PART A
Chapter 1

Mencius went to see King Hui of Liang. "Sir," said the king, "You have come all this distance, thinking nothing of a thousand *li*.[1] You must surely have some way of profiting my state?"

"Your Majesty," answered Mencius, "what is the point of mentioning the word *profit?* All that matters is that there should be benevolence and rightness. If Your Majesty says, 'How can I profit my state?' and the counselors say 'How can I profit my family?' and the gentlemen and commoners say, 'How can I profit my person?' then those above and those below will be trying to profit at the expense of one another and the state will be imperiled. . . . [I]f profit is put before rightness, there is no satisfaction short of total usurpation. No benevolent man ever abandons his parents, and no dutiful man ever puts his prince last. Perhaps you will now endorse what I have said, 'All that matters is that there should be benevolence and rightness. What is the point of mentioning the word *profit?*'"

●   ●   ●

Chapter 7

King Hsuan of Ch'i asked . . . "How virtuous must a man be before he can become a true king?"

[Mencius answered] "He becomes a true king by bringing peace to the people. This is something no one can stop."

"Can someone like myself bring peace to the people?"

"Yes."

"How do you know that I can?"

"I heard the following from Hu He: The king [Hsuan] was sitting in the upper part of the hall and someone led an ox through the lower part. The king noticed this and said, 'Where is the ox going?' 'The blood of the ox is to be used for consecrating a new bell.' 'Spare it. I cannot bear to see it shrinking in fear, like an innocent man going to the place of execution.' 'In that case, should the ceremony be abandoned?' 'That is out of the question. Use a lamb instead.' I wonder if this is true?"

"It is."

"The heart behind your action is sufficient to enable you to become a true king. The people all thought that you grudged the expense, but, for my part, I have no doubt that you were moved by pity for the animal." . . .

From *Mencius*, translated by D. C. Lau (Penguin Classics, 1970), copyright © D. C. Lau, 1970. Reprinted with permission of the publisher.

[1]About a third of a mile.

The king laughed and said, "What was really in my mind, I wonder? It is not true that I grudged the expense, but I *did* use a lamb instead of an ox. I suppose it was only natural that the people should have thought me miserly."

[Mencius said] "There is no harm in this. It is the way of a benevolent man. You saw the ox but not the lamb. . . . Your bounty is sufficient to reach the animals, yet the benefits of your government fail to reach the people. That a feather is not lifted is because one fails to make the effort; that a carload of firewood is not seen is because one fails to use one's eyes. Similarly, that peace is not brought to the people is because you fail to practice kindness. Hence your failure to become a true king is due to a refusal to act, not to an inability to act."

BOOK I, PART B
Chapter 8

King Hsuan of Ch'i asked, "Is it true that T'ang banished Chieh and King Wu marched against Tchou?"[2]

"It is so recorded," answered Mencius.

"Is regicide permissible?"

"A man who mutilates benevolence is a mutilator, while one who cripples rightness is a crippler. He who is both a mutilator and a crippler is an 'outcast.' I have indeed heard of the punishment of the 'outcast Tchou,' but I have not heard of any regicide."

BOOK II, PART A
Chapter 6

Mencius said, "No man is devoid of a heart sensitive to the suffering of others. Such a sensitive heart was possessed by the former kings and this manifested itself in compassionate government. With such a sensitive heart behind compassionate government, it was as easy to govern the empire as rolling it on your palm.

"My reason for saying that no man is devoid of a heart sensitive to the suffering of others is this. Suppose a man were, all of a sudden, to see a young child on the verge of falling into a well. He would certainly be moved to compassion, not because he wanted to get into the good graces of the parents, nor because he wished to win the praise of his fellow villagers or friends, nor yet because he disliked the cry of the child. From this it can be seen that whoever is devoid of the heart of compassion is not human, whoever is devoid of the heart of shame is not human, whoever is devoid of the heart of courtesy and modesty is not human, and whoever is devoid of the heart of right and wrong is not human. The heart

---

[2]Episodes in the traditional history of the earlier dynasties when tyrants had been forcibly overthrown.

of compassion is the germ of benevolence; the heart of shame, of dutifulness; the heart of courtesy and modesty, of observance of the rites; the heart of right and wrong, of wisdom. Man has these four germs just as he has four limbs. For a man possessing these four germs to deny his own potentialities is for him to cripple himself; for him to deny the potentialities of his prince is to cripple his prince. If a man is able to develop all these four germs that he possesses, it will be like a fire starting up or a spring coming through. When these are fully developed, he can take under his protection the whole realm within the four seas, but if he fails to develop them, he will not be able even to serve his parents."

BOOK III, PART A
Chapter 3

The Duke [Wen of T'eng] sent Pi Chan to ask about the well-field system.[3]

"Your prince," said Mencius, "is going to practice benevolent government and has chosen you for this mission. You must do your best. Benevolent government must begin with land demarcation. When boundaries are not properly drawn, the division of land according to the well-field system and the yield of grain used for paying officials cannot be equitable. For this reason, despotic rulers and corrupt officials always neglect the boundaries. Once the boundaries are correctly fixed, there will be no difficulty in settling the distribution of land and the determination of emolument.

"T'eng is limited in territory. Nevertheless, there will be men in authority and there will be the common people. Without the former, there would be none to rule over the latter; without the latter, there would be none to support the former. . . . Neither in burying the dead, nor in changing his abode, does a man go beyond the confines of his village. If those who own land within each *ching* befriend one another both at home and abroad, help each other to keep watch, and succor each other in illness, they will live in love and harmony. A *ching* is a piece of land measuring one *li* square, and each *ching* consists of nine hundred *mu*. Of these, the central plot of one hundred *mu* belongs to the state, while the other eight plots of one hundred *mu* each are held by eight families who share the duty of caring for the plot owned by the state. Only when they have done this

---

[3]Mencius believed that some of the ancient sage kings used a method of agricultural land distribution and taxation in which each plot of land one *li* square was subdivided into a grid resembling the Chinese character *ching*, which means "a well." The eight plots along the edges were allotted to peasant families, all of whom worked the center plot cooperatively for the benefit of the king. The historical use of the well-field system is problematic, but Mencius urged its adoption as a means to bring about fair distribution of enough land to ensure a decent livelihood for the people.

duty dare they turn to their own affairs. This is what sets the common people apart.

"This is a rough outline. As for embellishments, I leave them to your prince and yourself."

Chapter 4

[Mencius was in conversation with a man who argued that the prince should grow and prepare his own food, in order to avoid inflicting hardship on his people. Mencius led him to agree that even farmers buy goods produced by others, opening the way to the idea of a desirable specialization of labor.]

"Now, is ruling the empire such an exception that it can be combined with the work of tilling the land? There are affairs of great men, and there are affairs of small men. Moreover, it is necessary for each man to use the products of all the hundred crafts. If everyone must make everything he uses, the empire will be led along the path of incessant toil. Hence it is said, 'There are those who use their minds and there are those who use their muscles. The former rule; the latter are ruled. Those who rule are supported by those who are ruled.'[4] This is a principle accepted by the whole empire."

BOOK III, PART B
Chapter 8

Tai Ying-chih said, "We are unable in the present year to change over to a tax of one in ten and to abolish custom and market duties. What would you think if we were to make some reductions and wait till next year before putting that change fully into effect?"

"Here is a man," said Mencius, "who appropriates one of his neighbor's chickens every day. Someone tells him, 'This is not how a gentleman behaves.' He answers, 'May I reduce it to one chicken every month and wait until next year to stop altogether?'

"When one realizes that something is morally wrong, one should stop it as soon as possible. Why wait for next year?"

Chapter 9

"No sage kings have appeared since . . . [the era of Kings Wen and Wu]. Feudal lords do as they please; people with no official position are uninhibited in the

---

[4]For better than two thousand years, this passage was the standard justification for the existence and authority of a class of scholar–officials supported by the great mass of peasants and artisans. In the mid-twentieth century this bifurcation between intellectuals and workers became a target of the Communist effort to reshape Chinese society, and was one of the leading reasons for the categorical denunciation of Confucianism.

expression of their views, and the words of Yang Chu and Mo Ti fill the empire.[5] . . . Yang advocates everyone for himself, which amounts to a denial of one's prince; Mo advocates love without discrimination, which amounts to a denial of one's father. To ignore one's father on the one hand, and one's prince on the other, is to be no different from the beasts. Kung-ming Yi said 'There is fat meat in your kitchen and there are well-fed horses in your stables, yet the people look hungry and in the outskirts of cities men drop dead from starvation. This is to show animals the way to devour men.' If the way of Yang and Mo does not subside and the way to Confucius is not proclaimed, the people will be deceived by heresies and the path of morality will be blocked. When the path of morality is blocked, then we show animals the way to devour men, and sooner or later it will come to men devouring men. Therefore I am apprehensive. I wish to safeguard the way of the former sages against the onslaughts of Yang and Mo and to banish excessive views. Then advocates of heresies will not be able to rise. For what arises in the mind will interfere with policy, and what shows itself in policy will interfere with practice. Were there once more a sage, he would surely agree with what I have said." . . .

BOOK IV, PART A
Chapter 27

Mencius said, "The content of benevolence is the serving of one's parents; the content of dutifulness is obedience to one's elder brothers; the content of wisdom is to understand these two and hold fast to them; the content of the rites is the regulation and adornment of them; the content of music is the joy that comes of delighting in them. When joy arises how can one stop it? And when one cannot stop it, then one begins to dance with one's feet and wave one's arms without knowing it."

---

[5]Yang Chu was a fourth-century philosopher. His reputed remark that he would not give a hair of his body to gain the whole empire was in keeping with an egotistical attitude that held that one should do nothing to harm or diminish one's own life. Mencius misrepresented this as a selfish argument that one should not give a hair of one's body to save the empire. Mo Ti, or Mo Tzu, whose life roughly spanned the years between Confucius's death and Mencius's birth, taught a doctrine of universal love, not restricted by the Confucian emphasis on familial obligations. In this passage Mencius is guilty of implying that the social injustices of his time are somehow the fault of these philosophers from the previous century, largely on the grounds that they were heretics, i.e., that they failed to follow the Confucian way.

BOOK IV, PART B
Chapter 3

Mencius said to King Hsuan of Ch'i, "If a prince treats his subjects as his hands and feet, they will treat him as their belly and heart. If he treats them as his horses and hounds, they will treat him as a stranger. If he treats them as mud and weeds, they will treat him as an enemy."

Chapter 8

Mencius said, "Only when a man will not do some things is he capable of doing great things."

BOOK V, PART A
Chapter 5

Wang Chan said, "Is it true that Yao gave the empire to Shun?"

"No," said Mencius, "the emperor cannot give the empire to another."

"In that case, who gave the empire to Shun?"

"Heaven gave it to him."

"You say heaven gave it to him. Does this mean that heaven gave him detailed and minute instructions?"

"No. Heaven does not speak but reveals itself through its acts and deeds."

"How does heaven do this?"

"The emperor can recommend a man to heaven but he cannot make heaven give this man the empire; just as a feudal lord can recommend a man to the emperor but he cannot make the emperor bestow a fief on him. . . . In antiquity Yao recommended Shun to heaven and heaven accepted him; he presented him to the people and the people accepted him. Hence I said, 'Heaven does not speak but reveals itself by its acts and deeds.'"

"May I ask how he was accepted by heaven when recommended to it and how he was accepted by the people when presented to them?"

"When he was put in charge of sacrifices, the hundred gods enjoyed them. This showed that heaven accepted him. When he was put in charge of affairs, they were kept in order and the people were content. This showed that the people accepted him. Heaven gave it to him, and the people gave it to him. Hence I said, 'The emperor cannot give the empire to another.' Shun assisted Yao for twenty-eight years. This is something that could not be brought about by man, but by heaven alone. Yao died, and after the mourning period of three years, Shun withdrew to the south of Nan Ho, leaving Yao's son in possession of the field, yet the feudal lords of the empire coming to pay homage and those who were in litigation went to Shun, not to Yao's son, and ballad singers sang the praises of Shun, not of Yao's son. Hence I said, 'It was brought about by heaven.' Only then did Shun go to the Central Kingdoms and ascend the imperial throne. If he had just moved into Yao's palace and ousted his son, it would have been usurpation of the empire, not receiving it from heaven. The *T'ai shih*[6] says, 'Heaven sees with the eyes of its people. Heaven hears with the ears of its people.' This describes well what I meant."

BOOK VI, PART A
Chapter 8

Mencius said, "There was a time when the trees were luxuriant on the Ox Mountain. As it is on the outskirts of a great metropolis, the trees are constantly lopped by axes. Is it any wonder that they are no longer fine? With the respite they get in the day and in the night, and the moistening by the rain and dew, there is certainly no lack of new shoots coming out, but then the cattle and sheep come to graze upon the mountain. That is why it is as bald as it is. People, seeing only its baldness, tend to think that it never had any trees. But can this possibly be the nature of the mountain? Can what is in man be completely lacking in moral inclinations? A man's letting go of his true heart is like the case of the trees and the axes. When the trees are lopped day after day is it any wonder that they are no longer fine? If, in spite of the respite a man gets in the day and in the night and of the effect of the morning air on him, scarcely any of his likes and dislikes resemble those of other men, it is because what he does in the course of the day once again dissipates what he has gained. If this dissipation happens repeatedly, then the influence of the air in the night will no longer be able to preserve what was originally in him, and when that happens, the man is not far removed from an animal. Others, seeing his resemblance to an animal, will be led to think that he never had any native endowment. But can that be what a man is genuinely like? Hence, given the right nourishment there is nothing that will not grow, and deprived of it there is nothing that will not wither away. Confucius said, 'Hold on to it and it will remain; let go of it and it will disappear. One never knows the time it comes or goes, neither does one know the direction.' It is perhaps to the heart this refers."

---

[6]A portion of *The Book of History* that is now lost.

29

𝕰

Hsun Tzu

THE HSUN TZU

By the time Confucianism became the official philosophy of the Chinese state in the late second century B.C., the "idealistic Confucianism" of Mencius (Selection 28) had become the dominant version of the Sage's teaching. Over the next twenty-one centuries of the Confucian state and society, Mencius's interpretation held the commanding place. This fact tended to obscure the intellectual strength and prominence of other early schools of Confucian thought—none more significant in its day than the "realistic" or "naturalistic" Confucianism (given its classic statement by Hsun Tzu). Biographical facts regarding Master Hsun are limited. He was born in the small state of Chao (in what is now Shansi Province) and, although dates are uncertain, he evidently flourished between 298 and 238 B.C. It is believed that he was a wandering scholar who held minor positions in states other than his own. Other evidence indicates that he taught the last two great Legalist philosophers, Han Fei Tzu and Li Ssu, whose fatal association apparently began when they were fellow students under Hsun Tzu (see Selection 32).

The basic disagreement between Hsun Tzu and Mencius lay in their almost diametrically opposed assumptions about human nature. Confucius himself had relatively little to say on this issue, leaving his followers in later generations to let the logic of their inclinations drive them to extreme positions. The thirty-two chapters of The Hsun Tzu show a keen, logical mind at work on a number of practical, as well as philosophical, issues. Chapter 23, "The Nature of Man Is Evil," excerpted here, deals most directly and extensively with the question of human nature as the starting point of moral philosophy. At first, Hsun Tzu seems to be repetitious (to the point of a counter-productive tedium) in his assertion that "The nature of man is evil" and "his goodness is the result of his activity," a phrase repeated more than a dozen times in this selection. But careful reading reveals that he builds a complex argument, like the framing of a house, and that *each repetition of "the nature of man is evil" is another nail that holds the structure in place.*

His choice of the word evil *may strike the reader as too strong for the case he actually makes, implying a distinct desire to do wrong. However, he seems to be asserting the existence of a natural human inclination to self-gratification, unbound by consideration for the harm we may do to others, something like Sigmund Freud's view of the natural self. In the absence of instruction, discipline, and guidance, this natural amorality leads to evil actions. Hsun Tzu is no cynic, though. As a good Confucian, he believes there is good in the world, and the virtues of piety and righteousness are very real for him. But he rejects and clearly fears the consequences of Mencius's doctrine of innate human kindness and goodness. Hsun Tzu believes that kindness and goodness are essential qualities of the human character, but they are* acquired *qualities: "Man's goodness is the result of his activity."*

Hsun Tzu was more influential than Mencius in the century after his death, but his association with the hated Legalists, especially with Li Ssu, who was first minister under the tyrant emperor of the Ch'in Dynasty, was probably one reason why his writing fell into disfavor. It may be, too, that his harsh appraisal of human nature was simply less congenial to the Chinese spirit than Mencius's cheerful assumption that, at heart, we are all good.

CHAPTER 23
The Nature of Man Is Evil

The nature of man is evil; his goodness is the result of his activity. Now, man's inborn nature is to seek for gain. If this tendency is followed, strife and rapacity result and deference and compliance disappear. By inborn nature one is envious and hates others. If these tendencies are followed, injury and destruction result and loyalty and faithfulness disappear. By inborn nature one possesses the desires of ear and eye and likes sound and beauty. If these tendencies are followed, lewdness and licentiousness result, and the pattern and order of propriety and righteousness disappear. Therefore to follow man's nature and his feelings will inevitably result in strife and rapacity, combine with rebellion and disorder, and end in violence. Therefore there must be the civilizing influence of teachers and laws and the guidance of propriety and righteousness, and then it will result in deference and compliance, combine with pattern and order, and end in discipline. From this point of view, it is clear that the nature of man is evil and that his goodness is the result of activity.

Crooked wood must be heated and bent before it becomes straight. Blunt metal must be ground and whetted before it becomes sharp. Now the nature of man is evil. It must depend on teachers and laws to become correct and achieve propriety and righteousness and then it becomes disciplined. Without teachers and laws, man is unbalanced, off the track, incorrect. Without propriety and righteousness, there will be rebellion, disorder, and chaos. The sage-kings of antiquity, knowing that the nature of man is evil, and that it is unbalanced, off the track, rebellious, disorderly, and undisciplined, created the rules of propriety and righteousness and instituted laws and systems in order to correct man's feelings, transform them, and direct them so that they all may become disciplined and conform with the way. Now people who are influenced by teachers and laws, accumulate literature and knowledge, and follow propriety and righteousness are superior men, whereas those who give reign to their feelings, enjoy indulgence, and violate propriety and righteousness are inferior men. From this point of view, it is clear that the nature of man is evil and that his goodness is the result of his activity.

Mencius said, "Man learns because his nature is good." This is not true. He did not know the nature of man and did not understand the distinction between man's nature and his effort. Man's nature is the product of nature; it cannot be learned and cannot be worked for. Propriety and righteousness are produced by the sage. They can be learned by men and can be accomplished through work. What is in man but cannot be learned or worked for is his nature. What is in him and can be learned or accomplished through work is what can be achieved through activity. This is the difference between human nature and human activity. Now by nature man's eye can see and his ear hear. But the clarity of vision is not outside his eye and the distinctness of hearing is not outside his ear. It is clear that clear vision and distinct hearing cannot be learned. Mencius said, "The nature of man is good; it becomes evil because man destroys his original nature." This is a mistake. By nature man departs from his primitive character and capacity as soon as he is born, and he is bound to destroy it. From this point of view, it is clear that man's nature is evil.

By the original goodness of human nature is meant that man does not depart from his primitive character but makes it beautiful, and does not depart from his original capacity but utilizes it, so that beauty being inherent in his primitive character and goodness being inherent in his will are like clear vision being inherent in the eye and distinct hearing being inherent in the ear. Hence we say that the eye is clear and the ear is sharp. Now by nature man desires repletion when hungry, desires warmth when cold, and desires rest when tired. This is man's natural feeling. But now when a man is hungry and sees some elders before him, he does not eat ahead of him but yields to them. When he is tired he dares not seek rest because he wants to take over the work of the elders. The son yielding to or taking over the work of his father, and the younger brother yielding to or taking over the work of his elder brother—these two lines of action are contrary to original nature and violate natural feeling. Nevertheless, the way of filial piety is the pattern and order of propriety and righteousness. If one follows his natural feelings, he will have no deference or compliance. Deference and compliance are contrary to his natural feelings. From this point of view, it is clear that man's nature is evil and that his goodness is the result of his activity.

Someone may ask, "If man's nature is evil, whence come propriety and righteousness?" I answer that all propriety and righteousness are results of the activity of sages and not originally produced from man's nature. The potter pounds the clay and makes the vessel. This being the case, the vessel is the product of the artisan's activity and not the original product of man's nature. The artisan hews a piece of wood and makes a vessel. This being the case, the vessel is the product of the artisan's activity and not the original product of man's nature. The sages gathered together their ideas and thoughts and became familiar with activity, facts, and principles, and thus produced propriety and righteousness, and instituted laws and systems. This being the case, propriety and righteousness and laws and systems are the products of the activity of the sages and not the original products of man's nature.

As to the eye desiring color, the ear desiring sound, the mouth desiring flavor, the heart desiring gain, and the body desiring pleasure and ease—all these are products of man's original nature and feelings. They are natural reactions to stimuli and do not require any work to be produced. But if the reaction is not naturally produced by the stimulus but requires work before it can be produced, then it is the result of activity. Here lies the evidence of the difference between what is produced by man's nature and what is produced by his effort. Therefore the sages transformed man's nature and aroused him to activity. As activity was aroused, propriety and righteousness were produced, and as propriety and righteousness were produced, laws and systems were instituted. This being the case, propriety, righteousness, laws, and systems are all products of the sages. In his nature the sage is common with and not different from ordinary people. It is in his effort that he is different from and superior to them.

It is the original nature and feelings of man to love and profit and seek gain. Suppose some brothers are to divide their property. If they follow their natural feelings, they will love profit and seek gain, and thus will do violence to each other and grab the property. But if they are transformed by the civilizing influence of the pattern and order of propriety and righteousness, they will even yield to outsiders. Therefore, brothers will quarrel if they follow their original nature and feeling but, if they are transformed by righteousness and propriety, they will yield to outsiders.

People desire to be good because their nature is evil. If one has little, he wants abundance. If he is ugly, he wants good looks. If his circumstances are narrow, he wants them to be broad. If poor, he wants to be rich. And if he is in a low position, he wants a high position. If he does not have it himself, he will seek it outside. If he is rich, he does not desire more wealth, and if he is in a high position, he does not desire more power. If he has it himself, he will not seek it outside. From this point of view, it is clear that people desire to be good because their nature is evil.

Now by nature a man does not originally possess propriety and righteousness; hence he makes strong effort to learn and seeks to have them. By nature he does not know propriety and righteousness; hence he thinks and deliberates and seeks to know them. Therefore, by what is inborn alone, man will not have or know propriety and righteousness. There will be disorder if man is without propriety and righteousness. There will be violence if he does not know propriety and righteousness. Consequently by what is inborn alone, disorder and violence are within man himself. From this point of view, it is clear that the nature of man is evil and that his goodness is the result of activity.

Mencius said, "The nature of man is good." I say that this is not true. By goodness at any time in any place is meant true principles and peaceful order, and by evil is meant imbalance, violence, and disorder. This is the distinction between good and evil. Now do we honestly regard man's nature as characterized by true principles and peaceful order? If so, why are sages necessary and why are propriety and righteousness necessary? What possible improvement can sages make on true principles and peaceful order?

Now this is not the case. Man's nature is evil. Therefore the sages of antiquity, knowing that man's nature is evil, that it is unbalanced and incorrect, and that it is violent, disorderly, and undisciplined, established the authority of rulers to govern the people, set forth clearly propriety and righteousness to transform them, instituted laws and governmental measures to rule them, and made punishment severe to restrain them, so that all will result in good order and be in accord with goodness. Such is the government of sage-kings and the transforming influence of propriety and righteousness.

But suppose we try to remove the authority of the ruler, do away with the transforming influence of propriety and righteousness, discard the rule of laws and governmental measure, do away with the restraint of punishment, and stand and see how people of the world deal with one another. In this situation the strong would injure the weak and rob them, and the many would do violence to the few and shout them down. The whole world would be in violence and disorder and all would perish in an instant. From this point of view, it is clear that man's nature is evil and that his goodness is the result of his activity.

The man versed in ancient matters will certainly support them with evidences from the present, and he who is versed in the principles of nature will certainly support them with evidences from the world of men. In any discussion, the important things are discrimination and evidence. One can then sit down and talk about things, propagate them, and put them into practice. But now Mencius said that man's nature is good. He had neither discrimination nor evidence. He sat down and talked about the matter but rose and could neither propagate it nor put it into practice. Is this not going too far? Therefore if man's nature is good, sage-kings can be done away with and propriety and righteousness can be stopped. But if his nature is evil, sage-kings are to be followed and propriety and righteousness are to be greatly valued. For bending came into existence because there was crooked wood, the carpenter's square and ruler came into existence because things were not straight, and the authority of rule is instituted and propriety and righteousness are made clear because man's nature is evil. From this point of view, it is clear that man's nature is evil and that his goodness is the result of his activity. Straight wood does not depend on bending to become straight; it is straight by nature. But crooked wood must be bent and heated before it becomes straight because by nature it is not straight. Now, the nature of man is evil. It has to depend on the government of sage-kings and the transforming influence of propriety and right-eousness, and then all will result in good order and be in accord with goodness. From this point of view, it is clear that man's nature is evil and that his goodness is the result of his activity.

The questioner may say, "It is by the nature of man that propriety and right-eousness can be produced through accumulated effort and hence the sages can pro-duce them." I answer that this is not true. The potter pounds the clay and pro-duces the piece of pottery. Is the pottery inherent in the nature of the potter? The artisan hews wood and produces a vessel. Is the vessel inherent in the nature of the artisan? What the sages have done to propriety and righteousness is analogous to the potter's pounding and producing the pottery. This being the case, is it by the original nature of man that propriety and righteousness are produced through accumulated effort? With reference to the nature of man, it is the same in sage Emperors Yao and Shun, wicked King Chieh, and robber Chih. It is the same in the superior or inferior man. If propriety and righteousness are products of accu-mulated effort and to be regarded as inherent in man's nature, then why are Yao and Sage-King Yu highly honored, and why is the superior man highly honored? Yao, Yu, and the superior man are highly honored because they can transform nature and arouse effort. As effort is aroused, propriety and righteousness are pro-duced. Thus the relation between the sages and propriety and righteousness, pro-duced through accumulated effort, is like the potter pounding clay to produce the pottery. From this point of view, is it by the nature of man that propriety and right-eousness are produced through accumulated effort? Chieh, Chih, and the inferior man are despised because they give rein to their nature, follow their feelings, and enjoy indulgence, and lead to the greed for gain, to quarrels and rapacity. It is clear that man's nature is evil and that his goodness is the result of his activity.

Heaven is not partial to Tseng, Ch'ien, and Hsiao-i and negligent to the com-mon multitude. Then why did Tseng, Ch'ien, and Hsiao-i alone abundantly demonstrate the actuality of filial piety and preserve its good name? It is because they observed propriety and righteousness to the fullest extent. Heaven is not partial to the people of Ch'i and Lu and negligent to the people of Ch'in. Then why is it that in the righteous relation between father and son and the distinction of function between husband and wife, the people of Ch'in are inferior to those of Ch'i and Lu in filial piety and in the mutual respect between husband and wife? It is because the people of Ch'in give rein to their nature and feelings, enjoy indulgence, and neglect propriety and righteousness. Is it because their natures are different?

"Any man in the street can become Sage-King Yu." What does this ancient saying mean? I say that Yu became Sage-King Yu because he practiced humanity, righteousness, laws, and correct principles. This shows that these can be known and practiced. Every man in the street possesses the faculty to know them and the capacity to practice them. This being the case, it is clear that every man can be Yu.

Shall we consider humanity, righteousness, laws, and correct principles as basically impossible to be known or practiced? If so, even Yu could not have known or practiced them. Shall we consider every man in the street to be without the faculty to know them or the capacity to practice them? If so, at home he would not be able to know the righteous relation between father and son and outside he would not be able to know the correct relation between ruler and minister. But this is not the case. Every man in the street is capable of knowing the righteous relation between father and son at home and the correct relation between ruler and minister outside. It is clear, then, that the faculty to know them and the capacity to practice them are found in every man in the street. Now, if every man's faculty to know and capacity to practice are applied to the fact that humanity and righteousness can be known and practiced, it is clear that he can become Yu. If in his practices and studies day after day for a long time, he concentrates his mind, has unity of purpose, thinks thoroughly and discriminately, and accumulates goodness without stop, he can then be as wise as the gods, and form a trinity with heaven and earth. Thus the sage is a man who has reached this state through accumulated effort.

Someone may say, "The sage can reach that state through accumulated effort, but not everyone can do so. Why?" I answer that he can, but he does not do it. An inferior man can become a superior man, but he does not want to. A superior man can become an inferior man, but he does not want to. It is not that they cannot become each other. They do not do so because they do not want to. It is possible for every man to become Yu, but it does not follow that every man in the street is able actually to do so. However, the fact that he is not able actually to do so does not destroy the possibility of his doing so. It is possible for a man with feet to walk all over the world and yet so far there has not been any who is able actually to do so. It is possible for the artisan, farmer, or merchant to exchange their professions, and yet there has not been any who is able actually to do so. From this point of view, what is possible is not the same as what is able actually to be done. But not being able actually to be done does not destroy the possibility. There is a great difference between what is possible on the one hand, and what is able actually to be done, on the other. It is clear that they are not interchangeable. . . .

30

❧

Lao Tzu

THE TAO TE CHING

The Tao Te Ching, *usually translated as the "classic of the way and its power,"*
is one of the most beautiful and significant, but also one of the most enig-
matic, works of Chinese literature. It is a collection of eighty-one "chapters," each
one a poem, sometimes with interlarded prose passages. Together they embody
most of the ideas that lie at the heart of what has come to be called Taoism.
Virtually all Chinese philosophers spoke of and claimed to have discovered the
Tao or "way," but those who appropriated the title of Tao Chia (the "school of
the way") believed that its teachings brought one into proper harmony with the
force that animates all nature.

As with so many of the seminal writings from the period of the Hundred
Schools, authorship and date of composition of the Tao Te Ching are uncertain
and have become wrapped in myth. Tradition credits the poems to one Lao Tan
or Lao Tzu (the "old master" or "old philosopher"), a slightly older contemporary
of Confucius who served as archivist to the court of the Chou Dynasty in the late
sixth century B.C. Supposedly, Lao Tzu was about to leave China and "retire from
the world," but was persuaded by the Keeper of the Western Pass to set down his
thoughts before departing. In a short time he wrote all the "five thousand char-
acters" that make up this classic. Scholars for the past two millennia have been
skeptical about the historical reality of Lao Tzu and many have regarded him as
a mythical figure, but the association between the name of Lao Tzu and this book
is so pervasive as to create that familiar interchangeability of author with title,
so that we often find the Tao Te Ching referred to simply as The Lao Tzu.

Some strands of thought that make up the Tao Te Ching probably do come
down from the sixth or fifth century, but the book as we now know it seems more
like an anthology, probably collected in the late fourth or early third century B.C.,
representing segments written at different times and by different hands. Taoism,
a philosophy that became a religion, then became intertwined with Buddhism,

and which still exists in institutional form in China, has seen myriad reinterpre-
tations of the Tao Te Ching. *Its central theme is the all-embracing, transcendent*
nature of the Tao, *or the "one," a force that preceded the cosmos, created it,*
and sustains it. The Tao *is not its true name, nor can we describe it, because lan-*
guage is merely a part of creation, and cannot encompass it. The significance of
words in the Tao Te Ching *lies not in descriptions, but in the power of beautiful*
poetry to evoke a sense of the mystery of the Tao, *and to provoke reflection on the*
reordering of personal and public life necessary to reestablish a primal harmony
between mankind and nature.

   Taoism provided a useful counterbalance to the moral rigidity, formalism,
and social activism engendered by some forms of Confucianism. It appealed to
those who wished to achieve the peace and empowerment that comes from mov-
ing with the flow of the natural universe, rather than struggling against it. In
time, as Taoism came to be woven into the fabric of China's intellectual and spir-
itual life, it became a commonplace observation that a public man was "a
Confucian in office and a Taoist in retirement."

CHAPTER I

The way that can be told of is not the unvarying way;
The names that can be named are not unvarying names.
It was from the nameless that heaven and earth sprang;
The named is but the mother that rears the ten thousand creatures,[1]
      each after its kind.
Truly, "Only he that rids himself forever of desire can see the secret
      essences";
He that has never rid himself of desire can see only the outcomes.
These two things issued from the same mold, but nevertheless are
      different in name.
This "same mold" we can but call the mystery,
Or rather the "darker than any mystery,"
The doorway whence issue all secret essences.

●　　●　　●

From: Arthur Waley, *The Way and Its Power: A Study of the Tao Te Ching and Its Place in Chinese Thought* (New York: Grove Weidenfeld, 1958), pp. 141, 145, 149, 151, 155, 165–166, 174, 178, 183, 187, 192, 197, 215, 224, 238, 243.

[1]The physical world, especially human beings.

CHAPTER 3

If we stop looking for "persons of superior morality" to put in power, there will be no more jealousies among the people. If we cease to set store by products which are hard to get, there will be no more thieves. If the people never see such things as excite desire, their hearts will remain placid and undisturbed. Therefore the Sage rules

> By emptying their hearts
> And filling their bellies,
> Weakening their intelligence
> And toughening their sinews
> Ever striving to make the people knowledgeless and desireless.

Indeed he sees to it that if there be any who have knowledge, they dare not interfere. Yet through his actionless activity all things are duly regulated.

● ● ●

CHAPTER 6

> The valley spirit never dies.
> It is named the mysterious female,
> And the doorway of the mysterious female
> Is the base from which heaven and earth sprang.
> It is there within us all the while;
> Draw upon it as you will, it never runs dry.

● ● ●

CHAPTER 8

The highest good is like that of water. The goodness of water is that it benefits the ten thousand creatures; yet itself does not scramble, but is content with the places that all men disdain.[2] It is this that makes water so near the way.

> And if men think the ground the best place for building a house upon,
> If among thoughts they value those that are profound,
> If in friendship they value gentleness,
> In words, truth; in government, good order;
> In deeds, effectiveness; in actions, timelines—
> In each case it is because they prefer what does not lead to strife,
> And therefore does not go amiss.

---

[2]That is, water seeks the lowest level, while men scramble for the heights.

● ● ●

CHAPTER 11

We put thirty spokes together and call it a wheel;
But it is on the space where there is nothing that the usefulness of the
     wheel depends.
We turn clay to make a vessel;
But it is on the space where there is nothing that the usefulness of the
     vessel depends.
We pierce doors and windows to make a house;
And it is on these spaces where there is nothing that the usefulness of
     the house depends.
Therefore, just as we take advantage of what is, we should recognize the
     usefulness of what is not.

● ● ●

CHAPTER 18

It was when the great way declined
That human kindness and morality arose;
It was when intelligence and knowledge appeared
That the great artifice began.
It was when the six near ones were no longer at peace
That there was talk of "dutiful sons";[3]
Not till fatherland was dark with strife
Did we hear of "loyal slaves."[4]

CHAPTER 19

Banish wisdom, discard knowledge,
And the people will be benefited a hundredfold.
Banish human kindness, discard morality,
And the people will be dutiful and compassionate.
Banish skill, discard profit,
And thieves and robbers will disappear.
If when these three things are done they find life too plain and
     unadorned,

---

[3]The Confucian stress on filial piety and other structured relationships arises when natural human bonds are forgotten.

[4]Ministers to the monarch sometimes called themselves "loyal slaves."

Then let them have accessories;
Give them simplicity to look at, the uncarved block[5] to hold,
Give them selflessness and fewness of desires.

●   ●   ●

CHAPTER 25

There was something formless yet complete,
That existed before heaven and earth;
Without sound, without substance,
Dependent on nothing, unchanging,
All pervading, unfailing.
One may think of it as the mother of all things under heaven.
Its true name we do not know;
Way is the by-name that we give it.
Were I forced to say to what class of things it belongs I should call it
        great *(ta)*.
Now *ta* also means "passing on,"
And *passing on* means "going far away,"
And *going far away* means "returning."

Thus just as Tao has "this greatness" and as earth has it and heaven has it, so may the ruler also have it. Thus "within the realm there are four portions of greatness," and one belongs to the king. The ways of men are conditioned by those of earth. The ways of earth, by those of heaven. The ways of heaven, by those of Tao, and the ways of Tao by the self-so.[6]

●   ●   ●

CHAPTER 28

He who knows the male, yet cleaves to what is female
Becomes like a ravine, receiving all things under heaven,

---

[5]To the Taoist, the uncarved block symbolized what was naturally right and could only be distorted by "carving," i.e., by human intervention. The Taoists preferred a course of *wu wei*, or "non-action."

[6]That which is so by its nature.

And being such a ravine
He knows all the time a power that he never calls upon in vain.
This is returning to the state of infancy.
He who knows the white, yet cleaves to the black
Becomes the standard by which all things are tested;
And being such a standard
He has all the time a power that never errs,
He returns to the limitless.
He who knows glory, yet cleaves to ignominy
Becomes like a valley that receives into it all things under heaven,
And being such a valley
He has all the time a power that suffices;
He returns to the state of the uncarved block.
Now when a block is sawed up it is made into implements;
But when the Sage uses it, it becomes chief of all ministers.
Truly, "The greatest carver does the least cutting."

•   •   •

CHAPTER 32

Tao is eternal, but has no fame [name];
The uncarved block, though seemingly of small account,
Is greater than anything that is under heaven.
If kings and barons would but possess themselves of it,
The ten thousand creatures would flock to do them homage;
Heaven-and-earth would conspire
To send sweet dew,
Without law or compulsion, men would dwell in harmony.
Once the block is carved, there will be names,[7]
And so soon as there are names
Know that it is time to stop.
Only by knowing when it is time to stop can danger be avoided.
To Tao all under heaven will come
As streams and torrents flow into a great river or sea.

•   •   •

---

[7]There will be distinctions and categories, rather than the oneness that is the nature of the Tao.

CHAPTER 36

What is in the end to be shrunk
Must first be stretched.
Whatever is to be weakened
Must begin by being made strong.
What is to be overthrown
Must begin by being set up.
He who would be a taker
Must begin as a giver.
This is called "dimming" one's light.
It is thus that the soft overcomes the hard
And the weak, the strong.
It is best to leave the fish down in his pool;
Best to leave the state's sharpest weapons where none can see them.

•   •   •

CHAPTER 40

In Tao the only motion is returning;
The only useful quality, weakness.
For though all creatures under heaven are the products of being,
Being itself is the product of not-being.

•   •   •

CHAPTER 43

What is of all things most yielding[8]
Can overwhelm that which is of all things most hard.
Being substanceless it can enter even where there is no space;
That is how I know the value of action that is actionless.
But that there can be teaching without words,
Value in action that is actionless,
Few indeed can understand.

•   •   •

---

[8]Water, which in time can erode even the hardest things, such as rocks.

CHAPTER 60

Ruling a large kingdom is indeed like cooking a small fish. They who by Tao ruled all that is under heaven did not let an evil spirit within them display its powers. Nay, it was not only that the evil spirit did not display its powers; neither was the Sage's good spirit used to the hurt of other men. Nor was it only that his good spirit was not used to harm other men, the Sage himself was thus saved from harm. And so, each being saved from harm, their "powers" could converge toward a common end.

• • •

CHAPTER 66

How did the great rivers and seas get their kingship over the hundred
lesser streams?
Through the merit of being lower than they; that was how they got
their kingship.
Therefore the Sage
In order to be above the people
Must speak as though he were lower than the people.
In order to guide them
He must put himself behind them.
Only thus can the Sage be on top and the people not be crushed by his
weight.
Only thus can he guide, and the people not be led into harm.

Indeed in this way everything under heaven will be glad to be pushed by him and will not find his guidance irksome. This he does by not striving; and because he does not strive, none can contend with him.

• • •

CHAPTER 78

Nothing under heaven is softer or more yielding than water; but when it attacks things hard and resistant there is not one of them that can prevail. For they can find no way of altering it. That the yielding conquers the resistant and the soft conquers the hard is a fact known by all men, yet utilized by none. Yet it is in reference to this that the Sage[9] said, "Only he who has accepted the dirt of the country can be lord of its soil-shrines; only he who takes upon himself the evils of the

---

[9]Lao Tzu.

country can become a king among those who dwell under heaven." Straight words seem crooked.

• • •

CHAPTER 81

True words are not fine-sounding;
Fine-sounding words are not true.
The good man does not prove by argument;
And he who proves by argument is not good.
True wisdom is different from such learning;
Much learning means little wisdom.
The Sage has no need to hoard;
When his own last scrap has been used up on behalf of others,
Lo, he has more than before!
When his own last scrap has been used up in giving to others,
Lo, his stock is even greater than before!
For heaven's way is to sharpen without cutting,
And the Sage's way is to act without striving.

31

Chuang Tzu

THE CHUANG TZU

We have little knowledge of Chuang Tzu's life beyond his given name, Chou, and the fact that he once held minor public office. It is believed that he was a contemporary of Mencius (Selection 28), which means that he was active in the last half of the fourth century B.C. and into the early years of the third. The single book attributed to him typically uses his name as its title. The traditional view is that Chuang Tzu, interpreting Taoist thought two and a half centuries after Lao Tzu (Selection 30), bore a relationship to the "Old Philosopher" analogous to that which Mencius had with Confucius (Selection 26). Chuang Tzu does invoke the name of Lao Tzu in his writing, but his thought is not always in accord with that of the Tao Te Ching, and scholars in the last century have suggested that the two great Taoist texts may be more nearly contemporary, and may have drawn from a common source now lost.

The Chuang Tzu is certainly a different sort of book from the Tao Te Ching. Most obvious is the different form of the work, a collection of thirty-three chapters composed of prose essays and anecdotes. Many of the latter are philosophical "tall tales" in which Lao Tzu encounters Confucius, or Chuang Tzu encounters Mencius or some other philosopher of the time. In each of these invented conversations, the Taoist comes off as wiser and more intellectually agile, clearly the winner in a friendly contest of wits, while Confucius (or whoever) goes away a bit befuddled, the bubble of his intellectual and moral pretensions burst. Other fictional meetings involve a "simple" craftsman who responds to pompous questioning from a king or duke about his skill. The answer the craftsman gives demonstrates the shallowness of the questioner's mind, but also makes a point about the seamless relationship between a craftsman and his material, a metaphor for that central Taoist belief in mankind's oneness with all nature.

While this Taoist theme, which some have called a "nature mysticism," is a prominent motif of The Chuang Tzu; its governing passion is the quest for free-

dom, a freedom so far-reaching in its conception as to approach philosophical anarchy. The Tao Te Ching *also has unconventional things to say about the approach to and uses of political power, but it lies within the scope of those works of the Hundred Schools which see the maintenance of political order as a central problem. Chuang Tzu's view of public responsibility, on the other hand, is that it is a trap that the wise will avoid. In later years, in the troubled times that came again and again throughout Chinese history, this frankly anti-political strain in Chuang Tzu's thinking made his book a haven for the politically dispossessed, and the platform for a new life of retirement from the world.*

Even beyond this anti-political element, however, the stories and essays of The Chuang Tzu *are a call to intellectual freedom, to liberation of the mind from all conventional ways of seeing the world and of living and working in it. A number of passages in this selection illustrate this radical mode of thinking, perhaps none more so than those that deal with death. Chuang Tzu should not be understood as preaching a gospel of an afterlife in which, as in the Christian view, we are rewarded for our sufferings or virtues in this life. Rather, he sees death as the turning of another corner in a life characterized by many such turnings. One does not know what lies beyond that corner, but should approach it with a calm mind and without fear.*

Hui Tzu[1] said to Chuang Tzu, "I have a big tree of the kind men call *shu*. Its trunk is too gnarled and bumpy to apply a measuring line to, its branches too bent and twisty to match up to a compass or square. You could stand it by the road and no carpenter would look at it twice. Your words, too, are big and useless, and so everyone alike spurns them!"

Chuang Tzu said, "Maybe you've never seen a wildcat or a weasel. It crouches down and hides, watching for something to come along. It leaps and races east and west, not hesitating to go high or low—until it falls into the trap and dies in the net. Then again there's the yak, big as a cloud covering the sky. It certainly knows how to be big, though it doesn't know how to catch rats. Now you have this big tree and you're distressed because it's useless. Why don't you plant it in

From *The Complete Works of Chuang Tzu*, trans. Burton Watson (New York: Columbia University Press, 1968), pp. 35, 49, 116, 131, 152–153, 165–166, 187–189, 191–192, 193–194, 205–206, 244–245, 269, 357. Reprinted with permission of the publisher.

[1]Hui Tzu, a friend of Chuang Tzu, was one of the School of Logicians. He represents, in *The Chuang Tzu*, a stolid intellectualism in contrast to the claims of the imagination that Chuang Tzu advances. Yet the next-to-last excerpt in this selection is a touching posthumous tribute to Hui Tzu as a friend and worthy intellectual sparring partner.

Not-Even-Anything Village, or the field of Broad-and-Boundless, relax and do nothing by its side, or lie down for a free and easy sleep under it? Axes will never shorten its life, nothing can ever harm it. If there's no use for it, how can it come to grief or pain?"

● ● ●

Once Chuang Chou[2] dreamt he was a butterfly, a butterfly flitting and fluttering around, happy with himself and doing as he pleased. He didn't know he was Chuang Chou. Suddenly he woke up and there he was, solid and unmistakable Chuang Chou. But he didn't know if he was Chuang Chou who had dreamt he was a butterfly, or a butterfly dreaming he was Chuang Chou. Between Chuang Chou and a butterfly there must be *some* distinction! This is called the transformation of things.

● ● ●

Ts'ui Chu was questioning Lao Tan.[3] "If you do not govern the world, then how can you improve men's minds?"

Lao Tan said, "Be careful—don't meddle with men's minds! Men's minds can be forced down or boosted up, but this downing and upping imprisons and brings death to the mind. Gentle and shy, the mind can bend the hard and strong; it can chisel and cut away, carve and polish. Its heat is that of burning fire, its coldness that of solid ice, its swiftness such that, in the time it takes to lift and lower the head, it has twice swept over the four seas and beyond. At rest, it is deep-fathomed and still; in movement, it is far-flung as the heavens, racing and galloping out of reach of all bonds. This indeed is the mind of man!"

● ● ●

When Yao[4] ruled the world, Po-ch'eng Tzu-kao was granted land as one of his noblemen. But when Yao passed the throne to Shun, and Shun passed it to Yu,[5] Po-ch'eng Tzu-kao relinquished his title and took up farming. Yu went to see him

---

[2]That is, Chuang Tzu. This passage uses his given name, Chou, rather than the honorific Tzu, which means "master."

[3]That is, Lao Tzu.

[4]See Selection 10, *The Book of History.*

[5]Yu was another early emperor, credited with founding the Hsia Dynasty (2205?–1766? B.C.) and with devising a system to contain the devastating floods that afflicted China in his time. Unlike Yao and Shun, whose historical reality is questionable, Yu probably was an historical figure.

and found him working in the fields. Yu scurried forward in the humblest manner, came to a halt, and said, "In former times, when Yao ruled the world, sir, you served as one of his noblemen. But when Yao passed the throne to Shun, and Shun passed it to me, you relinquished your title and took up farming. May I be so bold as to ask why?"

Tzu-kao said, "In former times, when Yao ruled the world, he handed out no rewards and yet the people worked hard; he handed out no punishments and yet the people were cautious. Now you reward and punish, and still the people fail to do good. From now on virtue will decay, from now on penalties will prevail. The disorder of future ages will have its beginning here! You had better be on your way now—don't interrupt my work!" Busily, busily, he proceeded with his farm work, never turning to look back.

● ● ●

Duke Huan[6] was in his hall reading a book. The wheelwright P'ien, who was in the yard below chiseling a wheel, laid down his mallet and chisel, stepped up into the hall, and said to Duke Huan, "This book Your Grace is reading—may I venture to ask whose words are in it?"

"The words of the sages," said the duke.

"Are the sages still alive?"

"Dead long ago," said the duke.

"In that case, what you are reading there is nothing but the chaff and dregs of the men of old!"

"Since when does a wheelwright have permission to comment on the books I read?" said Duke Huan. "If you have some explanation, well and good. If not, it's your life!"

Wheelwright P'ien said, "I look at it from the point of view of my own work. When I chisel a wheel, if the blows of the mallet are too gentle, the chisel slides and won't take hold. But if they're too hard, it bites in and won't budge. Not too gentle, not too hard—you can get it in your hand and feel it in your mind. You can't put it into words, and yet there's a knack to it somehow. I can't teach it to my son, and he can't learn it from me. So I've gone along for seventy years, and at my age, I'm still chiseling wheels. When the men of old died, they took with them the things that couldn't be handed down. So what you are reading there must be nothing but the chaff and dregs of the men of old."

● ● ●

---

[6]Duke Huan of Ch'i, who reigned from 685 to 643 B.C., was among the first of the aggressive feudal rulers. He appears in four anecdotes of *The Chuang Tzu*. His imperious speech in this excerpt is in keeping with his reputed character.

Confucius said to Lao Tzu, "I have been studying the six classics—the Odes, the Documents, the Ritual, the Music, the Changes, and the Spring and Autumn, for what I would call a long time, and I know their contents through and through. But I have been around to seventy-two different rulers with them, expounding the ways of the former kings and making clear the path trod by the Dukes of Chou and Shao, and yet not a single ruler has found anything to excite his interest. How difficult it is to persuade others, how difficult to make clear the way!"

Lao Tzu said, "It's lucky you didn't meet with a ruler who would try to govern the world as you say. The six classics are the old worn-out paths of the former kings—they are not the thing which walked the path. What you are expounding are simply those paths. Paths are made by shoes that walk them, they are by no means the shoes themselves!

"The white fish hawk has only to stare unblinking at its mate for fertilization to occur. With insects, the male cries on the wind above, the female cries on the wind below, and there is fertilization. The creature called the *lei* is both male and female and so it can fertilize itself. Inborn nature cannot be changed, fate cannot be altered, time cannot be stopped, the way cannot be obstructed. Get hold of the way and there's nothing that can't be done; lose it and there's nothing that *can* be done."

Confucius stayed home for three months and then came to see Lao Tzu once again. "I've got it," he said. "The magpie hatches its young, the fish spit out their milt, the slim-waisted wasp has its stages of transformation, and when baby brother is born, big brother howls. For a long time now I have not been taking my place as a man along with the process of change. And if I do not take my own place as a man along with the process of change, how can I hope to change other men?"

Lao Tzu said, "Good, Ch'iu—now you've got it!"

• • •

Once, when Chuang Tzu was fishing in the P'u River, the king of Ch'u[7] sent two officials to go and announce to him: "I would like to trouble you with the administration of my realm."

Chuang Tzu held onto the fishing pole and, without turning his head, said, "I have heard that there is a sacred tortoise in Ch'u that has been dead for three thousand years. The king keeps it wrapped in cloth and boxed, and stores it in the ancestral temple. Now would this tortoise rather be dead and have its bones left behind and honored? Or would it rather be alive and dragging its tail in the mud?"

"It would rather be alive and dragging its tail in the mud," said the two officials.

Chuang Tzu said, "Go away! I'll drag my tail in the mud!"

---

[7]Ch'u was the largest of the warring states. The king is mentioned several times in *The Chuang Tzu,* more for his symbolism as a powerful figure than for any reflection on his character.

● ● ●

Chuang Tzu and Hui Tzu were strolling along the dam of the Hao River when Chuang Tzu said, "See how the minnows come out and dart around where they please? That's what fish really enjoy!"

Hui Tzu said, "You're not a fish—how do you know what fish enjoy?"

Chuang Tzu said, "You're not I, so how do you know I don't know what fish enjoy?"

Hui Tzu said, "I'm not you, so I certainly don't know what you know. On the other hand, you're certainly not a fish—so that still proves you don't know what fish enjoy!"

Chuang Tzu said, "Let us go back to your original question, please. You asked me *how* I know what fish enjoy—so you already knew I knew it when you asked the question. I know it by standing here beside the Hao."

● ● ●

Chuang Tzu's wife died. When Hui Tzu went to convey his condolences, he found Chuang Tzu sitting with his legs sprawled out, pounding on a tub and singing. "You lived with her, she brought up your children and grew old," said Hui Tzu. "It should be enough simply not to weep at her death. But pounding on a tub and singing—this is going too far, isn't it?"

Chuang Tzu said, "You're wrong. When she first died, do you think I didn't grieve like anyone else? But I looked back to her beginning and the time before she was born. Not only the time before she was born, but the time before she had a body. Not only the time before she had a body, but the time before she had a spirit. In the midst of the jumble of wonder and mystery a change took place and she had a spirit. Another change and she had a body. Another change and she was born. Now there's been another change and she's dead. It's just like the progression of the four seasons: spring, summer, fall, and winter.

"Now she's going to lie down peacefully in a vast room. If I were to follow after her bawling and sobbing, it would show that I don't understand anything about fate. So I stopped."

● ● ●

When Chuang Tzu went to Ch'u, he saw an old skull, all dry and parched. He poked it with his carriage whip and then asked, "Sir, were you greedy for life and forgetful of reason, and so came to this? Was your state overthrown and did you bow beneath the axe, and so came to this? Did you do some evil deed and were you ashamed to bring disgrace upon your parents and family, and so came to this? Was it through the pangs of cold and hunger that you came to this? Or did your springs and autumns pile up until they brought you to this?"

When he had finished speaking, he dragged the skull over and, using it for a pillow, lay down to sleep.

In the middle of the night, the skull came to him in a dream and said, "You chatter like a rhetorician and all your words betray the entanglements of a living man. The dead know nothing of these! Would you like to hear a lecture on the dead?"

"Indeed," said Chuang Tzu.

The skull said, "Among the dead there are no rulers above, no subjects below, and no chores of the four seasons. With nothing to do, our springs and autumns are as endless as heaven and earth. A king facing south on his throne could have no more happiness than this!"

Chuang Tzu couldn't believe this and said, "If I got the arbiter of fate to give you a body again, make you some bones and flesh, return you to your parents and family and your old home and friends, you would want that, wouldn't you?"

The skull frowned severely, wrinkling up its brow. "Why would I throw away more happiness than that of a king on a throne and take on the troubles of a human being again?" it said.

● ● ●

Woodworker Ch'ing carved a piece of wood and made a bell stand, and, when it was finished, everyone who saw it marveled, for it seemed to be the work of gods or spirits. When the marquis of Lu[8] saw it, he asked, "What art is it you have?"

Ch'ing replied, "I am only a craftsman—how would I have any art? There is one thing, however. When I am going to make a bell stand, I never let it wear out my energy. I always fast in order to still my mind. When I have fasted for three days, I no longer have any thought of congratulations or rewards, of titles or stipends. When I have fasted for five days, I no longer have any thought of praise or blame, of skill or clumsiness. And when I have fasted for seven days, I am so still that I forget I have four limbs and a form and body. By that time, the ruler and his court no longer exist for me. My skill is concentrated and all outside distractions fade away. After that, I go into the mountain forest and examine the heavenly nature of the trees. If I find one of superlative form, and I can see a bell stand there,[9] I put my hand to the job of carving; if not, I let it go. This way I am simply matching up 'heaven' with 'heaven.' That's probably the reason that people wonder if the results were not made by spirits."

---

[8]The feudal state of Lu was Confucius's home. Chuang Tzu's references to "the marquis of Lu" probably include several men who held this title over the years until Lu finally lost its independence and identity to larger, more aggressive states.

[9]This idea finds a fascinating parallel in the Neoplatonic belief of the Renaissance sculptor Michelangelo, that the figures he carved were virtually imprisoned within the marble, and that he was liberating them with his chisel.

• • •

The grand marshall's bucklemaker was eighty years old, yet he had not lost the tiniest part of his dexterity. The grand marshall said, "What skill you have! Is there a special way to this?"

"I have a way. From the time I was twenty I have loved to forge buckles. I never look at other things—if it's not a buckle, I don't bother to examine it."

Using this method of deliberately *not* using other things, he was able, over the years, to get some use out of it. And how much greater would a man be if, by the same method, he reached the point where there was nothing that he did not use! All things would come to depend on him.

• • •

Chuang Tzu was accompanying a funeral when he passed by the grave of Hui Tzu. Turning to his attendants, he said, "There was once a plasterer who, if he got a speck of mud on the tip of his nose no thicker than a fly's wing, would get his friend Carpenter Shih to slice it off for him. Carpenter Shih, whirling his hatchet with a noise like the wind, would accept the assignment and proceed to slice, removing every bit of mud without injury to the nose, while the plasterer just stood there completely unperturbed. Lord Yuan of Sung, hearing of this feat, summoned Carpenter Shih and said, 'Could you try performing it for me?' But Carpenter Shih replied, 'It's true that I was once able to slice like that—but the material I worked on has been dead these many years.' Since you died, Master Hui, I have had no material to work on. There's no one I can talk to any more."

• • •

Duke Ai of Lu said to Yen Ho,[10] "If I were to make Confucius my pillar and stanchion, do you think it would improve the health of the state?"

"Beware—that way lies danger! Confucius will deck things out in feathers and paint, and conduct his affairs with flowery phrases, mistaking side issues for the crux. He is willing to distort his inborn nature in order to make himself a model for the people, not even realizing that he is acting in bad faith. He takes everything to heart, submits all to the judgment of the spirit—how could such a man be worth putting in charge of the people? Does he meet with your approval? Would you like to provide for his support? It would be a mistake, but you may do it if you like. Yet one who would induce the people to turn their backs on reality and study hypocrisy is hardly fit to be made a model for the people. If we are to take thought for later ages, it would be best to drop the scheme." . . .

---

[10]A scholar of Lu in the early fifth century B.C. whom Chuang Tzu admired for his humility and good sense.

32

❧

Han Fei Tzu

THE HAN FE TZU

Han Fei Tzu (Master Han Fei, 280?–233 B.C.) stands apart from other major political philosophers of China's Hundred Schools in several important respects. Whereas the others belonged to the class of shih, or "knights," Han Fei was a prince of Han, one of the smaller and weaker of the warring states. Thus he knew the uses of political power and the burden of its responsibilities as did none of the others, a fact that undoubtedly shaped his skepticism about political theorizing and his hard-headed, utilitarian approach to the problems of government.

Moreover, in an age when the wandering scholars taught their disciples and sought to influence heads of state through persuasive oratory, Han Fei was a stutterer, unable to compete without embarrassment in the arena of public discourse. His venom is often directed against those "who put on a fair appearance and speak in elegant phrases." He turned instead to writing letters addressed to the kings of Han, whom he served. Eventually these were collected in a single volume, known in typical fashion as The Han Fei Tzu. To the good fortune of later readers, even those who have found his ideas repugnant, he developed a clear, forceful style of exposition.

Han Fei Tzu is credited with perfecting a strand of thought already several centuries in formation, the school of Fa-chia, known to us as "legalism," or "realism." A former student of Hsun Tzu (Selection 29), he began with that realistic Confucian's premise that "the nature of man is evil." To this he added the doctrines that the state exists for the benefit of the ruler, whose only obligation to the people is to ensure strength and stability; that society needs only farmers and fighters, others tend to be wasteful or troublesome; that the law must be clearly understood and ruthlessly enforced. These views, set in the context of a perceptive and wholly undeceived view of politics in his own age, make The Han Fei Tzu seem in many ways akin to the most influential work of Renaissance Italian polit-

ical realism, Machiavelli's The Prince *(Volume 3 of this series, Selection 2), with which it is often compared.*

Ironically, Han Fei Tzu fell victim to the power politics he so effectively articulated. In 234 B.C., the armies of Ch'in attacked his state of Han. The following year, he was sent as ambassador to Ch'in in a desperate last-minute attempt to stave off total destruction. The chief minister of Ch'in, Li Ssu, had been a fellow student under Hsun Tzu years before, but now saw the brilliant Han Fei as a possible rival. Han Fei was imprisoned. When Li Ssu sent him poison, Han Fei evidently realized he had fallen into a fatal trap, had no honorable way out, and ended his life.

Within twelve years Ch'in had conquered and united all China under the tyrant Emperor Chin Shih Hunag-ti. A string of edicts drafted by Li Ssu made real the terrible simplification of the state Han Fei Tzu had prescribed—regimentation of all aspects of life, elimination of useless social classes, and the burning of all but practical books. Just as Ch'in unification brought an end to the Warring States Period, Han Fei Tzu's death marked at least a symbolic end to the remarkable period of the Hundred Schools. This had been a three-centuries-long quest for political stability within the bounds of moral rectitude, a quest that ended with an act of treachery and the impending triumph of the absolute, amoral state.

FROM SECTION 49, "THE FIVE VERMIN"

There was a farmer of Sung[1] who tilled the land, and in his field was a stump. One day a rabbit, racing across the field, bumped into the stump, broke its neck, and died. Thereupon the farmer laid aside his plow and took up watch beside the stump, hoping that he would get another rabbit in the same way. But he got no more rabbits, and instead became the laughing stock of Sung. Those who think they can take the ways of ancient kings and use them to govern the people of today all belong in the category of stump-watchers.!

•   •   •

From *Han Fei Tzu: Basic Writings,* trans. Burton Watson (New York: Columbia University Press, 1964), pp. 97, 100–102, 105–107, 110–111, 116–117. Reprinted with permission of the publisher.

[1]One of the feudal states of the Chou Dynasty period, conquered by the expanding Ch'in state in 286 B.C.

Men of high antiquity strove for high moral value; men of middle times sought out wise schemes; men of today vie to be known for strength and spirit. Ch'i was once planning an attack on Lu. Lu dispatched Tzu-king to dissuade the men of Ch'i,[2] but they replied, "Your words are eloquent enough. But what we want is territory, and that is the one thing you have not mentioned." So in the end Ch'i called out its troops, attacked Lu, and fixed its boundary line only ten *li* away from the Lu capital gate.

King Yen practiced benevolence and righteousness and the state of Hsu was wiped out. Tzu-kung employed eloquence and wisdom and Lu lost territory. So it is obvious that benevolence, righteousness, eloquence, and wisdom are not the means by which to maintain the state. Discard the benevolence of King Yen and put an end to Tzu-kung's wisdom: build up the might of Hsu and Lu until they can stand face to face with a state of ten thousand war chariots—then Ch'i and Ching will no longer be able to do with them as they please!

Past and present have different customs; new and old adopt different measures. To try to use the ways of a generous and lenient government to rule the people of a critical age is like trying to drive a runaway horse without using reins or whip. This is the misfortune that ignorance invites.

Now the Confucians and the Mo-ists[3] all praise the ancient kings for their universal love of the world, saying that they looked after the people as parents look after a beloved child. And how do they prove this contention? They say, "Whenever the minister of justice administered some punishment, the ruler would purposely cancel all musical performances; and whenever the ruler learned that the death sentence had been passed on someone, he would shed tears." For this reason they praise the ancient kings.

Now if a ruler and subject must become like father and son before there can be order, then we must suppose that there is no such thing as an unruly father or son. Among human affections none takes priority over the love of parents for their children. But though all parents may show love for their children, the children are not always well behaved. And though the parents may love them even more, will this prevent the children from becoming unruly? Now the love of the ancient kings for their people was no greater than the love of parents for their children. And if such love cannot prevent children from becoming unruly, then how can it bring the people to order? . . .

Moreover, the people will bow naturally to authority, but few of them can be moved by righteousness. Confucius was one of the greatest sages of the world. He perfected his conduct, made clear the way, and traveled throughout the area

---

[2]Ch'i was one of the larger of the warring states. Lu, which was smaller and weaker, was Confucius's home state. Tzu-kung (c. 520–450 B.C.) was one of Confucius's leading disciples, noted for his eloquence.

[3]Mo Tzu (468?–376? B.C.) taught a philosophy of universal love.

within the four seas, but in all that area those who rejoiced in his benevolence, admired his righteousness, and were willing to become his disciples numbered only seventy. For to honor benevolence is a rare thing, and to adhere to righteousness is hard. Therefore within the vast area of the world only seventy men became his disciples, and only one man—he himself—was truly benevolent and righteous.

Duke Ai of Lu was a mediocre ruler, yet when he ascended the throne and faced south as sovereign of the state, there was no one within its boundaries who did not acknowledge allegiance to him. The people will bow naturally to authority, and he who wields authority may easily command men to submit; therefore Confucius remained a subject and Duke Ai continued to be his ruler. It was not that Confucius was won by the duke's righteousness; he simply bowed before his authority. On the basis of righteousness alone, Confucius would never have bowed before Duke Ai; but because Duke Ai wielded authority, he was able to make Confucius acknowledge his sovereignty.

•   •   •

The Confucians, with their learning, bring confusion to the law; the knights, with their military prowess, violate the prohibitions.[4] Yet the ruler treats both groups with respect, and so we have disorder. People who deviate from the law should be treated as criminals, and yet the scholars actually attain posts in the government because of their literary accomplishments. People who violate the prohibitions ought to be punished, and yet the bands of knights are able to make a living by wielding their swords in a private cause. Hence, those whom the law condemns, the ruler accepts, and those whom the magistrates seek to punish, the higher officials patronize. Thus law and practice, high official and lowly magistrate, are all set at odds, and there is no fixed standard. Under such circumstances even ten Yellow Emperors[5] could not bring the state to order. Those who practice benevolence and righteousness should not be praised, for to praise them is to cast aspersion on military achievements; men of literary accomplishment should not be employed in the government, for to employ them is to bring confusion to the law.

In the state of Ch'u[6] there was a man named Honest Kung. When his father stole a sheep, he reported the theft to the authorities. But the local magistrate, considering that the man was honest in the service of his sovereign but a villain to his own father, replied, "Put him to death!" and the man was accordingly sentenced

---

[4]By no means all of the *shih,* or "knights," of the Warring States Period became scholars. Many grouped together to sell their military services, ostensibly to offer protection in an increasingly lawless age, but often in fact to become local warlords in defiance of royal and feudal authority. For Han Fei Tzu, these were among the "vermin" of the state.

[5]The Yellow Emperor was the legendary founder of the Chinese state in antiquity.

[6]Largest of the warring states, it was fertile land occupying a large extent of the Yangtze River valley.

and executed. Thus we see that a man who is an honest subject of his sovereign may be an infamous son to his father.

There was a man of Lu who accompanied his sovereign to war. Three times he went into battle, and three times he ran away. When Confucius asked him the reason, he replied, "I have an aged father and, if I should die, there would be no one to take care of him." Confucius, considering the man filial, recommended him and had him promoted to a post in the government. Thus we see that a man who is a filial son to his father may be a traitorous subject to his lord.

The magistrate of Ch'u executed a man, and as a result the felonies of the state were never reported to the authorities; Confucius rewarded a man, and as a result the people of Lu thought nothing of surrendering or running away in battle. . . .

In ancient times when Ts'ang Chieh[7] created the system of writing, he used the character for "private" to express the idea of self-centeredness, and combined the elements for "private" and "opposed to" to form the character for "public." The fact that public and private are mutually opposed was already well understood at the time of Ts'ang Chieh. To regard the two as being identical in interest is a disaster which comes from lack of consideration.

If I were to give advice from the point of view of the private individual, I would say the best thing is to practice benevolence and righteousness and cultivate the literary arts. By practicing benevolence and righteousness, you become trusted, and when you have become trusted you may receive official appointment. Similarly, by cultivating the literary arts you may become an eminent teacher, and when you have become an eminent teacher you will win honor and renown. This is the highest goal of the private individual. But when this happens, then, from the point of view of the state, someone who has performed no meritorious service to the nation is receiving official appointment, and someone who holds no government title is enjoying honor and renown. If the government is conducted in this fashion, then the state will face certain disorder and the ruler will surely be in peril. Hence the interests of the individual and the state are mutually at odds, and both cannot prevail at the same time.

●   ●   ●

Farming requires a lot of hard work but people will do it because they say, "This way we can get rich." War is a dangerous undertaking but people will take part in it because they say, "This way we can become eminent." Now if men who devote themselves to literature or study the art of persuasive speaking are able to get the fruits of wealth without the hard work of the farmer, and can gain the advantages of eminence without the danger of battle, then who will not take up such pursuits? So for every man who works with his hands there will be a hundred devoting

---

[7]Ts'ang Chieh, reputed to have lived in the twenty-seventh century B.C., is credited in Chinese tradition with drafting the first written characters.

themselves to the pursuit of wisdom. If those who pursue wisdom are numerous, the laws will be defeated, and if those who labor with their hands are few, the state will grow poor. Hence the age will become disordered.

Therefore, in the state of an enlightened ruler there are no books written on bamboo slips;[8] law supplies the only instruction. There are no sermons on the former kings; the officials serve as the only teachers. There are no fierce feuds of private swordsmen; cutting off the heads of the enemy is the only deed of valor. Hence, when the people of such a state make a speech, they say nothing that is in contradiction to the law; when they act, it is in some way that will bring useful results; and when they do brave deeds, they do them in the army. Therefore, in times of peace the state is rich, and in times of trouble its armies are strong. These are what are called the resources of the ruler. The ruler must store them up, and then wait for an opening to strike at his enemy. He who would surpass the five emperors of antiquity and rival the three kings must proceed by this method.

● ● ●

An enlightened ruler will administer his state in such a way as to decrease the number of merchants, artisans, and other men who make their living by wandering from place to place, and will see to it that such men are looked down upon. In this way he lessens the number of people who abandon primary pursuits [agriculture] to take up secondary occupations. Nowadays, however, if a man can enlist the private pleading of someone at court, he can buy offices and titles. When offices and titles can be bought, you may be sure that merchants and artisans will not remain despised for long; and when wealth and money, no matter how dishonestly gotten, can buy what is in the market, you can be sure that the number of merchants will not remain small for long. When a man who sits back and collects taxes makes twice as much as the farmer and enjoys greater honor than the plowman or the soldier, then public-spirited men will grow few and merchants and tradesmen will increase in number.

These are the customs of a disordered state: Its scholars praise the ways of former kings and imitate their benevolence and righteousness, put on a fair appearance and speak in elegant phrases, thus casting doubt upon the laws of the time and causing the ruler to be of two minds. Its speechmakers propound false schemes and borrow influence from abroad, furthering their private interests and forgetting the welfare of the state's altars of soil and grain. Its swordsmen gather bands of followers about them and perform deeds of honor, making a fine name for themselves and violating the prohibitions of the five government bureaus. Those of its people who are worried about military service flock to the gates of private individuals and pour out their wealth in bribes to influential men who will

---

[8]Prior to the development of paper in China in the early centuries A.D., books were written on bamboo slips or on silk cloth.

plead for them, in this way escaping the hardship of battle. Its merchants and artisans spend their time making articles of no practical use and gathering stores of luxury goods, accumulating riches, waiting for the best time to sell, and exploiting the farmers.

These five groups are the vermin of the state. If the rulers do not wipe out such vermin, and in their place encourage men of integrity and public spirit, then they should not be surprised, when they look about the area within the four seas, to see states perish and ruling houses wane and die.

PART
III

CONSOLIDATION
AND EMPIRES

❧

In Selections 33 through 45 we see the continuing power of empires in
places as separate as Rome, India, and China. Travelers continue to
make the hazardous journeys between them. For example, in Selection 36,
The Periplus of the Erythraean Sea, a Greek-speaking Roman citizen journeys down the east coast of Africa, trading continually for goods in the
well-established markets there, and then sails across to the Persian Gulf
and on to India. The texts of Part III of this volume date mainly from the
second through the fifth centuries A.D. Although the African (Ethiopian)
texts (Selection 38) apparently were set down much later, their origins
date from this period.

In Plutarch's biography of Marcus Cato (Selection 33) we read of Cato's
conservative puritanical behavior that was idealized for generations of
Romans as the kind of lifestyle that was essential for the preservation of
Rome. Despite Cato's rigorous attempt to exclude all non-Roman influ-
ences, however, there is evidence, seen in the excerpt from *The Golden Ass*
(Selection 34), of the strong attraction for many Romans to the ancient
Egyptian religion of Isis and Osiris. Also competing with the Roman state
religion was the new religion of Christianity that advanced the doctrine of
a God who walked the earth, mainly in the remote province of Judaea, and
had been crucified there by Roman authorities. Growing out of Jewish
roots, Christianity added a New Testament (Selection 35), written in
Greek, to the already revered Old Testament (Selection 6), written in
Hebrew. After A.D. 313, when Christianity became a legal religion in
the Roman Empire, it still had many critics who blamed the weakened

condition of the Empire on its doctrine of heavenly salvation. The most significant defender of Christianity against this charge was Saint Augustine in his massive philosophical and historical work *The City of God* (Selection 37), where his integration of Greek philosophical form with Christian content is seen. The spread of the new religion up the Nile, deep into the African continent, is evidenced by the translation of the Bible into Ge'ez, an Ethiopian language, by the late fifth century, reinforcing the conversion of the great kingdom of Axum, whose chronicles are recorded (Selection 38). Not only did Christianity generate churches in Ethiopia, but a branch of Judaism flourished there into the twentieth century. An example of its literature also appears in Selection 38.

In the ancient world, the Greeks were not the only ones who theorized about literary forms. Bharata's *Natyashastra* (Selection 39) is a Sanskrit (Indian) work about the art of drama. Having its origin in the entertainments of the gods, according to Bharata, drama became a major source of entertainment and instruction for humans. Dramatic theory paralleled practice. As an example of Sanskrit drama, Kalidasa's *Shakuntala* (Selection 40) is an Indian play of about the fifth century A.D. whose dominant feeling is erotic love. The selections from Sanskrit literature end with a collection of short secular poems on love and other themes (Selection 41) and an influential exposition of Hindu philosophy (Selection 42).

The three final selections in Part III return the reader to China and the greatness of the Han Dynasty (206 B.C.–A.D. 220). In Tung Chung-shu's *Luxuriant Gems* (Selection 43), there is seen a further working out of Confucian philosophy. Ssu-ma Ch'ien (Selection 44) gives us a vast vista of Chinese history, full of biographical details and contemporary accounts, comparable to the work of the earlier Greek historian Herodotus (Selection 14). This volume ends with a selection of shorter poems from the Han Dynasty. They reveal both intense personal feelings and larger social themes.

꿏

33

Plutarch

LIVES

Greek literature did not end with the decline of the Greek city–state in the fourth century B.C. (See Selection 19 for Aristotle's view of the ideal city–state.) Literature continued to flourish, and, from the fourth century, a new form made its appearance: the short biography, presenting a specific person with unique traits. As Greek literature gained new admirers in the early Roman Empire, this sort of biographical writing became widely practiced and may even have provided a pattern for the Christian gospels. Certainly, the form reached its peak with Lucius Mestrius Plutarchus (ca. A.D. 46–124).

Little is known of Plutarch's own life. After his student days in Athens, he spent some years in Rome lecturing, in Greek, on philosophical and rhetorical subjects. An amiable man of wide interests, broad learning, and cultivated taste, he came to be on close terms with the "mighty"; there is, in fact, some evidence that the Emperor Trajan made him a consul and a provincial governor. Plutarch, however, preferred the life of a country gentleman; he returned to his native Chaeronea in Greece, where he happily filled its petty offices and priesthoods. It was then that he composed, in Greek, his best-known work, the Lives. It is a collection of biographical studies of famous Greek soldiers and statesmen, paired— for purposes of comparison—with their Roman counterparts. Twenty-three of these paired studies have come down to us, along with four single life studies. In general, Plutarch was more interested in portraying character than in systematically narrating the events of his subjects' lives. (Like most ancient writers, Plutarch saw personal character as fixed—not changing. He implied in the Lives that, perhaps, only acquired characteristics can be modified.) While remaining impartial in his comparisons, he intended to show that Greece, during its glorious past, produced men as great as the greatest of the now-dominant Romans. Plutarch embodies the upper class, conservative, Greco–Roman attitudes of his time. His view of life and history is essentially moral: the past must be studied for its ethical lessons.

The following selection from the Lives *is taken from Plutarch's biography of Marcus Porcius Cato (234–149* B.C.*), usually known as Cato the Elder, or the Censor. (Censors were elected high officials who made up the official list of Roman citizens used for such vital functions as military service and tax assessment; they also served as guardians of public law and morality.) As "social history," Plutarch's short biography of Cato offers a penetrating glimpse into the values and customs of the Roman Republic. But, foremost, it gives a memorable picture of one of the Republic's influential personalities and patriotic heroes who, throughout his private and public life, sought to stem the foreign cultural tide that was eroding the ancestral ways of the Roman people—once the most puritanical of antiquity. Cato remains, to this day, an admired model for advocates of conservative values and of personal striving for the public good; thus, the conservative Cato Institute (of Washington, D.C.) is named for him.*

If only because Plutarch's sources of information have not survived, his Lives *are vital to our knowledge of many Greek and Roman personalities. The wide popularity of the* Lives *across the centuries gives Plutarch first place among those Greek authors who shaped an image of the ancient world for later ages. Among many later influential writers, Shakespeare used Plutarch closely as a major source for his portrayals of classical characters.*

MARCUS CATO

The family of Marcus Cato, it is said, was of Tusculan[1] origin, though he lived, previous to his career as soldier and statesman, on an inherited estate in the country of the Sabines.[2] His ancestors commonly passed for men of no note whatever, but Cato himself extols his father, Marcus, as a brave man and a good soldier. He also says that his grandfather, Cato, often won prizes for soldierly valor, and received from the state treasury, because of his bravery, the price of five horses which had been killed under him in battle. The Romans used to call men who had no family distinction, but were coming into public notice through their own achievements, "new men," and such they called Cato. But he himself used to say that as far as office and distinction went, he was indeed new, but having regard to

---

Plutarch, *Lives,* trans. Bernadotte Perrin, Vol. II, "Marcus Cato" (London, 1914), pp. 303–321, 337, 343–351, 357–373, 379–383. Adapted by the editor.

[1]Tusculum was an ancient town about ten miles southeast of Rome.

[2]The Sabines were a tribal group living northeast of Rome in its earliest days. By 268 B.C., the Sabines had become fully Romanized and ceased to be a separate people.

ancestral deeds of valor, he was oldest of the old. His third name[3] was not Cato at first, but Priscus. Afterwards he got the surname of Cato for his great abilities. The Romans call a man who is wise and prudent: *catus.*

As for his outward appearance, he had reddish hair and keen grey eyes, as the author of the well-known epigram ill-naturedly gives us to understand:

> Red-haired, snapper and biter, his grey eyes
> > flashing defiance,
> Porcius, come to the shades, will be thrust back
> > by their Queen.[4]

His physical body—since he labored from the very first with his own hands, held to a temperate way of life, and performed military duties—was very serviceable, vigorous, and healthy. His eloquence—a second body, as it were, and an instrument with which to perform not only necessary, but also high and noble services—he developed and perfected in the villages and towns about Rome. There he served as advocate for all who needed him, and got the reputation of being first a zealous pleader, and then a capable orator. Thenceforth the weight and dignity of his character revealed themselves more and more to those who had dealings with him; they saw that he was bound to be a man of great affairs, and have a leading place in the state. For he not only gave his services in legal contests without fee of any sort, but did not appear to cherish even the reputation won in such contests. For he was more desirous of high reputation in battles and campaigns against the enemy, and while he was yet a mere youth had his breast covered with honorable wounds. He says himself that he made his first campaign when he was seventeen years old, at the time when Hannibal was consuming Italy with the flames of his successes.[5]

In battle, he showed himself effective in hand combat, sure and steadfast of foot, and with a fierce expression. With threatening speech and harsh cries he would advance upon the foe, for he rightly thought, and tried to show others, that often-times such action terrifies the enemy more than does the sword. On the march, he carried his own armor on foot, while a single servant followed in charge

---

[3]The Roman "third name," or *cognomen,* was an extra personal name that functioned originally like a nickname, indicating a characteristic of the bearer. Often, the *cognomen* was handed down from father to son and became the family name. (Cato's full name was Marcus Porcius Cato—the original family name having been Porcius.)

[4]That is, according to this writer, Cato is so ill-tempered that even the queen of the underworld will not admit him.

[5]Hannibal, pledged to undying hatred of Rome, was the most brilliant general of Carthage in its wars against Rome. His army devastated much of Italy, although he never succeeded in capturing Rome itself. The year was 217 B.C. when Cato fought against Hannibal's army.

of his camp provisions. With this man, it is said, he was never angry, and never scolded him when he served up a meal; he actually assisted in most of such preparations, provided he was free from his military duties. Water was what he drank on his campaigns, except that once in a while, in a raging thirst, he would call for vinegar, or, when his strength was failing, would add a little wine.

Near his fields was the cottage which had once belonged to Manius Curius, a hero of three triumphs.[6] To this he would often go, and the sight of the small farm and the simple dwelling led him to think of their former owner, who, though he had become the greatest of the Romans, had subdued the most warlike nations, and driven Pyrrhus[7] out of Italy. Nevertheless, he tilled this little patch of ground with his own hands and occupied this cottage, after three triumphs. Here it was that the ambassadors of the Samnites once found him seated at his hearth cooking turnips, and offered him much gold; but he dismissed them, saying that a man whom such a meal satisfied had no need of gold, and for his part he thought that a more honorable thing than the possession of gold was the conquest of its possessors. Cato would go away with his mind full of these things, and on viewing again his own house and lands and servants and way of life, would increase the labors of his hands and reduce his extravagances. . . .

There was at Rome a certain man of the highest birth and greatest influence, who had the power to discern excellence in the bud, and the grace to cultivate it and bring it into general esteem. This man was Valerius Flaccus. He had a farm next to that of Cato, and learned from Cato's servants of their master's laborious and frugal way of living. He was amazed to hear them tell how Cato, early in the morning, went on foot to the marketplace and pleaded the cases of all who wished his aid; then came back to his farm, where, clad in a working blouse if it was winter, and stripped to the waist if it was summer, he labored with his servants, then sat down with them to eat of the same bread and drink of the same wine. They told Valerius many other instances of Cato's fairness and moderation, quoting also sundry pithy sayings of his, until at last Valerius gave command that Cato be invited to dine with him. After this, discovering by converse with him that his nature was gentle and polite, and needed, like a growing tree, only cultivation and room to expand, Valerius urged and at last persuaded him to engage in public life at Rome. Accordingly, taking up his abode in the city, his own efforts as an advocate at once won him admiring friends, and the favor of Valerius brought him great honor and influence, so that he was made military tribune first, and then quaestor. After this, being now launched on an eminent and brilliant career, he

---

[6]When a Roman general won a great victory against foreign enemies, he was rewarded with a triumphal procession, by the authority of the Senate, at Rome. This elaborate celebration was the highest Roman military honor.

[7]A king of Epirus, northwest of Greece, distant cousin of Alexander the Great. Pyrrhus invaded Italy in 280 B.C.

shared the highest honors with Valerius, becoming consul[8] with him, and afterwards censor. . . .

The influence which Cato's oratory won for him increased, and men called him a Roman Demosthenes;[9] but his manner of life was even more talked about and carried abroad. For his oratorical ability set before young men not only a goal which many already were striving eagerly to attain, but a man who worked with his own hands, as his fathers did, and was contented with a cold breakfast, a frugal dinner, simple clothing, and a humble dwelling—one who thought more of rejecting the extras of life than of possessing them. Such a man was rare. The Roman commonwealth had now grown too large to keep its earlier integrity. The conquest of many kingdoms and peoples had brought a large mixture of customs, and the adoption of ways of life of every sort. It was natural, therefore, that men should admire Cato, when they saw that, whereas other men were broken down by labors and weakened by pleasures, he was victor over both. And this too, not only while he was still young and ambitious, but even in his old age, after consulship and triumph. Then, like some victorious athlete, he persisted in the regimen of his training, and kept his mind unaltered to the last.

He tells us that he never wore expensive clothing; that he drank the same wine as his slaves; that as for fish and meats, he would buy enough for his dinner from the public stalls—and even this for Rome's sake, that he might not live on bread alone, but strengthen his body for military service. He once inherited an embroidered Babylonian robe, but sold it at once; not a single one of his farmhouses had plastered walls; he never paid much for a slave, since he did not want them to be delicately beautiful, but sturdy workers, such as grooms and herdsmen. And these he thought it his duty to sell when they got old, instead of feeding them when they were useless; and that in general, he thought nothing cheap that one could do without. He said also that he bought lands where crops were raised and cattle herded, not those where lawns were sprinkled and paths swept for pleasure.

These things were thought by some to be the result of the man's stinginess; but others excused them in the belief that he lived in this way only to correct and moderate the extravagance of others. However, for my part, I regard his treatment of his slaves like beasts of burden, using them to the utmost, and then, when they were old, driving them off and selling them, as the mark of a very mean nature, which recognizes no tie between man and man but that of profit. . . . A kindly man will take good care even of his horses when they are worn out with age, and of his dogs, too, not only in their puppyhood, but when their old age needs nursing. . . .

---

[8]During the time of the Roman Republic, when Cato lived, two consuls were elected annually by the male citizens. They carried the judicial and military authority that had formerly been wielded by the kings. The Romans of that period even dated the years by the names of their consuls. (Cato was consul in 195 B.C.)

[9]An Athenian (383–322 B.C.), the most famous Greek orator.

We should not treat living creatures like shoes or pots and pans, casting them aside when they are bruised and worn out with service; but, if for no other reason, than for the sake of practice in kindness to our fellow men, we should accustom ourselves to mildness and gentleness in our dealings with other creatures. I certainly would not sell even an ox that had worked for me, just because he was old, much less an elderly man, removing him from his habitual place and customary life, as it were from his native land, for a paltry price, useless as he is to those who sell him and as he will be to those who buy him. But Cato, boasting of such things, says that he left in Spain even the horse which had carried him through his military campaign, that he might not tax the city with the cost of its transportation home. Whether these things should be set down to greatness of spirit or littleness of mind, is an open question.

But in other matters his self-restraint was beyond measure admirable. For instance, when he was in command of an army, he took for himself and his staff not more than three bushels of wheat a month, and for his beasts of burden, less than a bushel and a half of barley a day. He received Sardinia to govern as his province; and whereas his predecessors used to charge the public treasury for their tents, couches, and clothing while they oppressed the province with the cost of their large retinues of servants and friends, and of their lavish and elaborate banquets, his simple economy stood out in an incredible contrast. He made no demands whatever upon the public treasury, and made his circuit of the cities on foot, followed by a single public officer, who carried his robe and cup for libations to the gods. And yet, though in such matters he showed himself mild and lenient to those under his authority, in other ways he displayed a dignity and severity proper to the administration of justice. He carried out the edicts of the government in a direct and masterful way so that the Roman power never inspired its subjects with greater fear or affection.

● ● ●

He dealt with the Athenians through an interpreter. He could have spoken to them directly, but he always clung to his native ways, and mocked at those who were lost in admiration of anything that was Greek. . . . Moreover, he says the Athenians were astonished at the speed and pungency of his discourse. For what he himself set forth with brevity, the interpreter would repeat to them at great length and with many words; and on the whole he thought the words of the Greeks were born on their lips, but those of the Romans in their hearts.

● ● ●

Cato, who was ever rather generous, it would seem, in his own praises, and did not hesitate to follow up his great achievements with boastings equally great, is very pompous in his account of this exploit. He says that those who saw him at that time pursuing the enemy and hewing them down, felt convinced that Cato owed less to Rome than Rome to Cato; also that the consul Manius himself, flushed with victory, threw his arms about him, still flushed with his own victory, and embraced him a long time, crying out for joy that neither he himself nor the whole Roman people could fittingly requite Cato for his benefactions. Immediately after the battle he was sent to Rome as the messenger of his own triumphs. He had a fair passage to Brundisium, crossed the peninsula from there to Tarentum in a single day, traveled thence four days more, and on the fifth day after landing reached Rome, where he was the first to announce the victory. He filled the city full of joy and sacrifices, and the people with the proud feeling that it was able to master every land and sea.

These are perhaps the most remarkable features of Cato's military career. In political life, he seems to have regarded the impeachment and conviction of malefactors as a department worthy of his most zealous efforts. For he brought many prosecutions himself, assisted others in bringing theirs, and even instigated some to begin prosecutions, as for instance Petillius against Scipio. That great man, however, trampled the accusations against him under foot, as the splendor of his house and his own inherent loftiness of spirit prompted him to do, and Cato, unable to secure his capital conviction, dropped the case. But he so cooperated with the accusers of Lucius, Scipio's brother, as to have him condemned to pay a large fine to the state. This debt Lucius was unable to meet, and was therefore liable to imprisonment. Indeed, it was only at the intercession of the tribunes that he was at last set free.

We are also told that a certain young man, who had got a verdict of civil outlawry against an enemy of his dead father, was passing through the forum on the conclusion of the case, and met Cato, who greeted him and said: "These are the sacrifices we must bring to the spirits of our parents; not lambs and kids, but the condemnations and tears of their enemies." However, he himself did not go unscathed, but wherever in his political career he gave his enemies the slightest handle, he was all the while suffering prosecutions and running risk of condemnation. It is said that he was defendant in nearly fifty cases, and in the last one when he was eighty-six years of age. It was in the course of this that he uttered the memorable saying: "It is hard for one who has lived among men of one generation, to make his defence before those of another." And even with this case he did not put an end to his legal contests, but four years later, at the age of ninety, he impeached Servius Galba. Indeed, he may be said, like Nestor,[10] to have been vigorous and active among three generations. . . .

Ten years after his consulship, Cato was a candidate for the censorship. This office towered, as it were, above every other civic honor, and was, in a way, the high point of a political career. The variety of its powers was great, including that of examining into the lives and manners of the citizens. Its creators thought that

[10]An old and respected king, full of advice, in Homer's *Iliad* and *Odyssey*. (Because Plutarch used the Roman historian Livy as his source in the matter of Cato's age, he was mistaken. Cato lived "only" to the age of eighty-five.)

no one should be left to his own ways and desires, without inspection and review, either in his marrying, having children, ordering his daily life, or in the entertainment of his friends. Thinking that these things revealed a man's real character more than did his public and political career, they set men in office to watch, warn, and chastise, that no one should turn to vices and give up his native and customary way of life. They chose to this office one of the so-called patricians,[11] and one of the plebeians.[12] These officers were called censors, and they had authority to degrade a knight, or to expel a senator who led a wild and disorderly life. They also revised the assessments of property, and arranged the citizens in lists [for military service] according to their social and political classes. There were other great powers also connected with the office.

Therefore, when Cato became a candidate, nearly all the best-known and most influential men of the senatorial party united to oppose him. The men of noble parentage among them were moved by jealousy, thinking that nobility of birth would be trampled if men of lowly origin forced their way up to the summits of honor and power; while those who were conscious of base practices and of a departure from ancestral customs feared the severity of the man, which was sure to be harsh and unyielding in the exercise of power. Therefore, after due consultation and preparation, they put up in opposition to Cato seven candidates for the office, who sought the favor of the people with promises of mild conduct in office, supposing that they wanted to be ruled with a lax and indulgent hand. Cato, on the contrary, showed no inclination to be agreeable whatever, but plainly threatened wrongdoers in his speeches, and loudly cried that the city had need of a great purification. He urged the people, if they were wise, not to choose the most agreeable physician, but the one who was most in earnest. He himself, he said, was such a physician, and so was Valerius Flaccus, of the patricians. With him as colleague, and him alone, he thought he could cut the excessive luxury and effeminacy of the time. As for the rest of the candidates, he saw that they were all trying to force their way into the office in order to administer it badly, since they feared those who would administer it well. And so truly great were the Roman voters, and so worthy of great leaders, that they did not fear Cato's rigor and haughty independence, but rejected those candidates who, it was believed, would do everything to please them, and elected Flaccus to the office along with Cato.[13]

• • •

As censor, Cato paid not the slightest heed to his accusers, but grew still more strict. He cut off the pipes by which people conveyed part of the public water sup-

---

[11]Members of the Roman aristocratic, privileged class.

[12]The majority of citizens, like Cato, who were not patricians.

[13]In 184 B.C.

ply into their private houses and gardens; he upset and demolished all buildings that encroached on public land; he reduced the cost of public works to the lowest, and forced the rent of public lands to the highest possible figure. All these things brought much hatred upon him. Titus Flamininus headed a party against him which induced the Senate to annul as useless the outlays and payments which he had authorized for temples and public works, and incited the boldest of the tribunes to call him to account before the people and fine him two talents. The Senate also strongly opposed the erection of the basilica [large, rectangular public hall] which he built at the public cost below the council-house in the Forum, and which was called the Basilica Porcia.

Still, it appears that the people approved of his censorship to an amazing extent. At any rate, after erecting a statue to his honor in the temple of health, they commemorated in the inscription upon it, not the military commands nor the triumph of Cato, but, as the inscription may be translated, the fact "that when the Roman state was tottering to its fall, he was made censor, and by helpful guidance, wise restraints, and sound teachings, restored it again." . . .

He heaped high praise upon himself. He tells us that men of self-indulgent lives, when rebuked for it, used to say: "We ought not to be blamed; we are no Catos." Also that those who imitated some of his practices and did it clumsily, were called "left-handed Catos." Also that the Senate looked to him in the most dangerous crises as seafarers to their helmsman, and often, if he was not present, postponed its most serious business. These boasts of his are confirmed by other witnesses, for he had great authority in the city, alike for his life, his eloquence, and his age.

He was also a good father, a considerate husband, and a household manager of no little talent; nor did he give only a fitful attention to this, as a matter of little or no importance. Therefore, I think I ought to give suitable instances of his conduct in these relations. He married a wife who was of higher birth than she was rich, thinking that, although the rich and the high-born may be alike given to pride, still, women of high birth have such a horror of what is disgraceful that they are more obedient to their husbands in all that is honorable. He used to say that the man who struck his wife or child laid violent hands on the holiest of holy things. Also that he thought it more praiseworthy to be a good husband than a great senator, and there was nothing more to admire in Socrates of old than that he was always kind and gentle with his shrewish wife and stupid sons. After the birth of his own son, no business could be so urgent, unless it had a public character, as to prevent him from being present when his wife bathed and wrapped the babe. For the mother nursed it herself, and often gave her breast also to the infants of her slaves, that so they might come to cherish a brotherly affection for her son. As soon as the boy showed signs of understanding, his father took him under his own charge and taught him to read, although he had an accomplished slave, Chilo by name, who was a school-teacher, and taught many boys. Still, Cato thought it not right, as he tells us himself, that his son should be scolded by a slave or have his ears tweaked when he was slow to learn, still less that he should be indebted to his slave for such a priceless thing as education. He was therefore himself not only the boy's reading-teacher, but his tutor in law, and his athletic trainer, and he taught his son not merely to hurl the javelin and fight in armor and ride the horse, but also to box, to endure heat and cold, and to swim strongly through the eddies and billows of the Tiber. His "History of Rome," as he tells us himself, he wrote out with his own hand and in large characters, that his son might have in his own home an aid to acquaintance with his country's ancient traditions. He declares that his son's presence put him on guard against making indecencies of speech as if in the presence of the Vestal Virgins,[14] and that he never bathed with him. This, indeed, would seem to have been a general taboo with the Romans, for even fathers-in-law avoided bathing with their sons-in-law, because they were ashamed to uncover their nakedness. Afterwards, however, when they had learned from the Greeks their freedom in going naked before men, they in their turn infected the Greeks with the practice of doing so even before women.

So Cato worked at the task of molding his son to virtue. But since his body was rather too frail to endure much hardship, he relaxed somewhat the excessive rigidity and austerity of his own way of life. But his son, although frail, made a sturdy soldier, and fought brilliantly under Aemilius Paulus in the battle against Perseus.[15] On that occasion his sword either was knocked from his hand or slipped from his moist grasp. Distressed by this mishap, he turned to some of his companions for aid, and supported by them rushed again into the thick of the enemy. After a long and furious struggle, he succeeded in clearing the place, and found the sword at last among the many heaps of arms and dead bodies where friends and foes alike lay piled upon one another. Paulus, his commander, admired the young man's exploit, and there is still in existence a letter written by Cato himself to his son, in which he heaps extravagant praise upon him for this honorable zeal in recovering his sword. The son afterwards married Tertia, a daughter of Paulus and a sister of Scipio the Younger;[16] his admission into such a family was due no less to himself than to his father. Thus Cato's careful attention to the education of his son bore worthy fruit.

---

[14]The Vestals were virgin priestesses selected from noble families for terms of thirty years; they were expected to remain chaste and to tend the sacred fire in the temple of Vesta (Roman goddess of the family hearth).

[15]Aemilius Paulus was a consul who totally defeated Perseus, the last king of Macedonia, at the Battle of Pydna in 168 B.C. Twenty years after that decisive battle, Macedonia became a Roman province.

[16]This Scipio was adopted into the distinguished family of Scipio Africanus, conqueror of Hannibal, the Carthaginian general. Scipio the Younger later (146 B.C.) won the *final* victory for Rome against Carthage.

He owned many slaves, and usually bought those prisoners of war who were young and still capable of being reared and trained. Not one of his slaves ever entered another man's house unless sent there by Cato or his wife, and when any of them was asked what Cato was doing, he always answered that he did not know. A slave of his was expected either to be busy about the house, or to be asleep, and he preferred the sleepy ones. He thought these gentler than the wakeful ones, and that those who had enjoyed the gift of sleep were better for any kind of service than those who lacked it. In the belief that his slaves were led into most mischief by their sexual passions, he required that the males should have sex with the female slaves of the house at a fixed price, but should never approach any other woman.

At the outset, when Cato was still poor and in military service, he found no fault at all with what was served up to him, declaring that it was shameful for a man to quarrel with a servant over food and drink. But afterwards, when his circumstances were improved and he used to entertain his friends and colleagues at table, no sooner was the dinner over than he would flog those slaves who had been unsatisfactory in preparing or serving it. He was always arranging that his slaves should have feuds and disagreements among themselves; harmony among them made him suspicious and fearful of them. He had those who were suspected of some capital offence brought to trial before all their fellow servants, and, if convicted, put to death.

However, as he applied himself more strenuously to money-getting, he came to regard agriculture as more entertaining than profitable, and invested his money in business that was safe and sure. He bought ponds, hot springs, districts given over to fullers,[17] pitch factories, land with natural pasture and forest, all of which brought him large profits. He used to loan money also on ships, and his method was as follows. He required his borrowers to form a large company, and when there were fifty partners and as many ships for his security, he took one share in the company himself, and was represented by Quintio, a freedman of his, who accompanied his clients in all their ventures. In this way his entire security was not risked, but only a small part of it, and his profits were large. He used to lend money also to those of his slaves who wished it, and they would buy boys with it, and after training and teaching them for a year, at Cato's expense, would sell them again. Many of these boys Cato would retain for himself, counting to the credit of the slave the highest price bid for his boy by outsiders. He tried to persuade his son also to such investments, by saying that it was not the part of a man, but of a widow woman, to lessen his property. But surely Cato was going too far when he said that a man should be admired and glorified like a god if the

---

[17]Fuller's earth is an absorbent clay, used especially for removing grease from fabrics, as a filter, and as a dusting powder.

final inventory of his property showed that he had added to it more than he had inherited.

When he was now well on in years, there came as delegates from Athens to Rome, Carneades the Academic and Diogenes the Stoic philosopher[18] to beg the reversal of a certain decision against the Athenian people, which imposed upon them a heavy fine. Upon the arrival of these philosophers, the most studious of the city's youth hastened to wait upon them, and became their devoted and admiring listeners. The charm of Carneades especially, which had boundless power, and a fame not inferior to its power, won large and sympathetic audiences, and filled the city, like a rushing mighty wind, with the noise of his praises. Report spread far and wide that a Greek of amazing talent, who disarmed all opposition by the magic of his eloquence, had infused a tremendous passion into the youth of the city—in consequence of which they gave up their other pleasures and pursuits and were "possessed" about philosophy. The other Romans were pleased at this, and glad to see their young men lay hold of Greek culture and associate with such admirable men. But Cato, at the very outset, when this zeal for discussion came into the city, was distressed—fearing that the young men, by giving this direction to their ambition, should come to love a reputation based on mere words more than one achieved by military deeds. And when the fame of the visiting philosophers rose yet higher in the city, and their first speeches before the Senate were interpreted, at his own instance and request, by so conspicuous a man as Gaius Acilius, Cato determined, on some excuse or other, to rid the city of them all. So he rose in the Senate and condemned the city officials for keeping for so long a time a delegation composed of men who could easily secure anything they wished, so persuasive were they. "We ought," he said, "to make up our minds one way or another, and vote on what the delegation proposes, in order that these men may return to their schools and lecture to the sons of Greece, while the youth of Rome give ear to their laws and officials, as before."

This he did, not, as some think, out of personal hostility to Carneades, but because he was wholly opposed to philosophy, and made mock of all Greek culture and training, out of patriotic Roman zeal. He says, for instance, that Socrates was a mighty talker who attempted, as best he could, to be his country's tyrant by abolishing its customs and by enticing his fellow citizens into opinions contrary to the laws. He made fun of the school of Isocrates,[19] declaring that his pupils kept on studying with him till they were old men, as if they were to practice their

---

[18]This visit in 155 B.C. became quite famous as it drew the attention of many Romans to the Greek schools of philosophy. Carneades was called "the Academic" because he was head of the Academy founded by Plato (see introduction to Selection 18). Diogenes was the head of the Stoic school of philosophy.

[19]A student of Socrates and a famous orator, who established his own school in Athens.

arts and plead their cases before Minos[20] in Hades. And seeking to prejudice his son against Greek culture, he declared, in the tone of a prophet or a seer, that Rome would lose her empire when she had become infected with Greek literature. But time has certainly shown the emptiness of this pessimistic declaration, for while the city was at the height of its empire, she made every form of Greek learning and culture her own.

It was not only Greek philosophers that he hated, but he was also suspicious of Greeks who practiced medicine at Rome. He had heard, it would seem, of Hippocrates's[21] reply when the Great King of Persia sent for him, with the promise of a large fee, that he would never put his skill at the service of non-Greeks who were enemies of Greece. He said all Greek physicians had taken a similar oath, and urged his son to beware of them all. He himself, he said, had written a book of recipes, which he followed in the treatment of any who were sick in his family. He never required his patients to fast, but fed them on greens, or bits of duck, pigeon, or hare. Such a diet, he said, was light and good for sick people, except that it often causes dreams. By following such treatment he said he had good health himself, and kept his family in good health.

● ● ●

The last of his public services is supposed to have been the destruction of Carthage.[22] It was Scipio the Younger who actually brought the task to completion, but it was largely in consequence of the advice and counsel of Cato that the Romans undertook the war. Cato first became involved when sent on a mission to the Carthaginians and Masinissa the Numidian,[23] who were at war with one another, to inquire into the grounds of their quarrel. Masinissa had been a friend of the Roman people from the first, and the Carthaginians had entered into treaty relations with Rome only after the defeat which the elder Scipio [Africanus] had given them. The treaty deprived them of their empire, and imposed a heavy money tribute upon them. Cato, however, found the city by no means in a poor and lowly state, as the Romans supposed, but rather teeming with vigorous fighting men, overflowing with enormous wealth, filled with arms of every sort

---

[20]In Greco–Roman mythology, the judge of dead souls in the underworld.

[21]A famous Greek physician of the fifth century B.C.

[22]The powerful city on the African coast that rivalled Rome for control of the Mediterranean world. The Roman Republic fought three major wars against Carthage, ending in its capture and total destruction by Scipio the Younger in 146 B.C., three years after Cato's death.

[23]Numidia was a country of the African nomads lying immediately west and south of Carthage. Masinissa was the head of one of their tribal alliances.

and with military supplies, and not a little puffed up by all this. He therefore thought it no time for the Romans to be straightening out the affairs of Masinissa and the Numidians, but that they should repress the power of Carthage, which was becoming once again a deadly danger. Accordingly, he returned speedily to Rome, and advised the Senate that the former defeats of the Carthaginians had diminished not so much their power as their foolhardiness, and were likely to make them in the end not weaker, but more expert in war. He declared that their present contest with Numidia was but a prelude to a contest with Rome, while peace and treaty were mere names wherewith to cover their postponement of war till a proper occasion arose.

In addition to this, it is said that Cato purposely dropped an African fig in the Senate, as he shook out the folds of his toga; and then, as the senators admired its size and beauty, he said that the country where it grew was only three days' sail from Rome. And in one thing he was even more savage, namely, in adding to any speech of his whatsoever these words: "And, in my opinion, Carthage must be destroyed." . . . He saw, probably, that the Roman public, in its recklessness, was already guilty of many excesses—and in the pride of its prosperity, spurned the control of the Senate, and dragged the whole state with it, wherever its mad desires led it. He wished, therefore, that the fear of Carthage should continue to curb the public, like a bridle, believing Carthage not strong enough to conquer Rome, nor yet weak enough to be despised. What Cato dreaded was that the Roman people, sunk in their follies and excesses, faced a growing and sober external power that had always threatened them. That power ought to be done away with altogether, he thought, so that the Romans might be free to concentrate on a cure for their internal failings.

In this way Cato is said to have brought to pass the third and last war against Carthage. . . .

34

֍

Apuleius

THE GOLDEN ASS

By the second century A.D., many religions, including Christianity, were rivals for converts within the relatively tolerant Roman Empire. Among the most popular of those groups that—despite vigorous conservative opposition—attracted many initiates from the old Roman state religion was the cult of the Egyptian goddess Isis. She represented the female generative force of nature. With her brother–husband, Osiris, she was also ruler of the lower world of the dead. Some of the beliefs and customs relating to this Egyptian goddess were eventually transformed and given Christian meanings. The clearest description we have of this important religion's rituals can be found in The Metamorphoses, or The Golden Ass, by Lucius Apuleius (born ca. A.D. 125), Platonic philosopher, Latin orator, and novelist.

Apuleius, born in the city of Madaura in North Africa, was educated at nearby Carthage and in the philosophical schools of Athens. He traveled widely in the east where, apparently, he was initiated into the "mystery" religion of Isis–Osiris. Journeying to Rome, he made a living as a teacher of rhetoric and as a lawyer. After returning to Africa, Apuleius married a rich widow considerably older than himself. She was the mother of his friend. Some of her kinsmen prosecuted Apuleius on the charge that he gained the love of the widow through magical means and caused the death of her son, his friend. Apuleius's Apologia still survives as a dazzlingly learned and successful courtroom defence in the case. He was acquitted of all charges, although Apuleius's fascination with magic is clear in the episodes of The Metamorphoses. Subsequently settling in Carthage, Apuleius traveled extensively around the other cities of northern Africa, lecturing in Latin mainly on philosophical topics. His point of view, greatly admiring of the Platonic tradition (Selections 17 and 18), can be seen in the titles of two of his surviving speeches, "On the God of Socrates" and "On the Beliefs of Plato." Apuleius's fame was sufficient that statues of him were erected in Carthage and in his birthplace of Madaura.

The work for which Apuleius is best known is The Metamorphoses ("transformations"), or The Golden Ass, the only Latin novel to survive complete. In it, he tells the story of Lucius (his own name) who sets out on a journey through Thessaly, a region of northern Greece known for its witches. In the town of Hypata, he plunges into a wild sexual affair with his host's female servant, Fotis. She steals her mistress's magical ointment for Lucius in order to change her lover into the winged owl he wishes to become temporarily. As often happens to impulsive servants in the ancient stories, however, she makes a mistake and hands him the wrong ointment. Lucius's handsome physical appearance is transformed into that of an ugly beast of burden, a jackass (donkey), although he retains all his human thoughts and feelings.

Although the antidote is simply to eat roses, the asinine Lucius is dragged off by a violent band of robbers before Fotis can bring the fragrant cure to him. The rapid series of wild adventures that befall the transformed young man delights the reader with a variety of tales, from the licentious and the macabre to the spiritual. (The "Golden" of the title refers to the entertainment value of the tales, the most famous and beautiful one being that of "Cupid and Psyche.") After twelve miserable months in his ass's skin, from one rose season to the next, Lucius escapes at full gallop from the Corinthian arena where he is scheduled to be part of a sexual exhibition with a condemned murderess who will then be torn apart by wild beasts. With tears running down his hairy face, Lucius, incapable of human speech, offers a soundless prayer and falls asleep.

The following excerpt begins in an atmosphere of religious revelation as the Egyptian goddess Isis appears to him, identifies herself as the true source of all the forms of female divinity, and tells Lucius of his forthcoming return to human form. Lucius awakens, watches an elaborate procession of Isis-worshipers pass by, and eats the garland of roses held by her high priest. His bestial form is transformed back into his human form. Dedicating himself to his savior goddess, Lucius (in the concluding section that follows this excerpt) eventually goes to Rome, where he is initiated into the deepest mysteries of both Isis and Osiris. Like his creator, Apuleius, Lucius becomes a famous lawyer.

Although The Golden Ass is a work of fiction, the conversion scenes clearly reflect the author's deeply felt personal experiences. The symbolism is clear: when man serves his lusts, he becomes a brute animal like the lowliest ass; when man turns toward the spirituality represented by Isis, he achieves his truly human form. Later, Christians were to discuss Apuleius's meaning with some care. The great Saint Augustine, in his City of God (Selection 37), suggested that Apuleius might have actually turned into an ass, a victim of his own "demonic art or power."

THE GODDESS ISIS INTERVENES

When I had finished my prayer and poured out the full bitterness of my oppressed heart, I returned to my sandy hollow, where once more sleep overcame me. I had scarcely closed my eyes before the apparition of a woman began to rise from the middle of the sea with so lovely a face that the gods themselves would have fallen down in adoration of it. First the head, then the whole shining body gradually emerged and stood before me poised on the surface of the waves. Yes, I will try to describe this transcendent vision, for though human speech is poor and limited, the goddess herself will perhaps inspire me with poetic imagery sufficient to convey some slight inkling of what I saw.

Her long, thick hair fell in tapering ringlets on her lovely neck, and was crowned with an intricate chaplet in which was woven every kind of flower. Just above her brow shone a round disc, like a mirror, or like the bright face of the moon, which told me who she was. Vipers rising from the left-hand and right-hand partings of her hair supported this disc, with ears of corn bristling beside them. Her many-colored robe was of finest linen; part was glistening white, part crocus-yellow, part glowing red, and along the entire hem a woven border of flowers and fruit clung, swaying in the breeze. But what caught and held my eye more than anything else was the deep black lustre of her mantle. She wore it slung across her body from the right hip to the left shoulder, where it was caught in a knot resembling the boss of a shield; but part of it hung in innumerable folds, the tasselled fringe quivering. It was embroidered with glittering stars on the hem and everywhere else, and in the middle beamed a full and fiery moon.

In her right hand she held a bronze rattle, of the sort used to frighten away the God of the Sirocco;[1] its narrow rim was curved like a sword-belt and three little rods, which sang shrilly when she shook the handle, passed horizontally through it. A boat-shaped gold dish hung from her left hand, and along the upper surface of the handle writhed an asp with puffed throat and head raised ready to strike. On her divine feet were slippers of palm leaves, the emblem of victory.

All the perfumes of Arabia floated into my nostrils as the goddess deigned to address me: "You see me here, Lucius, in answer to your prayer. I am Nature, the universal mother, mistress of all the elements, primordial child of time, sovereign of all things spiritual, queen of the dead, queen also of the immortals, the single manifestation of all gods and goddesses that are. My nod governs the shining heights of heaven, the wholesome sea-breezes, the lamentable silences of the world below. Though I am worshiped in many aspects, known by countless

[1]The sirocco is a hot, dry, dust-laden wind blowing north from Africa.

names, and propitiated with all manner of different rites, yet the whole round earth venerates me. The primeval Phrygians call me Pessinuntica, mother of the gods; the Athenians, sprung from their own soil, call me Cecropian Artemis; for the islanders of Cyprus I am Paphian Aphrodite; for the archers of Crete I am Dictynna; for the trilingual Sicilians, Stygian Proserpine; and for the Eleusinians their ancient Mother of the Corn.

"Some know me as Juno, some as Bellona of the Battles; others as Hecate, others again as Rhamnubia, but both races of Aethiopians, whose lands the morning sun first shines upon, and the Egyptians who excel in ancient learning and worship me with ceremonies proper to my godhead, call me by my true name, namely, Queen Isis. I have come in pity of your plight, I have come to favor and aid you. Weep no more, lament no longer; the hour of deliverance, shone over by my watchful light, is at hand.

"Listen attentively to my orders.

"The eternal laws of religion devote to my worship the day born from this night. Tomorrow my priests offer me the first fruits of the new sailing season by dedicating a ship to me: for at this season the storms of winter lose their force, the leaping waves subside and the sea becomes navigable once more. You must wait for this sacred ceremony, with a mind that is neither anxious for the future nor clouded with profane thoughts; and I shall order the high priest to carry a garland of roses in my procession, tied to the rattle which he carries in his right hand. Do not hesitate, push the crowd aside, join the procession with confidence in my grace. Then come close up to the high priest as if you wished to kiss his hand, gently pluck the roses with your mouth and you will immediately slough off the hide of what has always been for me the most hateful beast in the universe.[2]

"Above all, have faith: do not think that my commands are hard to obey. For at this very moment, while I am speaking to you here, I am also giving complementary instructions to my sleeping high priest; and tomorrow, at my commandment, the dense crowds of people will make way for you. I promise you that in the joy and laughter of the festival nobody will either view your ugly shape with abhorrence or dare to put a sinister interpretation on your sudden return to human shape. Only remember, and keep these words of mine locked tight in your heart, that from now onwards until the very last day of your life you are dedicated to my service. It is only right that you should devote your whole life to the goddess who makes you a man again. Under my protection you will be happy and famous, and when at the destined end of your life you descend to the land of ghosts, there too in the subterrene hemisphere you shall have frequent occasion

---

[2]Isis particularly hates the ass because it was identified with the demonic god Seth, who murdered Osiris, brother–husband of the good Isis. Thus, in having been turned into an ass, Lucius had been captured by the black magic of evil forces.

to adore me. From the Elysian fields[3] you will see me as queen of the profound Stygian realm, shining through the darkness of Acheron[4] with a light as kindly and tender as I show you now. Further, if you are found to deserve my divine protection by careful obedience to the ordinances of my religion and by perfect chastity, you will become aware that I, and I alone, have power to prolong your life beyond the limits appointed by destiny."

With this, the vision of the invincible goddess faded and dissolved.

THE ASS IS TRANSFORMED

I rose at once, wide awake, bathed in a sweat of joy and fear. Astonished beyond words at this clear manifestation of her godhead, I splashed myself with sea water and carefully memorized her orders, intent on obeying them to the letter. Soon a golden sun arose to rout the dark shadows of night, and at once the streets were filled with people walking along as if in a religious triumph. Not only I, but the whole world, seemed filled with delight. The animals, the houses, even the weather itself reflected the universal joy and serenity, for a calm, sunny morning had succeeded yesterday's frost, and the songbirds, assured that spring had come, were chirping their welcome to the queen of the stars, the mother of the seasons, the mistress of the universe. The trees, too, not only the orchard trees but those grown for their shade, roused from their winter sleep by the warm breezes of the south and tasselled with green leaves, waved their branches with a pleasant rustling noise; and the crash and thunder of the surf was stilled, for the gales had blown themselves out, the dark clouds were gone and the calm sky shone with its own deep, blue light.

Presently the vanguard of the grand procession came in view. It was composed of a number of people in fancy dress of their own choosing: a man wearing a soldier's sword-belt; another dressed as a huntsman, a thick cloak caught up to his waist with a hunting knife and javelin; another who wore gilt sandals, a wig, a silk dress, and expensive jewelry, and pretended to be a woman. Then a man with heavy boots, shield, helmet, and sword, looking as though he had walked straight out of the gladiators' school; a pretended magistrate with purple robe and rods of office; a philosopher with cloak, staff, clogs, and billy-goat beard; a bird-catcher, carrying lime and a long reed; a fisherman with another long reed and a fish-hook. Oh, yes, and a tame she-bear, dressed like a woman, carried in a sedan chair; and an ape in a straw hat and a saffron-colored Phrygian cloak with a gold

---

[3]That place in the underworld (Hades) where dwell the spirits of those favored by the gods.

[4]The Styx ("Stygian realm") and the Acheron are rivers in Hades.

cup grasped in its paws—a caricature of Jupiter's[5] beautiful cup-bearer Gany-mede. Finally an ass with wings glued to its shoulders and a doddering old man seated on its rump; you would have laughed like anything at that pair, supposed to be Pegasus and Bellerophon.[6] These fancy-dress comedians kept running in and out of the crowd, and behind them came the procession proper.

At the head walked women crowned with flowers, who pulled more flowers out of the folds of their beautiful white dresses and scattered them along the road; their joy in the savioress appeared in every gesture. Next came women with pol-ished mirrors tied to the backs of their heads, which gave all who followed them the illusion of coming to meet the goddess, rather than marching before her. Next, a party of women with ivory combs in their hands who made a pantomime of combing the goddess's royal hair, and another party with bottles of perfume who sprinkled the road with balsam and other precious perfumes; and behind these a mixed company of women and men who addressed the goddess as "daugh-ter of the stars" and propitiated her by carrying every sort of light—lamps, torch-es, wax-candles, and so forth.

Next came musicians with pipes and flutes, followed by a party of carefully chosen choir-boys singing a hymn in which an inspired poet had explained the origin of the procession. The temple pipers of the great god Serapis were there, too, playing their religious anthem on pipes with slanting mouthpieces and tubes curving around their right ears; also a number of beadles and whifflers crying: "Make way there, way for the goddess!" Then followed a great crowd of the god-dess's initiates, men and women of all classes and every age, their pure white linen clothes shining brightly. The women wore their hair tied up in glossy coils under gauze headdresses; the men's heads were completely shaven, representing the god-dess's bright earthly stars, and they carried rattles of brass, silver, and even gold, which kept up a shrill and ceaseless tinkling.

The leading priests, also clothed in white linen drawn tight across their breasts and hanging down to their feet, carried the oracular emblems of the deity. The high priest held a bright lamp, which was not at all like the lamps we use at night banquets; it was a golden boat-shaped affair with a tall tongue of flame mount-ing from a hole in the center. The second priest held an *auxiliaria,* or "sacrificial pot," in each of his hands—the name refers to the goddess's providence in help-ing her devotees. The third priest carried a miniature palm tree with gold leaves, also the serpent wand of Mercury.[7] The fourth carried the model of a left hand with the fingers stretched out, which is an emblem of justice because the left hand, with its natural slowness and lack of any craft or subtlety, seems more im-

---

[5]Jupiter (Greek Zeus) is chief among the gods.

[6]Bellerophon is a mythical Greek hero, rider of Pegasus, the winged horse.

[7]Greek Hermes, winged messenger of the gods.

partial than the right. He also held a golden vessel, rounded in the shape of a woman's breast, from the nipple of which a thin stream of milk fell to the ground. The fifth carried a winnowing fan woven with golden rods, not osiers. Then came a man, not one of the five, carrying a wine-jar.

Next in the procession followed those deities that deigned to walk on human feet. Here was the frightening messenger of the gods of heaven, and of the gods of the dead: Anubis with a face black on one side, golden on the other, walking erect and holding his herald's wand in one hand and in the other a green palm-branch. Behind, danced a man carrying on his shoulders, seated upright, the statue of a cow, representing the goddess as the fruitful mother of us all. Then along came a priest with a box containing the secret implements of her wonderful cult. Another fortunate priest had an ancient emblem of her godhead hidden in the lap of his robe: this was not made in the shape of any beast, wild or tame, or any bird or human being, but the exquisite beauty of its workmanship no less than the originality of its design called for admiration and awe. It was a symbol of the sublime and ineffable mysteries of the goddess, which are never to be divulged: a small vessel of burnished gold, upon which Egyptian hieroglyphics were thickly crowded, with a rounded bottom, a long spout, and a generously curving handle along which sprawled an asp, raising its head and displaying its scaly, wrinkled, puffed-out throat.

At last the moment had come when the blessing promised by the almighty goddess was to fall upon me. The high priest in whom lay my hope of salvation approached, and I saw that he carried the rattle and the garland in his right hand just as I had been promised—but, oh, it was more than a garland to me, it was a crown of victory over cruel fortune, bestowed on me by the goddess after I had endured so many hardships and run through so many dangers! Though overcome with sudden joy, I refrained from galloping forward at once and disturbing the calm progress of the pageant by a brutal charge, but gently and politely wriggled my way through the crowd which gave way before me, clearly by the goddess's intervention, until at last I emerged at the other side. I saw at once that the priest had been warned what to expect in his vision of the previous night but was nonetheless astounded that the fulfilment came so pat. He stood still and held out the rose garland to the level of my mouth. I trembled and my heart pounded as I ate those roses with loving relish; and no sooner had I swallowed them than I found that the promise had been no deceit. My bestial features faded away; the rough hair fell from my body; my sagging paunch tightened; my hind hooves separated into feet and toes; my fore hooves now no longer served only for walking upon, but were restored as hands to my human uses. Then my neck shrank; my face and head rounded; my great hard teeth shrank to their proper size; my long ears shortened; and my tail, which had been my worst shame, vanished altogether.

A gasp of wonder went up and the priests, aware that the miracle corresponded with the high priest's vision of the great goddess, lifted their hands to heaven and with one voice applauded the blessing which she had vouchsafed me: this swift restoration to my proper shape.

When I saw what had happened to me I stood rooted to the ground with astonishment and could not speak for a long while, my mind unable to cope with so great and sudden a joy. I could find no words good enough to thank the goddess for her extraordinary, loving kindness. But the high priest, who had been informed by her of all my miseries, though himself taken aback by the weird sight, gave orders in dumb-show that I should be lent a garment to cover me; for as soon as I regained my human shape, I had naturally done what any naked man would do—pressed my knees closely together and put both my hands down to screen my private parts. Someone quickly took off his upper robe and covered me with it, after which the high priest gazed benignly at me, still wondering at my perfectly human appearance.

"Lucius, my friend," he said, "you have endured and performed many labors and withstood the buffetings of all the winds of ill luck. Now at last you have put into the harbor of peace and stand before the altar of loving kindness. Neither your noble blood and rank nor your education sufficed to keep you from falling a slave to pleasure; youthful follies ran away with you. Your luckless curiosity earned you a sinister punishment. But blind fortune, after tossing you maliciously about from peril to peril has somehow, without thinking what she was doing, landed you here in religious felicity. Let her be gone now and fume furiously wherever she pleases, let her find some other plaything for her cruel hands. She has no power to hurt those who devote their lives to the honor and service of our goddess's majesty. The jade! What use was served by making you over to bandits, wild dogs, and cruel masters, by setting your feet on dangerous stony paths, by holding you in daily terror of death? Rest assured that you are now safe under the protection of the true fortune, all-seeing providence, whose clear light shines for all the gods that are. Rejoice now, as becomes a wearer of white linen. Follow triumphantly in the train of the goddess who has delivered you. Let the irreligious see you and, seeing, let them acknowledge the error of their ways. Let them cry: 'Look, there goes Lucius, rescued from a dreadful fate by the intervention of the goddess Isis; watch him glory in the defeat of his ill luck!' But to secure today's gains, you must enroll yourself in this holy order as last night you pledged yourself to do, voluntarily undertaking the duties to which your oath binds you; for her service is perfect freedom."

When the high priest had ended his inspired speech, I joined the throng of devotees and went forward with the procession, an object of curiosity to all Corinth. People pointed or jerked their heads at me and said: "Look, there goes Lucius, restored to human shape by the power of the almighty goddess! Lucky, lucky man to have earned her compassion on account of his former innocence and good behavior, and now to be reborn as it were, and immediately accepted into her most sacred service!" Their congratulations were long and loud.

Meanwhile the pageant moved slowly on and we approached the seashore, at last reaching the very place where, on the previous night, I had lain down as an ass. There the divine emblems were arranged in due order and there with solemn prayers the chaste-lipped priest consecrated and dedicated to the goddess a beautifully built ship, with Egyptian hieroglyphics painted over the entire hull; but first he carefully purified it with a lighted torch, an egg, and sulphur. The sail was shining white linen, inscribed in large letters with the prayer for the goddess's protection of shipping during the new sailing season. The long fir mast with its shining head was now stepped, and we admired the gilded prow shaped like the neck of Isis's sacred goose, and the long, highly-polished keel cut from a solid trunk of citrus-wood. Then all present, both priesthood and laity, began zealously stowing aboard winnowing-fans heaped with aromatics and other votive offerings and poured an abundant stream of milk into the sea as a libation. When the ship was loaded with generous gifts and prayers for good fortune, they cut the anchor cables and she slipped across the bay with a serene breeze behind her that seemed to have sprung up for her sake alone. When she stood so far out to sea that we could no longer keep her in view, the priests took up the sacred emblems again and started happily back towards the temple, in the same orderly procession as before.

On our arrival the high priest and the priests who carried the oracular emblems were admitted into the goddess's sanctuary with other initiates and restored them to their proper places. Then one of them, known as the Doctor of Divinity, presided at the gate of the sanctuary over a meeting of the shrine-bearers, as the highest order of the priests of Isis are called. He went up into a high pulpit with a book and read out a Latin blessing upon "our liege lord, the Emperor, and upon the Senate, and upon the Order of Knights, and upon the Commons of Rome, and upon all sailors and all ships who owe obedience to the aforesaid powers." Then he uttered the traditional Greek formula, "Ploeaphesia," meaning that vessels were now permitted to sail, to which the people responded with a great cheer and dispersed happily to their homes, taking all kinds of decorations with them: such as olive boughs, scent shrubs, and garlands of flowers, but first kissing the feet of a silver statue of the goddess that stood on the temple steps. I did not feel like moving a nail's breadth from the place, but stood with my eyes intently fixed on the statue and relived in memory all my past misfortunes.

Meanwhile, the news of my adventures and of the goddess's wonderful goodness to me had flown out in all directions; eventually it reached my own city of Madaura,[8] where I had been mourned as dead. At once my slaves, servants, and close relatives forgot their sorrow and came hurrying to Corinth in high spirits to welcome me back from the Underworld, as it were, and bring me all sorts of presents. I was as delighted to see them as they were to see me—I had despaired of ever doing so—and thanked them over and over again for what they had brought

---

[8]Madaura is also the author's birthplace; the clear implication is that Apuleius, like his fictional Lucius, has become a worshiper of Isis.

me: I was especially grateful to my servants for bringing me as much money and as many clothes as I needed.

I spoke to them all in turn, which was no more than my duty, telling them of troubles now past and of my happy prospects; then returned to what had become my greatest pleasure in life—contemplation of the goddess. I managed to obtain the use of a room in the temple and took constant part in her services, from which I had hitherto been excluded. The brotherhood accepted me almost as one of themselves, a loyal devotee of the great goddess.

Not a single night did I pass, nor even doze off during the day, without some new vision of her. She always ordered me to be initiated into her sacred mysteries, to which I had long been destined. I was anxious to obey, but religious awe held me back, because after making careful enquiries I found that to take orders was to bind oneself to a very difficult life, especially as regards chastity: and that an initiate has to be continuously on his guard against accidental defilement. Somehow or other, though the question was always with me, I delayed the decision which I knew I must sooner or later take.

One night I dreamed that the high priest came to me with his lap full of presents. When I asked: "What have you there?" he answered: "Something from Thessaly. Your slave Candidus has just arrived." When I awoke, I puzzled over the dream for a long time, wondering what it meant, especially as I had never owned a slave of that name. However, I was convinced that whatever the high priest offered me must be something good. When dawn approached I waited for the opening of the temple, still in a state of anxious expectation. The white curtains of the sanctuary were then drawn and we adored the august face of the goddess. A priest went the round of the altars, performing the morning rites with solemn supplications and, chalice in hand, poured libations of water drawn from a spring within the temple precincts. When the service was over, a choir saluted the breaking day with the loud hymn that they always sing at the hour of prime.[9]

The doors opened and who should come in but the two slaves whom I had left behind at Hypata when Fotis by her unlucky mistake had put a halter around my neck. They had heard the tale of my adventures and brought me all my belongings. They had even managed to recover my white horse, after its repeated changes of hand, by identifying my brand on its haunch. Now I understood the meaning of my dream: not only had they brought me something from Thessaly, but I had recovered my horse, plainly referred to in the dream as "your slave Candidus"; for *Candidus* means "white."

Thereafter I devoted my whole time to attendance on the goddess, encouraged by these tokens to hope for even greater marks of her favor, and my desire for taking holy orders increased. I frequently spoke of it to the high priest, begging him to initiate me into the mysteries of the holy night. He was a grave man,

---

[9]Dawn.

remarkable for the strict observance of his religious duties, and checked my restlessness, as parents calm down children who are making unreasonable demands, but so gently and kindly that I was not in the least discouraged. He explained that the day on which a postulant might be initiated was always indicated by signs from the goddess herself, and that it was she who chose the officiating priest and announced how the incidental expenses of the ceremony were to be paid. In his view I ought to wait with attentive patience and avoid the two extremes of overeagerness and obstinacy; begin neither unresponsive when called nor importunate while awaiting my call. "No single member of the brotherhood," he said, "has ever been so wrong-minded and sacrilegious, in fact so bent on his own destruction, as to partake of the mystery without direct orders from the goddess, and so fall into deadly sin. The gates of the underworld and the guardianship of life are in her hands, and the rites of initiation approximate to a voluntary death from which there is only a precarious hope of resurrection. So she usually chooses old men who feel that their end is fast approaching yet are not too senile to be capable of keeping a secret; by her grace they are, in a sense, born again and restored to new and healthy life."

He said, in fact, that I must be content to await definite orders, but agreed that I had been foreordained for the service of the goddess by clear marks of her favor. Meanwhile I must abstain from forbidden food, as the priests did, so that when the time came for me to partake of their most holy mysteries I could enter the sanctuary with unswerving steps.

I accepted his advice and learned to be patient, taking part in the daily services of the temple as calmly and quietly as I knew how, intent on pleasing the goddess. Nor did I have a troublesome and disappointing probation. Soon after this she gave me proof of her grace by a midnight vision in which I was plainly told that the day for which I longed, the day on which my greatest wish would be granted, had come at last. I learned that she had ordered the high priest, . . . whose destiny was linked with mine by planetary sympathy, to officiate at my initiation.

These orders and certain others given me at the same time so exhilarated me that I rose before dawn to tell the high priest about them, and reached his door just as he was coming out. I greeted him and was about to beg him more earnestly than ever to allow me to be initiated, as a privilege that was now mine by right, when he spoke first. "Dear Lucius," he said, "how lucky, how blessed you are that the great goddess has graciously deigned to honor you in this way. There is no time to waste. The day for which you prayed so earnestly has dawned. The many-named goddess orders me to initiate you into her most holy mysteries."

He took me by the hand and led me courteously to the doors of the vast temple, and when he had opened them in the usual solemn way and performed the morning sacrifice he went to the sanctuary and took out two or three books written in characters unknown to me: some of them animal hieroglyphics, some of them ordinary letters protected against profane prying by having their tops and tails wreathed in knots or rounded like wheels or tangled together in spirals like vine tendrils. From these books he read me out instructions for providing the necessary clothes and accessories for my initiation.

I at once went to my friends the priests and asked them to buy part of what I needed, sparing no expense: the rest I went to buy myself.

In due time the high priest summoned me and took me to the nearest public baths, attended by a crowd of priests. There, when I had enjoyed my ordinary bath, he himself washed and sprinkled me with holy water, offering up prayers for divine mercy. After this he brought me back to the temple and placed me at the very feet of the goddess.

It was now early afternoon. He gave me certain orders too holy to be spoken above a whisper, and then commanded me in everyone's hearing to abstain from all but the plainest food for the ten succeeding days, to eat no meat and drink no wine.

I obeyed his instructions in all reverence and at last the day came for taking my vows. As evening approached a crowd of priests came flocking to me from all directions, each one giving me congratulatory gifts, as the ancient custom is. Then the high priest ordered all uninitiated persons to depart, invested me in a new linen garment and led me by the hand into the inner recesses of the sanctuary itself. I have no doubt, curious reader, that you are eager to know what happened when I entered. If I were allowed to tell you, and you were allowed to be told, you would soon hear everything; but, as it is, my tongue would suffer for its indiscretion and your ears for their inquisitiveness.

However, not wishing to leave you, if you are religiously inclined, in a state of tortured suspense, I will record as much as I may lawfully record for the uninitiated, but only on condition that you believe it. *I approached the very gates of death and set one foot on Proserpine's threshold,*[10] *yet was permitted to return, rapt through all the elements. At midnight I saw the sun shining as if it were noon; I entered the presence of the gods of the underworld and the gods of the upper-world, stood near and worshiped them.*

Well, now you have heard what happened, but I fear you are still none the wiser.

The solemn rites ended at dawn and I emerged from the sanctuary wearing twelve different stoles, certainly a most sacred costume but one that there can be no harm in my mentioning. Many uninitiated people saw me wearing it when the high priest ordered me to mount into the wooden pulpit which stood in the center of the temple, immediately in front of the goddess's image. I was wearing an outer garment of fine linen embroidered with flowers, and a precious scarf hung down from my shoulders to my ankles with sacred animals worked in color on every part of it; for instance Indian serpents and Hyperborean griffins, which are

---

[10]Proserpine (Greek Persephone) is the queen of the underworld.

winged lions generated in the more distant parts of the world. The priests call this scarf an Olympian stole. I held a lighted torch in my right hand and wore a white palm tree chaplet with its leaves sticking out all round like rays of light.

The curtains were pulled aside and I was suddenly exposed to the gaze of the crowd, as when a statue is unveiled, dressed like the sun. That day was the happiest of my initiation, and I celebrated it as my birthday with a cheerful banquet at which all my friends were present. Further rites and ceremonies were performed on the third day, including a sacred breakfast, and these ended the proceedings. However, I remained for some days longer in the temple, enjoying the ineffable pleasure of contemplating the goddess's statue, because I was bound to her by a debt of gratitude so large that I could never hope to pay it.

35

🦢

THE BIBLE
NEW TESTAMENT

The New Testament, first written in Greek, is a Christian addition to the Hebrew Old Testament. Christians believe that the appearance and teachings of Jesus represented a new covenant, or testament (the words are the same in Greek), superseding the old one between God and the Jews. (See Selection 6 for the old covenant on Mount Sinai.) The twenty-seven books that make up the New Testament were written independently during the late first century and early second century of the Christian era. They were among many Christian writings circulating at the time and were not defined as sacred, as were the scriptures of the Jews, until more than a century after Jesus's crucifixion. And it was not until A.D. 367 that the list (canon) of texts, as we know it now, was officially accepted by most Christian groups. The New Testament is thus the result of a winnowing-out process from a large body of early Christian writings. Although, as with the older Hebrew scriptures, the New Testament was not originally a product of Western thought, after centuries of historical development the Jewish–Christian tradition and Western culture have become inseparably interwoven.

The following passages deal with some of the most fundamental matters of Christian faith. They were highly colored, in those early centuries, by traditional thought-forms and language. Their place of origin is ancient Palestine, occupied at the time by Roman imperial forces. They focus on the life, teachings, and divine significance of a unique personality, Jesus of Nazareth.

The expression of the Christian story underwent changes from the outset. The gospel (the "good news" about Jesus's life) was first preached in a strictly Jewish atmosphere in the Roman-conquered provinces of Judea and Galilee, where ideas of a "Messiah," a "Kingdom of God," and a "Son of Man" were well-known. As the Christian movement shifted from its Jewish roots and became increasingly identified with non-Jews (Gentiles), its message was restated in a way more suited to the Greek-speaking peoples around the eastern Mediterranean. Such terms as "Savior," "Son of God," and "Body of Christ" then appeared. In general, the *earlier gospels emphasize Jesus's role as a human ethical teacher and prophet favored by God. These books are named for Mark, written ca. A.D. 70–80, and Matthew and Luke, both written ca. A.D. 90. The gospel named for John, written ca. A.D. 100, on the other hand, stresses the divine nature of Jesus.*

All the gospels should be read in the light of the disturbed political condition of Judea during the years between Jesus's crucifixion and the unsuccessful Jewish revolt against Rome, from A.D. 66 to 73. The Roman destruction of Jerusalem in A.D. 70 apparently destroyed the earliest Christian records (in the local languages of Hebrew and Aramaic). Thus, the gospels, as we know them now, were set down after the revolt failed, and they reflect the need to prove to the Roman officials that the Christians were separate from the rebellious Jews.

The first selection, the "Sermon on the Mount" from The Gospel According to Matthew, shows the ethical side of the Christian tradition. Jesus's teachings go beyond the Law of Moses (see Selection 6 from Exodus). They summon individuals to put inwardness of religious life before the outward forms. The three chapters of Matthew's twenty-eight included here are among the most popular in the Bible, despite the demands they make on those who have chosen to serve God rather than self.

The crucifixion of Jesus at first seemed to both his friends and enemies as the end of an ill-fated religious mission. His disciples, however, soon became convinced of his return from death and awaited him. Seven weeks after the reported resurrection (Easter Sunday), on the day of Pentecost in the Christian calendar, the disciples were "filled with the Holy Spirit." Thus, the Christian Church was born, and the disciples went forward with the worldwide work of converting others. The most influential of the apostles (earliest Christian missionaries) was Paul. Known at first by his Hebrew name of Saul, he was a vigorous convert to the new faith. He proved to be a fearless preacher and organizer, founding and guiding new congregations in Asia Minor and Greece and giving instructions through numerous visits and letters. Paul's letters, ca. A.D. 51–63, may be the earliest writings of the New Testament. One of his most significant letters, the second selection, is excerpted here. The letter of Paul to the Romans deals with such essential matters of doctrine as "justification by faith" and the relation of the old Jewish covenant to the new Christian covenant. Later, when established as part of the Holy Scripture, the letters of Paul would exercise immense and continuing influence on the philosophy and practices of all Christians.

⟡

THE GOSPEL ACCORDING TO MATTHEW[1]
The Sermon on the Mount[2]
4:23–7:29

And he went about all Galilee, teaching in their synagogues and preaching the gospel of the kingdom and healing every disease and every infirmity among the people. So his fame spread throughout all Syria, and they brought him all the sick, those afflicted with various diseases and pains, demoniacs, epileptics, and paralytics, and he healed them. And great crowds followed him from Galilee and the Decapolis[3] and Jerusalem and Judea and from beyond the Jordan.

Seeing the crowds, he went up on the mountain, and when he sat down[4] his disciples came to him. And he opened his mouth and taught them, saying:

"Blessed are the poor in spirit, for theirs is the kingdom of heaven.

"Blessed are those who mourn, for they shall be comforted.

"Blessed are the meek, for they shall inherit the earth.

"Blessed are those who hunger and thirst for righteousness, for they shall be satisfied.

"Blessed are the merciful, for they shall obtain mercy.

"Blessed are the pure in heart, for they shall see God.

"Blessed are the peacemakers, for they shall be called sons of God.

"Blessed are those who are persecuted for righteousness's sake, for theirs is the kingdom of heaven.

"Blessed are you when men revile you and persecute you and utter all kinds of evil against you falsely on my account. Rejoice and be glad, for your reward is great in heaven, for so men persecuted the prophets[5] who were before you.

The Scripture quotations contained herein are from the Revised Standard Version of the Bible, copyright 1946, 1952, 1971 by the Division of Christian Education of the National Council of the Churches of Christ in the USA. Used by permission.

[1]Of unknown authorship, this gospel may have acquired its title because the writer possibly used, as one of his sources, a collection of Jesus's sayings prepared by the disciple Matthew. Like the other gospels, it was written in Greek for a mainly non-Jewish audience after the Roman destruction of Jerusalem in A.D. 70. It attempts to distinguish the new religion of Christianity from its Jewish roots. Nevertheless, this gospel assumes the reader's knowledge of the Old Testament and of Jewish history and religious ideas. Many of Jesus's sayings in the gospels are, in fact, quotations or adaptations of the older Hebrew scriptures.

[2]This passage is often described as the essence of Christian ethical teaching. The sermon's delivery on a mountain suggests Jesus's relationship to the Law of Moses, delivered on Mount Sinai.

[3]A region—also occupied by Rome—just east of the Jordan River.

[4]The usual posture of Jewish rabbis (religious leaders) while teaching.

[5]The Jewish prophets of the Old Testament. (See, for example, Jeremiah, Selection 6).

"You are the salt of the earth; but if salt has lost its taste, how shall its saltness be restored? It is no longer good for anything except to be thrown out and trodden underfoot by men.

"You are the light of the world. A city set on a hill cannot be hid. Nor do men light a lamp and put it under a bushel, but on a stand, and it gives light to all in the house. Let your light so shine before men, that they may see your good works and give glory to your Father who is in heaven.

"Think not that I have come to abolish the law and the prophets; I have come not to abolish them but to fulfil them.[6] For truly, I say to you, till heaven and earth pass away, not an iota, not a dot, will pass from the law until all is accomplished. Whoever then relaxes one of the least of these commandments and teaches men so, shall be called least in the kingdom of heaven; but he who does them and teaches them shall be called great in the kingdom of heaven. For I tell you, unless your righteousness exceeds that of the scribes and Pharisees,[7] you will never enter the kingdom of heaven.

"You have heard that it was said to the men of old,[8] 'You shall not kill;[9] and whoever kills shall be liable to judgment.' But I say to you that everyone who is angry with his brother shall be liable to judgment; whoever insults his brother shall be liable to the council, and whoever says, 'You fool!' shall be liable to the hell of fire. So if you are offering your gift at the altar, and there remember that your brother has something against you, leave your gift there before the altar and go; first be reconciled to your brother, and then come and offer your gift. Make friends quickly with your accuser, while you are going with him to court, lest your accuser hand you over to the judge, and the judge to the guard, and you be put in prison; truly, I say to you, you will never get out till you have paid the last penny.

"You have heard that it was said, 'You shall not commit adultery.' But I say to you that everyone who looks at a woman lustfully has already committed adultery with her in his heart. If your right eye causes you to sin, pluck it out and throw it away; it is better that you lose one of your members than that your whole body be thrown into hell. And if your right hand causes you to sin, cut it off and throw it away; it is better that you lose one of your members than that your whole body go into hell.

"It was also said, 'Whoever divorces his wife, let him give her a certificate of divorce.' But I say to you that everyone who divorces his wife, except on the

---

[6]The relations of Jesus's message to the Jewish Law (given at Mount Sinai) obviously was of great concern to his followers, who were mostly of Jewish heritage. Here he clearly states the enduring force of that law.

[7]The Pharisees, one of the main Jewish sects in Jesus's time, became the principal interpreters of Judaism after the fall of Jerusalem. Their scribes (specialists in religious law) conducted prayers in the synagogues and explained the Hebrew bible.

[8]That is, the men who received the Law at Mount Sinai.

[9]Others translate: "murder."

ground of unchastity, makes her an adulteress; and whoever marries a divorced woman commits adultery.

"Again you have heard that it was said to the men of old, 'You shall not swear falsely, but shall perform to the Lord what you have sworn.' But I say to you, do not swear at all, either by heaven, for it is the throne of God, or by the earth, for it is his footstool, or by Jerusalem, for it is the city of the great King. And do not swear by your head, for you cannot make one hair white or black. Let what you say be simply 'Yes' or 'No'; anything more than this comes from evil.

"You have heard that it was said, 'An eye for an eye and a tooth for a tooth.' But I say to you, do not resist one who is evil. But if anyone strikes you on the right cheek, turn to him the other also; and if anyone would sue you and take your coat, let him have your cloak as well; and if anyone forces you to go one mile, go with him two miles. Give to him who begs from you, and do not refuse him who would borrow from you.

"You have heard that it was said, 'You shall love your neighbor and hate your enemy.' But I say to you, love your enemies and pray for those who persecute you, so that you may be sons[10] of your Father who is in heaven; for he makes his sun rise on the evil and on the good, and sends rain on the just and on the unjust. For if you love those who love you, what reward have you? Do not even the tax collectors do the same? And if you salute only your brethren, what more are you doing than others? Do not even the Gentiles[11] do the same? You, therefore, must be perfect, as your heavenly Father is perfect.

"Beware of practicing your piety before men in order to be seen by them; for then you will have no reward from your Father who is in heaven.

"Thus, when you give alms, sound no trumpet before you, as the hypocrites do in the synagogues and in the streets, that they may be praised by men. Truly, I say to you, they have received their reward. But when you give alms, do not let your left hand know what your right hand is doing, so that your alms may be in secret; and your Father who sees in secret will reward you.

"And when you pray, you must not be like the hypocrites; for they love to stand and pray in the synagogues and at the street corners, that they may be seen by men. Truly, I say to you, they have received their reward. But when you pray, go into your room and shut the door and pray to your Father who is in secret; and your Father who sees in secret will reward you.

"And in praying do not heap up empty phrases as the Gentiles do; for they think that they will be heard for their many words. Do not be like them, for your Father knows what you need before you ask him. Pray then like this:

> Our Father who art in heaven,
> Hallowed be thy name.

---

[10]That is, worthy followers of God's Law.

[11]Non-Jews, who did *not* receive the Law at Mount Sinai.

Thy kingdom come,
Thy will be done,
On earth as it is in heaven.
Give us this day our daily bread;
And forgive us our debts,
As we also have forgiven our debtors;
And lead us not into temptation,
But deliver us from evil.

For if you forgive men their trespasses, your heavenly Father also will forgive you; but if you do not forgive men their trespasses, neither will your Father forgive your trespasses.

"And when you fast, do not look dismal, like the hypocrites, for they disfigure their faces that their fasting may be seen by men. Truly, I say to you, they have received their reward. But when you fast, anoint your head and wash your face, that your fasting may not be seen by men but by your Father who is in secret; and your Father who sees in secret will reward you.

"Do not lay up for yourselves treasures on earth, where moth and rust consume and where thieves break in and steal, but lay up for yourselves treasure in heaven, where neither moth nor rust consumes and where thieves do not break in and steal. For where your treasure is, there will your heart be also.

"The eye is the lamp of the body. So, if your eye is sound, your whole body will be full of light; but if your eye is not sound, your whole body will be full of darkness. If then the light in you is darkness, how great is the darkness!

"No one can serve two masters; for either he will hate the one and love the other, or he will be devoted to the one and despise the other. You cannot serve God and *mammon*.[12]

"Therefore I tell you, do not be anxious about your life, what you shall eat or what you shall drink, nor about your body, what you shall put on. Is not life more than food, and the body more than clothing? Look at the birds of the air: they neither sow nor reap nor gather into barns, and yet your heavenly Father feeds them. Are you not of more value than they? And which of you by being anxious can add one cubit[13] to his span of life? And why are you anxious about clothing? Consider the lilies of the field, how they grow; they neither toil nor spin; yet I tell you, even Solomon in all his glory was not arrayed like one of these. But if God so clothes the grass of the field, which today is alive and tomorrow is thrown into the oven, will he not much more clothe you, O men of little faith? Therefore do not be anxious, saying, 'What shall we eat?' or 'What shall we drink?' or 'What shall we wear?' For the Gentiles seek all these things; and your heavenly Father

---

[12]A Semitic word meaning "money" or "material possessions."

[13]A measuring unit of about eighteen inches.

knows that you need them all. But seek first his kingdom and his righteousness, and all these things shall be yours as well.

"Therefore do not be anxious about tomorrow, for tomorrow will be anxious for itself. Let the day's own trouble be sufficient for the day.

"Judge not, that you be not judged. For with the judgment you pronounce you will be judged, and the measure you give will be the measure you get. Why do you see the speck that is in your brother's eye, but do not notice the log that is in your own eye? Or how can you say to your brother, 'Let me take the speck out of your eye,' when there is the log in your own eye? You hypocrite, first take the log out of your own eye, and then you will see clearly to take the speck out of your brother's eye.

"Do not give dogs what is holy; and do not throw your pearls before swine, lest they trample them underfoot and turn to attack you.

"Ask, and it will be given you; seek, and you will find; knock, and it will be opened to you. For everyone who asks receives, and he who seeks finds, and to him who knocks it will be opened. Or what man of you, if his son asks him for bread, will give him a stone? Or if he asks for a fish, will give him a serpent? If you then, who are evil, know how to give good gifts to your children, how much more will your Father who is in heaven give good things to those who ask him! So whatever you wish that men would do to you, do so to them; for this is the law and the prophets.

"Enter by the narrow gate; for the gate is wide and the way is easy, that leads to destruction, and those who enter by it are many. For the gate is narrow and the way is hard, that leads to life, and those who find it are few.

"Beware of false prophets, who come to you in sheep's clothing but inwardly are ravenous wolves. You will know them by their fruits. Are grapes gathered from thorns, or figs from thistles? So, every sound tree bears good fruit, but the bad tree bears evil fruit. A sound tree cannot bear evil fruit, nor can a bad tree bear good fruit. Every tree that does not bear good fruit is cut down and thrown into the fire. Thus you will know them by their fruits.

"Not everyone who says to me, 'Lord, Lord,' shall enter the kingdom of heaven, but he who does the will of my Father who is in heaven. On that day many will say to me, 'Lord, Lord, did we not prophesy in your name, and cast out demons in your name, and do many mighty works in your name?' And then will I declare to them, 'I never knew you; depart from me, you evildoers.'

"Everyone then who hears these words of mine and does them will be like a wise man who built his house upon the rock; and the rain fell, and the floods came, and the winds blew and beat upon that house, but it did not fall, because it had been founded on the rock. And everyone who hears these words of mine and does not do them will be like a foolish man who built his house upon the sand; and the rain fell, and the floods came, and the winds blew and beat against that house, and it fell; and great was the fall of it."

And when Jesus finished these sayings, the crowds were astonished at his teaching, for he taught them as one who had authority, and not as their scribes.[14]

THE LETTER OF PAUL TO THE ROMANS[15]
Salutation
1:1–7

Paul, a servant of Jesus Christ, called to be an apostle, set apart for the gospel of God which he promised beforehand through his prophets in the holy scriptures, the gospel concerning his Son, who was descended from David according to the flesh and designated Son of God in power according to the Spirit of holiness by his resurrection from the dead, Jesus Christ our Lord, through whom we have received grace[16] and apostleship to bring about the obedience of faith for the sake of his name among all the nations, including yourselves who are called to belong to Jesus Christ;

To all God's beloved in Rome, who are called to be saints;

Grace to you and peace from God our Father and the Lord Jesus Christ. . . .

Salvation through Faith Alone
1:16–32

For I am not ashamed of the gospel: it is the power of God for salvation to everyone who has faith, to the Jew first and also to the Greek.[17] For in it the righteousness of God is revealed through faith for faith; as it is written, "He who through faith is righteous shall live."

---

[14]That is, as one who speaks on his own responsibility, as did the prophets—*not* as one who conforms to earlier authorities, as did the scribes.

[15]Paul was a Greek-speaking Jew from Tarsus in Asia Minor. Originally employed as a persecutor of the Christians in Jerusalem and Damascus, ca. A.D. 36, he was converted to Christianity on the road to Damascus by a blinding vision. After his conversion, Paul traveled throughout the eastern part of the Roman-controlled Mediterranean world, spreading the Christian message (mainly to non-Jews). This letter, probably written from Corinth early in A.D. 57 tells of Paul's intention to visit Rome, where there was already a Christian community. Paul's religious thinking is here clearly set forth. He argues for the doctrine of "justification": forgiveness from the penalty of sin comes only through *faith in Christ*. Paul also deals with the role in the *new* covenant of his Jewish kindred, for justification applies equally to Jew and Gentile.

[16]The freely given, undeserved favor and love of God.

[17]That is, to non-Jews in general. The eastern end of the Mediterranean was culturally Hellenistic (Greek). Thus, the entire New Testament was written in the Greek language.

For the wrath of God is revealed from heaven against all ungodliness and wickedness of men who by their wickedness suppress the truth. For what can be known about God is plain to them, because God has shown it to them. Ever since the creation of the world his invisible nature, namely, his eternal power and deity, has been clearly perceived in the things that have been made. So they are without excuse; for although they knew God they did not honor him as God or give thanks to him, but they became futile in their thinking and their senseless minds were darkened. Claiming to be wise, they became fools, and exchanged the glory of the immortal God for images resembling mortal man or birds or animals or reptiles.

Therefore God gave them up in the lusts of their hearts to impurity, to the dishonoring of their bodies among themselves, because they exchanged the truth about God for a lie and worshiped and served the creature rather than the Creator, who is blessed forever! Amen.

For this reason God gave them up to degrading passions. Their women exchanged natural intercourse for unnatural, and in the same way also the men, giving up natural intercourse with women, were consumed with passion for one another. Men committed shameless acts with men and received in their own persons the due penalty for their error.

And since they did not see fit to acknowledge God, God gave them up to a debased mind and to things that should not be done. They were filled with every kind of wickedness, evil, covetousness, malice. Full of envy, murder, strife, deceit, craftiness, they are gossips, slanderers, God-haters, insolent, haughty, boastful, inventors of evil, rebellious toward parents, foolish, faithless, heartless, ruthless. They know God's decree, that those who practice such things deserve to die—yet they not only do them but even applaud others who practice them.

God Is for Every Person, Without Partiality

2:1–3:9

Therefore you have no excuse, O man, whoever you are, when you judge another; for in passing judgment upon him you condemn yourself, because you, the judge, are doing the very same things. We know that the judgment of God rightly falls upon those who do such things. Do you suppose, O man, that when you judge those who do such things and yet do them yourself, you will escape the judgment of God? Or do you presume upon the riches of his kindness and forbearance and patience? Do you not know that God's kindness is meant to lead you to repentance? But by your hard and impenitent heart you are storing up wrath for yourself on the day of wrath when God's righteous judgment will be revealed. For he will render to every man according to his works: to those who by patience in well-doing seek for glory and honor and immortality, he will give eternal life; but for those who are factious and do not obey the truth, but obey wickedness, there will be wrath and fury. There will be tribulation and distress for every human being who does evil, the Jew first and also the Greek,[18] but glory and honor and peace for everyone who does good, the Jew first and also the Greek. For God shows no partiality.

All who have sinned without the law will also perish without the law, and all who have sinned under the law will be judged by the law. For it is not the hearers of the law who are righteous before God, but the doers of the law who will be justified. When Gentiles who have not the law do by nature what the law requires, they are a law to themselves, even though they do not have the law. They show that what the law requires is written on their hearts, while their conscience also bears witness and their conflicting thoughts accuse or perhaps excuse them on that day when, according to my gospel, God judges the secrets of men by Christ Jesus.

But if you call yourself a Jew and rely upon the law and boast of your relation to God and know his will and approve what is excellent, because you are instructed in the law, and if you are sure that you are a guide to the blind, a light to those who are in darkness, a corrector of the foolish, a teacher of children, having in the law the embodiment of knowledge and truth—you then who teach others, will you not teach yourself? While you preach against stealing, do you steal? You who say that one must not commit adultery, do you commit adultery? You who abhor idols, do you rob temples? You who boast in the law, do you dishonor God by breaking the law? For, as it is written, "The name of God is blasphemed among the Gentiles because of you."

Circumcision indeed is of value if you obey the law; but if you break the law, your circumcision becomes uncircumcision.[19] So, if a man who is uncircumcised keeps the precepts of the law, will not his uncircumcision be regarded as circumcision? Then those who are physically uncircumcised but keep the law will condemn you who have the written code and circumcision but break the law. For he is not a real Jew who is one outwardly, nor is true circumcision something external and physical. He is a Jew who is one inwardly, and real circumcision is a matter of the heart, spiritual and not literal. His praise is not from men but from God.

Then what advantage has the Jew? Or what is the value of circumcision? Much in every way. To begin with, the Jews are entrusted with the oracles of God. What if some were unfaithful? Does their faithlessness nullify the faithfulness of God? By no means! Let God be true though every man be false, as it is written,[20]

---

[18]The Jew *first* because the special relationship granted to the people who had received the earlier covenant increased their responsibility. Both Jews and Gentiles, however, are *judged* equally by their actions, the Jews under the Law of Moses as found in the Old Testament, the Gentiles by the same standard as "written on their hearts."

[19]That is, the Jewish violator of the Law stands before God precisely where the pagan violator stands. (Circumcision is the physical symbol of God's covenant with the Hebrews, Genesis 17.)

[20]In Psalm 51.

"That thou mayest be justified in thy words,
and prevail when thou art judged."

But if our wickedness serves to show the justice of God, what shall we say? That
God is unjust to inflict wrath on us? (I speak in a human way.) By no means! For
then how could God judge the world? But if, through my falsehood, God's truthfulness abounds to his glory, why am I still being condemned as a sinner? And
why not do evil that good may come?—as some people slanderously charge us
with saying. Their condemnation is just.

What then? Are we Jews any better off? No, not at all; for I have already
charged that all men, both Jews and Greeks, are under the power of sin. . . .

Justification[21] through Faith by God's Grace—
Not through Works

3:21–31

But now the righteousness of God has been manifested apart from law, although
the law and the prophets bear witness to it, the righteousness of God through
faith in Jesus Christ for all who believe. For there is no distinction; since all have
sinned and fall short of the glory of God, they are justified by his grace as a gift,
through the redemption[22] which is in Christ Jesus, whom God put forward as an
expiation by his blood,[23] to be received by faith. This was to show God's righteousness, because in his divine forbearance he had passed over former sins; it was
to prove at the present time that he himself is righteous and that he justifies him
who has faith in Jesus.

Then what becomes of our boasting? It is excluded. On what principle? On
the principle of works? No, but on the principle of faith.[24] For we hold that a
man is justified by faith apart from works of law. Or is God the God of Jews only?
Is he not the God of Gentiles also? Yes, of Gentiles also, since God is one; and he
will justify the circumcised on the ground of their faith and the uncircumcised
through their faith. Do we then overthrow the law by this faith? By no means! On
the contrary, we uphold the law.

---

[21]Pardon—forgiveness by God of humans' sinful guilt—necessary for individual salvation.

[22]Payment (for sin), liberation, deliverance.

[23]Christ's death is a sacrificial atonement (expiation) for human sin; it is God's way of
cleansing away the sins of the faithful.

[24]That is, if salvation could be achieved by human "works" (deeds), there might be a reason for boasting; but since salvation is through *faith*, there is no reason for pride.

36

⚜

THE PERIPLUS OF THE
ERYTHRAEAN SEA

*T*he Periplus *is the first Western record of organized sea-trading with Africa
and the East. Whereas the earliest known trade had been located in the
region of the Persian Gulf, extending to Egypt in one direction and India in the
other, now Mediterranean centers of civilization were expanding, exploring, and
establishing commercial links to the south and east. Phoenician, Indian, and
Arab traders had long-standing networks that were followed by Greek and
Roman seamen.*

*From India came spices, especially cinnamon, sandalwood, gems, and muslin;
from Africa, gold, ivory, ostrich feathers, and oil; from the Arabian Gulf, frankincense and myrrh, and increasingly more and more items that fed the trade as
the Romans conquered Egypt and took control of the eastern Mediterranean. By
the time of the first Roman emperor, Augustus, around the beginning of the first
century A.D., overland trade to India remained in Parthian and Arab hands, but
sea routes were open to Roman merchants. Despite the opposition of existing Arab
kingdoms, the Romans were able to enlist the aid of the African kingdom of
Axum, and gradually made inroads into the Hindu and Arab monopolies.*

*Some time between A.D. 95 and 130 an anonymous Greek (or Greek-speak-
ing Egyptian) sailor, who was also a Roman subject, possibly sailing on an
Egyptian-made ship, recorded in Koine (a Greek dialect) his journey from Egypt
to India. Traveling down the Red Sea, hugging the Horn of Africa, his vessel then
headed east, around the Arabian peninsula, into the Persian Gulf and on to
India. The vast sea, comprising the Indian Ocean and its extensions up the Red
Sea and Persian Gulf, was given the name* Erythraean Sea *by the Greeks. His
record of the* periplus *("circumnavigation") gives details of importance to a merchant: items that were to be traded or bought, market and travel conditions, and
occasional glimpses into the peoples he encountered. The selection given here
details the coastal strip that extends south of the tip of the Horn, a region named
Azania (parts of present-day Somalia, Kenya, and Tanzania). The southernmost*

mart mentioned is Rhapta, located somewhere south of Zanzibar. This early account of the busy markets and sea trade along the East African coast testifies to the long-standing contact between ancient civilizations dating back to far more remote periods.

Beyond Tabae,[1] after four hundred stadia,[2] there is the village of Pano. And then, after sailing four hundred stadia along a promontory, toward which place the current also draws you, there is another market-town called Opone, into which the same things are imported as those already mentioned, and in it the greatest quantity of cinnamon is produced, and slaves of the better sort, which are brought to Egypt in increasing numbers; and a great quantity of tortoiseshell, better than that found elsewhere.

The voyage to all these far-side market-towns is made from Egypt about the month of July, that is *Epiphi*. And ships are also customarily fitted out from the places across this sea, from Ariaca and Barygaza, bringing to these far-side market-towns the products of their own places; wheat, rice, clarified butter, sesame oil, cotton cloth, and girdles, and honey from the reed called *sacchari*. Some make the voyage especially to these market-towns, and others exchange their cargoes while sailing along the coast. This country is not subject to a king, but each market-town is ruled by its separate chief.

Beyond Opone, the shore trending more toward the south, first there are the small and great bluffs of Azania,[3] this coast is destitute of harbors, but there are places where ships can lie at anchor, the shore being abrupt; and this course is of six days, the direction being southwest. Then come the small and great beach for another six days' course and after that in order, the Courses of Azania, the first being called Sarapion and the next Nicon; and after that several rivers and other anchorages, one after the other, separately a rest and a run for each day, seven in

---

From *The Periplus of the Erythraean Sea,* translated by Wilfred H. Schoff. New York: Longmans, Green, and Co., 1912. (Pp. 27–29.)

[1]Tabae and the names of the ports that follow, such as Opone, are the names of ancient seaports along the Red Sea and the East African coast. Most of these ports have long since vanished.

[2]The stade is a measure of distance equal to the length of the spring race in an ancient Greek stadium, about six hundred feet. Four hundred stadia, thus, would be about forty-five miles.

[3]Azania was, apparently, the eastern coast of present-day Somalia.

all, until the Pyralaae islands and what is called the channel; beyond which, a little to the south of southwest, after two courses of a day and night along the Ausanitic coast, is the island of Menuthias, about three hundred stadia from the mainland, low and wooded, in which there are rivers and many kinds of birds and the mountain-tortoise. There are no wild beasts except the crocodiles; but there they do not attack men. In this place there are sewed boats, and canoes hollowed from single logs, which they use for fishing and catching tortoise. In this island they also catch them in a peculiar way, in wicker baskets, which they fasten across the channel-opening between the breakers.

Two days' sail beyond, there lies the very last market-town of the continent of Azania, which is called Rhapta;[4] which has its name from the sewed boats already mentioned; in which there is ivory in great quantity, and tortoiseshell. Along this coast live men of piratical habits, very great in stature, and under separate chiefs for each place. The Mapharitic chief governs it under some ancient right that subjects it to the sovereignty of the state that is become first in Arabia. And the people of Muza now hold it under his authority, and send thither many large ships; using Arab captains and agents who are familiar with the natives and intermarry with them, and who know the whole coast and understand the language.

There are imported into these markets the lances made at Muza especially for this trade and hatchets and daggers and awls and various kinds of glass and, at some places, a little wine and wheat, not for trade, but to serve for getting the goodwill of the savages. There are exported from these places a great quantity of ivory, but inferior to that of Adulis, and rhinoceros horn and tortoiseshell (which is in best demand after that from India), and a little palm oil.

And these markets of Azania are the very last of the continent that stretches down on the right hand from Berenice; for beyond these places the unexplored ocean curves around toward the west, and running along by the regions to the south of Aethiopia and Libya and Africa, it mingles with the western sea.

---

[4]Rhapta is off the coast of present-day Tanzania and represented the southernmost point of the *periplus* ("circumnavigation").

37

※

Saint Augustine

THE CITY OF GOD

In the early fourth century (A.D. 313) Christianity achieved legal status among the other religions of the Roman Empire. Near the end of that same century (A.D. 381) Christianity became the official religion of the state, and worship of the old Greek and Roman gods was forbidden. That conflict with classical (Greek and Roman) culture was not only religious; there were also philosophical and social consequences. Paradoxically, as they were the heirs of classical civilization and were imbued with its forms of thought and expression, many fourth- and fifth-century Christians still thought of themselves as part of that more than a thousand-year-old tradition. Instead of turning their backs on classical civilization, some Christian writers struggled to give it a new moral and spiritual direction, thus achieving a kind of synthesis of Christianity and classicism. The most important of these comprehensive philosophers, the dominant Western "Father of the Church," was Aurelius Augustinus (A.D. 354–430).

Born in northern Africa near ancient Carthage, Augustine received the best education his middle-class father, a pagan, could afford. His mother was a devout Christian who influenced him greatly. After attending an advanced school at Carthage, Augustine became a teacher of rhetoric (literature and speech) at Carthage, then at Rome, and then Milan. There, impressed by Milan's learned and eloquent Bishop Ambrose, he was converted (A.D. 386) to Christianity. In his autobiography, Confessions, Augustine describes the errors of his youth, his intense spiritual and psychological struggles, and his philosophical path to conversion. A few years after his return to Africa from Milan, he was made bishop of Hippo Regius, a small coastal town near his birthplace. Even from there, his personality and constant flow of writings spread his fame so that he became the outstanding figure in the entire Western Church—his enduring influence second only to Saint Paul's.

Augustine's most important and longest work, The City of God, *written between 413 and 426, was meant to "combat the blasphemies and errors" of those who, bewildered by the collapse of their former security, laid the blame for the capture of Rome by the Visigoths (A.D. 410) on the Romans' official rejection of their old gods. Although he obviously rejected those pagan gods, Augustine was well read in the philosophies of that pagan world and admired much of it, especially Platonism. He answered Christianity's attackers with his idea of the "two cities." This, "the most famous of all philosophic meditations on history," as it has been called, is excerpted in the following passages.*

History, Augustine states, is the unfolding result of God's will—moving from Creation to the Last Judgment. Individuals choose one of the two communities that embrace all of humanity: the "heavenly city" or the "earthly city." But they make their choice in accordance with God's will (predestination) and God's grace (mercy). (For the reader's convenience, the original book and chapter numbers for these excerpts are shown in the subtitles. Augustine's favorite sources of biblical quotation—too many to footnote fully here—are the Psalms, the Gospels, and Paul's Letters.) In The City of God *we see clearly the intellectual process whereby Christianity became integrated into a new world-view equal in its comprehensiveness to the classical philosophies that it largely replaced.*

THE VICES OF THE ROMANS WHICH THE OVERTHROW OF THEIR COUNTRY DID NOT SERVE TO REFORM
Book I, Chapter 33

Are your minds bereft of reason? You are not merely mistaken; this is madness. Here are people in the East bewailing Rome's humiliation, and great states in remote regions of the earth holding public mourning and lamentation—and you Romans are searching for theaters, pouring into them, filling them, behaving more irresponsibly than ever before. It is this spiritual disease, degeneration, decline into immortality and indecency that Scipio[1] feared when he opposed the erection of theaters. He saw how easily ease and plenty would soften and ruin you. He did not wish you to be free from fear.

Saint Augustine, *The City of God*, trans. Demetrius B. Zema and Gerald G. Walsh (Washington, D.C.: The Catholic University of America Press, 1962–1964). Copyright 1950–1954. Reprinted by permission of the Catholic University of America Press.

[1]Publius Cornelius Scipio Nasica Serapio, a conservative Roman aristocrat, consul (138 B.C.), and general of the republican era.

He did not think that the republic could be happy while walls were standing, yet morals were collapsing. But, you were more attached to the seductions of foul spirits than to the wisdom of men with foresight. That is why you take no blame for the evil you do, but blame Christianity for the evil you suffer. Depraved by prosperity and unchastened by adversity, you desire, in your security, not the peace of the State but liberty for license. Scipio wanted you to have a salutary fear of the enemy, lest you should rot in debauchery. Though crushed by the enemy, you put no check on immortality, you learned no lessons from calamity; in the depths of sorrows you still wallow in sin.

AN INTRODUCTION TO THE PART OF THIS WORK IN WHICH THE RESPECTIVE ORIGINS AND THE ENDS OF THE TWO CITIES, THE HEAVENLY AND THE EARTHLY, ARE TO BE DISCUSSED

Book XI, Chapter 1

The expression, "City of God," which I have been using, is justified by that scripture whose divine authority puts it above the literature of all other people and brings under its sway every type of human genius—and that, not by some casual intellectual reaction, but by a disposition of divine providence. For, in this scripture, we read: "Glorious things are said of thee, O city of God"; and, in another psalm: "Great is the Lord, and exceedingly to be praised in the city of our God, in His holy mountain, increasing the joy of the whole earth"; and, a little later in the same psalm: "As we have heard, so have we seen, in the city of the Lord of hosts, in the city of our God: God hath founded it forever"; and in another text: "The stream of the river maketh the city of God joyful: the most high hath sanctified his own tabernacle. God is in the midst thereof, it shall not be moved."[2]

Through these and similar passages too numerous to quote, we learn of the existence of a City of God whose founder has inspired us with a love and longing to become its citizens. The inhabitants of the earthly city who prefer their own gods to the Founder of the holy City do not realize that he is the God of gods—though not, of course, of those false, wicked, and proud gods who, because they have been deprived of that unchangeable light which was meant for all, are reduced to a pitiful power and, therefore, are eager for some sort of influence and demand divine honors from their deluded subjects. He is the God of those rever-

---

[2]Augustine, as he often does, is quoting from the Old Testament's Book of Psalms. In this case, Psalms 87, 48, and 46.

ent and holy gods who prefer to obey and worship one God rather than to have many others obeying and worshiping them.[3]

In the ten preceding books, I have done my best, with the help of our Lord and King, to refute the enemies of this City. Now, however, realizing what is expected of me and recalling what I promised, I shall begin to discuss, as well as I can, the origin, history, and destiny of the respective cities, earthly and heavenly, which, as I have said, are at present inextricably intermingled, one with the other. First, I shall explain how these two cities originated when the angels took opposing sides.

THE ESSENTIAL DIFFERENCE BETWEEN THE TWO CITIES, BETWEEN WORLDLY SOCIETY AND THE COMMUNION OF SAINTS
Book XIV, Chapter 28

What we see, then, is that two societies have issued from two kinds of love. Worldly society has flowered from a selfish love which dared to despise even God, whereas the communion of saints is rooted in a love of God that is ready to trample on self. In a word, this latter relies on the Lord, whereas the other boasts that it can get along by itself. The city of man seeks the praise of men, whereas the height of glory for the other is to hear God in the witness of conscience. The one lifts up its head in its own boasting; the other says to God: "Thou art my glory, thou liftest up my head."

In the city of the world both the rulers themselves and the people they dominate are dominated by the lust for domination; whereas in the City of God all citizens serve one another in charity, whether they serve by the responsibilities of office or by the duties of obedience. The one city loves its leaders as symbols of its own strength; the other says to its God: "I love thee, O Lord, my strength." Hence, even the wise men in the city of man live according to man, and their only goal has been the goods of their bodies or of the mind or of both; though some of them have reached a knowledge of God, "they did not glorify him as God or give thanks but became vain in their reasonings, and their senseless minds have been darkened. For while professing to be wise" (that is to say, while glorying in their own wisdom, under the domination of pride), "they have become fools, and they have changed the glory of the incorruptible God for an image made like to

---

[3]By "those false, wicked, and proud gods" Augustine means the fallen angels who, in Christian teachings, rebelled against God. The earthly city originated with those rebellious angels, now demons, who caused people to believe in the old pagan gods, considered by Augustine to be mere fictions. "Those reverent and holy gods" are, of course, the good angels who remained faithful to God.

corruptible man and to birds and four-footed beasts and creeping things" (meaning that they either led their people, or imitated them, in adoring idols shaped like these things), "and they worshiped and served the creature rather than the creator who is blessed forever." In the City of God, on the contrary, there is no merely human wisdom, but there is a piety which worships the true God as He should be worshiped and has as its goal that reward of all holiness whether in the society of saints on earth or in that of angels of heaven, which is "that God may be all in all."

ON THE TWO LINES OF DESCENT, DISTINGUISHED BY THEIR RESPECTIVE DESTINIES, WHICH CAN BE TRACED, FROM THE BEGINNING ON, IN THE HISTORY OF MANKIND

Book XV, Chapter 1

Regarding the Garden of Eden, the happiness that was possible there, the life of our first parents, their sin, and their punishment, a great deal has been thought, said, and written.[4] In the foregoing books I myself have said something on these subjects, setting forth what can be found in the text of scripture and adding only such reflections as seemed in harmony with its authority. The discussion could be pursued in greater detail, but it would raise so many and such varied problems that I would need for their solution more books than our present purpose calls for; nor is there so much time at my disposal that I feel obliged to waste it in satisfying the curiosity of those persons with nothing to do who are more captious in putting their questions than capable of grasping the answers.

Actually, I think I have said enough on the really great and difficult problems concerning the origin of the world, the soul, and the human race. In regard to mankind I have made a division. On the one side are those who live according to man; on the other, those who live according to God. And I have said that, in a deeper sense, we may speak of two cities or two human societies, the destiny of the one being an eternal kingdom under God while the doom of the other is eternal punishment along with the Devil.

Of the final consummation of the two cities I shall have to speak later. Of their original cause among the angels whose number no man knows and then in the first two human beings, I have already spoken. For the moment, therefore, I must deal with the course of the history of the two cities from the time when chil-

---

[4]See Genesis, in Selection 6, from the Old Testament.

dren were born to the first couple until the day when men shall beget no more. By the course of their history, as distinguished from their original cause and final consummation, I mean the whole time of world history in which men are born and take the place of those who die and depart.

Now, the first man born of the two parents of the human race was Cain. He belonged to the city of man. The next born was Abel, and he was of the City of God. Notice here a parallel between the individual man and the whole race. We all experience as individuals what the Apostle [Paul] says: "It is not the spiritual that comes first, but the physical, and then the spiritual." The fact is that every individual springs from a condemned stock and, because of Adam, must be first cankered and carnal, only later to become sound and spiritual by the process of rebirth in Christ. So, too, with the human race as a whole, as soon as human birth and death began the historical course of the two cities, the first to be born was a citizen of this world and only later came the one who was an alien in the city of men but at home in the City of God, a man predestined by grace[5] and elected by grace. By grace an alien on earth, by grace he was a citizen of heaven. In and of himself, he springs from the common clay, all of which was under condemnation from the beginning, but which God held in his hands like a potter, to borrow the metaphor which the Apostle so wisely and deliberately uses. For, God could make "from the same mass one vessel for honorable, another for ignoble use." The first vessel to be made was "for ignoble use." Only later was there made a vessel for honorable use. And as with the race, so, as I have said, with the individual. First comes the clay that is only fit to be thrown away, with which we must begin, but in which we need not remain. Afterwards comes what is fit for use, that into which we can be gradually molded and in which, when molded, we may remain. This does not mean that everyone who is wicked is to become good, but that no one becomes good who was not once wicked. What is true is that the sooner a man makes a change in himself for the better the sooner he has a right to be called what he has become. The second name hides the first.

Now, it is recorded of Cain that he built a city, while Abel, as though he were merely a pilgrim on earth, built none. For, the true City of the saints is in heaven, though here on earth it produces citizens in whom it wanders as on a pilgrimage through time looking for the Kingdom of Eternity. When that day comes it will gather together all those who, rising in their bodies, shall have that kingdom given to them in which, along with their Prince, the King of Eternity, they shall reign forever and ever.

---

[5]In Christian theology, the freely given and undeserved favor and love of God.

ON PRUNING THE LOVE OF HUMAN PRAISE
BECAUSE THE GLORY OF THE SAINTS
IS ALL IN GOD
Book V, Chapter 14

. . . After the Apostles[6] came the martyrs[7] . . . a vast multitude of them with true piety and, therefore, with true virtue endured what other men made them suffer. It was different with pagan heroes. They were citizens of the earthly city, of a kingdom not in heaven but on earth, and the only purpose of all their duties was the city's temporal security. They knew nothing of everlasting life, but only of a succession of living and dying mortals. What other glory could they love but the fame by which, when they were dead, they might seem to live on the lips of those who praised them?

GOD'S TEMPORAL REWARD FOR THE
NATURAL MORALITY OF THE ROMANS
Book V, Chapter 15

For these pagan heroes there was not to be the divine grace of everlasting life along with His holy angels in his heavenly city, for the only road to this society of the blessed is true piety, that is, that religious service or *latreía* (to use the Greek word) which is offered to the One true God. On the other hand, if God did not grant them at least the temporal glory of a splendid Empire, there would have been no reward for the praiseworthy efforts or virtues by which they strove to attain that glory. When our Lord said: "Amen I say to you they have received their reward," He had in mind those who do what seems to be good in order to be glorified by men.

After all, the pagans subordinated their private property to the common welfare, that is, to the republic and the public treasury. They resisted the temptation to avarice. They gave their counsel freely in the councils of the state. They indulged in neither public crime nor private passion. They thought they were on the right road when they strove, by all these means, for honors, rule, and glory. Honor has come to them from almost all peoples. The rule of their laws has been imposed on many peoples. And in our day, in literature and in history, glory has been given them by almost everyone. They have no right to complain of the justice of the true and supreme God. "They have received their reward."

---

[6]The earliest Christian missionaries.

[7]Those who went to their deaths because of their service to Christ.

THE REWARD OF THE SAINTS WHO ARE CITIZENS OF THE ETERNAL CITY, AND FOR WHOM THE EXAMPLES OF ROMAN VIRTUES WERE NOT WITHOUT VALUE

Book V, Chapter 16

The reward of the saints[8] is altogether different. They were men who, while on earth, suffered reproaches for the City of God, which is so much hated by lovers of this world. That City is eternal. There, no one is born because no one dies. There, there reigns that true and perfect happiness which is not a goddess, but a gift of god—toward whose beauty we can but sigh in our pilgrimage on earth, though we hold the pledge of it by faith. In that City, the sun does not "rise upon the good and bad" for the Sun of Justice cherishes the good alone. There, where the Truth is a treasure shared by all, there is no need to pinch the poor to fill the coffers of the state.

It was, then, not only to reward the Roman heroes with human glory that the Roman Empire spread. It had a purpose for the citizens of the Eternal City during their pilgrimage on earth. Meditating long and seriously on those great examples, they could understand what love of their Heavenly Fatherland should be inspired by everlasting life, since a fatherland on earth has been so much loved by citizens inspired by human glory.

ON WAR AND PEACE IN THE ASSOCIATIONS OF EARTHLY MINDED MEN

Book XV, Chapter 4

As for the city of this world, it is neither to last forever nor even to be a city, once the final doom of pain is upon it. Nevertheless, while history lasts, it has a finality of its own; it reaches such happiness by sharing a common good as is possible when there are no goods but the things of time to afford it happiness. This is not the kind of good that can give those who are content with it any freedom from fear. In fact, the city of man, for the most part, is a city of contention with opinions divided by foreign wars and domestic quarrels and by the demands for victories which either end in death or are merely momentary respites from further war. The reason is that whatever part of the city of the world raises the standard of war, it seeks to be lord of the world, when, in fact, it is enthralled in its own wickedness. Even when it conquers, its victory can be mortally poisoned by pride, and if, instead of taking pride in the success already achieved, it takes account of

---

[8]All those whose first loyalty is to God.

the nature and normal vicissitudes of life and is afraid of future failure, then the victory is merely momentary. The fact is that the power to reach domination by war is not the same as the power to remain in perpetual control.

Nevertheless, it is wrong to deny that the aims of human civilization are good, for this is the highest end that mankind of itself can achieve. For, however lowly the goods of earth, the aim, such as it is, is peace. The purpose even of war is peace. For, where victory is not followed by resistance there is a peace that was impossible so long as rivals were competing, hungrily and unhappily, for something material too little to suffice for both. This kind of peace is a product of the work of war, and its price is a so-called glorious victory; when victory goes to the side that had a juster cause it is surely a matter for human rejoicing, and the peace is one to be welcomed.

The things of earth are not merely good; they are undoubtedly gifts from God. But, of course, if those who get such goods in the city of men are reckless about the better goods of the city of God, in which there is to be the ultimate victory of an eternal, supreme, and untroubled peace, if men so love the goods of earth as to believe that these are the only goods or if they love them more than the goods they know to be better, then the consequence is inevitable: misery and more misery.

THE CHRISTIAN VIEW OF THE SUPREME GOOD AND THE ULTIMATE EVIL, AS DISTINGUISHED FROM THE PHILOSOPHERS' VIEW THAT THE SUPREME GOOD IS IN MEN THEMSELVES
Book XIX, Chapter 4

If I am asked what stand the City of God would take on the issues raised and, first, what this City thinks of the supreme good and ultimate evil, the answer would be: She holds that eternal life is the supreme good and eternal death the supreme evil, and that we should live rightly in order to obtain the one and avoid the other. Hence the scriptural expression, "the just man lives by faith"[9]—by faith, for the fact is that we do not now behold our good and, therefore, must seek it by faith; nor can we of ourselves even live rightly, unless He who gives us faith helps us to believe and pray, for it takes faith to believe that we need His help.

Those who think that the supreme good and evil are to be found in this life are mistaken. It makes no difference whether it is in the body or in the soul or in both—or, specifically, in pleasure or virtue or in both—that they seek the

---

[9]See Selection 35 from the letter of Paul to the Romans.

supreme good. They seek in vain whether they look to serenity, to virtue, or to both; whether to pleasure plus serenity, or to virtue, or to all three; or to the satisfaction of our innate exigencies, or to virtue, or to both. It is in vain that men look for beatitude on earth or in human nature. Divine Truth, as expressed in the prophet's words, makes them look foolish: "The Lord knows the thoughts of men" or, as the text is quoted by St. Paul: "The Lord knows the thoughts of the wise that they are vain."

ON THE AREAS OF AGREEMENT AND DISAGREEMENT BETWEEN THE TWO CITIES
Book XIX, Chapter 17

While the homes of unbelieving men are intent upon acquiring temporal peace out of the possessions and comforts of this temporal life, the families which live according to faith look ahead to the good things of heaven promised as imperishable, and use material and temporal goods in the spirit of pilgrims, not as snares or obstructions to block their way to God, but simply as helps to ease and never to increase the burdens of this corruptible body which weighs down the soul. Both types of homes and their masters have this in common, that they must use things essential to this mortal life. But the respective purposes to which they put them are characteristic and very different.

So, too, the earthly city which does not live by faith seeks only an earthly peace, and limits the goal of its peace, of its harmony of authority and obedience among its citizens, to the voluntary and collective attainment of objectives necessary to mortal existence. The heavenly City, meanwhile—or, rather, that part that is on pilgrimage in mortal life and lives by faith—must use this earthly peace until such time as our mortality which needs such peace has passed away. As a consequence, so long as her life in the earthly city is that of a captive and an alien (although she has the promise of ultimate delivery and the gift of the Spirit as a pledge), she has no hesitation about keeping in step with the civil law which governs matters pertaining to our existence here below. For, as mortal life is the same for all, there ought to be common cause between the two cities in what concerns our purely human living.

Now comes the difficulty. The city of this world, to begin with, has had certain "wise men" of its own mold, whom true religion must reject, because either out of their own daydreaming or out of demonic deception these wise men came to believe that a multiplicity of divinities was allied with human life, with different duties, in some strange arrangement, and different assignments: this one over the body, that one over the mind; in the body itself, one over the head, another over the neck, still others, one for each bodily part; in the mind, one over the intelligence, another over learning, another over temper, another over desire; in the realities, related to life, that lie about us, one over flocks and one over wheat, one over wine, one over oil, and another over forests, one over currency, another over navigation, and still another over warfare and victory, one over marriage, a different one over fecundity and childbirth, so on and so on.[10]

The heavenly City, on the contrary, knows and, by religious faith, believes that it must adore one God alone and serve Him with that complete dedication which the Greeks call *latreía* and which belongs to Him alone. As a result, she has been unable to share with the earthly city a common religious legislation, and has had no choice but to dissent on this score and so to become a nuisance to those who think otherwise. Hence, she has had to feel the weight of their anger, hatred, and violence, save in those instances when, by sheer numbers and God's help, which never fails, she has been able to scare off her opponents.

So long, then, as the heavenly City is wayfaring on earth, she invites citizens from all nations and all tongues, and unites them into a single pilgrim band. She takes no issue with that diversity of customs, laws, and traditions whereby human peace is sought and maintained. Instead of nullifying or tearing down, she preserves and appropriates whatever in the diversities of divers races is aimed at one and the same objective of human peace, provided only that they do not stand in the way of faith and worship of the one supreme and true God.

Thus, the heavenly City, so long as it is wayfaring on earth, not only makes use of earthly peace but fosters and actively pursues along with other human beings a common platform in regard to all that concerns our purely human life and does not interfere with faith and worship. Of course, though, the City of God subordinates this earthly peace to that of heaven. For this is not merely true peace, but, strictly speaking, for any rational creature, the only real peace, since it is, as I said, "the perfectly ordered and harmonious communion of those who find their joy in God and in one another in God."

When this peace is reached, man will be no longer haunted by death, but plainly and perpetually endowed with life, nor will his body, which now wastes away and weighs down the soul, be any longer animal, but spiritual, in need of nothing, and completely under the control of our will.

This peace the pilgrim City already possesses by faith and it lives holily and according to this faith so long as, to attain its heavenly completion, it refers every good act done for God or for his fellow man. I say "fellow man" because, of course, any community life must emphasize social relationships.

---

[10]Augustine is referring to the many gods of the pre-Christian Greeks and Romans. Different gods had power over different aspects of humanity and the environment.

THE SOCRATIC SCHOOL OF PHILOSOPHY
Book VIII, Chapter 3

To Socrates goes the credit of being the first one to channel the whole of philosophy into an ethical system for the reformation and regulation of morals.[11] His predecessors without exception had applied themselves particularly to physics or natural science. I do not think that it can be definitely decided just why Socrates chose to follow this course. It has been suggested that he did so because he had become wearied of obscure and uncertain investigations, and preferred to turn his mind to a clean-cut objective, to that secret of human happiness which seems to have been the sole purpose of all philosophical research. Others have claimed, more kindly, that he did not think it right for minds darkened with earthly desires to reach out beyond their limits to the realm of the divine.

Socrates realized that his predecessors had been seeking the origin of all things, but he believed that these first and highest causes could be found only in the will of the single and supreme Divinity and, therefore, could be comprehended only by a mind purified from passion. Hence his conclusion, that he must apply himself to the acquisition of virtue, so that his mind, freed from the weight of earthly desires, might, by its own natural vigor, lift itself up to eternal realities and, with purified intelligence, contemplate the very nature of that immaterial and immutable light in which the causes[12] of all created natures abidingly dwell. Nevertheless, with his marvelous combination of wit and words, pungency and politeness, and with his trick of confessing ignorance and concealing knowledge he used to tease and poke fun at the folly of ignoramuses who talked as though they knew the answers to those moral problems in which he seemed wholly absorbed.

The result was that he incurred their enmity. He was falsely accused and condemned to death. However, the very city of Athens that had publicly condemned him began publicly to mourn his loss, and the wrath of the people was so turned against his two accusers that one[13] of them was killed by an angry mob and the other[14] escaped a similar death only by voluntary and perpetual exile.

Socrates was thus so highly distinguished both in life and in death that he left behind him numerous disciples. They rivaled one another in zealous discussions

---

[11] See Selection 17, the *Apology*, in which Socrates (469–399 B.C.) defends his life's philosophical work at his trial.

[12] Plato (429–347 B.C.), Socrates's most brilliant disciple, wrote of the eternal Forms or Ideas as "causes." See his "Allegory of the Cave," in Selection 18, the *Republic*.

[13] Meletus, prosecutor in the trial of Socrates.

[14] Anytus, the politician who remained in the background but pressed Meletus to carry on the prosecution. (Augustine's information on the fates of both of these accusers of Socrates is of doubtful accuracy.)

of those ethical problems where there is question of the supreme good and, hence, of human happiness.

In his discussions, Socrates had a way of proposing and defending his theories and then demolishing them. No one could make out exactly what he believed. Consequently, each of his followers picked what he preferred and sought the supreme good in his heart's desire.

Now the truth is that the supreme good is that which, when attained, makes all men happy. Yet, so varied in regard to this good were the views of the Socratics that it seems hardly credible that all of them were followers of one and the same master. . . .

ON THE MOST DISTINGUISHED DISCIPLE OF SOCRATES, PLATO, THE ONE WHO DIVIDED PHILOSOPHY INTO THREE PARTS
Book VIII, Chapter 4

Of the pupils of Socrates, Plato was so remarkable for his brilliance that he has deservedly outshone all the rest. He was born in Athens of a good family and by his marvelous ability easily surpassed all his fellow disciples. Realizing, however, that neither his own genius nor Socratic training was adequate to evolve a perfect system of philosophy, he traveled far and wide to wherever there was any hope of gaining some valuable addition to knowledge. Thus, in Egypt he mastered the lore which was there esteemed. From there he went to lower Italy, famous for the Pythagorean School, and there successfully imbibed from eminent teachers all that was then in vogue in Italian philosophy.

However, Plato's special affection was for his old master—so much so that in practically all the *Dialogues* he makes Socrates, with all his charm, the mouthpiece not only of his own moral arguments but of all that Plato learned from others or managed to discover himself.

Now, the pursuit of wisdom follows two avenues—action and contemplation. Thus, one division of philosophy may be called active; the other part, contemplative. The former deals with the conduct of life; that is to say, with the cultivation of morals. Contemplative philosophy considers natural causality and truth as such. Socrates excelled in practical wisdom; Pythagoras favored contemplation, and to this he applied his whole intelligence.

It is to Plato's praise that he combined both in a more perfect philosophy, and then divided the whole into three parts: first, moral philosophy which pertains to action; second, natural philosophy whose purpose is contemplation; third, rational philosophy which discriminates between truth and error. Although this last is necessary for both action and contemplation, it is contemplation especially which claims to reach a vision of truth. Hence, this threefold division in no way invalidates the distinction whereby action and contemplation are considered the constituent elements of the whole of philosophy. Just what Plato's position was in each of these three divisions—that is to say, just what he knew or believed to be the end of all action, the cause of all nature, the light of all reason—I think it would be rash to affirm and would take too long to discuss at length.

Plato was so fond of following the well-known habit of his master of dissimulating his knowledge of opinions that in Plato's own works (where Socrates appears as a speaker) it is difficult to determine just what views he held even on important questions. However, of the views which are set forth in his writings, whether his own or those of others which seemed to have pleased him, a few must be recalled and included here. In some places, Plato is on the side of the true religion which our faith accepts and defends. At other times he seems opposed; for example, on the respective merits of monotheism and polytheism in relation to genuine beatitude after death.

Perhaps this may be said of the best disciples of Plato—of those who followed most closely and understood most clearly the teachings of a master rightly esteemed above all other pagan philosophers—that they have perceived, at least, these truths about God: that in Him is to be found the cause of all being, the reason of all thinking, the rule of all living. The first of these truths belongs to natural, the second to rational, the third to moral philosophy.

Now, if man was created so that by his highest faculty he might attain to the highest of all realities, that is, to the one, true, and supreme God, apart from whom no nature exists, no teaching is true, no conduct is good, then let us seek Him in whom all we find is real, know Him in whom all we contemplate is true, love Him in whom all things for us are good.

38

✤

Ethiopian Writings

THE ROYAL CHRONICLE OF EZANA AND THE BOOK OF BARUCH

The African kingdom of Axum, ancient progenitor of Ethiopia, dates back to the first millennium B.C., when the highlands of present-day Ethiopia saw the creation of a state with its capital at Axum. Axum rose to a prominent position in the Horn of Africa by the third century B.C. During the first half of the fourth century A.D., the ruler of Axum, King Ezana (320–340) was converted to Christianity by an Egyptian monk from Alexandria named Frumentius. The links with the Egyptian Coptic Church account for the Monophysite doctrines embraced by the Ethiopian Christians, that is, the belief that there is only one, divine nature in the person of Christ, rather than one that is both human and divine.

The literature that developed in Axum celebrates two branches of its society— its monarchs and its religious faith. The accomplishments of Axum's kings were recorded from the earliest times, much as the Egyptians had done with tomb inscriptions. Stone inscriptions regarding King Ezana, included in the first of the readings in this selection, list the countries he ruled and record his many conquests. The deities mentioned in this inscription include the Greek Ares (god of war), the Ethiopian Astar, Beher, and Meder (representing the moon, the country, and the earth), as well as the Christian "Lord of Heaven."

By the second half of the fifth century A.D., Greek-speaking Monophysite monks from Syria undertook the task of converting the population of Axum and translated the Bible from Greek into Ge'ez, an Ethiopian language. By the end of the seventh century A.D., the work of translation had been completed, includ-

ing not only the Bible but also other Christian writings, along with the only complete extant version of the Book of Enoch.

Ultimately, the Ethiopian Christian Church generated a Jewish branch as well as the Christian Coptic one. The Jews were known locally as the Falasha *(meaning "wanderers" or "visitors"), although they called themselves the* Beta Israel *(Hebrew for "the house of Israel"). Although the evidence is not conclusive, it appears that the Falasha may represent an offshoot of the Ethiopian Christian Church of the fourteenth century. In recent years the remaining Falasha have emigrated from Ethiopia to Israel.*

Like most Ethiopian literature, initial Falasha compositions date from the fourteenth century; however, the textual sources undoubtedly date back to the time of the translations of the Greek Bible into Ge'ez. Falasha beliefs seem to support this theory. Although the first mention of the Falasha in Ethiopian sources dates to the royal Chronicles of Amda Tseyon *(1314–1344), there is no evidence of the Jewish traditions and religious writings that developed elsewhere in the post-biblical period, and that formed the basis for normative Jewish thought. Hebrew names for God are employed by the Falasha, as well as the title Lord of Land. Other names indicate an overlapping of the Judeo-Christian God with indigenous deities. The Falasha, like their Coptic Christian counterparts, believe in the existence of angels and devils, giving particular prominence to Michael as first among the archangels. The Falasha also believe in a messianic figure named Theodore, while both the Falasha and Christians believe in Elijah's immortality and his role in preparing for the coming of the messiah. Whereas the Coptic Christians venerate the Virgin Mary, the Falasha worship the personification of the Sabbath (also a female figure) who is an intercessor between the sinner and God.*

Falasha writings generally date from the fourteenth century. Their sources, however, are more ancient, and, as in the case of the apocalyptic Book of Baruch, *display complicated relations to earlier writings. For example, overtly Christian references were replaced by Jewish ones, so that the initial formula of the Ethiopian text, "In the name of the Father, the Son, and the Holy Ghost," became "Blessed be God, the Lord of Israel." References to Christ are replaced by the word* God, *and so on. Details concerning Heaven and Hell go back to an Ethiopic* Apocalypse of the Virgin, *itself an adaptation of the Apocalypse of Paul, written as early as the third century A.D. Paul's version has as its chief source the Apocalypse of Peter, written as early as the second century. Ethiopic apocalypses of Peter, of the Virgin, and of Baruch seem to be translations from Arabic sources translated from the Greek. Thus the Ethiopic* Book of Baruch *has roots in early Christian history, and apparently took shape at the time of the translations from the Greek texts in the seventh century. The Falasha version is an adaptation of these earlier Christian texts.*

THE ROYAL CHRONICLE OF EZANA

Ezana, King of Aksum and of Himyar and of Raydan and of Ethiopia and of Saba and of Salhen and of Tseyamo and of Bega and of Kasu, the King of Kings, the son of the invincible god, Ares.[1]

As the peoples of the Bega had rebelled, we sent our brothers Shaiazana and Hadefan to make war on them. And having laid down their arms, our brothers subdued them and brought them to us with their camp-followers and 3,112 cattle and 6,224 sheep and pack animals, giving them cattle and grain to eat, and beer, wine, and water to drink to the full, according to their number. They brought six tributary kings with their people, in number 4,400. They received each day 22,000 pieces of bread and wine for four months whilst they were bringing them to us. After giving them all kinds of food, as well as clothing, we allowed them to depart. They settled in a district called Matlia which belongs to our realm. And we commanded that food should be given to them, and we granted to the six kings 25,140 cattle.

To obtain the favor of my begetter, the invincible Ares, I have set up to him one statue of gold and one in silver and three in bronze.

Ezana, the son of Ella Amida, of the family of Halen, King of Aksum, and of Hemer [Himyar], and of Raydan, and of Sab, and of Salhen, and of Tseyamo, and of Bega, and of Kasu, the son of Mahrem.

He made war on the Tsarane, whose kingdom is Afan, after they had fought us and killed a merchant caravan. And then we made war upon them; first of all we sent armies, the army of Mahaza, and the army of Dakuen, and the army of Hara, and then we ourselves followed, and we encamped at the place where the troops were assembled and we made our soldiers set out from there. And they killed, and made prisoners, and despoiled them. And we attacked Sane and Tsawante, and Gema, and Zahtan, four peoples, and we took prisoner Alita with his two children. And a slaughter took place of the men of Afan, 503 men and 202

"Royal Chronicle of Ezana," from *The Ethiopian Royal Chronicles,* edited by Richard K. P. Pankhurst, copyright 1967, pp. 3–7. Reprinted by permission of Oxford University Press. "The Book of Baruch," from *Falasha Anthology,* edited and translated by Wolf Leslau, copyright 1979 (1951), pp. 64–76. Reprinted by permission of Yale University Press.

[1]Ezana, ruler of Axum (Aksum in the text), reigned in the fourth century A.D., and is renowned for having introduced Christianity to his kingdom. He ruled over an area now associated with Ethiopia, but the references to regions in this paragraph actually correspond only vaguely to present-day Ethiopia. The term *Ethiopia* in the chronicle refers to a region west of Aksum; Himyar and Raydan were situated across the Red Sea in South Arabia; Kasu was probably to the west of Aksum, in present-day Sudan; while the other places cannot be identified. The reference to Ares is to the Greek god of war, known to the Ethiopians as Mahrem.

women, in all 705. Of his camp-followers there were taken prisoner 40 men and 165 women and children, in all 205. As booty were carried off 31,957 cattle and 827 baggage animals. And the king returned in safety together with his people. And he set up a throne here in Shado, and committed himself to the protection of Astar and Beher and Meder. If there be anyone who would overthrow it and remove it, that person, and his land and his race, shall be overthrown and removed and be rooted out of his country. And he [the king] offered one hundred cattle and fifty prisoners as a thanks-offering to Mahrem who had begotten him. . . .

By the power of the Lord of Heaven who is mightier than everything which exists in heaven or on earth. Ezana, the son of Ella Amida, of the descent of Halen, King of Aksum and of Hemer, Raydan, Saba, Salhen, Tseyamo, Bega, and Kasu, King of Kings . . . and invincible to the enemy. By the might of the Lord of Heaven who has made me lord, who reigns as the perfect one for all eternity. . . .

By the might of the Lord of All I made war upon Noba, for the peoples of Noba had rebelled and made a boast of it. The peoples of Noba had said: "they (the Aksumites) will not cross the Takaze." And they were in the habit of attacking the peoples of Mangurto and Khasa and Barya and the blacks and of making war upon the red peoples. And two or three times they had broken their solemn oaths and had killed their neighbors mercilessly, and they had stripped bare and stolen the properties of our envoys and messengers which I had sent to them to inquire into their thefts, and had stolen from them their weapons of defence.

And as I have sent warnings to them, and they would not listen to me and refused to stop their evil deeds and heaped insults upon me and then took to flight, I made war upon them. And I rose up in the might of the Lord of the Land, and I fought them on the Takaze, at the ford of Kemalke. Thereupon they took to flight and would not make a stand. And I followed the fugitives for twenty-three days, killing and making prisoners and capturing booty wherever I stopped. My people who marched into the country brought back prisoners and booty.

Meanwhile I burnt their towns, both those built of brick and those built of reeds, and my soldiers carried off their food, as well as copper, iron, and brass; they destroyed the statues in their houses [i.e., temples], as well as their storehouses for food, and their cotton trees, casting them in the river Sida [the Nile]. And there were many men who died in the water, their number being unknown to me. The soldiers sank their ships crowded with people, men and women, in the river. And I captured two chieftains, who had come as spies riding on female camels. . . . And I captured an Angabenawi nobleman. . . . The chieftains who died were five in number. . . .

And I came to Kasu and I fought a battle and made prisoners of its people at the junction of the rivers Sida and Takaze. And the day after I arrived I sent out the army Mahaza and the army Hara, and Damawa and Falha and Sera, to raid the country upstream of Sida, and the cities built of brick and those of reeds. The names of the cities built of brick were Alwa and Daro. And they killed and captured prisoners and cast people into the water, and they arrived safe and sound having terrified their enemies and conquered them by the might of the Lord of the Land. And after that I sent the army of Halen and the army of Laken and the army of Sabarat, and Falha and Sera, down the Sida against the towns of Noba which are made of reeds. . . . The towns of brick which the Noba had taken were Tabito and Fertoti. And my people arrived at the frontier of the red Noba and they returned safe and sound, having captured prisoners and slain the Noba and taken booty from them by the might of the Lord of Heaven. And I set up a throne in that country at the place where the rivers Sida and Takaze join, opposite the town with brick houses. . . .

The things which the Lord of Heaven has given me are: men captives, 214; women captives, 415; total captives, 629. Men slain, 602; women and children slain, 156; total slain, 700. Total of prisoners and slain, 1,387. Booty, 10,560 cattle and 51,050 sheep.

And I set up a throne here in Shado by the might of the Lord of Heaven, who has helped me and given me sovereignty.

May the Lord of Heaven make my kingdom strong! And as He has this day conquered my enemy for me may He conquer for me wherever I go. As He has this day conquered for me, and overthrown my enemy, I will rule the people with righteousness and justice, and will not oppress them. And may they preserve this throne which I have set up for the Lord of Heaven, who has made me king, and the land upon which it lies. And if there shall be anyone who shall remove it, destroy it or overthrow it, he and his kinsfolk shall be rooted out and removed from the land. I have set up this throne by the might of the Lord of Heaven.

FALASHA WRITINGS: THE BOOK OF BARUCH

Blessed be God, the Lord of Israel.

We shall write that which God has revealed to the blessed, holy, and praised Abba Baruch.[2] When he was thirty-five years of age his parents took him to Jerusalem and put him in service with the high priest, named Eskendros.[3] The high priest associated him with the doorkeepers of Jerusalem, and he remained in service for thirty years. He prayed as follows: "Let me not see the destruction of Jerusalem." After the thirty-fifth year had gone by he went to draw water. He drew water and covered it with a fig leaf. A deep sleep overcame him and so he slept. Then God raised up Nebuchadnezzar, the king of Babylon, at the time of Manasseh, the king of Judah.[4] He captured Jerusalem and destroyed all its monuments, led away its priests and prophets, captured Zion,[5] took the precious stone that Solomon had made for it, and took captive its men and animals.

A great angel named Sutu'el appeared. He exalted Baruch heavenward and let him see all the hidden and manifest things. He brought him into the heavenly Jerusalem, and let him see established and high thrones, decorated places, shining crowns of various appearances, and white robes of various shapes.

I, Baruch, asked the angel who conducted me, and said to him: "Whose is this dwelling?" He answered and said to me: "It belongs to the martyrs who have despised and hated this ephemeral world, who have delivered themselves up to death for the sake of justice and eternal life, to those whose heads were cut and whose blood was shed."

Then he showed me the aspect of the heavenly Jerusalem. I said to him: "Was it made before or after the creation?" He said to me: "Before the creation of Adam. The names of all the just, from Adam up to the end of the world, are written on this golden column."

---

[2] Baruch, secretary and disciple of the Jewish prophet Jeremiah, has been the subject of a number of ancient writings, including one of the apocryphal books of the Old Testament. Differing versions—some in Hebrew, Aramaic, Greek, Syriac, Slavonic, Armenian, and Ethiopic—existed in ancient times. This version was Ethiopic, and has roots dating back to the early Christian period. It combines both Christian and Jewish themes, including the Christian emphasis on the purity of celibacy, and the Jewish emphasis on the purity of the Temple sanctuary in Jerusalem; the Jewish earthly messiah is combined with Christian otherworldly expectations.

[3] The Ethiopic name for Alexander.

[4] Nebuchadnezzar, king of Babylonia, conquered the kingdom of Judah and the city of Jerusalem, destroyed the Temple, and led the Jews into exile about 586 B.C. The text errs in dating the conquest to the reign of Manasseh, rather than Jehoiakim and Zedekiah.

[5] Zion is, presumably, the Temple in Jerusalem or the ark within the Temple containing the two tablets of "the Law."

Then he brought me into the middle where the column was and there I saw high and shiny seats and robes whiter than milk, the sun, the moon, and the stars. The place was full of fruit. I asked the angel who conducted me and said to him: "Who enters through this gate?" He who guided me answered and said to me: "Blessed are those who enter through this gate. Here the husband remains with his wife and the wife remains with her husband."

Then he showed me a golden bed, a couch of precious stones, garments, and purses. I said to my guide: "Are they for those who remained in their virginity from their youth?" He said to me: "Yes, for those who guarded their virginity from their youth."

Then he took me to a great city and brought me into this city. There I saw many plants, numbering 4,007, full of fruit. I said to my guide: "Who are those who enter into this house?" He answered and said to me: "Those who despised and hated the ephemeral world will enter through this gate that Adam built of old in this city. Many will hope for it, but few will enter through it."

Then he brought me to a stream of oil.[6] I said to my guide: "Who will enter through this gate?" "Those who despised and hated this ephemeral world from their youth until the end of their lives; those who, having taken the pure monastical garment, were continent and of pure flesh and spirit."

Then he brought me across this stream of oil and showed me a stream of milk, greater than the sea and the deep waters. I asked my guide and said to him: "Who will enter into this stream of milk?" He answered and said to me: "This stream is for the children who were chosen while still in their mothers' wombs, and for all who were killed by iniquity, too.[7] They will dwell in the end of days in the shadow of this stream of milk, together with their children. It is not for the children alone but also for the hermits, who were chosen in their mothers' wombs for the heavenly kingdom and did not mate with women from the day they put on the monastical cloth of chastity."

Then he brought me to a city which was white and shining, decorated with gold, hyacinth, and pearls, filled with fruit and plantations of almonds, nuts, and pomegranates. And I asked my guide: "Who are those who will enter into this city?" He said to me: "The kings and governors who observed justice; who did regard no man, rich or poor, small or big; those who loved the orphans, priests, and temples; and those who dressed them as well as the widows in fine raiment; those who loved justice and gave alms to the poor and indigent; those who fed the hungry and gave to the thirsty to drink. This then is the dwelling of the kings and governors."

---

[6]Other apocryphal writings state that there are four streams that run through Paradise, and they are of honey, milk, oil, and wine. This motif runs through Jewish, Christian, and Muslim writings.

[7]Various apocryphal writings speak of children killed in their mothers' wombs by Herod.

Then he brought me to a place facing this one, and the city I saw was brighter than the sun, the moon, and the stars ten million times over, decorated with pearls and filled with fruit and plants. I said to my guide: "Whose is this beautiful residence?" He answered and said to me: "Blessed is the man who will enter into this residence. It is for the mighty of the earth who killed no one, who were given not to idolatry, who confounded not one soul with another, who practiced neither magic nor sorcery. This then is their residence."

Then he took me opposite this place on a golden ship and brought me to the place of the City of God,[8] and showed me all the kingdoms of glory that do not pass away but grow and are glorified a million times. I said to my guide: "What is the name of this city?" He said to me: "The City of God." I said to him: "Who will enter into this city?" My guide said to me: "The meek who kept no vengeance in their hearts, who made peace with their neighbors, who did not repay evil to the villain who had done them evil, who blessed those who cursed them, who shared their bread with the hungry, their cup with the thirsty, their clothes with the naked, who redeemed the captives with their wealth and lent of their gold to the poor. This is their residence."

He took me away from this gate and brought me to another city named Aqraba, which means the "Land of the Living." There I saw Enoch and Elijah writing down the deeds of the just of the earth.[9]

In the days of this man the Holy Spirit will descend without cloud like rain for seven days and will be like oil. Without it man will not be purified from his sins and the drops of God's mercy will not be spread over the earth. In those days peace will reign and there will be no hatred, no agitation, and no robbery, but love, joy, offerings, and rejoicing. If someone asks but wood from his neighbor, he willingly will lend or give him all his wealth. In those days the fear of God will abound and the many churches that have previously been destroyed in the world will be rebuilt. Everything will be accomplished on the order of the king. Believers will abound and belief will be strong. In those days the priests will walk according to the prescribed laws and the ordinances of justice as did Melchizedek,[10] Moses, and Aaron, the holy priests. Like them they will please God during their lifetimes. In those days love will abound as well as peace, joy, exultation, and knowledge of the Lord. In those days there will be no sorrow or distress, no hunger or thirst, no murder or controversy. In those days people will have one feeling and one thought, and they will walk in the straight path of grace.

Then I saw a stream of honey, that flowed like the water of the sea. I asked my guide: "Who will enter into this stream?" He answered me: "The blessed prophets who prophesied of the good that would come at the end."

---

[8]The heavenly Jerusalem.

[9]Besides Enoch and Elijah, other heavenly scribes include Ezra, Metatron, and Messiah.

[10]Biblical high priest and king of Salem.

Then he showed me, opposite that stream of honey, a stream of wine that was like a torrent of sea water. I asked my guide: "Who will enter into this stream?" He said to me: "Those who despised the world, who were given to hospitality, and who loved their neighbors as themselves."

Then the angel took me to the east and showed me a golden column on which was engraved an inscription in a thin writing brighter than the sun, the moon, and the stars of the sky. I asked him: "What is this golden column and what is this writing on it that has the likeness of the sun, the moon, and the shining stars?" He answered me: "The names of the just are written for eternal life on this golden column, where they wax not old or corrupt." I said to him: "Are the names alone engraved upon it; are not the features of the face engraved upon it, too?" He answered and said: "All the features of the faces of the just are engraved for eternal life on this golden column, where they neither wax old nor become corrupt. They are engraved with a golden pen; the deeds of the sinners are engraved with an iron pen." I asked my guide: "Whose is this city?" He said to me: "The Land of the Living. Those in it are Enoch and Elijah, who write God's commandments, and who live there forever."

Then he took me to another area and I saw at its gates big trees full of fruit. Many hermits were scattered there, suffering from great hunger and thirst. A stream was also in this place. When they wished to eat from the tree it ascended to the sky, and when they rose in order to eat it descended to the earth. When they wished to drink from the stream it vanished and entered into the heart of the earth, and when they despaired of drinking the stream came out and reappeared to them. Sorrowfully I asked the angel who conducted me, and said to him: "Whose is this city and who are these men?" He answered and said to me: "This city belongs to the hermits. They were perfect in fasting, adoration, prayer, and purity of the body but they were boastful and haughty." I said to him: "Did their haughtiness prevent them from entering into the Heavenly Kingdom?" He said to me: "The root of sin is haughtiness and loftiness."

Then he showed me a city a thousand thousand times brighter than the sun, the moon, and the stars, full of fruit trees yielding thousands of blessed fruits every hour. There were also shining raiment, crowns adorned and bright, golden belts, garments of precious stones, clothes, and shoes at the right and the left, branches of olive trees and branches of palm trees, the odor of which ravishes the heart and the taste of which makes the soul go forth from the body. Its beginning and end are not perceived. None knows it but God. Even the angels of God know it not, and the priests do not use it to burn incense. I asked him: "Whose is this residence?" He said to me: "It is the residence of the hermits." I said to him: "Will not all of them enter into this dwelling?" He said: "No." I said to him: "Who, then, are those who will enter into this residence?" He said to me: "Those who did not mate with women after they retired from this world; those who did not smite their neighbors with their slander; those who did not ride on mules;[11] those who did not carry seats and sit on them; those who did not acquire gold and silver, the goods of this world and who did not like them; those who despised and hated this world; those who did not love office; who did not lie on a bed or on a couch in this world; who did not claim to be eating,[12] in fact, there is no joy for the hermits upon this earth, their pleasure begins when their soul leaves this world; those who did not like vain glory, who did not accept gold or silver or precious clothes from kings and princes, who did not set crowns upon their heads, and who did not take bribes to the disadvantage of the innocent. All these will enter into this residence." Having heard this I praised the Lord.

Then he took me to the west. There I saw a column of fire on which was writing by a pen of fire. The writing was thin and compact and the column of fire was greater than the column of gold. I asked him: "What is that written on the column of fire?" He said to me: "The names of the sinners."

Opposite that column I saw virgins clothed in darkness, and the guide said to me: "These are mad virgins who were avaricious." I said to him: "Do they stay in this land of suffering because of their avarice?" He said to me. "Yes."

Then I saw a stream of fire, with many men seated upon thrones of fire. I asked him: "Who are those who undergo such punishment?" he said to me: "They are priests." I said to him: "Why are they punished so severely?" he said to me: "This is the punishment of priests and high priests who introduced improper things into the temple and accepted bribes for the priesthood." I said to him: "As a matter of fact they introduced improper things into the sanctuary for bribes: children of the divorced, stutterers, the dumb and the deaf, the blind, the broken-handed, and the leprous, children of Kedar,[13] the rich but not the poor. Therefore these priests are punished."

Then he showed me a big sea of fire, by which many people were being swallowed. I said to him: "Who are these that are being punished so severely?" He said to me: "Priests and teachers." I said to him: "Why are they punished?" He said to me: "Because they alone ate the firstlings in the sanctuary; they alone ate the tithe of the sanctuary;[14] they ate the funeral meal of the poor and buried them not with honor; they walked not in the path of life; they taught not the glory of the Sabbath, saying, 'Honor it, and introduce not into the dwellings donkeys, mules, oxen, sheep, goats, or even hens.' As for the teachers, they did not rebuke their children, neither sons nor daughters. Therefore will they be punished."

---

[11]Riding mules or horses was considered a sign of arrogance.

[12]That is, those who did not use eating as a pretext for not having the time to do good deeds in the world.

[13]Kedar is one of the sons of Ishmael; this reference may refer to the Bedouins.

[14]Instead of giving to the needy.

Then he showed me an abyss of fire, full of people who scoured burning charcoals with their hands and drew the streams of fire with their fingers. The streams of fire swallowed them entirely, so that none could recognize their mouths or lips. I said to him: "Who are these who are punished like this?" He said to me: "Those who have lost their virginity in deserted places, without their parents giving them in marriage."

I also saw an abyss and a big pit of fire, and people without number were in it. The fire devoured some of them up to their knees, others up to their breasts, others up to their necks, others up to their mouths, and still others entirely. I said to him: "Who are these who undergo such severe punishment?" He said to me: "Those swallowed up to the knees uttered vehement words in the sanctuary. Those swallowed up to the reins fornicated with women in the house of God. Those swallowed up to their breasts slandered their neighbors in the sanctuary. Those devoured up to their necks spoke after their offering to God without cooling off the bread or the water. Those devoured entirely fornicated with man as with woman."

Then I saw an abyss and a pit of fire the depth of which was equal to 11,007 cubits. I said to him: "Who are these who go down into this stream?" He said: "Those who fornicated with a woman in childbed or with a woman in her uncleanness or with an ignominious woman; those who married the wife of one who died[15] or the wife of a brother; those who fornicated with a daughter or with a sister or with the daughter of a brother; those who fornicated with domestic animals or with wild beasts. This is their punishment."

Then I saw big rocks of fire, and there I saw many men scattered through the fire. I said to him: "Who are these who are punished in this abyss of fire and in these rocks of fire?" He said to me: "Those who worshiped stones. Therefore their punishment is by stones of fire."

Then I saw big trees, all of fire. Many men were suspended from them, and serpents of fire and dogs of fire devoured them. I said to him: "Who are these who undergo this terrible punishment?" He said to me: "Priests, and widows who, being pregnant, drank medicines to kill the conceived being. The killed beings cried unto God saying: 'O Lord, O Lord, we might have been good or bad but they did not let us grow; some of us were eaten by dogs, others by beasts.' God ordered that the children be given to Temleyakos;[16] as for their parents, they undergo this punishment."

Then I saw a big caldron of fire in which there were many of the mighty kings, governors, and princes. I said to him: "Who are these who are punished like this?" He said to me: "The mighty kings, governors, and princes, who ate of

---

[15]Probably referring to a priest, thus following biblical law that forbade priests to marry widows.

[16]An angel who places children in a beautiful place.

the offerings and laid waste the sanctuary, who robbed the dwellings of the priests and laid desolate the land, who loved not the orphans and gave not alms from what God had given them. Woe unto you who spoil the world! Woe unto you who eat of the offerings! Woe, for your punishment will be severe! Woe unto you who spoil with a razor God's creatures! Woe unto you, kings and governors, who build sanctuaries to please the eye of man, but in your hearts you like not the priests and chanters! You are like a bee with no honey or a pitcher with no water. Woe unto you, kings and governors, who do not save the oppressed and the poor. You foolish ones, do you think that you will enter the heavenly kingdom because of your great riches? All the glory of your house will not go down with you and your terrestrial kingdom will be forgotten, for the existence of this world is ephemeral. The world is ephemeral and its concupiscence as well. Everything is ephemeral and wears out like a garment, and like linen clothes that you change and they are changed, for the existence of this world is ephemeral. Blessed are the kings who pleased God during their lifetimes. Blessed are the kings who loved the poor and the miserable. Blessed are those who made wisdom their mother. Blessed are the kings who gave all their wealth to the poor and miserable as ransom for their souls, knowing that the existence of this world is ephemeral, that gold and silver deteriorate and garments wear out. Woe unto you, kings, you who are creatures and yet exalt yourselves over other creatures. Woe unto you, kings and governors, you are dust; and why do you exalt yourselves over the dust? Woe unto you, kings and governors, you are clay; and why do you exalt yourselves over the clay? Woe unto you, kings and governors, who cut off the creatures of God with the razor and the sword; you can make neither white nor black even a single hair of your head. Heard you not what scripture said: 'One man is more honorable than ninety-nine angels'?[17] Woe unto you, kings and governors, who rob the sanctuary and rebuke not your subordinates that they may not corrupt the world. If your governors corrupt the world and you rebuke them not, I shall require their blood of you, says God."

I, Baruch, saw horrible and great judgments, and each of them was terrifying. I saw great mountains of fire full of pitch and sulphur, a terrifying caldron full of the great governors and princes engulfed in a sea of fire. I said to the angel Sutu'el who conducted me: "Who are these men who undergo this terrible punishment?" He said to me: "The wicked kings who corrupted the world and defiled the sanctuary."

Then I saw a large pit of fire full of princes and wealthy people, men and women. Serpents of fire were suspended on their garments and devoured them, vipers of fire stung them, dogs of fire bit and devoured them, angels of fire pierced them, rocks of fire fell upon them, and the pit of fire engulfed them up to their heads. I asked the angel. "Who are these who are punished so severely?" He said

---

[17]That is, a righteous man surpasses the angels.

to me: "These are the hermits who were supposed to despise this world but despised it not and purified not their thoughts. They were like other men of the world, they had relations with women and married and forgot God during their lifetimes. They resemble the dog that returns to his own vomit, or the sow that was washed and returns to the mire, or Absalom who transgressed the commandments of his father.[18] They resemble Lot's wife who became a pillar of salt. All things are vain."

Then I saw many men whom they made to run on burning sand. I said to him: "Who are these whose punishment is like this?" He said to me: "Deacons who did not promptly bring the offerings into the sanctuary."

Then I saw people suspended by burning ropes, their feet upward and their heads downward. I said to him: "Who are these who are punished like this?" He said to me: "Priests who did not offer Sunday sacrifices to God at sunrise; the rest day of the temple comes from God. Therefore they are punished."

Then I saw people whom they made to touch fire and to whom they gave cups of fire to drink. I said to him: "Who are these who are punished like this?" He said to me: "Priests and deacons who did not offer sacrifices with a pure heart, those who, being bound by the priesthood, transgressed it. This is their punishment."

Then I saw men whose hands were cut off. I said to him: "Who are these maimed people?" He said to me: "Those who wrote magic texts and carved. This is their punishment."

Then I saw people from whose mouths came fire and sulphur. I said to him: "Who are these who are punished like this?" He said to me: "The tailors who sewed garments and kept for themselves even a small piece of thread."

Then I saw people brought in with cords of fire and searing flame. All kinds of fruit and limpid water passed in front of them, but when they wished to drink the water fled from them. I said to him: "Who are these who are punished like this?" He said to me: "Those who broke the fast and those who hastened to eat?"[19]

All this the angel Sutu'el showed to me.

Then I saw a terrible punishment, sealed with seven seals. He said to me: "O Baruch, wilt thou be strong enough to see this terrible and frightful punishment?" I said to him: "Speak, O Lord." Then he commanded the angel of Gehenna[20] and said: "Show the seal of Gehenna to Baruch, the beloved of God." And he opened the seal and, behold, a great torment called Gehenna appeared, and a great cold, and snow. From the time of the creation of heaven and earth until the end of the world, the shining sun would be unable to heat it. Those who are thrown into it will no more be mentioned among the living, and those who enter into it will remain there. As the prophet David says: "Therefore the wicked will not rise from

---

[18]That is, who did not obey King David, his father.

[19]The Falasha fast every Thursday.

[20]That is, the angel of hell.

hell and the sinners will not remain in the congregation of the righteous." He also says: "Like the dust which the wind drives away from the surface of the earth."

Then I, Baruch, saw what he showed me: bad years, and numerous good years during which there will be love, corn, wheat, honey, and milk. The Holy Spirit will go down like the dew of the rain season; fast and prayer will please God. The husband will speak agreeably with his wife, the daughter-in-law with her mother-in-law, the monk with his disciple, and the disciple with his teacher, the brother with his brother, the daughter with her mother, and the mother with her daughter, the father with his son, and the son with his father, the relative with his relatives, and the friend with his friends.

In the four-hundred-and-seventieth cycle, the six-thousandth year, and the fifth day, a queen[21] will reign and there will be great joy. Qostantinos[22] and Teodros,[23] the orthodox, will reign, and in their days there will be love and peace. They will build God's house which Diyoqletyanos,[24] the heretic, destroyed. In their time five hundred and thirty years will be added to Gabra Masqal,[25] the king of Aksum, because of his orthodoxy.

Then every year love will decrease. Small foxes will rise; they will destroy the whole world and they will exalt the ark of God into the heavenly Zion. Wheat will grow less and water will flow four times less.[26] Those who bring offerings, incense, and sacrifices to God's house will go up to heaven. There will be good priests and bad priests. Those who minister in God's house will be the slothful, the foolish, the silly, and the scorners. At that time slothful teachers will be created. They will reduce everything to schemes. They will not be saved nor will they save their children. They will profane the Sabbath and violate the festivals.

In the twenty-fourth year of mercy the trees of the fields will rejoice, the mountains and hills will be joyful, as will creatures, man, and beast. Everything will go back to its first condition.

Then a righteous man will reign. Righteousness shall be the girdle of his loins and faithfulness the girdle of his reins. Justice shall spring out in his days. He will reign thirty years in the five-hundred-and-forty-eighth cycle.

---

[21]Probably referring to Helena, wife of the Roman Emperor Constantius I and mother of Constantine the Great.

[22]Constantine the Great (A.D. 285–337), the Roman emperor who converted to Christianity.

[23]Perhaps Emperor Theodosius the Great (A.D. 345–395), during whose time Christianity became the official religion of the empire.

[24]Diocletian (A.D. 245–313), the Roman emperor who persecuted Christians.

[25]The second son of Kaleb, the king of Ethiopia. He was a devout Christian and succeeded the throne in A.D. 550, suggesting a lower limit to the date of *The Book of Baruch*.

[26]Drought and famine were thought to be the chief plagues that would prevail at the time of the Antichrist of Christian tradition.

After that the false messiah will come. He will say: "I am God," and will perform numerous signs and wonders. He shall cause the sun to rise in the west and the moon toward Elam; his right eye will be blended with blood, his right foot will be thin; the nails of his hands will be distorted and those of his hands and feet will be like scythes; his right hand will be for extermination and his left hand for death. He will reign seven years.

Then God will cause the false messiah to cease. The lion will then reign seven years or sixty-seven in the count of the cycles. He will summon a council of priests, monks, believers, and numerous armies. He will say to the Cross:[27] "Take away all this," and the Cross will take it and ascend to heaven. All of them will weep bitterly and will die; the king will die with them. Michael and Gabriel[28] will come with their armies and will take them into the garden of joy. Then the demon Qoleyon[29] will come with thirty thousand and seventy-seven others and will reign. They will eat rocks like reeds, will swallow fire, and will drink the blood of women in their impurity. They will reign seven years.

Then the eagle[30] will reign and will reside in Jerusalem. He will devour ten thousand girls each evening, and ten thousand each morning. He will reign seven years.

Then the winds[31] will reign. They will destroy God's houses and will unearth the bones of men. They will reign seven years.

The holy Michael will blow the horn for thirty years, and all the bones will assemble. Then he will sound the trumpet for the second time for thirty years. The bones will be sewn up again with flesh and all the bodies will assemble. The holy Michael, the archangel, will blow the trumpet for the third time for thirty years, and all the dead will be resurrected in the twinkling of an eye. The glory of some of them will be greater than the sun, others will stand up in honor, still others in misery. Then the King of Heaven and Earth will come and will reward all men according to their deeds. Praise and glory be to Him forever. Amen.

If I, Baruch, were to tell you everything I saw and heard all the books would not contain it. The spirit of God dictated it to Absalom and Abimelech, the priests of Jerusalem. He gave it to King Masfeyanos,[32] who fears the Lord. Glory to God forever. Amen.

---

[27]That is, the messiah.

[28]Angels who lead the fight against the Antichrist.

[29]That is, Apolyon, angel of the bottomless pit.

[30]Perhaps representing the Babylonian kingdom.

[31]Perhaps representing the Nubians, a people of the upper Nile River, known for their ferocity.

[32]Identity unknown.

39

爱

Bharata

NATYASHASTRA

Natyashastra *is an ancient Indian Sanskrit work about the art of drama. The Sanskrit word* natya *has been customarily translated into English as "drama." The word* shastra *means "science" or "treatise." The* Natyashastra *is, therefore, known in English as* A Treatise on Dramaturgy. *This is only an approximate translation, because, as discussed below,* natya, *although it has similarities with Western drama, is different from it in some significant ways. Except for this difference, the* Natyashastra, *as a work on the theory and practice of drama, is comparable in its importance in world literature to the* Poetics *of the ancient Greek philosopher Aristotle (fourth century* B.C.*). Both of these works, based as they are on the study of drama as it existed in their respective cultures, arrive at conclusions of a universal nature on the art of drama.*

The Natyashastra *is attributed to Bharata, also called Bharata Muni (Muni is an honorific that means "an accomplished sage"). According to the consensus among scholars, Bharata probably lived sometime between the second century* B.C. *and the second century* A.D.*, although at least one scholar, the author of the translation used for this selection, pushes the date as far back as the fifth century* B.C. *In any case, Bharata's historical existence is so covered with fictional embellishment that we know him more as a semi-mythical figure than as a real human being. However, there is no doubt about the fact that he did exist. The great Indian playwrights of the first millennium* A.D. *knew him as the greatest authority on drama and were influenced by his work. The* Natyashastra *also served as the most important subject of interpretation and commentaries by the foremost critics of the time.*

Bharata begins the Natyashastra *with a description of the origin of* natya *as follows: The gods, headed by Indra, approached Brahma, the lord of creation, and requested him to create an object of diversion that should be both audible and vis-*

ible. Granting their request, Brahma concentrated on the four existing Vedas *(see Selection 8) and drew from them a fifth* Veda, *the* Natyaveda *("knowledge" or "book of natya"). It consisted of semi-historical tales (known as* itihasa*) that were conducive to duty, management of wealth, success, and fame, as they provided guidance to people in all their actions. The tales were rich with teachings from all the learned texts and contained a review of all the arts and crafts. Brahma then offered the* Natyaveda *to Indra, asking him to have the stories in it dramatized and acted by gods. But Indra told Brahma that the gods were not capable of understanding or using the* Natyaveda; *only the sages, who had lived a pious life and knew the mystery of the* Vedas, *could receive, maintain, and practice it. So Brahma asked "the sinless" Bharata to put the* Natyaveda *to use. Bharata learned it from Brahma and made his one hundred sons study it and learn to make proper use of it. At Bharata's request, Brahma provided him with further necessities— music, singing, graceful celestial nymphs, beautiful dresses, and the like—for dramatic performances. Bharata staged the first play for the enjoyment of the gods before establishing drama as an art for everyone's entertainment.*

The significance of this myth lies in its demonstration of the fact that drama and, for that matter, all art had a high place in the ancient Hindu culture. The Hindu system of values was governed by a view of human life that divided its ends into four categories. These were dharma *("religious and ritual obligations");* artha *("management of material wealth and other worldly affairs," which included family life and all economic and political activities);* kama *("personal enjoyment," including the gratification of the senses and the enjoyment of art); and* moksha *("spiritual perfection in the form of the realization of one's true and eternal self" as explained in the* Upanishads *[Selection 20]). The ultimate goal of life was considered to be* moksha. *Requirements and expected behavior in each of the four areas of activities were all meant to lead to this final goal. Thus, art, including drama, was intended to serve an end higher than itself. It did so in two ways: through moral lessons presented in its content, and, more profoundly, through the esthetic experience provided by artistic form. This esthetic experience, by its uplifting effect, provided release from the mundane world and brought one closer to one's spiritual true self. Bharata's treatment of the art of drama in the* Natyashastra *shows both these aspects of its usefulness.*

The Natyashastra *is a long work, containing six thousand verses, besides some prose, in thirty-six chapters. It deals exhaustively with all aspects of* natya *from the standpoint of both the content of plays and their staging. It contains directions for the writers of plays as well as for actors and producers. Topics covered include the construction of a playhouse; ceremonies preliminary to a performance; choreographic elements, such as dance, conventional gestures, and movements of different parts of the body; costumes and makeup; classification of plays and analysis of their structure; poetic aspects of plays; instrumental music and singing and their use in plays; classification of roles and characters and the training of actors; the training and qualifications of other members of the profession; and criticism of dramatic performances. Besides these principal topics, many minor ones come up for consideration in passing.*

Bharata defines natya *as "A mimicry of the exploits of gods, the Asuras (a class of demigods), kings as well as of householders in this world. . . ." This definition is somewhat similar to Aristotle's view of art, including drama, as imitation* (mimesis) *of life. However, there is a very significant difference between the manner of imitation in Aristotle and that in* natya. *Whereas Aristotle gives little specific information as to how the imitation is to be effected in drama, the* Natyashastra *lays down elaborate rules for its achievement. Because of these rules and the effectiveness of mimicry achieved through them, the theorists of* natya *later than Bharata called it "a poem to be seen," thus distinguishing it from epic or narrative poetry and fiction as preeminently a spectacle. This makes* natya *fundamentally different from Aristotle's view of drama, because, according to him, although spectacle is one of the elements of drama, it is only an element of minor importance. He prefers that drama achieve its effects without emphasis on spectacle. Dependence on spectacle, in his view, shows lack of art in a dramatist. In* natya, *in contrast, spectacle is the essence of art. It is, therefore, to be enhanced and reinforced with music, song, dance, and evocation of an appropriate atmosphere.*

The most central and unique feature of Bharata's treatment of natya *is the theory of* rasa *(which, in the context of* natya, *means "sentiments"). The Sanskrit word* rasa *means "juice" or "the enjoyment of tasting juice," which serves as a metaphor for the evocation and savoring of certain sentiments in the spectator's mind. Such evocation and such savoring are the purpose and function of* natya. *The evocation of sentiments is accomplished by the presentation in a play of situations charged with particular feelings, or "psychological states" as Bharata calls them. The presentation produces in the spectator's mind a sentiment corresponding to the particular feeling with which the depicted situation is charged. The sentiment produced in the spectator's mind parallels, but is not identical with, the feeling as it is in real life. The spectator experiences it in freedom, that is, without the compulsion to act in response to it as one would in real life. The spectator's experience is thus related to, but is qualitatively different from, that of real life. It is an esthetic experience.* Rasa, *used as a technical term, thus means "esthetic experience."*

According to Bharata, all human beings have eight enduring, or fundamental, feelings: love, mirth, sorrow, anger, heroism, fear, disgust, and wonder. Corresponding to these are eight possible rasas. *In addition to the fundamental feelings, there are thirty-three complementary, or passing, feelings, such as weakness, apprehension, envy, indolence, etc. Treatment of complementary feelings reinforces one or another fundamental feeling in the evocation of a particular* rasa. *Each play should have one dominant* rasa—*other* rasas *are necessary, but they must be subordinate to and enhance the dominant* rasa *in order to assure the harmony of a play.*

The following excerpt, drawn from Chapter Six of the Natyashastra, *which, according to many scholars, is the most important chapter of the work, focuses on the theory of* rasa. *It discusses the emotional content of plays and describes what actors should do to represent various feelings.*

EIGHT SENTIMENTS[1]

The eight sentiments recognized in drama are as follows: erotic, comic, pathetic, furious, heroic, terrible, odious, and marvellous.

These eight are the sentiments named by Brahma.[2] I shall now speak of the durable and the complementary psychological states and the *sattvika* ones.[3]

Durable Psychological States

The durable psychological states are known to be the following: love, mirth, sorrow, anger, energy, terror, disgust, and astonishment.

The thirty-three complementary psychological states are known to be the following: discouragement, weakness, apprehension, envy, intoxication, weariness, indolence, depression, anxiety, distraction, recollection, contentment, shame, inconstancy, joy, agitation, stupor, arrogance, despair, impatience, sleep, epilepsy, dreaming, awakening, indignation, dissimulation, cruelty, assurance, sickness, insanity, death, fright, and deliberation. . . .

Eight *Sattvika* States

Paralysis, perspiration, horripilation,[4] change of voice, trembling, change of color, weeping, and fainting are the eight *sattvika* states.

From Manomohan Ghosh, trans. *The Natyashastra* (Calcutta: Manisha Granthalaya Private Limited, 1967. First published 1951), pp. 102–103, 105–117. Printed with permission.

[1]"Sentiment" here is the translation of the term *rasa*, which, in *Natyashastra,* means "esthetic experience." Sentiment is related to, but is qualitatively different from, "feeling" in real life. It is the experience produced in the spectator's mind by the portrayal of a feeling in drama.

[2]Brahma is the Hindu god of creation. In the opening of the *Natyashastra,* Bharata says that drama was created by and taught to him by Brahma.

[3]Psychological states are emotions, or feelings. Bharata divides them into three categories: fundamental, or durable, feelings; complementary, or passing, feelings; and *sattvika* ("involuntary") feelings.

[4]A bristling of the hair on the head and the body because of terror, cold, or illness. Also called gooseflesh.

SENTIMENTS EXPLAINED

In that connection I shall first of all explain the sentiments *(rasa).* No poetic meaning proceeds from speech without any kind of sentiment. Now the sentiment is produced from a combination of determinants,[5] consequents,[6] and complementary psychological states. Is there any instance parallel to it? Yes, it is said that, as taste *(rasa)* results from a combination of various spices, vegetables, and other articles, and as six tastes are produced by articles, such as raw sugar or spices or vegetables, so the durable psychological states, when they come together with various other psychological states, attain the quality of a sentiment [i.e., become sentiment]. Now one enquires, "What is the meaning of the word *rasa?*" It is said in reply [that *rasa* is so called] because it is capable of being tasted. "How is *rasa* tasted?" In reply it is said that just as well-disposed persons, while eating food cooked with many kinds of spice, enjoy its tastes and attain pleasure and satisfaction, so the cultured people taste the durable psychological states while they see them represented by an expression of the various psychological states with words, gestures, and the *sattva,* and derive pleasure and satisfaction. . . .

Just as connoisseurs of cooked food, while eating food which has been prepared from various spices and other articles, taste it, so the learned people taste in their heart the durable psychological states (such as love, sorrow, etc.) when they are represented by an expression of the psychological states with gestures. Hence these durable psychological states in a drama are called sentiments.

RELATION BETWEEN SENTIMENTS AND PSYCHOLOGICAL STATES

Now one enquires, "Do the psychological states come out of the sentiments or the sentiments come out of the psychological states?" On this point, some are of opinion that they arise from their mutual contact. But this is not so. Why?

It is apparent that the sentiments arise from the psychological states and not the psychological states from the sentiments. For on this point there are traditional couplets, such as [the following].

The psychological states are so called by experts in drama, for they make one feel the sentiments in connection with various modes of dramatic representation. Just as by many articles of various kinds, auxiliary cooked eatable [meat and fish] is brought forth, so the psychological states, along with different kinds of histrionic representation will cause the sentiments to be felt.[7]

---

[5]Determinants are the causes or factors bringing about certain feelings.

[6]Consequents are the visible signs accompanying particular feelings.

[7]Histrionic representation is dramatic representation by acting.

There can be no sentiment prior to (without) the psychological states, and no psychological states without the sentiments following it, and during the histrionic representations they result from their interaction. . . .

Just as a tree grows from a seed, and flowers and fruits from a tree, . . . likewise the psychological states exist as the source of all the sentiments.

EIGHT SENTIMENTS FROM FOUR ORIGINAL ONES

Now we shall describe the origin, colors, presiding deities,[8] and examples of these sentiments. Sources of these eight sentiments are the four original sentiments (i.e., erotic, furious, heroic, and odious).

The comic sentiment arises from the erotic, the pathetic from the furious, the marvellous from the heroic, and the terrible from the odious.

A mimicry of the erotic sentiment is called the comic, and the result of the furious sentiment is the pathetic, the result of the heroic sentiment is called the marvellous, and that which is odious to see, results in the terrible.

The erotic sentiment is light green; the comic sentiment, white; the pathetic sentiment, grey; the furious sentiment, red; the heroic sentiment, yellowish; the terrible sentiment, black; the odious sentiment, blue; and the marvellous sentiment, yellow.

PRESIDING DEITIES OF SENTIMENTS

Vishnu is the god of the erotic, Pramathas of the comic, Rudra of the furious, Yama of the pathetic, Mahakala (Shiva) of the odious, Kala of the terrible, Indra of the heroic, and Brahma of the marvellous sentiments.[9]

Thus have been described the origin, colors, and deities of these sentiments. Now we shall explain the determinants, the consequents, the complementary psychological states, and their combination, definition, and examples.

We shall now enumerate the durable psychological states in different sentiments.

---

[8]These deities are all Hindu gods. Vishnu is the god who preserves creation; Rudra, the god of storms; Yama, the god of death and the underworld; Shiva, the destroyer and fertility god; Kala, the god of time; and Indra, a king in the heavens.

[9]Bharata lists the various feelings conventionally associated with the different gods and other mythical figures in the Hindu pantheon. Vishnu, Shiva, or Mahakala and Brahma are the highest Hindu gods. Pramathas are a class of demi-gods, or fiends, attendant on Shiva. Rudra is a very complex deity embodying many contradictory qualities of good and evil. One main aspect in which he is visualized is as the god of storms, called the howler, roarer, or terrible. Yama is the god of death; Kala, the god of time; and Indra, the great king of the heavens.

The Erotic Sentiment

Of these, the erotic sentiment proceeds from the durable psychological state of love, and it has as its basis [soul] a bright attire; for whatever in this world is white, pure, bright, and beautiful is appreciated in terms of the durable psychological state of love. For example, one who is elegantly dressed is called a lovely person. Just as persons are named after the profession of their father, mother, or family in accordance with the traditional authority, so the sentiments, the psychological states, and other objects connected with drama are given names in pursuance of the practice and the traditional authority. Hence the erotic sentiment has been so named on account of its usually being associated with a bright and elegant attire. It owes its origin to men and women and relates to the fullness of youth. It has two bases: union and separation. Of these two, the erotic sentiment in union arises from determinants like the pleasures of the season, the enjoyment of garlands, unguents, ornaments, the company of beloved persons, objects of senses, splendid mansions, going to a garden and enjoying oneself there, seeing the beloved one, hearing his or her words, playing and dallying with him or her. It should be represented on the stage by consequents such as clever movement of eyes, eyebrows, glances, soft and delicate movement of limbs, and sweet words, and similar other things. Complementary psychological states in it do not include fear, indolence, cruelty, and disgust. The erotic sentiment in separation should be represented on the stage by consequents, such as indifference, languor, fear, jealousy, fatigue, anxiety, yearning, drowsiness, sleep, dreaming, awakening, illness, insanity, epilepsy, inactivity, fainting, death, and other conditions.

Now it has been asked, "If the erotic sentiment has its origin in love, why does it sometimes manifest itself through pathetic conditions?" In reply to this it is said, "It has been mentioned before that the erotic sentiment has its basis in union as well as in separation. Authorities on *ars amatoria (vaisikasastra)*[10] have mentioned ten conditions of the persons separated from their beloved ones, which are pathetic. . . . The pathetic sentiment relates to a condition of despair owing to the affliction under a curse, separation from dear ones, loss of wealth, death, or captivity; while the erotic sentiment, based on separation, relates to a condition of retaining optimism arising out of yearning and anxiety. Hence the pathetic sentiment and the erotic sentiment in separation differ from each other. And this is the reason why the erotic sentiment includes conditions available in all other sentiments.

And the sentiment called erotic is generally happy, connected with desired objects, enjoyment of seasons, garlands and similar other things, and it relates to the union of man and woman.

---

[10] *Vaisikasastra* means "the art of love."

There are besides two *aryas* related to the preceding *sutra:*[11]

The erotic sentiment arises in connection with favorable seasons, garlands, ornaments, enjoyment of the company of beloved ones, music and poetry, and going to the garden and roaming there. It should be represented on the stage by means of composure of the eyes and the face, sweet and smiling words, satisfaction and delight, and graceful movements of limbs.

The Comic Sentiment

Now the comic has as its basis the durable psychological state of laughter. This is created by determinants, such as showing unseemly dress or ornament, impudence, greediness, quarrel, defective limb, use of irrelevant words, mentioning of different faults, and similar other things. This (the comic sentiment) is to be represented on the stage by consequents like the throbbing of the lips, the nose, and the cheek, opening the eyes wide or contracting them, perspiration, color of the face, and taking hold of the sides. Complementary psychological states in it are indolence, dissimulation, drowsiness, sleep, dreaming, insomnia, envy, and the like. This sentiment is of two kinds: self-centered and centered in others. When a person himself laughs, it relates to the self-centered (comic sentiment), but when he makes others laugh, it (the comic sentiments therein) is centered in others.

There are two traditional *aryas* here:

As one laughs with an exhibition of oddly placed ornaments, uncouth behavior, words and dress and strange movements of limbs, it is called the comic sentiment.

As this makes other persons laugh by means of his uncouth behavior, words, movement of the limbs, and strange dress, it is known as the comic sentiment.

This sentiment is mostly to be seen in women and men of the inferior type, and it has six varieties of which I shall speak presently.

They are: slight smile, smile, gentle laughter, laughter of ridicule, vulgar laughter, and excessive laughter. Two by two they belong respectively to the superior, the middling, and the inferior types of persons.

In Persons of the Superior Type

To persons of the superior type belong the slight smile and the smile; to those of the middling type, the gentle laughter and the laughter of ridicule; and to those of the inferior type, the vulgar laughter and the excessive laughter.

There are *slokas* on this subject:[12]

The slight smile of the people of the superior type should be characterized by slightly blown cheeks and elegant glances, and in it teeth are not to be made visible.

---

[11]*Aryas* are verses. *Sutras* are principles, rules, or precepts.

[12]*Sloka* is a type of verse.

Their smile should be distinguished by blooming eyes, face, and cheeks, and in it teeth should be slightly visible.

In Persons of the Middling Type

The gentle laughter should have slight sound and sweetness and should be suitable to the occasion, and in it eyes and cheeks should be contracted and the face joyful.

During the laughter of ridicule the nose should be expanded, eyes should be squinting, and the shoulder and the head should be bent.

In Persons of the Inferior Type

The laughter on occasions not suitable to it, the laughter with tears in one's eyes, or with the shoulder and the head violently shaking, is called the vulgar laughter.

The excessive laughter is that in which the eyes are expanded and tearful sound is loud and excessive, and the sides are covered by hands.

Comic situations which may arise in the course of a play, for persons of the superior, middling, or inferior type are thus to be given expression to. . . .

The Pathetic Sentiment

Now the pathetic sentiment arises from the durable psychological state of sorrow. It grows from determinants such as affliction under a curse, separation from dear ones, loss of wealth, death, captivity, flight accidents, or any other misfortune. This is to be represented on the stage by means of consequents such as shedding tears, lamentation, dryness of the mouth, change of color, drooping limbs, being out of breath, loss of memory, and the like. Complementary psychological states connected with it are indifference, languor, anxiety, yearning, excitement, delusion, fainting, sadness, dejection, illness, inactivity, insanity, epilepsy, fear, indolence, death, paralysis, tremor, change of color, weeping, loss of voice, and the like.

On this point there are two *aryas:*

The pathetic sentiment arises from seeing the death of a beloved person, or from hearing something very unpleasant, and these are its determinants.

This is to be represented on the stage by consequents like weeping loudly, fainting, lamenting and bewailing, exerting the body, or striking it.

The Furious Sentiment

Now the furious sentiment has as its basis the durable psychological state of anger. It owes its origin to *raksasas, danavas,*[13] and haughty men, and is caused by fights.

---

[13] *Raksasas* and *danavas* are demonic beings of an evil nature.

This is created by determinants such as anger, rape, abuse, insult, untrue allegation, exorcizing, threatening, revengefulness, jealousy, and the like. Its actions are beating, breaking, crushing, fighting, drawing of blood, and similar other deeds. This is to be represented on the stage by means of consequents such as red eyes, knitting of eyebrows, defiance, biting of the lips, movement of the cheeks, pressing one hand with the other, and the like. Complementary psychological states in it are presence of mind, determination, energy, indignation, restlessness, fury, perspiration, trembling, horripilation, choking voice, and the like.

Now one enquires, "Is it to be assumed from the above statement about *raksasas* that they only give rise to the furious sentiment, and that this sentiment does not relate to others?" [Reply] "No, in case of others too, this sentiment may arise. But in case of *raksasas* it is to be understood as their special function. They are naturally furious, for they have many arms, many mouths, standing and unkempt hairs of brown color, and prodigious physical frame of black complexion. Whatever they attempt, be it their speech, movement of limbs or any other effort, is by nature furious. Even in their love-making they are violent. It is to be easily inferred that persons who imitate them give rise to the furious sentiment from their fights and battles.

On these points there are two *aryas:*

The furious sentiment is created by striking, cutting, mutilation, and piercing in fights, and tumult of the battle, and the like.

It should be represented on the stage by special acts, such as the release of many missiles, cutting off the head, the trunk and the arms.

Such is the furious sentiment viewed by experts, it is full of conflict of arms, and in it words, movement, and deeds are terrible and fearful.

The Heroic Sentiment

Now the heroic sentiment relates to the superior type of persons and has energy as its basis. This is created by determinants, such as presence of mind, perseverance, diplomacy, discipline, military strength, aggressiveness, reputation of might, influence, and the like. It is to be represented on the stage by consequents such as firmness, patience, heroism, charity, diplomacy, and the like. Complementary psychological states in it are contentment, judgment, pride, agitation, energy, determination of purpose, indignation, remembrance, horripilation, and the like. There are two *aryas* [on these points]:

The heroic sentiment arises from energy, perseverance, optimism, absence of surprise, and presence of mind, and such other special conditions of the spirit.

This heroic sentiment is to be properly represented on the stage by firmness, patience, heroism, pride, energy, aggressiveness, influence, and censuring words.

The Terrible Sentiment

Now the terrible sentiment has as its basis the durable psychological state of fear. This is created by determinants like hideous noise, sight of ghosts, panic, and anxiety due to untimely cry of jackals and owls,[14] staying in an empty house or forest, sight of death or captivity of dear ones, or news of it, or discussion about it. It is to be represented on the stage by consequents such as trembling of the hands and the feet, horripilation, change of color, and loss of voice. Its complementary psychological states are paralysis, perspiration, choking voice, horripilation, trembling, loss of voice, change of color, fear, stupefaction, dejection, agitation, restlessness, inactivity, fear, epilepsy and death, and the like.

On these points there are two traditional *aryas:*

The terrible sentiment is created by hideous noise, sight of ghosts, battle, entering an empty house or forest, and offending one's superiors or the king.

Terror is characterized by looseness of the limbs, the mouth, and the eyes; paralysis of the thighs; looking around with uneasiness; dryness of the drooping mouth; palpitation of the heart; and horripilation.

This is the character of natural fear; the artificially shown fear also should be represented by these conditions. But in case of the feigned fear all efforts for its representation should be milder.

This terrible sentiment should be always represented by tremor of hands and feet; paralysis; shaking of the body; palpitation of the heart; dryness of the lips, the mouth, the palate, and the throat.

The Odious Sentiment

Now the odious sentiment has as its basis the durable psychological state of disgust. It is created by determinants like hearing of unpleasant, offensive, impure, and harmful things or seeing them or discussing them. It is to be represented on the stage by consequents such as stopping movement of all the limbs, narrowing down of the mouth, vomitting, spitting, shaking the limbs [in disgust], and the like. Complementary psychological states in it are epileptic fit, delusion, agitation, fainting, sickness, death, and the like. On these points there are two traditional *aryas:*

The odious sentiment arises in many ways from disgusting sight, tastes, smell, touch, and sound which cause uneasiness.

This is to be represented on the stage by narrowing down the mouth and the eyes, covering the nose, bending down the head, and walking imperceptibly.

---

[14]The howling of jackals and the hooting of owls were considered to be ominous sounds foreboding disaster.

The Marvellous Sentiment

The marvellous sentiment has as its basis the durable psychological state of astonishment. It is created by determinants such as sight of heavenly beings or events, attainment of desired objects, entry into a superior mansion, temple, audience hall, and seven-storied palace, and seeing illusory and magical acts. It is to be represented on the stage by consequents such as wide opening of eyes; looking with fixed gaze; horripilation; tears of joy; perspiration; joy; uttering words of approbation; making gifts; crying incessantly "ha, ha, ha"; waving the end of *dhoti* or *sari*;[15] and movement of fingers and the like. Complementary psychological states in it are weeping, paralysis, perspiration, choking voice, horripilation, agitation, hurry, inactivity, death, and the like.

On this point there are two traditional *aryas:*

The marvellous sentiment is that which arises from words, character, deed, and personal beauty.

This is to be represented on the stage by a gesture of feeling; sweet smell; joyful shaking of limbs; and uttering "ha, ha, ha" sounds; speaking words of approbation; tremor; choking voice; perspiration; and the like.

---

[15]A *dhoti* is a sheet of material worn below the waist, usually by men. A *sari*, too, is a long sheet of cloth, part of it wrapped around the waist and part covering the head and the rest of the upper body, usually worn by women.

40

❦

Kalidasa

SHAKUNTALA

A ncient India had a long and well-established dramatic tradition. The
Sanskrit poet and playwright Kalidasa, who flourished in the fifth century
A.D., was the greatest dramatist of his time. In fact, Kalidasa is regarded as the
foremost playwright of India and among the best in the world. When the English
scholar Sir William Jones translated Kalidasa's play Shakuntala into English in
1789 (the first time it had been translated into a Western language), it was
received with great enthusiasm throughout Europe. It was particularly admired
by the famous German poet and philosopher Johann Wolfgang von Goethe
(1749–1832). Since then, of all Sanskrit writers, Kalidasa has remained the one
whose work has been most frequently translated and presented on the stage in the
Western world. In India, too, Kalidasa has been more widely read for the last fifteen hundred years than any other writer of Sanskrit. As the seventh-century
Sanskrit novelist Bana says:

> Where find a soul that does not thrill
> In Kalidasa's verse to meet
> The smooth, inevitable lines
> Like blossom-clusters, honey-sweet?

Kalidasa was the author of at least six works—three dramas, two epics, and
one elegiac poem. These works have been preserved through the ages in numerous
editions and through commentaries by other writers. He was perhaps also the
author of a seventh work, a descriptive poem about the seasons. Despite the abundant information about his writings, however, little is known with certainty
about his life, except what we can gather from his writings. From his style it is
often inferred that he probably lived in the fifth century A.D. A fact that emerges
most obviously from the content and quality of his writings is that he was a man
of extensive and well-rounded education. To begin with, he possessed a perfect

knowledge of the Sanskrit language. He had mastered the Sanskrit grammar, regarded by the Hindus as the "chief of all sciences." He had equally mastered the works of rhetoric and dramatic theory, subjects that also received great attention from learned men of the time. Kalidasa was well-grounded in the ancient Indian systems of philosophy and possessed considerable knowledge of law as well as astronomy. He combined his wide learning with close observation of the life around him, his observation of nature being particularly accurate and sensitive.

It is obvious from Kalidasa's education and refined sensibility that he belonged to the cultured elite of his time. Tradition associates him with the court of King Vikramaditya of the Gupta Dynasty (ca. A.D. 320–550). It has not been possible to identify Vikramaditya exactly, but there is no doubt that he existed. He ruled from the city of Ujjain, in west central India, which, during his reign, was a "most brilliant capital." Internal evidence from one of his poems suggests that Ujjain might have been Kalidasa's home. Vikramaditya was a great patron of learning and the arts who gathered at his court many distinguished artists and scholars. The nine most eminent among them were known as the "nine gems." Kalidasa was probably one of these "gems."

The courtly culture of Vikramaditya's reign marked the peak of the cultural achievements of the Gupta kings, whose reign, mainly because of the flowering of culture under their rule, is known as the golden, or classical, age of Hinduism. Under the Guptas, the arts were both prized and highly developed. There had evolved in this period well-defined standards of excellence governing both the form and content of works of art and their appreciation. These rules were incorporated into elaborate theories of art and esthetic enjoyment. While the artists were expected to follow these theories in their practice, it was also expected that their audiences have the right sensibility and knowledge about the nature of art to be able to appreciate it properly. The courtiers of the Gupta kings comprised an audience of this kind. They were individuals of cultivated esthetic taste, with deep knowledge and experience of the artistic process. Whether he was himself a courtier or not, such was the audience for which Kalidasa wrote.

Of central importance in the art and art criticism of the classical period was the theory of rasa. *The Sanskrit word* rasa *literally means "juice" or enjoyable savoring of it. When used as critical terminology, it referred to the esthetic experience that a work of art contains and produces. Although the theory of* rasa *came to subsume all the fine arts, it pertained primarily to drama. In brief, the theory is as follows: All art (for example, drama) represents situations that evoke feelings of one kind or another. In all, there are eight fundamental and thirty-three subsidiary feelings. The fundamental feelings are: love, mirth, sorrow, anger, heroism, fear, disgust, and wonder. In each work of art, such as a play, one fundamental feeling dominates the content. Other feelings, fundamental or subsidiary, are included, but they are subordinate to and help intensify the evocation of the dominant feeling. Feelings, as portrayed in art, parallel but are not exactly the same as their counterparts in real life. They are but the esthetic equivalents of real-life feelings. The audience can savor them in freedom, without the compulsion to act in response to them as one would in the real world. That is why all feelings, pleasant or unpleasant when experienced in the real world, produce enjoyment when appropriately presented in art.*

Besides conformity to the theory of rasa, *some of the other features of the Indian classical drama were as follows. It was conceived within a religious world view, according to which goodness always came to a happy ending. Therefore, although a play might have tragic elements, it could not have a tragic ending. Sanskrit drama thus contrasted sharply with Western drama in this respect. Characters generally were defined by their social roles. They were not, as a rule, tragic individuals struggling against their destiny. Nothing considered disagreeable, such as physical violence or pornography, even kissing, was to be shown on stage. Women performed the female roles. Stage properties were spare and simple. Music was used lavishly and lyrical digressions were common. Long monologues were avoided. For their subjects and stories, plays usually drew upon history, legend, and, above all, mythology and longer works of literature. Kalidasa observed all these conventions of the classical Sanskrit drama.*

Kalidasa's Shakuntala *is considered to be his best play. He adapted the story for it from an episode in the* Mahabharata *(Selection 25). The plot of the play is the story of King Dushyanta, who, on a hunt in the forest, comes upon a hermitage, a place considered very holy in Hindu culture. Here he sees the young and beautiful Shakuntala, who was born of a union between a great sage, Kaushika, and a celestial nymph, Menaka. Abandoned at birth, she is raised as a foster child by Father Kanva, the head of the hermitage. At the time we first meet Shakuntala, Father Kanva is away on a pilgrimage. Dushyanta and Shakuntala fall in love and exchange nuptial vows by a "voluntary ceremony." Dushyanta then leaves for his capital, it being assumed that Shakuntala will join him there later. One day, after the king has left, an irascible sage, Durvasas, announces himself as a guest at Father Kanva's cottage. Absorbed in thoughts of Dushyanta, Shakuntala fails to notice him. Durvasas feels insulted and puts a curse on Shakuntala that her lover will not remember her when she goes to join him. A friend of Shakuntala implores Durvasas to take the curse back. He partially relents, saying that the curse will be lifted when the king sees a gem in a ring he has left as a token with Shakuntala. Unfortunately, on her way to the king's court, she accidentally drops the ring while saying a prayer beside a river. Thus, the king fails to recognize and accept her as his wife. Shakuntala is saved from humiliation by her mother's intervention and is carried to the semi-celestial hermitage of the ancient sage Kashyapa. There she gives birth to her and Dushyanta's son. Meantime, the ring lost by Shakuntala is found inside a fish's stomach by a fisherman and it reaches the king who, now remembering Shakuntala, is struck with remorse. He is finally reunited with Shakuntala when he happens to stop at Kashyapa's hermitage on his way back from the heavens after having defeated the demons in their war against the god Indra.*

Kalidasa builds on this simple plot an imaginary world of such wondrous beauty that, for fifteen centuries, it has never ceased to enchant his audiences. It is a world suffused with the love of nature, of human beings, especially of women (in the person of Shakuntala), and of the deep goodness of their conduct. Although the action is touched by sadness and potential tragedy in the king's rejection of Shakuntala, it quickly recovers from the setback. The play exudes an expansive feeling of joy that fills the universe from the earth to the heavens and from the heavens to the earth.

The following excerpts, from the earlier part of the story, illustrate how Kalidasa depicts situations evoking particular feelings and the rasas associated with them. The first excerpt in this selection opens with King Dushyanta in his chariot on a hunt, chasing a deer with great energy and speed. The scene is charged with feelings of power and heroism. These are quickly followed by feelings of serenity and holiness associated with the hermitage. The excerpt ends with the arousal of love between Dushyanta and Shakuntala at their first meeting. In the second excerpt, their love reaches a fever pitch and comes near sexual consummation. The third excerpt depicts the sadness at the hermitage at the time of Shakuntala's departure to join the king. The dominant rasa of the play is that of erotic love. The other rasas reinforce and enhance, by contrast or blending, this central rasa.

☙

ACT I
The Hunt

(Enter, in a chariot, pursuing a deer, KING DUSHYANTA, *bow and arrow in hand, and a charioteer.)*

   CHARIOTEER *(looking at the king and the deer)*
   Your Majesty,

> I see you hunt the spotted deer
>   With shafts to end his race,
> As though God Shiva should appear
>   In his immortal chase.[1]

From Arthur W. Ryder, trans. *Shakuntala and Other Writings* (New York: E. P. Dutton & Co., Inc., 1959. First published 1912), pp. 5–12, 14–16, 27–38, 44–50.

[1]Shiva is a major Hindu god. In one of his aspects, he is the guardian of the animal kingdom as well as a hunter.

KING

Charioteer, the deer has led us on a long chase. And even now

> His neck in beauty bends
> As backward looks he sends
> At my pursuing car
> That threatens death from far.
> Fear shrinks to half the body small;
> See how he fears the arrow's fall!

> The path he takes is strewed
> With blades of grass half-chewed
> From jaws wide with the stress
> Of fevered weariness.
> He leaps so often and so high,
> He does not seem to run, but fly.

(In surprise.) Pursue as I may, I can hardly keep him in sight.

CHARIOTEER

Your Majesty, I have been holding the horses back because the ground was rough. This checked us and gave the deer a lead. Now we are on level ground, and you will easily overtake him.

KING

Then let the reins hang loose.

CHARIOTEER

Yes, your Majesty. *(He counterfeits rapid motion.)* Look, your Majesty!

> The lines hang loose; the steeds unreined
> 　　Dart forward with a will.
> Their ears are pricked; their necks are strained;
> 　　Their plumes lie straight and still.
> They leave the rising dust behind;
> They seem to float upon the wind.

KING *(joyfully)*

See! The horses are gaining on the deer.

> As onward and onward the chariot flies,
> The small flashes large to my dizzy eyes.
> What is cleft in twain, seems to blur and mate;
> What is crooked in nature, seems to be straight.
> Things at my side in an instant appear
> Distant, and things in the distance, near.

A VOICE BEHIND THE SCENES

O King, this deer belongs to the hermitage, and must not be killed. . . .

KING *(hastily)*

Stop the chariot. . . . Charioteer, drive on. A sight of the pious hermitage will purify us.

CHARIOTEER

Yes, your Majesty. *(He counterfeits motion again.)*

KING *(looking about)*

One would know, without being told, that this is the precinct of a pious grove.

CHARIOTEER

How so?

KING

Do you not see? Why, here

> Are rice-grains, dropped from bills of parrot chicks
> Beneath the trees; and pounding-stones where sticks
> A little almond oil;[2] and trustful deer
> That do not run away as we draw near;
> And river paths that are besprinkled yet
> From trickling hermit-garments, clean and wet.

Besides,

> The roots of trees are washed by many a stream
> That breezes ruffle; and the flowers' red gleam
> Is dimmed by pious smoke;[3] and fearless fawns
> Move softly on the close-cropped forest lawns.

CHARIOTEER

It is all true.

KING *(after a little)*

We must not disturb the hermitage. Stop here while I dismount.

CHARIOTEER

I am holding the reins. Dismount, your Majesty.

KING *(dismounts and looks at himself)*

One should wear modest garments on entering a hermitage. Take these jewels and the bow. . . .

A VOICE BEHIND THE SCENES

This way, girls!

KING *(listening)*

I think I hear someone to the right of the grove. . . . *(He conceals himself.)*

---

[2]Almond oil was considered good for application on the skin and hair. The hermits used it in preference to other oils.

[3]Smoke rising from sacrificial fires.

SHAKUNTALA[4]

Oh, Anusuya! Priyamvada has fastened this bark dress so tight that it hurts.[5] Please loosen it. *(ANUSUYA does so.)*

PRIYAMVADA *(laughing)*

You had better blame your own budding charms for that.

KING

She is quite right.

> Beneath the barken dress
> > Upon the shoulder tied,
> In maiden loveliness
> > Her young breast seems to hide,
>
> As when a flower amid
> > The leaves by autumn tossed—
> Pale, withered leaves—lies hid,
> > And half its grace is lost.

Yet in truth the bark dress is not an enemy of her beauty. It serves as an added ornament. For

> The meanest vesture glows
> > On beauty that enchants:
> The lotus lovelier shows
> > Amid dull water plants;
>
> The moon in added splendor
> > Shines for its spot of dark;
> Yet more the maiden slender
> > Charms in her dress of bark.

SHAKUNTALA *(looking ahead)*

Oh, girls, that mango tree is trying to tell me something with his branches that move in the wind like fingers. I must go and see him. *(She does so.)*

PRIYAMVADA

There, Shakuntala, stand right where you are a minute.

SHAKUNTALA

Why?

PRIYAMVADA

When I see you there, it looks as if a vine were clinging to the mango tree.

---

[4]While concealed, the king has gathered from the conversation among the women that Shakuntala is the foster daughter of the head of the hermitage, Father Kanva.

[5]Everyone living in a hermitage wore hermit clothes made from the bark of such plants as flax or jute.

SHAKUNTALA

I see why they call you the flatterer.

KING

But the flattery is true.

> Her arms are tender shoots; her lips
> Are blossoms red and warm;
> Bewitching youth begins to flower
> In beauty on her form.

ANUSUYA

Oh, Shakuntala! Here is the jasmine vine that you named Light of the Grove. She has chosen the mango tree as her husband.

SHAKUNTALA *(approaches and looks at it, joyfully)*

What a pretty pair they make. The jasmine shows her youth in her fresh flowers, and the mango tree shows his strength in his ripening fruit. *(She stands gazing at them.)*

PRIYAMVADA *(smiling)*

Anusuya, do you know why Shakuntala looks so hard at the Light of the Grove?

ANUSUYA

No. Why?

PRIYAMVADA

She is thinking how the Light of the Grove has found a good tree, and hoping that she will meet a fine lover.

SHAKUNTALA

That's what you want for yourself. *(She tips her watering pot.)*

ANUSUYA

Look, Shakuntala! Here is the spring-creeper that Father Kanva tended with his own hands—just as he did you. You are forgetting her.

SHAKUNTALA

I'd forget myself sooner. *(She goes to the creeper and looks at it, joyfully.)* Wonderful! Wonderful! Priyamvada, I have something pleasant to tell you.

PRIYAMVADA

What is it, dear?

SHAKUNTALA

It is out of season, but the spring-creeper is covered with buds down to the very root.

THE TWO FRIENDS *(running up)*

Really?

SHAKUNTALA

Of course. Can't you see?

PRIYAMVADA *(looking at it joyfully)*

And I have something pleasant to tell *you*. You are to be married soon.

SHAKUNTALA *(snappishly)*

You know that's just what you want for yourself.

PRIYAMVADA

I'm not teasing. I really heard Father Kanva say that this flowering vine was to be a symbol of your coming happiness.

ANUSUYA

Priyamvada, that is why Shakuntala waters the spring-creeper so lovingly.

SHAKUNTALA

She is my sister. Why shouldn't I give her water? *(She tips her watering-pot.)* . . .

SHAKUNTALA *(excitedly)*

Oh, oh! A bee has left the jasmine vine and is flying into my face. *(She shows herself annoyed by the bee.)*

KING *(ardently)*

> As the bee about her flies,
> Swiftly her bewitching eyes
> > Turn to watch his flight.
> She is practicing today
> Coquetry and glances' play
> > Not from love, but fright.

(Jealously.)

> Eager bee, you lightly skim
> O'er the eyelid's trembling rim
> > Toward the cheek aquiver.
> Gently buzzing round her cheek,
> Whispering in her ear, you seek
> > Secrets to deliver.

> While her hands that way and this
> Strike at you, you steal a kiss,
> > Love's all, honeymaker.
> I know nothing but her name,
> Not her caste, nor whence she came—
> > You, my rival, take her.

SHAKUNTALA

Oh, girls! Save me from this dreadful bee!

THE TWO FRIENDS *(smiling)*

Who are we, that we should save you? Call upon Dushyanta. For pious groves are in the protection of the king.

KING

A good opportunity to present myself. Have no—*(He checks himself. Aside.)* No, they would see that I am the king. I prefer to appear as a guest.

SHAKUNTALA

He doesn't leave me alone! I am going to run away. *(She takes a step and looks about.)* Oh, dear! Oh, dear! He is following me. Please save me.

KING *(hastening forward)*

Ah!

> A king of Puru's mighty line
>   Chastises shameless churls;
> What insolent is he who baits
>   These artless hermit-girls?

(The girls are a little flurried on seeing the king.)

ANUSUYA

It is nothing very dreadful, sir. But our friend *(indicating* SHAKUNTALA*)* was teased and frightened by a bee.

KING *(to* SHAKUNTALA*)*

I hope these pious days are happy ones. (SHAKUNTALA's *eyes drop in embarrassment.)*

ANUSUYA

Yes, now that we receive such a distinguished guest.

PRIYAMVADA

Welcome, sir. Go to the cottage, Shakuntala, and bring fruit. This water will do to wash the feet.

KING

Your courteous words are enough to make me feel at home.

ANUSUYA

Then, sir, pray sit down and rest on this shady bench.

KING

You, too, are surely wearied by your pious task. Pray be seated a moment.

PRIYAMVADA *(aside to* SHAKUNTALA*)*

My dear, we must be polite to our guest. Shall we sit down? *(The three girls sit.)*

SHAKUNTALA *(to herself)*

Oh, why do I have such feelings when I see this man? They seem wrong in a hermitage.

KING *(looking at the girls)*

It is delightful to see your friendship. For you are all young and beautiful.

PRIYAMVADA *(aside to* ANUSUYA*)*

Who is he, dear? With his mystery, and his dignity, and his courtesy? He acts like a king and a gentleman.[6]

---

[6]At this first meeting, King Dushyanta conceals his true identity.

ANUSUYA

I am curious too. I am going to ask him. *(Aloud.)* Sir, you are so very courteous that I make bold to ask you something. What royal family do you adorn, sir? What country is grieving at your absence? Why does a gentleman so delicately bred submit to the weary journey into our pious grove?

SHAKUNTALA *(aside)*

Be brave, my heart. Anusuya speaks your very thoughts.

KING *(aside)*

Shall I tell at once who I am, or conceal it? . . .

PRIYAMVADA *(approaching* SHAKUNTALA*)*

. . . You mustn't go.

SHAKUNTALA

. . . Why not?

PRIYAMVADA

You owe me the watering of two trees. You can go when you have paid your debt. *(She forces her to come back.)*

KING

It is plain that she is already wearied by watering the trees. See!

> Her shoulders droop; her palms are reddened yet;
> > Quick breaths are struggling in her bosom fair;
> The blossom o'er her ear hangs limply wet;
> > One hand restrains the loose, dishevelled hair.

I therefore remit her debt.

(He gives the two friends a ring. They take it, read the name engraved on it, and look at each other.)

KING

Make no mistake. This is a present—from the king.

PRIYAMVADA

Then, sir, you ought not to part with it. Your word is enough to remit the debt.

ANUSUYA

Well, Shakuntala, you are set free by this kind gentleman—or rather, by the king himself. Where are you going now?

SHAKUNTALA *(to herself)*

I would never leave him if I could help myself.

PRIYAMVADA

Why don't you go now?

SHAKUNTALA

I am not *your* servant any longer. I will go when I like.

KING *(looking at* SHAKUNTALA. *To himself)*

Does she feel toward me as I do toward her? At least, there is ground for hope.

> Although she does not speak to me,
>   She listens while I speak;
> Her eyes turn not to see my face,
>   But nothing else they seek.

A VOICE BEHIND THE SCENES

Hermits! Hermits! Prepare to defend the creatures in our pious grove. King Dushyanta is hunting in the neighborhood.

> The dust his horses' hoofs have raised,
>   Red as the evening sky,
> Falls like a locust swarm on boughs
>   Where hanging garments dry.

KING *(aside)*

Alas! My soldiers are disturbing the pious grove in their search for me. . . .

ANUSUYA *(to* SHAKUNTALA*)*

Shakuntala dear, Mother Gautami will be anxious.[7] We must hurry and find her.

SHAKUNTALA *(feigning lameness)*

Oh, oh! I can hardly walk. . . . Anusuya, my foot is cut on a sharp blade of grass, and my dress is caught on an amaranth twig. Wait for me while I loosen it. *(She casts a lingering glance at the king and goes out with her two friends.)*

KING *(sighing)*

They are gone. And I must go. The sight of Shakuntala has made me dread the return to the city. I will make my men camp at a distance from the pious grove. But I cannot turn my own thoughts from Shakuntala.

> It is my body leaves my love, not I;
>   My body moves away, but not my mind;
> For back to her my struggling fancies fly
>   Like silken banners borne against the wind.

(Exit.)

•   •   •

ACT III
Love-Making

KING

Where shall I go now to rest from my weariness? *(He sighs.)* There is no rest for me except in seeing her whom I love. *(He looks up.)* She usually

---

[7]Gautami is the most senior lady at the hermitage.

spends these hours of midday heat with her friends on the vine-wreathed banks of the Malini.[8] I will go there. *(He walks and looks about.)* I believe the slender maiden has just passed through this corridor of young trees. For

> The stems from which she gathered flowers
> > Are still unhealed;
> The sap where twigs were broken off
> > Is uncongealed.

(He feels a breeze stirring.) This is a pleasant spot, with the wind among the trees.

> Limbs that love's fever seizes,
> > Their fervent welcome pay
> To lotus-fragrant breezes
> > That bear the river-spray.

(He studies the ground.) Ah, Shakuntala must be in this reedy bower. For

> In white sand at the door
> > Fresh footprints appear,
> The toe lightly outlined,
> > The heel deep and clear.

I will hide among the branches, and see what happens. *(He does so joyfully.)* Ah, my eyes have found their heaven. Here is the darling of my thoughts, lying upon a flower-strewn bench of stone, and attended by her two friends. I will hear what they say to each other.

(He stands gazing. Enter SHAKUNTALA *with her two friends.)*

THE TWO FRIENDS *(fanning her)*

Do you feel better, dear, when we fan you with these lotus-leaves?

SHAKUNTALA *(wearily)*

Oh, are you fanning me, my dear girls? *(The two friends look sorrowfully at each other.)*

KING

She is seriously ill. *(Doubtfully.)* Is it the heat, or is it as I hope? *(Decidedly.)* It *must* be so.

> With salve upon her breast,
> > With loosened lotus-chain,
> My darling, sore oppressed,
> > Is lovely in her pain

---

[8]The name of a river.

> Though love and summer heat
>   May work an equal woe,
> No maiden seems so sweet
>   When summer lays her low.

PRIYAMVADA *(aside to* ANUSUYA*)*

Anusuya, since she first saw the good king[9], she has been greatly troubled. I do not believe her fever has any other cause.

ANUSUYA

I suspect you are right. I am going to ask her. My dear, I must ask you something. You are in a high fever.

KING

It is too true.

> Her lotus-chains that were as white
> As moonbeams shining in the night,
> Betray the fever's awful pain,
> And fading, show a darker stain.

SHAKUNTALA *(half rising)*

Well, say whatever you like.

ANUSUYA

Shakuntala dear, you have not told us what is going on in your mind. But I have heard old, romantic stories, and I can't help thinking that you are in a state like that of a lady in love. Please tell us what hurts you. We have to understand the disease before we can even try to cure it.

KING

Anusuya expresses my own thoughts.

SHAKUNTALA

It hurts me terribly. I can't tell you all at once.

PRIYAMVADA

Anusuya is right, dear. Why do you hide your trouble? You are wasting away every day. You are nothing but a beautiful shadow.

KING

Priyamvada is right. See!

> Her cheeks grow thin; her breast and shoulders fail;
> Her waist is weary and her face is pale:
> She fades for love; oh, pitifully sweet!
> As vine-leaves wither in the scorching heat.

SHAKUNTALA *(sighing)*

I could not tell anyone else. But I shall be a burden to you.

---

[9]Since their first meeting, the girls have recognized that the guest is their king.

THE TWO FRIENDS

That is why we insist on knowing, dear. Grief must be shared to be endured.

KING

> To friends who share her joy and grief
> > She tells what sorrow laid her here;
> She turned to look her love again
> > When first I saw her—yet I fear!

SHAKUNTALA

Ever since I saw the good king who protects the pious grove—*(She stops and fidgets.)*

THE TWO FRIENDS

Go on, dear.

SHAKUNTALA

I love him, and it makes me feel like this.

THE TWO FRIENDS

Good, good! You have found a lover worthy of your devotion. But of course, a great river always runs into the sea.

KING *(joyfully)*

I have heard what I longed to hear.

> 'Twas love that caused the burning pain;
> 'Tis love that eases it again;
> As when, upon a sultry day,
> Rain breaks, and washes grief away.

SHAKUNTALA

Then, if you think best, make the good king take pity upon me. If not, remember that I was. . . .

PRIYAMVADA *(aside to* ANUSUYA*)*

Anusuya, she is far gone in love and cannot endure any delay.

ANUSUYA

Priyamvada, can you think of any scheme by which we could carry out her wishes quickly and secretly?

PRIYAMVADA

We must plan about the "secretly." The "quickly" is not so hard.

ANUSUYA

How so?

PRIYAMVADA

Why, the good king shows his love for her in his tender glances, and he has been wasting away, as if he were losing sleep.

KING

It is quite true.

The hot tears, flowing down my cheek
 All night on my supporting arm
And on its golden bracelet, seek
 To stain the gems and do them harm.

The bracelet slipping o'er the scars
 Upon the wasted arm, that show
My deeds in hunting and in wars,
 All night is moving to and fro.

PRIYAMVADA *(reflecting)*

Well, she must write him a love-letter. And I will hide it in a bunch of flowers and see that it gets into the king's hand as if it were a relic of the sacrifice.[10]

ANUSUYA

It is a pretty plan, dear, and it pleases me. What does Shakuntala say?

SHAKUNTALA

I suppose I must obey orders. . . . Well, I thought out a little song. But I haven't anything to write with.

PRIYAMVADA

Here is a lotus-leaf, glossy as a parrot's breast. You can cut the letters in it with your nails.

SHAKUNTALA

Now listen, and tell me whether it makes sense.

THE TWO FRIENDS

Please.

SHAKUNTALA *(reads)*

I know not if I read your heart aright;
 Why, pitiless, do you distress me so?
I only know that longing day and night
 Tosses my restless body to and fro,
 That yearns for you, the source of all its woe.

KING *(advancing)*

Though Love torments you, slender maid,
 Yet he consumes me quite,
As daylight shuts night-blooming flowers
 And slays the moon outright.

THE TWO FRIENDS *(perceive the king and rise joyfully)*

Welcome to the wish that is fulfilled without delay. (SHAKUNTALA *tries to rise.*)

---

[10]That is, ritual sacrifice.

KING

Do not try to rise, beautiful Shakuntala.

> Your limbs from which the strength is fled,
> That crush the blossoms of your bed
> And bruise the lotus-leaves, may be
> Pardoned a breach of courtesy.

SHAKUNTALA *(sadly to herself)*

Oh, my heart, you were so impatient, and now you find no answer to make.

ANUSUYA

Your Majesty, pray do this stone bench the honor of sitting upon it. (SHAKUNTALA *edges away.)*

KING *(seating himself)*

Priyamvada, I trust your friend's illness is not dangerous.

PRIYAMVADA *(smiling)*

A remedy is being applied and it will soon be better. It is plain, sir, that you and she love each other. . . . *(aside to* ANUSUYA*)* Look Anusuya! See how the dear girl's life is coming back moment by moment—just like a peahen in summer when the first rainy breezes come. . . .

SHAKUNTALA

Are my friends gone?[11]

KING *(looking about)*

Do not be anxious, beautiful Shakuntala. Have you not a humble servant here, to take the place of your friends? Then tell me:

> Shall I employ the moistened lotus-leaf
> To fan away your weariness and grief?
> Or take your lily feet upon my knee
> And rub them till you rest more easily?

SHAKUNTALA

I will not offend against those to whom I owe honor.[12] *(She rises weakly and starts to walk away.)*

KING *(detaining her)*

The day is still hot, beautiful Shakuntala, and you are feverish.

> Leave not the blossom-dotted couch
> To wander in the midday heat,

---

[11]Shakuntala's friends, in order to leave her alone with the king, have left with the excuse that they must help a lost fawn.

[12]It was considered discourteous to put one's feet on a person one should respect.

> With lotus-petals on your breast,
>> With fevered limbs and stumbling feet.

(He lays his hand upon her.)

SHAKUNTALA

Oh, don't! Don't! For I am not mistress of myself. Yet what can I do now?
I had no one to help me but my friends.

KING

I am rebuked.

SHAKUNTALA

I was not thinking of your Majesty. I was accusing fate.

KING

Why accuse a fate that brings what you desire?

SHAKUNTALA

Why not accuse a fate that robs me of self-control and tempts me with
the virtues of another?

KING *(to himself)*

> Though deeply longing, maids are coy
>> And bid their wooers wait;
> Though eager for united joy
>> In love, they hesitate.

> Love cannot torture them, nor move
>> Their hearts to sudden mating;
> Perhaps they even torture love
>> By their procrastinating.

(Shakuntala moves away.)

KING

Why should I not have my way? *(He approaches and seizes her dress.)*

SHAKUNTALA

Oh, sir! Be a gentleman. There are hermits wandering about. . . .

SHAKUNTALA *(takes a step, then turns with an eager gesture)*

O King, I cannot do as you would have me. You hardly know me after
this short talk. But oh, do not forget me.

KING

> When evening comes, the shadow of the tree
>> Is cast far forward, yet does not depart;
> Even so, beloved, wheresoe'er you be,
>> The thought of you can never leave my heart.

SHAKUNTALA *(takes a few steps. To herself)*

Oh, oh! When I hear him speak so, my feet will not move away. I will hide in this amaranth hedge and see how long his love lasts. *(She hides and waits.)*

KING

Oh, my beloved, my love for you is my whole life, yet you leave me and go away without a thought.

> Your body, soft as siris-flowers,
> Engages passion's utmost powers;
> How comes it that your heart is hard
> As stalks that siris-blossoms guard?

SHAKUNTALA

When I hear this, I have no power to go.

KING

What have I to do here, where she is not? *(He gazes on the ground.)* Ah, I cannot go.

> The perfumed lotus-chain
>   That once was worn by her
> Fetters and keeps my heart
>   A hopeless prisoner.

(He lifts it reverently.)

SHAKUNTALA *(looking at her arm)*

Why, I was so weak and ill that when the lotus-bracelet fell off, I did not even notice it.

KING *(laying the lotus-bracelet on his heart)*

Ah!

> Once, dear, on your sweet arm it lay,
> And on my heart shall ever stay;
> Though you disdain to give me joy,
> I find it in a lifeless toy.

SHAKUNTALA

I cannot hold back after that. I will use the bracelet as an excuse for my coming. *(She approaches.)*

KING *(seeing her. Joyfully)*

The queen of my life! As soon as I complained, fate proved kind to me.

> No sooner did the thirsty bird
>   With parching throat complain,
> Than forming clouds in heaven stirred
>   And sent the streaming rain.

SHAKUNTALA *(standing before the king)*

When I was going away, sir, I remembered that this lotus-bracelet had fallen from my arm, and I have come back for it. My heart seemed to tell me that you had taken it. Please give it back, or you will betray me, and yourself too, to the hermits.

KING

I will restore it on one condition.

SHAKUNTALA

What condition?

KING

That I may myself place it where it belongs.

SHAKUNTALA *(to herself)*

What can I do? *(She approaches.)*

KING

Let us sit on this stone bench. *(They walk to the bench and sit down.)*

KING *(taking* SHAKUNTALA'S *hand)*

Ah!

> When Shiva's anger burned the tree
> Of love in quenchless fire,[13]
> Did heavenly fate preserve a shoot
> To deck my heart's desire?

SHAKUNTALA *(feeling his touch)*

Hasten, my dear, hasten.

KING *(joyfully to himself)*

Now I am content. She speaks as a wife to her husband. *(Aloud.)* Beautiful Shakuntala, the clasp of the bracelet is not very firm. May I fasten it in another way?

SHAKUNTALA *(smiling)*

If you like.

KING *(artfully delaying before he fastens it)*

See, my beautiful girl!

> The lotus-chain is dazzling white
> As is the slender moon at night.

---

[13]This is a reference to a myth about Shiva, a Hindu god of great powers, including the power of destruction. In one aspect, he is an ascetic contemplative god. Once, the other gods wanted him to fall in love with the divine daughter of the Himalaya Mountain and have children. Kama, the god of love, was asked to arouse the feeling of love in Shiva's heart as he sat in his meditative trance. When Kama tried to perform his task, Shiva became angry and opened his third eye, which is in his forehead, and with it burnt down Kama and the tree of love that Kama was planting in his heart.

Perhaps it was the moon on high
That joined her horns[14] and left the sky,
Believing that your lovely arm
Would, more than heaven, enhance her charm.

SHAKUNTALA

I cannot see it. The pollen from the lotus over my ear has blown into my eye.

KING *(smiling)*

Will you permit me to blow it away?

SHAKUNTALA

I should not like to be an object of pity. But why should I not trust you?

KING

Do not have such thoughts. A new servant does not transgress orders.

SHAKUNTALA

It is this exaggerated courtesy that frightens me.

KING *(to himself)*

I shall not break the bonds of this sweet servitude. *(He starts to raise her face to his.* SHAKUNTALA *resists a little, then is passive.)*

KING

Oh, my bewitching girl, have no fear of me. *(*SHAKUNTALA *darts a glance at him, then looks down. The king raises her face. Aside.)*

Her sweetly trembling lip
    With virgin invitation
Provokes my soul to sip
    Delighted fascination.

SHAKUNTALA

You seem slow, dear, in fulfilling your promise.

KING

The lotus over your ear is so near your eye, and so like it, that I was confused. *(He gently blows her eye.)*

SHAKUNTALA

Thank you. I can see quite well now. But I am ashamed not to make any return for your kindness.

KING

What more could I ask?

It ought to be enough for me
    To hover round your fragrant face;
Is not the lotus-haunting bee
    Content with perfume and with grace?

---

[14]The corners of the crescent moon.

SHAKUNTALA

But what does he do if he is not content?

KING

This! This! *(He draws her face to his.)*

A VOICE BEHIND THE SCENES

O sheldrake bride,[15] bid your mate farewell. The night is come.

SHAKUNTALA *(listening excitedly)*

Oh, my dear, this is Mother Gautami, come to inquire about me. Please hide among the branches. *(The king conceals himself. Enter* GAUTAMI, *with a bowl in her hand.)*

GAUTAMI

Here is the holy water, my child. . . . *(Sprinkling* SHAKUNTALA *with the holy water)* May you live long and happy, my child. Has the fever gone down? *(She touches her.)*

SHAKUNTALA

There is a difference, mother.

GAUTAMI

The sun is setting. Come, let us go to the cottage.

●　　●　　●

ACT IV

Shakuntala's Departure

(Enter KANVA, *returning after his ablutions.)*

KANVA

> Shakuntala must go today;
> 　　I miss her now at heart;
> I dare not speak a loving word
> 　　Or choking tears will start.
>
> My eyes are dim with anxious thought;
> 　　Love strikes me to the life:
> And yet I strove for pious peace—
> 　　I have no child, no wife.
>
> What must a father feel, when come
> The pangs of parting from his child at home?

(He walks about.) . . .

---

[15]Sheldrake is a species of duck. Gautami is telling the female sheldrake to bid farewell to her mate. This means that the day is over and it is time for everyone to come home. Unknown to Gautami, her call to the sheldrake bride functions as a metaphor for Shakuntala's situation. She too must leave her mate and go home.

GAUTAMI

My child, here is your father. The eyes with which he seems to embrace you are overflowing with tears of joy. You must greet him properly. (SHAKUNTALA *makes a shamefaced reverence.*) . . .

KANVA

My daughter, walk from left to right about the fires in which the offering has just been thrown.[16] *(All walk about.)*

> The holy fires around the altar kindle,
> And at their margins sacred grass is piled;
> Beneath their sacrificial odors dwindle
> Misfortunes. May the fires protect you, child!

(SHAKUNTALA *walks about them from left to right.*)

KANVA

Now you may start, my daughter. *(He glances about.)* Where are Sharngarava and Sharadvata? *(Enter the two pupils.)*

THE TWO PUPILS

We are here, Father.

KANVA

Sharngarava, my son, lead the way for your sister. . . . O trees of the pious grove, in which the fairies dwell,

> She would not drink till she had wet
> Your roots, a sister's duty,
> Nor pluck your flowers; she loves you yet
> Far more than selfish beauty.
>
> 'Twas festival in her pure life
> When budding blossoms showed;
> And now she leaves you as a wife—
> Oh, speed her on her road!

SHARNGARAVA *(listening to the song of koil-birds)*[17]
Father,

> The trees are answering your prayer
> In cooing cuckoo-song,
> Bidding Shakuntala farewell,
> Their sister for so long.

---

[16]Father Kanva is performing a fire sacrifice to bid Shakuntala farewell.

[17]A species of the cuckoo-bird.

INVISIBLE BEINGS

> May lily-dotted lakes delight your eye;
>> May shade-trees bid the heat of noonday cease;
> May soft winds blow the lotus-pollen nigh;
>> May all your path be pleasantness and peace.

(All listen in astonishment.)

GAUTAMI

My child, the fairies of the pious grove bid you farewell. For they love the household. Pay reverence to the holy ones.

SHAKUNTALA *(does so. Aside to* PRIYAMVADA*)*

Priyamvada, I long to see my husband, and yet my feet will hardly move. It is hard, hard to leave the hermitage.

PRIYAMVADA

You are not the only one to feel sad at this farewell. See how the whole grove feels at parting from you.

> The grass drops from the feeding doe;
>> The peahen stops her dance;
> Pale, trembling leaves are falling slow,
>> The tears of clinging plants.

SHAKUNTALA *(recalling something)*

Father, I must say good-bye to the spring-creeper, my sister among the vines.

KANVA

I know your love for her. See! Here she is at your right hand.

SHAKUNTALA *(approaches the vine and embraces it)*

Vine sister, embrace me too with your arms, these branches. I shall be far away from you after today. Father, you must care for her as you did for me.

KANVA

> My child, you found the lover who
>> Had long been sought by me;
> No longer need I watch for you;
> I'll give the vine a lover true,
>> This handsome mango tree.

And now start on your journey.

SHAKUNTALA *(going to the two friends)*

Dear girls, I leave her in your care too.

THE TWO FRIENDS

But who will care for poor us? *(They shed tears.)*

KANVA

Anusuya! Priyamvada! Do not weep. It is you who should cheer Shakuntala. *(All walk about.)*

SHAKUNTALA

Father, there is the pregnant doe, wandering about near the cottage. When she becomes a happy mother, you must send someone to bring me the good news. Do not forget.

KANVA

I shall not forget, my child.

SHAKUNTALA *(stumbling)*

Oh, oh! Who is it that keeps pulling at my dress, as if to hinder me? *(She turns round to see.)*

KANVA

> It is the fawn whose lip, when torn
>> By kusha-grass,[18] you soothed with oil;
> The fawn who gladly nibbled corn
>> Held in your hand; with loving toil
> You have adopted him, and he
> Would never leave you willingly.

SHAKUNTALA

My dear, why should you follow me when I am going away from home? Your mother died when you were born and I brought you up. Now I am leaving you, and Father Kanva will take care of you. Go back, dear! Go back! *(She walks away, weeping.)*

KANVA

Do not weep, my child. Be brave. Look at the path before you.

> Be brave, and check the rising tears
>> That dim your lovely eyes;
> Your feet are stumbling on the path
>> That so uneven lies. . . .

ANUSUYA

My dear, there is not a living thing in the whole hermitage that is not grieving today at saying good-bye to you. Look!

> The sheldrake does not heed his mate
>> Who calls behind the lotus-leaf;
> He drops the lily from his bill
>> And turns on you a glance of grief. . . .

---

[18]A species of grass with sharp leaves, used as an ingredient in sacrificial ritual.

SHAKUNTALA *(throwing her arms about her father)*

I am torn from my father's breast like a vine stripped from a sandal tree on the Malabar hills.[19] How can I live in another soil? *(She weeps.)* . . .

KANVA

Child, you interrupt my duties in the pious grove.

SHAKUNTALA

Yes, Father. You will be busy in the grove. You will not miss me. But oh! I miss you.

KANVA

How can you think me so indifferent? *(He sighs.)*

> My lonely sorrow will not go,
>> For seeds you scattered here
> Before the cottage door, will grow;
>> And I shall see them, dear.

Go. And peace go with you. *(Exit* SHAKUNTALA, *with* GAUTAMI, SHARN-GARAVA, *and* SHARADVATA.*)*

THE TWO FRIENDS *(gazing long after her mournfully)*

Oh, oh! Shakuntala is lost among the trees.

KANVA

Anusuya! Priyamvada! Your companion is gone. Choke down your grief and follow me. *(They start to go back.)*

THE TWO FRIENDS

Father, the grove seems empty without Shakuntala.

KANVA

So love interprets. *(He walks about, sunk in thought.)* . . .

---

[19]Hills on the west coast of India.

41

🦂

POEMS FROM THE SANSKRIT

Speaking about the ancient Indian secular poetry in Sanskrit, known as Kavya, an early twentieth-century British Sanskrit scholar, Arthur Berriedale Keith, said that "The Kavya literature includes some of the great poetry of the world. . . . It is in the great writers of Kavya, headed by Kalidasa (Selection 40), that we find depth of feeling for life and nature matched with perfection of expression and rhythm." The secular Sanskrit poetry of ancient India, therefore, merits the attention of all students of world literature. However, unfortunately, it has not received the attention it deserves, either outside India or even within India, in the centuries after the ancient period. Part of the reason for this neglect outside India has been the spiritual image of India created by an emphasis on the religious–philosophical works, such as the Upanishads *(Selection 20) and the* Bhagvad Gita *(Selection 25), in the early Western studies of Indian culture. Even in the case of the classical Indian drama, which is strongly secular and humanistic in spirit, its appreciation in the Western world was considerably biased by a stress on the religious world view behind it. Within India too, after the ancient period, since Sanskrit was the language of the Hindu scriptures, it was increasingly perceived as primarily the language of sacred literature. The awareness about the great secular literature in Sanskrit, therefore, decreased steadily. Under colonialism, the influence of the Western bias toward religion in the study of Sanskrit literature reinforced this trend. Only in recent times has this attitude begun to change and secular Sanskrit literature been given due recognition.*

The great creative period of Sanskrit poetry ranged from the second to the tenth century A.D. In fact, most of the extant poems that can be dated with some certainty were written from the fourth century onward. The poetry of the period has come down to us in the form of collections from ancient and medieval times. Of the ancient collections, two—one ascribed to Bhartrhari and the other to Amaru—are better known. Both of them consist of individual stanzas, each stanza apparently comprising a poem by itself. Most probably, both collections are anthologies containing the works of many different poets, although it is possible that either collection is actually the work of the individual after whom it is named. It is generally assumed that both Bhartrhari and Amaru were themselves poets, not just anthologists. Aside from the association of their names with the collections, however, nothing else is known about them.

From the medieval period, there have survived several very large anthologies of ancient Sanskrit poetry, the three best-known among them being the Subhasita-ratna-kosa *("a treasury of fine verses"),* Subhasitavali *("a necklace of fine verses"), and the* Paddhati *("manual" or simply "anthology"). The last of these, however, contains many verses that cannot be considered poetry by any critical criterion. Apparently, they were included for the information they provided on various subjects. The medieval anthologies name hundreds of poets, but many poems are not ascribed to anyone. When the names are given, often they are not completely reliable. The poems in these anthologies are arranged by subject matter, not by author. These subjects are somewhat similar from one anthology to another. They include gods, especially the god of love, and other mythical figures; each of the six Indian seasons; stages in a young woman's life, such as adolescence and maturity; on being in love; love-making; signs, such as biting and scratching, that love-making has occurred; each of the many different wild animals; parts of a girl's body, each part a separate subject; different aspects of nature; and precious stones and jewels. Love, in its multifarious forms, is a subject dearest to the Sanskrit poets' hearts. In their treatment of it, they are often very frank and uninhibited. They give details of physical passion difficult to find in other languages. Yet they eschew vulgarity and almost invariably show good taste in their portrayal of sexual love.*

The best poetry preserved in these ancient and medieval anthologies is highly sophisticated, complex, and marked with subtlety. It owes these qualities to two main factors: the nature of the language in which it is written and the learning and refined sensibility of its authors. Sanskrit is endowed with an immense capacity for inflection and for building very long compound words using inflection. This gives the language a power of compression and condensation difficult to match in other languages. A few lines of Sanskrit poetry can contain what would require in another language a poem several times longer. Sanskrit is also extremely rich in synonyms. For instance, where English has just one word for "lotus," Sanskrit has about fifty. Another conspicuous feature of Sanskrit is its exceptional capacity for double meanings of words and phrases, which allow punning on a very large scale. Poets could write long epics in such a way that the same words could be interpreted as telling two different stories.

The authors of the poetry in question were, as a rule, very learned individuals. They belonged to and wrote for a cultural elite, often a part of a courtly circle. Both the poets and their audiences were steeped in knowledge of many different kinds, including, above all, a knowledge of the established techniques of writing and of appreciation of poetry. The audience was expected to have a cultivated taste for proper appreciation, just as the poets needed to go through a rigorous training and needed to possess a refined sensibility for writing poetry. In his book, An Inquiry into Poetry, *a tenth-century writer, Rajasekhara, prescribes the training that a poet must have. It includes the study of dictionaries, and of treatises on meter and poetic theory, besides a sound general education in culture. Rajasekhara goes on to* say that the poet needs to have a healthy constitution, inspiration and natural talent, regular and assiduous practice, and frequent company of other literary persons of good taste. A poet should be clean and pure in both body and mind, and live amidst comfortable and tranquil surroundings. Rajasekhara prescribes for the poet an elaborate daily routine for all hours of the day and night. The routine includes study, writing, socializing with literary friends, revision of daily writing, and proper rest and personal care. All this was considered necessary for the nurturing of the poet's creativity and sensibility.

Not every poet could measure up to Rajasekhara's ideal. But the ideal did have a basis in reality. As a rule, a poet had to be a learned and a highly cultured person, with a finely attuned poetic sensibility. During the period in which these poems were written, the Sanskrit language had become a language only for the learned. It had always been a literary language, a heightened form of the common speech of the Aryans. Over the centuries, the gap between the language of literature and common, everyday speech widened so much that, by the time of the classical period (ca. A.D. 300–700), Sanskrit had become purely a language of the learned. In the hands of the writers of the classical age, it achieved perfection in the beauty and elegance of its literary forms and modes of expression. Separated from the language of everyday life, classical Sanskrit was already a "dead" language even in the classical age, but, paradoxically, it continued as the flourishing vehicle of a most vital literature for many centuries after the classical age. Its situation in ancient India was thus somewhat akin to that of Latin in relation to the vernacular languages of medieval Europe.

Classical Sanskrit poetry had extremely well-established rules and conventions in its forms and modes of expression. The poets of our period faithfully conformed to these rules and conventions, but the best among them could always make a fresh use of the conventional modes of poetry with their inventiveness and imagination, thus transforming them into an effective means of communicating an original experience. They did not allow conventional practice to become stale and lifeless, but rather kept it continuously infused with life. A case in point is the conventional use of stock comparisons—the poets used them profusely. A beautiful woman's face is always like the moon, her tresses like black clouds, her eyes like lotuses, her lips sweet nectar, her arms like gold, her breasts like mountain slopes, and so on. The better poets never use any comparison in this repertory without giving it an original touch to make it an expression of a genuine sentiment. Convention is harnessed into the service of an honest portrayal of life.

Somewhat in the manner of the medieval anthologies of ancient Sanskrit poetry, the poems in the following selection are arranged in groups according to their subject. These poems are taken from John Brough's Poems from the Sanskrit. Brough translated his selections from the medieval anthologies and from various other sources, as documented in his book.

ON POETRY

I

Of what use is the poet's poem,
Of what use is the bowman's dart,
Unless another's senses reel
When it sticks quivering in the heart?

2

Fate, give me any other ill you please;
I will bear it gladly. But I live among
Men who are philistines: do not mark me then
To be a poet, do not mark me, do not mark me.

3

Patience, better than armor, guards from harm.
And why seek enemies, if you have anger?
With friends, you need no medicine for danger.
With kinsmen, why ask for fire to keep warm?
What use are snakes when slander sharper stings?
What use is wealth where wisdom brings content?
With modesty, what need for ornament?
With poetry's Muse, why should we envy kings?

4

These wooden-hearted critics, how can they
Know anything of poets' poetry
Fresh as a jasmine bud? But come,
Forget this nonsense, hearken to my rune:
For poetry's moonray nectar melts a stone.

WOMAN'S BEAUTY

I

She is sweet to enjoy, she is fair, she is fine,
Pretty girl, and in love, she is lovely and more.
Oh, she lives in my heart, she's the one I adore;
Never fasting or prayers won such a heaven mine.

From John Brough, trans. *Poems from the Sanskrit* (Hammondsworth: Penguin Books Ltd., 1968), poems 2, 63, 70, 219, 159, 194, 43, 47, 72, 45, 12, 182, 207, 158, 20, 193, 79, 6, 7, 24, 25, 139, 5, 10, 135, 122, 170, 157, 162, 37, 229, 211, 250, 17, 143, 40, 78, 230, 191, 203, 248, 260, 26, 166, 185, 8, 18, 51, 179, 4, 141, 253, 54, 134, 251, 68, 241, 216, 212, 120, 244, 91. Reproduced by permission of Penguin Books, Ltd.

2

A lover reunited with her darling,
The bee clings close and kisses the mango blossom.

3

All men alike have suffered theft;
If a man sees her, she steals his heart;
If he sees her not, what has he left
Worth looking at?

4

Although I have a lamp and fire,
Stars, moon, and sun to give me light,
Unless I look into her eyes,
All is black night.

LOVE

I

Love made a magic snare—
My lady's arms. When they are not there,
My breath comes short, I pant and choke with pain;
But when they tighten around my neck, I live again.

2

A hundred times I learned from my philosophy
To think no more of love, this vanity,
This dream, this source of all regret,
This emptiness.
But no philosophy can make my heart forget
Her loveliness.

3

The clear bright flame of man's discernment dies
When a girl clouds it with her lamp-black eyes.

4

I burn with anguish when we are apart,
When he returns, with jealous fear;
And when I see him, he assaults my heart;
I faint when he is near.
No single moment can I capture bliss,
When he is gone, when he is here.
What in this world can be more strange than this?
And yet he is my dear.

5

Such bitter grief as this has cracked my heart,
Which still has not burst apart;
And from my body, fainting from the smart,
The senses do not depart.
Internal fires within my body blaze,
And yet I am not consumed:
Fortune has cleft me with a mortal wound,
Yet still I live out my days.

6

Take not in hand your mango-feathered heart,[1]
Love, do not string your bow
To strike in thoughtless sport my fainting mind—
Surely heroic prey!
Why do you, Love? Already in my heart
Blazing from long ago
The fire was lit by her soft glance, unkind,
And burned that heart away.

7

Love goes a fishing with the rod Desire,
Baiting his hook with Woman for delight.
Attracted by the fish, the man-fish bite.
He hauls them in and cooks them in his fire.

8

Surely the god of love became her willing slave,
Obedient to the orders that her glances gave.

9

Although I conquer all the earth,
Yet for me there is only one city.
In that city there is for me only one home;
And in that home, one room only;
And in that room, a bed.
And one woman sleeps there,
The shining joy and jewel of all my kingdom.

---

[1]The Hindu god of love is Kama. Like his Greek and Roman counterparts, Eros and Cupid, he is visualized as a young boy with a bow and arrows. His bow is strung with bees and his arrows are flowers. Whosoever he shoots with his arrows falls helplessly in love.

10

"Do not go," I could say; but this is inauspicious.
"All right, go" is a loveless thing to say.
"Stay with me" is imperious. "Do as you wish" suggests
Cold indifference. And if I say "I'll die
When you are gone," you might or might not believe me.
Teach me, my husband, what I ought to say
When you go away.

11

Today adds another day
And still your father is unkind.
The darkness closes up the path.
Come, little son, let us go to bed.

12

You are pale, friend moon, and do not sleep at night,
And day by day you waste away.
Can it be that you also
Think only of her, as I do?

13

Has God no pity, while he counts away
The endless hours of every weary day,
The endless nights, when still my sad head lies
Unpillowed by the breast of Lotus-eyes?

14

The lotus-flower, that once was proud
To match your eyes, is drowned and out of sight.
The moon, reflector of your beauty's light,
Has hid herself behind a cloud.
The wild geese, eager to express
Your grace, have flown away. My grudging Fate
Denies me even such inadequate
Reminders of your loveliness.

15

Blow wind, to where my loved one is,
Touch her, and come and touch me soon:
I'll feel her gentle touch through you,
And meet her beauty in the moon.
These things are much for one who loves—
A man can live by them alone—

That she and I breathe the same air,
And that the earth we tread is one.

16

Although my mind is sick with love, I find
I have acquired the gift of magic sight.
Though she is far away, and it is night,
I see her in a foreign land
From where I stand.

17

"Well, but you surely do not mean to spend
Your whole life pining? Show some spirit.
Are there no other men? What is the merit
Of faithfulness to one?" But when her friend
Gave her this advice, she answered, pale with fear,
"Speak soft. My love lives in my heart, and he will hear."

18

Pure logic may convince a lover's heart
That ampler blessings flow when we're apart.
When she is here, my lady is but one:
When she's away, in all things I see her alone.

19

"Go if you must," she said, "and I shall pray
That Heaven may guard you on your way;
And I shall be reborn, I swear,
Wherever you may be, my dear."

LOVE-MAKING

I

When the fever is caused by her looks and her voice,
The treatment of choice
Is a thrice-daily sip
Of her honey-sweet lip.
To avoid further harm,
And to keep the heart warm,
This follow-up treatment is known to be best:
The soothing and gentle warm touch of her breast.

2

When his mouth faced my mouth, I turned aside
And steadfastly gazed only at the ground;
I stopped my ears, when at each coaxing word
They tingled more; I used both hands to hide
My blushing, sweating cheeks. Indeed I tried.
But oh, what could I do, then, when I found
My bodice splitting of its own accord?

3

You're off to meet your lover in some haste,
With tinkling necklaces and bangles,
A merry girdle clinking at your waist,
While at each step an anklet jangles.
(You glance around in constant trepidation,
Fearful of coming under observation.)

4

When we have loved, my love,
Panting and pale from love,
Then from your cheeks, my love,
Scent of the sweat I love:
And when our bodies love
Now to relax in love
After the stress of love,
Ever still more I love
Our mingled breath of love.

5

When he had filled her with the joy of love,
He tried to pull aside her slipping dress
So as to gaze upon her loveliness:
But still her girdle shone with gems above,
And so he did not quite succeed to see,
Nor could she modestly retreat: her lover
Failed to unveil her nakedness, while she,
No more successful, strove herself to cover.

6

When in love's fight they came to grips,
'Neath wounds of teeth and nails she sank;
And might have died—save that she drank
Ambrosia from her lover's lips.

WHEN LOVE IS DEAD

I

In former days we'd both agree
That you were me, and I was you.
What has now happened to us two,
That you are you, and I am me?

2

She never turned away, nor yet began
To speak harsh words, nor did she bar the door;
But looked at him who was her love before
As if he were an ordinary man.

WOMAN—MAN'S PERFECT BLISS AND GRIEF

I

The moon tries every month in vain
To paint a picture of your face;
And, having failed to catch its grace,
Destroys the work, and starts again.

2

Flaunt your proud head, moon. Nightingale, arise
And sing. Wake, lotus, spread your petals wide.
My lady who has vanquished all your pride
Is gently sleeping, silent, with closed eyes.

3

Mere lotuses I can no longer prize;
The sweetest honey I must criticize;
I laugh at nectar's sweetness—What is this?
For I have drunk a stronger Draught of bliss:
The deadly glances of her loving eyes.

4

Soft as a bud her betel-scarlet lips,
Skin stained with sandal paste, and brimming eyes
Running eye-shadow as the fountain sprays:
Damp hair, flower-scented, dripping dress that grips
And shows her body all. What charms arise
From Beauty bathing late on summer days!

5

He marvelled at her breasts, and when he'd seen them
He shook his head, to disengage his gaze
Trapped in between them.

6

Her hand upon her hip she placed,
And swayed seductively her waist;
With chin upon her shoulder pressed,
She stretched herself to show her breast:
With sapphire pupils burning bright
Within the pearly orbs of white,
Her eyes with eagerness did dance,
And threw me a come-hither glance.

7

Her breasts are high,
Her waist lies low;
And next, an upthrust hip:
If on uneven ground you go—
Why, any man might trip.

8

No, but look here now, this is just absurd,
The way our famous poets talk of girls
As weak and winsome. Weak? Is this a word
To use of those who, with a shake of curls
And with the triumph of a modest glance,
Can lead the very gods a merry dance?

9

In this vain world, when men of intellect
Must soil their souls with service, to expect
A morsel at a worthless prince's gate,
How could they ever hope to renovate
Their spirits?—were it not that fate supplies
The swinging girdles and lotus eyes—
Women, with swelling breasts that comfort soon,
Wearing the beauty of the rising moon.

10

It is the jewels that are bedecked by women,
Not women who are beautified by them:
A woman unbejewelled will still enrapture,
But who looks twice at any girl-less gem?

11

No single plant in this world's garden-plot
Bears such sweet fruit, such bitter fruit as she:
Ambrosial are the apples on her tree
When she is in love, and poison when she's not.

12

This is God's truth, good folks, no lie;
I have no need to lie. In heaven, on earth, or in hell,
Woman is man's bliss and his whole joy;
Woman is also his only grief.

13

It may be hard enough to do,
But if you try, you'll find
A way to pin down quicksilver,
But not a woman's mind.

14

Nor gifts, nor honor, righteousness, nor praise,
Learning nor force, can mend a woman's ways.

ON BEING HUMAN

1

A man lives long who lives a hundred years:
Yet half is sleep, and half the rest again
Old age and childhood. For the rest, a man
Lives close companion to disease and tears,
Losing his love, working for other men.
Where can joy find a space in this short span?

2

The pieces move, now few, now more:
Here many, where before was one,
Here none, where many stood before.
Time, with the goddess Death at play,
Sits at the checkerboard and rolls
Alternate dice of night and day,
And takes the pieces: living souls
Of all that dwell beneath the sun.

3

Untimely, cut by Fate:
But in the hearts of friends

Memories,
Like a great bell, reverberate.

4

Those whom the gods would keep
In safety, they protect,
Not as a shepherd guards his sheep,
But by the gift of a wise intellect.
Nor do the gods appear
In warrior's armor clad
To strike men down with sword or spear.
Those whom they would destroy, they first make mad.

5

At dawn the old man, slowly, painfully,
Managed to stand, but trembling at the knees
Clutching hard fist over stick, while tears met
The dribble from the corner of his mouth,
His scorched and fragment rags barely concealing
A tattered loin-cloth. Forcing crooked legs
To give their utmost paralytic speed,
He started on another day's long road,
Shivering, half-conscious of the bitter wind.

6

This life on earth's a poison tree,
And yet with two fruits sweet:
Ambrosia of poesy,
And joy when true friends meet.

NATURE

I

The summer sun, who robbed the pleasant nights,
And plundered all the water of the rivers,
And burned the earth, and scorched the forest-trees,
Is now in hiding; and the autumn clouds,
Spread thick across the sky to track him down,
Hunt for the criminal with lightning-flashes.

2

With tumbled hair of swarm of bees,
And flower-robes dancing in the breeze,
With sweet, unsteady lotus-glances,
Intoxicated, Spring advances.

3

With tail-fans spread, and undulating wings
With whose vibrating pulse the air now sings,
Their voices lifted and their beaks stretched wide,
Treading the rhythmic dance from side to side,
Eyeing the raincloud's dark, majestic hue,
Richer in color than their own throats' blue,
With necks upraised, to which their tails advance,
Now in the rains the screaming peacocks dance.

SOCIAL THEMES

1

Still in the hamlets of this wretched land
Some families exist, though thin and torn
By harsh oppression of a landlord's hand,
Yet loath to leave the homes where they were born.
And now the mongoose wanders where he will
Where only broken thatch and walls remain;
From their pale, liquid throats, the pigeons still
Murmur with beauty, to assuage the pain.

2

A use can be found
For rotten wood,
And infertile ground
May produce some good.
Kings, when they fall,
Have no uses at all.

3

Hand in clasped hand and side pressed close to side,
Silently stand some children of the poor,
And shyly, hungry eyes half-turned aside,
Observe the eater through the open door.

CRITICS

1

The fire of envious critics' tongues
Refines the true poetic gold.
Should we not celebrate in cheerful song
Poor fools who give us benefits untold?

42

ॐ

Shankara

UPADESHASAHASRI

*S*hankara *(ca. eighth century A.D.), reverently referred to as Shankara* Acharya *("the teacher"), is regarded as the greatest interpreter of the Hindu religion. He is known for his exposition of the Vedanta, a philosophical system based on the interpretation of the* Upanishads *(Selection 20). The Vedanta is one of the many systems of Hindu philosophy, which include the six orthodox Hindu systems and several unorthodox ones, such as the philosophies of Buddhism (Selection 21). The view of the Vedanta that Shankara propounded is known as the* Advaita *("non-dualist") Vedanta. The Advaita Vedanta postulates an uncompromising monism—the idea that all existence has one underlying reality, besides which nothing else truly exists. Shankara's exposition of the Vedanta established it as the dominant philosophy of India up until the present day. The Vedanta is also the Hindu philosophy best known in Europe and America, where it has been an important influence on literature and religion during the nineteenth and the twentieth centuries.*

The term Vedanta *means the "end of the Veda," that is, the* Upanishads. *As the name of a school of philosophy, the term* Vedanta *first came to be applied to certain texts that attempted to formulate and synthesize the teachings of the* Upanishads *systematically. A most important text of this kind, the* Brahmasutra *(also known as the* Vedantasutra*), attributed to Badarayana (first century B.C.), actually incorporated the work of many different scholars and was completed in the early fifth century A.D. The* Brahmasutra *systematically summarized, arranged, criticized, and compiled different and often conflicting interpretations of the* Upanishads. *Another major text that synthesized the content of the* Upanishads *was the* Bhagvad Gita *("the song of the Lord") in the* Mahabharata *(Selection 25). The* Bhagvad Gita, *presenting as it does the concept of duty as enjoined in the social–religious structure of Hinduism, made the teaching of the* Upanishads *the foundation of its message. As the Vedanta emerged as a philo-*

sophical system, the Upanishads, *the* Bhagvad Gita, *and the* Brahmasutra *came to be regarded as its threefold textual foundation.*

The fundamental postulate of the Vedanta philosophy is that true reality exists both at the universal level and at the level of the individual self. The underlying reality of all existence is referred to as the Brahman and that of the individual self is called Atman. The crucial question in the Vedantic philosophy always has been the relationship between Brahman and Atman. It is now generally agreed in the Vedantic philosophy that the two differ only in name, but are, in essence, identical. In the early history of the Vedanta, however, there was no clearly common acceptance of this monistic position.

In the early centuries of its history, the Vedanta was overshadowed by another system of Hindu philosophy, the Sankhya, and later by the philosophical ideas of Mahayana Buddhism. The Bhagvad Gita *regarded as a major text of the Vedanta, itself subscribes to a dualist view of the world, reflecting the influence of the Sankhya. This dualistic view posits the existence of two entities: spirit and matter. Spirit alone is considered to be intelligent; matter is nonsentient. Hence, the phenomenal world is a manifestation of matter, which goes through evolution because of the proximity of spirit. The spirit is reflected in these evolved forms of matter—intellect, ego, mind, and senses—but itself remains an uninvolved spectator of the processes involved in matter. True knowledge, in this dualistic philosophy, consists of the recognition of spirit as distinct from matter and seeing all worldly activities as material in nature. Such knowledge brings release from material bondage and the suffering that comes with this bondage.*

The Brahmasutra, *however, aiming to strengthen the position of the Vedanta, rejected the dualism of the Sankhya and its influence on the Vedanta. It took instead a monistic stand on the nature of reality, positing Brahman alone as the ultimate cause of the universe. But it did not equate Atman with Brahman, considering Atman only as a portion of Brahman. Besides, the monism of the* Brahmasutra *was not categorical. It wavered between two opposite views, both present in the* Upanishads—*one being that Atman and Brahman are different from each other and the other that they are not different—and took a compromising stand by accepting both these points of view, the "difference-and-non-difference" position.*

During the centuries preceding the life of Shankara, the Vedanta came under the strong influence of the philosophical ideas of Mahayana Buddhism (Selections 21 and 22). The influence was so strong that works ostensibly interpreting the Vedanta began to have little to do with the Vedanta and virtually became Buddhist texts. Two main philosophical views of Mahayana Buddhism deserve mention. According to one of these, the phenomenal world has only a qualified reality, in the same manner as a near-sighted monk might see nonexistent flies in his empty bowl. The reality of the phenomenal world exists only while the illusion of it lasts. The only abiding reality is, paradoxically, the Void, or Emptiness. The second view is somewhat similar to the first, though not exactly the same.

According to this view, too, the universe exists only in the mind of its perceiver. All perceptions can be explained as the projection of a person's mind. However, this view posits that there exists a pure being, independent of human thought and without characteristics or predicates. This being is referred to as Suchness. Salvation is attained by exhausting the store of one's human consciousness and becoming the pure being itself. Vedantic thought, before Shankara, was overshadowed by Buddhist ideas such as these.

Shankara reversed the situation. Mastering both the Vedantic literature and Buddhist thought, he adapted the latter for the purpose of consolidating Vedantic thought. He accepted the Buddhist concepts, such as Emptiness and Suchness, giving them a Vedantic character in the form of the already-existing concepts of Atman and Brahman. He devised new concepts, the concepts of avidya *("nescience," or "ignorance") and* parmartha *("highest truth") being the most important among them, to assimilate the Buddhist ideas of illusion and reality into the Vedanta. He integrated Buddhist philosophy into the Vedanta so extensively that some of his rival Vedantists dubbed him a "crypto-Buddhist." However, by the way he used Buddhist ideas in his exposition of the Vedanta, he established the supremacy of the Vedanta in Indian philosophy.*

The main points of Shankara's philosophy are as follows. The only true reality is Brahman. Atman and Brahman are wholly identical. The reality of Atman–Brahman cannot be negated. The phenomenal world, that is, the world of transmigratory existence from life to life in the continuous cycle of birth, death, rebirth, and death again, is an illusion caused by avidya. *The "knowledge"* (vidya) *of the highest truth ("I [Atman] am the supreme and absolute reality, Brahman," in the words of Shankara) removes the illusion of transmigratory existence and provides eternal release from it. Shankara describes the experience of this knowledge: "When the knowledge* (vidya) *of Brahman is firmly grasped, it is conducive to one's own beatitude and the continuity of the knowledge of Brahman. And the continuity of the knowledge of Brahman is helpful to people as a boat is helpful to one wishing to get across a river." The absolute oneness of Brahman and its identity with Atman, as postulated in Shankara's system, is known as the Advaita Vedanta. Advaitic ideas existed long before Shankara, but it was he who established the Advaita tradition permanently as the main current of the Vedanta by basing it on his concept of* avidya.

All of Shankara's works except one are commentaries on other texts. The exception is the Upadeshasahasri *("a thousand verses of teachings") from which the following excerpt is extracted. The* Upadeshasahasri *is an independent work on the Advaita Vedanta. It has two parts, a metrical first part followed by a prose part. The prose is entirely pedagogical, explaining how the means of final release should be taught. The metrical part discusses the basic issues of the Advaita Vedanta. To drive his lesson home, Shankara returns to the treatment of the central issues again and again, so that the different chapters can be read almost independently of one another, as can the individual verses in each chapter. The main topic throughout is the identity of Brahman and the self. The chapter selected here focuses on the "right thought" that, according to Shankara, leads to the knowledge of the true self and to release from the cycle of transmigration.*

RIGHT THOUGHT

1. Since nothing else exists, it is certainly the highest Atman,[1] all-knowing, all-seeing, and pure, which is the Atman to be known. Salutation to this Atman which one should know.

2. I ever bow down to those who, by their knowledge of words, sentences, and means of knowledge, have like lamps illumined Brahman,[2] the secret doctrine of the *Vedas*.[3]

3. Paying homage to those teachers whose words have reached me and destroyed my sins as the sunbeam reaching and destroying the darkness, I shall state the conclusion about the knowledge of Brahman.

4. There is no other attainment higher than that of Atman, for the sake of which attainment exist the words of the *Vedas* and of the *Smritis* as well as actions.[4]

5. Whatever attainment may be desired for the sake of happiness, even though it be for one's own sake, is contrary to happiness.[5] So the knowers of Brahman have declared the attainment of Atman to be the highest one on account of its eternity.

Adapted from Sengaku Mayeda, trans. *A Thousand Teachings: The Upadeshasahasri of Sankara* (Tokyo: University of Tokyo Press, 1979), pp. 160–168. Printed with permission.

[1] Atman is one's true self. In the philosophy of the Vedanta, it is believed to be eternal and immortal.

[2] Brahman is the ultimate true reality of all existence. According to the Vedanta, Brahman and Atman are essentially identical.

[3] The *Vedas* are the most sacred scripture of Hinduism. They are regarded as literature received through divine revelation. The doctrine referred to here is that of the *Upanishads* (Selection 20), which comprise the last part of the *Vedas*. It is called the secret doctrine, because it is meant to be taught only to those who are worthy of it.

[4] Literally, *Smritis* means "lawbooks." Actually, they include many different kinds of works, including the great epics, such as the *Mahabharata* (Selection 25), works which contain the rules by which one is supposed to live. Actions, also known as works, are the ritual requirements of religion.

[5] The implication here is that the pursuit of worldly happiness is contrary to the highest form of happiness, which is the attainment of Atman.

6. And as Atman is by nature self-attained, attainment of it does not depend upon anything else. But any attainment which depends upon something else arises from seeing a difference between Atman and Brahman.[6]

7. Seeing difference is nescience.[7] Its cessation is called final release. And this cessation can arise not through action but through knowledge alone,[8] since that is incompatible with nescience.

8. A result of action is inconstant, since it has nescience and desire as its cause. It is said that the *Vedas* alone are the right means to acquire knowledge with regard to Atman.

9. As the *Vedas* are devoted to one object only (i.e., the knowledge of Brahman), the wise know that they consist of one sentence only.[9] The oneness of Atman and Brahman should indeed be known through the understanding of the meaning of this one sentence.

10. But difference between Atman and Brahman is falsely assumed on the ground of difference of meaning, which is understood in the two different words *Atman* and *Brahman;* even the meaning which is referred to is falsely understood on hearing the word *Atman.*[10] Therefore, this triad, *viz.,*

---

[6]Atman is self-existent. It does not depend on anything else outside itself for its being. In fact, nothing besides Atman (which, here, is the same as Brahman) truly exists. Atman–Brahman is the totality of all reality, unchanging and characterized by oneness. The notion of an entity, whose attainment or being depends upon something other than itself, arises from the assumption of a difference between Atman and Brahman or, more precisely, between Atman as the true self and self seen as separate from it. This separation implies the assumption of diversity, instead of unity, in existence. Given the illusion of diversity, it is also possible to assume that one entity can depend on another.

[7]The difference explained in footnote 6 comes from nescience, or ignorance (*avidya* in Sanskrit). According to Shankara, *avidya* is the cause of the erroneous belief that the phenomenal world, that is, the world of ordinary experience, exists. Actually, the phenomenal world is an illusion. Seeing an individual as confined to the phenomenal world, and, therefore, as separate from the ultimate reality, Brahman, is ignorance.

[8]Release from ignorance and bondage to the illusory world comes only from the knowledge of Atman–Brahman, and not from action. The results of action are not dependable, because action is caused by nescience and desire. This is so because, in the state of ignorance, the self is not aware of itself as Atman and, therefore, is subject to desire for something outside itself.

[9]That one sentence is "Thou are that," meaning that the true self (Atman) of every individual is also Brahman.

[10]That is, the difference between Atman and Brahman is falsely assumed on the basis of the difference between the meanings of the two terms, one meaning the reality of the self and the other of the universe. Even the term *Atman* by itself is misunderstood, being seen not as the true self but rather the self in the phenomenal world.

form, name, and action, is mentioned as constituting the world in the *Shruti*.[11]

11. As this triad is falsely assumed to be interdependent, it is unreal, like a figure which is described in word and painted elsewhere outside of the intellect.[12]

12. And just as the form-and-color, which is seen located outside of the intellect, is expressed in word through the intellect, so this whole is falsely assumed by the confused intellect.

13. Therefore it is reasonable that this triad is unreal; Atman which is nothing but being-pure consciousness only is not what is falsely assumed. Atman is at once the primal knowledge and the object of knowledge, but everything else is falsely assumed.

14. That *atman*[13] by which one knows everything in the dreaming state is knowledge but that knowledge is due to its *maya*.[14] That by which one sees and hears in the dreaming state is called the eye and the ear respectively.

15. That by which one speaks in the dreaming state is called speech, and likewise, it has the names nose, tongue, sense of touch, other organs, and the mind.

16. On account of the limiting adjuncts which are falsely constructed on Atman, this very knowledge is different in many ways, just as difference appears in one and the same gem on account of difference of limiting adjuncts such as blue and yellow.[15]

---

[11]The triad of form, name, and action sums up the fundamental attributes of everything in the phenomenal world. *Shruti* is "revealed knowledge" and another name for the *Vedas*.

[12]That is, all parts of the triad—form, name, and action—seem to be interdependent and, therefore, real, but they are neither interdependent nor real. For instance, a figure's description in words and likeness in a picture may seem interdependent, but actually they are separate from one another and are falsely assumed by the mind to be interdependent and real.

[13]The fivefold *atman* is not the Atman discussed previously, but rather "the worldly self." Atman–Brahman is superior to this self and it is invisible.

[14]According to Shankara, there are three states of consciousness: the waking state; the dreaming state; and the state of deep, dreamless sleep. All these states are states of illusion. Their root cause is nescience. In all these states, there is experience of knowledge. The only knowing agent is Atman. In the dreaming state, knowledge is perceived not directly by Atman, but through its reflection in the organs of perception, such as the eye, ear, etc., which, by themselves, are not capable of knowledge. This reflection of Atman is called its *maya* ("magic").

[15]An adjunct is something joined to another thing but not to be equated with it. Just as the color of a gem is only the adjunct of a gem and not the gem itself, the adjuncts of

17. In like manner the knowledge of one when in the waking state is falsely assumed to have difference. Atman in the waking state makes manifest the object in the intellect,[16] and because of this confused idea performs actions which arise from desire.

18. As in dream so in waking, something external and internal is produced by the notion of interdependence,[17] just as a thing written and the reading of it come from the notion of their interdependence.

19. His atman falsely constructing the difference, desires it, and then wills to obtain it. Willing its desires, it obtains the results of what it has done.

20. Everything comes from nescience. This world is unreal, for it is seen by one who has nescience and is not perceived in the state of deep sleep.

21. It is indeed declared to us in the *Shruti* that knowledge is the notion of the oneness of Atman and Brahman and nescience is the notion of the difference of Atman from Brahman. Therefore knowledge is affirmed in the scripture with all vigor.

22. When the mind becomes pure like a mirror, knowledge shines forth; therefore the mind should be purified. The mind is purified by abstention, the permanent rites, sacrifices, and austerities.[18]

23. The best austerities of the body, etc., should be performed to purify the mind. The concentration of the mind, etc., and the emaciation of the body in this and that season should be performed.[19]

24. Sense-perception should be known as the waking state, memory as the dreaming state, the absence of both as the state of deep sleep, and one's own Atman as the highest state.

Atman in the world of nescience, such as the eye, ear, nose, etc., are not Atman itself. The knowledge perceived through the adjuncts is limited and of different kinds rather than being complete and unified.

[16]The intellect, like the eye, nose, etc., also perceives knowledge by the reflection of Atman, which makes objects manifest in it. The self, confusing itself with the intellect as the knower, performs actions caused by desire and obtains the results of its actions, which hold it in bondage.

[17]That is, the interdependence between what is perceived (external) and what perceives (internal). Both the perceiver and the perceived, as well as the interdependence between them, are unreal.

[18]Although release comes only from knowledge of Atman–Brahman and not from the works of religion, such as austerities, rituals, etc., the works do help in preparing the mind for knowledge.

[19]Various austerities, or rituals, were required at certain times of the year.

25. The darkness called deep sleep is ignorance and it is the seed of the dreaming and waking states.[20] If it is burned up by the knowledge of one's own Atman, like a seed that has been scorched it has no power of germinating.

26. That single *maya* seed is to be known as repeatedly and successively changing in these three ways.[21] Atman, though one and changeless, is as the bearer of *maya,* knowable in many ways, like the sun in the water.

27. Just as one and the same seed becomes different in accordance with differences of vital air,[22] dreaming state, etc., so Atman, like the moon on the water, becomes different in bodies in the dreaming and waking states.

28. Just as a magician comes and goes riding on an elephant created by his magic, so the Atman, though motionless, is related to vital air, dreaming state, and the like.

29. Just as there is neither elephant nor rider, but there stands the magician different from them, so there are neither vital air and the like, nor a seer of them, but the knower, the seeing, different from them, always exists.

30. Neither for one whose sight is not bound, nor for the magician, is there any magical illusion. This magical illusion exists only for him whose sight is bound. Therefore in fact there is no magician at all.

31. Atman should be directly known according to the *Shruti* which says that Atman is directly present, for the *Shruti* says, "The knot of the heart is loosened . . . when He is seen. . . . If here he does not know it, there is great loss," and the like.

32. Because of its being soundless, etc., it cannot be perceived by the sense-organs. Likewise, as it is different from pleasure, etc., how can it be perceived by the intellect?

33. Just as Rahu,[23] though he is invisible, is perceived in the moon during an eclipse and just as a reflection of the moon, etc., is seen in the water, so Atman, though all-pervading, is perceived there in the intellect.

---

[20] That is, the darkness of the state of deep sleep is ignorance *(avidya)* by itself. This darkness is the root cause ("seed") of the dreaming as well as of the waking state. The "three ways" (see verse 26) are ignorance (or deep sleep), the dreaming state, and the waking state.

[21] Although *maya* (literally, "magic," or "illusion") manifests itself in these three ways, ultimately, it is a reflection of Atman, like the sun in the water.

[22] The "vital air" *(prana* in Sanskrit, literally meaning the "breath of life") is the entity by which one lives. Here, it could mean one's life in the world or the state of deep sleep.

[23] This is a reference to a myth, according to which a demon, Rahu, swallows the sun or the moon from time to time, thus causing their eclipses. The story goes that, once upon a time, when the gods churned the ocean to produce the nectar of life, Rahu assumed a disguise and stole some of the nectar and drank it. The sun and the moon detected him and informed the god Vishnu, who cut off Rahu's head. So Rahu wreaks vengeance on the sun and the moon by occasionally swallowing them.

34. Just as the reflection and heat of the sun are perceived in the water but do not belong to the water, so knowledge, though in the intellect, is not a quality of it, since it differs in nature from the intellect.

35. Atman, whose seeing never fails, sees a modification of the intellect connected with the eyes, and is the seer of seeing and similarly the hearer of hearing—so says the *Shruti*.

36. Seeing a modification of the mind which is isolated from the senses, it is the thinker of thinking, unborn. Likewise, it is the understander of understanding since it has unfailing power. Therefore the scripture says, "For there is no cessation of the seeing of the seer." . . .

37. It is changeless. . . . "It appears to meditate" and "It appears to move about."[24] . . . It is pure . . . "There a thief is not a thief" . . . and "It is not followed by good, it is not followed by evil."[25] . . .

38. As its power never fails, it is the knower in the state of deep sleep as well as in the waking state, for it is changeless. But the distinction is supposed only as regards the object of knowledge since the *Shruti* says, "Where there seems to be another, there the one might see the other."[26] . . .

39. As mediated by time, space, etc., the ordinary seeing by non-Atman, such as the eye, is indeed indirect. As seeing is the nature of Atman it has been said that Brahman is directly known.

40. No second lamp is necessary for illuminating a lamp; similarly no knowledge other than Atman is required for knowing Atman, since knowledge is the nature of Atman.

41. It is not accepted that Atman is an object, or changeable, or manifold. Therefore Atman is not to be discarded or accepted by something other than Atman.

42. Atman includes the exterior and the interior,[27] is unscathed, and beyond birth, death, and old age. What does one fear who knows, "I am Atman"?

---

[24]That is, Atman may appear to change, but is actually unchanging.

[25]Atman is beyond everything in the world, including a person's identity, such as the identity of a thief or of anyone else, or good and evil as known in the world.

[26]Atman alone is the knower and the subject of knowledge. It exists by itself; nothing besides it exists. Other entities may appear to exist, but they do not truly exist. For something to be an object of knowledge as distinct from the knower, its separate existence must be assumed. Since nothing besides Atman truly exists, anything other than Atman, which becomes an object of knowledge, has only an appearance of existence. So when something appears to exist in this manner, one sees it as a distinct entity and makes it an object of knowledge.

[27]See footnote 26. The notions of the exterior and the interior and the differentiation between them manifest themselves only in the illusory world. In Atman, there is no such differentiation.

43. There is action *(karman)* only until injunction to attain Atman, since notions of belonging to a caste, etc., are then removed; their removal results from the conclusion "Thou art that"[28] . . . based on the scriptural teaching "It is neither gross nor subtle."[29] . . .

44. Since in abandoning the body in the previous life one has given up lineage and the like, lineage and the like belong to the body. Thus the body is also non-Atman.

45. Therefore the notions of "mine" and "I" which apply to the non-Atman such as the body, etc., are nescience. It (= nescience) should be abandoned by means of knowledge of Atman since the *Shruti* says, "For this is the doctrine of the demons."[30] . . .

46. Just as the duties of observing ten-day periods of impurity come to an end at the time of entering the life of a wandering ascetic,[31] the actions based upon lineage and the like come to an end at the time of attaining knowledge.

47. But, willing his desires, an ignorant man obtains the results of what he has done. When desires are cast off by him who sees his own Atman, he becomes immortal.

48. The injunction to attain the nature of Atman results in the cessation of actions and the like. Atman is neither an object to be accomplished nor a means of accomplishment; it is held to be eternally content as the *Shruti* says.

49. Actions result in things being produced, obtained, changed, or purified. There are no results of action other than these. Therefore one should abandon actions together with their requisites.

---

[28]*Karman*, or *karma*, is a well-known concept in Indian philosophy and religion. The term literally means "action," but, more importantly, it refers to the consequences of action. The theory is that all actions performed with a desire to obtain something produce results that bind the performer of action. The individual performing such actions must reap their results, if not in the present life, then in a subsequent one. For it is believed that one goes through a continuous cycle of transmigration from life to life. In fact, it is also believed that the identity and circumstances of a person in a particular life are the consequences of their actions in the present or in a previous life. The chain of actions and their consequences, as well as the cycle of transmigration, ends only when one attains Atman.

[29]Grossness or subtlety describe the attributes of the things of the limited, unreal world. They are inadequate for describing the nature of Atman–Brahman.

[30]The doctrine subscribing to the notions of "mine" and "I" associated with the unreal self is the doctrine of demons, a class of evil-natured beings.

[31]A reference to the Indian belief that certain events, such as a birth or a death in a family, render the family impure for a number of days. This impurity does not affect those who have become wandering ascetics.

50. Concentrating upon Atman the love which is now set on external things—for they end in suffering, are inconstant and exist for Atman—a seeker after the truth should resort to a teacher

51. who is tranquil, wise, released, actionless, and established in Brahman, since the *Shruti* says, "One who has a teacher knows . . ." and the *Smriti* also says, "Learn to know this by obeisance, by questioning, by serving."[32]

52. If a student is disciplined and properly qualified, the teacher should immediately transport him over his great interior ocean of darkness in the boat of the knowledge of Brahman.

53. Seeing, touching, hearing, smelling, thinking, knowing, and other powers, though they are of the nature of pure consciousness, are differentiated by limiting adjuncts.[33]

54. As the sun always shines, without destroying or creating anything by its rays, so does it (Atman) always know all, being all-pervading, all-seeing, and pure.

55. Through nescience Atman abiding in the body is regarded as the seeing of something other than itself, and as being the same size as the body and possessed of the qualities of the body, by such comparisons as that of the moon in the water and the like.[34]

56. Having seen an external object, one shuts the eyes and remembers it in the dreaming state and then abandoning it in the state of deep sleep, one opens up the seeing of Atman, reaches Brahman, and does not travel along any path.[35]

57. He who has thus given up the triad, *viz.,* the vital air (= the state of deep sleep), goes across the great ocean of ignorance, for he is by nature abiding in his own Atman, attributeless, pure, awakened, and released.

58. When he has realized, "I am unborn, undying, deathless, free from old age, fearless, all-knowing, all-seeing, and pure," he is not born again.

59. He who knows the oneness of Atman and Brahman concludes that the above-mentioned darkness-seed does not exist. How should he be born again when it does not exist?

60. Just as clarified butter, extracted from milk, does not become the same as before if thrown back into it, so the knower once discriminated from the

---

[32]That is, by obeisance to and by questioning and serving the teacher.

[33]That is, although all the faculties mentioned here derive their powers from the pure consciousness of Atman, they are not Atman and are differentiated from it by limiting qualities.

[34]It is because of ignorance that Atman is seen as and equated with something other than itself, such as the body, in the same way as the reflection of the moon in the water may be equated with the moon.

[35]As noted earlier, the state of deep sleep is still a state of ignorance. It is only by shedding the veil of this ignorance that one sees and reaches Atman–Brahman.

untrue such as the intellect never becomes the same embodied Atman as before.

61. One becomes free from fear realizing, "'I am Brahman' . . . which is 'the real, knowledge, and the infinite' . . . which is superior to the fivefold atman such as the atman consisting of the essence of food, etc., and which is declared in the scripture to be 'invisible.'"

62. A man who knows the truth, i.e., the bliss of that Atman, from fear of which speech, mind, fire, and the like carry out their functions, does not fear anything at all.

63. If a knower of Atman abides in his own infinite and non-dual kingdom, which is superior to name and the like, then whom should he salute? Then there is no need for action.

64. When Atman is external it is called *Viraj* or *Vaisvanara*. When it remembers within, it is called *Prajapati*. But when everything vanishes it is called *Prajna* or *Avyakrta*.[36]

65. As they are merely verbal handles, however, the triad, namely, the state of deep sleep, etc., are unreal. A man who thus covers himself with the truth, "I am the true and the knower," is released.

66. As the sun has light as its nature, it has neither day nor night. In like manner I have neither knowledge nor ignorance since I have pure consciousness as my nature, without distinctions in it.

67. As the scripture is not to be doubted, one should remember, "I am always Brahman; as I am Brahman, I have nothing to reject or accept."

68. He is not born again who sees thus, "I am the one in all beings just as the ether and all beings are in me."[37]

69. There is nothing else but one's own Atman anywhere, outside, within or inside, since the *Shruti* says, "This Brahman is . . . without an outside, without an inside." It is therefore pure and self-effulgent.

70. According to such scriptural passages as "Not thus![38] Not so!" Atman is "the quiescence of the pluralistic universe and non-dual.". . . And according to such scriptural passages as, "That imperishable . . . is the unknown knower." . . . It should not be known in any way other than that.

---

[36]The external and the internal aspects of Atman mentioned here parallel the waking and dreaming states described earlier. They do not have a permanent existence and vanish with the realization of Atman.

[37]In Indian philosophy, ether is an entity that permeates all existence. It is the metaphysical analogue of space.

[38]This is a reference to a method of exposition in the Vedanta philosophy where the reality of Atman–Brahman is suggested negatively by pointing to other things and noticing, "it is not this, it is not this."

71. If one has come to know the supreme Brahman, realizing, "I am the Atman of all," one becomes the Atman of all beings, since the *Shruti* says, "Whoever thus knows 'I am Brahman' becomes this all; even the gods have no power to prevent his becoming thus, for he is their Atman." . . .

72. If a living being clearly knows his Atman as the highest Atman, as God, he is to be worshiped by the gods and ceases to be domestic animal for the gods.[39]

73. As a killer of the unreal thus covers himself with the truth, "I am the real-Atman and the knower, but, like ether, I am empty of anything else," he is not bound again.

74. They are pitiable who know the supreme Brahman differently from this. "The gods would be under the power of him" . . . who is a self-ruler, a seer of non-difference, and abiding in himself.

75. Abandoning your relationship with lineage, etc., and other words along with actions and saying, "Om,"[40] you attain your own Atman, which is all, pure,

76. the bulwark of all that is established,[41] devoid of day, night, and the like, and is to the sides, above, below, all, ever-shining, and free from disease.

77. One should know one's Atman to be the highest One which is devoid of merit and demerit, free from past and future, free from cause and effect and free from all bondage.

78. While being pure and not acting, Atman does all; while standing, it goes past those who are running. As it is almighty through its *maya,* it is thought to be manifold, though really it is unborn.

79. While causing the world to turn around, I, Atman, am actionless, non-agent and non-dual for, like a king, I am merely the witness of the world, and like a magnet, merely close to it.

80. One should bear in mind, "I am that Brahman which is attributeless, actionless, eternal, free from the pairs of opposites,[42] free from disease, pure, awakened, and released."

81. Having properly known bondage, final release, and all the causes from which all this and both bondage and final release result; the one (= the state of deep sleep) and the two (= the dream and waking states) which are to be rejected; and the only, pure, and highest truth which transcends the knowable and the unknowable, which has been studied and which is spoken of by the *Shruti*

---

[39]"Domestic animal" here implies a lowly inferior.

[40]In Hinduism, the syllable "Om" is believed to be the eternal sound from which the universe was created.

[41]"Established" here means eternal and unchanging.

[42]The phenomenal world is made of opposites, such as right and wrong, high and low, darkness and light, beginning and end, and so on.

and sages,—having known all this one would become a knower of Brahman who has transcended sorrow and delusion, who is all-knowing, all-doing, free from the fear of existence, and who has completed all that has to be done.

82. Atman itself does not become something to be rejected nor is it to be accepted by itself or anything else. Nothing else becomes something to be rejected or to be accepted by itself (Atman); this is true thought as has been mentioned above (stanza 67).

83. This true thought leads people to understand Atman and has all the *Upanishads* as its field; so, having come to know this, they are released from all the bonds of transmigratory existence.

84. As it is the supreme means of purification that is the secret doctrine of all the *Vedas* and is the highest secret doctrine even for the gods, it has been expounded here.

85. This secret and supreme knowledge should not be given to a student who is not tranquil but should be taught to a student who is dispassionate and obedient.

86. And there is no actionless one other than the teacher who is offering the knowledge of Atman. Therefore, a student who is seeking after knowledge should always qualify himself with the qualities of a student.

87. Salutation to that knowledge-Atman which is all-knowing and almighty and besides which there is nothing else, neither knowledge, nor object of knowledge, nor knower.

88. Salutation to the all-knowing teachers by whom through knowledge we have been led across the great ocean of birth and death filled with ignorance.

43

⚹

Tung Chung-shu

LUXURIANT GEMS OF THE SPRING AND AUTUMN ANNALS

Establishment of the Han Dynasty (206 B.C.–A.D. 220) brought a period of strength and stability to China after centuries of feudal warfare and the brief but traumatic Ch'in Dynasty (221–206 B.C.). It was a time of consolidating the political unification harshly accomplished by the Ch'in. Han emperors and their ministers began to work out the rudiments of a remarkable balance in a government Legalist in the spirit of its centralized power, yet tempered by Confucian humanism. That balance was to characterize Chinese imperial government at its best for more than two millennia and was the secret of its durability.

The term "Han Synthesis" has been applied to Chinese philosophy during this dynasty. It is a period in the history of thought that shows a remarkably different face from that which we have seen during the period of the Hundred Schools (Selections 26 through 32). The age of creativity and passionate, sharp-witted diversity was over. In its stead there came a tendency to move all thought toward a melding of ideas, with a consequent blurring of what had once been clearly defined distinctions among the various schools. No doubt this tendency to consolidation in philosophy reflects the unity achieved in Han times, not only in political but in the whole spectrum of economic, social, and cultural life. It probably also reflects the fact that the book burning and the execution of scholars during the Ch'in Dynasty disrupted the generation-to-generation continuity of disciples within the major schools, and so weakened them almost to the point of extinction.

The synthesizing tendency of Han thought is well-illustrated by the following selection. Its author, Tung Chung-shu (ca. 179–104 B.C.) described himself as a Confucian, and was the philosopher most responsible for persuading Wu Ti, sixth emperor of the Han, to adopt Confucianism as the official doctrine of the state in

136 B.C. Yet there is little here that will seem familiar to those acquainted with the thought of Confucius and Mencius (Selections 26 and 28). Rather, the emphasis is on two sets of ideas that come down from much earlier Chinese thought. One of these is the yin/yang duality: yin is "the moon, the feminine, the negative," while yang is "the sun, the male, the positive." Yin/yang speculation had found a place, though not a central one, in Taoist thought, especially with the notion that the interplay between these forces underlies all processes in nature, and that harmony or disharmony are caused by the balance or imbalance between them. Speculation involving the "five agents" was also rooted in an earlier time, and parallels some strands of pre-Socratic Greek thought about the basic material of all creation. But by the time the five agents are worked into what has come to be called Yin Yang Confucianism, they are really metaphors for whole ranges of non-material phenomena.

Taken literally, Tung Chung-shu's thoughts about the five agents, and about the resemblance between the human body and the heavens, seem far-fetched. They should rather be seen as a metaphoric working out in detail of the idea of a dynamic interrelationship among all things, of an all-embracing cosmic harmony. In the history of Chinese thought, the Han was not a high point of either creativity or clarity. However, the pervasive desire to "see the world steadily and see it whole" was a revealing characteristic of the age of China's imperial consolidation, and like so much else that emerged from that age, the Han Synthesis left its mark on the Chinese tradition down to the early years of the twentieth century.

CHAPTER 42
The Meaning of the Five Elements

Heaven has five agents (i.e., elements): the first is wood; the second, fire; the third, earth; the fourth, metal; and the fifth, water. Wood is the beginning of the cycle of the five agents, water is its end, and earth is its center. Such is their natural sequence. Wood produces fire, fire produces earth, earth produces metal, metal produces water, and water produces wood. Such is their father-and-son relationship.[1] Wood occupies the left, metal occupies the right; fire occupies the front, water occupies the rear; and earth occupies the center. Such is their order

---

[1]This is only one among many instances of Tung Chung-shu's efforts to find reflections of Confucian virtues—in this case filial piety—in the cosmic scheme symbolized by the five agents.

as that of father and son, and the way in which they receive from one another and spread out. Therefore wood received from water; fire, from wood; earth, from fire; metal, from earth; and water, from metal. Those that give are fathers and those that receive are sons. It is the way of heaven that the son always serves his father. Therefore when wood is produced, fire should nourish it; and after metal perishes, water should store it. Fire enjoys wood and nourishes it with yang, but water overcomes metal and buries it with yin. Earth serves heaven with the utmost loyalty. Therefore the five agents are the actions of filial sons and loyal ministers. The five agents are so-called because they are tantamount to five actions. That is how the term was derived. The sage knows this and therefore he shows much love and little sternness, and is generous in supporting the living and serious in burying the dead. This is to follow the system of heaven. It is the function of the son to receive and to fulfill. For him to support is like fire enjoying wood, to bury one's father is like water overcoming metal, and serving the ruler is like earth showing respect to heaven. People like these may be said to be good in their actions.

Each of the five agents succeeds the others according to its order. Each of them performs its official function by fulfilling its capacity. Thus wood occupies the eastern quarter and controls the forces of spring, fire occupies the southern quarter and controls the forces of summer, metal occupies the western quarter and controls the forces of autumn, and water occupies the northern quarter and controls the forces of winter. For this reason, wood controls production, metal controls destruction, fire controls heat, water controls cold. It is the course of nature that people must be employed according to their order and officials appointed according to their capacity. Earth occupies the center and is the natural benefactor.[2] It is the helper of heaven. Its character is abundant and beautiful and cannot be identified with the affairs of any single season. Therefore, among the five agents and the four seasons, earth includes them all. Although metal, wood, water, and fire each have their own functions, their positions would not be established were it not for earth. . . .

CHAPTER 56

The Correspondence of Man and the Numerical Categories of Heaven

Heaven is characterized by the power to create and spread things, earth is characterized by its power to transform, and man is characterized by moral principles.

---

[2] The five agents were seen, among other things, as metaphors for historical change, in which each of the dynasties was equated with an element and its characteristic attributes. The Han Dynasty was equated with earth and had taken for its ceremonial regalia earth's color, yellow. In this passage Tung Chung-shu is paying homage to the imperial dynasty through the symbolism of earth among the five agents.

The material force of heaven is above, that of earth below, and that of man in between. Spring produces and summer grows, and all things flourish. Autumn destroys and winter stores, and all things are preserved. Therefore there is nothing more refined than material force, richer than earth, or more spiritual than heaven. Of the creatures born from the refined essence of heaven and earth, none is more noble than man. Man receives the mandate from heaven and is therefore superior to other creatures. Other creatures suffer troubles and defects and cannot practice humanity and righteousness; man alone can practice them. Other creatures suffer troubles and defects and cannot match heaven and earth; man alone can match them. Man has 360 joints, which match the number of heaven.[3] His body, with its bones and flesh, matches the thickness of earth. He has ears and eyes above, with their keen sense of hearing and seeing, which resemble the sun and moon. His body has its orifices and veins, which resemble rivers and valleys. His heart has feelings of sorrow, joy, pleasure, and anger, which are analogous to the spiritual feelings [of heaven]. As we look at man's body, how much superior it is to that of other creatures and how similar to heaven! Other creatures derive their life from the yin and yang of heaven in a non-erect way, but man brilliantly shows his patterns and order. Therefore, with respect to the physical form of other creatures, they all move about in a non-erect and incumbent position. Man alone stands erect, looks straight forward, and assumes a correct posture. . . . From this we can see that man is distinct from other creatures and forms a trinity with heaven and earth.

Therefore, in the body of man, his head rises up and is round and resembles the shape of heaven.[4] His hair resembles the stars and constellations. His ears and eyes, quick in their senses, resemble the sun and moon. The breathing of his nostrils and mouth resembles the wind. The penetrating knowledge of his mind resembles the spiritual intelligence [of heaven]. His abdomen and womb, now full and now empty, resemble the myriad things. The myriad things are nearest to the earth. Therefore the portion of the body below the waist corresponds to earth. As the body resembles heaven and earth, the waist serves as a sash. What is above the neck is noble and majestic in spirit, which is to manifest the feature of heaven and its kind. What is below the neck is full and humble, comparable to the soil. The feet are spread out and square, resembling the shape of the earth. Therefore, in wearing ceremonial sash and girdle, the neck must be straight to distinguish it from the heart. What is above the sash (the waist) is all yang and what is below

---

[3]This statement represents a strained numerology, in which an inaccurate count of the joints of the human body is argued to correspond with a rounded-off count of the days in a year.

[4]The Chinese traditionally thought of heaven as round, earth as square. The standard form of Chinese coinage for two millennia featured a raised circular rim and a square hole cut from the center, symbolizing "all under heaven."

the sash is all yin, each with its own function. The yang is the material force of heaven, and the yin is the material force of the earth. Therefore when yin and yang become operative and cause man to have ailment in the foot or numbness in the throat, for example, the material force of the earth rises to become clouds and rain. Thus there is resemblance in the correspondence. The agreement of heaven and earth and the correspondence between yin and yang are ever found complete in the human body. The body is like heaven. Its numerical categories and those of heaven are mutually interwoven, and therefore their lives are interlocked. Heaven completes the human body with the number of days in a full year. Consequently the body's 366[5] lesser joints correspond to the number of days in the year, and the twelve larger joints correspond to the number of months. Internally the body has five viscera, which correspond to the number of the five agents. Externally, there are the four limbs, which correspond to the four seasons. . . . In what may be numbered, there is correspondence in number. In what may not be numbered, there is correspondence in kind. They are all identical and correspond to heaven. Thus heaven and man are one. Therefore present the formed so as to make manifest the formless and get hold of what may be numbered to make manifest what may not be numbered. Spoken of in this way, it is quite proper for things to correspond to each other in kind. It is like the form of the body. Its correspondence to heaven is correct by virtue of its numerical categories.

---

[5]The disparity between the numbers in this body/calendar linkage and those given earlier in the same chapter is difficult to explain. It may be a useful reminder that Tung Chung-shu was not a scientific philosopher but a metaphysician whose starting and ending point was his belief in the harmony of all phenomena.

44

꣠

Ssu-ma Ch'ien

RECORDS OF THE HISTORIAN

The writing of history, long established as a major element of Chinese literature (see Selection 10), developed great professionalism and intellectual sophistication during the Han Dynasty. Major figures in this development were a father-and-son team of official dynastic historians, Ssu-ma T'an (170?–110 B.C.) and Ssu-ma Ch'ien (145–90? B.C.). While Ssu-ma Tan was responsible for its grand conception, his son went on to complete a work that encompassed no less than the entire history of the world—which, of course, meant principally China and the world as seen from China—from the founding of the state by the legendary Yellow Emperor in the twenty-seventh century B.C. down to his own time. Ssu-ma Ch'ien's completion of this monumental task is all the more remarkable because of a disaster that befell him in 98 B.C. Having spoken favorably of a Han general who had surrendered to the northern barbarians, Ssu-ma Ch'ien was held in disgrace at the court of Emperor Wu Ti (ruled from 140 to 87 B.C.). In his fury, the emperor offered Ssu-ma Ch'ien a choice between death and castration. Not because he feared death, but because, as he wrote to a friend, "I grieve that I have things in my heart that I have not been able to express fully . . . ," he chose the degradation of becoming a palace eunuch. But it left him the time he needed to complete his great work.

Organizing the vast mass of material he had collected on extensive tours of the emperor's domains and in the imperial library was a major challenge. Ssu-ma Ch'ien's solution to the problem is worth noting because it became the pattern for the twenty-five official dynastic histories that followed the Shi Chi ("records of the historian") over the next two millennia. There are five main subdivisions of the Shi Chi. The first, the Basic Annals, in twelve chapters, sets forth a summary of the entire historical period. The second subdivision, in ten chapters, contains chronological tables giving the names and dates of royal and feudal officials over the same period. The third subdivision is composed of eight chapters, each of which analyses a topic, such as rituals, the calendar, or the economy. The fourth, in thirty chapters, gives the histories of the great Chou Dynasty families. The fifth consists of seventy chapters of biography, the final chapter being his own autobiography.

It is impossible to overestimate the importance of the Records of the Historian. For one thing, it is the principal, and often the only, source we have for many major historical developments and for the lives of such giants of the Chinese tradition as Confucius, Mencius, and other masters of the Hundred Schools. For another, Ssu-ma Ch'ien sets a standard for objective history by frequently including the relevant contemporary document—a decree, letter, speech, or the like—which puts us in touch with the mind of the historical character and with the flavor of the historical moment. Last, and by no means least, he is a splendid prose writer, capable of bringing his actors and their actions alive and making them memorable. His role as the shaper of China's historiographic tradition has led to comparisons with the Greek historian Herodotus (Selection 24).

The excerpts below are selected from Ssu-ma Ch'ien's account, in the first section of his Records, of the man who rose from a peasant village lay-about to found the mighty Han Dynasty. Obviously, Ssu-ma Ch'ien had to treat Kao-tsu with respect. He includes, though largely without comment, the stories of early signs and portents of future greatness. Above all, he clearly portrays the founding emperor as the hero of this turn of the "dynastic cycle," the drama of a man gaining the "mandate of heaven" and establishing a new regime to replace one that had lost its moral bearings. But while Kao-tsu comes through these pages as a hero, he is neither superman nor plaster saint. We come away from this biography with a feeling of having met a thoroughly plausible human being moving toward his destiny.

SHI CHI
Chapter 8

The Basic Annals of the Emperor Kao-tsu

Kao-tsu[1] was a native of the community of Chun-yang in the city of Feng, the district of P'ei. His family name was Liu and his polite name Chi. His father was known as the "Venerable Sire" and his mother as "Dame Liu."

Before he was born, Dame Liu was one day resting on the bank of a large pond when she dreamed that she encountered a god. At this time the sky grew dark and was filled with thunder and lightning. When Kao-tsu's father went to look for her, he saw a scaly dragon over the place where she was lying. After this she became pregnant and gave birth to Kao-tsu.

Kao-tsu had a prominent nose and a dragon-like face, with beautiful whiskers on his chin and cheeks; on his left thigh he had seventy-two black moles.[2] He was kind and affectionate with others, liked to help people, and was very understanding. He always had great ideas and paid little attention to the business the rest of his family was engaged in.

When he grew up he took the examination to become an official and was made village head of Ssu River. He treated all the other officials in the office with familiarity and disdain. He was fond of wine and women and often used to go to Dame Wang's or old lady Wu's and drink on credit. When he got drunk and lay down to sleep, the old women, to their great wonder, would always see something like a dragon over the place where he was sleeping. Also, whenever he would drink and stay at their shops, they would sell several times as much wine as usual. Because of these strange happenings, when the end of the year came around the old women would always destroy Kao-tsu's credit slips and clear his account.

•   •   •

From *Records of the Historian: Chapters from the* Shih Chi *of Ssu-ma Ch'ien,* trans. Burton Watson (New York and London: Columbia University Press, 1969), pp. 105–106, 109, 114–118, 132–133, 135–136, 140–143, 145–146. Reprinted with permission of the publisher.

[1]The emperor's family and given names were Liu Pang, but, while Ssu-ma Ch'ien refers to the family name, he never uses the personal name Pang. Here he uses the official posthumous title, which means "exalted ancestor," and in other passages is careful to use whatever title the emperor held at any point during the course of his rise from obscurity to power: governor of P'ei, king of Han. Likewise, although he makes it clear that Empress Lu started life in humble circumstances, even working beside her husband in the fields, he always accords her the imperial title.

[2]A mystic number, therefore a sign of special providence.

The First Emperor of Ch'in,[3] repeatedly declaring that there were signs in the southern sky indicating the presence of a "son of heaven," decided to journey east to suppress the threat to his power. Kao-tsu, suspecting that he himself was the cause of the visit, fled into hiding among the rocky wastes of the mountains and swamps between Mang and Tang. Empress Lu and others who went with her to look for him, however, were always able to find him. Kao-tsu, wondering how she could do this, asked her and she replied, "There are always signs in the clouds over the place where you are. By following these we manage to find you every time." Kao-tsu was very pleased in his heart. When word of this circulated among the young men of the district of P'ei, many of them sought to become his followers.

$$\bullet \quad \bullet \quad \bullet$$

[As the confused civil war broke out following the Ch'in emperor's death, Kao-tsu was elevated, evidently by popular acclaim, to the office of Governor of P'ei District.] King Huai's[4] elder generals all advised him, saying, "Hsiang Yu[5] is by nature extremely impetuous and cruel. When he attacked and conquered the city of Hsiang-ch'eng, he butchered every one of the inhabitants without mercy. Wherever he passed he has left behind him destruction and death. . . . This time it would be better to send a man of true moral worth who, relying on righteousness, will proceed west and make a proclamation to the elders of Ch'in. The

---

[3]The state of Ch'in, on the northwest frontier of late Chou Dynasty China, developed its military power over generations and, by 221 B.C., completed its conquest and consolidation of the other feudal states. Its king assumed the title Ch'in Shih Huang-ti (First Emperor of the Ch'in) and, guided by Legalist advisers, proceeded to impose a ruthless regime of harsh laws, forced movement of peoples, massive building projects such as the Great Wall, and book-burning. He was hated and feared in his own time, and became the classic example of tyranny for all subsequent Chinese history. His death in 210 B.C. touched off the scramble for power among ambitious military and civilian officials from which Kao-tsu emerged as victor and founder of the Han Dynasty (206 B.C.–A.D. 220), the longest-lived of all the imperial dynasties. It is Ch'in Shih Huang-ti's tomb that is still guarded by the vast army of life-sized clay soldiers near the modern city of Sian.

[4]Partly as a holdover from the late days of the Warring States Period when heads of the remaining feudal states assumed kingly titles, partly too as a result of military men establishing territorial bases during the civil war, many men at this time claimed the title of king. Kao-tsu himself for several years was designated king of Han, before he consolidated his power to establish the imperial dynasty of the same name.

[5]Hsiang Yu was one of the generals, perhaps the most capable of the lot, contending for power as the Ch'in Dynasty collapsed. Ssu-ma Ch'ien, as Han Dynasty court historian, had to walk a fine line in characterizing Kao-tsu's greatest rival. Hsiang Yu is frequently described as impetuous and cruel, but he is also seen as a worthy opponent, always brave and skillful.

men of Ch'in have long suffered under their rulers. Now if we can send a truly worthy man who will not come to them with rapine and violence in his heart, we can surely persuade them to submit. . . . Only the governor of P'ei [Kao-tsu], who from the first has shown himself to be a man of tolerance and moral stature, is worthy to go."

In the end, King Huai . . . dispatched only the governor of P'ei who, gathering up the scattered remnants of Ch'en She's and Hsiang Liang's armies, marched out of Tang to seize the region to the west. Proceeding to Ch'eng-yang and Chiang-li, he threw his weight against the Ch'in fortifications and defeated both garrisons.

●　　●　　●

The governor of P'ei was about to lead his troops on to the west, but . . . [one of his advisers] cautioned him, saying, "Although you wish to enter the pass as soon as possible, there are a great many soldiers of Ch'in holding the strong points. Now if you march on without seizing the city of Yuan, Yuan will attack you from behind. With the power of Ch'in awaiting you ahead, your way will be fraught with danger!" Accordingly, the governor of P'ei led his troops back by another road at night, changed his flags and pennants, and just before dawn encircled the city of Yuan with several bands of his troops. . . . Ch'en Hui, [one of the officers defending the town, came secretly to Kao Tsu and said,] "Our officers believe that if they surrender they will certainly be put to death and therefore they have all mounted the walls and are firmly guarding the city. Now if you wear out your days remaining here attacking the city, many of your men are bound to suffer injury and death, while if you lead your troops away from Yuan, Yuan will surely pursue you from behind. Should you choose the former course you will never reach Hsien-yang in time to take advantage of the agreement,[6] while should you choose the latter you will be bedeviled by the power of Yuan. If I were to suggest a plan for you, I would say it is best to promise to enfeoff the governor [appoint him under authority of King Huai] if he surrenders. Then you may leave him behind to guard the city for you while you lead his troops with you to the west. When the other cities that have not submitted hear of your action, they will hasten to open their gates and await your coming, so that your passage will be freed from all hindrance."

---

[6]An agreement among the rebel generals that whoever reached Hsien-yang first should become king of its territory. Kao-tsu's dilemma, which the officer from the besieged city points out in this passage, was common enough in a war involving so many independent armies moving across the face of China. The choice of a political, rather than a military, solution was also common, and here, as in other passages, the Grand Historian characterizes Kao-tsu as a prudent man, always willing to listen to sensible advice, even from an enemy.

The governor of P'ei approved this idea and accordingly made the governor of Yuan marquis of Yin and enfeoffed Ch'en Hui with a thousand households.

• • •

In the tenth month of the first year of Han [late in 207 B.C.] the governor of P'ei finally succeeded in reaching Pa-shang ahead of the other leaders. Tzu-ying, the king of Ch'in, came in a plain carriage drawn by a white horse, wearing a rope about his neck,[7] and surrendered the imperial seals and credentials by the side of Chih Road. Some of the generals asked that the king of Ch'in be executed, but the governor of P'ei replied, "The reason King Huai first sent me upon this mission was that he sincerely believed I was capable of showing tolerance and mercy. Now to kill a man who has already surrendered would bring only bad luck!" With this he turned the king of Ch'in over to the care of his officials. Then he proceeded west and entered Hsien-yang. . . . [He later] summoned all the distinguished and powerful men of the districts and addressed them, saying:

> Gentlemen, for a long time you have suffered beneath the harsh laws of Ch'in. Those who criticized the government were wiped out, along with their families; those who gathered to talk in private were executed in the public market. I and the other nobles have made an agreement that he who first enters the pass[8] shall rule over the area within. Accordingly I am now king of this territory within the pass. I hereby promise you a code of laws consisting of three articles only; He who kills anyone shall suffer death; he who wounds another or steals shall be punished according to the gravity of the offence; for the rest I hereby abolish all the laws of Ch'in. Let the officials and people remain undisturbed as before. I have come only to save you from further harm, not to exploit or tyrannize over you. Therefore do not be afraid!

---

[7]Technically, Tzu-ying was the third emperor of Ch'in, but had scaled back his own title in view of the weakness of his position. Here he comes to Kao-tsu in mourning and in total submission. What follows in this passage is further particularization of Kao-tsu's moderation, his determination to end the tyranny of Ch'in's harsh laws, and the popular support this won him. It is clear that Ssu-ma Ch'ien is writing into his account of Kao-tsu the characteristics of the humane ruler familiar to any reader of Confucius and Mencius.

[8]The pass referred to often in this chapter includes part of the course of the Yellow River, and connects the North China Plain on the east with the higher country to the west. It lies mostly in modern Honan Province. The Ch'in state, lying west of the pass, had been able to defend and strengthen itself in part because of its protected geographical position. The pass became the pivotal region for military activity in the war that destroyed the Ch'in and led to establishment of the Han Dynasty.

He sent men to go with the Ch'in officials and publish this proclamation in the district towns and villages. The people of Ch'in were overjoyed and hastened with cattle, sheep, wine, and food to present to the soldiers. But the governor of P'ei declined all such gifts, saying, "There is plenty of grain in the granaries. I do not wish to be a burden to the people." With this the people were more joyful than ever and their only fear was that the governor of P'ei would not become king of Ch'in.

• • •

[Kao-tsu did not become king of Ch'in. Hsiang Yu, still clearly the most power-ful leader among the contending generals, broke the agreement that this kingship should go to the first to enter Hsien-yang, but did accord Kao-tsu the title of king of Han. Relations between the two men deteriorated, Hsiang Yu permitted the murder of the last Ch'in emperor, fought a series of engagements with Kao-tsu's forces, and, at one point, even took Kao-tsu's parents, wife, and children prison-er in their home province of P'ei. The showdown between the two came in 202 B.C.] In the fifth year, the king of Han, with the forces of the other leaders, joined in an attack on the army of Ch'u,[9] fighting with Hsiang Yu for a decisive victory at Kai-hsia. Han Hsin led a force of three hundred thousand to attack the center, with General K'ung leading the left flank and General Pi leading the right flank, while the king of Han followed behind. Chou P'o, the marquis of Chiang, and General Ch'ai followed behind the king. Hsiang Yu's forces numbered some one hundred thousand.[10] Han Hsin advanced and joined in combat but, failing to gain the advantage, retired and allowed General K'ung and General Pi to close in from the sides. When the Ch'u forces began to falter, Han Hsien took advantage of their weakness to inflict a great defeat at Kai-hsia. The soldiers of Hsiang Yu, hearing the Han armies singing the songs of Ch'u, concluded that Han had already conquered the whole land of Ch'u. With this, Hsiang Yu fled in despair, leaving his soldiers to suffer total defeat. The king of Han dispatched the cavalry general Kuan Ying to pursue and kill Hsiang Yu at Tung-ch'eng. After cutting off the heads of eighty thousand of the enemy, he overran and conquered the land of Ch'u. . . .

In the first month, the various nobles and generals all joined in begging the king of Han to take the title of emperor, but he replied, "I have heard that the

---

[9]Ch'u, which encompassed most of the lower valley of the Yangtze River, was the largest and southernmost of the former warring states. It was the region from which Hsiang Yu drew most of his military strength.

[10]Numbers of troops in this and other engagements may be exaggerated. However, it is clear that the size of armies and the scale of military operations had increased dramati-cally in the period of the warring states. The human and economic devastation of con-tinual warfare increased correspondingly.

position of emperor may go only to a worthy man. It cannot be claimed by empty words and vain talk. I do not dare to accept the position of emperor."

His followers all replied, "Our great king has risen from the humblest beginnings to punish the wicked and violent and bring peace to all within the four seas. To those who have achieved merit he has accordingly parceled out land and enfoeffed them as kings and marquises. If our king does not assume the supreme title, then all our titles as well will be called into doubt. On pain of death we urge our request!"

The king of Han three times declined and then, seeing that he could do no more, said, "If you, my lords, consider it a good thing, then it must be to the good of the country." On the day *chia-wu* [February 28, 202 B.C.][11] he assumed the position of supreme emperor on the north banks of the Ssu River.

● ● ●

The sixth year [201 B.C.]: Every five days Kao-tsu would go to visit his father, the "Venerable Sire," observing the etiquette proper for an ordinary son toward his father.[12] The steward of his father's household spoke to the Venerable Sire, saying, "As heaven is without two suns, so the earth has not two lords. Now although the emperor is your son, he is the ruler of men, and although you are his father, you are his subject as well. How does it happen then that the ruler of men is doing obeisance to one of his subjects? If this is allowed to continue, the emperor's majesty will never prevail upon the world!"

The next time Kao-tsu came to visit, his father, bearing a broom in his hands as a sign of servitude, went to the gate to greet him and stood respectfully to one side. Kao-tsu in great astonishment descended from his carriage and hastened to his father's side. "The emperor is the ruler of men," his father said. "How should he on my account violate the laws of the empire?" With this Kao-tsu honored his father with the title Grand Supreme Emperor and, because he was secretly pleased with the advice of his father's steward, he awarded the man five hundred catties [approximately 600 grams] of gold.

● ● ●

In the tenth month of the twelfth year [195 B.C.] Kao-tsu had already attacked Ch'ing Pu's army at Kuei-chui, and Ch'ing Pu was in flight.[13] Kao-tsu dispatched

---

[11]The official dating for the Han Dynasty, however, started from the year 206 B.C., when Kao-tsu assumed the title of king of Han.

[12]The episode described in this passage constitutes another point in the characterization of Kao-tsu as a good Confucian.

[13]Defeat of Hsiang Yu and proclamation of Kao-tsu as emperor did not end the fighting. In fact, Kao-tsu spent most of the few years of life left to him in warfare against rebellious feudal lords and against barbarians on the northern frontier.

a special general to pursue him, while he himself started back to the capital, passing through his old home of P'ei on his way. Here he stopped and held a feast at the palace of P'ei, summoning all his old friends and the elders and young men to drink to their heart's content. He gathered together a group of some one hundred and twenty children of P'ei and taught them to sing and, when the feast was at its height, Kao-tsu struck the lute and sang a song which he had composed:

> A great wind came forth;
> The clouds rose on high.
> Now that my might rules all within the seas,
> I have returned to my old village.
> Where shall I find brave men
> To guard the four corners of my land?

He made the children join in and repeat the song, while he rose and danced. Deeply moved with grief and nostalgia, and with tears streaming down his face, he said to the elders of P'ei, "The traveler sighs for his old home. Though I have made my capital within the pass, after I have departed this life my spirit will still think with joy of P'ei. From the time when I was governor of P'ei, I went forth to punish the wicked and violent until at last the whole world is mine. It is my wish that P'ei become my bath-town.[14] I hereby exempt its people from all taxes. For generation after generation, nothing more shall be required of you." Then for over ten days the old men and women and Kao-tsu's former friends of P'ei spent each day drinking and rejoicing, reminiscing, and joking about old times.

● ● ●

When Kao-tsu was fighting against Ch'ing Pu, he was wounded by a stray arrow and on the way back he fell ill. When his illness continued to grow worse, Empress Lu sent for a skilled doctor. The doctor examined Kao-tsu and, in answer to his question, replied, "This illness can be cured." With this, Kao-tsu began to berate and curse him, saying, "I began as a commoner and with my three-foot sword conquered the world. Was this not the will of heaven? My fate lies with heaven. Even P'ien Ch'ueh, the most famous doctor of antiquity, could do nothing for me!" In the end he would not let the doctor treat his illness, but gave him fifty catties of gold and sent him away. . . .

In the fourth month, the day *chia-ch'en* [June 1, 195 B.C.], Kao-tsu passed away in the Palace of Living Joy. . . .

---

[14]A town or district whose tax obligations to the imperial government were permanently remitted, on the understanding that the money would be used for "bath water," i.e., for private local purposes. There is a nice sense of kindness-for-kindness in this passage when one remembers how the old women who kept the wine shops in P'ei used to forgive the young Kao-tsu his apparently considerable drinking debts.

• • •

The Grand Historian remarks: The government of the Hsia Dynasty[15] was marked by good faith, which in time deteriorated until mean men had turned it into rusticity. Therefore the men of Shang who succeeded to the Hsia reformed this defect through the virtue of piety. But piety degenerated until mean men had made it a superstitious concern for the spirits. Therefore the men of Chou who followed corrected this fault through refinement and order. But refinement again deteriorated until it became in the hands of the mean a mere hollow show. Therefore what was needed to reform this hollow show was a return to good faith, for the way of the three dynasties of old is like a cycle, which, when it ends, must begin over again.

It is obvious that in late Chou and Ch'in times the earlier refinement and order had deteriorated. But the government of Ch'in failed to correct this fault, instead adding its own harsh punishments and laws. Was this not a grave error?

Thus when the Han rose to power it took over the faults of its predecessors and worked to change and reform them, causing men to be unflagging in their efforts and following the order properly ordained by heaven. It held its court in the tenth month and its vestments and carriage tops were yellow, with plumes on the left sides of the carriages.

---

[15]Ssu-ma Ch'ien concludes his account of Kao-tsu with a brief summary of the traditional view of the earlier dynasties, stressing the cyclical nature of political regimes founded in good faith, which, in time, deteriorated. Dating of all these early dynasties is still disputed, but acceptable—sometimes overlapping—provisional dates are: Hsia, 2205–1766 B.C.; Shang, 1766–1122 B.C.; Chou, 1122–256 B.C.; period of the warring states, 481–221 B.C.

45

꒰

POETRY OF THE HAN DYNASTY

T*he importance of poetry in Chinese life, already noted in relation to* The Book of Songs *(Selection 11), in no way diminished during the harsh years of war and social and political dislocation between about 481 and 221* B.C., *known as the period of the warring states. Scholars of Chinese culture disagree as to whether the Han Dynasty (206* B.C.–A.D. *220) deserves the title of "a golden age," as do some later dynasties. However, the Han did produce a rich and varied body of poetry and witnessed the development to maturity of one new poetic form and the vigorous recasting of another.*

This selection opens with translations of thirteen of the lyrics from a collection that came to be known as the "Nineteen Old Poems" of the Han. They are anonymous and undated, although students of this literature believe they were written by a member, or members, of the literati sometime in the second century A.D. *They are composed in a lyric form, the* shih, *first encountered in the Chou Dynasty's* Book of Songs. *In that earlier work,* shih *poetry always was written with a terse four-character line, but the revival of the form that began in early Han times utilized either five or seven characters, giving the lines greater flow and flexibility. Many of the themes familiar from the* Book of Songs *appear again in the "Nineteen Old Poems," but there is greater complexity in their treatment, and a darker emotional tone. A good example is the fourth poem, whose first eight lines echo the joyous songs of clan feasts from the* Book of Songs, *but whose last six lines turn to reflection on the brevity of human life and an almost desperate call to strive for fame and wealth while life lasts.*

Other lyrics in this selection, two of them by the great Han "Martial Emperor" Wu Ti (ruled from 140–87 B.C.), *need little explication. However, the final excerpt, Yang Hsiung's "Poverty," does require particular mention because it represents a form of poetic composition, the* fu, *or "rhyme-prose," which was relatively new in the years of the Han Dynasty and that saw its greatest development and elaboration in that age. A* fu *is really a poetic essay, often introduced by and interspersed with prose passages. Even its poetic lines are usually written in a longer line than that of typical lyric poetry. These* fu *are often highly descrip-*

tive, or discursive, works, frequently fanciful in their vision of the world and teaching a moral lesson through their narrative, as is the case in the "Poverty" fu presented here.

SELECTIONS FROM THE NINETEEN OLD HAN POEMS

I

On and on, going on and on,
away from you to live apart,
ten thousand *li*[1] and more between us,
each at opposite ends of the sky.
The road I travel is steep and long;
who knows when we meet again?
The Hu[2] horse leans into the north wind;
the Yueh bird nests in southern branches:
day by day our parting grows more distant;
day by day robe and belt dangle looser.
Shifting clouds block the white sun;
the traveler does not look to return.
Thinking of you makes one old;
years and months suddenly go by.
Abandoned, I will say no more
but pluck up strength and eat my fill.[3]

Selections from "The Nineteen Old Poems" from Burton Watson, *Chinese Lyricism: Shih Poetry from the Second to the Twelfth Century, with Translations* (New York and London: Columbia University Press, 1971), pp. 20, 23–30. Reprinted with permission of the publisher. Other selections from Arthur Waley, *Chinese Poems* (London: George Allen & Unwin Ltd., 1946), pp. 42–43, 45–48, 52–54. Reprinted by permission of the copyright holder, HarperCollins Publishers.

[1]One *li* is approximately one-third of a mile.

[2]Hu designates an area on the northern frontiers of Han China. Yueh in the next line originally meant the region near the mouth of the Yangtze River, but came more generally to mean "the south." The two lines exemplify a verbal parallelism between the two lines of a couplet, a common characteristic of the revised *shih* form.

[3]It is possible to translate the last two lines in exactly the opposite way, i.e., to convey the speaker's sense that the abandoned wife or lover left at home should "pluck up strength" and take care of herself.

2

Green green, river bank grasses
thick thick, willows in the garden;
plump plump, that lady upstairs,
bright bright before the window;
lovely lovely, her red face-powder;
slim slim, she puts out a white hand.
Once I was a singing-house girl,
now the wife of a wanderer,
a wanderer who never comes home—
It's hard sleeping in an empty bed alone.

3

Green green the cypress on the ridge,
stones heaped about in mountain streams:
between heaven and earth our lives rush past
like travelers with a long road to go.
Let this measure of wine be our merriment;
value it highly, without disdain.
I race the carriage, whip the lagging horses,
roam for pleasure to Wan and Lo.[4]
Here in Lo-yang, what surging crowds,
capped and belted ones chasing each other;
long avenues fringed with narrow alleys,
the many mansions of princes and peers.
The Two Palaces[5] face each other from afar,
paired towers over a hundred feet tall.
Let the feast last forever, delight the heart—
then what grief or gloom can weigh us down.

4

We hold a splendid feast today,
a delight barely to be told in words.
Strike the lute, raise joyful echoes,
new notes of ghostly beauty.
Let the talented sing fine phrases;
he who knows music will understand.

---

[4]Lo-yang was the capital of the Restored, or Eastern Han, Dynasty after A.D. 25; Wan, southeast of Lo-yang, was the home of the Eastern Han's founder, Emperor Kuang-wu, and was noted for its magnificence.

[5]Palaces of the reigning emperor and of the heir-apparent, located in the northern and southern quarters of Lo-yang, respectively.

One in mind, we share the same wish,
though the thought within remains unspoken:
> Man lives out his little sojourn,
> scudding by like a swirl of dust.
> Why not whip up your high-stepping horses,
> be first to command the road to power?
> What profit to stay poor and unhonored,
> floundering forever in bitterness!

5

Northwest the tall tower stands,
its top level with floating clouds,
patterned windows webbed in lattice,
roofs piled three stories high.
From above, the sound of strings and song;
what sadness in that melody!
Who could play a tune like this,
who but the wife of Ch'i Liang?[6]
The clear *shang*[7] mode drifts down the wind;
halfway through it falters and breaks,
one plucking, two or three sighs,
longing, a grief that lingers on—
It is not the singer's pain I pity,
but few are those who understand the song!
If only we could be a pair of calling cranes,
beating wings, soaring to the sky!

7

Clear moon brightly shining in the night,
crickets chirping by the eastern walls;
the jade bar[8] points to early winter;
crowding stars, how thick their ranks!
White dew soaks the wild grasses,
cycle of the seasons swiftly changing;
autumn locusts cry among the trees;
dark swallows, where did they go?
Once we were students together;

---

[6]Ch'i Liang's widow is supposed to have played mournful lute music before drowning herself after her husband's death in battle in 550 B.C.

[7]*Shang*: one of the five modes of Chinese music, one associated with autumn.

[8]The handle of the Big Dipper, which can also be thought of as the hand of a seasonal clock.

you soared on high, beating strong wings,
no longer recalling the hand of friendship;
you've left me behind like a forgotten footprint.
Southern Winnow, Dipper in the north,
Draught Ox[9] that will not bear a yoke—
truly, with no rock to underpin them,
what good are empty names?

8

Frail frail, lone growing bamboo,
roots clasping the hill's edge;
to join with my lord now in marriage,
a creeper clinging to the moss.
Creepers have their time to grow,
husband and wife their proper union.
A thousand miles apart we made our vow,
far far—mountain slopes between us,
Thinking of you makes one old;
your canopied carriage, how slow its coming!
These flowers sadden me—orchis and angelica,
petals unfurled, shedding glory all around;
if no one plucks them in blossom time
they'll wilt and die with the autumn grass.
But if in truth you will keep your promise,
how could *I* ever be untrue?

9

In the garden a strange tree grows,
from green leaves a shower of blossoms bursting.
I bend the limb and break off a flower,
thinking to send it to the one I love.
Fragrance fills my breast and sleeves,
but the road is far—it will never reach you.
Why is such a gift worth giving?
Only because I remember how long ago we parted.

---

[9]The "Nineteen Old Poems" are rich in astronomical allusions. The Winnow, Dipper, and
Ox "that will not bear a yoke" are probably symbols for things that, like the hollow
friendship which is the poem's subject, have impressive names but no substance.

10

Far far away, the Herdboy Star;[10]
bright bright, the Lady of the River of Heaven;
slim slim, she lifts a pale hand,
clack clack, playing the shuttle of her loom,
all day long—but the pattern's never finished;
welling tears fall like rain.
The River of Heaven is clear and shallow;
what a little way lies between them!
only the span of a single brimming stream—
They gaze and gaze and cannot speak.

11

I turn the carriage, yoke and set off,
far far over never-ending roads.
In the four directions, broad plain on plain;
east wind shakes the hundred grasses.
Among all I meet, nothing of the past;
what can save us from sudden old age?
Fullness and decay, each has its season;
success—I hate it, so late in coming!
Man is not made of metal or stone;
how can he hope to live for long?
Swiftly he follows in the wake of change;
a shining name—let that be the prize!

13

I drive my carriage from the upper east gate,[11]
scanning the graves far north of the wall;
silver poplars, how they whisper and sigh;
pine and cypress flank the broad lane.
Beneath them, the ancient dead,
black black there in the long night,
sunk in sleep beneath the Yellow Springs;[12]

---

[10]References are to a poignantly beautiful bit of Chinese astronomical lore. The Herdboy, corresponding roughly to the Western constellation Aquila, and the Weaving Lady, corresponding to the star Vega and two others in the Constellation Lyra, are lovers separated by the River of Heaven, the Milky Way. One night a year, kindly magpies form a bridge of their wings to permit the two lovers to meet.

[11]Of Lo-yang.

[12]The abode of the dead.

a thousand years pass but they never wake.
Times of heat and cold in unending succession,
but the years heaven gives us are like morning dew.
Man's life is brief as a sojourn;
his years lack the firmness of metal or stone.
Ten thousand ages come and go
but sages and wise men discover no cure.
Some seek long life in fasts and potions;
many end by poisoning themselves.
Far better to drink fine wine,
to clothe ourselves in soft white silk![13]

15

Man's years fall short of a hundred;
a thousand years of worry crowd his heart.
If the day is short and you hate the long night,
why not take the torch and go wandering?
Seek out happiness in season;
who can wait the year to come?
Fools who cling too fondly to gold
earn no more than posterity's jeers.
Prince Ch'iao,[14] that immortal man—
small hope we have of matching him!

17

First month of winter: cold air comes,
north winds sharp and cruel.
I have many sorrows, I know how long the night is,
looking up to watch the teeming ranks of stars.
Night of the fifteenth: a bright moon full;
twentieth night: toad and hare[15] wane.
A traveler came from far away,

---

[13]There are interesting parallels between the expressions of this "eat, drink, and be merry, for tomorrow we die" theme of the "Nineteen Old Poems" and the Epicurean poems being written in Rome in the same years. This is but one of a number of striking similarities between the Roman and Han Empires.

[14]Originally noted for longevity, in Han times Prince Ch'iao may have become a figure in a cult of immortal spirits.

[15]Animal figures that the Chinese believed could be perceived in the delineation between dark and light areas on the moon, comparable to the "man in the moon" familiar to the West.

put a letter into my hand;
at the top it spoke of "undying remembrance,"
at the bottom of "parting long endured."
I tucked it away inside my robe;
three years—not a word has dimmed.
With whole heart I offer my poor love,
fearful you may not see its worth.

OTHER SELECTED POEMS
OF THE HAN DYNASTY

Wu Ti
THE AUTUMN WIND

Autumn wind rises: white clouds fly.
Grass and trees wither; geese go south.
Orchids, all in bloom; chrysanthemums smell sweet.
I think of my lovely lady; I never can forget.
Floating–pagoda boat crosses Fen River;
Across the mid-stream white waves rise.
Flute and drum keep time to sound of rowers' song;
Amidst revel and feasting sad thoughts come;
Youth's years how few, age how sure!

Wu Ti
LI FU-JEN

The sound of her silk skirt has stopped.
On the marble pavement dust grows.
Her empty room is cold and still.
Fallen leaves are piled against the doors.
  Longing for that lovely lady
How can I bring my aching heart to rest?

Hsi-chun

LAMENT OF HSI-CHUN[16]

My people have married me
In a far corner of earth;
Sent me away to a strange land,
To the king of the Wu-sun.
A tent is my house,
Of felt are my walls;
Raw flesh my food
With mare's milk to drink.
Always thinking of my own country,
My heart sad within.
Would I were a yellow stork
And could fly to my old home!

Anonymous (First Century A.D.?)

FIGHTING SOUTH OF THE RAMPARTS

They fought south of the ramparts,
They died north of the wall.
They died in the moors and were not buried.
Their flesh was the food of crows.
"Tell the crows we are not afraid;
We have died in the moors and cannot be buried,
Crows, how can our bodies escape you?"
The waters flowed deep
And the rushes in the pool were dark.
The riders fought and were slain;
Their horses wander neighing.
By the bridge there was a house.
Was it south, was it north?

---

[16]Although Emperor Wu Ti launched vigorous military campaigns against the barbarians beyond China's northern frontiers, he also engaged in forms of diplomacy that involved "gifts," including the presentation to barbarian chieftains of beautiful women of good family. In 105 B.C. Lady Hsi-chun was sent to join the harem of a Central Asian nomadic king, who proved to be aged and infirm, and with whom she could not even converse. Stories and poems of women suffering Hsi-chun's fate became staples of Chinese literature in the imperial era. See: Yuan Drama, *Autumn in Han Palace,* vol. II, Selection 46, in this *World Literature and Thought* series.

The harvest was never gathered.
How can we give you your offerings?
You served your prince faithfully,
Though all in vain.
I think of you, faithful soldiers;
Your service shall not be forgotten,
For in the morning you went out to battle
And at night you did not return.

Anonymous
THE OTHER SIDE OF THE VALLEY

I am a prisoner in the hands of the enemy,
Enduring the shame of captivity.
My bones stick out and my strength is gone
Through not getting enough to eat.
My brother is a Mandarin[17]
And his horses are fed on millet.
Why can't he spare a little money
To send and ransom me?

Anonymous (First Century A.D.?)
OLD AND NEW

She went up the mountain to pluck wild herbs;
She came down the mountain and met her former husband.
She knelt down and asked her former husband
"What do you find your new wife like?"
"My new wife, although her talk is clever,
Cannot charm me as my old wife could.
In beauty of face there is not much to choose,
But in usefulness they are not alike.
My new wife comes in from the road to meet me;
My old wife always came down from her tower.
My new wife weaves fancy silks;
My old wife was good at plain weaving.
Of fancy silk one can weave a strip a day;
Of plain weaving, more than fifty feet.
Putting her silks by the side of your weaving
I see that the new wife will not compare with the old."

17An imperial official.

Yang Hsiung (52 B.C.–A.D. 18)
POVERTY

I, Yang Tzu, hid from life,
Fled from the common world to a lonely place,
Where to the right a great wilderness touched me
And on the left my neighbor was the Hill of Sung.
Beggars whose tenements
Lie wall to wall, though they be tattered and poor,
Rough-used, despised and scorned, are yet in companies
And sociable clans conjoined. But I in my despair
Called Poverty to me, saying: "Long ago
You should have been cast out, driven far away,
Press-ganged, or pilloried as man's fourth curse.
Yet not in childhood only, in infancy
When laughing I would build
Castles of soil or sand, were you
My more than neighbor, for your roof
Touched mine and our two homes were one;
But in manhood also weighed I with the great,
Lighter, because of you
Than fluff or feather; more frail my fortunes
Than gossamer, who to the state submitting
Great worth found small employ;
Withdrawing, heard no blame.

"What prompts you, Poverty,
So long to linger, an unwanted guest?
Others wear broidered coats; my homespun is not whole.
Others eat millet and rice, I boil the goosefoot seed.
No toy nor treasure is mine,
Nor aught to make me glad.
Clans gather at the feast
In great ease and gladness,
But I abroad the world
Trudge out afoot with panniers on my back,
Sell my day-labor for a coat to cover me.
Servant of many masters
Hand-chafed I dig, heel-blistered hoe,
Bare-backed to the wind and rain.
And that all this befell me,
That friends and favorites forsook me,
That up the hill of state so labored was my climb

Who should bear blame? Who but you, O Poverty,
Was cause of all my woe?

"I fled you high and far, but you across the hills of heaven
Like a hawk did follow me.
I fled you among the rocks, in caverns of stone I hid;
But you up those huge steeps
Did follow me.
I fled you to the ocean, sailed that cypress ship
Across the storm, but you
Whether on wave-crest or in the hollows of the sea,
Did follow me.
And if I move, you too are stirring;
If I lie down, you are at rest.
Have you no other friend in all the world?
What would you seek of me?
Go, Poverty! and pester me no more."

Then said Poverty: "So be it, my master:
I am dismissed. Yet though men say,
'Much chatter, little wit,' listen! I too
Have a heart that is full and a tale that must be told.

"My father's father, long, long ago
Was illustrious in the land; of virtue so excellent
That by the king's throne in council he stood,
Admonishing the rulers how to make statutes and laws.
Of earth were the stairs, roofed over with thatch,
Not carved nor hung.
But when the world in latter days
Was given over to folly, fell about in darkness,
Then gluttons gathered together; by ill means the covetous
Fastened upon their prey;
Despised my grand-dad, they were so insolent and proud,
Built arbors of onyx, terraces of jade,
And huge halls to dwell in; lapped lakes of wine.
So that at last I left them
Suddenly as a swan that soars
And would not tread their court.
Thrice daily I look into my heart
And find I did no wrong.
As for your home, mighty are the blessings I brought,
Stacked high as the hills.
Your small woes you remember;

But my good deeds you have forgot.
Did I not teach you
By gradual usage, indifferent to endure
Summer's heat and winter's cold?
(And that which neither heat nor cold can touch—
Is it not eternal as the gods?)

"I, Poverty,
Turned from you the envy of the covetous, taught you to fear
Neither Chieh the Tyrant nor the Robber Chih.
Others, my master,
Quake behind bolt and bar, while you alone
Live open to the world.
Others by care
And pitiful apprehension are cast down,
While you are gay and free."
Thus spoke Poverty, and when his speech was ended,
Stern of countenance and with dilated eye,
He gathered up the folds of his garment and rose from where he sat,
Passed down the stairway and left my house.

"Farewell," said Poverty, "for now I leave you.
To that hill I take my way
Where sheltering, the Lord of Ku-chu's sons
Have learnt to ply my trade."
Then I, Yang Tzu, left the mat where I lay
And cried: "O Poverty, let my crooked words
Be as unspoken; forget that I have wronged you.
I have heard truth, O Poverty, and received it.
Live with me always, for of your company
I shall not weary till I die."
Then Poverty came back and dwelt with me,
Nor since has left my side.